COLLECTIBLES
HANDBOOK & PRICE GUIDE

TURBOTRAIN

COLLECTIBLES
HANDBOOK & PRICE GUIDE

Judith Miller

MILLER'S

Miller's Collectibles Handbook & Price Guide 2019-2020
By Judith Miller

First published in Great Britain in 2018 by Miller's, a division of Mitchell Beazley,
imprints of Octopus Publishing Group Ltd., Carmelite House,
50 Victoria Embankment, London, EC4Y 0DZ
www.octopusbooks.co.uk

An Hachette UK Company
www.hachette.co.uk

Distributed in the US by Hachette Book Group
1290 Avenue of the Americas, 4th and 5th Floors, New York, NY 10104

Distributed in Canada by Canadian Manda Group
664 Annette St., Toronto, Ontario, Canada, M6S 2C8

Miller's is a registered trademark of Octopus Publishing Group Ltd.
www.millersguides.com

Copyright © Octopus Publishing Group Ltd. 2018

While every care has been taken in the compilation of this guide, neither the publishers nor the
author can accept any liability for any financial or other loss incurred by reliance placed on the
information contained in Miller's Collectibles Price Guide 2019-2020.

ISBN 978 1 78472 420 7

A CIP catalog record for this book is available from the British Library.

Set in Frutiger

Printed and bound in China

1 3 5 7 9 10 8 6 4 2

Publisher Alison Starling
Editorial Co-ordinator Katie Lumsden
Proofreader John Wainwright
Indexer Hilary Bird
Designer Ali Scrivens, TJ Graphics
Senior Production Manager Peter Hunt

Photographs of Judith Miller by Chris Terry

CONTENTS

LIST OF CONSULTANTS

CERAMICS

Will Farmer
Fieldings Auctioneers
www.fieldingsauctioneers.co.uk

Wayne Chapman
Lynways
www.lynways.com

Steven Moore
Burleigh Pottery

John Newton
John Newton Antiques
www.johnnewtonantiques.com

David Rago
Rago Arts, USA
www.ragoarts.com

CAMERAS

James Spiridion
Adam Partridge Auctioneers
www.adampartridge.co.uk

COINS

Timothy Medhurst
Duke's
www.dukes-auctions.com

COMICS

Phil Shrimpton
Phil Comics
www.phil-comics.com

Luke Kennedy
Astons Auctioneers
www.astonsauctioneers.co.uk

COSTUME JEWELRY

Gemma Redmond
www.gemmaredmond
vintage.co.uk

DOLLS

Sue Brewer
www.britishdollshowcase.co.uk

GLASS

Will Farmer
Fieldings Auctioneers
www.fieldingsauctioneers.co.uk

Mike & Debby Moir
M & D Moir
www.manddmoir.co.uk

Wayne Chapman
Lynways
www.lynways.com

INUIT

Duncan McLean
Waddington's, Canada
www.waddingtons.ca

SCIENTIFIC INSTRUMENTS

Charles Miller
Charles Miller Ltd
www.charlesmillerltd.com

SPORTING

Graham Budd
Graham Budd Auctions
www.grahambuddauctions.co.uk

We'd also like to thank our friends and colleagues who have helped and supported us in many ways with this book including: Laura Genders from Adam Partridge, Ian Jackson from Bearnes, Hampton and Littlewood, Rachel Morgan from Bellmans, Lauren Bertoia-Costanza from Bertoia, Hannah Daly and Lucinda Blythe from Bloomsbury, Rachael Williams from Brightwells, Leigh Gotch from C&T Auctions, Patricia Durdikova from Cheffins, Carol Johnson from Dee, Atkinson & Harrison, Marc Tielemans from Dominic Winter, Victoria Billington from Dreweatts, Daisy Jones from Ewbank's, Alexandra Whittaker and Liam Bolland from Fellows, Alison Snowdon from Fieldings, Lara Bell from Great Western Auctions, Emma Cranberry and Jill Gallone from Hansons, Emma from Hartleys, Mark Grant and James Welch from John Nicholson's, Gayle Stephens from Keys, Geoff from Kingham & Orme, Helen Robson from Lacy Scott Knight, Rachael Salter from Lawrences, Chris Elmy from Lockdales, Blair Cowan and Alex Dove from Lyon & Turnbull, Sharon Sparrow from Peter Wilson, Hannah Kelleher from Pook & Pook, Kathy Plaskitt from Potteries Auctions, Nadine Becker from Quittenbaum, Anthony Barnes from Rago Arts, Gemma Redmond Vintage, Alexandra Nelson from Swann Auction Galleries, Diane Baynes from Sworders, Katie Smithson from Tennants, Tim Brophy from W&H Peacock, Susan Lower from Wallis & Wallis, and Tamzin Corbett from Woolley & Wallis; and Julie Brooke, for her help updating our Directory of Auctioneers.

HOW TO USE THIS BOOK

Subcategory heading Indicates the sub-category of the main heading.

Page tab This appears on every page and identifies the main category heading as identified in the Contents List on pages 5-6.

Judith Picks Items chosen specifically by Judith, either because they are important or interesting, or they might be a good investment.

Caption The description of the item illustrated, including when relevant, the period, the maker or factory, medium, the year it was made, dimensions and condition. Many captions have **footnotes** which explain terminology or give identification or valuation information.

The price guide These price ranges give a ballpark figure for what you should pay for a similar item. The great joy of collectibles is that there is not a recommended retail price. The price ranges in this book are based on actual prices, either what a dealer will take or the full auction price.

Quick reference Gives key facts about the factory, maker or style, along with stylistic identification points, value tips and advice on fakes.

The object The collectibles are shown in full color. This is a vital aid to identification and valuation. With many objects, a slight color variation can signify a large price differential.

Source code Every item has been specially photographed at an auction house, a dealer, an antiques market or a private collection. These are credited by a code at the end of each caption, and can be checked against the Key to Illustrations.

Closer Look Does exactly that. Here we show identifying aspects of a factory or maker, point out rare colors or shapes, and explain why a particular piece is so desirable.

INTRODUCTION

Welcome to the new 'Miller's Collectibles Handbook and Price Guide', in which I am proud to present over 4,000 completely new, specially selected collectibles. Representative of the domestic and international market, they range from advertising to automobilia, metalware to militaria, paperweights to posters, teddy bears to tribal art. All collecting fields, tastes and passions are catered for.

Preceded by a list of Contents, and a user-friendly explanation of How To Use This Book, every collectible depicted has a descriptive caption and a price guide. Many are also accompanied by specially written footnotes that highlight interesting aspects of the item. You will also find a wealth of additional information in the 'Closer Look' and 'Judith Picks' features, as well as in the 'Quick Reference' boxes, which provide helpful introductions to particular collecting areas, designers or makers. And at the back of the book, the practical aspects of collecting - buying and selling - are supported by directories of auction houses, specialists, fairs and societies.

So, what has happened in the Collectibles market since our last guide? What's 'on trend', and what isn't, and what can we learn from this? One stand-out collecting area in terms of demand and prices paid has been 20thC posters, especially travel-related examples featuring steam trains and/or idyllic destinations. As with the comics market, much of this is fueled by increasing recognition of the sheer quality of the artwork available - artwork that, of course, can be decoratively displayed around

A rare West German salt-glazed jug, made in the studios of Klotilde Giefer-Bahn. c1945 12.5in (32cm) high $850-900 JNEW

the home - but it's also driven by nostalgia for a stylish, dynamic but decidedly less frenetic bygone age.

Certainly, nostalgia underpins many developments in the Collectibles market. For example, modern First Editions - think J.K. Rowling - are evermore valuable. While much of this can be attributed to the personal nostalgia of younger collectors who grew up with the Harry Potter books, I think there is also a significant element of nostalgia for 'hard copy' and the printed word, as 'virtual' communication via the internet becomes the 'norm'. Of course, one generation's nostalgia isn't necessarily another's: Dinky Toy cars were played with in one childhood, Corgi cars in a subsequent one - which does much to explain changing trends in the Toys market. In these areas, condition in vital; collectors aim to buy mint examples.

Nostalgia, however, isn't the be all and end all. There is also the small matter of changing aesthetics. What once appeared fresh and pleasing to the eye gradually diminishes, and is replaced by a different 'look'. Ultimately this is a matter of fashion and explains why, for example, the naturalistic form and decoration of Victorian ceramics and glass is generally fetching lower prices, while more geometric or abstract Art Deco and Mid-Century Modern equivalents, especially Scandinavian pieces, are forging ahead. Meanwhile, 18thC blue and white porcelain from factories such as Caughley is growing increasingly affordable.

Of course, at some point this may all start to about-turn. Predicting that tipping point is far from an exact science. In the indeterminate interim, the best advice I can give is: to maximise the chances of making a good investment, always buy the best example of something you can afford - but more importantly, to maximise the pleasure of collecting, always buy the best example of something you love. Happy Collecting!

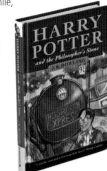

Rowling, J.K., 'Harry Potter and the Philosopher's Stone', first edition, first issue. 1997 $70,000-80,000 BLO

Judith Miller.

A Corgi Toys 'STUDEBAKER GOLDEN HAWK', no.211, in original box. $150-200 LSK

A Clarice Cliff shape 360 vase, 'Orange Roof Cottage' pattern. c1932 8.25in (21cm) high $1,200-1,300 FLD

A Vistosi glass bird, designed by Alessandro Pianon. c1960 10.5in (26.5cm) high $6,500-8,000 GWA

A glass petrol pump globe, for Blaydon Petrol.

11.5in (29cm) diam

$1,000-1,200   DA&H

A single-sided enamel advertising thermometer/sign, for Duckhams Motor Oil.

35.75in (91cm) high

$550-650   DA&H

An early 20thC 'The Sportsman's BP Ethyl' enamel advertising sign, for Ethyl Gasoline Corporation, minor repairs.

36in (91.5cm) wide

$400-550   LOCK

A 1970s Gulf petrol 3D forecourt plastic sign.

42.5in (108cm) square

$250-350   DA&H

QUICK REFERENCE - SHELL

- Shell began in 1891 as the trademark for kerosene shipped by the firm Marcus Samuel and Co. The logo had its roots in the company's history as merchants of antiques and seashells.
- In 1897, Samuel formed the Shell Transport and Trading Company, which later merged with the Royal Dutch Petroleum Company to become the Royal Dutch Shell Group. Shell went on to become a leading multinational oil and gas company and remains so today.
- Throughout the 20thC, Shell funded widespread marketing campaigns, creating postcards, posters, enamel signs, petrol pumps, valentine cards and books. The Shell Heritage Art Collection, featuring items from many of Shell's advertising campaigns, is on display at the National Motor Museum in Hampshire, England.

A porcelain enamel single-sided Mobiloil sign, 'Gargoyle'.

25in (61cm) wide

$300-400   DA&H

A Shell Diesoline petroleum pump glass globe.

17in (43cm) high

$750-850   DA&H

A Shell petroleum pump glass globe.

17in (43cm) high

$600-650   DA&H

A 1950s Shell clam 3D forecourt plastic sign.

43.25in (110cm) wide

$350-400   DA&H

A set of four Avon motorcycle tire insert cardboard advertising signs, for Speedmaster, Trials Supreme, Sidecar Triple Duty and S.M.

$350-400   **DA&H**

An enamel double-sided advertising sign, for Michelin Cycle Tyres.

20.5in (52cm) high

$350-400   **DA&H**

QUICK REFERENCE - THE MICHELIN MAN

Michelin was founded in 1889 by brothers André and Edouard Michelin and went on to become one of the world's leading tire manufacturers. Mr Bibendum, usually referred to as the Michelin Man, has been one of the most iconic advertising symbols of the last hundred years. It was thought up by the Michelin brothers in the 1890s and designed by poster artist O'Galop, pseudonym of Marius Rossillon. Since the 1890s, the Michelin Man has been constantly reimagined, changing design and style with the time.

A 1950s Plastic Michelin Man/Mr Bibendum advertising figure.

15in (38cm) long

$150-200   **LOCK**

A Michelin Man/Mr Bibendum promotional suit.

$250-350   **DA&H**

An unissued advertising figure of Michelin Man/Mr Bibendum, with stand.

18.5in (47cm) high

$130-200   **APAR**

A rare Stepney Tyres pictorial enamel sign, depicting a British Bull Dog stood astride a tire, by Imperial Enamel, with gloss finish.

The Stepney spare wheel was invented by Thomas Morns Davies in Llanelli in 1904; before this, early motorcars were made without spares. The firm moved to Walthamstow in 1922 and renamed itself Stepney Tyres. The term 'stepney' is still used in India to refer to a spare tire. A larger version of this sign, with a height of 59.75in (152cm), was sold for £9,400 ($12,600) by Richard Edmonds Auctions in 2015.

29in (73.5cm) high

$6,500-8,000   **RE**

A BP Motor Spirit double-sided porcelain enamel advertising sign.

24in (61cm) wide

$350-400   **DA&H**

QUICK REFERENCE - ADVERTISING

- Most of the advertising memorabilia available to collectors today dates from the 20thC. Advertising can provide fascinating insights into the design trends, commercial markets and social history of that period.

- In general, collectors tend to focus either on a particular kind of advertising item - such as enamel signs or posters - or a particular brand or range of products. Food and drink advertising remains popular, as does tobacco advertising. Signs, especially those in mint condition, tend to fetch the highest prices.

- The advertising collectibles market is driven by a combination of nostalgia and availability. The brands that collectors know well, such as Cadbury's Chocolate or Colman's Mustard, are often popular, as are large brands such as Coca Cola, Shell or Michelin, which have produced a large range of advertising items over a long period of time.

- Items that clearly represent a subject area, artistic movement or time period are also highly collectible, whether from a well-known brand or not. Late 19thC and early 20thC Art Nouveau and 1920s-30s Art Deco advertising items are very popular. 1950s-60s 'vintage' pieces have increased in popularity over the past decade. A design by a major artist will also increase an item's value.

- While good condition does increase value, advertising items have often been used over many years, sometimes in outdoor settings, so condition should be consistent with age and use. Reproductions are common in this market, so examine items especially carefully. The way a piece was made can help identify it as an original or a reproduction.

An AA double-sided porcelain enamel advertising sign.

24.5in (62cm) high

$250-350   DA&H

A Commercial Motor Users Association Official Caterer single-sided porcelain enamel advertising sign.

17.75in (45cm) diam

$350-400   DA&H

A Jaguar Sales & Service double-sided illuminated hanging sign, boxed.

30in (76cm) wide

$550-600   PW

A porcelain enamel single-sided sign, for East Yorkshire Motor Services Ltd.

19.75in (50cm) wide

$400-450   DA&H

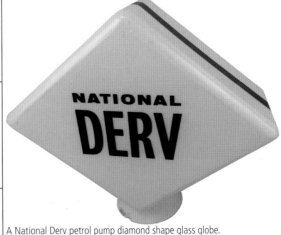

A National Derv petrol pump diamond shape glass globe.

19in (48cm) high

$650-750   DA&H

A Lotus single-sided advertising sign, in an aluminum mount.

20in (51cm) square

$250-350   DA&H

A Morris dealers double-sided porcelain enamel advertising sign.

28.25in (72cm) diam

$450-550   DA&H

A Pratt's enamel double-sided advertising sign.

20.75in (53cm) wide

$350-400   DA&H

ADVERTISING

An early to mid-20thC Castle
Tobacco Factory Nottingham
'Country Life Smoking Mixture'
tobacco tin, by John Player & Sons.
5.5in (14cm) high
$150-200   **LOCK**

A late 19thC Cope's Cigarettes
advertising showcard, signed to
lower left 'A. Piot', framed and
glazed.
20.25in (15.5cm) high
$450-550   **LOCK**

An original confectioner double-
sided enamel sign, promoting
Park Drive 'Plain & Corked Tipped'
cigarettes, some light rust.
16.25in (41cm) wide
$150-200   **W&W**

A rare life-size model of a woman,
inscribed '1942, Flowers and
Tobacco Woodbines and John
Players'.
72in (183cm) high
$3,500-4,000   **MEA**

An original 'Turf, Virginia
Cigarettes' enamel advertising sign.
36in (91.5cm) high
$250-350   **LOCK**

Judith Picks

Garryowen was born in 1876, bred
by H.S. Moore of Dublin, sired
by Champion Palmerston out of
Champion Belle. He was owned by
James J. Giltrap, a legal agent. From
his first entry in a dog show, he won prizes. Garryowen's
portrait was commissioned by Col. J.K. Millner, from
William Osborne RHA and is in the collection of the
National Gallery of Ireland. Spillane's was a well-known
Limerick family of tobacco manufacturers established in
1829 who named its Plug tobacco after the famous dog.
The logo for the brand shows him resplendent in the
collar decorated with some of his prize medals. Large metal
advertising signs
featuring the
logo and the
words 'Smoke
Garryowen Plug
it satisfies' were
a familiar sight
all over Ireland.

A 'Smoke Garryowen' enamel advertising sign, the Irish red setter
'Garryowen' wearing his champion's collar.
36.5in (92.5cm) wide
$800-950   **WHYT**

An enamel double-sided advertising
swinging sign, for Major.
39.25in (100cm) high
$350-400   **DA&H**

A framed chromolithograph poster,
advertising 'Wills Star cigarettes' in
original frame.
22.5in (57cm) wide
$250-350   **K&O**

ADVERTISING

A 1950s fibreglass advertising cow, from an Ashbourne ice cream shop, some damage to one ear.

$200-250   HAN

An early 20thC J&J Colman Ltd. advertising mirror, depicting King Edward VII, framed.

21.25in (54cm) high

$250-350   **LOCK**

A scratchbuilt wooden shop display model of a Bakery Articulated Lorry, advertising Cottage Loaf Bakery of Ipswich.

$60-80   **LSK**

A CLOSER LOOK AT A COLMAN'S SIGN

Established in 1814 and still operational today, Colman's is a desirable brand.

This wooden sign is in the form of a shield.

It depicts a tin of Colman's Mustard and a bull's head, which has been the company's trademark and logo since 1855.

This sign is believed to be the work of the painter A.J. Munnings (1878-1959), which adds to the value.

An early 20thC original Colman's Mustard wooden advertising sign, stamped to reverse 'J. & J. Colman, 108 Cannon Street, London E.C.'.

26in (66cm) high

$4,000-5,500   **LOCK**

An original 'Fry's Five Boys, Milk Chocolate' color lithograph advertising sign, on paper/card, contemporary framed and glazed.

J.S. Fry & Sons was founded in the mid-18thC and went on to become one of Britain's best-known chocolate companies. In 1847, Fry's produced the first solid chocolate bar. Their 'Five Boys' bar was released in 1902, with a wrapper depicting a boy's face in five differing expressions, 'Desperation', 'Pacification', 'Expectation', 'Acclamation', and 'Realization'. Fry's became a division of Cadbury's in 1919. The original Fry's factory closed down after the takeover of Cadbury's by Kraft Foods in 2010.

19.25in (49cm) high

$250-350   **LOCK**

A Royal Doulton 'Gordon Highlander' character jug, for Grants Whisky, still full (750ml @ 43% ABV) and with paper tab over red finial to Glengarry, Style One (four barrel handle), backstamped 'C', in its original red plush box with booklet.

This was issued in 1987 in a limited edition of 2,500 to commemorate the centenary of Grant's Whisky.

1987

$100-120   **FELL**

A late 19thC Huntley & Palmers Biscuits color advertising showcard, framed and glazed.

29.5in (75cm) high

$1,600-2,000   **LOCK**

An Art Deco hanging double-sided advertising clock, for Kingston Cream.

36.25in (92cm) high

$1,600-2,000   **DA&H**

A rare and possibly unique Royal Doulton flambé 'Old Crow' decanter.

This was originally made for Old Crow Kentucky Bourbon Whiskey, National Distillers Corp. The base is marked with a black patch cancelling the logo, there are several firing cracks and resulting hairlines to the base, and pock marks to the glaze from poor firing, these factory faults are possibly why the logo has been cancelled by the black patch of glaze.

c1954

$900-1,000   *12.25in (31cm) high*   **PW**

A mid-20thC plastic and cardboard Golly shop advertising figure, possibly for Robertson's, reading 'Golly it's good!', back of figure stamped 'Sal Display Colford Glos'.

17in (43cm) high

$100-120   **LOCK**

A mid-20thC cardboard shop display sign, reading 'Golly its good! Robertson's Mincemeat'.

19in (48.5cm) high

$150-200   **LOCK**

A CLOSER LOOK AT AN AIRCRAFT BISCUIT TIN

This is an extremely rare William Crawford & Sons A1 'Pride of London' airliner aircraft biscuit tin.

It would have been expensive in its day - hence the rarity.

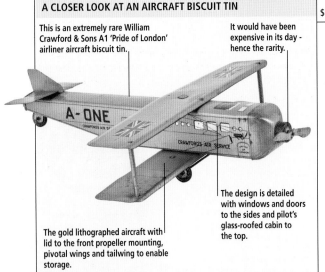

The gold lithographed aircraft with lid to the front propeller mounting, pivotal wings and tailwing to enable storage.

The design is detailed with windows and doors to the sides and pilot's glass-roofed cabin to the top.

A biscuit tin, by William Crawford & Son, with 'A-ONE Crawford's Air Service' to either side.

c1920

$2,000-2,500   *16.5in (42cm) long*   **MART**

A large Whitbread India Pale Ale advertising bottle, with paper label.

23in (59cm) high

$200-250   **TEN**

An original 'Wincarnis' color lithograph advertising sign, reading 'Wincarnis, The Wine of Life, Look Mummy Here Comes Your Wincarnis', glazed, with contemporary frame.

19.75in (50cm) high

$200-250   **LOCK**

A rare advertising brochure, 'MATCHMAKING', for Bryant and May, by the Curwen Press, color lithograph cover by Paul Nash (1889-1946), photographs by Francis Bruguière, text by E.P. Leigh-Bennett, 55 pages, minor marks, staples removed from spine.

1931   *13.25in (33.5cm) wide*

$550-600   **DW**

A Canterbury Belts Ltd. advertising figure, as a wooden handpainted Hussar.

26in (66cm) high

$400-450   **LOCK**

An original 'We Play Dunlop' golf advertising figure.

15.75in (40cm) high

$400-450   **APAR**

A Beswick pottery Dulux dog paint advertisement.

13in (35.5cm) high

$300-400   **HT**

ADVERTISING

QUICK REFERENCE - HMV

HMV has been a leading specialist retailer of music since the early 20thC. The company was founded in 1908 and its first shop opened in 1921. HMV stands for 'His Master's Voice', the name of the painting by Francis Barraud that HMV uses as its trademark. The painting, which depicts a dog listening to a gramophone, has also been used in a range of HMV advertising.

A mid-20thC jointed wooden Mazda valves Ediswan Radio advertising doll.

15in (38cm) high

$300-400   **LOCK**

An early 20thC HMV advertising cut out.

22.75in (58cm) wide

$200-250   **K&O**

An HMV Victrola advertising jigsaw, glazed and framed.

$80-100   **K&O**

ADVERTISING

An early 20thC HMV ('His Masters Voice') enamel advertising sign, some areas of restoration.

19.75in (50cm) wide

$350-400   K&O

An Irish Times enamel sign.

19.5in (49.5cm) wide

$350-400   WHYT

An original 'Jones' Sewing Machines enamel advertising sign, reading 'Busy'.

The Jones Sewing Machine Company was founded in 1860 by William Jones and Thomas Chadwick. Thomas Chadwick soon left the partnership, but Jones continued his work alongside his brother, John Jones, and by the 1890s they presided over one of the largest sewing machine factories in England. Today Jones survives as part of Brother Industries of Japan.

34.25in (87cm) wide

$550-600   LOCK

A painted pine double-sided trade sign, possibly made for Hotel Main in Washington, PA, USA which was then known as 'The Sign of the Crossed Keys', dated.

1826   *62in (157.5cm) high*

$2,000-2,500   POOK

A Penfold Golf Ball vulcanised rubber advertising figure and a reproduction 'We Play Dunlop' figure.

22in (56cm) high

$450-550 the two   TEN

A 1970s Power 3D forecourt plastic sign.

41.75in (106cm) high

$25-35   DA&H

A Royal Daylight Oil double-sided porcelain enamel advertising sign.

Royal Daylight Oil was used for cooking, heating and paraffin lamps.

21.75in (55cm) wide

$200-250   DA&H

QUICK REFERENCE - STEPHENS INK

Stephens' Ink Company was one of the most important ink producers of the 19thC and 20thC. It was founded by Dr Henry Stephens in 1832 and later inherited by his son, Henry Charles 'Inky' Stephens, MP for Hornsey and Finchley. Stephens was acquired by the Royal Sovereign Pencil Company Ltd. in 1967. The final Stephens factory closed in 1985. Stephens advertised widely in newspapers, in magazines, on bus tickets and outside high-street shops. Stephens advertising thermometers even made appearances in films such as 'Passport to Pimlico', 1949, and 'Brief Encounter', 1945. The Stephens Collection in Finchley holds a wide selection of Stephens artefacts and memorabilia.

A large tin enamel Stephens Inks shop advertising thermometer, signed by Jordan Bilston, numbered '5/14', small chips to the edges of the sign.

61.5in (156cm) high

$1,600-2,000   PW

A large late 19thC 'Sunlight Soap, £1000, Guarentee of Purity' enamel advertising sign.

36in (91.5cm) wide

$350-400   LOCK

An unusual milkmaid creamer, advertising Thomas Smith, dated, firing crack and restored handle.

1843   *11.5in (29cm) wide*

$300-400   K&O

A color lithographic publicity flyer, by Alphonse Mucha (1860-1939), for The West End Review, with an 8-page stapled booklet of press reviews for the West End Review, original printed boards in glassine dust jacket, torn without loss.

Mucha designed a poster for this magazine in 1897 that was one of his largest lithographic works, forming a nine-sheet poster measuring 10 feet by 7 feet. The periodical was published between June 1897 and September 1899 and this image was used for a number of the magazine's covers.

1898   *flyer 14in (36cm) high*

$1,300-1,500   DW

A late 19thC Weekly Telegraph enamel tin advertising sign, signed 'Alfred Leeseo'.

20.5in (51.5cm) high

$300-350   LOCK

An enamel advertising sign for 'WEBBS SEEDS, WORDSLEY STOURBRIDGE', some damage.

36.25in (92cm) high

$2,500-3,000   FLD

A double-sided porcelain enamel advertising sign, for 'White Rose Oil, Purest and Best', stamped 'P.3/34'.

21.75in (55cm) wide

$450-550   DA&H

QUICK REFERENCE - IRIDESCENCE

- The ancient Roman glass seen today often appears opaque, with marbled colors. However, it was not originally produced like this and most glass would have been clear in Roman times.
- Many Roman glass vessels were buried underground in the intervening centuries since their production, and long exposure to sand, soil, heat and minerals has caused iridescence. This creates the rainbow effect so often seen on the surface of ancient glass.
- The iridescence on ancient glass influenced many 20thC glass companies and designers, including Loetz, Lalique, Steuben and Tiffany.

An unguentarium glass bottle, possibly late Roman, with purple and green iridescence.

3.5in (9cm) high

$150-200 **ROS**

A Roman bottle, with open neck and bulbous body.

1st-3rdC AD   *2.5in (6.5cm) high*

$90-110 **LOCK**

A Roman glass bowl, of yellow color.

1st-3rdC AD   *6in (15cm) wide*

$80-100 **LOCK**

A Roman glass bowl, the iridescent bowl with wide lip and bowed base.

1st-3rdC AD   *4.75in (12cm) wide*

$250-350 **LOCK**

A Roman glass bottle, with iridescent color.

1st-3rdC AD   *3.25in (8cm) high*

$80-100 **LOCK**

A Roman candlestick-type glass unguentarium, excavated in the Phoenician/Sprian area, good patina and iridescence.

1stC AD   *5.25in (13cm) high*

$150-200 **HAN**

A Roman glass flask, excavated in the Phoenician/Spirian area, good patina and iridescence.

1stC AD   *6in (15cm) high*

$250-300 **HAN**

A Roman skillet with handle.

5in (3cm) diam

$350-400 **LOCK**

An Egyptian blue glazed ushabti figure, holding fly whisks, unnamed.

4in (10cm) high

$400-550 **GWA**

A pair of mid-4thC BC Gnathian-ware prochous, Greek/South Italy, one has been broken off at the neck and put back together, some wear to the black ground generally.

7.75in (19.5cm) high

$800-1,000 **DN**

A CLOSER LOOK AT A PENNY ARCADE MACHINE

This is a rare Edwardian Penny Arcade machine, 'The Belvedere', from the 1900s.

It is decorated with faded green velvet backing with silver Art Nouveau lilies.

It appears to be in working order, which increases the value.

The player inserts a penny to fire a ball-bearing along a steel track toward 7 cups: 5 are green for 'WIN', 2 red for 'LOSE'.

An Edwardian Penny Arcade machine, possibly produced in Saxony, glazed access door in an oak case with substantial brass fittings.

23.5in (59.5cm) high

$800-1,000   W&W

A rare 1900s Edwardian 'The Gypsy' Penny Arcade machine, the Gypsy surrounded by a dial showing the fortunes, requiring a penny to spin the fortune teller's wheel which randomly points to readings such as 'A Proposal', 'A Lover' or 'An offer of Marriage', apparently in working order.

23.5in (60cm) high

$650-800   W&W

An Edwardian 'The Clown' Penny Arcade machine, possibly produced in Saxony, product no.1566, operating a ball-bearing game involving the player moving a clown to catch the ball-bearing, apparently in working order.

c1905   23.5in (60cm) high

$130-200   W&W

QUICK REFERENCE - TABLE FOOTBALL

Early precursors to table football developed in the 1880s-90s in Spain, France, Germany and other European countries, where it was chiefly used as a parlor game. Table football as we know it today had developed by the 1920s. There is some disagreement over who invented table football, but Lucien Rosengart (1881-1976), Alejandro Finisterre (1919-2007) and Harold Searles Thornton are all thought to have produced early designs; Harold Searles Thornton patented his in the UK in November 1923. While table football games were produced in 1920s-30s, they did not achieve widespread popularity until the 1960s-70s, making this fairly early model rarer and more desirable.

A Brooklands Totalisator old penny-operated fruit machine, the die-cast front with traces of red and green paint and payout list, oak case and base and locking steel back with key.

24.75in (63cm) high

$650-800   DA&H

A 1920s-30s Italian table football, of wooden construction, with green linoleum, rubber, aluminum and other metals.

56in (142cm) long

$12,000-15,000   QU

ARCADE MACHINES

A mid-20thC table football game, probably Spanish, with painted metal figures, sloped pitch and coin operated mechanism, with applied brass plaque, 'Cordoba Football Table Barcelona', restored.

65.5in (166cm) long

$3,500-4,000

ROS

A 1950s British 'Strike'Em' Penny Arcade machine, involving the player firing a ball-bearing along a plated steel track that ends in 10 individual winning cups, all oak construction, apparently in working order.

35in (89cm) high

$1,600-2,000

W&W

A 20thC pinball machine, 'Cosmic Gunfight' later mounted in a polished steel frame.

The 'Cosmic Gunfight' pinball machine was produced by Williams Electronics Inc. in 1982. Williams Electronics released over 200 different arcade machines in the 1960s-80s. 'Cosmic Gunfight' allows four players to play at once. It was designed by Barry Oursler, with artwork by Doug Watson and Larry Day. It is estimated that about 1,000 'Cosmic Gunfight' pinball machines were built.

42.5in (108cm) wide

$800-1,000

BELL

A late 20thC 'Futbolin' stained oak table football game, probably Spanish, with painted metal players, sloping pitch to center circle and with coin operated mechanism.

68in (173cm) wide

$1,300-1,600

BELL

A Data East 'Star Trek' pinball machine, coin operated, on metal legs.

This pinball machine was produced 1991-92 by Data East Cooperation (also known as DECO), a Japanese video games and electronic engineering company that has been producing games since the 1970s. The 'Star Trek' pinball machine was designed by Joe Kaminkow and Ed Cebula, with artwork by Margaret Hudson and Kevin O'Connor. Approximately 4,400 were built.

1991   *52in (132cm) high*

$600-750

FLD

QUICK REFERENCE - FRANZ BERGMAN

- From the 19thC onward, the creation of bronze figures flourished in Vienna, Austria. Franz Bergman (1861-1939) was one of the most important makers.
- The Bergman factory was founded in 1860 by his father (also called Franz Bergman, 1838-94), and was taken over by Franz Bergman junior after his father's death.
- Bergman was one of the key instigators of the 'Vienna bronze boom' in the late 19thC and early 20thC. His factory produced a range of bronze sculptures, including Oriental figures, birds and animals, and a line of 'erotic' models. The bronzes were highly detailed and cold-painted with vibrant colors.
- Bergman bronzes were stamped with a capital 'B' within a twin-handled urn or vase. Like many other Austrian bronzes of the time, Bergman models were often inscribed 'Geschutzt', German for 'protected' or 'copyrighted'. Erotic figures were sometimes marked 'Namgreb', which is Bergman backward.

A late 19thC to early 20thC bronze figure of a female blackbird, by Franz Bergman, with maker's marks.

6.75in (17cm) long

$1,200-1,600   L&T

A matched pair of Austrian cold-painted bronze models of golden pheasants, by Franz Bergman, modeled as a cock and hen, both stamped 'B' in a vase.

c1920   *9in (23cm) high*

$1,600-2,000   BELL

An Austrian cold-painted bronze owl, probably by Franz Bergman, on an onyx base, marks obscured by base, some surface scratches.

c1930   *5.5in (14cm) high*

$1,600-2,000   BELL

A late 19thC to early 20thC Austrian cold-painted bronze bird inkwell, by Franz Bergman, modeled as a thrush, its neck hinged to reveal a ceramic liner, stamped 'BERGMAN', 'GESCHUTZT' twice and 'A59 459'.

6.75in (17cm) long

$900-1,000   WW

An early 20thC Austrian cold-painted bronze model of an eagle, by Franz Bergman, the underside stamped with a 'B' in a vase, 'GESCHUTZT' and numbered '4485'.

14.5in (37cm) wide

$2,500-3,500   WW

A cold-painted bronze model of a starling, by Franz Bergman, impressed marks to underside of tail feathers.

4.5in (11.5cm) high

$1,300-2,000   FLD

A cold-painted bronze model of a woodcock, by Franz Bergman, impressed mark to underside of tail feathers.

7in (17.5cm) high

$2,500-3,500   FLD

AUSTRIAN BRONZES

An early 20thC Austrian cold-painted orientalist bronze figure of an Arab, by Franz Bergman, stamped twice with 'B' in a vase and 'GESCHÜTZT 2746'.

4.25in (10.5cm) high

$900-1,100   WW

An Austrian cold-painted bronze seated figure, by Franz Bergman, on a wooden plinth, stamped mark 'Gesch', signs of paint loss.

2.75in (7cm) high

$200-250   HAN

An Austrian bronze figural candlestick, by Franz Bergman, in the form of a nude maiden, stamped with amphora 'B' mark, 'Gesch' and numbered '5070'.

8.25in (21cm) high

$800-950   ROS

An Austrian cold-painted bronze model of a nude maiden, by Franz Bergman, mounted on a shallow marble bowl, stamped 'B' in vase mark.

6.75in (17cm) high

$250-400   ROS

A 19thC Austrian cold-painted 'erotic' bronze figure, by Franz Bergman, in the form of a seated female reading a book.

5.5in (14cm) high

$1,600-2,000   HANN

A 19thC Austrian cold-painted bronze desk stand, by Franz Bergman, modeled as a female playing a harp.

15.75in (40cm) wide

$1,600-2,000   HANN

A 19thC Austrian cold-painted 'erotic' bronze figure, by Franz Bergman, modeled as an Arabic male holding a cloth and a cat, opening to reveal a nude female.

5.5in (14cm) high

$2,000-2,500   HANN

A 19thC Austrian cold-painted 'erotic' bronze figure, by Franz Bergman, modeled as an Arabic male holding a cloth, opening to reveal a nude female.

5.5in (14cm) high

$2,000-2,500   HANN

A late 19thC Austrian bronze grouse desk stand, by Rudolf Winder, the hinged tail opening to reveal twin inkwell recess, the hinged head enclosing a pen wipe, signed 'R. Winder'.

9.75in (25cm) high

$750-800   BELL

A late 19thC Austrian cold-painted bronze parrot.

11in (28cm) long

$1,700-2,000   SWO

An Austrian cold-painted bronze chaffinch, unmarked, minor casting flaw to breast.

3.5in (9cm) long

$250-400   FELL

An Austrian cold-painted bronze Cockatoo, stamped 'Geschutzt 33053', with Bergman vase stamp.

11.75in (30cm) high

$1,000-1,300   BE

A late 19thC to early 20thC Austrian cold-painted bronze grouse, stamped 'GESCHUTZT'.

3.5in (9cm) high

$450-600   WW

A late 19thC to early 20thC Austrian cold-painted bronze snipe, on a Blue John ashtray base.

4.75in (12cm) wide

$250-400   WW

A late 19thC to early 20thC Austrian cold-painted bronze bird and nest inkwell, the bird's neck hinged, stamped 'GESCHUTZT' and '29'.

6.75in (17cm) wide

$400-550   WW

An Austrian cold-painted bronze model of a bird.

8.25in (21cm) high

$250-350   LHA

AUSTRIAN BRONZES

An Austrian cold-painted bronze bulldog, unstamped, paint loss to head and upper body.

7in (18cm) long

$350-400   **BE**

A late 19thC Austrian cold-painted bronze vesta, cast as a cat upon a hinged barrel confronted by a terrier.

6in (15cm) wide

$850-900   **L&T**

An early 20thC Austrian cold-painted bronze and onyx inkstand, modeled with a pointer, with a pair of hinged inkwell compartments and a pen tray, on leather feet.

12.25in (31cm) long

$650-750   **WW**

A late 19thC Austrian cold-painted bronze hound desk paper clip, on a walnut base.

12.5in (32cm) long

$550-650   **BELL**

A late 19thC to early 20thC Austrian cold-painted fox, in the manner of Bergman, the underside of the tail stamped 'GESCHUTZT'.

7in (18cm) long

$1,000-1,200   **WW**

An Austrian cold-painted bronze and agate squirrel pin dish.

c1930   *3.5in (9cm) long*

$60-80   **HAN**

A late 19thC to early 20thC Austrian cold-painted bronze hind deer, the underside of its belly stamped 'GESCHUTZT'.

5.5in (14cm) long

$650-800   **WW**

A late 19thC to early 20thC Austrian bronze camel, the panniers on his back opening to reveal ink holders.

6in (15cm) high

$100-130   **ROS**

An Austrian cast bronze group of two Iguanas, on hardwood base.

6.25in (16cm) wide

$750-850   **ECGW**

An Austrian bronze model, 'Lovers Reclining', by Siegfried Charoux (1896-1967), signed 'Charoux' to the lower right.

14.25in (36cm) wide

$750-850   BELL

A CLOSER LOOK AT A SEIFERT BRONZE

This bronze figure is by Victor Heinrich Seifert (1870-1953).

He is more famous for his post-World War I sculptures, while his earlier bronzes are comparatively rare.

The figure is entitled 'Trinkendede Frauenakt', German for 'Nude Woman Drinking'.

She is presented on a circular bronze base and turned circular pink marble base.

A 19th/20thC Austrian bronze patinated figure of a nude maiden, signed.

27.25in (69cm) high

$4,500-5,500   ROS

A 19thC cold-painted bronze, after Waagen, modeled as an Arab girl leaning against an urn, on a marble base.

34in (86.5cm) high

$2,500-4,000   JN

An Austrian bronze figure of a snake dancer.

17.5in (44.5cm) high

$2,500-3,000   LHA

An Austrian cold cast group, man riding a camel, on a marble base.

15in (38cm) high

$350-400   JN

An Austrian cold-painted bronze lamp, cast as an Arabic woman, with palm tree shade.

c1900   *12.25in (31cm) high*

$900-1,100   L&T

An Austrian cold-painted bronze figural lamp.

16in (40.5cm) high

$3,500-4,000   LHA

An Austrian cold-painted bronze figural table lamp.

16in (40.5cm) high

$2,000-2,500   LHA

QUICK REFERENCE - AUTOMOBILIA

- Automobilia can refer to any motoring memorabilia. There is a market for car badges, fuel cans, advertising signs, scale models, car accessories, instruction manuals and much more. Car mascots, especially interwar Art Deco models, are also popular with collectors.
- Car mascots are small sculptural models fitted to the front of a car, often to the radiator grill. Car mascots were popular from the 1920s to 1950s. They were chiefly made of glass or metal, usually zinc, pewter or aluminum. They declined in popularity in the 1960s due to safety restrictions.
- While some car mascots were added by owners to personalize their cars, many were produced by car manufacturers themselves and fitted as standard to new models. Manufacturers commissioned sculptors and designers to create mascots to become part of the company's brand. Distinctive examples include the Ford greyhound, the Pakard swan and the Rolls Royce 'Spirit of Ecstasy'.
- For advertising automobilia, see pages 9-11.

A winged/flying 'B' car mascot, by Joseph Fray, fitted to Bentley Cars in the 1920s, stamped 'Jo's Fray B.Ham' to base.

6.75in (17cm) high

$250-350   ECGW

A 1920s 'Icarus' mascot, designed by Frederick Gordon Crosby, signed.

6in (15cm) high

$900-1,000   ECGW

A silvered bronze Hispano Suiza desk piece, 'Cicogne', by Frederick Bazin, modeled as a stylized stork, on a wooden base.

An example of this car mascot features in Dominique Pascal's 'Bouchons de Radiator' on the front cover and on page 247.

4.25in (11cm) high

$400-550   ECGW

A 'Leaping Lion' car mascot, on a seven-sided cap, stamped 'Inskip', offered with cars supplied by J.S. Inskip of New York, possibly re-plated.

6.25in (16cm) wide

$250-350   ECGW

A 1930s chrome leopard car mascot, by Desmo.

7.25in (18.5cm) wide

$350-400   APAR

A CLOSER LOOK AT A LALIQUE CAR MASCOT

'Coq Nain' was first introduced in February 1928 at the price of 440 francs.

It is modeled as a cockerel in a crouched pose with a high plumed tail.

The fine detail to the feathers would have been hand finished.

Despite a small chip to the tail, the price remains relatively high, as Lalique is a desirable maker.

A Rene Lalique car mascot, 'Coq Nain', no.1135, in a deep topaz tint, engraved marks.

7.75in (20cm) high

$2,000-2,500   FLD

A Rene Lalique 'Sanglier' molded smoke glass boar car mascot, stamped 'R. Lalique, France', small chips to snout.

During the 1920s and 30s, Lalique introduced a series of sculpted radiator covers and car mascots, featuring classical deities and animal figures. By 1932, Lalique was selling 46 different mascot designs. For other Lalique glass, see page 223.

2.25in (6cm) high

$1,300-1,600   ECGW

An 'Indian Lookout'/Scout car mascot, designed by Giulliaume Laplagne, signed.

4.75in (12cm) high excluding base

$1,300-2,000   ECGW

A 'La Renomée' Ballot Moteur car mascot, by Emile Edmond Peynot, France, the 'Trumpeting Angel' in silvered bronze, the tip of the trumpet able to unscrew.

1923-26   *4in (10cm) high*

$400-550   ECGW

A Rolls Royce 'Spirit of Ecstasy' car mascot, stamped 'R.R. Ltd. 6.2.11'.

1929-30   *4.75in (12cm) high*

$200-250   ECGW

A large 'Spirit of Ecstasy' figure, mounted on a marble base, probably used as a car showroom display model.

14.5in (37cm) high

$150-200   ECGW

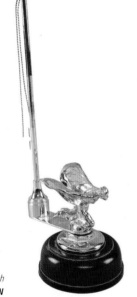

A Rolls Royce 'Schneider 56B Seaplane' mascot, marked 'Rolls Royce Ltd' on float.

1929   *4in (10cm) high*

$800-950   ECGW

A kneeling 'Spirit of Ecstasy' car mascot, incorporating a chrome-plated flag post.

13.75in (35cm) high

$1,000-1,300   ECGW

One of a pair of 1920s French 'Winged Sphinx' mascots, by Ruffony, mounted as a pair or bookends, plated hollow-cast white metal figure, each signed.

3.5in (9cm) high

$400-550 pair   ECGW

A 'Leaping Greyhound' car mascot, on a radiator cap, possibly from a 1930s Lincoln.

base 11in (28cm) wide

$550-650   ECGW

A late 1920s 'Pierce Arrow Archer' car mascot.

base 10.25in (26cm) wide

$550-650   ECGW

A 1920s 'British Girl Facing Wind' car mascot, also known as 'Windswept' or 'Goddess of Freedom'.

6in (15cm) high

$400-550   ECGW

A Jaguar 160 MPH Smiths speedometer, untested.
$150-200   DA&H

A pair of Morris Minor duotone front seats, in Porcelain Green and Beige.
c1962-64
$40-50   DA&H

An early 20thC 'King of the Road' car lamp, by Joseph Lucas Ltd. of Birmingham.
$130-200   WHP

A London Transport Buffer Stop lamp.
$70-80   LSK

A 1950s Sirram car picnic set for lunch and tea, fitted with plates, cutlery, whicker and glass bottles, a kettle and containers, with an ivorine plaque inscribed 'SIRRAM REGISTERED TRADE MARK M, LTD, B.', in a leatherette covered case with leather strap handles.
24.75in (63cm) wide
$650-800   WW

A Bugatti car radiator decanter, by Ruddspeed.
7.75in (20cm) high
$550-650   ECGW

A Ruddspeed Rolls Royce grill decanter, the reverse scratched 'Xmas 1965', with case.
case 7.75in (20cm) long
$350-400   DA&H

A model of the 'Ferrari Dino 268 SP' car, built by Modellismo Leonardo, in a 1:12 scale, no.112 of a limited edition of 499, in a Perspex display case.

The original car was driven by Pedro Rodriquez and competed in the Nurburgring 1000km in 1962.

17.25in (44cm) wide

$1,600-2,000   ECGW

A Javan Smith '1964 Ferrari 250 LM' hand built model car, in 1:8 scale, in a Perspex display case.

23.5in (60cm) wide

$1,600-2,000   ECGW

A Javan Smith hand built model of the iconic 'Sharknose' Ferrari 156 F1 car, hand signed by Phil Hill, in a special Phil Hill Perspex display case.

case 23.5in (60cm) wide

$2,500-3,500   ECGW

A model of the 'Mercedes W196' car, hand built, in 1:8 scale, in a Perspex display case.

22.75in (58cm) wide

$2,500-3,500   ECGW

A BARC Brooklands Member's car badge, stamped 'Spencer London', 'no.1019' and 'This Badge is the property of the Brooklands Automobile Racing Club'.   *4in (10cm) high*

$400-550   ECGW

A silver-plated inkwell, with fitted blue liner, mounted on wood stand, of Bentley car interest, flying 'B' motif to top.

$350-400   ECGW

A Rolls Royce silver-plated presentation piece, in the shape of a cap with braided peak, with a glass liner, engraved 'Rolls Royce Xmas 1925', the lid with a 'Spirit of Ecstasy' figure handle.

5in (13cm) high

$550-650   ECGW

QUICK REFERENCE - BOOKS

- First editions may have multiple print runs (or impressions), but the first print run will always be the most valuable. A copy from the first print run of a first edition of a hardback book is called a 'true' first edition.
- Paperback first editions can also be collectible but tend not to fetch as high prices.
- The quantity of the first print run of a book affects the value of its first editions. Iconic and famous titles may well be sought-after, but more obscure works or those from an author's early career, which were printed in smaller quantities, are often more expensive.
- There are several ways of identifying a first edition. Check that the publishing date and copyright date match, and confirm the original publishing date and publisher with a reliable source. Look for the number '1' in the series of numbers on the imprint/copyright page.
- An author's signature often adds value to a first edition. Personal dedications are less desirable, unless the recipient is famous or connected to the author.
- Condition is important. The first editions that fetch the highest prices are undamaged and come with the original dust jacket. A hardback missing the dust jacket can be worth as little as half the price of a hardback with the dust jacket intact. If the price has been 'clipped' or cut away from the jacket, this can also reduce the price.

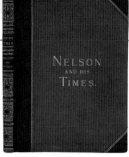

Beresford, Lord Admiral Charles and Wilson, H.W. 'NELSON AND HIS TIMES', published by Harmsworth, London, with marbled endpapers, quarter calf red morocco binding with gilt titles and decoration.
1897   *13in (33cm) high*
$600-750   CM

Bruce, Leo, 'Case Without a Corpse', first edition, published by Geoffrey Bles, price-clipped, a little rubbed and soiled.
1937
$450-550   DW

Chadwick, Philip George, 'The Death Guard', first edition, published by Hutchinson & Co., 52 pages, publisher's catalog at end, some spotting and toning, inscribed to front endpaper: 'To Roy, Boom! Zuzzoo-oo! Not even Trenchmen could stop this other idea of yours! Philip'.

'Apocalyptic science fiction horror novel of the creation of artificial life. The discovery is used to build a huge army of synthetic troops. The novel enjoys a reputation of being a superior work of its kind. It is, however, an exceedingly uncommon book; in all probability, most of the stock was destroyed in the blitz.' - George Locke, 'Spectrum of Fantasy I', page 49.
1939
$2,000-2,500   DW

Burroughs, William, 'The Naked Lunch', first edition, published by Olympia Press, Paris, 'Francs 1500' on back cover, fraying to ends of spine and edge of covers.
1950
$450-600   BLO

Christie, Agatha, 'The Body in the Library', first edition, crease mark to page 49, previous owner inscriptions '1944' at front, professionally restored dust jacket.
1942
$350-450   DW

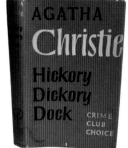

Christie, Agatha, 'Hickory Dickory Dock', first edition, published by Collins, London, inscribed by the author 'for Len with love from Agatha', in stained dust wrapper.
1955
$1,700-2,000   CHEF

Dickens, Charles, 'The Posthumous Papers of the Pickwick Club', first edition in the original 19/20 parts, published by Hatton & Cleaver, engraved title and 42 plates, lacking almost all advertisements, with some repair and restoration, green morocco-backed box, 8vo.

The first edition original serialized parts of Victorian novels tend to fetch higher prices than the first bound book-form editions. A first book-form edition of 'The Pickwick Papers' would likely fetch $250-500.
1836-37
$1,000-1,300   BLO

Dostoyevsky, Fyodor, 'Crime and Punishment: A Russian Realistic Novel', first English language edition, published by Vizetelly & Co., no.XIII in Vizetelly's One-Volume Novels series.

This was found by the vendor in a job lot of books acquired elsewhere at auction for £14 ($20). This 1885 first English language edition was probably translated from the Russian by the Russian-born but British-nationalized novelist Frederick Wishaw. It was also published in the USA in the same year. Only one copy of either version has been seen at auction and that was 25 years ago.
1886
$20,000-24,000 DW

Judith Picks

This is just a little glimpse into the involvement of T.S. Eliot in his plays, which have always been inspirational. T.S. Eliot had a minor correspondence with Miss Woodliffe which appears in the collected letters of T.S. Eliot volume 6. She was an actress and a receipt to her addressed to Sadler's Wells Theatre in London is included with this book. 'The Rock' was written as part of a fundraising campaign to assist the Forty-Five Churches Fund to build new churches in London's suburbs. 'The Rock' expresses Eliot's thoughts on community and tradition which he later elaborated more famously in, for example, 'Murder in the Cathedral'.

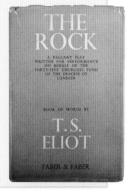

Eliot, T.S., 'The Rock: A Pageant Play', published by Faber & Faber, inscribed to Miss Phyllis Woodliffe, who had played the part of 'Mrs Bert' in the play, signed and dated by T.S. Eliot.
1934
$1,000-1,200 APAR

Durrell, Lawrence, 'Justine', first edition, a few light spots to foredges, original cloth, price-clipped dust jacket, fading to spine.
1957
$900-1,100 DW

Fleming, Ian, 'Thunderball', first edition, published by Jonathan Cape, London, hard cover with dust jacket, outer dust jacket design by Richard Chopping, some wear, torn.
1961
$400-550 MOR

Fleming, Ian, 'The Man with the Golden Gun', first edition, published by Jonathan Cape, London, hard cover with dust jacket, dust jacket design by Richard Chopping.
1965
$250-400 MOR

Fleming, Ian, 'The Spy Who Loved Me', first edition, original cloth, dust jacket, one or two light spots to rear panel, 8vo.
1962
$750-850 DW

Fleming, Ian, 'Octopussy and the Living Daylights', published by Jonathan Cape, London, hard cover and dust jacket, dust jacket designed by Richard Chopping.
1966
$130-200 MOR

Greene, Graham, 'The Name of Action', first edition, second issue, 3/6 dust jacket, a few minor spots, chip and loss at head of spine and upper panel.
This is the author's second novel. It was so poorly received by critics that Greene refused to let the publishers reprint it. 'The Name of Action' has been out of print since the 1930s and is a rare find.
1930
$1,300-2,000 DW

Hughes, Ted, 'The Hawk in the Rain', first edition, published by Faber & Faber.

This is the author's first book.
1957
$400-550 DW

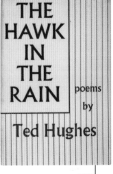

BOOKS

Joyes, James, 'Ulysses', published by Slocum & Cahoon A23, one of 900 copies on japon vellum paper.
1936
$1,200-1,500   BLO

Joyce, James, 'Finnegans Wake', first edition, published by Faber & Faber, some spotting to endpapers.
1939
$1,000-1,200   DW

Spark, Muriel, 'The Go-Away Bird, with Other Stories', first edition, published by Macmillan & Co. Ltd., London, inscribed by Spark 'Lots of love to dear Dad & Mum from Muriel', dust-jacket not price clipped but with some soiling and light wear.
1958
$11,500-12,000   L&T

Judith Picks

Being a Scot I could hardly not love the brilliantly written 'The Prime of Miss Jean Brodie', published in 1961, which is probably Muriel Spark's best-known novel. She reminds me of many teachers at the Galashiels Academy I attended in the 1960s. The book focuses on the character of Miss Jean Brodie, the fascinating and eccentric 1930s schoolmistress of Marcia Blaine School, who dazzles her pupils with her glamour and ideals. Miss Jean Brodie is said to have been based partly on Christina Kay, one of Spark's schoolteachers at James Gillespie's School for Girls in Edinburgh.

This is a very special copy. It is a first edition, with cover art by Victor Reinganum (1907-95), who illustrated the dust jackets of several of Spark's books. Still more importantly, it is dedicated to Spark's son, Samuel 'Robin' H.L. Spark, from whom she later became estranged. The front reads 'To Robin, Love & wonkies Mummy xxx'.

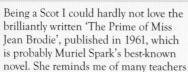

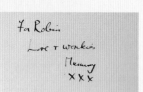

Spark, Muriel, 'The Prime of Miss Jean Brodie', first edition, published by Macmillan & Co. Ltd., London, original green cloth gilt, some soiling and bumping to the dust jacket.
1961
$30,000-35,000   L&T

QUICK REFERENCE - MURIEL SPARK AND ROBIN

This was Muriel Spark's first novel and this copy comes from the estate of the late Mr Samuel H.L. Spark, known as Robin, the son Muriel bore in 1938 during an unhappy, short-lived marriage. Most of the books in Robin's large collection were inscribed either to her parents or to Robin. Muriel Spark later broke of all relations with her son Robin and disinherited him. The fact that Muriel had converted to Catholicism, whereas Robin adopted his grandparents' orthodox Judaism, was one early cause of the breakdown, and Muriel also accused him of seeking publicity in their relationship to advance his career as a painter. Matters continued to deteriorate and long before her death in Italy in 2006, Muriel had made certain that Robin would not be a beneficiary of her estate and instead left her substantial fortune to Penelope Jardine, her companion of many years.

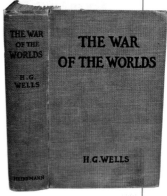

Spark, Muriel, 'The Comforters', first edition, published by Macmillan & Co. Ltd., London, 8vo, inscribed by Spark to front free-endpaper 'Robin with love from Mummy Feb. 1957' and signed 'Muriel Spark' to title-page.
1957
$4,000-4,500   L&T

Spark, Muriel, 'The Ballad of Peckham Rye', first edition, published by Macmillan & Co. Ltd., London, inscribed by Spark to 'Robin darling - This is your book - with love from Mummy' and signed 'Muriel Spark'.
1960
$10,000-11,500   L&T

Wells, H.G., 'The War of the Worlds', first edition, first issue, published by Heinemann, London, inscribed by the author to E.J. Sullivan, with signed angelic caricature by Wells below.

Provenance: E.J. Sullivan and then by family descent. Edmund Joseph Sullivan (1869-1933) was a British book illustrator, known for his illustrations of Thomas Carlyle's 'Sartor Resartus' in 1898 and of Well's 'A Modern Utopia' in 1905.
1898
$20,000-27,000   CHEF

Anderson, Anne, (illustrator), 'The Fairy Tales of Grimm & Anderson', published by Collins Clear Type Press, 16 color plates, tear and loss at top margin of rear panel, light creasing and one or two nicks.
c1930
$400-550   DW

Caroll, Lewis (AKA Dodgson, Charles Lutwidge), 'Alice's Adventures in Wonderland', illustrated by Harry Rountree, ink inscription, 92 color illustrations including 14 full-page illustrations.
1908
$1,300-2,000   FOR

Crompton, Richmal, 'Just - William', first edition, published by George Newnes Ltd., London, illustrations by Thomas Henry, 4 pages advertisements at rear, extremities of cover lightly bumped and scuffed, the dust-jacket creased, soiled and browned.

This 1922 publication was the book that launched the famous William series, which went on to feature 38 books between the 1920s-70s. First editions are exceedingly rare. Another copy was sold for £260 ($350) at Donhams in 2010, but no other first editions of 'Just - William' have been sold within the last 40 years.
c1922   *6.75in (17cm) high*
$2,000-2,500   TOV

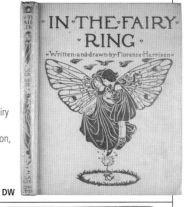

The Brothers Grimm, 'Hansel and Gretel and Other Stories', published by Hodder and Stoughton, signed and illustrated by Kay Nielsen, limited edition, numbered '133/600', 12 mounted color and 10 black and white plates, 276 pages.
c1925
$2,500-4,000   PSA

Harrison, Florence, 'In the Fairy Ring: Written and drawn by Florence Harrison', first edition, published by Blackie & Son, twenty-four colored plates.
1908
$900-1,000   DW

Kipling, Rudyard, 'Just So Stories, for little children', first edition, published by Macmillan and Co., London, 22 plates, original cloth, repairs to plate verso, pages 81, 95 and 178-9 with sellotape.
1902
$250-400   L&T

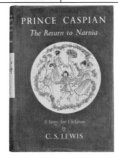

Lewis, C.S., 'Prince Caspian', first edition, color frontispiece and illustrations by Pauline Bayney, professionally restored.

The Chronicles of Narnia, by C.S. Lewis (1898-1963), were published 1950-56 and consisted of seven books set in the fantasy world of Narnia. The series enjoys continual success today, with 'The Lion, The Witch and the Wardrobe' perhaps the most popular.
1951
$1,000-1,200   DW

Lewis, C.S., 'The Voyage of the Dawn Treader', first edition, illustrations by Pauline Baynes, one or two light spots, price-clipped professionally restored, 8vo.
1952
$900-1,100   DW

Milne, A.A., 'When we were very Young', first edition, second issue (with 'ix' printed on relevant page), published by Methuen, London, illustrations by E.H. Shepard, 'presentation copy' stamp on title.
1924
$550-650   L&T

Milne, A.A., 'The House At Pooh Corner', first edition, published by Methuen, with decorations by Ernest H. Shepard.
1928
$550-650   DW

QUICK REFERENCE - BEATRIX POTTER

Helen Beatrix Potter (1866-1943) was an English writer and illustrator. She learnt to draw and paint from an early age, practising by painting her family pets, two rabbits named Benjamin Bouncer and Peter Piper. After several rejections from publishers, Potter published her first book, 'The Tale of Peter Rabbit' herself, printing 250 copies with the private printers Strangeways. The book's success encouraged Frederick Warne & Co. to publish her. They reprinted 'The Tale of Peter Rabbit' in color in 1902. Potter then returned to Strangeways and paid for a private edition of 500 copies of 'The Tailor of Gloucester' to be printed. It was re-published by Warne the following year, alongside 'The Tale of Squirrel Nutkin'. Beatrix Potter remains one of the world's best-loved children's authors today.

Potter, Beatrix, 'The Story of Miss Moppet', first edition, first issue, 'London & New York' on the back of wallet, comprising 14 color illustrations.

This is a scarce variant red binding. As the model for Miss Moppet, Potter borrowed a kitten belonging to a local mason. She wrote in a letter, 'It is very young and pretty and a most fearful pickle.'
1906
$2,500-3,500   FOR

Potter, Beatrix, 'The Roly-Poly Pudding', first edition, second impression, published by Frederick Warne & Co., London.
1908
$200-250   KEY

Potter, Beatrix, 'The Tailor of Gloucester', first privately printed edition, published by Strangeways, color frontispiece and fifteen color plates, inscribed 'For Mr Carr from Leslie Linder July 27th 1970'.

Provenance: Given by Leslie Linder to the current owner's husband in the 1970s in lieu of payment - at his request - for legal work which he carried out for Beatrix Potter's bibliographer. Only 500 copies of this book were printed. This Strangeways edition differs considerably in both text and illustration from Warne's later edition of 1903. Of all her books 'The Tailor of Gloucester' remained Beatrix Potter's own favorite.
1902
$6,500-8,000   DW

QUICK REFERENCE - HARRY POTTER

- To date, over 450 million copies of the Harry Potter books have sold worldwide, in over 79 languages. Rare and first edition Harry Potter books are now highly collectible.
- First editions, especially of the 'Harry Potter and the Philosopher's Stone' and 'Harry Potter and the Chamber of Secrets', can be very valuable. Editions with rare covers, limited editions, large-print or proof editions, are highly sought-after. First foreign editions can also be valuable.
- J.K. Rowling's signature immediately increases the value of a Harry Potter book. A signed first edition of 'Harry Potter and the Philosopher's Stone' recently sold at Bonhams for a record £106,250 ($140,000). Collectors should always be wary of fake signatures.
- The most valuable Harry Potter book is the first impression of the first hardback edition of the first book. Only 500 of these were published, 300 of which went straight into libraries. They can be identified by the number sequence '10 9 8 7 6 5 4 3 2 1' in the imprint page, the crediting of 'Joanne Rowling', not 'J.K. Rowling', and the repetition of

'1 wand' on page 53. This last error occurs in multiple printings but was corrected in later editions.
- 26 June 2017 marked the 20-year anniversary of the publication of the first Harry Potter book.

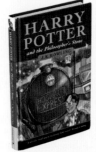

Rowling, J.K., 'Harry Potter and the Philosopher's Stone', first edition, first issue, with '1 wand' mistakenly appearing twice in list on page 53, original pictorial boards.
1997
$70,000-80,000   BLO

Robinson, W. Heath, 'The Adventures of Uncle Lubin', first edition, published by Grant Richards, color frontispiece.

This was the author's first book.
1902
$900-1,100   DW

Smith, Dodie, 'The Hundred and One Dalmatians', published by Heinemann, London, first edition, illustrated by Janet and Anne Grahame-Johnstone.
1956
$200-250   L&T

Spark, Muriel, 'The Very Fine Clock', first edition, Alfred A. Knopf, New York, inscribed by Spark to an initial leaf, 'Love to Very Fine Robin from his Mum. xxx Edinburgh 16th October 1968'.

Provenance: From the estate of the Late Mr Samuel H.L. Spark, known as Robin (see page 32).
1968
$6,500-8,000   L&T

Wain, Louis, 'Two Cats at Large, A Book of Surprises', with verses by Sidney Chawner Woodhouse, first edition, George Routledge, London, with 20 large colored illustrations.

See page 297 for examples of Louis Wain postcards.
1910
$350-400   KEY

'The New Adventures of Rupert', first edition, published by Daily Express Publications, the first Rupert Bear annual, duotone illustrations.
1936
$250-400   DW

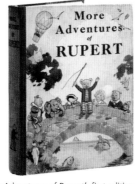

'More Adventures of Rupert', first edition, published by Daily Express Publications, the second Rupert Bear annual, duotone illustrations.
1937
$200-250   DW

Lee, Robert, and Tyndall, Robert, 'Noddy taking Mr Marvel Monkey to the police station', a 20thC watercolor, showing Noddy in his car with Mr Marvel Monkey outside the police station, with Big Ears and Mr Plod, and Miss Fluffy Cat and Sally Skittle.
1957   *7in (17.5cm) high*
$450-550   DW

BOXES

QUICK REFERENCE - BOXES

- Although the market for traditional 'brown' furniture from the Georgian and Victorian periods is going through a difficult time, the prices of smaller pieces have remained steady. Antique boxes, being useful as well as decorative, remain popular purchases.
- Value depends on the type of box, its age, condition and the quality of its materials and craftsmanship. Look for decorative appeal and unusual patterns and forms.
- Tea caddies tend to fetch the highest prices. Most on the market are from the 18thC and 19thC, when it was common to lock up tea to prevent spillage or theft by servants. Tea was still a relative luxury, meaning that many tea caddies were produced to high standards and made of expensive materials such as ivory, tortoiseshell and exotic woods.
- It is always worth checking the condition of boxes carefully. Replaced locks, panels or hinges can reduce the value. Prestigious makers or high-quality locks often add value, so examine locks, makers' names or labels carefully.

A 18thC black japanned tea caddy, the interior with three divisions, with a secret base drawer.

10in (25.5cm) wide

$400-550   WW

A George III satinwood and marquetry inlaid tea caddy, crossbanded in rosewood, the interior fitted with twin lidded compartments.

8.25in (21cm) wide

$600-650   MOR

A George III papier mâché tea caddy, attributed to Henry Clay, with a lidded interior.

Henry Clay (d.1812) was an 18thC artist and inventor. He founded Clay & Company in 1770 and developed a new and more durable form of papier mâché. This 'heat-resisting paperware', patented in 1772, could be carved, cut, lacquered and japanned just like wood or metal. Clay was also a key figure in Birmingham's japanning industry. Japanning was the process of varnishing and decorating a papier mâché piece to create a shiny black surface, which could then be painted.

4.75in (12cm) wide

$1,300-1,600   WW

A George III ivory tea caddy, inlaid with tortoiseshell stringing, with a part foil lined interior with a tortoiseshell lid, the front with a painting of a lady beside a tomb within a silver mount.

5in (12.5cm) high

$1,600-2,000   WW

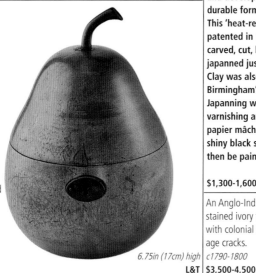

A late 18thC George III fruitwood pear-shaped tea caddy, with a stem finial and metal escutcheon.

6.75in (17cm) high

$1,500-2,500   L&T

An Anglo-Indian Vizagapatam stained ivory tea caddy, decorated with colonial buildings in landscapes, age cracks.

c1790-1800   *11in (28cm) wide*

$3,500-4,500   BE

A Regency tortoiseshell tea caddy, with two covered tea wells with ivory knop handles.

6in (15cm) wide

$650-800   L&T

An early 19thC tortoiseshell tea caddy, two lidded compartments within, some minor defects.

6.5in (16.5cm) wide

$550-650   KEY

An early Victorian tortoiseshell tea caddy, opening to reveal two lidded compartments, on bun feet.

10in (25.5cm) wide

$900-1,100   L&T

An early 19thC shagreen dressing table case, fitted with plated jars and tools.

11.75in (30cm) wide

$250-350   **FLD**

An Edwardian silver and tortoiseshell quatrefoil dressing table trinket box, by J. Batson & Son, London, slight play to the hinge.

1906   *8.25in (21cm) wide*

$650-800   **DN**

An Edwardian silver and tortoiseshell dressing table trinket box, by Ollivant & Botsford, London.

1908   *7.5in (19cm) long*

$1,000-1,300   **DN**

An Edwardian silver and tortoiseshell dressing table trinket box, by William Comyns & Sons, London.

1910   *6.25in (16cm) wide*

$900-1,100   **DN**

An Edwardian silver mounted jewelry box, hallmarked for A. & J. Zimmerman Ltd., Birmingham, hallmarks noticeably worn.

1908   *3.5in (9cm) long*

$70-80   **FELL**

An Edwardian silver mounted jewelry box, hallmarked for George Nathan & Ridley Haynes, Birmingham.

1906   **FELL**

$200-250

A George V silver dressing table box, Birmingham, indistinct maker's mark.

1918   *7.25in (18.5cm) wide*

$300-400   **MOR**

A 1920s silver mounted jewelry or trinket box, the circular body with hinged cover, decorated with aqua green guilloché enamel, hallmarked for Albert Carter, Birmingham, hallmarks worn.

1925   *3.5in (9cm) diam*

$350-400   **FELL**

A silver mounted jewelry or trinket box, decorated with green guilloché enamel, hallmarked for Adie Brothers Ltd., Birmingham, hallmarks worn but legible, hinge pin out to one side.

1931   *3.25in (8cm) diam*

$250-300   **FELL**

QUICK REFERENCE - SEWING BOXES

Until the second half of the 20thC, sewing was a large part of the lives of many upper and middle class women. Baskets and boxes for holding thread, pincushions, thimbles and other sewing tools would have been common. In the 18thC, the demand for finely made sewing boxes for wealthy ladies lead to the production of impressive boxes made from rare woods, leather, ivory or precious metals. In the mid-19thC, industrialization and the increasing numbers of the middle classes prompted the production of less expensive and more durable sewing boxes.

A George III mahogany and walnut sewing box, the lid with central color print of a cherub and sleeping child, original paper lining with removable pin cushion, needle book and ivory acorn tape measure.

7.25in (18.5cm) wide

$250-350   BLEA

A rosewood sewing box, with a central painted panel of a woman, over a matching lidded and compartmentalized tray, with key.

c1830   10in (25.5cm) wide

$350-400   BLEA

A 19thC Vizagapatam ivory sewing box, with black line decoration, the cover opening to reveal a compartmentalized interior.

$450-600   FLD

A rosewood Tunbridge ware sewing box, with panels and bandings in stickware, the interior with ruched silk panel, over a compartmentalized tray, with box form pincushion.

c1840   8.75in (22cm) wide

$550-600   BLEA

An early 19thC Palais Royal sewing box, in painted tin with gilt-metal mounts, the lid lined with a mirror over a velvet flush fitted tray, with mother-of-pearl accessories: a folding rule, a pair of scissors, a pair of reels, a matched needlecase with gilt and enamel pansy motif, a thimble, a matched writing pen, a cut glass scent bottle, and two reel tops, with key.

Palais Royal refers to the area of Paris around the Royal Palace, which in the 18thC and 19thC specialized in the production of small and elaborate art objects. Palais Royal sewing boxes and tools were often intricately carved or engraved and incorporated mother-of-pearl elements. Some wares were marked with a small gilt and enamel motif of a blue pansy against a gold background. The quality of workmanship on Palais Royal items is usually very high.

7.75in (19.5cm) wide

$600-650   BLEA

An early 19thC painted Tunbridge ware reel box, in the form of a cottage, the sliding lid revealing paper lined interior with divisions.

3.75in (9.5cm) wide

$2,500-3,500   BLEA

Judith Picks

What I love about these rare early Tunbridge ware boxes is the imagination that went into the design and the exquisite detail. This cottage has five diamond trellis windows and a stable door with two trees to the front, the sides and back with conforming decoration below a tiled pitched roof with chimney. It is the perfect depiction of a rural idyll, transported into an upper class drawing room.

An early 19thC painted Tunbridge ware sewing box, the blue painted interior lacking divisions, fitted with a drawer to one end.

6in (15cm) wide

$4,500-5,500   BLEA

BOXES

A CLOSER LOOK AT A SEWING BOX

This sewing box is in the novelty shape of a grand piano. The frame is made of flame mahogany, the keyboard of ivory.

When opened, it plays two melodies after Chopin.

The interior is fitted with a mirror to the lid and a purple velvet tray to the base.

The tray contains an embroidered pincushion, a quiver-form needlecase, a stiletto, a tambour hook, steel scissors, tweezers, a thimble, a reel, two pairs of snowflake winders, a pearl-handled folding knife and a cut glass scent bottle.

A good Palais Royal-style musical sewing box, in the form of a grand piano, one pair of scissors lacking, the musical movement stamped 'M. Bordier / 10365', with key.

c1840   *11.5in (29cm) long*

$1,000-1,300   **BLEA**

A Victorian mahogany sewing box, with a pull-out fitted tray, with six mother-of-pearl and bone cotton reels, various mother-of-pearl implements, cotton winders, a thimble and other bone and ivory pieces.

10.75in (27.5cm) wide

$450-550   **WW**

A mid-Victorian papier mâché sewing box, painted with flowers, the interior with original lidded and compartmentalized tray in red silk and velvet with a selection of tools and accessories, lock stamped 'VR Patent', with key.

12in (30.5cm) wide

$400-550   **BLEA**

A papier mâché book form sewing box, commemorating The Great Exhibition of 1851, titled tooled leather spine, the lid with reverse glass panel depicting the exhibition building, the compartmentalized interior in red silk and paper with a few accessories.

8.75in (22.5cm) long

$400-550   **BLEA**

A late Victorian papier mâché sewing box, with gilt and mother-of-pearl decoration, the interior in paper and silk with tool card with some mother-of-pearl and other tools, with key.

9.75in (25cm) wide

$200-250   **BLEA**

A French split and colored straw work sewing box, the lid with a house, the interior with two pin cushions and three floral decorated lids, one dated, general losses and wear.

1883   *8.5in (21.5cm) wide*

$60-100   **BLEA**

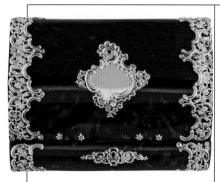

A late Victorian silver-mounted tortoiseshell stationery casket and matching blotting folder, by William Comyns & Sons, London.

1897   *11.25in (29cm) wide*

$900-1,000   DN

A Victorian inlaid walnut Tunbridge ware-style walnut writing box, with fitted interior.

11.75in (30cm) wide

$80-100   FLD

A Victorian inlaid amboyna writing box, with white metal cartouche, inscribed to 'Norman Liversidge from his Uncle and Aunt George 29th November 1890', interior fitted with tooled blue velvet writing surface.

16.25in (41cm) wide

$150-200   MOR

An 18thC fruitwood bible box, the front later hinged.

$50-60   MOR

An Art Deco-style cigarette box, inlaid in amboyna with ivory borders.

$80-100   MOR

9in (23cm) wide

An A.E. Jones copper cigarette box and cover, set with enamel roundel, cedar lined, unsigned.

6in (15cm) wide

$250-400   WW

A late 18thC French tortoiseshell snuff box, with engine turned decoration and gold mounts, with a shell thumbpiece.

2.25in (6cm) wide

$650-800   WW

An early 19thC mahogany apothecary's box, with fitted interior with fourteen glass bottles and stoppers, with various labels and with a drawer containing a glass pestle and mortar and a set of scales.

9.5in (24cm) high

$650-800   WW

A pair of late 18thC George III mahogany knife boxes, with chequer banding and boxwood line inlay, with silvered mounts and brass handles to the sides, with void interiors.

15.75in (40cm) high

$800-950 **L&T**

A late 19thC rosewood and brass mounted box, the interior later fitted with two silver lidded boxes and a bottle, hallmarks for London.

1861 *6.5in (16.5cm) wide*

$200-250 **BLEA**

A late 19thC Anglo-Indian ebony and ivory box, probably Bombay.

5in (12.5cm) wide

$350-400 **WW**

A burr maple string box, in the form of an apple with a brass stalk.

4.75in (12cm) high

$550-650 **WW**

A Victorian novelty oak box, modeled as a dog kennel, with a cast metal panel modeled as the head of a dog, some splitting.

8.75in (22cm) high

$250-350 **FELL**

An Austro-Hungarian silver and enamel box, Austro-Hungarian hallmarks for Vienna.

c1872-1922 *1.75in (4.5cm) diam 1.87oz*

$150-200 **FELL**

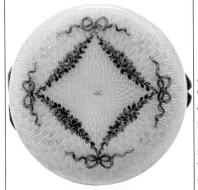

A Continental silver and enameled box, stamped '800', in a fitted box.

2.25in (5.5cm) diam

$450-550 **BE**

An early 19thC French Vernis Martin box, decorated with flowers.

Vernis Martin was a kind of japanning or lacquer used widely in 18thC and early 19thC France to decorate furniture and smaller items such as fans and boxes. It was developed chiefly by the Martin family, an 18thC French family of artists. It was designed to imitate East Asian lacquer and was produced in several colors, most distinctively green and golden red.

2.25in (6cm) diam

$150-200 **BLEA**

An early 19thC gold-mounted ivory toothpick box, with three toothpicks.

c1800-20 *3.25in (8cm) long*

$200-250 **WW**

QUICK REFERENCE - LEICA

- In 1849 in Wetzlar, Germany, Carl Kellner founded the Optical Institute to produce optical microscopes. It was later taken over by Ernst Leitz, who renamed the company Ernst Leitz Optical Institute.
- In 1914, Leitz developed its first camera, the Ur-Leica. It was invented by designer Oskar Barnack and was the first fully functional camera using 35mm perforated film. This was much smaller than the film used in earlier cameras; negatives were produced at a reduced size, then expanded when developed.
- A revised version of this camera, the Leitz Camera or Leica, was released to the public in 1925. The Leica camera was compact and portable, and featured mechanisms to prevent overexposure, ensuring that the camera could be used outdoors.
- Since the early 20thC, Leica has been a leading figure in the development of photography and camera technology. It is still operational today.

A Leica I camera, serial no.65670, with Hektor f=5cm.1:2,5 lens.
1931
$750-800   APAR

A Leica IIIg camera, serial no.880330, with Leitz Wetzlar Summitar f2, 50mm lens.
$650-800   TEN

A Leica Leitz Wetzlar Leicaflex camera, serial no.1172797, with a 1:2/50 lens no.2191536, with original case.
$250-350   LOCK

A Leica II (model D), camera, with Leitz Elmar 1:3.5 F=50mm lens, with associated leather case.
1933
$400-450   CHEF

A Leica III camera, serial no.139142, with Jupiter-8 lens, in associated leather case.
1934
$200-250   APAR

A Leica IIIA camera, serial no.193057, with a Elmar f=5cm 1:3, 5 lens, with lens cap.
1936
$200-250   APAR

A Leica IIIB camera, serial no.288134, with a Summar f=5cm 1:2, no.484347 lens.
1938-39
$250-350   APAR

A Leica IIIF camera, serial no.605089, with a Summarit f=5cm 1:1,5 Nr.951650 lens, in a leather case.
1951-52
$550-600   APAR

A CLOSER LOOK AT A LEICA LENS

The Thambar is a rare lens. It was produced by Leica 1934-40 and only 3,000 or so were ever made.

The serial number '226247' indicates that this particular lens was made within the first year of production.

The lens is in good condition, with the original lens cap present, which increases the value.

If the lens was in an original branded box, it would fetch an even higher price.

A Leica Ernst Leitz Wetzlar Thambar lens f=9cm 1:2,2 no.226247.
c1934
$3,000-3,500   APAR

A Bolex H16 Reflex 16mm cine camera.
$550-600   CHEF

A Contaflex TLR camera, serial no.Y84316, with Carl Zeiss Jena Sonnar f/1.5 50mm lens.
$900-1,000   GWA

A Corfield Periflex camera, with screw fit Lumar 1:3.5/50 lens, with ever-ready case, the mechanism seized up and unable to shoot.
$200-250   PW

A Gandolfi mahogany plate-camera, with a C.P. Goerz, Berlin lens, lenses marked 'No. 320869' with ivory plaque to front 'Gandolfi, London, Patent', with one dark slide and a box of Ilford Chrome Plates.
$550-650   HAN

A Rolleiflex 3.5F camera, serial no.2219964, with Carl Zeiss Planar f3.5, 75mm lens, in original leather case, with flash, lens hood, lens filter and booklet.
$550-600   TEN

A Sanderson regular model plate camera, mahogany with brass mounts and black leather bellows, with ivorine plaque for 'Sanderson H Ltd London', with further brass plaque and Regular Model.

Cambridge-born Frederick Herbert Sanderson was a cabinet maker and wood carver by trade, but his passion was architectural photography. Unable to find a model to suit his needs, Sanderson took out a patent for a 'hand & stand' form camera in 1895 and designed his own.
c1900   *9in (23cm) wide*
$250-350   LSK

An early 20thC mahogany and brass folding half-plate field camera, two black metal double dark slides and sliding quarter plate adaptor with three brass and mahogany double dark slides, in canvas carrying bag.
$200-250   DA&H

A brass photographic 50mm iris lens, by Emil Busch, case engraved 'Rapid Aplanat Number 5 Foc. 18ins, R.O.J.A.vorm Emil Busch, Rathenow', slide adjuster reading '8, 11, 16, 22, 32, 45, 84'.
$250-350   MART

A Nikon Nikkor f1.4, serial no.222421, 85mm lens.
$550-600   TEN

A gentleman's 'Dandy Stick', the ivory knop with piqué decoration, the stepped malacca haft with brass ferrule.
c1700   *45.25in (115cm) long*
$2,000-2,500   **TEN**

An 18thC gentleman's walking cane, the ivory mushroom knop with piqué decoration, the silver collar engraved 'B D', with tapering malacca haft, cut-down.
c1700   *35.25in (89.5cm) long*
$900-1,100   **TEN**

An 18thC gentleman's walking cane, the ivory and tortoiseshell piqué work handle with yellow and white metal inlaid decoration, the applied white metal collar engraved 'Edward Pool 1741', handle and cane possibly associated, top of handle possibly associated, losses to inlay, denting and creasing to white metal band.
35in (89cm) long
$650-800   **FELL**

A 19thC walking stick, the snakewood shaft with steel handle engraved 'Admiral Duff to Rev. J.D. Hull, 1844'.
35.75in (90.5cm) long
$60-80   **DW**

A 19thC 'Flick' stick, the malacca shaft with gilt-metal collar, with horn ferrule.
35.75in (91cm) long
$350-400   **DW**

QUICK REFERENCE - HENRY BYAM MARTIN

Admiral Sir Henry Byam Martin KCB (1803-65) was a senior Royal Navy officer and watercolor artist. He first went to sea in October 1818 and by 1840 was Captain in charge of H.M.S. Carysfort, with which he was involved in action off Tartus during the Syrian War and took part in the capture of Acre in November 1840. His actions earned him an appointment as a Commander of the Order of the Bath. From 1846-47 he was sent to the Society Islands in the South Pacific to spy on the Franco-Tahitian War and investigate the sovereignty claim of Queen Pomare IV over the Leeward Islands. He was promoted to Rear-Admiral in 1854 and was appointed as a Knight Commander of the Order of the Bath for his work during the war with Russia in 1855.

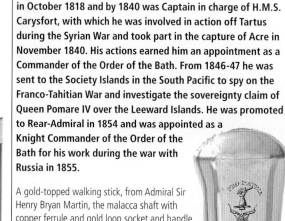

A gold-topped walking stick, from Admiral Sir Henry Bryan Martin, the malacca shaft with copper ferrule and gold loop socket and handle inscribed 'HENRY BYAM MARTIN 1865'.
1865   *36in (91.5cm) long*
$650-800   **CM**

A walking stick, carved with Cecil Rhodes, the handle formed by a lion on a crocodile, the shaft serpent entwined.
1889   *14.25in (36cm) long*
$1,000-1,200   **TRI**

A 19thC walking cane, with ivory knop, carved as a Napoleonic period soldier, on ebony shaft with silver collar, Birmingham.
1899   35.75in (91cm) long
$400-450   **DW**

A 19thC carved ivory walking cane, the handle as a bulldog with glass eyes and growling mouth, on a silver collar, some damage, London.
1897   36.25in (92cm) long
$350-400   **FELL**

A 19thC carved wooden walking cane, with a bulldog with inset green eyes.
34in (86.5cm) long
$200-250   **FELL**

A 19thC walking cane, modeled as a dog with glass eyes, elements associated.
35.5in (90cm) long
$200-250   **FELL**

A Victorian carved wooden walking stick, modeled as a dog with glass eyes, with white metal collar and bamboo cane, possibly associated.

36in (91.5cm) long

$150-200 **FELL**

A 19thC walking cane, modeled as a dog with glass eyes, on metal collar and malacca cane, possibly associated, crack to head.

35in (89cm) long

$120-130 **FELL**

An early 20thC carved wooden-handled walking cane, modeled as a hound with glass eyes and painted detail, on an ebonized cane, possibly associated.

32.25in (82cm) long

$150-200 **FELL**

A thornwood walking cane, modeled as a dog with glass eyes, with silver collar, possibly associated, London.

1974 *33in (84cm) long*

$200-250 **FELL**

An Art Nouveau silver cane handle, modeled as a snake, entwined around the shaft, stamped marks.

c1915 *4.75in (12cm) wide*

$1,300-2,000 **WW**

A silver-mounted walking stick, modeled as a mallard duck, with glass eyes, on ebonized wooded cane with a brass ferrule, possibly associated, London.

1905 *35in (89cm) long*

$550-650 **FELL**

A rhinoceros horn wood walking stick, with a metal collar, carved as a parrot with inlaid eyes.

34in (86.5cm) long

$600-650 **JN**

A Japanese Meiji period ivory cane handle, with a bear attacking two monkeys.

3in (7.5cm) long

$150-200 **FELL**

An Edwardian rosewood walking stick, carved as a boot with laces.

38.25in (97cm) long

$200-250 **DW**

A hardwood walking cane, with boot handle.

36.5in (93cm) long

$100-130 **PW**

A 19thC walking stick, with whalebone shaft with scrimshaw whale's tooth handle engraved with mermaid and a whale, the root end with silver cap, with iron ferrule.

39in (99cm) long

$550-650 **DW**

An Irish bog oak walking cane, with scrolling vines, shamrocks and serpent in relief, the jeweled finial on gilt-metal.

37in (94cm) long

$1,000-1,300 **MEA**

An Indian white metal mounted 'Ashoka Column' walking cane, with a black lacquered shaft simulating holly wood.

35.5in (90cm) long

$150-200   BRI

A hardwood walking cane, decorated with Indian Hindu Gods, Ganesha, Shiva, Krishna, with animals in color on the ivory handle.

$400-450   PW

A malacca cane walking stick, the Chinese silver top embossed with figures.

34in (86.5cm) long

$200-250   PW

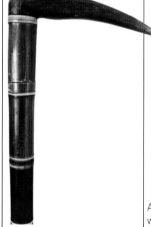

A Victorian mariner's walking cane, with a braided twine handle and Turk's head pommel.

34.75in (88cm) long

$200-250   PW

A 19thC white metal-handled walking cane, handle with scaly dragons, on stained wooden cane, with a brass ferrule, possibly associated.

36in (91.5cm) long

$250-300   FELL

A rhinoceros horn walking stick.

35.75in (91cm) long

$350-400   JN

A 19thC Folk Art carved crooked wood cane, the handle carved with two grotesque heads.

35.75in (91cm) long

$400-450   DW

A mid-19thC Folk art holly and penwork walking cane, decorated with figures, birds and animals.

33.5in (85cm) long

$300-400   WW

A late 19thC 'Cheroot Gun' cane, modeled as an old cannon on a rosewood shaft with brass ferrule.

This cane is believed to have been carried by gamblers in the American Wild West. If accused of card cheating, they could ignite the cannon with a lit cheroot for self defense.

35.5in (90cm) long

$250-350   DW

A Victorian novelty 'Gamer's' walking stick, the silver wirework ball handle inset with small Victorian silver coin, unscrewing to reveal a compartment for dice, with ebony shaft and ferrule.

37.5in (95cm) long

$400-450   DW

An early 20thC cherrywood cane, possibly from Austria, the bowl unscrews to reveal a nickel and composite mouth piece, metal ferrule.

36.25in (92cm) long

$200-250   DW

A parasol, with ceramic medallion painted with a lady, to a bamboo shaft, the canopy marked 'PARAGON LAURUS S. FOX & CO. LIMITED', the canopy requiring replacement.

35.25in (89.5cm) long

$400-550 FELL

A Continental porcelain-handled parasol, decorated with courting couples, one stretcher marked 'La Capuella', the cane tip with brass ferrule.

33in (84cm) long

$200-250 FELL

A Continental porcelain-handled parasol, painted with a cherub, the malacca shaft with collars stamped '18CT G.P.', one stretcher marked 'PARAGON - S. FOX & CO. LIMITED', silk-effect fabric is a replacement.

36.25in (92cm) long

$300-350 FELL

A carved wooden-handled parasol or umbrella, modeled as a fox with glass eyes, to a cane handle, tip and brass ferrule, marked 'THE ARMSTRONG REG'D BRITISH MAKE'.

37.75in (96cm) long

$130-200 FELL

A late Victorian rhinoceros horn hunting whip, with an antler horn handle with a button inscribed 'SWAINE & CO. LONDON', with a silver colored ferrule inscribed 'Violet 1883'.

24.25in (61.5cm) long

$750-800 WW

A rhinoceros horn sidesaddle whip, with silver handle and mounts, hallmarked for London.

1899   27.25in (69cm) long

$650-750 WW

A late 19thC rhinoceros horn sidesaddle whip, with an engraved gilt-brass handle.

25.5in (64.5cm) long

$1,600-2,000 WW

A late 19thC rhinoceros horn sidesaddle whip, with a gilt-brass handle.

26in (66cm) long

$1,500-2,000 WW

A late 19thC rhinoceros horn hunting whip, by Swaine, the antler horn handle above a silver ferrule, inscribed 'SWAINE' with indistinct hallmarks.

79in (201cm) long

$1,200-1,500 WW

A late 19thC rhinoceros horn sidesaddle whip, inscribed 'SWAINE & ADENEY LONDON'.

27.75in (70.5cm) long

$1,500-1,700 WW

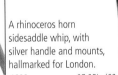

An early 20thC bamboo horse measuring stick, with a silver button revealing a boxwood measure, originally with a spirit level.

37in (94cm) long

$600-650 WW

CERAMICS

QUICK REFERENCE - BESWICK POTTERY

- The Beswick Pottery was founded in Loughton, Staffordshire, in 1894, by James Wright Beswick and his sons John and Gilbert. It initially focused on tableware and vases, then began to produce figurines from 1900.
- Beswick was sold to Royal Doulton in 1969, but production continued under the name 'Beswick' until 1989, when Beswick and Doulton animal figurines were combined as 'Royal Doulton'. The name 'Beswick' returned to use in 1999, until the factory closed in 2002.
- Beswick's animal figurines remain its most sought-after wares. The Beatrix Potter figurines, produced from 1946, and Disney figurines, produced from 1952, are also popular.
- Prices for Beswick wares rose after the closure of the factory in 2002 and, while they have fallen in the present economic climate, prices for rare figurines remain high. Early pieces, limited edition or prototype figurines fetch the highest prices. However, it is difficult to identify early pieces, as figurines were not back-stamped or numbered until 1934.

A Beswick 'Shire Mare', designed by Arthur Gredington, model no.818, in black gloss.

Over 15 colorways of the 'Shire Mare' were introduced. The rarest are blue and iron gray.

8.5in (21.5cm) high

$600-750   FLD

A Beswick 'Grazing Shire', designed by Arthur Gredington, model no.1050, in brown colorway, gloss-glazed.

The rarest colorway variant of this model is the rocking horse gray, produced c1947-62.

5.25in (13.5cm) high

$40-50   K&O

A Beswick 'Grazing Shire', designed by Arthur Gredington, model no.1050, in dapple gray, with circle mark.

1962-70   5.5in (14cm) high

$400-450   FLD

A Beswick 'Susie Jamaica', model no.1347, modeled riding upon a donkey.

1954-75   7in (17.5cm) high

$60-80   FELL

A Beswick 'Mountie on a Dark Brown/Black Horse', designed by Arthur Gredington, model no.1375, gloss-glazed.

1955-76   8.25in (21cm) high

$550-600   WHP

A Beswick 'Cowboy on a Palomino Horse', designed by Graham Orwell, model no.1377, gloss-glazed.

The horse ridden by the cowboy is the same horse as in model no.1374.

1955-73   9in (23cm) high

$650-750   WHP

A Beswick skewbald 'American Indian Chief on Horseback', designed by Graham Orwell, model no.1391, gloss-glazed.
1955-90   *8.5in (21.5cm) high*
$300-400   **PW**

A rare Beswick 'Huntsman', on a painted white horse, designed by Arthur Gredington, model no.1501, gloss-glazed.

This model was also produced in brown, chestnut, gray, opaque, palomino, rocking horse gray and white. The rarest of these is the rocking horse gray, which was produced c1958-62 and fetches much higher prices than the other colorways.
1958-71   *8.25in (21cm) high*
$750-850   **PSA**

A rare Beswick 'Imperial Horse', in a painted white colorway, designed by Albert Hallam and James Hayward, model no.1557, gloss-glazed.

This model was also produced in brown, chestnut, gray, opaque, palomino, rocking horse gray and white. The most highly sought after colorways are rocking horse gray and painted white. This horse was also used in model no.1546, with Queen Elizabeth as rider.
1958-67   *8.25in (21cm) high*
$250-350   **PSA**

A Beswick 'The Duke of Edinburgh on a Alamein', designed by Edward Folkard, model no.1588, gloss-glazed, in light dapple gray.
1958-81   *10.5in (27cm) high*
$400-450   **WHP**

A Beswick 'Lifeguard on a Light Dapple Gray Horse', designed by Arthur Gredington, model no.1624, gloss-glazed.
1959-77   *5.75in (14.5cm) high*
$450-500   **WHP**

A Beswick 'Exmoor Pony Heatherman', designed by Arthur Gredington, model no.1645, gloss-glazed.
1961-83   *6.5in (16.5cm) high*
$60-80   **K&O**

A Beswick 'Highwayman on a Rearing Horse', designed by Albert Hallam, model no.2210, mat-glazed, on a turned wooden base.
1970-75   *13.75in (35cm) high*
$250-350   **WHP**

A CLOSER LOOK AT AN ARAB STALLION

The dapple gray 'Arab Stallion' is much rarer and more valuable than the 'Arab Stallion' in brown.

The colorful saddle, which the brown 'Arab Stallion' does not wear, adds to the interest of this model.

The model is mat-glazed, which also increases its value.

Like other models in the 'Connoisseur Horses' series, the 'Arab Stallion' is modeled on a stand.

A Beswick dapple gray 'Arab Stallion', designed by Albert Hallam, model no.2269, on a wooden plinth.
1970-75
$2,000-2,500   **PSA**

A Beswick 'Black Beauty' and 'Black Beauty Foal', designed by Graham Tongue, model no.2466 and no.2536, mat-glazed.

The 'Black Beauty' no.2466 and 'Black Beauty Foal' no.2536 were issued separately, and then released together for a special edition commissioned by Lawleys by Post in 1998 to celebrate the centenary of Beswick's Gold Street factory. As these models lack a stand, they were probably originally purchased separately.

larger 7in (18cm) high

$60-80   **K&O**

A Beswick 'Lipizzaner and Rider', designed by Graham Tongue, model no.2467 (second version), gloss-glazed.

In the first version, the horse's hind legs (but not its tale) are attached to an circular base; in the second version, the horse's hind legs and tail are attached to an oval base.

9.5in (24cm) high

$400-450   **WHP**

A Beswick 'Steeplechaser', designed by Graham Tongue, model no.2505, gloss-glazed.

1975-81   *8.5in (21.5cm) high*

$350-400   **WHP**

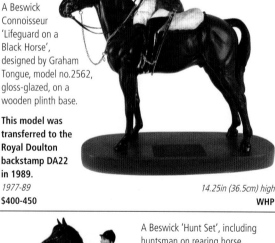

A Beswick Connoisseur 'Lifeguard on a Black Horse', designed by Graham Tongue, model no.2562, gloss-glazed, on a wooden plinth base.

This model was transferred to the Royal Doulton backstamp DA22 in 1989.

1977-89

$400-450

14.25in (36.5cm) high

WHP

A prototype Beswick 'Indian Chief on Horse', with a green and black glaze, the horn on the headdress re-stuck, the other horn tip missing.

10.25in (26cm) high

$350-450   **PSA**

A Beswick 'Hunt Set', including huntsman on rearing horse, two foxes and four hounds, the 'Huntsman' with two small minor glaze flakes to his sleeve, one running fox with a restored leg, one hound with restoration, the three other hounds with re-stuck tails.

$200-250   **PW**

A limited edition Beswick 'Huntsman and hounds' Tableau piece, from 'The Hunt' collection exclusive for Sinclair's, on a ceramic base, with certificate.

$550-650   **PSA**

QUICK REFERENCE - ANIMALS

- Beswick produced animal figurines from 1900. By 1930 these figurines were very successful and a major part of the factory's production.
- Notable designers of Beswick animal figurines include Arthur Gredington, Colin Melbourne, Graham Tongue, Albert Hallam and Alan Maslankowski.
- Collectors usually focus on one type of animal; for example, farm animals, wild animals, dogs, cattle or horses.
- Cattle are currently very popular, with rare bulls especially sought-after. Calves tend to be less valuable than adult cattle, but nonetheless are often bought by collectors to match their bulls and cows.
- Beswick animal figurines have been known to fetch high prices. Potteries Auctions sold a rare red strawberry roan 'Hereford Bull' for £5,500 ($7,400). The record remains a 'Spirit of Whitfield' pony, modeled by Graham Tongue, which sold for £9,500 ($12,700) at Bonhams in 2003.
- Color, glaze, form and position all affect value, with colors such as 'roan' and 'rocking horse gray' generally more valuable than brown or white. Mat glazes tend to be more valuable than gloss. Even differently positioned legs and tails can affect value.
- Condition dictates value for Beswick pieces, so all collectors aim to buy at mint condition, unless the figurine is extremely rare. It is always worth examining protruding horns, thin legs and tails for breakages.

A Beswick 'Hereford bull', designed by Arthur Gredington, model no.949.

c1941-57　　　*5.5in (14.5cm) high*

$150-200　　　**WHP**

A rare Beswick 'Aberdeen Angus Calf', designed by Arthur Gredington, model no.1249, in Belted Galloway colors, numbered '38' on its foot, without factory stamp.

$750-800　　　**PSA**

A Beswick 'Shorthorn Bull', designed by Arthur Gredington, model no.1504.

1957-73　　　*5in (12.5cm) high*

$550-650　　　**PSA**

A Beswick 'Black Galloway Bull', designed by Arthur Gredington, model no.1746A, gloss-glazed.

1962-69　　　*4.5in (12cm) high*

$800-950　　　**PSA**

A Beswick 'Silver Dunn Galloway Bull', designed by Arthur Gredington, model no.1746C, gloss-glazed.

1962-69　　　*4.5in (12cm) high*

$900-1,000　　　**PSA**

Judith Picks

In the 1970s I worked for some months as a clerical assistant in the Ministry of Agriculture, Fisheries and Food. I worked with vets who were involved in the Brucellosis Eradication Scheme. I remember being particularly impressed by, ie frightened of, the belted Galloway bulls. So this figure is a firm favorite!

A Beswick 'Belted Galloway Bull', designed by Arthur Gredington, model no.1746B, gloss-glazed.

1963-69　　　*4.5in (12cm) high*

$1,300-2,000　　　**PSA**

A set of Beswick 'Limousins', comprising a bull, cow and calf, model nos.2463B, 3075B and 1827E.

The 'Limousin' design was a special colorway produced for the Beswick Collectors Club. The 'Limousin' bull, cow and calf were issued in 1998 in limited editions of 653, 656 and 711 respectively. The Club's 'B.C.C.' backstamp appears alongside the usual Beswick stamp on each of these three models.

1998　　　*bull 5in (12.5cm) high*

$750-800　　　**PSA**

CERAMICS

A rare large Beswick 'Penguin', designed by Mr Owen, model no.450A, in black colorway, gloss-glazed.

The Beswick 'Penguin' was also produced in blue.

1936-54   *8.25in (21cm) high*
$300-350   K&O

A Beswick 'Zebra', in tan and white, designed by Arthur Gredington, model no.845A.

This model's colorway is rarer than the black and white zebra, model no.845B.

7in (18cm) high
$200-250   WHP

A Beswick 'Yellow Budgie', designed by Arthur Gredington, model no.1216B, gloss-glazed.

This model was also produced in green and in blue. The blue colorway is a common piece, worth roughly $60-140; the green colorway is slightly less common, worth $200-400. The yellow colorway is the rarest.

1970-72   *7in (18cm) high*
$800-950   PSA

A Beswick 'Merino Ram', in cream colorway, designed by Arthur Gredington, model no.1917.

1964-67   *4.25in (11cm) high*
$1,000-1,300   PSA

A Beswick 'Bronze Turkey', designed by Albert Hallam, model no.1957, gloss-glazed.

White examples of this model were also produced and are rarer than the bronze.

1964-69   *7.5in (18.5cm) high*
$400-450   WHP

A Beswick 'Pair of Partridges', designed by Albert Hallam, model no.2064, gloss-glazed.

1966-75   *6in (15.5cm) high*
$300-400   WHP

A Beswick 'Seated Unicorn', designed by Graham Tongue, model no.2094, gloss-glazed.

This is a replica of a Staffordshire figure produced in 1820 to commemorate the Coronation of George IV.

1967-71   *6in (15cm) high*
$90-120   WHP

A Beswick 'Pony Express', designed by Harry Sales, modeled by David Lyttleton, model no.2789A (first variation), in gray colorway, gloss-glazed.

Beswick produced another 'Pony Express', model no.2789B (second variation), with a bay horse, the rider in a red jacket and yellow jodhpurs.

1983-89   *4.25in (10.5cm) high*
$120-150   **K&O**

A Beswick 'Marlin', designed by Arthur Gredington, model no.1243, gloss-glazed.

1952-70   *5.5in (14cm) high*
$350-450   **WHP**

A Beswick 'Black Bass', designed by Colin Melbourne, model no.1485, gloss-glazed.
1957-68   *5.5in (14.5cm) high*
$150-200   **WHP**

A set of three Beswick 'Kingfisher' wall plaques, designed by Arthur Gredington, model no.729, some minor damage.

1939-71   *largest 6.75in (17cm) high*
$80-100   **WHP**

A set of three Beswick 'Kingfisher' wall plaques of graduated size, with green colorway, model no.729, versions 1, 2 and 3.
1939-71   *largest 7.5in (19cm) high*
$250-350   **HAN**

A set of three Beswick 'green woodpecker' wall plaques, designed by Graham Orwell, model no.1344, versions 1, 2, 3.
1954-68   *largest 6.5in (16.5cm) high*
$250-350   **WHP**

CERAMICS

A Beswick Beatrix Potter 'Duchess Holding a Pie' figure, designed by Graham Tongue, model no.2601, stamped 'BP3B'.

1979-82 *4in (10cm) high*

$100-130 PSA

A Beswick Beatrix Potter 'Simpkin' figure, modeled by Alan Maslankowski, model no.2508, stamped 'BP3B'.

1975-83 *4in (10cm) high*

$120-160 PSA

A rare Beswick Beatrix Potter 'Duchess with Flowers' figure, designed by Graham Orwell, model no.1355, stamped 'BP2A'.

This is rarer than the similar model no.2601, 'Duchess holding a Pie' (see right), and usually fetches a much higher price.

1955-67 *3.75in (9.5cm) high*

$1,200-1,500 PSA

A Beswick Beatrix Potter 'Ginger' figure, modeled by David Lyttleton, model no.2559, stamped 'BP3B'.

Depending on the individual model, Ginger's jacket varies from light to dark green.

1976-82 *3.75in (9.5cm) high*

$120-150 PSA

A Beswick Beatrix Potter 'Susan' figure, modeled by David Lyttleton, model no.2716, stamped 'BP3C'.

'Susan' version BP6A is a rarer version of this model and usually fetches higher prices.

1983-89 *4in (10cm) high*

$100-130 PSA

A Beswick figure 'Alice' from the Alice in Wonderland series, designed by Albert Hallam and Graham Tongue, model no.2476, gloss-glazed.

An alternative Beswick model of Alice, no.LC2 (3952), modeled by Martyn Alcock, was produced in 1999 as a limited edition of 2,500.

1973-83 *4.75in (12cm) high*

$60-80 PSA

A rare Beswick 'Snow White', designed by Arthur Gredington, model no.1332A (first version), with yellow and purple dress, red cape and white collar.

This was remodeled in 1955 as no.1332B, a Snow White with straighter hair. This second version was produced 1955-67 and is in less demand than the rarer 1332A.

1954-55 *5.5in (14cm) high*

$600-750 BRI

A Beswick 'Heron Yacht', model no.1634, with a red hull.

9in (22.5cm) high

$100-130 **WHP**

A Beswick 'Bell Yacht' wall plaque, model no.1632, with a turquoise hull.

7.75in (19.5cm) high

$200-250 **WHP**

A Beswick jug modeled as a 'Mayor', advertising Worthington's.

9in (23cm) high

$50-70 **WHP**

A Beswick figure modeled as a 'poodle and a bulldog', advertising Dubonnet.

17in (17.5cm) high

$200-250 **WHP**

A Beswick jug modeled as a 'running gentleman', advertising Double Diamond, model no.1517.

8.25in (21cm) high

$100-130 **WHP**

A Beswick vase, of a ridged ovoid form, decorated in brown and orange glazes, mold no.429.

11in (28cm) high

$40-50 **WHP**

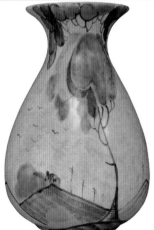

A Beswick vase, painted with village scene.

c1940 *9.75in (25cm) high*

$40-50 **K&O**

QUICK REFERENCE - ENGLISH PORCELAIN

- Porcelain is thought to have been invented in China during the Han Dynasty, (c206 BC-AD 220). Hard paste porcelain is made by firing a mixture of kaolin and petuntse at 1350°C.
- Hard paste porcelain was first developed in Europe in 1708 by Johann Friedrich Böttger. The following year, his patron set up the Meissen factory in Germany.
- Porcelain production spread to England in the 1740s. The factories of Chelsea, Bow and Lund's of Bristol began production, soon followed by Derby, Longton Hall, Lowestoft, Worcester and Plymouth. Many English porcelain pieces, especially those of the Worcester, Caughley (see pages 65-67), Lowestoft and Liverpool factories, were decorated in blue and white, mirroring the Oriental style.
- If you appreciate 18thC blue and white porcelain, now is a great time to buy.

A Lowestoft porcelain plate, decorated with a Chinese garden scene.
c1765　　　*9in (23cm) diam*
$550-600　　　**KEY**

A Lowestoft sparrow-beak jug, transfer-printed with the 'Good Cross Chapel' design.

This print is unique to Lowestoft porcelain. It is named after a chapel in South Lowestoft ruined in the 16thC and appears to include a light-house with a lamp room above, known locally as the High Light.
c1780　　　*3.5in (9cm) high*
$650-750　　　**KEY**

A Derby porcelain pierced basket, with a chinoiserie landscape, a couple of fine hairline cracks to the trellis.
c1760　　　*10.75in (27cm) long*
$550-600　　　**DN**

An early 19thC porcelain jug, transfer-printed with fruit and leaves.
　　　3.5in (9cm) high
$80-100　　　**DA&H**

A Worcester porcelain mug, transfer-printed with a European landscape, blue hatched crescent mark.
c1770　　　*5in (12cm) high*
$200-250　　　**BELL**

QUICK REFERENCE - TRANSFER-PRINTED WARES

- Transfer-printing was developed in the mid-18thC as a cheaper and quicker alternative to painting ceramics by hand. The technique was used by factories such as Worcester, Spode, Davenport, Copeland & Garett, amongst others.
- The design would be engraved onto a copper plate, which was then covered in ink. The design was transferred to the ceramic surface using paper, then sealed under a clear glaze.
- Transfer-printed wares are traditionally blue and white, as an underglaze of cobalt blue was at the time the only one that could withstand the heat of the kiln.
- Transfer-printed pieces can usually be recognized on close examination by the cross-hatching or dots created by the copper plate engraving, and the lack of raised lines usually created when painting by hand.
- Prices currently remain very flat, although rare patterns, such as Spode's 'Indian Sporting Series' and 'The Durham Ox' do achieve higher prices. The 'Willow' pattern is probably the most common, with all but the rare shapes selling for very little. With prices low and many auctions selling blue and white wares in large job lots, now is an excellent time to start a collection.

An early 19thC armorial plate, by Hicks, Meigh & Johnson, bearing the Arms and Motto of the Salters Company, the crest reading 'Sal Sapit Omnia' (Salt Savours All), mark verso.
　　　10.25in (26cm) diam
$100-160　　　**KEY**

A 19thC Staffordshire black transfer-printed plate, with portrait center, the front inscribed 'Norfolk's Pride, the patriot Coke', the back inscribed 'Lovick's China and Glass Emporium, Norwich' small hairline crack.

Thomas William Coke was born in 1754 and was a prime mover in the agricultural revolution, holding shows at his Holkham Estate from 1776. He represented Norfolk for the Whigs from 1776 to 1833 and in 1837 was raised to the peerage.
　　　10.25in (26cm) diam
$100-130　　　**KEY**

A large 19thC soup tureen and cover, by John and Richard Riley, printed with Gracefield House in Queen's County, Ireland, printed mark, minor faults.

This is after the engraving by Robert Wallis.

13.5in (34cm) high

$400-550   WW

A Rogers supper set, comprising a footed bowl and cover and four curved dishes and covers, printed with figures before Eastern buildings, the covers surmounted with lion finials, set into a wooden tray, some damages.

c1830   21.75in (55cm) wide

$400-550   WW

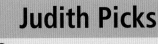

Judith Picks

This type of shaped chamber pot was named after the French Jesuit priest Father Bourdalou, who, at the time of Louis XIV, preached such interminably long sermons that ladies began to bring these pots into church concealed in their muffs, so that they could be secretly used in emergency under their wide dresses. The alternative story is that he was such an inspirational preacher that people queued for hours to hear him. Either way a discreet chamber pot was needed! They were also useful on long coach journeys.

A late 18thC or early 19thC Spode pearlware transfer-printed Bourdalou, in 'Princess Adelaide' pattern, impressed factory mark and 'M' to base.

9.25in (23.5cm) long

$150-200   MART

A Spode pottery meat plate, 'Shooting a Leopard', from the 'Indian Sporting Series', titled to rear, impressed 'SPODE' mark, crazed and stained, small chip to the rim, heavy surface wear to the underside.

This is such a high quality service that even with damage this plate is still desirable.

c1820   20.75in (52.5cm) wide

$800-950   BELL

An early to mid-19thC transfer-printed dish or stand, of a tiger hunt, the unfortunate cat being set upon by a pack of hounds, while a figure on the back of an elephant fires his gun.

This was most likely a small Staffordshire factory copying the vastly popular Spode 'Indian Sporting Series', but it lacks the technical quality of the Spode examples (see left).

14.25in (36.5cm) diam

$100-160   WW

A rare Turner & Co. stone china custard cup and cover, printed in the Chinese manner with two figures on a bridge in a pagoda landscape.

c1800   3.5in (9cm) high

$450-550   WW

A 19thC transfer-printed soup bowl, with the arms of the City of London, a shield quartered by the cross of St George, containing the sword of St Paul, above a banner titled 'Domine Dirige Nos'.

9in (23cm) diam

$100-130   WW

A rare early to mid-19thC Staffordshire dish, with transfer decoration of a view of 'Gunton Hall'.

The scene is a view from the west with some similarity to Ladbrooke's lithograph of 1822.

9.5in (24cm) wide

$1,000-1,300   KEY

A 19thC Staffordshire 'Alms House, Boston' platter, impressed 'Stevenson'.

The 19thC 'American' Staffordshire wares, produced in England and sold in the USA, were transfer-printed with scenes of American history and landscape. The designs were taken from prints and drawings by American and European artists. Some of the original artworks came from publications on the history and topography of the USA. Others were from the works of English painter William Henry Bartlett or the Irish artist William Guy Wall.

16.5in (42cm) long
$1,000-1,300   POOK

A 19thC Staffordshire 'Arms of New Jersey' platter, with blue eagle mark on underside.
19.75in (49cm) long
$2,000-2,500   POOK

A 19thC Staffordshire 'Bank of Savannah' small tray.
6.75in (17cm) long
$1,300-2,000   POOK

A 19thC Staffordshire 'Chillicothe, Ohio' platter, mis-marked 'Albany'.
9in (24cm) wide
$2,500-3,500   POOK

A 19thC Staffordshire 'Columbus' platter.
14.5in (37cm) long
$2,000-2,500   POOK

A 19thC Staffordshire 'Detroit' platter.
18.75in (47.5cm) long
$4,000-4,500   POOK

A 19thC Staffordshire 'Louisville' platter.
12.5in (32cm) long
$2,000-2,500   POOK

A 19thC Staffordshire 'Sandusky' platter.
16.5in (42cm) wide
$1,000-1,300   POOK

A Staffordshire 'Tappan Bay from Greenburgh' open vegetable plate, marked 'E. Wood & Sons'.
8.75in (22cm) wide
$1,600-2,000   POOK

A 19thC Staffordshire 'Highlands North River' plate.

10.25in (25.5cm) diam

$2,000-2,500 POOK

A 19thC Staffordshire 'New York City Hotel' plate, with medallion portraits of Washington and Lafayette.

8.75in (22.5cm) diam

$1,000-1,300 POOK

A 19thC Staffordshire 'Entrance to the Erie Canal into the Hudson at Albany' plate.

10.25in (26cm) diam

$1,000-1,300 POOK

A Staffordshire 'Niagara' medallion plate, with images of Jefferson, Lafayette, Clinton and Washington, and a view of the 'Entrance of the Canal into the Hudson at Albany', marked 'EA. Stevenson'.

10in (25.5cm) diam

$5,500-6,000 POOK

A 19thC Staffordshire 'The Eddistone Light House' reticulated basket.

11in (28cm) wide

$2,000-2,500 POOK

A 19thC Staffordshire 'Washington Independence' pitcher and basin.

pitcher 9.25in (23.5cm) high

$2,000-2,500 POOK

A 19thC Staffordshire 'Seal of United States' pitcher.

5.75in (14.5cm) high

$1,000-1,300 POOK

A 19thC Staffordshire 'Hartford State House' handled cup.

$900-1,000 POOK

CERAMICS

QUICK REFERENCE - BORDER FINE ARTS

- Border Fine Arts was founded by John Hammond in 1974 in an 18thC farmhouse near Langholm, Scotland. The company specialized in highly detailed and accurately painted figurines and figural groups, focusing on wildlife and rural farming scenes.
- For the first few years, the company consisted of three people - founder John Hammond and sculptors Victor Hayton and Ray Ayres. However, it grew quickly and won the Scottish Business Achievement Award in 1986.
- The Langholm factory closed down in 2016 after a decline in sales.
- Borders Fine Art figures were first modeled in wax. A mold was then produced by shaping silicone around the wax, then removing the wax original and filling the mold with 'Thorionware', a resin that would react under pressure to create a white porcelain-like casting. The resulting models were then painted by hand. This means that no two pieces are identical.
- Limited edition models with original boxes and certificates are the most highly sought after by collectors.

A Border Fine Arts 'Off to the Smithy' model, no.B0955, from a limited edition of 950.
$400-450   K&O

A Border Fine Arts 'Lacking Horse Power' model, no.B0985, from a limited edition of 950.

4in (10cm) high

$180-220   K&O

A Border Fine Arts 'Carrying Burdens' model, no.B0892, from a limited edition of 950, boxed with certificate.
$200-250   K&O

A Border Fine Arts '3 Mile Back up t' Road' model, no.B1001, from a limited edition of 500, boxed with certificate.
$300-400   K&O

A Border Fine Arts 'Bought at Market' model, no.B1140, from a limited edition of 600, boxed with certificate.
$300-400   K&O

A Border Fine Arts 'Country Air' model, no.B1163, from a limited edition of 750, boxed with certificate.
$400-450   K&O

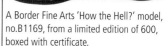

A Border Fine Arts 'How the Hell?' model, no.B1169, from a limited edition of 600, boxed with certificate.
$250-350   K&O

A Border Fine Arts 'A Show Day to Remember' model, no.B1204, from a limited edition of 500, boxed with certificate.

$650-750   **K&O**

A Border Fine Arts 'Keep on Running' model, no.B1207, from a limited edition of 750.

$100-130   **K&O**

A Border Fine Arts 'Left Behind' model, no.B1215, from a limited edition of 500, boxed with certificate.

$150-200   **K&O**

A Border Fine Arts 'Taking to the Tup' model, no.B1243, from a limited edition of 500, boxed with certificate.

$200-250   **K&O**

A Border Fine Arts 'Getting the Feed Out' model, no.B1250, from a limited edition of 500, boxed with certificate.

$300-350   **K&O**

A Border Fine Arts 'Farmyard Antics' model, no.B1303, from a limited edition of 500, boxed with certificate.

$1,000-1,300   **K&O**

A Border Fine Arts 'Standing Firm' model, no.B1382A, from a limited edition of 350, boxed.

$250-300   **K&O**

A Border Fine Arts 'Checking the Hill Ewes' model, no.B1513, from a limited edition of 350, boxed.

$400-550   **K&O**

A Border Fine Arts 'The Country Doctor' model, by Ray Ayres, no.JH63, from the 'All Things Wise and Wonderful' series, from a limited edition of 1,250, on a wooden plinth, marked 'JA63' boxed.

8in (20.5cm) wide

$100-130   **PSA**

CERAMICS

QUICK REFERENCE - BURMANTOFTS

- In 1881, James Holroyd opened an art pottery studio in Leeds, as a side project to his company Wilcocks. This new venture in handthrown and handpainted ceramics was called Burmantofts Faience Pottery.

- Burmantofts was strongly influenced by the Aesthetic Movement and produced a range of detailed and beautifully designed ceramics between 1881 and 1904.

- Many wares were hand modeled, often using the French Barbotine technique, where thick slip is used to paint and model ceramics. Some lines, such as the fantastical grotesques and 'Partie-Colour' were made from molds, then embellished and painted by hand. Burmantofts monochrome wares of blue, red and orange-yellow are especially distinctive.

- Holroyd was closely involved in the company but left his designers free to explore their own ideas. This is shown in the breadth and variation of Burmantofts design.

A Burmantofts faience wall plate, by Joseph Walmsley, painted with a scaly fish inside scroll border in luster on a ruby luster ground, impressed marks, painted 'JW' monogram.

10.25in (26cm) diam

$450-550   **WW**

A Burmantofts Faience Pottery wall plaque, by Harold Leach, model no.1124, impressed marks, incised 'HL' monogram.

18in (45.5cm) diam

$400-550   **WW**

A CLOSER LOOK AT A FAIENCE CHARGER

This charger was designed and handpainted by Leonard King in a Persian-inspired style.

The border is patterned with fish, jellyfish, shells, eels and seaweed in shades of blue, turquoise, yellow and cream.

The well depicts Venus riding on the waves, while a young child holding a bird looks on.

This is a rare, large and intricately detailed piece, which increases its value.

A Burmantofts faience charger, impressed marks, painted 'LK' monogram, painted shell mark and '87', minor glaze loss to the rim.

24.75in (63cm) diam

$25,000-30,000   **WW**

An early 20thC Burmantofts Art Pottery shape 140 vase, impasto decorated with a relief molded mouse, impressed mark, restored.

12.25in (31cm) high

$100-120   **FLD**

A Burmantofts faience 'Anglo-Persian' solifleur vase, by Leonard King, impressed marks, painted monogram and 'D.160'.

10.25in (26cm) high

$1,200-1,600   **WW**

An early 20thC Burmantofts Art Pottery vase, impasto decorated with a fish, signed 'Thinp', impressed mark, restored.

11in (28cm) high

$150-250   **FLD**

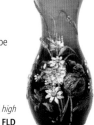

A Burmantofts faience 'Dragon' vase, modeled in relief with a dragon attacking a dragonfly, impressed marks, 'WH' monogram, stress cracks to neck, restored chips to the spine of the dragon.

15.5in (39.5cm) high

$4,000-4,500   **WW**

A Burmantofts faience 'Partie-Colour' vase, model no.2204, impressed and painted marks.

11.25in (28.5cm) high

$750-850   **WW**

An early 20thC Burmantofts shape no.1768 vase, impressed marks, impressed 'White'.

6.75in (17cm) high

$150-250   **FLD**

A late 19thC to early 20thC Burmantofts footed jug, impressed mark.

6.75in (17cm) high

$160-220   **FLD**

A Burmantofts faience floor vase, model no.412, impressed marks, hairline crack to top rim, chip to base, minor glaze frits to high points.

An example of this vase was illustrated in the 1899 Burmantofts Faience catalog.

30.75in (78cm) high

$200-250   **WW**

A Burmantofts faience jardinière and stand, model no.2018, decorated with swans swimming on a river, impressed marks.

34.75in (88cm) high

$300-400   **WW**

A large Burmantofts faience Pottery 'Veritas' oil stove and cover, with pierced Moorish dome cover, stamped 'D' to base, minor glaze chips to feet.

See Jason Wigglesworth, 'The History of the Burmantofts Pottery', private press, page 68, for an example of a glazed blue stove.

38.25in (97cm) high

$650-800   **WW**

A Burmantofts faience 'Fijian' dish, model no.1802, with applied glass eyes, impressed marks.

Christopher Dresser (see pages 192-193) produced a variation of this dish for Linthorpe Pottery. The dish is based on examples of Fijian ceremonial wooden dishes that were included in national museum collections including the British Museum. See Michael Whiteway, 'Christopher Dresser: A Design Revolution', V&A, page 93, plate 114, for a Linthorpe example next to an original Fijian dish from the British Museum collection.

7.5in (19cm) wide

$1,000-1,200   **WW**

A Burmantofts faience model of a tortoise, model no.1997, with applied glass eyes, impressed marks.

9in (23cm) wide

$650-800   **WW**

A Burmantofts faience model of a monkey, model no.796, impressed marks, some light glaze frits to the high points.

6in (15.5cm) wide

$650-800   **WW**

A Burmantofts faience frog figure, impressed mark 'no.461'.

5.5in (14cm) high

$250-350   **BRI**

CERAMICS

QUICK REFERENCE - CARLTON WARE

- The Wiltshaw & Robinson Company was founded in 1890 in Stoke. From 1894 onward, it operated under the trade name 'Carlton Ware'.
- The founder's son, Frederick Cuthbert Wiltshaw, took over in 1918. With the help of design director Horace Wain and later Enoch Boulton, Wiltshaw launched a range of luster projects featuring flower and animal designs.
- The 'Handcraft' range was introduced in the late 1920s, with mat glazes and simple floral designs. The 1929 'Oven to Table' series and the 1960s 'Walking Ware' range were also successful.

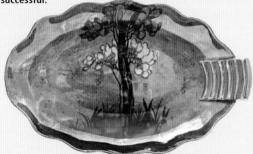

A Carlton Ware 'Rabbits at Dusk' or 'Shadow Bunnies' luster dish, with stepped handle, numbered '1608/2', impressed 'Mr8 / 1306 4247'.

10.25in (26cm) long

$150-200   **HAN**

A Carlton Ware 'Orbit' pattern part coffee and dinner service, comprising a coffee pot and cover, two milk jugs, sugar bowl, six cups and saucers, three gravy jugs and a stand, a three piece cruet and a bottle and stopper, printed backstamps.

c1950-60

$200-250   **BE**

A Carlton Ware 'Jazz Stitch' vase, pattern no.3655, printed and painted with a geometric design on a mottled luster ground, printed and painted marks.

10.5in (26.5cm) high

$450-550   **WW**

A Carlton Ware Art Deco dish, decorated and enameled with flowers and gilt.

11.75in (30cm) wide

$130-200   **K&O**

A Carlton Ware vase, 'Palm Blossom' design, pattern no.4278.

7.75in (20cm) high

$450-500   **PSA**

A Carlton Ware Guinness lamp base and shade, modeled with a toucan, with advertising verse printed around the base, with printed mark.

The shade is a valuable feature.

base 9.5in (24cm) high

$650-800   **PW**

A Carlton Ware 'Fantasia' vase, decorated with exotic birds, printed marks to base, overall fine crazing, occasional glaze scratches.

7in (18cm) high

$600-650   **PW**

A Carlton Ware jug, 'Secretary Bird' design, pattern no.4018, some wear to gilding on top rim and handle.

7.75in (20cm) high

$150-200   **PSA**

A set of three graduated advertising Carlton Ware Guinness pottery wall plaques.

largest 9.75in (25cm) long

$150-250   **FELL**

QUICK REFERENCE - CAUGHLEY PORCELAIN

- Caughley Works, first known as 'Salopian China Manufactory' began in the 1750s, when Ambrose Gallimore leased a pottery at Caughley, Shropshire. From the early 1770s onward, Gallimore worked with Thomas Turner on 'soft-paste' porcelain, made with soapstone and china clays imported from Devon and Cornwall.
- Caughley specialized in transfer-printed blue and white wares, emulating imported Chinese porcelain. From 1780 onward, the wares also have a noticeable French influence.
- Caughley produced a range of tea services, dinner services and other household wares, as well as a small range of miniature 'toy' wares.
- Caughley wares were decorated in blue and white, with a clear glaze that can glow orange in the light. Gilded and enameled details were sometimes added. The most famous Caughley patterns include 'Fisherman' and 'Willow', both of which were adopted by other subsequent factories, including Worcester.
- Wares are often marked either 'S' for Salopian or 'C' for Caughley.
- The Caughley works was bought in 1799, by John Rose of the Coalport factory, who had himself once trained at Caughley.

A Caughley dessert plate, painted with the 'Bright Sprigs' pattern, impressed 'Salopian' mark.
c1784-92   *6.5in (16.5cm) diam*
$300-350   **HALL**

A Caughley dessert dish, painted with the 'Carnation' pattern within a basket weave border, unmarked, chipped.

This is a late shape, rarer than the earlier square dish. This pattern was later repeated by both Derby and Coalport. See, The Caughley Society, 'Caughley Blue and White Patterns', 2012, page 72.
c1788-93   *9.25in (23.5cm) wide*
$90-120   **HALL**

A very rare Caughley inkwell and liner, transfer-printed with the 'Bell Toy' pattern, unmarked, chipped, cracked, repaired.
c1777-88   *2.75in (7cm) high*
$900-1,100   **HALL**

A Caughley butter pot, stand and cover, transfer-printed with the 'Fence' pattern, the cover with elaborate relief floral terminal, 'C' mark, one handle re-stuck.
c1778-88   *4.5in (11.5cm) diam*
$400-450   **HALL**

A Caughley tea canister and cover, transfer-printed with the 'Fenced Garden' pattern, unmarked.
c1786-90   *5in (12.5cm) high*
$150-200   **HALL**

A CLOSER LOOK AT A FISHERMAN' MUG

The border of this mug is not, in general, associated with the normal 'Fisherman' pattern; it is usually part of the 'Sunflower' pattern.

This is the first known dated piece in the 'Fisherman' pattern and is a relatively early date.

'James Bullock' may refer to one James, son of Joseph and Elizabeth Bullock, who was baptised on 19 May 1757 in Kidderminster.

The tiger at the base of the mug is very rare, adding to the value.

A Caughley mug, transfer-printed with the 'Fisherman' and very rare 'Tiger' pattern, named and dated 'James Bullock, 1779', 'S' mark.
5.5in (14cm) high
$4,000-4,500   **HALL**

A Caughley egg cup, transfer-printed with the 'Fisherman' or 'Pleasure Boat' pattern, unmarked, restored chip.

This egg cup cost 8d at the time, which was not inexpensive.
c1780-90   *2.25in (6cm) high*
$800-950   **HALL**

CERAMICS

Judith Picks

Having collected English blue and white porcelain for many years, it is sad to see prices struggling. Many common patterns are now sold at auction as 'job lots'. So it really is an excellent time to buy! Ladles and spoons are more desirable, especially in pristine, unrestored condition. So many have been discarded or restored. Always check for restoration. Some clues to age or telltale signs of repair aren't easily visible to the naked eye, but will fluoresce under ultraviolet light.

A Caughley tureen ladle, transfer-printed with the 'Fisherman' or 'Pleasure Boat' pattern, unmarked.
c1780   7in (17.5cm) long
$400-450   **HALL**

A Caughley tureen and cover, printed with the 'Gillyflower 5' pattern, 'C' mark, cover cracked, though possibly some cracks from manufacture.

This is a very heavy piece and any attempts to lift up the lid by the handle would have undoubtedly have led to breakages, meaning that it is a rare piece.
c1780-85   14.5in (37cm) diam
$750-850   **HALL**

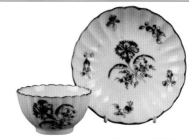

A Caughley butter boat, painted with the 'Gillyflower 1' pattern, unmarked.

This pattern is mainly found on tea wares, but can appear on pickle leaf dishes, mugs, dessert plates, baskets and dishes. 'Gillyflower 1' is a direct copy of the Worcester pattern of the same name, although the original inspiration is most likely from a French source.
c1780   2.75in (7cm) long
$400-550   **HALL**

A Caughley tea bowl and saucer, painted with the 'Gillyflower 1' pattern, 'C' mark.
c1776-78   saucer 5in (12.5cm) diam
$250-350   **HALL**

A Caughley toy teapot with cover, painted with the 'Island' pattern, 'S' mark.

The cover may not be associated with this teapot, and was most likely intended for a coffee pot.
c1780-92   2.75in (7cm) high
$200-250   **HALL**

A Caughley toy guglet or water bottle, painted in underglaze blue with the 'Island' miniature pattern, 'S' mark.

'Toys' are particularly desirable for collectors. This is also a rare desirable shape. A miniature bowl would have been originally intended to go with this guglet. A similar example sold for £1,920 ($2,600) at Bonhams on 12 March 2008.
c1780-90   2.25in (6cm) high
$2,000-2,500   **HALL**

A Caughley toy mug, painted with the 'Island' pattern, 'S' mark, has been in pieces.
c1780-90   1.5in (4cm) high
$550-650   **HALL**

A Caughley coffee pot and cover, transfer-printed with the 'Pagoda' pattern, unmarked, crack to body.
c1784-91   10in (25.5cm) high
$300-350   **HALL**

A Caughley basket, transfer-printed with the 'Pine Cone' pattern, 'C' mark and impressed 'To' mark.

This basket is significant because of its comparatively small size.

c1778-86　　　　　　7.25in (18.5cm) wide

$750-850　　　　　　　　　**HALL**

A Caughley mug, transfer-printed with 'Stalked Fruit and a Fox', 'S' mark.

This is a very early example which is slightly misshapen, with no glaze to the base and featuring a fuzzy pattern as was sometimes the case with early pieces. Not only is this print the rarer, earlier version of the 'Stalked Fruit' pattern, but the addition of the 'Fox' is exceptionally rare, with only four examples known.

c1776-80　　　　　　5in (12.5cm) diam

$2,000-2,500　　　　　　　　　**HALL**

An important Caughley mask-head jug, printed in blue on both sides with a 'Severn Trow' passing underneath the Shropshire Ironbridge, dated, and initialed 'JH' or possibly 'IH'.

The initials may refer to John Hill (1769-1814), a member of the Hill family of Hawkstone, who was 21 in 1790. He was the son of John Hill, 3rd Baronet (1740-1824) and father of Rowland Hill, 1st Viscount. The Hills of Hawkstone are well known as patrons of both Caughley and Coalport.

1790　　　　　　7.25in (18.5cm) high

$6,000-6,500　　　　　　　　　**HALL**

A Caughley dessert plate, transfer-printed with the 'Temple' pattern, 'Sx' mark, central star crack.

c1784-92　　　　　　8in (20cm) diam

$60-100　　　　　　　　　**HALL**

A Caughley vase, painted with the 'Three Boats' pattern, hairline crack.

This vase is the only example known in this pattern and of this shape.

c1780-90　　　　　　14.25in (11cm) high

$2,500-3,500　　　　　　　　　**HALL**

A Caughley custard cup and cover, transfer-printed with the 'Willow Nankin' pattern, unmarked, small chip to cover.

c1784-92　　　　　　3.25in (8.5cm) high

$350-400　　　　　　　　　**HALL**

A Caughley wine taster, transfer-printed with a rare fruit pattern, unmarked, faint hairline.

This is the only one recorded in this pattern. Whilst known as a wine taster, the actual function is still somewhat disputed. It could equally be a caddy spoon.

c1780-85　　　　　　bowl 2in (5cm) diam

$650-800　　　　　　　　　**HALL**

A Caughley plate, painted with a fan-paneled landscape within powder blue ground, impressed 'Salopian' and painted faux Chinese mark.

c1777-85　　　　　　8in (20cm) diam

$600-650　　　　　　　　　**HALL**

CERAMICS

QUICK REFERENCE - CLARICE CIFF

- Clarice Cliff (1899-1972) was born in Stoke-on-Trent and began her career as an apprentice enameller at Linguard Webster & Co. in 1912.
- In 1916 she moved to A.J. Wilkinson. In the mid-1920s, Wilkinson gave Cliff her own studio, Newport Pottery.
- Her 'Bizarre' range was launched in 1927, shortly followed by 'Fantasque'. Each covered a range of patterns and shapes. The majority of her wares were tableware, although she also designed vases, candlesticks, figurines and other items.
- She trained a group of dedicated decorators, mostly women, to paint her designs by hand. They became known as the 'Bizarre Girls'.
- Clarice Cliff wares were handpainted in thickly applied bright colors, often with thin black outlines. Her bold designs include stylized floral patterns, landscapes, geometric and abstract shapes. Many patterns come in a variety of colors. There is often variation within one pattern, as the 'Bizarre Girls' had some freedom to vary the designs.
- In general the market for Clarice Cliff has remained strong, especially for rarer shapes and patterns. Rare landscapes such as the 'Applique' range, 'May Avenue', 'Luxor' and unusual color variants of classic patterns such as 'Red Autumn' or 'Green House' continue to perform well. Geometric patterns such as 'Café', 'Sunspots', 'Football' and 'Tennis' remain strong. While floral patterns can fetch lower prices, patterns such as 'Apples' and 'Butterfly' have risen in popularity in recent years.
- Unusual shapes, such as 'YoYo' vases or finned vases, tend to fetch higher prices. Interest in large examples, such as 'Lotus' jugs and 'Mei Pings', has plateaued in recent years, but classic shapes such as 365, 362, 358 and 360 are proving very popular with collectors.

A Clarice Cliff and Billie Waters 'Bon Jour' teapot, milk and sugar, 'Abstract' pattern, for the 1934 Harrods 'Art in Industry' Exhibition, handpainted, 'Billie Waters' signature and 'Bizarre' mark, teapot restored.
1934
$800-950 FLD

A Clarice Cliff 'Perth' shape jug, 'Allsorts' pattern, handpainted, 'FANTASQUE' mark.
c1929   4.5in (11.5cm) high
$600-650 FLD

A Clarice Cliff shape 460 'Stamford' vase, 'Alton Green' pattern, handpainted with a stylized castle, 'FANTASQUE' and 'Bizarre' mark.
c1933   6in (15cm) high
$600-650 FLD

A Clarice Cliff single-handled 'Lotus' jug, 'Anemone' pattern, gray script signature.
c1937   11.75in (30cm) high
$350-400 FLD

A Clarice Cliff 'Bon Jour' teapot, 'Applique Crinoline Lady' pattern, handpainted 'Applique' and 'Bizarre' mark.
c1933   5in (13cm) high
$750-850 FLD

A Clarice Cliff 'Apple' shaped preserve pot, 'Apples' pattern, handpainted, 'Bizarre' mark.
c1931   8in (20.5cm) high
$400-450 FLD

A Clarice Cliff shape 365 vase, 'Apples' pattern, handpainted with stylized fruit and foliage with a piano keyboard motif, 'FANTASQUE' and 'Bizarre' mark, restored.
c1931   7.75in (20cm) high
$5,500-6,000 FLD

A Clarice Cliff 'Bon Jour' milk jug, 'Applique Crinoline Lady' pattern, handpainted, 'Bizarre' mark.
c1933   2.5in (6.5cm) high
$250-350 FLD

A Clarice Cliff Bizarre 'Art in Industry' plate, designed by Billie Walters, with a printed factory mark.

This plate was designed for the 'Artists in Industry' exhibition held in 1934.

1934 7.75in (20cm) diam
$90-120 WW

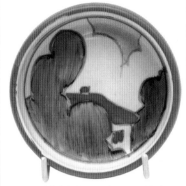

A Clarice Cliff dish, 'Autumn' pattern, black printed 'Newport Bizarre / Fantasque' mark.

3.5in (9cm) diam
$90-100 KEY

A Clarice Cliff pin dish, 'Blue Autumn' pattern, handpainted with a partial image of a cottage, 'FANTASQUE' and 'Bizarre' mark.

c1930 3in (7.5cm) wide
$120-130 FLD

Judith Picks

Clarice Cliff radically changed the output of the Staffordshire potteries in the Art Deco period. She and her paintresses were based at the Newport Pottery warehouse. The team first used old Newport blanks, which they covered in the brightly-colored and distinctive designs that were launched in 1927 as the Bizarre range. The associated Fantasque range evolved between 1928 and 1934 and mainly featured abstracts or landscapes of cottages and trees. She was an excellent marketeer and had to overcome tremendous cynicism to develop her distinctive range. One reason why Clarice Cliff pottery has been so attractive to collectors is that there is enough of it around to make it available to a large collecting base. And as some ranges and patterns were produced in much smaller quantities than others, that lends the ceramics a definite price structure. I admire her style, her bravery in a very male-dominated industry - much as I am not a collector!

A Clarice Cliff shape 206 vase, 'Green Autumn' pattern, handpainted with a stylized tree and cottage landscape, 'FANTASQUE' and 'Bizarre' mark.

c1930 6in (15.5cm) high
$600-750 FLD

A Clarice Cliff 'Conical' shape jug, 'Pastel Autumn' pattern, 'FANTASQUE' and 'Bizarre' mark.

c1930 4.5in (11.5cm) high
$200-250 FLD

A Clarice Cliff shape 341 vase, 'Berries Cafe au Lait' pattern, 'CAFE AU LAIT' and 'Bizarre' mark.

c1931 5in (13cm) high
$600-650 FLD

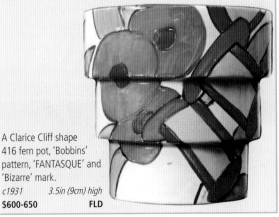

A Clarice Cliff shape 416 fern pot, 'Bobbins' pattern, 'FANTASQUE' and 'Bizarre' mark.

c1931 3.5in (9cm) high
$600-650 FLD

A Clarice Cliff 'Daffodil' shape preserve pot and cover, 'Bridgewater' pattern, handpainted with a stylized tree, cottage and bridge landscape, 'Bizarre' mark.

c1933 4.75in (12cm) high
$450-550 FLD

CLARICE CLIFF MARKS

FANTASQUE
HAND-PAINTED
Bizarre by Clarice Cliff
NEW PORT POTTERY
ENGLAND.

'FANTASQUE' and 'Bizarre' used c1930 onward.

CERAMICS

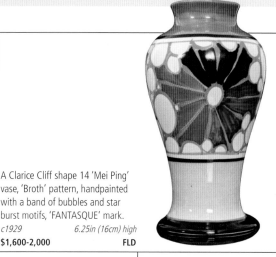

A Clarice Cliff shape 14 'Mei Ping' vase, 'Broth' pattern, handpainted with a band of bubbles and star burst motifs, 'FANTASQUE' mark.
c1929   *6.25in (16cm) high*
$1,600-2,000   **FLD**

A Clarice Cliff shape 362 vase, 'Broth' pattern, gold 'FANTASQUE' and 'Lawleys' marks.
c1929   *7.75in (20cm) high*
$1,500-2,500   **FLD**

A Clarice Cliff shape 690 preserve pot, 'Capri' pattern, 'Bizarre' mark.
c1935   *5.5in (14cm) high*
$350-400   **FLD**

A Clarice Cliff conical sugar sifter, 'Blue Chintz' pattern, 'FANTASQUE' and 'Bizarre' mark, restored.

In a 'soft' market, collectors often shy away from restoration unless it is a rare pattern.
c1932   *5.5in (14cm) high*
$250-350   **FLD**

A Clarice Cliff shape 478 bomb form biscuit barrel, 'Orange Chintz' pattern, with a chrome-plated cover and swing handle, 'Bizarre' mark.
c1932   *6.75in (17cm) high*
$400-450   **FLD**

A Clarice Cliff 'Conical' shape coffee pot, 'Circle Tree (RAF Tree)' pattern, 'FANTASQUE' mark.
c1929   *7in (17.5cm) high*
$900-1,000   **FLD**

A Clarice Cliff 'Biarritz' side plate, 'Coral Firs' pattern, large script signature and 'Biarritz' mark.
c1936   *6.5in (16.5cm) wide*
$130-200   **FLD**

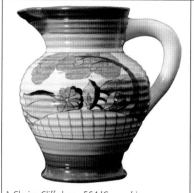

A Clarice Cliff shape 564 'George' jug, 'Cornwall' pattern, handpainted with a stylized garden landscape, 'FANTASQUE' and 'Bizarre' mark.
c1933   *6.75in (17cm) high*
$550-650   **FLD**

A Clarice Cliff 'Bon Jour' preserve pot and cover, 'Blue Cowslip' pattern, 'Bizarre' mark.
c1930   *4in (10cm) high*
$350-400   **FLD**

A Clarice Cliff 'Athens' teapot and cover, 'Crocus' pattern, printed factory mark, professional restoration to rim of the teapot.

5.5in (14cm) high

$200-250   WW

A Clarice Cliff sandwich plate, 'Crocus' pattern, 'CROCUS' and 'Bizarre' mark.

The collecting market for Clarice Cliff pottery is complex. It is still possible to find examples of 'Crocus', Cliff's longest produced pattern (1928-64) and some of the more pedestrian relief-molded wares such as 'Celtic Harvest', for as little as $40-100, but rare combinations of shape and pattern attract very high prices at auction.

c1931   *10.75in (27cm) wide*

$60-100   FLD

A Clarice Cliff shape 310 chamber stick, 'Diamonds' pattern, 'Bizarre' mark.

c1929   *2.75in (7cm) high*

$350-400   FLD

A Clarice Cliff shape 269 vase, 'Double V' pattern, 'Bizarre' mark.

c1929   *6in (15cm) high*

$850-900   FLD

A CLOSER LOOK AT A 'DOUBLE D' VASE

This shape 465 'Double D' vase is an absolute Art Deco classic. It was produced from 1931-c1934. _____

The 'Green Erin' pattern is very desirable. _____

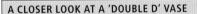

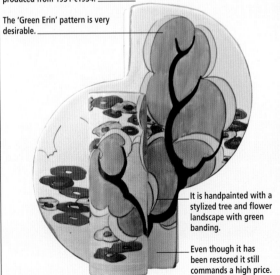

It is handpainted with a stylized tree and flower landscape with green banding.

Even though it has been restored it still commands a high price.

A Clarice Cliff vase, 'Bizarre' mark, restored.

c1933   *7.5in (19cm) high*

$2,000-2,500   FLD

A Clarice Cliff shape 200 vase, 'Double V Variant' pattern, handpainted with graduated V forms in green, purple and orange with stylized leaves, large 'Bizarre' mark.

c1929   *7.5in (19cm) high*

$850-900   FLD

A Clarice Cliff small 'Isis' vase, 'Eating Apples' pattern, 'Bizarre' mark, restored.

c1935   *6in (15cm) high*

$90-110   FLD

A Clarice Cliff shape 566 vase, 'Orange Erin' pattern, 'Bizarre' mark.

c1933   *4.75in (12cm) high*

$450-550   FLD

A Clarice Cliff 'Isis' jug, 'Farmhouse' pattern, handpainted with a stylized tree and cottage landscape, double image, 'FANTASQUE' and 'Bizarre' mark.

c1931   *9.75in (25cm) high*

$2,000-2,500   FLD

A Clarice Cliff preserve pot, 'Feathers and Leaves' pattern, partial 'Bizarre' mark.
c1929 8.5in (21.5cm) high
$350-400 **FLD**

A Clarice Cliff open preserve pot, 'Floreat' pattern, 'FANTASQUE' mark.
c1930 8.5in (21.5cm) high
$400-550 **FLD**

Judith Picks

This piece is an excellent example of the enduring popularity of Clarice Cliff. The shape is a classic, being a single-handled 'Isis' vase which displays the pattern extremely well. The 'Football' pattern, handpainted in an abstract block and line design with stylized net motifs between, blue and orange banding, is dramatic and instantly screams Art Deco.

A Clarice Cliff vase, large 'Bizarre' mark.
c1929 9.75in (25cm) high
$4,000-4,500 **FLD**

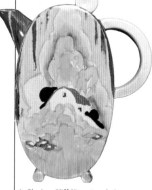

A Clarice Cliff 'Bon Jour' shape coffee pot, 'Forest Glen' pattern, handpainted with a stylized cottage landscape below a tonal red 'Delecia' sky, large script signature.
c1935 18.5in (47cm) high
$600-750 **FLD**

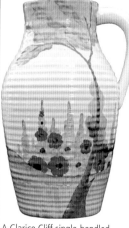

A Clarice Cliff single-handled 'Lotus' jug, 'Fragrance' pattern, large script signature.
c1936 11.75in (30cm) high
$650-800 **FLD**

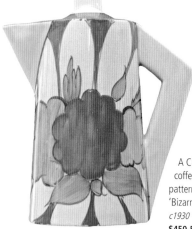

A Clarice Cliff 'Conical' coffee pot, 'Fruitburst' pattern, 'FANTASQUE' and 'Bizarre' marks.
c1930 7in (18cm) high
$450-550 **FLD**

A Clarice Cliff shape 358 vase, 'Orange Gardenia' pattern, 'FANTASQUE' mark.
c1931 7.75in (20cm) high
$2,500-3,500 **FLD**

A Clarice Cliff shape 265 vase, 'Red Gardenia' pattern, 'FANTASQUE' and 'Bizarre' marks.
c1931 6in (15cm) high
$800-950 **FLD**

A Clarice Cliff shape 362 vase, 'Gibraltar' pattern, handpainted with sailing boats at sea, 'FANTASQUE' and 'Bizarre' marks.

c1931   7.75in (20cm) high

$3,500-4,000   FLD

A Clarice Cliff shape 376 vase, 'Gloria Garden' pattern, 'Bizarre' mark.

c1930 7in (17.5cm) high

$400-450   FLD

A Clarice Cliff shape 362 vase, 'Honolulu' pattern, handpainted with a stylized tree with 'Zebra' stripe trunk, 'FANTASQUE' and 'Bizarre' mark.

c1933   7.75in (20cm) high

$3,000-4,000   FLD

A Clarice Cliff 'Apple' preserve pot, 'House and Bridge' pattern, with lid, 'FANTASQUE' and 'Bizarre' marks, a few slight chips to lid.

3.75in (9.5cm) high

$250-350   LOCK

A Clarice Cliff 'Drum' preserve pot, 'House and Bridge' pattern, 'FANTASQUE' and 'Bizarre' mark.

c1932   9.5in (24cm) high

$250-350   FLD

A Clarice Cliff shape 420 cigarette holder, 'Orange House' pattern, double image, 'FANTASQUE' and 'Bizarre' mark.

c1931   3.25in (8cm) high

$350-450   FLD

A Clarice Cliff shape 342 vase, 'Orange House' pattern, 'FANTASQUE' and 'Bizarre' mark.

c1930   7.75in (20cm) high

$1,300-2,000   FLD

A Clarice Cliff shape 358 vase, 'Inspiration Knight Errant' pattern, handpainted 'INSPIRATION' and 'Bizarre' mark, restored.

Due to the volatility of the mat glazes, a separate small team of 'Bizarre Girl' decorators was created and trained by Cliff to specialize on this range. This 'Knight Errant' pattern is handpainted with a knight on horseback in front of a castle, with a flowering bough to the opposing side. It is a complex design and is unusual and rare. Hence the value despite the restoration.

c1930   7.75in (20cm) high

$2,500-3,000   FLD

Judith Picks

While collecting Clarice Cliff can seem rather daunting, focusing on plates can be a good place to start. Plates tend to show the pattern well, are easy to display and tend to be more affordable as more were made and they are more plentiful on the market today. At most Antiques Roadshows we see quite a few examples, particularly, of course, the more common patterns.

A Clarice Cliff plate, 'Blue Japan' pattern, handpainted with a stylized pagoda and tree landscape with stippled 'Cafe au Lait' effect sky and ground, 'Bizarre' mark.
c1934   9in (23cm) wide
$200-250   **FLD**

A large Clarice Cliff 'Bon Jour' shape teapot, 'Jonquil' pattern, handpainted with a 'Delecia' streaked ground, 'Bizarre' mark.
c1935   6.5in (16.5cm) high
$350-400   **FLD**

A Clarice Cliff 'Bizarre' large sabot, 'Kew' pattern, impressed marks.
5.25in (13.5cm) long
$400-550   **WW**

A Clarice Cliff 'Greek' shape jug, 'Kew' pattern, handpainted with a 'Pagoda' in a garden setting, 'Bizarre' mark.
c1932   9in (23cm) high
$1,600-2,000   **FLD**

A small Clarice Cliff octagonal side plate, 'Latona Dahlia' pattern, handpainted with stylized flowers, handpainted 'LATONA' and 'Bizarre' mark.
c1930   5.75in (14.5cm) wide
$200-250   **FLD**

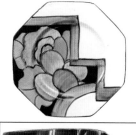

A Clarice Cliff shape 374 'Archaic' vase, 'Lightning' pattern, 'Bizarre' mark, some damage.
c1930   12.25in (31cm) high
$2,500-3,000   **FLD**

A Clarice Cliff 'Stamford' sugar bowl, 'Limberlost' pattern, unmarked.
c1932   2.5in (6.5cm) high
$130-200   **FLD**

A Clarice Cliff 'Conical' shape jug, 'Marigold' pattern, handpainted 'MARIGOLD' and 'Bizarre' mark.
c1930   6in (15cm) high
$1,500-2,000   **FLD**

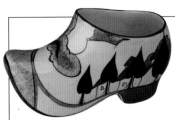

A Clarice Cliff sabot, 'May Avenue' pattern, handpainted with a stylized landscape with cottages behind spade-form trees with a large tree to the foreground with blue banding, 'Bizarre' mark.

The 'May Avenue' pattern embodies many of the features that Clarice Cliff collectors covet - bold designs and semi-abstraction. A 'May Avenue' charger realized £20,500 ($27,000) at the Fieldings Clarice Cliff Collectors' Club auction in May 2009.

c1933
$2,000-2,500   LOCK

A CLOSER LOOK AT A SUGAR CASTER

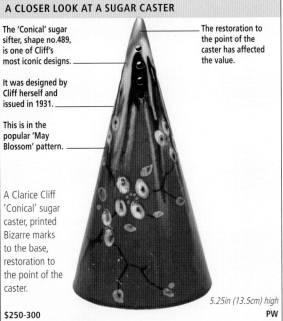

The 'Conical' sugar sifter, shape no.489, is one of Cliff's most iconic designs.

It was designed by Cliff herself and issued in 1931.

This is in the popular 'May Blossom' pattern.

The restoration to the point of the caster has affected the value.

A Clarice Cliff 'Conical' sugar caster, printed Bizarre marks to the base, restoration to the point of the caster.

5.25in (13.5cm) high
$250-300   PW

A Clarice Cliff 'Athens' teapot and cover, 'Melon' pattern, 'FANTASQUE' and 'Bizarre' mark.
c1929   6in (15cm) high
$650-800   FLD

A Clarice Cliff octagonal plate, 'Melon' pattern, 'FANTASQUE' mark.
c1930   9in (23cm) wide
$450-550   FLD

A Clarice Cliff shape 14 'Mei Ping' vase, 'Moonflower' pattern, 'Bizarre' mark, restored.

c1933   6in (15cm) high
$400-450   FLD

A Clarice Cliff shape 353 goblet vase, 'Moonlight' pattern, 'Bizarre' mark.
c1933   6in (15cm) high
$650-800   FLD

A large Clarice Cliff 'Bee Hive' honey pot, 'Mountain' pattern, handpainted with a stylized tree and cottage landscape before a mountain, 'FANTASQUE' and 'Bizarre' mark, base restored.
c1931   4in (10cm) high
$300-400   FLD

A Clarice Cliff shape 336 biscuit barrel, 'Nasturtium' pattern, 'Bizarre' mark.
c1932   6.75in (17cm) high
$400-450   FLD

CERAMICS

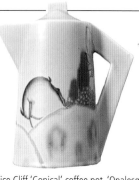

A Clarice Cliff 'Conical' coffee pot, 'Opalesque Stencil Deer' pattern, 'Bizarre' mark, some damage.

c1934   *7in (18cm) high*
$350-400   **FLD**

A Clarice Cliff 'Conical' shape teapot, 'Oranges' pattern, 'Bizarre' mark.

c1931   *4.25in (11cm) high*
$900-1,100   **FLD**

A Clarice Cliff 'Tankard' shape coffee can and saucer, 'Original Bizarre' pattern, handpainted red 'Bizarre' mark, cup restored.

c1928
$200-250   **FLD**

A CLOSER LOOK AT A VASE

This is an early Newport Pottery vase in the 'Original Bizarre' pattern.

It is decorated in the Oriental taste with domed cover and 'Dog of Fo' finial.

These initial 'Bizarre' designs incorporated crude handpainted interlocking triangles, between yellow, rust red and green banding.

A Clarice Cliff vase, numbered '180', large 'Bizarre' mark.
c1928   *11.75in (30cm) high*
$1,000-1,200   **FLD**

A Clarice Cliff 'Bon Jour' teapot, milk jug and sugar bowl, 'Delecia Pansies' pattern, 'Bizarre' mark, some damage.
c1932   *teapot 5in (13cm) high*
$800-950   **FLD**

A small Clarice Cliff 'Isis' vase, 'Passionfruit' pattern, large blue script signature.
c1936   *6in (15.5cm) high*
$250-300   **FLD**

A large Clarice Cliff dish form wall plaque, 'Patina Garden' pattern, handpainted with a splatter effect ground, 'PATINA' and 'Bizarre' mark.
c1932   *13.25in (33.5cm) wide*
$550-650   **FLD**

A Clarice Cliff shape 234 vase, 'Pebbles' pattern, 'FANTASQUE' mark.
c1929   *4.25in (11cm) high*
$800-950   **FLD**

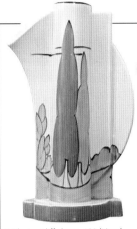

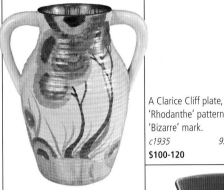

A Clarice Cliff plate, 'Rhodanthe' pattern, 'Bizarre' mark.

c1935   *9.75in (25cm) wide*

$100-120   **FLD**

A Clarice Cliff shape 469 'Liner' vase, 'Poplar' pattern, 'FANTASQUE' and 'Bizarre' mark.

c1932   *8.25in (21cm) high*

$2,500-3,500   **FLD**

A Clarice Cliff twin-handled 'Lotus' vase, 'Rhodanthe' pattern, printed marks, heavily restored and cracked.

11.75in (30cm) high

$550-600   **CHEF**

A Clarice Cliff advertising plaque, 'Orange Roof Cottage' pattern, handpainted marks.

c1932   *6in (15cm) high*

$2,000-2,500   **FLD**

A Clarice Cliff shape 360 vase, 'Orange Roof Cottage' pattern.

c1932   *8.25in (21cm) high*

$1,200-1,300   **FLD**

A Clarice Cliff shape 120 vase, 'Red Roofs' pattern, 'FANTASQUE' and 'Bizarre' mark.

c1931   *10.25in (26cm) high*

$2,500-3,500   **FLD**

A Clarice Cliff shape 335 biscuit barrel, 'Red Roofs' pattern, 'FANTASQUE' and 'Bizarre' mark, with original handle.

c1931   *6.25in (16cm) high*

$550-650   **FLD**

A Clarice Cliff plate, 'Red Roofs' pattern, with 'FANTASQUE' and 'Bizarre' marks.

9in (23cm) diam

$400-550   **HAN**

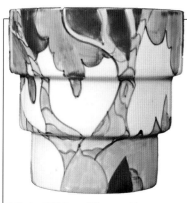

A Clarice Cliff shape 421 stepped fern pot, 'Rudyard' pattern, 'Bizarre' mark.

c1933   *6in (15cm) high*

$450-550   **FLD**

A Clarice Cliff shape 450 'Daffodil' bowl, 'Rudyard' pattern, 'FANTASQUE' and 'Bizarre' mark.

This is an unusual and desirable shape.

c1933   *13in (33cm) wide*

$1,600-2,000   **FLD**

A Clarice Cliff 'Coronet' shape jug, 'Sandon' pattern, 'Bizarre' mark.

c1935   *6in (15cm) high*

$300-400   **FLD**

A Clarice Cliff cake plate, 'Secrets' pattern, with a chrome-plated carry handle, 'Bizarre' mark.

c1933   *8.5in (21.5cm) wide*

$300-400   **FLD**

A Clarice Cliff 'Heath' shape fern pot, 'Sharks Teeth' pattern, 'Bizarre' mark.

c1929   *3.75in (9.5cm) high*

$1,000-1,300   **FLD**

A Clarice Cliff 'Isis' vase, 'Sliced Fruit' pattern, restored.

c1930   *10in (25.5cm) high*

$300-400   **FLD**

A Clarice Cliff shape 230 double ogee form preserve pot, 'Solitude' pattern, with berry finials, 'FANTASQUE' and 'Bizarre' marks.

3.25in (8.5cm) high

$300-400   **HAN**

A Clarice Cliff shape 472 bon-bon dish, 'Solitude' pattern, 'FANTASQUE' and 'Bizarre' mark.

c1933   *9.5in (24cm) wide*

$300-400   **FLD**

A Clarice Cliff shape 566 vase, 'Spire' pattern, large script signature.

c1937   *5in (12.5cm) high*

$400-450   **FLD**

A Clarice Cliff shape 186 vase, 'Summerhouse' pattern.

6.25in (16cm) high
$1,300-2,000   **HAN**

A Clarice Cliff tea plate, 'Summerhouse' pattern, with printed factory mark.

6in (15cm) diam
$400-450   **WW**

A Clarice Cliff shape 365 vase, 'Summerhouse' pattern, 'FANTASQUE' and 'Bizarre' marks.

c1931   *7.75in (20cm) high*
$1,700-2,000   **FLD**

A Clarice Cliff shape 14 'Mei Ping' vase, 'Summerhouse' pattern, 'FANTASQUE' and 'Bizarre' marks.

c1932   *9in (23cm) high*
$2,500-3,500   **FLD**

A CLOSER LOOK AT A 'LOTUS' JUG

A 'Lotus' jug's is amongst the most characteristic shapes associated with Cliff. It was actually designed by John Butler in 1919.

It is handpainted with an abstract landscape with sun burst, skyscrapers and birds.

Classic Art Deco subject matter.

The orange and black display the oily sheen present on original Cliff.

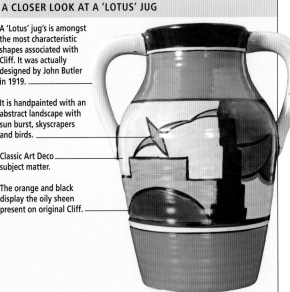

A Clarice Cliff 'Crown' shaped jug, 'Sunrise' pattern, 'FANTASQUE' mark with gold 'Lawleys' backstamp, restored.

c1930   *3.75in (9.5cm) high*
$400-450   **FLD**

A Clarice Cliff double-handled 'Lotus' jug, 'Sunray (Night and Day)' pattern, 'Bizarre' mark.

c1929   *11.5in (29cm) high*
$2,500-4,000   **FLD**

A Clarice Cliff 'Chester' fern pot, 'Blue Sunrise' pattern, 'FANTASQUE' mark.

c1929   *3.5in (9cm) high*
$600-750   **FLD**

A Clarice Cliff 'Isis' vase, 'Red Sunrise' pattern, 'FANTASQUE' mark.

c1929   *9.75in (25cm) high*
$1,000-1,200   **FLD**

A Clarice Cliff 'Heath' shape fern pot, 'Swirls' pattern, 'Bizarre' mark.

c1929   *7in (18cm) high*
$600-750   **FLD**

CERAMICS

A Clarice Cliff 'Crown' shape jug, 'Blue Trees and House' pattern, 'FANTASQUE' and 'Bizarre' mark, banding refreshed.
c1930   *3.75in (9.5cm) high*
$250-300   **FLD**

A large Clarice Cliff 'Conical' jug, 'Orange Trees and House' pattern, 'FANTASQUE' mark, restored.
c1930   *18in (45.5cm) high*
$750-800   **FLD**

A large Clarice Cliff shape 383 'Conical' bowl, 'Red Trees and House' pattern, 'Bizarre' mark.
c1930   *9.25in (23.5cm) wide*
$1,200-1,600   **FLD**

A Clarice Cliff 'Athens' shape jug, 'Red Tulip' pattern, 'FANTASQUE' and 'Bizarre' mark, some damage.
c1931   *6in (15.5cm) high*
$250-300   **FLD**

A Clarice Cliff 'Leda' shape preserve dish, 'Tulips' pattern, 'Bizarre' mark.
c1933   *5.25in (13.5cm) wide*
$200-250   **FLD**

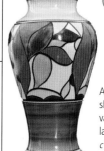

A Clarice Cliff shape 204 vase, 'Umbrellas' pattern, 'FANTASQUE' mark.
c1929   6in (15.5cm) high
$750-800   **FLD**

A large Clarice Cliff shape 14 'Mei Ping' vase, 'Whisper' pattern, large 'Bizarre' mark.
c1929 11.75in (30cm) high
$1,300-2,000   **FLD**

A Clarice Cliff 'Conical' coffee service, 'Umbrellas and Rain' pattern, 'FANTASQUE' mark.
c1930
$4,000-4,500   **FLD**

A Clarice Cliff 'Bizarre Fantasque' cake plate, 'Windbells' pattern.
c1930s   *8.75in (22cm) diam*
$250-350   **LOCK**

A Clarice Cliff 'Stamford' shape early morning breakfast set, 'Windbells' pattern, 'Bizarre' marks.

c1933

$3,500-4,000   FLD

A Clarice Cliff dish, decorated with the 'Woman's Journal' pattern, black printed Wilkinson's 'Bizarre' mark.

7.5in (19cm) diam

$200-250   KEY

A Clarice Cliff 'Bon Jour' teapot, 'Xavier' pattern, handpainted with a 'Cafe au Lait' stippled yellow ground, 'Bizarre' mark, restored.

c1933   5in (13cm) high

$850-900   FLD

A Clarice Cliff figure, of a seated Arab, 'Wilkinson Ltd' mark only.

4.75in (12cm) high

$100-130   FLD

A Clarice Cliff water lily planter.

8.75in (22cm) long

$80-100   LOCK

A Wilkinson fish ashtray, designed by Clarice Cliff, the fins fluted for cigarettes.

5in (13cm) wide

$80-100   HAN

A Clarice Cliff shape 424 novelty flower block, 'Angel Fish', partial 'Bizarre' mark.

7.75in (20cm) high

$750-800   FLD

A modern Wedgwood 'Age of Jazz' table centerpiece, originally designed by Clarice Cliff, with printed marks.

8in (20.5cm) high

$150-200   WW

CERAMICS

QUICK REFERENCE - CHARLOTTE RHEAD

- Charlotte Rhead (1885-1947) was the daughter of pottery designer Frederick Rhead (see page 162 and 163). She attended Fenton Art School, then worked as a decorator and designer at a number of potteries, including Wardle & Co., Burgess & Leigh and most notably A.G. Richardson.
- A.G. Richardson & Co. was founded in 1915. Its 'Crown Ducal Ware' pottery range included dinner, tea and breakfast services in a variety of patterns.
- Charlotte Rhead joined the factory in 1931. She introduced the 'tube-lining' technique of decoration, where outlines are piped onto a ceramic surface, leaving a low relief outline design where spaces can be filled with colored glazed. Her distinctive patterns, such as 'Rhodian', 'Indian Tree', 'Golden Leaves' and 'Wisteria', were influenced by the Art Deco movement. She left the factory in 1942 and worked at H.J. Wood until her death in 1947.

A Crown Ducal charger, designed by Chalotte Rhead, in the 'Persian Rose' design, pattern no.4040.

14.25in (36.5cm) diam

$60-100   HAN

A Crown Ducal wall charger, by Charlotte Rhead, in the 'Carnation' design, pattern no.4924.

12.5in (32.5cm) diam

$550-650   PSA

A Crown Ducal charger, by Charlotte Rhead, in the 'Wisteria' design, pattern no.2954.

12.75in (32.5cm) diam

$250-350   PSA

A Crown Ducal wall charger, by Charlotte Rhead, in the 'Arabian Scroll' design, pattern no.4926.

12.75in (32.5cm) diam

$130-200   PSA

A Crown Ducal wall charger, by Charlotte Rhead, in the 'Caliph' design, pattern no.5411.

12.75in (32.5cm) diam

$150-200   PSA

A Crown Ducal vase, designed by Charlotte Rhead, in the 'Wisteria' design, in ribbed shouldered form, no.2124954, signed to base.

7.5in (19cm) high

$90-110   HAN

A Crown Ducal pottery vase, by Charlotte Rhead, decorated with scaly dragons upon a green ground, signature and printed marks to underside, with crazing and rubbing

6.75in (17cm) high

$80-100   FELL

A Crown Ducal 'War Against Hitlerism' teapot.

8.25in (21cm) long

$90-100   LOCK

QUICK REFERENCE - DENNIS CHINAWORKS

- Dennis Chinaworks was founded in Somerset, England, in 1993, by husband and wife Richard Dennis and Sally Tuffin. The company produces ceramic vessels with a small in-house team of hand-decorators. The patterns often take inspiration from the natural world, with designs incorporating animals and plants.
- Sally Tuffin studied at Walthamstow Art School and the Royal Collage of Art. From 1961-72, she co-ran a fashion design business, Foale & Tuffin. She also worked as design director for Moorcroft Pottery 1986-93 (see pages 107-118).
- Richard Dennis trained with Sotheby's, before establishing an antique glass and ceramic business and later a publishing house producing books for collectors.
- Today, the majority of Dennis Chinaworks wares are designed by Sally Tuffin and their son, Buchan Dennis.
- Many works have been commissioned for prestigious galleries and museums, including the Pugin Exhibition at the Victoria & Albert Museum, the Andrew Lloyd Webber Collection at the Royal Academy of Arts and the Durer Exhibition at the British Museum.
- Many wares are made in limited editions. The most sought after pieces tend to be trial pieces or those from limited editions of less than 50.

A Dennis Chinaworks trial bottle shape vase, designed by Buchan Dennis, with the 'Tumbling Blocks' design, printed and painted marks.
2014   *12.5in (32cm) high*
$1,300-2,000   **WW**

A Dennis Chinaworks 'Football' limited edition vase, designed by Buchan Dennis, painted by Adam White, thrown by Rory Mcleod, dated, painted marks.
2010   *7in (18cm) high*
$200-250   **WW**

A limited edition Dennis Chinaworks vase, designed by Sally Tuffin, with the 'Lobster' design, printed and painted marks.

For Sally Tuffin's work for Moorcroft, see page 118.
2003   *11in (28cm) high*
$650-800   **WW**

A limited edition Dennis Chinaworks 'Thisbe' vase, designed by Sally Tuffin, after a design by William Morris, painted by Vanessa Whitemore, thrown by Rory Mcleod, dated, painted marks.
1997   *9.5in (24cm) high*
$550-650   **WW**

A Dennis Chinaworks 'Jousting Tent' trial jar and cover, designed by Sally Tuffin, painted by Adam White, thrown by Rory Mcleod, dated, painted marks, trial 5.
2010   *9.75in (25cm) high*
$750-800   **WW**

A Dennis Chinaworks limited edition 'Zebra' vase, designed by Sally Tuffin, impressed and painted marks, light star crack to base, dated.
1999   *9in (23cm) high*
$250-350   **WW**

A Dennis Chinaworks 'Klimt Kiss' limited edition sidestep vase, designed by Sally Tuffin, painted by Heidi Warr, thrown by Rory Mcleod, painted in a unique colorway on a yellow ground, dated, painted marks.
2006   *9.75in (25cm) high*
$550-650   **WW**

A Dennis Chinaworks limited edition vase, 'Klimt Dancer', designed by Sally Tuffin, painted by Theresa Blackmore, thrown by Rory Mcleod, painted marks, one-off color variation, dated.
2015   *12.25in (31cm) high*
$400-550   **WW**

CERAMICS

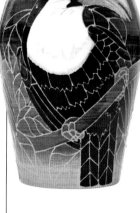

A Dennis Chinaworks vase, designed by Sally Tuffin, impressed and painted marks.

6.75in (17cm) high

$200-250 FLD

A limited edition Dennis Chinaworks 'Black Cat' vase, designed by Sally Tuffin, painted by Natasha Chapman-Cox, thrown by Rory Mcleod, dated, painted marks.

2014 *11.5in (29cm) high*

$400-450 WW

A Dennis Chinaworks vase, designed by Sally Tuffin, decorated with tube-lined toucans, impressed and painted marks.

6.25in (16cm) high

$90-110 FLD

A Dennis Chinaworks lidded box, 'Blue Snowdrop' pattern, designed by Sally Tuffin, the knop formed as a bumble bee, impressed marks, some damage.

4.25in (11cm) high

$60-80 FLD

A large Dennis Chinaworks vase, by Sally Tuffin, decorated with polar bears on a glacier, dated.

2003 *14.25in (36cm) high*

$200-250 PSA

A Dennis Chinaworks vase, 'Carp' pattern, designed by Sally Tuffin, in the purple colorway, impressed and painted marks.

8.75in (22cm) high

$250-350 FLD

A Dennis Chinaworks 'Corn and Poppy' limited edition flask and lid, designed by Sally Tuffin, painted by Natasha Chapman-Cox, thrown by Rory Mcleod, the lid with mouse finial, dated, with painted marks.

2011 *8.5in (21.5cm) high*

$350-400 WW

A Doulton & Watts 'Mr and Mrs Caudle' reform flask, molded with Robert William Jerrold's characters Mr and Mrs Caudle in bed to the front above the quote 'No! Mr Caudle, I shall not go to sleep like a good soul, see Punch', the reverse with Mrs Prettyman, impressed factory marks to the base.

7in (18cm) high

$130-200   LA

An Aesthetic Movement Doulton Lambeth stoneware water jug, designed by Hannah Barlow, incised with cattle, incised monogram and marks '766'.

1878   9in (23cm) high

$450-550   HAN

QUICK REFERENCE - DOULTON LAMBETH

- The Doulton Factory was founded in Lambeth, London, in 1815 by John Doulton, Martha Jones and John Watts. Doulton first focused on everyday stoneware such as inkwells and bottles.
- When John Doulton's son Henry joined the firm in 1835, the business expanded. It began to make and supply drainpipes to various cities around the world. Henry's success allowed the factory to switch their focus to decorative wares from 1871.
- Doulton worked closely with the Lambeth School of Art, and many Doulton pieces were designed and decorated by students. These 'Doulton Lambeth' pieces are often in the Art Nouveau style.
- Most are signed with artists' monograms. Significant designers include the Tinworth brothers, Arthur (dates unknown) and George (1843-1913), and the Barlow siblings, Hannah (1859-1913), Florence (d.1909) and Arthur (d.1909).
- Doulton prices have declined over the past 15 years, especially for late 19thC and early 20thC Victorian-style stoneware. The most valuable pieces tend to be those by notable designers, such as Mark Marshall or the Barlow or Tinworth siblings. Unusual patterns, shapes, sizes or styles, especially Moorish or Art Nouveau-style pieces, can also fetch high prices.

An Aesthetic Movement Doulton Lambeth stoneware biscuit barrel, designed by Hannah Barlow, incised with horses, mounted with a Mappin Brothers collar, lid, and handle, monogram and marks 'b78'.

1879   6.25in (16cm) high

$600-650   HAN

A Doulton Lambeth lemonade jug, by Hannah Barlow, depicting milkmaid, cattle and buildings in the background, impressed marks, dated.

1879   8.75in (22.5cm) high

$1,000-1,300   K&O

A rare Doulton Lambeth teapot and lid, by Hannah Barlow, sgraffito decorated with two large oval panels of cats and four circular mouse panels, with incised floral and foliate design to the body.

c1880   6.5in (16.5cm) high

$2,000-2,500   K&O

A pair of Doulton stoneware vases, by Hannah Barlow, incised with cattle, marked to base '463' and monograms.

11in (28cm) high

$800-950   HAN

A large Doulton Lambeth 'The Waning of the Honeymoon' group, attributed to Mark Marshall.

1895   6.75in (17cm) high

$2,000-2,500   K&O

A large Doulton jardinière, by Bessie Newberry, Gothic reform-style floral design in relief, stamped marks and incised 'B N', some scratching to glaze.

13in (33cm) long

$120-160   ECGW

CERAMICS

A rare Doulton Lambeth cashpot, by George Tinworth, modeled with young tennis players at each corner, signed 'GT', impressed marks, professional restoration to some figures.

In a fairly depressed Doulton market, prices for George Tinworth stoneware have remained relatively high.

	4.75in (12cm) high
$1,600-2,000	**K&O**

A rare Doulton Lambeth match striker, by Harry Simeon, modeled as a man with tricorn hat, seated next to a drum, marked 'Doulton Lambeth England'.

c1920	5.5in (14cm) high
$1,200-1,600	**K&O**

A Doulton Lambeth 'Aspreys' flask, designed by Harry Simeon, complete with original stopper, impressed marks.

c1890	9.5in (24cm) high
$350-400	**K&O**

A Doulton Lambeth stoneware vase and cover, by Eliza Simmance, signed.

c1890	11.5in (29cm) high
$400-550	**K&O**

A Doulton Lambeth 'Musician', by George Tinworth, depicting a mouse standing, playing a horn, dated, incised monogram, one ear with large chips, broken from the base and re-glued.

1885	4.25in (11cm) high
$800-950	**LA**

A very rare Doulton Lambeth 'The Cockneys at Brighton' group, by George Tinworth, impressed with the 'GT' monogram and Doulton mark.

c1885	3.75in (9.5cm) high
$7,500-8,500	**K&O**

A CLOSER LOOK AT A TINWORTH MOUSE GROUP

This early Doulton stoneware mouse group predates the 'HN' series by nearly thirty years.

This model was designed by George Tinworth (1843-1913), who worked for Doulton from 1866.

In the 1880s, George Tinworth modeled many mice groups, all with characterful expressions. Over twenty of these were 'mouse musicians'.

The stand is inscribed 'A little of it is all very well', calling into question the quality of the mice's music!

A Doulton Lambeth 'Pianist, Horn Player and Singer' mouse group, with Doulton rosette mark.

c1895	3.25in (8cm) high
$6,000-6,500	**K&O**

A rare Doulton Lambeth 'Crossing the Channel' group, by George Tinworth, signed on the back with the 'GT' monogram, with impressed mark.

c1885	4.75in (12cm) high
$4,000-5,500	**K&O**

A Doulton Lambeth 'Photography' group, by George Tinworth, signed 'GT' to the rear, impressed marks.

c1885	3.75in (9.5cm) high
$4,000-4,500	**K&O**

QUICK REFERENCE - ROYAL DOULTON FIGURINES

- Doulton first produced figurines in the 1880s under George Tinworth, then under Charles Noke from 1889 onward. From 1912, all figurines were assigned a 'HN' number. 'HN' stood for Harry Nixon, who ran the painting department. Over time, more than 4,000 HN numbers were assigned.

- By 1912, Doulton was known as Royal Doulton, after receiving a royal warrant in 1901. The first model to be assigned a HN number, HN1, was called 'Darling', because Queen Mary had called the figurine 'a darling' on a visit to the factory in 1913.

- Significant designers of Royal Doulton figurines include Leslie Harradine, who worked closely with Noke in the 1920s-50s, Mary Nicoll and Peggy Davies, who produced the majority of the figurines in the 1950s-60s, and Alan Maslankowski, who worked at Royal Doulton from 1968-2006.

- In general, collectors focus on type, color or designer. Figurines that were produced only for a short time are rarer and more valuable, as are those with an unusual colorway. Many Royal Doulton figurines were produced in a range of colorways, which can vary dramatically in price.

- In general, the most desirable and sought after figurines are those produced before World War II. Particular ranges or themes, such as 'Middle Earth' or 'Bunnykins', have also proved popular.

A Royal Doulton 'Lady of the Georgian Period', designed by E.W Light, no.HN41, black painted mark to the base 'Georgian Lady / C.J Noke SC / Potted by Doulton Co', with printed green mark and HN number.

Alternative versions of the 'Lady of the Georgian Period' exist in HN311, HN444, HN690 and HN702. HN41 was the first.

1914-36   *10.5in (27cm) high*

$550-650   **FLD**

A Royal Doulton 'Guy Fawkes' figurine, in a red cloak, black hat and robes, designed by C.J. Noke, HN98.

Two variations of this 'Guy Fawkes' figurine exist. 'Guy Fawkes' in a green cloak, no.HN445, was produced 1921-38. 'Guy Fawkes' in a brown cloak, no.HN347, was produced 1919-38. Both are extremely rare.

1918-49   *10.5in (26.5cm) high*

$650-800   **PSA**

A large Royal Doulton 'King Charles' figurine, designed by C.J. Noke and Harry Tittensor, HN404, inscribed 'King Charles' in gilt, with green printed factory mark.

'King Charles' was later reproduced as HN2084 with a yellow base, 1952-92, and in 1992 as HN3459 in a red, dark blue and purple coat in a limited edition of 350.

1920-51   *16.5in (42cm) high*

$800-1,000   **BE**

A Royal Doulton 'Helen' figurine, HN157.

8in (20.5cm) high

$250-350   **WHP**

An early Royal Doulton 'The Bather' figurine, designed by Leslie Harradine, HN687, with blue robe, inscribed 'Potted by Doulton & Co' to the base.

This model was made with a variety of colorways, as HN597, HN781, HN782, HN1238, HN1708. The rarest two models are HN781, where 'The Bather' wears a blue and green robe, and HN782, with a purple and black robe. Both were produced 1926-38.

1924-49   *9.75in (25cm) high*

$200-250   **APAR**

A Royal Doulton 'Modern Piper' figurine, designed by Leslie Harradine, HN756, inscribed on the base 'Pied Piper potted by Doulton & Co', restoration to base and back of cloak.

1925-40   *8.5in (21.5cm) high*

$650-800   **PSA**

A Royal Doulton 'Quality Street' figurine, HN1211, in crinoline dress in shades of pink and purple, with painted and printed marks to base.

1926-36   *7.25in (18.5cm) high*

$200-250   **GWA**

A Royal Doulton 'Baba' figurine, in green and orange, designed by Leslie Harradine, HN1248, with minor patches of crazing, glued at the head join, minor glaze losses.

A range of differently colored 'Babas' were made, nos.HN1230, HN1243, HN1244, HN1245, HN1246 and HN1247. They are all of roughly equal value.

1927-38   *3in (8cm) high*

$300-400   **PW**

CERAMICS

A Royal Doulton 'Sweet & Twenty' figurine, by Leslie Harradine (1887-1965), HN1298, painted maker's marks 'SWEET AND TWENTY / POTTED BY DOULTON & CO / HN1298 / HA' and printed and impressed factory marks, dated.

This figurine was produced in a range of different colors, in HN1360, HN1437, HN1438, HN1549, HN1563, and HN1649. The rarest is probably HN1563, the black and light pink variation, produced 1933-38.

1929   *7in (18cm) wide*

$250-300   **L&T**

A Royal Doulton 'Flower-seller's Children' figurine group, in purple, red and yellow, designed by Leslie Harradine, HN1342, underglaze painted, printed backstamp and painted marks verso.

Variations include HN525, HN551, HN1206 and HN1406. HN525 and HN551, the 'Flower-seller's Children' in green and blue, and in blue, orange and yellow respectively, are exceedingly rare, with few surviving examples known to exist.

7.75in (19.5cm) high

$60-80   **LSK**

A Royal Doulton 'The Windmills Lady' porcelain figurine, HN1400, designed by Leslie Harradine (1887-1965), painted, printed and impressed maker's marks, dated.

1931   *8.25in (21cm) high*

$900-1,000   **L&T**

A Royal Doulton earthenware 'Margery' figurine, in maroon and purple, designed by Leslie Harradine, HN1413.

1930-49   *10.5in (27cm) high*

$35-40   **LOCK**

A Royal Doulton 'The Potter' figurine, in brown, designed by C.J. Noke, HN1493, underglaze painted, printed backstamp and painted marks verso.

'The Potter' also comes in the rarer green, HN1518, or green and purple, HN1522.

6.75in (17cm) high

$80-100   **LSK**

A Royal Doulton 'Modena' figurine, in blue and pink, designed by Leslie Harradine, HN1845, overall fine crazing, two dark colored lines to the glaze.

No.HN1846 is an alternative 'Modena' in a red and green dress.

1938-49   *7.5in (19cm) high*

$250-350   **PW**

A Royal Doulton 'Bon Jour' figurine, in a green dress, designed by Leslie Harradine, HN1879.

No.HN1888 is an alternative 'Bon Jour' in red; both models are of roughly the same rarity.

1938-49   *6.75in (17cm) high*

$200-250   **PSA**

A Royal Doulton 'The Jester' figurine, designed by C.J. Noke, HN2016, in brown and mauve, with green printed marks.

'The Jester' comes in 15 different variations. The first was HN45, a jester in black and white, first issued in 1915.

10in (25cm) high

$60-80   **FELL**

A Royal Doulton 'Princess Badoura' Prestige figurine, designed by Harry Tittensor, H.E. Stanton and F. Van Allen Phillip, HN2081.

An alternative 'Princess Badoura' Prestige figurine exists in blue, red and gold, no.HN3921.

21.75in (55cm) high

$4,500-5,500   **PSA**

A Royal Doulton 'Giselle' figurine, in blue and white, designed by Peggy Davies, HN2139.
1954-69   *6in (15cm) high*
$50-70   **FLD**

A Royal Doulton 'Noelle' figurine, in orange, white and black, designed by Peggy Davies, HN2179.
1957-67   *7in (17.5cm) high*
$35-45   **WHP**

A Royal Doulton figurine of Omar Khayyam, designed by M. Nicoll, HN2247, non-original writing to base.
1965-83   *6in (16cm) high*
$45-55   **LOCK**

A Royal Doulton 'Queen of Sheba' figurine, from 'Les Femmes Fatales' range, designed by Peggy Davies, HN2328, no.668 of a limited edition of 750, with box and certificate.
1982   *9.5in (24cm) high*
$250-350   **PW**

A Royal Doulton 'St George and the dragon' Prestige figurine, designed by W.K. Harper, HN2856, signed 'PS 1982 Not for sale', one gold tassel missing from rear.
1982   *16in (40.5cm) high*
$2,000-2,500   **PSA**

A Royal Doulton 'Helen of Troy' figurine, from 'Les Femmes Fatales' range, designed by Peggy Davies, HN2387, no.663 of a limited edition of 750, with box and certificate.
1981   *9.5in (24cm) high*
$350-400   **PW**

A Royal Doulton 'Sir Winston Churchill' figurine, designed by A. Hughes, HN3057.
10.25in (26cm) high
$90-100   **WHP**

A Royal Doulton 'Dick Turpin on rearing black horse' model, designed by Graham Tongue, HN3272, from a limited edition of 5,000, commissioned by Lawleys By Post, with its certificate.
1989   *12in (30.5cm) high*
$130-200   **PSA**

A Royal Doulton 'General Lt General Uylsses S Grant' Prestige figurine, designed by Robert Tabbenor, HN3403, from a limited edition of 5,000, a marked artist's copy, with signature, without number.

1993   *11.75in (30cm) high*

$750-850   **PSA**

A Royal Doulton 'General Robert E Lee' Prestige figurine, designed by Robert Tabbenor, HN3404, from a limited edition of 5,000, a marked artist's copy, with signature, without number.

1993   *11.5in (29cm) high*

$800-950   **PSA**

A Royal Doulton 'Vice Admiral Lord Nelson' Prestige figurine, designed by Alan Maslankowski, HN3489, from a limited edition of 950, a marked artist's copy, with signature, without number.

1993   *12.5in (32cm) high*

$600-750   **PSA**

A Royal Doulton Archives 'Hebe, Handmaiden to the Gods' Prestige figurine, by Alan Maslankowski, HN4079, from a limited edition of 250, from the 'Immortals' collection, marked 'Artists Copy' to base.

2000   *14in (35cm) high*

$550-650   **PSA**

A Royal Doulton 'St George' prestige figurine, designed by Alan Maslankowski, HN4371, from a limited edition of 50, from the Classics collection, marked 'Artists Copy' and signed in gold on base, boxed, with certificate by Alan Maslankowski.

Provenance: the personal collection of Alan Maslankowski. Maslankowski worked at Royal Doulton from 1968-2006 and had written into his contract that he was to retain one piece of each model that was put into production.

2001   *17in (43cm) high*

$10,000-11,000   **PSA**

A Royal Doulton 'Alexander The Great' prestige figurine, designed by Alan Maslankowski, HN4481, from a limited edition of 50 from the Classics collection, marked 'Artists Copy' and signed in gold on base, with certificate by Alan Maslankowski.

2002   *18.25in (46cm) high*

$8,000-9,500   **PSA**

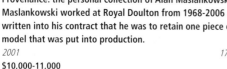

A Royal Doulton 'Spike & Tyke' figurine, from a from a limited edition of 500.

2000   *6in (15cm) high*

$40-50   **WHP**

A small Royal Doulton 'Jester' face mask, HN1611.

3in (7.5cm) high

$200-250   **K&O**

A Royal Doulton Bunnykins 'Artist' figurine, designed by Walter Hayward, modeled by Alan Maslankowski, DB13.

1975-82   *3.75in (9.5cm) high*
$40-50   **PSA**

A pair of Royal Doulton Bunnykins figurines, 'Footballer' DB119 and 'Goalkeeper' DB118, designed by Denise Andrews, modeled by Warren Platt, both limited editions of 250 each.

1991   *4.5in (12cm) high*
$250-350   **PSA**

A Royal Doulton Bunnykins 'The Milkman' figurine, designed by Graham Tongue, modeled by Amanda Hughes-Lubeck, DB125, from a special edition of 1,000.

1992   *4in (12cm) high*
$120-160   **PSA**

A Royal Doulton Bunnykins 'Clown' figurine, in white with black stars and pompoms, red squares on the trousers and a red ruff, designed by Denise Andrews, modeled by Warren Platt, DB128, from a special edition of 750.

An alternative Royal Doulton Bunnykins 'Clown' figurine, DB129, with red stars and pompoms, black squares to the trousers and a black ruff, was also released in 1992 as a special edition of 250.

1992   *4.25in (11cm) high*
$150-200   **PSA**

A Royal Doulton Bunnykins 'Trick or Treat' figurine, designed by Denise Andrews, modeled by Amanda Hughes-Lubeck, DB162, from a special edition of 1,500.

A rarer and more valuable prototype colorway of the Bunnykins 'Trick or Treat' figurine is known to exist.

1995   *4.5in (12cm) high*
$200-250   **PSA**

A Royal Doulton Bunnykins 'Trumpet Player', with green and yellow colorway, designed by Kimberly Curtis, modeled by Shane Ridge, DB210A, from a limited edition of 2,500 in total, 100 in this colorway, boxed with certificate.

This figurine was made to commemorate the 75th Anniversary of Bunnykins.

2000   *5in (12.5cm) high*
$45-55   **PSA**

A Royal Doulton Bunnykins 'Drummer', in black and red colorway, designed by Kimberly Curtis, modeled by Shane Ridge, DB250A, from a limited edition of 2,500 in total, 200 in this colorway, boxed with certificate.

This figurine was made to commemorate the 75th Anniversary of Bunnykins.

2001   *4.5in (11cm) high*
$60-80   **PSA**

A rare 1930s Royal Doulton Bunnykins 'Mary' figurine, designed by Charles Noke, D6002.

'Mary' was one of the first Bunnykins figurines ever produced.

6.5in (16.5cm) high
$550-600   **PSA**

A rare Royal Doulton Bunnykins teapot, the lid modeled as a rabbit's head, printed Bunnykins Royal Doulton marks.

7.75in (20cm) long
$250-400   **GWA**

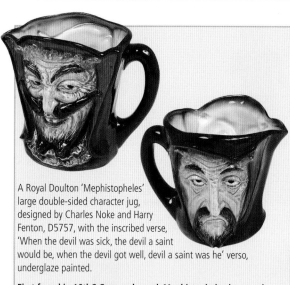

A Royal Doulton 'Mephistopheles' large double-sided character jug, designed by Charles Noke and Harry Fenton, D5757, with the inscribed verse, 'When the devil was sick, the devil a saint would be, when the devil got well, devil a saint was he' verso, underglaze painted.

First found in 16thC German legend, Mephistopheles became best known in Johann von Goethe's drama, 'Faust' (1808), where he is portrayed as an evil spirit or devil to whom Faust sells his soul.

1937-48   *6in (15cm) high*
$400-450   **LSK**

A Royal Doulton 'Auld Mac' small character jug, designed by Harry Fenton, D5824, in all white variation, small crack to edge.

This piece was inspired by a comedy song by Sir Harry Lauder, 'Bang Went Sixpence', about a Scotsman named Mac.
1937-85   *3.25in (8.5cm) high*
$40-50   **PSA**

A large Royal Doulton 'Old King Cole' musical character jug, designed by Harry Fenton, D6014, with a brown crown.

This jug plays the nursery rhyme 'Old King Cole was a Merry Old Soul'.
1939   *7.5in (19cm) high*
$400-550   **PSA**

A rare Royal Doulton 'Old King Cole' small character jug, designed by Harry Fenton, D6037, with a yellow crown.

An alternative variation of 'Old King Cole', D6037, with a brown crown, was introduced in 1939.
1938-39   *3.5in (9cm) high*
$600-650   **PSA**

A rare Royal Doulton 'Hatless Drake' large character jug, designed by Harry Fenton, D6115, in a red colorway.

An alternative 'Drake' character jug, wearing a hat, D6115, was produced 1940-60.
1940-41   *5.75in (14.5cm) high*
$1,300-2,000   **PSA**

Judith Picks

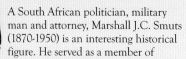

A South African politician, military man and attorney, Marshall J.C. Smuts (1870-1950) is an interesting historical figure. He served as a member of the British War Cabinet in World War I. He was Prime Minister of South Africa from 1919-24 and from 1939-48. He was the only man to sign both of the peace treaties ending World War I and World War II. Although Smuts had originally advocated racial segregation and opposed the enfranchisement of black Africans, he supported the Fagan Commission's recommendation that restrictions on black Africans in urban areas should be liberalized. Smuts subsequently lost the 1948 election to hard-line Afrikaners who created apartheid. He continued to work for reconciliation and emphasized the British Commonwealth's positive role until his death in 1950.

A large Royal Doulton 'Field Marshall J C Smuts' character jug, designed by Harry Fenton, D6198.
1946-48   *6.5in (16.5cm) high*
$650-800   **PSA**

A Royal Doulton 'Beefeater' large character jug, designed by Harry Fenton, D6206, variation with yellow highlights to the handle, with 'GR' cipher for King George VI.
1947-53   *6.5in (16.5cm) high*
$350-400   **PSA**

A large Royal Doulton 'White Haired Clown' character jug, designed by Harry Fenton, D6322. **This colorway is one of four variations of 'The Clown': Doulton also produced a red-haired clown, D5610, a brown-haired clown, D5610 and a black-haired clown, D6322.**

1951-55   *7.5in (19cm) high*

$250-350   PSA

A large Royal Doulton 'Ard Of 'Earing' character jug, designed by David D. Biggs, D6588.

1964-67   *7.5in (19cm) high*

$400-550   PSA

A rare Royal Doulton 'The Jockey' small character jug, designed by David B. Biggs, D6629.

While the large 'Jockey' character jug was widely produced, small and miniature sized jugs were test piloted but not produced, making this item far rarer.

1974   *4in (10cm) high*

$1,000-1,200   PSA

A Royal Doulton 'Guardsman' small character jug, designed by Stanley J. Taylor, D6771, in a white colorway.

1987-99   *4in (10cm) high*

$100-120   PSA

A Royal Doulton rare 'Sir Jack Hobbs' small character jug, D7131, designed by Stanley J. Taylor, from the Cricketers series, from a limited edition of 5,000.

1999   *4in (10cm) high*

$800-1,000   PSA

A Royal Doulton 'Don Quixote' large prototype character jug, with purple colored helmet, marked underneath with Royal Doulton stamp 'Royal Doulton tableware not for sale' in gold.

The 'Don Quixote' character jug was eventually produced in three sizes, large (D6455), small (D6460) and miniature (D6511).

$250-350   PSA

A rare Royal Doulton 'Blue Pearly Boy' small character jug, designed by Harry Fenton, with opaque buttons.

The 'Pearly Boy' character jug has no D number, but is a variation of 'Arry', D6235, with pearly buttons.

1949   *3.5in (9cm) high*

$1,300-1,700   PSA

A rare Royal Doulton 'The Yachtsman' small character jug.

The small 'Yachtsman' character jug was piloted but never put into production. The large 'Yachtsman' character jug, D6626, was produced 1971-80.

$800-950   PSA

CERAMICS

A rare Royal Doulton 'Pearly Girl' miniature character jug, designed by Harry Fenton, with a green feather hat, in brown colorway.

The 'Pearly Girl' character jug has no D number, but is a variation of 'Arriet', D6250, dressed in her finest.

1946   *2.5in (6.5cm) high*

$450-600   **PSA**

A rare Royal Doulton 'Pearly Girl' large character jug, designed by Harry Fenton, in white colorway, with a painted natural face.

6.5in (16.5cm) high

$1,600-2,000   **PSA**

A middle-sized Royal Doulton prototype 'The Miller' character jug, stamped 'not for re-sale' to the back.

This was sold with a certificate from Phillips 'The Marriage of Art and Industry' sale, 1999, lot 456.

$6,500-8,000   **PSA**

A middle-sized Royal Doulton prototype 'The Wife of Bath' character jug, stamped 'not for re-sale' to the back.

This was sold with a certificate from Phillips 'The Marriage of Art and Industry' sale, 1999, lot 456.

$6,500-7,500   **PSA**

A set of four Royal Doulton character jugs, comprising The King and Queen of Clubs, D6999, of Spades, D7087, of Hearts, D7037, and of Diamonds, D6969, designed by Stanley J. Taylor, from a limited edition of 2,500 of each, boxed with certificates.

1994-97   *5in (12.5cm) high*

$100-130   **FLD**

A set of rare 1990s Royal Doulton 'Dads Army' small prototype character jugs, comprising Sergeant Arthur Wilson, Captain George Mainwaring, Lance Corporal Jack Jones and Private James Frazer, all with 'not for re-sale' backstamp, impressed sample to base.

This set was sampled during the 1990s but never put into full production.

$8,500-10,000   **PSA**

A CLOSER LOOK AT A DOUBLE CHARACTER JUG

This double character jug depicts the literary characters Heathcliff and Cathy from Emily Brontë's 'Wuthering Heights'.

The right handle is engraved 'C' for Cathy and 'WH' for Wuthering Heights; the reverse is engraved 'TG' for Thrushcross Grange.

Each handle is cleverly designed to depict an element of the book. One is a tree, representing the Yorkshire moors; one shows the window of Wuthering Heights, which features in a key scene at the start of the book.

This model is a prototype, never put into production. This increases the value.

A Royal Doulton prototype 'Heathcliff and Cathy from Wuthering Heights' double character jug.

$2,500-3,500   **PSA**

A Royal Doulton 'Stalking Tiger' Prestige figurine, designed by Charles Noke, HN2646, signed 'JC'.
1955-92   *13.5in (34cm) long*
$400-450   PSA

A Royal Doulton flambé 'Stalking Tiger' Prestige figurine, designed by Charles Noke, HN2646, minor glaze scratches to the legs.
1950-96   *13.5in (34cm) long*
$250-350   PW

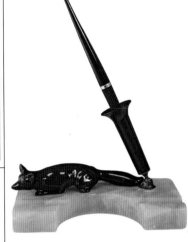

A Royal Doulton flambé fox, on an onyx pen stand.
c1930
$200-250   K&O

A Royal Doulton large flambé 'Leaping Salmon' model, designed by Charles Noke, model no.666.

This model was also produced in a Chinese Jade glaze c1930.
c1940-50   *12.5in (32cm) high*
$300-400   PSA

A large Royal Doulton flambé 'Seated Owl' model, designed by Alan Maslankowski, model no.2249.
1973-96   *12.25in (31cm) high*
$250-350   PSA

A large Royal Doulton flambé 'Seated Cat' model, by Alan Maslankowski, model no.2269, signed 'AM' to the base.
1977-96   *11.75in (30cm) high*
$250-350   PSA

A Royal Doulton flambé 'Year of the Pig' Burslem Artwares figurine, BA78.
$400-550   PSA

A Royal Doulton flambé 'Year of the Rat' Burslem Artwares figurine, BA79.
$250-350   PSA

A Royal Doulton flambé 'Year of the Ox' Burslem Artwares figurine, BA86.
$350-400   PSA

CERAMICS

QUICK REFERENCE - 'BLUE CHILDREN' SERIES

- The 'Blue Children' series, also known as 'Babes in the Wood', was produced at Doulton's Burslem studios from the 1890s.
- 'Blue Children' wares are decorated in midnight blue on a white bone china ground. They depict pastoral scenes, chiefly showing children and young ladies in turn-of-the-century dress taking part in outdoor activities, such as having picnics, playing games and gathering flowers. There are 24 different scenes in total, which appear on a range of wares, including plates, chargers and vases.
- The wares were decorated using the 'Flow Blue' technique, which involved adding lime or cobalt of ammonia during firing to make the colors flow. This resulted in the soft effect and muted colors of the 'Blue Children' wares. Burslem studio artists then added handpainted details to the central design, such as trees, flowers and birds.
- Key artists who worked on the 'Blue Children' range include Percy Curnock and Joseph Hanock.

A Royal Doulton 'Blue Children' vase, the lid missing.
c1895   14.5in (37cm) high
$350-400   **K&O**

A very large Royal Doulton 'Blue Children' vase, impressed marks on base.
c1915   21.75in (55cm) high
$400-550   **K&O**

A Royal Doulton pumpkin-shaped 'Blue Children' vase, depicting a girl with her mother.
c1915   7.75in (20cm) high
$300-400   **K&O**

A large Royal Doulton 'Blue Children' vase, impressed marks.
c1915   21.25in (54cm) high
$250-300   **K&O**

A Royal Doulton 'Blue Children' vase, 'Blind Mans Bluff'.
c1915   7.5in (19cm) high
$150-200   **K&O**

A Royal Doulton 'Blue Children' plaque.
c1915   14.25in (36cm) diam
$80-100   **K&O**

A Royal Doulton 'Blue Children' vase.
c1915   13.5in (34cm) high
$200-250   **K&O**

QUICK REFERENCE - LOVING CUPS

- These loving cups were produced at Doulton's Burslem Pottery during the 1930s. The majority of cups within the range were limited editions, produced in numbers of between 200 and 2,000.
- The loving cups were modeled by Charles Noke. The body was slip cast in low relief, then painted in underglaze colors.
- Many designs are commemorative, celebrating important royal or historical events. Others celebrate important historical figures, such as Captain Cook, Admiral Lord Nelson, George Washington and Charles Dickens.
- Several loving cups that depicted folklore heroes and literary characters were also produced. The designs included many characters that were also used as models for Royal Doulton Character Jugs.

A Royal Doulton 'The Village Blacksmith' loving cup, no.46 of a limited edition of 600.
c1935   *8.5in (21.5cm) high*
$130-200   **K&O**

A Royal Doulton 'The Regency Coach' loving cup, no.323 of a limited edition of 500.
c1935   *9.5in (24cm) high*
$250-350   **K&O**

A large Royal Doulton 'The Pied Piper' loving cup, from a limited edition of 600.
$400-550   **PSA**

A Royal Doulton 'The Three Musketeers' loving cup, no.182 of a limited edition of 600.
c1935   *9.75in (25cm) high*
$250-350   **K&O**

A Royal Doulton 'Sir Francis Drake' loving cup, with a hairline crack

This market is particularly averse to damage.
c1935   *11in (28cm) high*
$100-160   **K&O**

A Royal Doulton 'John Peel' two-handed loving cup, from a limited edition of 500.
c1935   *9in (23cm) high*
$650-800   **PSA**

A pair of Royal Doulton 'Moorland Ewers', painted and embossed with hunting scenes.
10.25in (26cm) high
$200-250   **PSA**

CERAMICS

QUICK REFERENCE - FULPER

- In 1860, Abram Fulper bought Samuel Hill's pottery in Flemington, NJ, USA, where he focused on utilitarian stoneware. His sons Charles, William, George and Edward Fulper took over after his death and incorporated the Fulper Pottery Company in 1899.
- Fulper moved into art pottery in the early 20thC. In 1909, Fulper introduced the new 'Vasekraft' line, where art glazes were applied over a traditional stoneware clay body at a low temperature. Many shapes were inspired by ancient Asian and European forms.
- In 1930, the firm was purchased by J. Martin Stangl, a German glaze chemist and designer for Fulper. He focused his efforts on red clay tableware and closed the original Fulper factory in 1935.

A 1910s-20s Fulper vase, with purple and pink flambé glaze, unmarked, factory drill hole and post-manufacture drill hole to base.

The fact that this vase is unmarked and has two drill holes severely affects the price.

16in (40.5cm) high

$200-250   DRA

A Fulper urn, with a mirror black, Chinese blue and famille rose flambé glaze, with a raised racetrack mark, professional restoration around foot.

1915-20s   *11in (28cm) high*

$350-400   DRA

A rare 1910s Fulper 'Vasekraft' vase, with a café-au-lait glaze, of spherical form, with handles, a rectangular ink stamp, a few minor grinding chips to edge of foot ring, some minor burst glaze bubbles to body.

10.25in (26cm) wide

$2,500-3,500   DRA

A 1920s Fulper vase, decorated with maidens, in a cucumber crystalline glaze, impressed with a horizontal 'Fulper' mark.

12.5in (32cm) high

$800-950   DRA

A Fulper hammered urn, in a cucumber crystalline glaze, stamped.

c1920   *11.5in (29cm) high*

$350-400   DRA

An early 20thC bullet-shaped Fulper earthenware vase, with a copperdust crystalline glaze and mirror black flambé glaze, vertical impressed mark.

13in (33cm) high

$1,200-1,300   DRA

An early 20thC Fulper vase, mat purple glazed earthenware, with raised vertical racetrack mark.

8.5in (21.5cm) diam

$350-400   DRA

An early 20thC Fulper vase, unmarked, extensive restoration to rim and one foot of base.

16.5in (42cm) high

$250-350   DRA

QUICK REFERENCE - HANCOCK & SONS

- Sampson Hancock & Sons was founded in 1857 in Tunstall, Staffordshire. It specialized in affordable tableware, home wares and crested china.
- Designs were tube-lined and so often resemble the work of William Moorcroft (see pages 107-118). From the end of World War I until the company's closure in 1937, the majority of designs were the work of George Cartlidge, F.X. Abraham and Edith Gater.
- Hancock & Son's richly colored and complexly patterned Art Nouveau 'Morrisware' has increased in popularity in recent years.

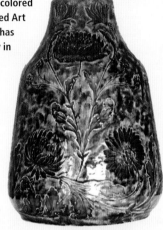

An early 20thC Hancock & Sons 'Morrisware' vase, by George Cartlidge, model no.C11-1, printed mark, signed.

11in (28cm) high

$600-650   **FLD**

A Hancock & Sons 'Morrisware' vase, designed by George Cartlidge, model no.C3-4, printed factory mark, facsimile signature.

7in (18cm) high

$400-450   **WW**

An early 20thC S. Hancock & Sons 'Morrisware' vase, designed by George Cartlidge, model no.C28-3, printed mark, signed in green, some damage.

14.5in (37cm) high

$550-600   **FLD**

A Hancock & Sons 'Morrisware' vase, designed by George Cartlidge, printed mark, signed.

9.75in (25cm) high

$450-550   **FLD**

A Hancock & Sons 'Morrisware' vase, designed by George Cartlidge, model no.C63-6, printed factory mark, facsimile signature.

6in (15cm) high

$450-550   **WW**

A Hancock & Sons 'Morrisware' candlestick, designed by George Cartlidge, model no.C20-1, printed factory mark.

13in (33cm) high

$600-650   **WW**

A Hancock & Sons 'Morrisware' vase, designed by George Cartlidge, model no.C81-1, printed factory mark, facsimile signature, chips to base rim.

12.25in (31cm) high

$200-250   **WW**

An early 20thC Hancock & Sons 'Morrisware' vase, by George Cartlidge, model no.C72-1, printed mark, signed.

12in (30.5cm) high

$350-400   **FLD**

A Hancock & Sons 'Morrisware' bowl, designed by George Cartlidge, model no.C16-27, tube-line decorated, impressed and painted marks, professional restoration.

9.5in (24.5cm) diam

$200-250   **WW**

CERAMICS

QUICK REFERENCE - KEVIN FRANCIS

- Kevin Francis was founded in 1985 by Kevin Pearson and Francis Salmon.
- It specialized in figurines and Toby jugs. Each model was handpainted and every design was produced in a limited edition.
- At first, Kevin Francis relied on commissions from Royal Doulton. However, it soon entered into an exclusive partnership with Peggy Davies Ceramics, which had been founded in 1981 by Royal Doulton modeller Peggy Davies and her son Rhodri. The companies worked closely together at the same studios.
- Today, Kevin Francis is owned by Peggy Davies Ceramics, which continues to produce figurines, vases and other ceramics.

A limited edition Kevin Francis 'Dancing Nymph' figurine, by Geoff Blower, modeled as a nude lady.
$300-350   PSA

A Kevin Francis 'Moulin Rouge' figurine, in artist's proof colorway.
$100-130   PSA

An unusual Kevin Francis 'Art Deco Lady Clarice Cliff' figurine, by John Michael, signed.
$150-200   PSA

An unusal Kevin Francis 'Erotic Nude Lady' figurine, by John Michael, in artist's proof colorway, signed.
$400-450   PSA

A limited edition Kevin Francis/Peggy Davies Ceramics 'Isadora' erotic figurine.
$200-250   PSA

A limited edition Kevin Francis/Peggy Davies Ceramics erotic 'Femme Fatale' figurine, by Victoria Bourne, artist's proof.
$450-500   PSA

A limited edition Kevin Francis/Peggy Davies Ceramics erotic 'The Temptress' figurine, by Victoria Bourne, artist's proof.
$350-400   PSA

A limited edition Kevin Francis 'Winston Churchill' two-handled character jug.
$50-60   PSA

A Kevin Francis 'Churchill' bust, no.22 of a limited edition of 100.
11in (28cm) high
$150-200   K&O

A Lenci Pottery figure of a dancer, inscribed 'Lenci, Made in Italy Torino LE', with Lenci Torino label, right hand restored.

9.75in (25cm) high

$650-800   SWO

QUICK REFERENCE - LENCI

- The Lenci factory was founded in Turin, Italy, in 1919, by Helen (Elena) Konig Scavini and her husband Enrico. 'Lenci' is an acronym for the company's motto 'Ludus Est Nobis Constanter Industria' ('Play is Our Constant Work'), and possibly also a corruption of Konig Scavini's nickname 'Helenchen' or 'Lenchen'.

- The factory began producing felt dolls (see page 189), then extended its range to earthenware and ceramics figurines in 1928. Many figurines were designed by Helen Konig Scavini herself, with contributions also from Giovanni Grande, Abele Jacopi and Sandro Vachetti.

- The company was taken over in 1937 and ceramic production ceased in 1964. Lenci's large Art Deco figurines remain highly sought-after by collectors today.

A Lenci Pottery model of a woman holding a young child, 'La Moglie del Soldato', designed by Helen Konig Scavini, impressed 'Lenci' mark, painted marks to base, some repaired damage.

12.75in (32.5cm) high

$200-250   WW

A Lenci Pottery model, 'Lucania', designed by Abele Jacopi, painted marks, small glaze frit to goat's ear.

17.75in (45cm) high

$1,300-2,000   WW

A rare Lenci Pottery 'Mama Sirena' sculptural group, designed by Helen Konig Scavini, model no.305, modeled as a mermaid and child riding a large tortoise, impressed number, painted marks, professional restoration.

12.5in (31.5cm) high

$4,000-4,500   WW

Judith Picks

When it comes to design innovation, there are few Art Deco figurines that encapsulate the style as well as Lenci. Helen Konig Scavini's remarkable talent ensured that she instilled the same sense of playfulness into each piece that was already evident in the Lenci doll designs. The ceramic figurines carried much of the fashionable Art Deco style along with the individual designers own personal distinctive traits. Throughout the ceramic manufacturing phase of the Lenci factory much of the success was largely due to the talents and foresight of the factories founder. Her lyrical and expressive creations showed just what a remarkable talent she had for design.

A Lenci Pottery figure of a lady, looking at a dog on the hem of her dress, inscribed 'Lenci, Italia'.

13.75in (35cm) high

$2,000-2,500   SWO

A Lenci Pottery badger, modeled after the original by Felice Tosalli, painted factory marks, 'Lenci, Made in Italy, Torino, 12-11-32'.

9.75in (25cm) long

$900-1,100   BE

A Lenci Pottery Seagull wall plaque, 'Albatros', designed by Principessa Bona Sancipriano, impressed signature, painted 'Lenci' marks, original paper label with price, minor glaze frits and repair to wing tip.

26.25in (66.5cm) wide

$900-1,100   WW

A Lenci Pottery plaque, 'Targa Madonna della Quiete', designed by Giovanni Grande, model no.437, impressed signature 'Grande', painted 'Lenci' mark, small glaze chip to border.

12.5in (32cm) high

$1,300-2,000   WW

A rare Lenci Pottery figure, 'Nella', designed by Helen Konig Scavini, painted marks, professional restoration to hand.

9in (23cm) high

$5,500-6,500   WW

CERAMICS

QUICK REFERENCE - LLADRO

- The Lladro Company was founded in 1953 in Valencia, Spain, by brothers Juan, José and Vicente Lladró. It produced stylized porcelain figurines.
- In 1962, Lladro opened its own Professional Training School. In 1969, Lladro opened the 'City of Porcelain', a large complex of factories, offices, gardens and leisure facilities for Lladro workers.
- Lladro is still operational today and has subsidiaries in several countries. Over its history, Lladro has created over 4,000 figurines.
- Early figurines from 1954 to the mid-1960s are stamped with decimal point serial numbers and are amongst the rarest Lladro pieces.

A Lladro 'Romeo and Juliet' figurine, designed by Antonio Ruiz, no.01004750.
1971-92   *17.75in (45cm) high*
$200-250   SWO

A Lladro 'Anticipation' figurine, designed by Regino Torrijos, no.01006608, in original box.
1999-2000   *13in (33cm) high*
$100-130   PSA

A Lladro 'Afternoon Promenade' figurine, designed by José Puche, no.01007636, in original box.
1995-98   *11in (28cm) high*
$100-120   PSA

A Lladro 'The Muse' figurine, designed by Francisco Polope, no.01007703, from a limited edition of 1,500 for the Privilege Gold Society, in original box.
2004   *10.5in (27cm) high*
$130-200   PSA

A Lladro 'Lamplighter' figurine, designed by Salvador Furió, no.01005205.
issued 1984   *19in (48cm) high*
$200-250   SWO

A Lladro 'An Evening Out' figurine, designed by Francisco Catalá, no.01005540.
1989-91   *12.5in (32cm) high*
$200-250   SWO

A Lladro 'Twilight Years' figurine, designed by Francisco Catalá, no.01005677.
1990-2004   *10.75in (27cm) high*
$200-250   SWO

A Lladro 'Checking The Time' prestige figurine, designed by Salvador Furió, no.01005762, in original box.
1991-95   *11.5in (29cm) high*
$150-200   PSA

A CLOSER LOOK AT A LLADRO FIGURINE

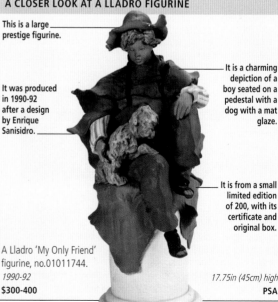

This is a large prestige figurine.

It was produced in 1990-92 after a design by Enrique Sanisidro.

It is a charming depiction of a boy seated on a pedestal with a dog with a mat glaze.

It is from a small limited edition of 200, with its certificate and original box.

A Lladro 'My Only Friend' figurine, no.01011744.
1990-92   *17.75in (45cm) high*
$300-400   PSA

QUICK REFERENCE - LORNA BAILEY

- Lorna Bailey (b.1978) began her career as a painter at her father's firm, LJB Ceramics, in Burslem, Staffordshire.
- Her abstract designs, inspired by the Art Deco works of Clarice Cliff, were noticed by Old Ellgreave Pottery, who put her 'House and Path' and 'Sunburst' patterns into full production when Bailey was just 17 years old.
- In 2003, LJB Ceramics changed its name to Lorna Bailey Artware. It produced a range of handcrafted, handpainted pieces, including domestic wares such as vases and teapots and decorative works such as animal and human figurines. Each design was produced for a short time and in limited numbers.
- Lorna Bailey Artwork closed down in 2008 when Bailey took early retirement.

A Lorna Bailey Art Deco 'Lady' jug, no.34 of a limited edition of 100.

$250-300   HAN

A Lorna Bailey 'Flame' vase, for Old Ellgreave.

$130-200   HAN

A Lorna Bailey 'Iris' teapot and water jug.

$150-250   HAN

A limited edition Lorna Bailey 'K9' teapot.

$100-130   HAN

A Lorna Bailey 'Ghost' teapot, no.27 of a limited edition of 60.

$200-250   HAN

A Lorna Bailey 'Ocean Liner' teapot, no.20 of a limited edition of 50.

$100-130   HAN

Judith Picks

Fred Dibnah MBE was born in Bolton in 1938. He was a steeplejack and television personality, with a keen interest in mechanical engineering.

As a child he was fascinated by the steam engines which powered the many textile mills in Bolton, but he paid particular attention to chimneys and the men who worked on them. From age 22, he served for two years in the armed forces. Once demobilized, he returned to steeplejacking and was asked to repair Bolton's parish church. In 1978, while making repairs to Bolton Town Hall, Dibnah was filmed by a regional BBC news crew. The BBC then commissioned an award-winning documentary, which followed him as he worked on chimneys and talked about his favorite hobby - steam. He proved popular with viewers and featured in a number of television programs. Toward the end of his life, with a decline in his steeplejacking business, Dibnah increasingly came to rely on after-dinner speaking.

In 1998, he presented a program on Britain's industrial history and went on to present a number of series, largely concerned with the Industrial Revolution. He died in 2004.

A Lorna Bailey 'Windmill' teapot, no.2 of a limited edition of 60.

$100-130   HAN

A Lorna Bailey 'Fiery Fred' teapot, no.3 of a limited edition of 100.

$150-200   HAN

A Lorna Bailey 'Fred and His Lanny' teapot, no.5 of a limited edition of 100.

$150-200   HAN

CERAMICS

QUICK REFERENCE - MARTIN BROTHERS

- Martin Brothers began in 1873 with a kiln at the brothers' family home in Fulham. In 1877 they moved into a disused soap works in Southall, where production continued until 1923.
- They used salt glaze stoneware to produce their handcrafted and unusual designs.
- Two of the brothers, Robert and Edwin, had been apprenticed at the Doulton Lambeth factories.
- Each brother took on a different role in the business. Robert Wallace Martin modeled the figures; the grotesques and face jugs were chiefly his work. Walter threw the pots. Edwin painted and decorated them. Charles, the youngest brother, ran the shop and gallery in Holborn. He often hid his favorite pots to prevent them being purchased.

A Martin Brothers tyg, by Robert Wallace Martin, incised with roundels of birds, before a full moon titled 'Morn', 'Noon' and 'Night', incised 'C8 R W Martin London SW'.

1879   *6in (15cm) high*

$1,600-2,000   **WW**

A Martin Brothers vase, with a crane flying amongst prunus and hills, silver-plated collar, inscribed 'R W Martin, Southall and London'.

c1880-90   *8.5in (22cm) high*

$900-1,000   **SWO**

A Martin Brothers vase, relief decorated with fish amongst seaweed, base inscribed 'R.W. Martin / 26.1.80 / 512'.

1880   *9.75in (25cm) high*

$600-750   **WHP**

A Martin Brothers vase, incised with stylized floral designs, inscribed 'R W Martin & Bros. London and Southall', restored.

c1890-1900   *9.5in (24cm) high*

$550-650   **SWO**

A Martin Brothers vase, incised with dragonflies, insects and plants, incised 'Martin Bros London & Southall'.

1898   *9in (23cm) high*

$900-1,100   **SWO**

A CLOSER LOOK AT A MARTIN BROTHERS VESTA

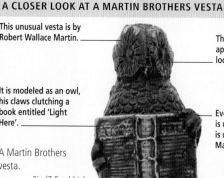

This unusual vesta is by Robert Wallace Martin.

The owl has an appealing rustic look.

It is modeled as an owl, his claws clutching a book entitled 'Light Here'.

Even though it is unsigned, it is unmistakably Martin Brothers.

A Martin Brothers vesta.

3in (7.5cm) high

$2,500-3,500   **WW**

A Martin Brothers miniature 'Aquatic' vase, by Edwin and Walter Martin, incised to each side with a jelly fish, incised '1902 Martin Bros London & Southall'.

1902   *2in (5cm) high*

$2,500-3,000   **WW**

A Martin Brothers vase, decorated with incised poppy heads and foliate scrolls, incised 'London & Southall' mark.

1906   *5in (13cm) high*

$900-1,000   **FLD**

A Martin Brothers vase, decorated with incised mistletoe leaves and berries, unmarked other than incised '28.4 iSI'.

4in (10cm) high

$550-600   **FLD**

QUICK REFERENCE - MINTON

- Minton was established in 1793 by Thomas Minton and Joseph Poulson. After his death, Thomas Minton was succeeded by his son Herbert. In 1845, Michael Hollins, a partner in the firm, opened the subsidiary company, Minton, Hollins & Company, to produce tiles. Minton was renamed 'Mintons Ltd.' in 1873.
- Léon Arnoux became art director in 1849. He introduced the 'majolica' range, which mirrored brightly colored Italian 'maiolica' wares of the 16thC. In the second half of the 19thC, Minton also experimented with new decorative techniques such as acid gilding and pâte-sur-pâte.
- Léon Solon became art director at the start of the 20thC. He and his assistant John W. Wandsworth created the Secessionist Ware range of ornamental tableware. These tube-lined and molded wares were partly inspired by Viennese Art Nouveau style.
- Although Mintons was slower to adopt Art Deco trends, some Art Deco tablewares were produced between the wars. Mintons also produced Art Deco figurines by Doris Linder, Richard Bradbury and Eric Owen.
- Mintons became a part of the Royal Doulton Tableware Group in 1968.

An 1860s Minton pottery tile, depicting a female portrait with foliate garland to her hair, detailed 'Minton Hollins & Co' to the rear.

8in (20.5cm) square

$550-600   **BELL**

A pair of Aesthetic Movement pâte-sur-pâte vases, attributed to Louis Solon for Minton, decorated with storks amongst reeds, unmarked.

Louis Solon was famous for his use of the French technique of slip glazed, cameo type porcelain. His son, Léon, pioneered the tube-lined Secessionist range.

5.5in (14cm) high

$300-400   **HAN**

A late 19thC Mintons novelty teapot, impressed mark to base, 'Mintons 1838' with impressed arrow.

1884   *7in (18cm) wide*

$150-200   **APAR**

A Minton's Pottery Secessionist jardinière, designed by Léon Solon and John Wadsworth, decorated in low relief with Poppy flowerheads, printed factory mark.

10.75in (27cm) high

$900-1,000   **WW**

MINTON MARKS

Mark used c1891-1910.

Mark used c1891-1902.

Mark used c1873-91.

Mark used 1951-

A Minton's Secessionist stick stand, decorated with poppies, printed and impressed maker's marks.

c1900   *22.5in (57cm) high*

$450-600   **L&T**

A Minton's Secessionist toilet set, designed by John Wadsworth and Léon Solon, with printed factory marks.

candlestick 6.25in (16cm) high

$100-140   **WW**

CERAMICS

A CLOSER LOOK AT A MINTON SECESSIONIST JARDINIÈRE

This jardinière was designed by Léon Solon and John Wadsworth.

It is of ovoid shape, with a collar rim. Even with the star crack to the base, it is a striking piece.

It is designed in the distinctive Secessionist style, tube-lined with stylized carnation flowers in red, green and salmon pink on a cream ground.

There are impressed and printed factory marks to the base.

A Minton Pottery Secessionist jardinière, star crack to base.

10.25in (26cm) high

$600-750   **WW**

A Minton Secessionist spill vase, the body tube-lined with geometric abstract design, restored and repaired.

12in (30.5cm) high

$150-200   **KEY**

A Minton Secessionist vase, tube-lined with stylized flora, printed marks to base, shape no.33, overall crazing.

7in (18cm) high

$300-400   **PW**

A Minton Secessionist vase, tube-lined with stylized flora, printed marks to base, shape no.29, overall crazing.

11in (28cm) high

$300-400   **PW**

A Mintons Ltd. Secessionist jardinière, with panels of stylized rose trees, printed maker's marks 'MINTONS LTD'.

c1905   *35in (88cm) high*

$1,000-1,300   **L&T**

A Mintons Ltd. Secessionist jardinière-on-stand, decorated with scrolling hearts and plum flowerheads and ocher leaves, printed maker's marks 'MINTONS LTD', registered pattern number 'RD.NO.616446' to base.

c1910   *40.25in (102cm) high*

$650-800   **L&T**

A Minton Archive Collection cat and mouse teapot, from a limited edition of 2,500.

8.25in (21cm) high

$150-250   **K&O**

A Minton Gilded 'Monkey' model, a 2004 edition for the year of the monkey, with 'Artists Copy' marked to the base, and signed in gold by Alan Maslankowski, with original box and paperwork.

$130-200   **PSA**

CERAMICS

QUICK REFERENCE - MOOCROFT

- William Moorcroft (1872-1945) studied at the Royal College of Art, London. He began his career at the Staffordshire pottery manufacturers James Macintyre & Co. in 1897, and soon ran the company's art pottery studio. His early designs included the distinctive 'Aurelian' and 'Florian' wares, decorated with stylized floral and foliate Art Nouveau designs.
- He founded W. Moorcroft Ltd. in 1913. With the backing of Liberty of London and other major retailers, the company was quickly successful. In 1928 William Moorcroft was appointed 'Potter to H.M. The Queen'.
- Moorcroft patterns were often inspired by the natural world. The designs were produced through 'tube-lining'. Outlines of a pattern were piped onto the surface, leaving a low relief outline design. The spaces within the pattern were then filled in with colored glazed.
- On William's death, his son Walter (1917-2002) took over the company. Moorcroft is still open today and operates from the same factory in Stoke-on-Trent where it was originally founded.
- Early ranges from the 1900s-20s, such as 'Florian' or 'Claremont' tend to be the most valuable, while common patterns, such as 'Anemone' and 'Pomegranate' are in general more affordable. Many collectors are increasingly interested in contemporary pieces from the 1990s onward, by designers such as Rachel Bishop, Emma Bossons, Philip Gibson, Sian Leeper and Sally Tuffin. Large pieces from limited editions tend to fetch the highest prices.

A Moorcroft Macintyre 'Florian' ware teapot.

4.75in (12cm) high

$130-200   SWO

A Moorcroft Burslem two-handled 'Florian' ware vase, on a green ground, restored.

The market is very sensitive to restoration. This vase would have fetched double this a few years ago.

10.5in (27cm) high

$400-550   BELL

A James Macintyre & Co. 'Florian' ware bowl, 'Tulip' pattern, designed by William Moorcroft, with a printed factory mark, and painted green signature.

7in (17.5cm) diam

$650-750   WW

A Macintyre Moorcroft vase, tube-lined and painted with the 'Pansy' pattern, printed mark in brown, signed in green and numbered '1161', impressed '160'.

1911-13   *8in (20.5cm) high*

$2,500-3,000   HT

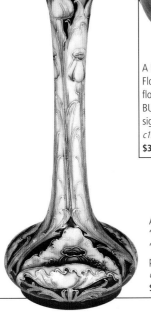

An early Macintyre Moorcroft 'Florian' ware solifleur vase, 'Poppy' pattern, painted and printed marks.

c1900   *9.75in (25cm) high*

$3,500-4,000   CHEF

A Moorcroft MacIntyre 'Late Florian' bowl, tube-lined with flowers, impressed 'MOORCROFT BURSLEM', with a green printed signature.

c1915   *13in (33cm) wide*

$350-400   MAB

A William Moorcroft Macintyre tobacco jar and cover, 'Revived Cornflower' pattern, brown printed factory mark and green painted monogram, impressed '965', two chips to the jar.

c1912   *4in (10cm) wide*

$800-950   TEN

EARLY MOORCROFT MARKS

James Macintyre & Co.,
Burslem, Staffordshire,
c1860-1928.
Mark used c1891-1900.

CERAMICS

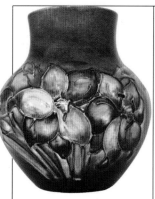

A mid-20thC Moorcroft pottery vase, 'African Lily' pattern, impressed marks.

introduced c1950s   4.75in (12cm) high

$200-250   **BELL**

A Moorcroft vase, 'Anemone' pattern, impressed 'MOORCROFT MADE IN ENGLAND', with blue painted initials.

c1950   10.75in (27.5cm) high

$60-100   **MAB**

A Moorcroft vase, 'Anemone' pattern.

introduced 1920s   4.25in (11cm) high

$130-200   **LOC**

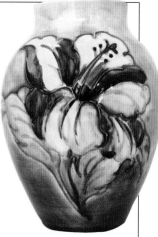

An early 20thC Moorcroft pottery vase, 'Anemone' pattern, paper label to base.

introduced 1920s   4.75in (12cm) high

$100-130   **BELL**

A Moorcroft bowl, 'Claremont' pattern, numbered 'M7', impressed marks and blue signature, restored.

introduced 1903   7.25in (18.5cm) diam

$300-400   **SWO**

A pair of Moorcroft 'Flamminian Ware' vases, for Liberty & Co., with inscribed signature, printed 'Made for Liberty's', restored.

introduced 1905   6in (15cm) high

$450-550   **SWO**

A Moorcroft 'Flamminian Ware' vase, for Liberty & Co., with tube-lined roundels, 'W Moorcroft' signature.

Moorcroft had worked closely with Liberty since the early days of Florian Ware. Liberty was also a major outlet for Moorcroft's first range of monochrome and luster glazes, Flamminian Wares, produced 1905-15. These wares were glazed in bright red, green and blue and decorated simply by Celtic or Japanesque foliate roundels.

introduced 1905   9in (22.5cm) high

$450-550   **SWO**

A Moorcroft pottery floating bowl, 'Claremont' pattern, designed by William Moorcroft, painted green signature, hairline crack to rim.

introduced 1903   11.5in (29cm) diam

$900-1,100   **WW**

A Moorcroft vase, 'Clematis' pattern, impressed facsimile signature and 'Potter to H.M. the Queen', with green painted initials.

c1950   9.5in (24cm) high

$80-100   **MAB**

Judith Picks

This is one of my favorite Moorcroft patterns. This was the first Moorcroft landscape design and was registered in September 1902, in shades of blue, as part of the Florian Ware range, and mainly sold by Liberty. It was given the name 'Hazledene'. By the end of the year a green version was also produced. From 1904 the colors became darker and by 1910 the design had dark trees on an olive green ground. This dark version was produced at the Washington Works and at Cobridge.

A Moorcroft 'Flamminian Ware' vase, with a sang-de-boeuf glaze and tube-lined roundels, incised 'W Moorcroft' and '8:05', crack to rim.
c1905   *15.25in (38.5cm) high*
$800-950   **SWO**

A Moorcroft pottery vase, 'Freesia' pattern, blue signature with original paper label.
introduced 1920s   *9.75in (24.5cm) high*
$300-350   **GWA**

A Moorcroft jardinière, 'Hazeldene' pattern, green signature and printed 'Liberty & Co Rd No.397964', fine crazing, a chip near base.
     8.25in (21cm) high
$1,600-2,000   **LA**

A Moorcroft bottle vase, in 'Hibiscus' pattern, with a paper label to the base.
introduced c1960s   *8.75in (22cm) high*
$90-110   **LOC**

A Moorcroft flambé vase, 'Leaf and Berries' pattern.
introduced 1928   *7in (17.5cm) high*
$600-650   **PSA**

A William Moorcroft jug, 'Leaf and Berry' pattern.
introduced 1928   *7.5in (19cm) high*
$130-200   **LOC**

A Moorcroft vase, 'Moonlit Blue' pattern, impressed 'Moorcroft'.
introduced 1922   *2.5in (7cm) high*
$600-750   **SWO**

A Moorcroft vase, 'Moonlit Blue' pattern, no.189, green signature, impressed marks.
introduced 1922   *4in (10cm) high*
$1,000-1,200   **SWO**

A composed pair of Moorcroft bottle vases, 'Moonlit Blue' pattern, painted and impressed marks, one with original paper trade label.
introduced 1922   *9in (23cm) high*
$2,500-3,500   **CHEF**

A Walter Moorcroft flambé vase, 'Orchid' pattern.

introduced c1937   *8.25in (21cm) high*

$550-650   **PSA**

A Moorcroft flambé frilled lamp base, 'Orchid' pattern, designed by William Moorcroft, impressed marks, painted green signature and paper label.

introduced c1937   *12.5in (32cm) high*

$450-550   **WW**

A Moorcroft bowl, 'Orchid' pattern, with impressed and painted marks.

c1940   *7.5in (19cm) diam*

$250-350   **BELL**

A Moorcroft flambé frilled vase, 'Orchid' pattern, impressed mark and monogrammed in blue.

introduced c1937   *5in (13cm) high*

$450-550   **FLD**

A Walter Moorcroft frilled shallow dish, 'Orchid' pattern, impressed marks with blue flash initials.

introduced c1937   *8.75in (22cm) diam*

$130-200   **FLD**

A Walter Moorcroft flambé frilled shallow plate, 'Orchid' pattern, impressed marks with flash initials.

introduced c1937   *10.25in (26cm) diam*

$350-400   **FLD**

A Moorcroft jug, 'Pansy' pattern.

introduced 1911   *4.25in (11cm) high*

$130-200   **LOC**

A Moorcroft vase, 'Pansy' pattern, of high shouldered form, impressed Burslem mark and signed in green, some damage.

introduced 1911   *8.75in (22cm) high*

$200-250   **FLD**

A large Moorcroft vase, 'Peacock Feathers' pattern, blue script mark and impressed mark.

c1930   *9.5in (24cm) high*

$1,000-1,200   **JN**

A CLOSER LOOK AT A MOORCROFT VASE

This range is part of the new ranges of lighter and more subdued color - to reflect contemporary taste.

It is typically tube-lined and painted in shades of green, blue and yellow on a cream ground.

This is a typical 1930s palette and shape - of flared cylindrical form with rounded shoulders and slightly everted rim.

It is well decorated with peacock feathers within incised bands.

A 1930s Moorcroft vase, 'Peacock Feathers' pattern, impressed mark, signed in blue.

7in (18cm) high

$1,000-1,200   **HT**

A Moorcroft vase, 'Pomegranate' pattern, green signature, impressed marks.

introduced 1910   8.5in (21.5cm) high

$400-550   **SWO**

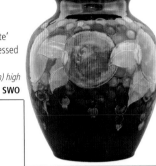

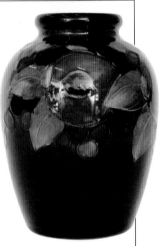

A Moorcroft biscuit barrel, 'Pomegranate' pattern, for Liberty, the planished pewter mount stamped 'Moorcroft Tudric 1328'.

introduced 1910   5in (13cm) high

$550-650   **ECGW**

An early 20thC Moorcroft burslem pottery vase, 'Pomegranate' pattern, shape no.80, impressed mark, signed in green.

introduced 1910 10.25in (26.5cm) high

$650-800   **HT**

A Moorcroft vase, 'Pomegranate' pattern, impressed signature mark.

introduced 1910   6.75in (17cm) high

$450-600   **FLD**

A Moorcroft tobacco jar and cover, 'Pomegranate' pattern, impressed 'Burslem' mark, signed in green.

introduced 1910   4in (10cm) high

$450-600   **FLD**

A Moorcroft ginger jar, 'Pomegranate' pattern, marked 'Moorcroft, Burslem', signed.

c1913   8.75in (22cm) high

$900-1,100   **K&O**

A Moorcroft three-handled bowl, 'Pomegranate Ocher' pattern, marked 'Moorcroft, Burslem, England', signed.

The 'Pomegranate' design was introduced in 1910 and sold at first by Liberty under the trade name 'Murena'. This is an excellent early example of this popular pattern.

c1914   7in (18cm) wide

$3,500-4,000   **K&O**

A pair of Moorcroft candlesticks, 'Pomegranate' pattern, designed by William Moorcroft, with impressed marks, professional restoration.

introduced 1910   *5in (13cm) diam*

$650-800   **WW**

A Moorcroft two-handled footed bowl, 'Spanish' pattern.

introduced 1910   6.75in (17cm) high

$1,000-1,300   **PSA**

A Moorcroft vase, 'Poppy' pattern, blue ground.

c1920   6.25in (16cm) high

$200-250   **BELL**

A Moorcroft vase, 'Spanish' pattern, designed by William Moorcroft, impressed Burslem mark and painted green signature, minor over-painting to base rim.

introduced 1910   10.5in (26.5cm) high

$1,600-2,000   **WW**

A Moorcroft 'Hesperian' bowl with crimped rim, 'Tulip' pattern, for Osler of London, full underglaze green signature and 'Osler' mark.

introduced 1900s

$1,300-2,000   *8.75in (22cm) diam*

                                    HAN

A Moorcroft vase, 'Tulip' pattern, signed in green 'W. Moorcroft des.', one crack to the neck.

introduced 1900s   11.5in (29cm) high

$1,000-1,200   **LA**

A Moorcroft vase, 'Weeping Willow and Beech' pattern, signature and impressed marks.

c1930   10.25in (26cm) high

$550-650   **BELL**

A 1940s Moorcroft vase, 'Wisteria' pattern.

6.75in (17cm) high

$350-400   **LOC**

A Moorcroft jardinière, in green and blue floral pattern, signed in green 'W. Moorcroft des.', printed 'Made for Liberty & Co.', some chips.

6.75in (17cm) high

$550-650   **LA**

A limited edition Moorcroft vase, 'Dent De Lion' pattern, designed by Rachel Bishop.

Rachel Bishop studied at Staffordshire University and joined Moorcroft in 1993, as the fourth ever Moorcroft senior designer, after William Moorcroft, Walter Moorcroft and Sally Tuffin. She still works at Moorcroft today.

14.25in (36cm) high

$450-550   PSA

A Moorcroft vase, 'Kyoto' pattern, designed by Rachel Bishop, marked 'R.J.B Des. 21.2.95' and '57/100', signed 'John Moorcroft', some crazing.

1995   *24in (61cm) high*

$1,500-2,500   CHEF

A Moorcroft vase, 'Sunflower' pattern, designed by Rachel Bishop, boxed.

c1995   *7.5in (19cm) high*

$450-550   BELL

A Moorcroft vase, 'Oberon' pattern, designed by Rachel Bishop, with a printed backstamp 'Moorcroft Made in England', and artist monogrammed and dated verso, factory second.

1993   *10.25in (26cm) high*

$150-200   LSK

A large Moorcroft vase, 'Poppy' pattern, designed by Rachel Bishop, impressed marks, painted 'R.J. Bishop' signature.

17in (43cm) high

$450-550   CHEF

A Moorcroft ginger jar and cover, 'Noah's Ark' pattern, designed by Rachel Bishop, Moorcroft Collectors Club no.682, dated.

1996   *6.25in (16cm) high*

$250-350   WHP

A Moorcroft prestige vase, 'Queen's Choice' pattern, designed by Emma Bossons.

Emma Bossons (b.1976) joined Moorcroft at the age of 20 and continues to work there. Her designs 'Hepaticia' and 'Queen's Choice' have been especially popular and her Golden Jubilee design was part of the Royal Collection.

17in (43cm) high

$1,200-1,300   PSA

MOORCROFT MARKS

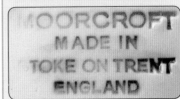

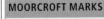

Mark used 1986 onward.

CERAMICS

A Moorcroft prestige vase, 'Vase of Smiles' pattern, designed by Emma Bossons, inspired by the designs of William De Morgan, trial, dated.
2014   *15in (38cm) high*
$900-1,100   **PSA**

A Moorcroft prestige vase, 'Queen's Choice' pattern, designed by Emma Bossons.
     13.5in (34cm) high
$750-850   **PSA**

A Moorcroft vase, 'Queens Choice' pattern, designed by Emma Bossons, boxed, dated.
2000   *7.25in (18.5cm) high*
$250-350   **BELL**

A Moorcroft vase, 'Spiraxia' pattern, designed by Emma Bossons, no.166 of a limited edition of 300, boxed.
c1998   *3.5in (9cm) high*
$400-450   **BELL**

A Moorcroft vase, 'Hidden Dreams' pattern, after an original by Emma Bossons, impressed 'Moorcroft Made in Stoke on Trent England', painted signatures for 'Emma Bossons' and 'Rachel Bishop', numbered '29/50', dated.
2005   *26.75in (68cm) high*
$2,000-2,500   **BE**

A Moorcroft tea set, 'Hepatica' pattern, designed by Emma Bossons, boxed.
$400-550   **PSA**

A Moorcroft ginger jar and cover, 'Cheetahs' pattern, designed by Anji Davenport, no.79 of a limited edition of 150, boxed, dated.
2003   *8.25in (21cm) high*
$400-550   **WHP**

A Moorcroft name tile, 'Queens Choice' pattern, designed by Emma Bossons, boxed, dated.
2001   *7.25in (18.5cm) wide*
$90-100   **WHP**

A Moorcroft vase, 'Woodside Farm' pattern, designed by Anji Davenport.

Anji Davenport has been a painter for Moorcroft for over 20 years. She has also created several designs, including 'Woodside Farm', which is based on her childhood home in Cheshire.

1999   *21.25in (54cm) high*
$1,600-2,000   **K&O**

A Moorcroft dish and cover, 'Juneberry' pattern, designed by Anji Davenport, boxed, dated.
2000   *5in (12.5cm) diam*
$90-110   **WHP**

A Moorcroft vase, 'Mountain Kingdom' pattern, designed by Philip Gibson, no.8 of a limited edition of 100, boxed, dated.

Philip Gibson studied at Newcastle School of Art and has worked as an in-house designer for both Wedgwood and Moorcroft. He is now a freelance designer based at his own studio in Staffordshire.

2004   *16.25in (41.5cm) high*
$1,000-1,200   **WHP**

A Moorcroft jug, 'Kingfisher' pattern, designed by Philip Gibson, no.30 of a limited edition of 300, boxed, dated.
2001   *7.5in (19cm) high*
$350-400   **WHP**

A Moorcroft vase, 'Wuthering Heights' pattern, designed by Philip Gibson for MacIntyre Pottery, no.12 of a limited edition of 150, boxed, dated.
2003   *5.5in (14cm) high*
$130-200   **WHP**

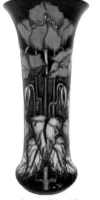

A Moorcroft vase, 'Blue Rhapsody' pattern, designed by Philip Gibson for the Collectors Club, signed to base, with impressed and painted marks, boxed.
2001   *10in (25.5cm) high*
$300-400   **GWA**

A Moorcroft trial vase, 'Highland Stag' pattern, designed by Kerry Goodwin, impressed and painted marks, dated.

Kerry Goodwin has worked at Moorcroft as a painter and designer since 2000.
2012   *20.75in (52.5cm) high*
$250-350   **WW**

A Moorcroft miniature dish, 'Hartgring' pattern, designed by Kerry Goodwin, boxed, dated.
2003   *4.75in (12cm) diam*
$90-110   **WHP**

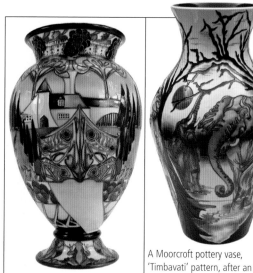

A Moorcroft Prestige vase, 'The Home Eventide' pattern, designed by Kerry Goodwin.

15.75in (40cm) high

$1,300-2,000   **PSA**

A Moorcroft pottery vase, 'Timbavati' pattern, after an original by Kerry Goodwin, tube-lined with elephants watering in an African landscape, impressed 'Moorcroft Made in Stoke on Trent England', painted signature, numbered '6/50', dated.

2007   *24.75in (63cm) high*

$2,500-3,500   **BE**

A CLOSER LOOK AT A MOORCROFT VASE

This was designed by Kerry Goodwin and dated 2009.

It is in the striking 'Town of Flowers' pattern.

Although using traditional Moorcroft techniques, this is a thoroughly modern design.

The pattern is well adapted to the shape, with the flowers adding mystery to the town.

A Moorcroft vase, 'Town of Flowers' pattern, impressed and painted marks, dated.

2009   *18.25in (46.5cm) high*

$1,000-1,200   **WW**

A Moorcroft vase, 'Meadow Cranesbill' pattern, designed by Shirley Hayes, no.8 of a limited edition of 100, boxed, signed, dated.

Shirley Hayes began at Moorcroft Pottery in 1992 as a painter and designed several ranges from 1999 onward, including 'Palmata', 'Pheasants Eye' and 'Venice.' She left Moorcroft in 2005 to set up her own studio.

2002   *8in (20.5cm) high*

$200-250   **WHP**

A Moorcroft bottle vase, 'Pheasants Eye' pattern, designed by Shirley Hayes, boxed, dated.

2000   *8.25in (21cm) high*

$200-250   **WHP**

A Moorcroft vase, 'Coming to America' pattern, designed by Paul Hilditch.

Paul Hilditch has worked at Moorcroft since 1999. He began as a painter and became a designer in 2008. His designs are highly detailed and pictorial, often depicting historical scenes.

2015   *10.75in (27cm) wide*

$800-950   **K&O**

A Moorcroft vase, 'Launching Liberty' pattern, designed by Paul Hilditch.

2016   *11.5in (29cm) high*

$400-550   **K&O**

A Moorcroft vase, 'Up, Up and Away' pattern, by Paul Hilditch, no.167 of a limited edition of 200.

2011   *9.5in (24cm) high*

$400-550   **K&O**

A Moorcroft vase, 'Ranthambore' pattern, designed by Sian Leeper, boxed, dated.
2002   *10.25in (26cm) high*
$800-850   **WHP**

A Moorcroft jar and cover, 'Otter' pattern, designed by Sian Leeper, no.13 of a limited edition of 150, impressed, signed.
2004   *8in (20cm) high*
$550-600   **HT**

A Moorcroft jug, 'Shimba Hills' pattern, designed by Sian Leeper, no.117 of a limited edition of 300, boxed.
2005   *12.25in (31cm) high*
$650-750   **K&O**

A Moorcroft vase, 'Puffins' pattern, designed by Carole Lovatt, boxed, dated.
1998   *5.25in (13.5cm) high*
$200-250   **WHP**

A limited edition Moorcroft lidded pot, 'Bredon Hill' pattern, designed by Vicky Lovatt.
3.5in (9cm) high
$250-500   **PSA**

A Moorcroft ginger jar, 'Treetops' pattern, by Vicky Lovatt.

A Moorcroft trial vase, 'Autumn Toadstool' pattern, designed by Vicky Lovatt, dated.
2014   *11.75in (30cm) high*
$550-600   **PSA**

2015   *3.5in (9.5cm) high*
$450-550   **K&O**

A Moorcroft vase, 'Maypole' pattern, designed by Wendy Mason, no.128 of a limited edition of 150, boxed.
c1997   *14.5in (37cm) high*
$1,000-1,200   **BELL**

CERAMICS

A Moorcroft ginger jar, 'Coral Reef' pattern, designed by Jeanne McDougall, printed and impressed marks, boxed.

2005   *9.5in (24cm) high*
$750-850   K&O

A Moorcroft 'Peter the Pig', modeled by Roger Mitchell, impressed marks, overall crazing, some tube lining missing.

This model is unusual as it has blue painted eyes, as opposed to the brown painted eyes seen on the standard version.

11.75in (30cm) long
$550-600   PW

A Moorcroft Collectors Club vase, 'Cloths in Heaven' pattern, by Nicola Slaney, no.229 of a limited edition of 250, impressed, boxed, marks to base.

Nichola Slaney has designed for Moorcroft since 1998.

2004   *10.5in (27cm) high*
$350-400   PW

A Moorcroft pottery owl, 'Model of Wisdom', by Rob Tabbenor, impressed mark highlighted in blue, initialed 'LH' (?) in blue, indistinctly signed, boxed.

2008   *5.5in (14cm) high*
$400-450   HT

QUICK REFERENCE - SALLY TUFFIN

- Sally Tuffin (b.1938) studied at Walthamstow Art School and the Royal Collage of Art.
- In the 1960s and 70s, she co-ran a fashion design business, Foale & Tuffin, with her colleague Marion Foale. Foale & Tuffin designed a range of colorful, bright dresses, skirts, tops and trousers for young women, which were sold at their shop in Carnaby Street and later at department stores.
- In 1986, in an attempt to preserve the security of Moorcroft Pottery, Sally Tuffin, her husband Richard Dennis, and their friends Hugh and Maureen Edwards jointly purchased a 76% stake in the company. From 1986-93, Tuffin worked as Art Director and designer for Moorcroft. Her numerous pattern designs include 'Balloons', 'Bramble', 'Peacock' and 'Sunflower'.
- In 1993, she founded Dennis Chinaworks with her husband, Richard Dennis (see pages 83-84).

A Moorcroft vase, 'Windsor Carnation' pattern, designed by Sally Tuffin, commissioned by Talents of Windsors, no.293 of a limited edition of 300, boxed.

c1993   *11.5in (29.5cm) high*
$250-350   BELL

A Moorcroft vase, 'Carp' pattern, designed by Sally Tuffin, boxed.

1994   *13in (33cm) high*
$800-1,000   BELL

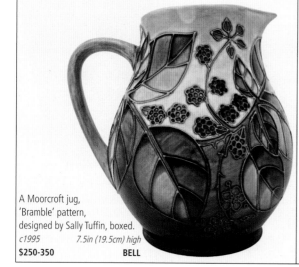

A Moorcroft jug, 'Bramble' pattern, designed by Sally Tuffin, boxed.

c1995   *7.5in (19.5cm) high*
$250-350   BELL

A Moorcroft vase, 'Sunflower' pattern, designed by Sally Tuffin, printed and impressed marks, dated.

1988   *26.75in (68cm) high*
$1,600-2,000   K&O

QUICK REFERENCE - GEORGE OHR

- George Ohr (1857-1918), the self-styled 'Mad Potter of Biloxi', MS, USA, is today known for his eccentric behavior as well as his unconventional pottery. Although he did not receive much acclaim during his lifetime, his wares are now highly sought after.

- Ohr made his unusual vessels, his 'mud babies', from clay that he dug by hand from the banks of the Tchoutacabouffa River. He then shaped the vessels by folding, squashing and denting, giving his pottery an exaggerated, asymmetrical and abstract appearance.

- His wares are often marked with unusual engravings, such as 'Mary had a little Lamb & Ohr has a little Pottery.' Ohr sometimes signed himself 'George Ohr, MD' - 'MD' standing for 'Mud Dauber' - and referred to his workshop as a 'Pot-Ohr-E'.

- The Ohr-O'Keefe Museum of Art in Biloxi was designed by artist and architect Frank Gehry and opened in 2014. It contains one of the largest collections of George Ohr wares in the world. The unusual architectural design of the museum pays tribute to Ohr's unusual creations.

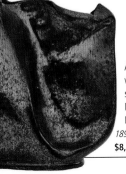

A vessel with crimped rim, by George Ohr, Biloxi, MS, with gunmetal and green glaze, stamped 'G.E. OHR BILOXI', a few flecks to rim.

1895-96   5in (12.5cm) wide
$5,500-6,500   DRA

A vase, by George Ohr, with in-body twist, orange, green and brown speckled glaze, stamped 'G.E. OHR Biloxi, Miss.', glazed-over chip to slightly misshapen rim in making of.

1897-1900   7.5in (19cm) high
$5,500-6,000   DRA

A pitcher, by George Ohr, with a gunmetal glaze, stamped 'G.E. OHR Biloxi, Miss.', incised 'OHR BILOXI'.

1897-1900   6in (15cm) high
$8,500-9,500   DRA

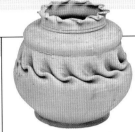

A bisque vase, by George Ohr, with a ruffled rim and in-body twist, with script signature.

1896-1910   6in (15cm) high
$4,500-5,500   DRA

A pitcher, by George Ohr, with twisted ribbon handle, with a brown and ocher speckled glaze, stamped 'G.E. OHR Biloxi, Miss.'.

1897-1900   4.5in (11.5cm) high
$5,500-6,000   DRA

A vase, by George Ohr, with a folded rim, an ocher and green glaze, stamped 'G.E. OHR Biloxi, Miss.'.

1897-1900   5in (12.5cm) wide
$5,500-6,000   DRA

A crumpled vase, by George Ohr, with a green and gunmetal speckled glaze, marked 'G.E. OHR Biloxi, Miss.', professional restoration to a chip.

1897-1900   4.25in (11cm) wide
$5,500-6,000   DRA

A CLOSER LOOK AT A JEFFERSON MUG

The mug is formed with an in-body twist and a crumpled, twisted handle.

The raspberry and indigo glaze has been sponged-on.

The mug is incised 'Rear Admiral Schley at Santiago July 3rd -1898 Here's to your good health and your family's and may they live long and prosper - J'.

Despite some professional restoration to the rim and to one hairline crack, the value remains high for this unusual piece.

A Jefferson mug, by George Ohr, some professional restoration, several touch-ups.

1896
$7,500-8,000   DRA

CERAMICS

A vessel, by George Ohr, with pinched rim and sides, green and brown speckled glaze, stamped 'G.E. OHR Biloxi, Miss.;'.

1897-1900   *5in (12.5cm) wide*

$4,000-5,000   **DRA**

An inkwell, by George Ohr, with a ruffled rim, green and ocher glaze, stamped 'G.E. OHR Biloxi, Miss.', professional restoration to one of the two mounds and to several ruffles.

1897-1900   *10in (25.5cm) wide*

$1,300-2,000   **DRA**

A vessel with ruffled rim, by George Ohr, with green and gunmetal sponged-on glaze, stamped 'G.E. OHR Biloxi, Miss.'.

1897-1900   *5in (12.5cm) wide*

$5,500-6,000   **DRA**

A squat pitcher, by George Ohr, with folded rim, gunmetal over ocher glaze, with script signature.

1898-1910   *6.5in (16.5cm) wide*

$5,500-6,000   **DRA**

A sculptural bisque vase, by George Ohr, with ruffled rim, with script signature, several chips to ruffles.

1898-1910   *10in (25.5cm) wide*

$4,500-5,500   **DRA**

A bisque pitcher, by George Ohr, with in-body twists, script signature, small chip under rim.

1898-1910   *7in (18cm) high*

$8,500-9,500   **DRA**

A pitcher, by George Ohr, with indigo blue and green sponged-on glaze, stamped 'G.E. OHR Biloxi, Miss.'.

c1900   *6.5in (16.5cm) high*

$2,500-3,500   **DRA**

A corseted vase, by George Ohr, with indigo glaze, stamped 'G.E. OHR Biloxi, Miss.', professional restoration to rim.

c1900   *7.5in (19cm) high*

$2,000-2,500   **DRA**

A cabinet vase, by George Ohr, with purple glaze, stamped 'G.E. OHR, Biloxi Miss.'.

c1900   *4in (10cm) high*

$2,000-2,500   **DRA**

QUICK REFERENCE - POOLE POTTERY

- Poole Pottery began as Carter and Co. in Poole, Dorset in 1873. It opened a subsidiary pottery in 1921. Formally Carter, Stabler & Adams, this subsidiary was known as Poole Pottery and renamed in 1963.
- The company combined traditional hand-throwing techniques with handpainted colorful modern designs. It produced many successful ranges, such as the 1920s 'Handcraft' line, Truda Carter's 1940s 'Twintone', 1950s 'Contemporary', and Tony Morris and Guy Sydenham's 1960s 'Delphis'.
- The Poole factory closed in 2006, but the brand continues as part of Lifestyle Holdings.
- Interest in 1920s-30s pieces is growing, but limited edition 1960s-70s pieces still tend to fetch the highest prices. Modern pieces are also collectible, especially those by Janice Tchalenko and Sir Terry Frost.

An unusual Carters Poole Pottery tile, 'Love Birds', probably designed by John Adams, unmarked, small glaze chip.

6in (15cm) square

$550-650   WW

A Poole Pottery 'Comical Hare' model, designed by Marjorie Drawbell, covered in an apple green glaze, impressed marks.

6.5in (16.5cm) high

$450-550   WW

A Poole Pottery 'Freeform' shape 698 bottle vase, glazed in lime green, printed marks.

15.25in (39cm) high

$90-110   FLD

A Poole Pottery 'PKT Freeform' baluster vase.

10in (25.5cm) high

$250-350   FLD

A Poole Pottery 'Freeform' shape 719 vase, in ice blue, printed marks.

12.5in (32cm) high

$80-100   FLD

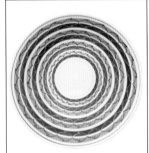

A Poole Pottery 'Freeform' footed bowl, 'ROC' pattern, printed and painted marks.

12.5in (32cm) diam

$90-120   FLD

A Poole Pottery shape 673 lamp base, impressed and painted marks.

10.25in (26cm) high

$100-130   FLD

A Poole 'Freeform' Harlequin 'HOL' pattern vase, designed by Ruth Pavel, painted by Diane Holloway.

'Freeform' is the name given to the Scandinavian-influenced asymmetrical and elliptical shaped vases conceived in the early 1950s and produced from 1956. A.B. Read is credited with the initial design, in conjunction with Guy Sydenham. The design policy at this time involved close co-operation between designer, thrower and artist. Painted designs by Ruth Pavely were informal and well adapted to the irregular curved surfaces of the 'Freeform' range. The vases were very popular for flower arranging and, in the words of Guy Sydenham, 'we couldn't make enough of them'.

c1955   *10.25in (26cm) high*

$400-550   HAN

CERAMICS

A Poole Pottery 'Delphis' charger, by Jean Millership, shape no.5, printed and painted factory marks.

14.5in (36.5cm) diam

$130-200　　WW

A 1960s Poole Pottery studio bottle vase, designed by Robert Jefferson, printed 'Poole Studio England' backstamp.

17.75in (45cm) high

$900-1,000　　LSK

A Poole Pottery vase, with dolphin stamp to base.

7.75in (19.5cm) high

$50-70　　LOCK

A 1960s Poole Pottery plaque, by Robert Jefferson, formed as a stylized bird, printed mark.

7.5in (19cm) long

$200-250　　FLD

QUICK REFERENCE - ROBERT JEFFERSON

The Poole Studio and Delphis ranges mark Robert Jefferson's most significant contribution to Pottery at Poole. He also designed table and kitchen wares. After graduating from the Royal College of Art in 1954, he became a resident designer at Poole in 1958. Jefferson was a great innovator, introducing new technology to the factory and reinvigorating the Poole catalog with new shapes and styles in keeping with a new decade. He also designed the 'Contour' tableware range and 'Black Pebble' pattern shown in the Twintone Gallery, together with Helios table lamps. He left Poole Pottery in 1966, after he had reputedly 'designed himself out of a job'. One-off pieces by Robert Jefferson and Tony Morris have shot up over the last couple of years and continue to rise.

A 1960s Poole Pottery studio bottle vase, designed by Robert Jefferson, printed 'Poole England' backstamp, with chip to top rim.

18in (45.5cm) high

$650-800　　LSK

A 1960s Poole Pottery vase, painted in black over blue with sgraffito line decoration, printed mark.

7.75in (20cm) high

$80-100　　FLD

A Poole Pottery table lamp, by Susan Russell, with typical bright colored floral stylized decoration, Poole England factory stamp and further inscription 'Hand-Painted at Poole Pottery by Susan Russell'.

12.5in (32cm) high

$80-100　　LSK

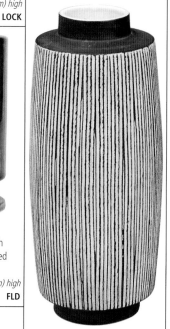

A 1960s Poole Pottery studio vase, designed by Robert Jefferson, with two Poole Studio TV backstamps.

12.25in (31cm) high

$1,300-2,000　　LSK

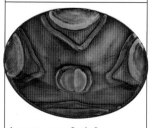

A contemporary Poole Pottery 'Delphis' bowl, printed marks.

10.25in (26cm) diam

$90-120　　FLD

QUICK REFERENCE - REG JOHNSON

- Reginald Johnson (1909-69) began his career at Royal Doulton in 1923 at the age of 14. He studied under Charles Noke and went on to become a design director for Royal Doulton, working chiefly on the Paragon and Royal Albert brands.
- In his own studio, he modeled character figurines, often in the style of Royal Doulton. These were individually potted and handpainted. Many were inspired by Arabian designs and dress, while others were influenced by famous artists such as Rembrandt and Gainsborough.
- His studio figures can be hard to find today, making his studio work often more valuable than his Royal Doulton pieces.

A Reg Johnson Studio Pottery 'Seated Cavalier' figurine.

9in (23cm) high

$250-300   PSA

A Reg Johnson Studio Pottery 'Seated Falstaff' figurine.

8.5in (21.5cm) high

$200-250   PSA

A Reg Johnson Studio Pottery 'Armenian Dice Thrower' figurine.

6in (15cm) high

$250-300   PSA

A Reg Johnson Studio Pottery 'Omar Khayyam' figurine.

8.75in (22cm) high

$90-110   PSA

A Reg Johnson Studio Pottery 'Mandarin' figurine.

8in (20.5cm) high

$130-200   PSA

A Reg Johnson Studio Pottery 'Embroiderer of Kashmir' figurine.

7.5in (19cm) high

$130-200   PSA

A Reg Johnson Studio Pottery 'Cobbler of Baghdad' figurine.

7in (18cm) high

$120-160   PSA

A Reg Johnson Studio Pottery 'Wolfgang Amadeus Mozart' figurine.

In general the musician figurines are less desirable than those with an Arabian and Oriental inspiration.

7.75in (20cm) high

$90-100   PSA

A Reg Johnson Studio Pottery 'Ludvig Van Beethoven' figurine.

8.25in (21cm) high

$90-100   PSA

CERAMICS

QUICK REFERENCE - ROOKWOOD

- In Cincinnati, OH, USA, in 1880, a wealthy young lady, Maria Longworth Nichols Storer, founded the Rookwood pottery. It began as a hobby but, with the help of Production Manager William Watts Taylor, soon became a great success.
- Rookwood produced many distinctive designs, including the yellow-tinted 'Standard' glaze, developed by Laura Fry in the 1880s, and the 'Iris', 'Sea Green' and 'Aerial Blue' glazes created in the 1890s. The mat 'Vellum' glaze was patented in 1904.
- Rookwood's commercial 'Production' ware, mass-produced for a cheaper market, was richly glazed and simply designed. These pieces lack the usual artists' monograms.
- Rookwood suffered heavily during the Depression. It filed for bankruptcy in 1941, although production continued until the mid-1960s.

An early Rookwood pitcher, by Laura Fry (1857-1943), decorated in the Japanesque style, impressed 'ROOKWOOD' stamp, date and artist cipher, poorly filled chip to spout.

1883   *7in (18cm) high*

$850-900   **DRA**

A Rookwood 'Standard Glaze' vase, by Matt Daly (1860-1937), painted with witch hazel, impressed 'Rookwood' stamp, date, model and artist cipher.

1886   *9.5in (24cm) diam*

$650-800   **DRA**

A Rookwood 'Dull Finish' pitcher with roses, by Artus Van Briggle (1869-1904), with flame mark '495A / W / ARV / S', firing line to top of handle.

1888   *10in (25.5cm) high*

$450-550   **DRA**

A Rookwood 'Sea Green' vase, by Constance Baker, with poppies, flame marked 'III / 900C / G / CAB', overall crazing.

1903   *8in (20.5cm) high*

$900-1,100   **DRA**

A Rookwood 'Iris Glaze' vase, with clover flowers, by Fred Rothenbusch (1876-1937), with flame mark, date, model and artist's cipher, interior X-shaped hairline, heavy crazing.

1903   *7.25in (18.5cm) high*

$450-600   **DRA**

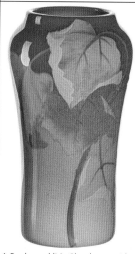

A Rookwood 'Iris Glaze' vase with autumn leaves, by Sara Sax (1870-1949), flame marked 'III / 935D / SX', overall fine crazing.

1903   *7.5in (19cm) high*

$800-950   **DRA**

A Rookwood 'Modeled Mat' vase, with irises, by Rose Fechheimer (1874-1961), with flame mark 'V / 952E / E.T.H'.

1905   *7in (18cm) high*

$400-550   **DRA**

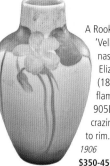

A Rookwood 'Vellum' vase, with nasturtium, by Elizabeth Lincoln (1876-1957), with flame mark 'VI / 905D / V / L.N.L', crazing, glaze drips to rim.

1906   *8.25in (21cm) high*

$350-450   **DRA**

A Rookwood 'Modeled Mat' vase, by Rose Fechheimer, with maple seeds, flame marked 'VI / S00D', one short, deep crazing line at rim.

1906   *6.5in (16.5cm) high*

$750-800   **DRA**

A CLOSER LOOK AT A VELLUM VASE

This vase was designed by Sarah Elizabeth 'Sallie' Coyne (1876-1939), who worked as a decorator at Rookwood 1891-1936.

The mat 'Vellum' glaze gives the vase its hazy, frosted appearance, adding to the wintry atmosphere.

It is decorated with a 'Winter Scenic' landscape.

It is flame marked 'XX / 918E / V / SEC': 'XX' for the year 1920, '918' for the vase's shape, 'E' for the size, 'V' for 'Vellum', and 'SEC' for the artist.

A Rookwood 'Vellum' vase, overall fine crazing.
1920   *6.25in (16cm) high*
$1,000-1,300   **DRA**

A Rookwood 'Vellum' vase, with magnolias, by Sara Sax, with flame mark 'IX / 942B / V / SX', crazing, tight 1in (2.5cm) hairline from rim.
1909   *8.25in (21cm) high*
$450-600   **DRA**

A Rookwood 'Vellum' vase, by Lorinda Epply (1874-1951), decorated with poppies, flame marked 'X / 907E / V / LE', overall fine crazing.
1910   *9.25in (23.5cm) high*
$1,300-2,000   **DRA**

A Rookwood 'Iris Glaze' vase, by Ed Diers (1871-1947), with wild roses, flame marked 'X / 917B / ED / W', overall crazing.
1910   *9.25in (23.5cm) high*
$1,000-1,200   **DRA**

A Rookwood 'Scenic Vellum' vase, by Lenore Abury (1866-1933), flame marked, date, model and artist cipher, moderate crazing.
1915   *8.25in (21cm) high*
$1,000-1,200   **DRA**

A Rookwood bowl, painted with violets, by Ed Diers, with flame mark, signed, dated, numbered '957C', crazing overall.
1916   *8in (20cm) diam*
$250-350   **DRA**

A tall Rookwood 'Scenic Vellum' vase, by Lenore Ashbury), Cincinnati, OH, flame marked 'XXII / 2032D / V / LA', overall crazing.
1922   *10in (25.5cm) high*
$800-950   **DRA**

A Rookwood 'Vellum' glaze bowl, with poppies, by Lenore Asbury, with flame mark 'XXX / 2260D / L.A. / V'.
1930   *7.75in (19cm) high*
$350-450   **DRA**

QUICK REFERENCE - KATARO SHIRAYAMADANI

Kataro Shirayamadani (1865-1948), was a Japanese ceramics painter who worked for Rookwood Pottery in Cincinnati, OH, USA, from 1887 until 1948. Shirayamadani was born in Tokyo. He was already an accomplished painter of porcelain when he came to the United States. He was working in Boston for the Fujiyama porcelain-decorating workshop when he first met Maria Longworth Nichols Storer, the founder of Rookwood Pottery, in 1886. She hired him to work for her at Rookwood in May, 1887. He lent an authentic influence to the pottery when Japanese design was extremely fashionable. A vase he designed won a Grand Prize at the 1900 Paris Exposition Universelle. The vase was acquired by the Philadelphia Museum of Art in 1901 and is still in its collection. He decorated table lamp bases that were combined with stained glass shades made by Tiffany Studios.

A Rookwood corseted vase in 'Decorated Mat' and 'Double Vellum' glaze, by Kataro Shirayamadani, with dogwood branches, flame marked with date and artist cipher.
1940   *8in (20.5cm) high*
$1,300-2,000   **DRA**

CERAMICS

QUICK REFERENCE - ROSEVILLE

- The Roseville Pottery was founded in Roseville, OH, USA, in 1890. It initially produced utilitarian wares and launched its first Art Pottery range, 'Rozane', in 1900.
- Frederick Hurten Rhead (brother of Charlotte Rhead, see page 82, and son of Frederick Rhead, see page 162 and 163) worked at Roseville 1904-08 and created several ranges, including the popular 'Della Robbia'. Other notable designers include Frank Ferrell and glaze-maker George Kraus.
- In 1908, as the demand for expensive wares fell, Roseville began several mass-produced, molded ranges, many of which were based on natural imagery.
- The pottery closed in 1954.

A Roseville stoneware pitcher with grazing bull in low relief, unmarked.

The crazing throughout, multiple chips along the base and rim and a heavy section of glaze chipping to handle severely affects the value.

c1910   7.75in (19.5cm) high
$40-50   DRA

A Roseville 'Carnelian I' urn, ink stamped 'R'.

1910-15   12.5in (32cm) high
$60-80   DRA

A pair of Roseville vases, one 'Egypto' and one 'Chloron', the first with Rozane Ware 'Egypto' raised seal, small bruise to the rim of one.

1905   5.5in (14cm) high
$550-650   DRA

An early 20thC Roseville 'Rozane' ware royal vase, with impressed mark.

5.25in (13.5cm) high
$250-350   DRA

A 1920s Roseville 'Blue Snowberry' jardinière and pedestal, both marked and numbered.

pedestal 17in (43cm) high
$350-400   DRA

A Roseville 'Rozane' vase, painted with elk, stamped 'ROZANE 832 RPCO', over-painting all around rim and top part of neck.

20.5in (52cm) high
$450-550   DRA

A Roseville 'Velmoss' vase, unmarked.

1927-35   11.75in (30cm) diam
$450-550   DRA

A Roseville 'Blue Iris' two-handled vase, marked and numbered, crazing throughout.

1932-37   15in (38cm) high
$450-550   DRA

A Roseville 'Cherry Blossom' floor vase, ink stamped '#628', original foil label.

1933   15.25in (38.5cm) high
$550-650   DRA

QUICK REFERENCE - ROYAL CROWN DERBY

- Derby has a long history of porcelain production. The original Derby factory, founded in 1750, closed in 1848; several other factories opened in its wake, including Crown Derby, which was established in 1876 by Edward Phillips and William Litherland. Litherland was already head of a family china and glass business in Liverpool.
- The company's popularity grew in the 1880s under the direction of Richard Lunn, attracting talented artists such as James Rouse senior, Count George Holtzendorf and Désiré Leroy. Its delicate porcelain and detailed gilded designs were highly popular. The company received a warrant from Queen Victoria in 1890 and became Royal Crown Derby.
- Its popularity continued into the 20thC. After World War II, it incorporated animal figurines and statuettes into its range.
- It was acquired by the Lawley Group in 1964 and subsequently by Royal Doulton in 1973. Its 1980s range of animal and bird paperweights, designed by Robert Jefferson, has proved especially popular. Today it is owned by Kevin Oakes.

A pair of Royal Crown Derby handpainted vases, by C. Gresley, signed on each panel, with date code.

1919   *7.25in (18.5cm) high*

$1,000-1,300   **K&O**

A Royal Crown Derby pedestal dish, pattern no.1128, marked to underside 'XLIII'.

$750-800   **HAN**

A Royal Crown Derby porcelain 'Imari' pattern jug vase or ewer, pattern no.1128, red printed marks with date code.

1974   *9.75in (24.5cm) high*

$350-400   **FELL**

One of a pair of Royal Crown Derby porcelain 'Imari' pattern bowls, pattern no.1128, red printed marks with date code, one bowl with thermal shock cracks around foot rim.

1974   *larger 11.5in (29cm) diam*

$550-600 pair   **FELL**

A pair of Royal Crown Derby porcelain 'Imari' pattern candlesticks, pattern no.1128, red printed marks with date code.

1974   *10.5in (26.5cm) high*

$750-800   **FELL**

A Royal Crown Derby 'Millenium Globe Clock', no.543 of a limited edition of 1000, boxed.

$350-400   **HAN**

A pair of Royal Crown Derby 'Mansion House' dwarfs.

larger 6.75in (17cm) high

$130-200   **LOCK**

A Royal Crown Derby 'Imari' elephant, with silver stopper.

8.25in (21cm) high

$400-450   **HAN**

CERAMICS

QUICK REFERENCE - ROYAL CROWN DERBY PAPERWEIGHTS

- Royal Crown Derby introduced the first six paperweights in September 1981 at Chatsworth House, Derbyshire. These paperweights were the Duck, Owl, Penguin, Quail, Rabbit and Wren.

- The company decided that sculptures of birds and animals would have greatest appeal. The range would be in a style that appealed to contemporary tastes whilst the decoration would continue the Derby traditions of rich decoration. It was felt important to incorporate the 'Imari' patterns.

- Robert Jefferson, a freelance sculptor who had previously worked for the Poole Pottery Studio in Dorset (see page 122), was asked to come up with some ideas for the range. Brian Branscombe, Art Director at Derby, and his wife June, who was also a designer at the Derby Art Studio, were asked to design the decoration for the paperweights, using the traditional 'Imari' color palette.

- The range became extremely successful and would also help to transform the overall prospects of Royal Crown Derby in the 1990s.

A Royal Crown Derby 'Golden Pheasant' paperweight, from the 250 Collection, with gold stopper, boxed.

$350-400   HAN

A Royal Crown Derby 'Chameleon' paperweight, with gold stopper.

$60-70   PSA

A Royal Crown Derby 'Spirit of Peace' paperweight, no.72 of a limited edition of 150, boxed, with certificate.

$800-950   HAN

A boxed Royal Crown Derby 'Frog' paperweight, no.441 of a limited edition of 500, stamped to the base 'Fine china and crystal specialists, Mulberry Hall York', gold stopper.

2.25in (6cm) high

$250-350   FLD

A Royal Crown Derby 'Sherwood Stag' paperweight, no.103 of a limited edition of 395, boxed, with certificate.

$400-450   HAN

A Royal Crown Derby 'Endangered Species White Rhinoceros' paperweight, no.257 of a limited edition of 1000, signed to base, boxed, with certificate.

$300-400   HAN

A limited edition Royal Crown Derby 'Irish Blue Kerry' paperweight, boxed, missing stopper.

$60-80   PSA

A Royal Crown Derby 'Snow Leopard' paperweight, no.89 of a limited edition of 250, with wooden stand and gold stopper, boxed.

$250-350   HAN

A Royal Crown Derby 'Winston Churchill Cat' paperweight, 'Jock VI of Chartwell', no.63 of a limited edition of 750, boxed, with certificate, with gold stopper.

$150-200   HAN

QUICK REFERENCE - ROYAL WORCESTER

- The Worcester factory was founded in 1751. It received a royal warrant from George III in 1788 and was known as Royal Worcester from 1862.
- The factory produced a range of ceramics, including tableware and figurines. Their designs and forms were often inspired by Oriental porcelain. Key artists included modeller James Hadley and sculpture Charles Toft.
- Royal Worcester continued throughout the 19thC, but sales fell sharply at the start of the 20thC, and the company declared bankruptcy in 1930. It was bought up by C.W. Dyson Perrins and continues to sell ceramics today.
- Many traditional Royal Worcester ceramics have largely gone out of fashion. Values for 19thC and 20thC pieces tend to be stagnant, although rare pieces, and pieces by painters such as John Freeman and the Stintons, can still fetch higher prices.

A Royal Worcester porcelain plate, by Reed, painted with apples and blackberries, within gilt-enriched borders, signed, gold printed mark, in card box.

10.75in (27cm) diam

$200-250   **FELL**

A Royal Worcester porcelain plate, by English, painted with plums and green grapes, within gilt relief-enriched mazarin blue borders, signed, gold printed mark, in original card box.

10.75in (27cm) diam

$450-550   **FELL**

A Royal Worcester porcelain pot pourri jar, cover and liner, by Freeman, shape no.1286, painted with apples, grapes, cherries, plums and gooseberries, signed, black printed mark.

10in (25.5cm) high

$1,200-1,600   **FELL**

A Royal Worcester porcelain vase, by Freeman, shape no.1969, painted with peaches, grapes, cherries and gooseberries, signed, black printed mark, minor gilt tarnishing to base of neck.

12in (30.5cm) high

$1,600-2,000   **FELL**

A Royal Worcester porcelain plate, by Freeman, shape no.1286, painted with apples, blackberries and cherries, signed, black printed mark, in original card box.

John Freeman was born in 1911 and joined the Royal Worcester factory in 1925. He became an extremely talented fruit and still-life painter and was probably the most prolific of all the fruit painters of his time. He stayed at the Royal Worcester factory throughout his long working life and became the senior fruit painter in the mens' painting room.

9.5in (24cm) diam

$800-950   **FELL**

A Royal Worcester jug, with strainer lip and simulated bamboo handle and knop, date code.

1890   *8.75in (22cm) high*

$150-200   **DA&H**

A Royal Worcester vase, painted with pheasants, by James Stinton, shape no.G706, signed, with date code.

James Stinton was the youngest son of John Stinton senior and brother of John Stinton Junior. He began at Graingers in 1889 moving to Royal Worcester in 1902, specializing in game birds. He also did a large number of watercolor paintings of game birds.

1903   *6in (15.5cm) high*

$750-800   **K&O**

A Royal Worcester pot pourri jar, shape no.1313, reg. no.112588, with pierced cover and inner lid, date code.

1898   *7.75in (20cm) high*

$250-350   **DA&H**

A Royal Worcester jug, painted with a kingfisher, by Billy Powell, signed, with date code.

Billy Powell was at the factory 1900-50, specializing in English birds. He was a hunchback and dwarf and had a tall seat to reach his painting desk. The factory put him to work with the gilders so that the public could see a painter, as they were not allowed into the mens' painting department.

1934   *3.25in (8cm) high*

$250-350   **K&O**

CERAMICS

QUICK REFERENCE - DORIS LINDNER

Doris Lindner was born in Llanyre in Radnorshire, South Wales in 1896. She studied sculpture at St Martin's School of Art in London, the British Academy in Rome and at Calderon's Animal School in London. From 1931 Doris Lindner's first models for Royal Worcester were of dogs, other small animals and Art Deco figure studies, followed by a series of zoo babies. In 1935 she started a number of horse group models that proved very successful including 'At the Meet' and 'Huntsman and Hounds'. In 1948, Doris Lindner modeled Princess Elizabeth on Tommy, which was issued as the very first equestrian limited edition, establishing her reputation. In the 1960s, Doris Lindner modeled a series of horses, equestrian studies and bulls. She traveled widely to gather information about her subjects. She consulted breeding societies and journeyed to America to study champion cattle in Texas. Miss Lindner worked in plasticine; she cut her models into sections before bringing them to the factory. The Limited Editions designed and modeled by Miss Lindner reached the height of popularity in the 1960s and she worked untiringly until she was over 80 years old. Doris Lindner died in 1979.

A Royal Worcester 'Two Calves' group, modeled by Doris Lindner, RW3146, inscribed.

1936-c50s   *4.75in (12cm) high*
$800-950   **SWO**

A Royal Worcester 'Suffolk Punch' figure, modeled by Doris Lindner, RW3825, on a hardwood stand, with leather framed certificate, no.383 of a limited edition of 500, black printed mark and title.

Lindner's model for this study was 'Beccles Warrener' owned by Mr G.E. Colson of Long Melford Suffolk.

1969   *9.75in (25cm) high*
$350-400   **MAB**

A limited edition Royal Worcester 'Stroller and Marion Coakes' figure, modeled by Doris Lindner, RW3872, from a limited edition of 750, on a wooden plinth.

1968   *11.25in (28.5cm) high*
$600-650   **PSA**

A Royal Worcester porcelain 'Nijinsky' model, modeled by Doris Lindner, RW3893, black printed marks, no.435 of a limited edition of 500, with wooden plinth.

1971   *9.75in (25cm) high*
$550-650   **FELL**

A Royal Worcester 'Labrador Revtriever' figure, modeled by Doris Lindner, RW3233, with mat black finish, with wooden plinth.

1975   *7in (18cm) long*
$200-250   **FELL**

A Royal Worcester 'Jersey Bull' figure, modeled by Doris Lindner, RW3776A, from the 'Prize Cattle' series, from a limited edition of 500, on a hardwood stand, a black printed mark and title.

Lindner's model for this study was the champion Leeburn Carlisle II, owned by Mr Carter of Hartpary, Gloucestershire.

1965   *7.75in (20cm) high*
$200-250   **MAB**

A Royal Worcester 'Captain Raimondo D'Inzeo on Merano' figure, modeled by Doris Lindner, RW3745, from a limited edition of 500, on a wooden plinth.

1962   *11in (28cm) high*
$550-650   **PSA**

A Royal Worcester 'Percheron Stallion' figure, by Doris Lindner, RW3786, from a limited edition of 500, on a wooden plinth, in a box.

1965   *9.5in (24cm) high*
$550-650   **LOC**

A CLOSER LOOK AT NAPOLEON BONAPARTE

This figurine of Napoleon Bonaparte was modeled by Bernard Winskill as part of the 'Military Commanders' series.

This piece comes with its box and certificate, which increases the value.

The horse and rider are made of bona china. Napoleon wears a red cape, dark blue coat and his distinctive hat.

It is mounted on a wooden plinth with a plaque reading 'Napoleon'.

A Royal Worcester 'Napoleon Bonaparte on horseback', RW3860, no.731 of a limited edition of 750.

An alternative version of this model was created in bronze in a limited edition of 15.

1969   *15in (38cm) high*
$1,000-1,300   **PW**

A Royal Worcester 'Monsieur Reynard' candle snuffer, modeled as a fox dressed as a lawyer, printed marks and date code.

1903 4in (10cm) high

$550-650 WW

A Royal Worcester 'Hadley' figure, no.960.

9in (23cm) high

$130-200 JN

A Royal Worcester 'Confidence' candle snuffer, of the singer Jenny Lind as a nightingale, printed marks and date code.

Jenny Lind first visited the Worcester porcelain factory in 1849, and settled close to Worcester following her retirement. This snuffer, along with its pair, 'Diffidence', is believed to have been made as a tribute in recognition of the charitable concerts held by Lind to raise money for the local hospital.

1919 4.25in (10.5cm) high

$750-800 WW

A Royal Worcester candle snuffer, 'Diffidence'.

1929 4in (10cm) high

$250-350 K&O

A pair of Royal Worcester Kate Greenaway-style figures, modeled by Hadley, no.1070, date code.

1886 10in (25.5cm) high

$250-350 K&O

A Royal Worcester 'Take Cover' group, modeled by Eileen A. Soper, RW3351, from the 'Wartime' Series, printed marks, dated.

1941 4.75in (12cm) high

$1,000-1,200 K&O

A Royal Worcester figurine of a violin player, no.1487, puce mark, date code.

1931

$550-600 K&O

A Royal Worcester 'City Imperial Volunteer' figure, modeled by George Evans, RW2106, from the 'Boer War' series, date code.

1900 7.5in (19cm) high

$1,000-1,200 BELL

A Royal Worcester 'Sister, The London Hospital' Figure, modeled by Ruth Van Ruyckevelt (1931-88), RW3662, no.183 of a limited edition to 500, black printed mark and title, with certificate and original box.

1963 6.75in (17cm) high

$900-1,000 MAB

CERAMICS

QUICK REFERENCE - RUSKIN

● Ruskin pottery was established Birmingham in 1897-98 by Edward Richard Taylor and his son William Howson Taylor.

● Early products included a range of ornamental and useful ware, including vases, tableware, buttons, cuff links and jewelry. Many early shapes were hand thrown.

● Howson Taylor experimented with a number of glaze techniques. Some were gradations of two colors; others were textured multicolor patterns. They included misty soufflé glazes, ice crystal effect glazes - 'crystalline', luster glazes resembling metallic finishes, and the most highly regarded of all, sang-de-boeuf and flambé glazes which produced a blood red effect. The sang-de-boeuf glazes were created using reduction of copper and iron oxides at high temperature. This was a difficult technique, first developed in China in the 13thC and reinvented by several art potters in Europe in the late 19thC. His glazes and colors were leadless and the decoration painted by hand.

● The factory struggled in the economic depression of the 1920s-30s. When the studio finally closed in 1935 the formulae for the glazes and all the pottery documentation were deliberately destroyed, so that the unique Ruskin products could never be replicated.

An early 20thC Ruskin Pottery soufflé glaze vase, impressed 'West Smethwick Ruskin Pottery' mark, dated.
1909   *10.25in (26cm) high*
$600-650   **FLD**

A Ruskin Pottery vase, the red-blue glaze running with mottled green, impressed mark 'Ruskin Pottery', dated.
1910   *8.75in (22cm) high*
$1,200-1,300   **LA**

A Ruskin Pottery brown glazed jug, with handpainted ivy leaves and grapes, the whiplash handle in pewter with two bands inset to the body, painted scissor mark, some damage.
                    9in (23cm) high
$1,300-2,000   **FLD**

An Arts and Crafts Ruskin cabouchon pendant, set within a hammered white metal square, with suspension loop to one corner, marked to the back 'W & M, Registration 521583'.
                    1in (2.5cm) square
$100-130   **HAN**

A Ruskin high-fired vase, in blue glaze, impressed marks.
c1910   *9.5in (24cm) high*
$2,000-2,500   **K&O**

A Ruskin vase, decorated with blue drip glaze, impressed marks and date to base, some glaze scratches.
1911   *9.75in (25cm) high*
$250-350   **PW**

A Ruskin vase, with mottled orange egg shell iridescent glaze, impressed 'Ruskin', dated.
1913   *11.5in (29.5cm) high*
$250-350   **BRI**

A Ruskin vase, with liver red and gray mottled glaze, impressed mark 'Ruskin England', dated.
1920   *10.25in (26cm) high*
$650-800   **LA**

Judith Picks

This interesting rare early piece was badly damaged round the neck. As my friend and colleague on the 'Antiques Roadshow', Will Farmer, who sold this piece at Fieldings, said, 'With regard to the vase, the value is simply down to rarity! The vase is a great shape and an early version of the mallet vase which he developed to become a classic mainstay of his rarer pieces and which was usually rolled out for the better glazes. Add to that the mark which was a very early impressed Taylor mark only used in the early years and then round it all off with the very unusual seaweed decoration to a soufflé glaze. We were incredibly cautious with the estimate owing to the level of damage around the upper section of the neck but it just goes to show that the super rare items will perform well with collectors. It was a proper academic piece which was seriously fought out by a couple of top end collectors all keen to own such an early experimental piece.'

A Ruskin Pottery mallet vase, impressed 'Taylor' mark and painted glaze codes to the base, damaged.
                    8.75in (22cm) high
$2,500-3,500   **FLD**

A Ruskin Pottery tazza, by William Howson Taylor, with a streaked blue luster glaze, impressed factory marks and date.
1923   *7.25in (18.5cm) high*
$350-400   **WW**

A Ruskin high-fired flambé vase, impressed marks.
c1920   *9.5in (24cm) high*
$1,800-2,200   **K&O**

A Ruskin high-fired vase, multiple colors including purples, reds and greens, impressed marks on base, dated.
1923   *14.5in (37cm) high*
$4,500-5,500   **K&O**

A Ruskin high-fired vase, red and purple-blue mottled glaze, impressed mark 'Ruskin England', dated.
1924   8.5in (21.5cm) high
$1,000-1,200   **LA**

A Ruskin Pottery vase, decorated in a streaked and mottled soufflé glaze in shades of brown and red, impressed marks, dated, some damage.
1926   9.75in (25cm) high
$1,500-2,000   **FLD**

A large Ruskin ginger jar and stand, in blue Crystaline glaze, impressed marks.
c1925   *14.25in (36cm) high*
$900-1,100   **K&O**

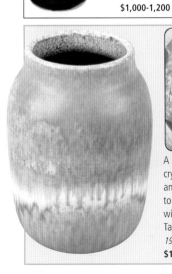

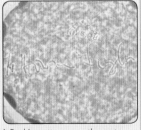

A Ruskin pottery vase, the mat crystalline glaze upon a blue, green and cream ground, impressed to base 'Ruskin England', dated, with incised signature 'W Howson Taylor', some surface wear.
1932   *9in (23cm) high*
$150-200   **FELL**

A Ruskin Pottery crystalline glaze vase, glazed in yellow over orange, impressed marks.
6.25in (16cm) high
$100-140   **HAN**

CERAMICS

A 1950s Michael Andersen and Sons vase, handmade and hand decorated, design no.5453.

7in (18cm) high

$200-250   LYN

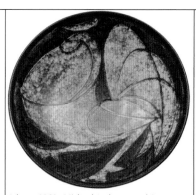

A large 1960s Michael Andersen and Sons 'Persia' glaze wall hanging dish, designed by Marianne Starck, decorated with a cockerel, design no.4106/1.

14.5in (37cm) diam

$250-300   LYN

A 1950s Michael Andersen and Sons tribal series vase, handmade, the design cut by hand, design no.5534.

8.5in (21.5cm) high

$200-220   LYN

An Arabia Finnish vase, with geometric zig-zag design, marked 'BH'.

4in (10cm) high

$35-45   HAN

A Gustavsberg 'Argenta' ware vase, by Wilhelm Kage, the body with a silver overlay crosshatch pattern, printed and impressed marks.

6.75in (17cm) high

$250-300   FLD

A 1950s Nymolle 'Spring Season' plate, by Bjørn Wiinblad.

11in (28cm) diam

$50-70   LYN

A Rosenthal Christmas wall plate, by Bjørn Wiinblad.

1987   *11.5in (29cm) diam*

$60-100   LYN

A Royal Copenhagen 'Fano/Faro' figurine, no.12413.

5.5in (14cm) high

$90-120   LOCK

A Royal Copenhagen 'Fairy Tale III' porcelain figural group, by Gerhard Henning, modeled as a turbaned man kissing a female nude on gilt oval base, marked and dated.

1962   *8.25in (21cm) high*

$750-850   ECGW

QUICK REFERENCE - ROYAL COPENHAGEN

- Royal Copenhagen began in Denmark in 1775 as the Royal Porcelain Factory, under the patronage of the Royal family.
- In the 1860s, the factory moved into private hands. It was acquired by the Alumina Factory in 1882.
- Royal Copenhagen continued to succeed into the 20thC. In 1972 it acquired the Georg Jensen Silversmithy. In 1985 it merged with Holmegaard Glassworks (see page 235) under the name Royal Copenhagen A/S. It is now part of the Royal Scandinavia group, and continues to produce ceramics.
- Royal Copenhagen marks often bear multiple features, as can be seen here. The crown 'Juliane Marie' mark was given to the factory by the Danish Royal family in 1775. The three wavy lines are the general Royal Copenhagen mark and are to be found on all pieces. Many pieces are also marked with the painter's mark, here to the right of the wavy lines; the design number, here to the top left of the wavy lines; the shape number, here to the bottom left of the wavy lines; the glaze type, below the lines; and the mark of the designer and range, at the bottom of the mark.

A Royal Copenhagen ceramic tray, the interior with crystalline glaze, the polar bear surmount, with painted marks '21-7-1924' to base.

12.5in (31.5cm) diam

$4,000-4,500   **FELL**

A Royal Copenhagen porcelain full lace part dinner and tea service, comprising 21 dessert plates, 12 teacups, 13 lobed saucers, 4 serving dishes (one lidded), a shell dish, a sugar bowl, 3 platters and 2 biscuits stands, some damage.

c1900-30s   *plates 6.75in (17cm) diam*

$3,500-4,000   **FELL**

A Royal Copenhagen bottle-shaped vase, by Kari Christensen, design no.181, shape no.2878.

7.5in (19cm) high

$100-150   **LYN**

A Royal Copenhagen chimney-shaped vase, by Johanne Greber, design no.805, shape no.3259.

9in (23cm) high

$140-160   **LYN**

A Royal Copenhagen chimney-shaped vase, by Johanne Greber, design no.780, shape no.3455.

7.5in (19cm) high

$100-120   **LYN**

A mid-1950s Royal Copenhagen vase, by Berte Jessen, from the 'Tenera' range, design no.206, shape no.2942.

7.5in (19cm) wide

$150-170   **LYN**

An early 1960s Royal Copenhagen barrel-form vase, by Marianne Johnson, design no.417, shape no.3115.

8in (20.5cm) high

$150-170   **LYN**

An early 1960s Royal Copenhagen 'eye' vase, by Inge Lise Koefed, from the 'Tenera' range, design no.138, shape no.2878.

7.5in (19cm) high

$200-250   **LYN**

A Royal Copenhagen pillow-shaped vase, by Ellen Malmer, design no.635, shape no.3121.

7.5in (19cm) high

$140-160 **LYN**

An early 1960s Søholm pitcher, by Maria Phillipi, from the 'Northern Lights' series, shape no.3312.

12.5in (32cm) high

$150-170 **LYN**

A Søholm vase, designed by Holm Sorensen, hand made, marked with Holm Sorensen's cipher.

6in (15cm) high

$100-130 **LYN**

A Søholm Burgundia vase, shape by Holm Sorensen, decoration by Svend Aage Jenen, base marked with factory name and shape number.

$200-250 **LYN**

A 1950s Søholm Art Deco Revival vase, designed by Holm Sorensen, based marked with designer's cipher and Søholm factory mark.

6in (15cm) high

$130-170 **LYN**

A Søholm Burgundia teardrop-shaped bowl, shape by Holm Sorensen, decoration and glaze by Svend Aage Jensen, shape no.2069.

16in (40.5cm) long

$130-150 **LYN**

An Uksala Ekeby Pottery dish, by Mari Simmulson, decorated with a naïve half-length study of a young girl, impressed 'LF4158 Sweden' to back.

10.5in (26.5cm) long

$160-200 **KEY**

A Bjørn Wiinblad own studio 'Spring Season' figure.

These figures were all individually decorated, meaning that no two are the same.

14.5in (37cm) high

$550-600 **LYN**

A Bjørn Wiinblad own studio 'Queen of Sheba' elephant candelabra, complete with plinth.

15.5in (39.5cm) high

$1,600-1,800 **LYN**

QUICK REFERENCE - ALDERMASTON POTTERY

Aldermaston Pottery was a pottery located in the Berkshire village of Aldermaston, England. It was founded in 1955 by Alan Caiger-Smith and was known for its tin-glaze pottery and particularly its luster ware. Alan Caiger-Smith worked with almost sixty assistants over a period of forty years at the pottery. The pottery scaled back its production in June 1993 when Caiger-Smith partially retired and stopped hiring assistants. It continued to be operated commercially until it was sold in 2006.

An Aldermaston Pottery tin-glazed plate, by Alan Caiger-Smith MBE (b.1930), painted and resist-decorated with a central flower, inside shell border, painted artist mark, dated.

1979   10.75in (27cm) diam

$600-750   WW

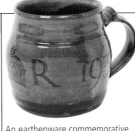

An earthenware commemorative tankard, by Michael Cardew, commemorating the silver jubilee of the Coronation of King George V, impressed seal, incised with crown, 'GR' and '1910-1935'.

1935   5in (13cm) high

$800-950   WW

A large Wenford Bridge Pottery footed bowl, by Michael Cardew, glazed in ash, impressed seal marks to side of foot.

12.25in (31cm) diam

$550-650   WW

QUICK REFERENCE - MICHAEL CARDEW

In 1926 Michael Cardew (who had trained under Bernard Leach for three years) rented the Becketts Pottery buildings, including the bottle kiln, and reopened it as the Winchcombe Pottery. Cardew's ambition was to make pottery for everyday use and at a price that ordinary people could afford, in the 17thC English slipware tradition. Using the clay on site and firing the pots in the bottle kiln, the range and skills quickly developed and in 1935 Charlie Tustin joined the team, followed in 1936 by Ray Finch (see page 139). Three years later Cardew left to set up Wenford Bridge, leaving Finch to run Winchcombe Pottery.

A salt glazed jug, by Michael Casson (1925-2003), with incised wave decoration, impressed seal mark.

Michael Casson OBE was born in London. He studied art and woodwork at Shoreditch College, and ceramics at Hornsey College of Art. He was one of the founding potters of the Craft Potters' Association, a co-operative that acquired a shop and gallery in central London in 1958.

10.75in (27cm) high

$400-450   CHEF

A Winchcombe Pottery slipware jug, by Michael Cardew (1901-83), probably made to commemorate a wedding, incised with date and initials 'BM' and 'EJM', marks to base and side of base.

1935   11in (28cm) high

$900-1,000   WW

A porcelain bottle vase and plate, by Poh Chap Yeap (1927-2007), the vase in a rich, dark tenmoku glaze, the plate covered in a deep green glaze with turquoise splashes, incised 'Yeap', fine hairline to plate.

vase 5.5in (14cm) high

$130-200   WW

A Hook Norton Pottery mottled blue and green bottle vase, by Russell Collins, with pierced lugs, impressed mark.

10.75in (27cm) high

$70-80   CHOR

A Hook Norton Pottery tenmoku and wood ash part glazed stoneware bottle, by Russell Collins, impressed mark.

16.5in (42cm) high

$90-110   CHOR

CERAMICS

QUICK REFERENCE - JOANNA CONSTANTINIDIS

Joanna Constantinidis (1927-2000) was born in York and studied fine art and ceramics at Sheffield College of Art. She specialized in hand-thrown pottery. From 1951 until her retirement in 1989, she taught at Chelmsford technical college, while working on her pottery in her spare time. Her early work often resembles Bernard Leach in style. Her 1970s-80s work was increasingly experimental in form and glaze.

A rare early plate, by Joanna Constantinidis, impressed early seal mark, painted date.

1950   *12.5in (32cm) diam*

$350-400   **WW**

A porcelain vase, by Joanna Constantinidis, with pale celadon glaze and trailed rust-brown, impressed seal mark.

6in (15cm) high

$650-800   **WW**

A stoneware vase, by Waistel Cooper (1921-2003), glazed dry white and dark manganese brown, painted 'Waistel', repaired neck.

8.75in (22cm) high

$550-600   **WW**

A stoneware thistle form vase, by Hans Coper, textured body with manganese and white slip highlights, impressed seal mark.

Provenance: This vase was bought directly from Lucie Rie's studio at Albion Mews in c1958.

6in (15cm) high

$35,000-40,000   **WW**

QUICK REFERENCE - HANS COPER

- Hans Coper (1920-81) was a highly influential mid-20thC potter.
- He was born in Chemnitz, Germany, in 1920 and came to Britain as a refugee in 1939. After serving in the Pioneer Corps in World War II, he found work with Austrian potter Lucie Rie in 1946, despite having little prior experience in ceramics. They worked together at her pottery in London, first focusing on ceramic buttons, then moving to domestic and tableware.
- In 1958 he set up his own studio. He taught for many years at the Camberwell School of Art and the Royal College of Art. Coper and Rie remained friends until his death in 1981.

A 20thC ovoid-volume vase, by Hans Coper, stoneware layered with white porcelain slips and engobes, over textured and incised body, the interior with manganese glaze, impressed seal mark.

This example, from the Sainsbury Collection, was used as the front cover for 'Hans Coper 1920-1981' retrospective exhibition catalog.

7.25in (18.5cm) high

$40,000-45,000   **WW**

A pottery 'Herring Gulls' figure, by Stella R. Crofts (1898-1964), incised 'Stella R Crofts'.

See Paul Hughes, 'Stella's Ark: Stella Crofts', private press, page 86, for another example dated 1928.

1926   *11.25in (28.5cm) high*

$750-800   **WW**

A small dish, by Marianne de Trey (1913-2016), painted with a fish, impressed seal mark.

Marianne de Trey was born in 1913 and studied at the Royal College of Art, London. In 1938, she married ceramist Sam Haile (see page 139). After her husband's death in a road accident in 1948, Marianne de Trey lived in Dartington, Devon, until her death in 2016 at the age of 102. She was awarded a CBE in 2006.

5.75in (14.5cm) long

$150-200   **CHEF**

A stoneware vase, by Mike Dodd (b.1943), covered in a thick ash glaze with incised decoration, impressed seal to base.

17in (43cm) high

$350-400   **WW**

A Winchcombe Pottery charger, by Ray Finch (1914-2012), glazed rust red painted to the well with two stylized fish, impressed seal mark.

15in (38cm) diam

$200-250 WW

A studio pottery vase, by Sheila Fournier, the brown glazed ground decorated with a textured white trailed and black spotted glaze, applied monogram seal to base.

7in (18cm) high

$200-250 FELL

A 1950s Guido Gambone faience jug, dark purple and blue on white, marked 'Donkey, GAMBONE ITALY'.

4.75in (12cm) high

$650-800 QU

A stoneware peep-hole bowl, by Ian Godfrey (1942-92), internally modeled with a village and animals, unsigned.

8.5in (21.5cm) diam

$800-950 WW

A rare slipware dish, by Thomas 'Sam' Haile (1909-48), decorated with a fish, impressed seal mark to underside, some light crazing.

This came with accompanying publication 'Sam Haile, Potter and Painter 1909-1948'. Sam Haile was born in 1909 and studied ceramics under William Staite Murray at the Royal College of Art. Haile's ceramics and paintings were highly influenced by the Surrealist movement. In 1938, he married Marianne de Trey (see page 138). His promising career was cut short when he died in a road accident in 1948.

17.5in (44.5cm) long

$900-1,100 CHEF

QUICK REFERENCE - PETER HAYES

- Peter Hayes (b.1946) studied at the Moseley School of Art and Birmingham College of Art.
- His highly sculptural pottery is influenced by his extensive travels and studies in Africa, where he made ceramics with various tribes and village potters, experimenting with new techniques and tools. He has also traveled widely in India, Nepal, Japan and New Mexico, adopting new techniques and ideas.
- He set up his own studio in Bath in 1982. His distinctive surfaces and glazes, some of which use raku firing, are often finished unusually. One piece was submerged in the Cornish sea for a few weeks. Another was washed over time in a river near his studio.

A slab-built stoneware bottle, by Shoji Hamada (1894-1978), covered with a rich tenmoku glaze and simple green brush design, unsigned.

7.75in (20cm) high

$3,500-4,000 WW

An early Lesotho stoneware pot, by Peter Hayes, incised with a frieze of warriors holding spears and shields, incised 'Peter Hayes 74' to base, minor chips to top rim.

1974 *10in (25.5cm) high*

$200-250 WW

A rare and early Lesotho pot, by Peter Hayes, incised with a band of warrior figures holding shields, signed and dated to base.

1979 *9in (23cm) high*

$250-400 WW

CERAMICS

A Lesotho stoneware vase, by Peter Hayes, incised and painted with a band of warriors holding shields and spears, impressed seal mark, signed and dated.

1979　　　　　　*11in (28cm) high*

$250-350　　　　　　　　**WW**

A white bone china porcelain arrowhead form, by Peter Hayes, wire mounted to raku base, etched 'Peter Hayes'.

7.5in (19cm) high

$250-350　　　　　　　　**WW**

A large raku sack-form vase, by Peter Hayes, with solifleur neck, textured burnished surface, impressed seal mark.

20.75in (53cm) high

$1,000-1,200　　　　　　**WW**

A stoneware unomi, by Ewen Henderson, covered in porcelain slips, the rim with pale blue glaze, unsigned.

Ewen Henderson (1934-2000) was born in Staffordshire and studied at Goldsmith's College and then Camberwell College of Arts, where he was taught by Hans Coper and Lucie Rie (see pages 138 and 143). His clay wares are distinctive for their complex forms and unusual glazes and oxides. He taught at Camberwell College of Arts for over 30 years.

4.25in (11cm) high

$1,600-2,000　　　　　　**WW**

A stoneware unomi, by Ewen Henderson, with applied slips, unsigned.

4.25in (10.5cm) high

$1,000-1,200　　　　　　**WW**

A vase, by Ewen Henderson, with applied porcelain and stoneware slips, unsigned.

See Lucie Rie, Hans Coper and their Pupils, 'Sainsbury Centre for Visual Arts', page 44, catalog no.70, for a comparable vase.

8.75in (22cm) high

$750-800　　　　　　　　**WW**

A tall pot, by Ewen Henderson, hand-built stoneware with applied mixed laminates and slips, unsigned.

Exhibited at 'Ewen Henderson Potter - A Retrospective View 1970-1986', British Crafts Centre; this actual vase was illustrated on the Private View invite.

26.25in (67cm) high

$6,000-6,500　　　　　　**WW**

A salt-glazed stoneware teapot and cover, by Walter Keeler (b.1942), covered in a pale blue speckled glaze, impressed seal mark, small nick to spout.

8.5in (21.5cm) high

$550-650　　　　　　　　**WW**

QUICK REFERENCE - BERNARD LEACH

Bernard Leach (1887-1979) grew up in Hong Kong, Japan and England. He opened the Leach Pottery in 1920 in St Ives, Crownwall, with his colleague Shoji Hamada (1894-1978, see page 139). Influenced by his upbringing and time spent studying and teaching in Japan, Leach aimed to ally the British Arts and Crafts movement with Oriental influences. He combined traditional 17thC and 18thC English slip glazes with Oriental forms and patterns. All of his pottery was made by hand.

A Leach Pottery stoneware vase, designed by Bernard Leach, impressed decoration, covered to the base with a tenmoku glaze, impressed seal marks, repaired chip to top rim.

5in (13cm) high

$250-350   WW

A stoneware 'Leaping Fish' bottle vase, by Bernard Leach, in tenmoku on a gray ground two impressed seal marks.

12.5in (32cm) high

$9,500-10,000   WW

A Lowerdown Pottery stoneware teapot and cover, by David Leach, impressed seal mark.

6.75in (17cm) high

$200-250   CHEF

A tenmoku tall bottle vase, by David Leach, decorated with weeping willow brushwork, personal seal, some fine crazing.

David Leach (1911-2005) was the eldest son of Bernard Leach. He was apprenticed at his father's Leach Pottery in Cornwall, where he was taught both by his father and by Shoji Hamada. In 1955, he set up his own pottery in Bovey Tracey, South Devon.

18in (46cm) high

$650-800   LA

A reclining pine cone box, by Kate Malone, stoneware covered in a crystalline glaze, incised signature, dated, minor professional restoration.

2012   *11.5in (29cm) wide*

$900-1,100   WW

A stoneware sculpture, 'Winged Angel', by John Maltby (b.1936), formed as a winged head with metal legs, signed in pen to the plinth base.

John Maltby is a British ceramist known for his wheel-thrown pottery and hand-formed figurative sculptures. He was born in Lincolnshire in 1936 and studied at Leicester College of Art and Goldsmith's College, London. He worked with David Leach before starting his own pottery at Stoneshill, Devon, in 1964.

9.5in (24cm) high

$350-400   FLD

A stoneware sculpture of a seated figure, by John Maltby, signed and titled to base.

10.25in (26cm) high

$800-950   WW

A stoneware vase with collar rim, by William Bill Marshall (1923-2007), covered in a transparent, running nuka glaze to the foot with patches of copper to the shoulder, with impressed trellis decoration, impressed 'WM' seal.

15.75in (40cm) high

$2,000-2,500   WW

CERAMICS

A Rorke's Drift stoneware jar and cover, by Dinah Molefe (b.1927), with applied strapping and three crenulated handles, glazed blue and silver over tenmoku, with painted signature, marked '178/74', dated.

Rorke's Drift Art and Craft Center is a center for the Arts and Crafts, including fine art, print-making, pottery and weaving, located in KwaZulu-Natal, South Africa. Dinah Molefe and several other women from the neighbouring Shiyane-Nqutu region joined the Pottery Workshop from the start. They were already expert ceramists and hand-builders, accustomed to using traditional Zulu and Sotho coiling methods in the making of domestic izinkamba (beer pots). Dinah Molefe worked at Rorke's Drift 1969-83.

1974   14.5in (37cm) high
$600-750   WW

QUICK REFERENCE - LISE B. MOORCROFT

- Lise B. Moorcroft (b.1965) is the granddaughter of William Moorcroft and daughter of Walter Moorcroft (see pages 107-118). She studied at London's Central School of Art and Design before setting up her own independent studio in Stoke, England, in the mid-1980s.
- Lise sketches her design in pencil directly onto the clay, making each piece unique. The design is then completed using tube-lining, the favorite technique of Moorcroft pottery. Her wares are then fired, perhaps as many as ten times, and applied with numerous layers of underglazes, handpainted glazes and lusters.
- All of Lise's work is signed. Her work has been exhibited in many galleries throughout the UK and beyond.

An art pottery luster charger, 'Butterfly Wing' design, by Lise B. Moorcroft, multi-glaze, with Poole studio backstamp, signed and dated.

2001   16.25in (41cm) diam
$120-160   PSA

An art pottery luster vase, 'Clownfish' design, by Lise B. Moorcroft, hand thrown, multi-glaze, signed and dated.

2003   11in (28cm) high
$250-400   PSA

An art pottery luster vase, 'Sunflowers' design by Lise B. Moorcroft, hand thrown, multi-glaze, signed and dated.

2005   12.25in (31cm) high
$250-400   PSA

An art pottery luster vase, 'Froggies' design, by Lise B. Moorcroft, cast, multi-glaze.

15.75in (40cm) high
$250-350   PSA

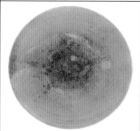

A flaring porcelain bowl, by Margaret O'Rorke (b.1938), covered in a pitted turquoise green glaze, unsigned.

15in (38cm) diam
$200-250   WW

A Richard Parkinson Pottery cockerel, model no.23, designed by Susan Parkinson, resist decorated in blue on a white ground, impressed marks to base.

See Carol Cashmore and Tim Smith-Vincent, 'Susan Parkinson and the Richard Parkinson Pottery', page 23, for a comparable example.

12in (30.5cm) high
$250-350   WW

A Richard Parkinson Pottery owl, designed by Susan Parkinson, resist decorated in blue on a white ground, impressed marks to foot.

8.5in (21.5cm) high
$250-350   WW

Judith Picks

I believe Lucie Rie to be the most inspirational and talented 20thC potter. She was born in Vienna in 1902 and studied at the Vienna Kunstgewerbeschule. She set up her own pottery studio in Vienna in 1925 but was forced to flee Austria in 1938. She then moved to London, where she established a new studio. From 1946-58, she worked with the ceramist Hans Coper (see page 138). Her wares are elegant and angular in shape, decorated simply and finished with a variety of glazes. In 1981 she received the CBE and in 1991 she became a Dame. Since her death in 1995, her work has continued to rise in value.

A stoneware vase, by Dame Lucie Rie (1902-95), with a streaked mat mushroom and ocher glaze, impressed seal mark.

6.75in (17cm) high

$5,500-6,000 **WW**

A fine early porcelain bowl, by Dame Lucie Rie, glazed yellow to the foot and interior, with a broad band of manganese, sgraffito decorated with dots and borders, impressed seal mark.

See John Houston, 'Lucie Rie', Crafts Council, page 39, color plate 9, for a comparable illustration; also Tony Birks, 'Lucie Rie' Alphabooks, page 105, for a comparable stem bowl illustrated from c1957.

4.25in (11cm) diam

$55,000-60,000 **WW**

An American Raku large winged-form sculpture, by Paul Soldner, on a metal base, numbered '978'.

Paul Soldner (1921-2011) was an American ceramist most notable for his development of the technique 'American raku'. The traditional Japanese raku technique involves firing a pot in a kiln at a lower temperature, then plunging the pot into water. American raku involves firing the piece then plunging it into flammable materials such as sawdust or newspapers instead of water.

37in (95cm) wide

$650-800 **WW**

A hand built stoneware vase, by John Ward (b.1938), impressed seal mark.

7.75in (19.5cm) wide

$3,500-4,000 **WW**

A stoneware pot, by Robert J. Washington, painted with two female figures, in red iron oxide, painted 'W' to base.

1965   20.75in (52.5cm) high

$1,000-1,200 **WW**

A handpainted pottery charger, by Elizabeth Mary Watt (1886-1954), marked 'EMW' to base.

12.5in (31.5cm) diam

$800-950 **GWA**

A large Totem form tube vase, by Robin Welch (b.1936), constructed in four sections, painted with white, red and black bands, impressed seal mark.

91.75in (233cm) high

$1,600-2,000 **WW**

A hand-built stoneware bowl, by Robin Welch (b.1936), with painted panel decoration, painted 'Robin Welch' signature, exhibition paper label to side.

9in (23cm) high

$900-1,100 **WW**

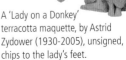

A 'Lady on a Donkey' terracotta maquette, by Astrid Zydower (1930-2005), unsigned, chips to the lady's feet.

Zydower studied at Sheffield School of Art from 1947-52.

17in (43cm) wide

$250-400 **WW**

CERAMICS

QUICK REFERENCE - TROIKA

- Troika was founded in 1962 in St Ives, Cornwall, England, by potter Benny Sirota, painter Lesley Illsley and architect Jan Thompson. Thompson left in 1965.
- Troika wares were slip-molded and decorated by hand. Early pieces had gloss glazes, but textured mat finishes were predominant from 1974.
- A range of vases, dishes, bowls and lamp bases were produced, along with some sculptural pieces. The shapes were clean-lined and modern. Designs were influenced by Scandinavian ceramics and the Cornish landscape and decorated with muted earthy colors.
- Prices vary considerably with shape, size, decoration, decorator and period. Condition is paramount, as even a hairline crack considerably decreases value. Many items have the artist's initials on the base.

A Troika pottery 'Double Base' vase, by Avril Bennet, modeled in low relief with geometric panels, with a painted monogram.

13.75in (35cm) high

$550-650   **WW**

A Troika Pottery 'Double Bass' vase, by Honor Curtis, painted 'St Ives' mark.

14in (35.5cm) high

$600-750   **FLD**

A 1970s Troika pottery vase, with typical geometric stylized opposing decoration, unsigned.

6.75in (17cm) high

$130-200   **LSK**

A blue and beige Troika coffin vase, by Sue Lowe.

6.75in (17cm) high

$150-250   **HAN**

A Troika coffin vase, by Annette Walters, in turquoise, blue and cream.

7in (17.5cm) high

$150-250   **HAN**

A blue Troika art pottery vase, by Anne Jones, signed to base 'Troika, Cornwall, AJ'.

8.25in (21cm) high

$50-80   **LOCK**

A brown Troika art pottery vase, by Alison Brigden, signed to base 'Troika, Cornwall, AB'.

8.25in (21cm) high

$50-80   **LOCK**

A Troika chimney vase or flask, by Marilyn Pascoe, blue and beige with white glazed edge, painted marks.

7.75in (20cm) high

$250-300   HAN

A large Troika cuboid vase, by Anne Jones, square section with shouldered rim.

13in (33cm) high

$250-300   HAN

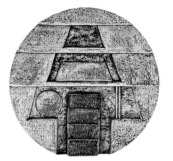

A Troika wheel vase, molded and textured with geometric molding in high relief, with three openings, signed and artist monogram to underside.

13in (33cm) high

$650-800   HAN

A Troika marmalade jar, signed to base.

3.5in (9cm) high

$50-70   LOCK

A Troika Pottery dish, by Stella Benjamin, in a tenmoku glaze with blue green tints, painted 'St Ives' mark, some damage.

12in (30.5cm) long

$80-100   FLD

A Troika Pottery 'Urn' vase, by Honor Curtis, painted 'St Ives' mark, some damage.

10.5in (26.5cm) high

$80-100   FLD

A CLOSER LOOK AT A TROIKA FACE MASK

Each side of the mask is modeled with a different face. The front is a detailed carving, while the back is a simplified abstract face with its eyes closed.

The design is inspired by Aztec paintings and face masks.

The base is signed 'Troika', with indistinguishable letters beneath. The artist is unknown.

Troika sculptural pieces are relatively rare, increasing the mask's value.

A Troika Pottery face mask, signed 'Troika'.

10.25in (26cm) high

$800-950   K&O

CERAMICS

QUICK REFERENCE - WADE

- The Wade group of potteries dates from the 19thC and originally included three separate potteries: A.J. Wade Ltd., Wade Heath & Co. and George Wade & Son.
- These three potteries expanded their production in the 1920s-30s to include a range of decorative and novelty wares, ranging from ornamental tea sets to figurines inspired by fairytale and literary characters.
- Wade Heath & Co.'s modernist mat-glazed 'Flaxman Ware' was popular during the 1930s. The company also acquired the rights to produce figurines of many Disney characters.
- Ornamental and novelty lines continued after World War II.
- The three potteries merged as Wade Potteries in 1958.

A Wade 'Pavlova' figurine.

9.5in (24cm) high

$90-100　　　　　WHP

A Wade Art Deco 'Argentina' cellulose figurine, with some restoration.

9.75in (25cm) high

$80-100　　　　　PSA

A Wade 'Snow White and the Seven Dwarfs' set, first version, with cellulose glaze.

This set was issued to coincide with the release of the Walt Disney film in 1938.

issued 1938　　　　*Snow White 7in (18cm) high*

$550-650　　　　　PSA

A rare Wade 'Old Nannie' figurine, dated, marked to base.

1939　　*9in (23cm) high*

$400-450　　　　APAR

A 1950s Wade 'Goldilocks' figurine.

This figurine was released in a set with the three bears.

1953-c58　*4in (10cm) high*

$150-200　　　　　PSA

A Wade 'Pair Budgerigars' figurine, by Faust Lang, underglaze, dated.

1939　*7.75in (19.5cm) high*

$250-350　　　　　PSA

A Wade 'Grebe' figurine, by Faust Lang, underglaze, dated.

1939　*9.75in (25cm) high*

$600-650　　　　　PSA

A Wade 'Brown Bear' figurine, by Faust Lang, underglaze, dated.

1939　*9in (24cm) high*

$900-1,000　　　　PSA

A large Wade Heath 'Walt Disney Donald Duck' teapot.

$250-350　　　　　PSA

QUICK REFERENCE - WEDGWOOD

- The Wedgwood pottery was founded in Staffordshire in 1759 by Josiah Wedgwood, who was soon joined by his business partner Thomas Bentley.
- Creamware, later known as 'Queensware' due to the patronage of Queen Charlotte, was introduced from c1762.
- 'Jasperware' was developed c1774-75. These pieces included white low-relief friezes of Classical scenes on blue, black or green bases and were highly successful.
- The 20thC saw the introduction of Daisy Makeig-Jones's (1881-1945) distinctive Fairyland luster wares. Other key 20thC designers include Keith Murray (1892-1981), John Skeaping (1901-81) and Eric Ravilious (1903-42).

A Wedgwood tea service for two, by Eric Ravilious, detailed with monochrome vignettes with typical Ravilious designs, some very minor rubbing to cup and jug base rim.

$5,500-6,000   **WM**

A Wedgwood mottled pink glazed vase, by Norman Wilson, impressed and printed marks.

Norman Wilson (1902-85) was a potter and designer who worked at Wedgwood from 1927, first as Works Manager, then Production Director and ultimately as Joint Managing Director from 1961.

5in (12.5cm) high

$400-450   **HAN**

A Wedgwood covered bowl or powder pot, by Norman Wilson, impressed and printed marks.

5in (13cm) high

$250-350   **HAN**

A Wedgwood vase, by Alfred Powell, painted with flowering vine on a trellis, printed 'Wedgwood' mark, painted artist cipher and '183'.

9.5in (24cm) high

$1,600-2,000   **WW**

A Wedgwood vase, by Keith Murray, shape no.3805, printed factory mark, 'KM' monogram, minor professional restoration to base rim.

11in (28cm) high

$400-450   **WW**

A 20thC Wedgwood Jasperware plaque.

7in (18cm) high

$50-70   **K&O**

A Wedgwood earthenware vase, designed by Keith Murray, in mat green, printed factory mark, and facsimile signature.

See Andrew Casey, '20th Century Ceramic Designers in Britain', ACC books, page 192, catalog 210, for a comparable example in Straw Yellow.

6in (15.5cm) high

$400-450   **WW**

A Wedgwood moonstone footed vase, by Keith Murray, facsimile mark.

6.25in (16cm) high

$550-650   **HAN**

A Wedgwood polar bear, by John Skeaping, in celadon glaze.

7.5in (19cm) high

$350-400   **PSA**

CERAMICS

QUICK REFERENCE - WEMYSS WARE

- In the 1880s, Robert Methven Heron launched the Wemyss range of the Fife Pottery. These new animal figurines and tableware pieces were aimed at the wealthy middle and upper middle classes.

- Designs were created and painted by Karel Nekola and patronized by Dora Wemyss of Wemyss Castle. Nekola died in 1915 and was succeeded by Edwin Sandland.

- The Fife Pottery closed in 1930 due to pressures from the economic depression. The production of Wemyss Ware then moved to Bovey Tracey Pottery Company Ltd., where it was supervised by Joseph Nekola, Karel Nekola's son.

- Joseph Nekola trained several apprentices at the Bovey Tracey Potteries, including Esther Weeks (née Clark) who took over as head decorator after his death in 1952.

- The production of Wemyss Ware at this site ended in 1957. Wemyss Ware was eventually acquired by Royal Doulton.

- Since 1985, Wemyss Ware has been produced at the Griselda Hill Pottery, Fife.

An early 20thC Wemyss Ware 'Dog Roses' egg cup, impressed maker's marks, twice 'WEMYSS', trace painted mark 'WEMYSS'.

2.25in (5.5cm) high

$550-650   **L&T**

A Wemyss Ware 'Dog Roses' napkin ring.

c1900   *1.75in (4.5cm) diam*

$250-350   **L&T**

A Wemyss Ware cabaret set, decorated with hearts and ribbons, bearing cipher with initials 'EAW', impressed maker's marks 'WEMYSS WARE / R.H.& S'.

c1895   *tray 17.5in (44cm) wide*

$1,600-2,000   **L&T**

A Wemyss Ware 'Geese' small tyg, impressed maker's marks 'WEMYSS WARE / R.H.&S'.

c1900   *4.25in (11cm) diam*

$250-350   **L&T**

A Wemyss Ware 'Violets' matchbox cover, printed retailer's mark.

c1900   *3.25in (8cm) long*

$650-800   **L&T**

A Wemyss Ware 'Cabbage Roses' button, impressed maker's mark 'WEMYSS'.

c1900   *1.25in (3cm) diam*

$550-650   **L&T**

An early 20thC Wemyss Ware 'Brown Cockerel' low pomade, impressed marks 'WEMYSS', printed retailer's mark.

3.5in (9cm) diam

$550-650   **L&T**

A post-1930 Wemyss Ware small 'Shamrocks' pig figure, painted and printed maker's marks 'WEMYSS / MADE IN ENGLAND'.

6.25in (16cm) long

$250-300   **L&T**

A small post-1930 Wemyss Ware black and white pig, painted maker's mark 'WEMYSS'.

6.25in (16cm) long

$350-450   **L&T**

QUICK REFERENCE - WESTERWALD STONEWARE

- Westerwald stoneware is a type of salt-glazed pottery from the Ransbach-Baumbach and Höhr-Grenzhausen areas of Westerwaldkreis in Rheinland-Pfalz, West Germany.
- The Westerwaldkreis area of Germany has large clay quarries of unusually rich and pure quality. These quarries have long prompted those who live in the region to turn to pottery, and there is evidence of ceramic production in the area since as far back as 1000 BC.
- Traditional salt-glazing first developed in the mid-15thC, when changing technology allowed kilns to be heated to higher temperatures. Jugs, vases and other vessels were molded, stamped or painted with dyes, then fired. The vessel would usually be decorated in cobalt blue, as few other colors could withstand the hot temperature of the kiln. While the vessel was being fired, table salt was thrown into the kiln, where it would vaporize and bond with the quartz in the clay, creating a shiny gray glaze.
- Ceramic production declined after the end of the 17thC, but has nonetheless continued throughout the region's history. The 1960s-70s saw a revival of traditional stoneware. These new designs were influenced by Japanese and other Oriental ceramics and combined modern designs with traditional techniques.
- Key artists of the mid to late 20thC movement include Elfriede Balzar-Kopp, Klothilde Giefer-Bahn, Görge Hohlt, Walburga Külz, Wim Mühlendyck, Gisela Schmidt-Reuther and Wendelin Stahl.
- Many significant Westerwald pottery wares from throughout history are on display at the Keramik Museum in Höhr-Grenzhausen, which was founded in 1976.

A rare 1960s Westerwald pottery figure of a ram, decorated in the studios of Elfriede Balzar-Kopp, with a stylized design in sgraffito and traditional salt-glaze and enamels.

$1,000-1,200   JNEW

A scarce 1960s Westerwald pottery charger, decorated in the studios of Elfriede Balzar-Kopp, with a 'retro' fish design in sgraffito and traditional salt-glaze and enamels.

14.5in (37cm) wide

$450-600   JNEW

A scarce 1960s Westerwald pottery figure, decorated in the studios of Elfriede Balzar-Kopp, modeled as a candleholder, with cobalt and traditional salt-glaze and enamels, signed 'B.K'.

8.75in (22cm) high

$400-450   JNEW

A scarce 1960s Westerwald pottery charger, decorated in the studios of Elfriede Balzar-Kopp, with a 'retro' bird design in sgraffito and traditional salt-glaze and enamels.

14.5in (37cm) diam

$450-550   JNEW

A scarce 1960s Westerwald pottery jug, decorated in the studios of Elfriede Balzar-Kopp, with a 'retro' stag design in sgraffito and traditional salt-glaze and enamels.

8.25in (21cm) high

$450-550   JNEW

CERAMICS

QUICK REFERENCE - ELFRIEDE BALZAR-KOPP

Elfriede Balzar-Kopp (1904-83) was a celebrated German ceramic potter. She was born as Elfriede Kopp in Berdorf, Luxembourg, in 1904. She studied at the State Engineering and Ceramic college in Höhr-Grenzhausen 1924-26, then at the State Majolica Factory Karlsruhe under Professor Konig 1926-27. In c1927 she married, changing her name to Balzar-Kopp, and opened her own studio. She completed her Masters degree in 1938, and received honors at the World Expo Paris and a crafts exhibition in Berlin. She went on to win several awards and medals, including the Silver Medal of the exhibition 'Ceramique International' in Prague, 1962 and the Federal Cross of Merit in 1974. Throughout her career, she collaborated closely in pottery and glaze techniques with potter Wim Mühlendyck.

A large rare 1960s-70s Westerwald pottery floor vase, decorated in the studios of Elfriede Balzar-Kopp, with a 'retro' bird design in sgraffito and traditional enamels, 'BK' to base.

17in (43cm) high

$750-850   JNEW

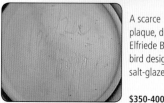

A scarce 1960s Westerwald pottery plaque, decorated in the studios of Elfriede Balzar-Kopp, with a 'retro' bird design in sgraffito and traditional salt-glaze and enamels.

14.5in (37cm) diam

$350-400   JNEW

A large rare 1960s-70s Westerwald pottery floor vase, decorated in the studios of Elfriede Balzar-Kopp, with a 'retro' horse design in sgraffito and traditional enamels, unmarked.

18in (46cm) high

$750-800   JNEW

A CLOSER LOOK AT AN ELFRIEDE BALZAR-KOPP JUG

The stylized bird and simple floral background show a mix of modern and traditional influences.

The bird has been painted with a cheerful expression.

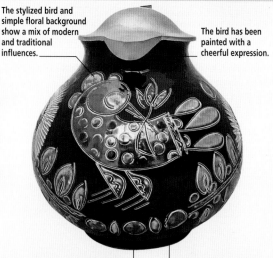

The design is done through 'sgrattifo'. Like salt-glazing, this is a very old technique. Balzar-Kopp has painted the jug with two contrasting coasts, then scratched through the surface to reveal the lower layer of color.

The colors of cobalt blue and dark brown are traditional in salt-glazed Westerwald pottery, as only certain colors could originally survive the high temperatures required for salt-glazing.

A scarce 1960s Westerwald pottery jug, decorated in the studios of Elfriede Balzar-Kopp, with a 'retro' bird design in sgraffito and traditional salt-glaze and enamels.

7.75in (20cm) high

$450-550   JNEW

A scarce 1960s-70s Westerwald pottery jug, decorated in the studios of Elfriede Balzar-Kopp, with a 'retro' bird design in sgraffito and traditional enamels, marked 'BK'.

9in (23cm) high

$200-250   JNEW

A scarce 1960s-70s Westerwald pottery floor vase, decorated in the studios of Elfriede Balzar-Kopp, with a 'retro' design in traditional enamels, signed 'Balzar Kopp'.

15.75in (40cm) high

$600-750   JNEW

A scarce 1960s-70s Westerwald pottery figure group, decorated in the studios of Elfriede Balzar-Kopp, with cobalt and traditional salt-glaze and enamels, signed to the base.

9.75in (25cm) high

$1,000-1,200   JNEW

A Westerwald pottery flask, decorated in the studios of Elfriede Balzar-Kopp, with a 'retro' fish design in sgraffito and traditional salt-glaze and enamels.

c1970   9.5in (24cm) high

$200-250   JNEW

QUICK REFERENCE - KLOTHILDE GIEFER-BAHN

Klothilde Giefer-Bahn (1924-2008) was born in Koblenz, Germany, in 1924, and studied in Höhr-Grenzhausen as an apprentice at the Elfriede Balzar-Kopp studio. In 1947, she completed her Masters training as a ceramicist, and shortly afterwards opened her own studio. From then on, she exhibited widely and has won many awards, participating in many national and international expositions. Today her son Roland continues the pottery, and examples of Klothilde Giefer-Bahn's work can be seen in museums and private collections around the world.

A Westerwald salt-glazed wall plate, decorated by Elfriede Balzar-Kopp, with a bird design in sgraffito, signed on the reverse.

c1970   11.75in (30cm) diam

$350-400   JNEW

A rare early salt-glazed jug, made in the studios of Klotilde Giefer-Bahn, Höhr-Grenzhausen, Rhineland-Palatinate, decorated in sgraffito with a modernist folklore scene, signed.

c1945   12.5in (32cm) high

$850-900   JNEW

A 1960s salt-glaze liquor flask, made in the studios of Klothilde Giefer-Bahn, decorated in sgraffito with a delightful stylized design, signed to the base.

6in (15cm) high

$200-250   JNEW

A 1960s salt-glaze jug, made in the studios of Klothilde Giefer-Bahn, decorated in sgraffito with a 'retro' Fish design, signed to the base.

8.25in (21cm) high

$400-450   JNEW

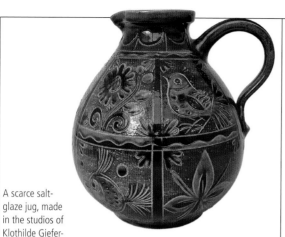

A scarce salt-glaze jug, made in the studios of Klothilde Giefer-Bahn, decorated in sgraffito with a traditional yet modernist design, signed and dated.

1976   *10.5in (26.5cm) high*

$600-650   **JNEW**

A rare salt-glaze vase, made in the studios of Klothilde Giefer-Bahn, decorated with stylized flowers in sgraffito and enamels, signed and dated to the base.

1978   *18.5in (47cm) high*

$1,000-1,200   **JNEW**

A 1940s-50s Westerwald salt-glazed jug, by Wim Mühlendyck (1905-86), decorated in sgraffito with a stylized modernist design, signed to the base.

Wim Mühlendyck was born on 1 March 1905 in Porz-Cologne. He attended the Hoehr-Grenzhausen Ceramic School 1927-30. From 1931, he ran his own workshop and pottery in Hoehr-Grenzhausen, until its closure in the 1970s. He was considered the reviver of Westerwalder ceramics and won many awards in his life. He died on 10 April 1986.

9.75in (25cm) high

$450-550   **JNEW**

A 1950s Westerwald salt-glazed pottery plaque, by Wim Mühlendyck, decorated in sgraffito, with an atmospheric study of leaping horse, signed to the base.

14.5in (37cm) high

$650-800   **JNEW**

A fine 1960s German salt-glaze flask, by Wim Mühlendyck, decorated in scraffito with a stylized flower design.

9.5in (24cm) high

$200-250   **JNEW**

A tactile studio bulbous pottery jug, made by Wendelin Stahl (1922-2000), with a pewter lid and superb crystalline glaze.

c1970   *15.75in (40cm) high*

$450-550   **JNEW**

A Terry Abbots tribute conical sugar sifter, in the 'Blue Autumn' pattern, after the Clarice Cliff original, handpainted mark, dated.
2012 *5.5in (14cm) high*
$35-40 **FLD**

A Terry Abbots tribute conical sugar sifter, in the 'Orange Autumn' pattern after a Clarice Cliff original, handpainted mark, dated.
2008 *5.5in (14cm) high*
$35-40 **FLD**

A pair of early 20thC Amphora 'Jugendstil' vases, the neck with four curled handles, impressed marks.
11.5in (29cm) high
$350-400 **FLD**

A 19thC Ashworth's ironstone 'Imari' part dinner service, with 15 dinner plates, 10 soup plates, 8 dessert plates, 2 covered tureens, a covered sauce tureen and stand, 3 graduated platters and a roast drainer, impressed and printed marks.
plate 10.5in (26.5cm) diam
$1,600-2,000 **L&T**

An Art Nouveau Amphora Pottery vase, model no.3882, with four angled handles and a pierced neck, highlighted in gilt, impressed marks.
11.5in (29cm) high
$50-70 **WW**

QUICK REFERENCE - BO'NESS

The town and former port of Bo'ness (Borrowstounness) stands on the southern shore of the River Forth, ten miles west of the Forth Bridge. In the 18thC, Bo'ness was one of the most thriving towns on the east coast. Among the town's many booming industries was pottery production and Bo'ness soon became established as one of the main pottery producing areas in Scotland. Pottery production in the town lasted for almost 200 years and reached its heyday at the end of the 19thC when three factories were operating simultaneously at Bo'ness, Grangepans and Bridgeness. The last pottery closed in 1958.

A post-war Biot earthenware jug, by Roland Brice and decorated by Fernand Léger, signed 'R.BRICE BIOT.AM'.
c1950 *6in (15.5cm) high*
$550-650 **FLD**

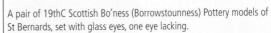

A pair of 19thC Scottish Bo'ness (Borrowstounness) Pottery models of St Bernards, set with glass eyes, one eye lacking.
12.75in (32.5cm) long
$100-160 **WW**

CERAMICS

QUICK REFERENCE - BOCH FRÈRES KERAMICS

Boch Frères Keramics was founded in Belgium in 1841 and is still operational today. In the 19thC it specialized in affordable, mid-market stoneware, but in the early 20thC the company shifted its focus to artistic wares. Charles Catteau (1880-1966) was design director from 1907 to 1948, and introduced the 1920s Art Deco line, notable for its clean-lined stylized forms and brightly colored patterns. Boch Frères' Art Deco pieces, especially those by Charles Catteau himself, remain the pottery's most valuable pieces today.

A pair of Boch Frères Keramics spill vases, by Charles Catteau, some damage.

6in (15cm) high

$100-140   LOC

A Bossons Fraser Artware wall plaque, 'Running Borzoi Dog', unmarked.

The W.H. Bossons Company was founded in 1946 by W.H. and Ray Bossons. The father and son team designed and sold character wall masks, figurines, wall plaques, lamp bases, bookends and other ceramic items, including their popular 'Fraser Art' range. The company closed in 1996.

15.25in (39cm) long

$130-200   PSA

A Bossons wall plaque, 'Mont Orgueil Castle, Jersey', embossed, some slight wear.

10.25in (26cm) diam

$20-25   PSA

A Boch Frères Keramis stoneware vase, painted with flowers and foliage, impressed mark and painted 'BFK 73'.

6.25in (16cm) high

$350-400   WW

A pair of late 19thC to early 20thC Boch Frères Keramics jars and covers, in the 'Iznik' style, the covers with lion finials, painted marks to base.

17in (43cm) high

$450-600   ROS

A late 19thC to early 20thC Boch Frères Keramics ewer, in the 'Mamluk' style, on eau-de-nil ground, signed to base 'B F K, 213 15'.

9.75in (25cm) high

$400-550   ROS

A C.H. Brannam jar and cover, applied with colored slips and sgraffitto, incised 'C.H. Brannam, Barum, 1889' with monogram for James Dewdney.

17.25in (44cm) high

$550-600   BE

A C.H. Brannam 'Puffin' jug, by William Baron, with inset glass eyes, professional restoration to claws.

5in (13cm) high

$450-550   BE

CERAMICS

A pair of Art Nouveau Brantjes Purmerend vases, painted with flowers and stylized foliage, painted marks, some chips.

The Brantjes Company was founded in 1895 by Clementine Brantjes and Egbert Estié, who was probably artistic director. Brantjes was located in the old factory of the former tile factory on the Neckerstraat. In 1895, the company had 46 employees, of which 35 were painters.

8.75in (22cm) high

$450-550 WW

An early 20thC Bretby pottery stick stand, modeled as a bear cub with inset glass eyes climbing a tree trunk, significant loss under base, rim chip.

26.5in (67cm) high

$350-400 BE

QUICK REFERENCE - BURLEIGH WARE

- Established in 1851 and still in existence today, Burleigh Ware, made by Burgess & Leigh, is known and collected worldwide.
- Famous for its blue and white designs, two of its most popular patterns, 'Asiatic Pheasants' and 'Arden' (originally 'Hawthorn'), have been in continuous production since 1862. They are made using Burleigh's now unique tissue transfer decoration.
- The 1930s range of yellow glazed flower jugs, designed by Ernest Bailey, especially the rare 'Tennis', 'Golf' and 'Cricket' jugs, are highly collectible, as is the rare Art Deco 'Guardsman' jug. Collectors should beware of copies made in the 2000s, which can usually be identified by a date for '2000' or '2001' under the mark.
- Charlotte Rhead (see page 82) worked at Burleigh from 1926-31. Her pieces are not seen very often and her large plaques are rare and desirable.
- Burleigh Ware is always marked. The well-known 'Beehive' mark was used throughout the 1930s with a leaf border. Post-war versions have no leaves.

A Burgess & Leigh Burleigh Ware 'Cricket' jug, handpainted.

7.5in (19cm) high

$200-250 PSA

A Burgess & Leigh Burleigh Ware 'Golf' jug, handpainted.

7.5in (19cm) high

$100-120 PSA

A Burgess & Leigh Burleigh Ware 'Guardsman' jug, handpainted.

7.75in (20cm) high

$250-350 PSA

A limited edition Coalport 'Marlena' figure, from the English Rose collection, boxed.

$70-80 PSA

A Cobridge stoneware vase, decorated with a sunset landscape with storks in trees, signed 'BL'.

11in (28cm) high

$100-140 HAN

QUICK REFERENCE - COMPTON POTTERY

In 1900 Mary Watts founded the Compton Potter's Arts Guild. The Guild followed the popular Arts & Crafts model of a medieval guild, with workmen being given the opportunity to create their own handiwork. In 1901 the Compton Pottery was built at the bottom of the hill beneath Limnerslease. Rapid expansion followed and when plans for Watts Gallery were drawn up in 1903, accommodation for twelve apprentice potters was included in the design. The Compton Pottery prospered throughout the beginning of the 20thC. Liberty & Co. on Regent Street stocked their works. The pottery became well known for its ornamental pots, birdbaths, garden ornaments and sundials. Architectural commissions were received from Clough Williams-Ellis for his Italianate village at Portmeirion and Gertrude Jekyll commissioned a garden pot that was subsequently marketing as the 'Jekyll model'. The Compton Pottery closed in 1956.

A Compton Pottery 'Dolphin' electric lamp base, modeled as three classical dolphins, unmarked, minor frits.

See Hilary Calvert, 'Compton Pottery', Watts Gallery publication, page 36, for a comparable example.

8.75in (22cm) high

$200-250 WW

CERAMICS

A Crown Devon model of a woman, probably designed by Kathleen Parsons, model no.224, with printed mark and impressed model number.

See Susan Hill, 'Crown Devon Jazz Publications', page 169, for an example of this figure.

9.5in (24cm) high

$200-250   WW

A Della Robbia shape 24 waisted 'Tall Lion' vase, by Violet Woodhouse, incised and painted marks to base, restored foot chips, overall crazing, glaze fault to rim.

See Peter Hyland, 'The Della Robbia Pottery Birkenhead 1894-1906', figure 258.

c1900   *11.75in (30cm) high*

$900-1,000   PW

A Delphin Massier Vallauris pottery vase, by J. Niolett, painted marks to base, signed to the side, hairline to rim.

4.5in (11.5cm) high

$150-200   WW

A massive Devonmoor advertising Toby jug, wearing a green coat over a claret waistcoat, with ruddy nose and cheeks.

Only a handful of these out-sized jugs are believed to have been made at Devonmoor, probably during the factory's second period of manufacture after 1922.

c1930   *23.5in (60cm) high*

$2,000-2,500   WW

A massive Devonmoor advertising Toby jug, a rim crack to the back of the hat.

Damage can severely effect the value of ceramic collectibles, even though this is a rarity.

c1930   *23.5in (60cm) high*

$450-600   WW

QUICK REFERENCE - ELTON WARE

- Sir Edmund Elton, 8th baronet (1846-1920), was an artist and studio potter. After inheriting his uncle's title and estate in Clevedon in 1883, he founded the Sunflower Pottery, where he designed and potted many Arts and Crafts wares.
- Elton produced simple red earthenware forms, decorated with gold or silver-colored 'crackle glazes', created by adding real gold or platinum during the firing process.
- After Elton's death, the pottery was taken over by William Fishley Holland until its closure in 1922.
- Elton Ware pieces are often signed 'Elton' to the base. They tend to be very fragile, so signs of damage or restoration considerably decrease the value.

An Elton Ware Sunflower Pottery vase, by Sir Edmund Elton, slip decorated with flower repeat, painted 'Elton', minor glaze loss to top rim.

5in (13cm) wide

$130-200   WW

A large Elton Ware vase, by Sir Edmund Elton, in gold crackle luster glaze.

c1900   *20.5in (52cm) high*

$800-950   K&O

An early 20thC Elton Ware vase, by Sir Edmund Elton, of globe and shaft form with four loop handles, decorated in a gold craquelure glaze over a green ground, incised signature.

$1,300-2,000   FLD

A large Ewenny Pottery model of a cat, with incised features, in a speckled green glaze, unmarked, minor glaze loss.

15.25in (38.5cm) high

$1,000-1,200   **WW**

A Fulham Pottery umbrella stand, by Jean-Charles Cazin, incised 'Fulham' and 'JC' monogram to base.

Cazin was active at the Fulham Pottery from 1872-74.

25.25in (64cm) high

$400-550   **ECGW**

A C.J.C. Bailey Fulham stoneware vase, by Edgar Kettle, incised with goats and figures, incised marks, some minor firing imperfections.

13in (34.5cm) high

$450-550   **CHEF**

A 1930s Goldscheider earthenware Art Deco figure, 'Butterfly Girl', impressed marks, initialed in black.

The excellent decoration on this piece adds to its value. The pose is typical of Goldscheider figures of this period but the brown cloche hat, fur collar and brown and orange marked cape are particularly striking.

12.5in (32cm) high

$1,600-2,000   **HT**

QUICK REFERENCE - GRUEBY

William Henry Grueby (1867-1925) founded the Grueby Faience Company in Boston, Massachusetts, in 1894. Pottery was handmade and decorated by a team of young women. Grueby experimented with glazes and developed a distinctive mat finish, in contrast to the glossy glazes most popular at the time. Grueby received much critical acclaim for his art pottery, but the company struggled financially and closed in 1911. He then founded the Grueby Faience and Tile Company, which closed in 1920.

A small Grueby vase, with leaves, with a glazed-over circular stamp, incised 'LHS', with original paper label.

c1905   *5.25in (13.5cm) high*

$1,200-1,300   **DRA**

A Grueby squat vessel with leaves, with a circular pottery stamp, incised 'ERF 7-26'.

c1905   *6in (15cm) wide*

$800-950   **DRA**

A CLOSER LOOK AT A GRUEBY TILE

Grueby tiles are particularly collectible.

This piece has highly desirable decoration with the goat and flowers.

It has its original paper label.

Even with a small glaze flake to one back corner and some light overall surface wear, the tile remains collectible.

A Grueby tile, with goat and flowers, original paper label.

c1905   *6in (15cm) square*

$2,500-3,000   **DRA**

A framed Grueby tulip tile, signed 'D.C.'.

c1910   *6in (15cm) square*

$1,700-2,000   **DRA**

CERAMICS

A Hornsea 'Summertime' cheese dish, designed by John Clappison.

For a wide variety of Hornsea pieces, see 'Miller's Collectibles Handbook & Price Guide 2016-17', pages 86-100.

1962   *base 8in (20cm) diam*

$45-55   **RHA**

A Karlsruhe terracotta wall tile, cast in low relief with fish swimming in an aquarium, impressed 'Karlsruhe', painted 'M', small chip to back edge.

8.75in (22.5cm) wide

$200-250   **WW**

A handpainted pottery mug, by Jessie M. King, painted 'JMK', rabbit and gate mark to base.

Jessie M. King (1875-1949) was a Scottish illustrator and painter. She trained at Glasgow School of Art and went on to illustrate books and design pottery, jewelry and wallpaper. Her handpainted pottery was sold exclusively through Paul Jones's Tea Rooms in Kirkcudbright, Fife. Her work is notable for its underglaze colors and fairytale-inspired designs.

4.5in (11.5cm) high

$900-1,000   **GWA**

A handpainted pottery jug, by Jessie M. King, with stylized floral decoration amongst wave and dot banded borders, painted 'JMK', rabbit and gate mark to base.

3.5in (9cm) high

$900-1,000   **GWA**

An earthenware fruit bowl, by Jessie M. King, painted with fish swimming amidst water lilies, painted 'JMK' and 'Green Gate'.

c1925   *8in (20.5cm) diam*

$450-600   **L&T**

An earthenware child's mug, by Jessie M. King, painted with floral frieze with a duck and inscription 'MARGARET', marked 'JMK' with gate and rabbit motifs.

c1920   *3.25in (8.5cm) high*

$800-950   **L&T**

A large Longpark 'Motto Ware' teapot and cover, slip decorated, printed factory mark, inscribed 'Youll ave a cup a Jay now waantee'.

13.75in (35cm) wide

$200-250   **WW**

A Maling luster bowl.

c1930   *9in (23cm) wide*

$35-40   **K&O**

A later 20thC Longwy earthenware vase, by Danillo Curetti, incised and crackle enamel decorated with a stylized figure of a female water carrier in the Art Deco taste, no.4 of a limited edition of 100, printed and handpainted marks to the base, 'F3168', 'Le Verseau'.

c1985   *9.75in (25cm) high*

$350-400   **FLD**

A 1910s Marblehead cabinet vase, with stylized roses, impressed ship mark 'MP'.

The Marblehead Pottery began in Massachusetts in 1904 when Herbert Hall established a pottery course as therapy for women with nervous disorders. This soon grew into a formal pottery, with Arthur E. Baggs as director. Key designers and decorators included Maude Milner, Arthur Hennessey and Sarah Tutt. It closed in 1936.

3.5in (9cm) high

$1,000-1,200   **DRA**

A 1910s Marblehead humidor, stamped ship mark 'MP', with original paper label, firing line to lid, Y-shaped line to body.

6in (15.5cm) wide

$400-450   **DRA**

A tall early 20thC Marblehead vase, stamped ship mark.

9in (23cm) high

$750-800   **DRA**

A Midwinter 'Fashion' shape part coffee and dinner service, 'Zambesi' pattern, after a design by Jessie Tait, comprising a coffee pot and cover, milk jug, 2 cream jugs, sugar bowl, 8 cups, 8 saucers, a bowl and a vegetable dish and cover, black backstamps.

c1955-60

$250-350   **BE**

A 19thC Mason's ironstone part dessert service, in the 'Imari' palette, comprising a comport, a pair of covered sauce tureens, 5 shell shaped dishes, a shaped dish, 15 dessert plates, and a saucer, with black printed or impressed marks 'MASON'S PATENT IRONSTONE CHINA'.

plates 8.5in (21.5cm) diam

$1,000-1,200   **L&T**

CERAMICS

QUICK REFERENCE - MIDWINTER

- Midwinter Pottery was founded as by William Robinson Midwinter in Burslem, Stoke-on-Trent, in 1910. By the late 1930s it was one of England's largest potteries.
- On a sales trip to North America in 1952, Roy Midwinter met with a disappointing response to his - and indeed all - Staffordshire wares. A second fruitless sales meeting with Simpson's in Canada prompted a radical departure from Midwinter's previous traditional shapes and designs. Roy Midwinter worked with designers such as Jessie Tait, Terence Conran, Hugh Casson, Eva Zeisel, Russel Wright and Raymond Loewy to revolutionize Midwinter's wares. They produced rimless and coupe plates, jugs and pots with fluid, organic shapes, all in brighter and cleaner colorways. Two new ranges, 'Fashion' and 'Stylecraft', were launched.
- Midwinter was taken over by J. & G. Meakin in 1968, which was in turn bought out by Wedgwood in 1970. The Midwinter factory closed in 1987.

A Midwinter 'Fashion' shape tea, coffee and part dinner service, 'Savanna' pattern, after a design by Jessie Tait, comprising teapot and cover, coffee pot and cover, milk jug, cream jug, sugar bowl, 6 teacups, 6 coffee cups and 12 saucers, 6 side plates, vegetable dish and cover and bowl, printed backstamps, interior stain to teapot, small bowl crazed.
c1955-60
$200-250   BE

A Midwinter 'Stylecraft' 'Fashion' shape coffee and part dinner service, 'Cannes' pattern, after a design by Hugh Casson, comprising 3 coffee pots and covers, 3 cream jugs, 2 sugar bowls, 12 cups, 12 saucers, vegetable dish and cover, gravy boat, 2 bowls and a sectional hors d'oeuvres dish, printed backstamps.
c1955-60
$250-350   BE

A Bernard Moore flambé vase, with foliage decoration, signed 'Bernard Moore'.

In 1905 Bernard Moore set up his own pottery works, which lasted from 1905 to 1915. It was after he went solo that Bernard began to produce technically remarkable pieces with flambé and sang-de-boeuf glazes, catering to an international market. He was particularly interested in recreating oriental glazes from the Ming Dynasty period.
c1910   9.5in (24cm) high
$400-550   K&O

A Bernard Moore flambé vase, with grapes and vine leaves decoration, signed 'Bernard Moore'.
c1910   9.5in (24cm) high
$400-550   K&O

A Bernard Moore flambé model rabbit, marked 'BM'.
c1910   3.25in (8cm) high
$400-450   K&O

A complete set of five Natwest piggy banks, comprising a father, mother, son, daughter and a baby pig, each with a stopper.
$50-70   LOCK

CERAMICS

QUICK REFERENCE - NEWCOMB

H. Sophie Newcomb Memorial College was a women's college founded in 1886 in New Orleans, LA, USA, with the aim of instructing young women in the liberal arts. Under the direction of Ellsworth Woodward, William Woodward and Mary Given Sheerer, the students of Newcomb College produced distinctive Arts and Crafts pottery, typically with underglaze floral designs. Key designers included Henrietta Bailey, Sadie Irvine, Leona Nicholson and A.F. Simpson. Production ceased in 1940.

An early Newcomb College vase, decorated with oleander, marked 'NC / AB51 / Lonnegan'.
1904   *8in (20cm) high*
$8,000-8,500   **DRA**

A Newcomb College transitional pitcher, by A.F. Simpson, decorated with freesias, marked 'NC / IX41 / JM / AFS'.
1917   *5in (13cm) high*
$1,300-2,000   **DRA**

An Art Deco majolica figure group of a woman with deer, signed in cast 'POLBERT'.
21in (53cm) wide
$80-100   **HAN**

A tin-glazed earthenware charger, by Patrick Swift (1927-83), signed 'P Swift, Porches'.

Patrick Swift was an acclaimed Irish artist. In 1968, he cofounded Porches Pottery with Lima de Freitas in Porches, Portugal.
15.25in (39cm) diam
$600-750   **CHOR**

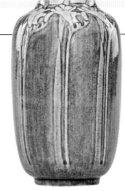

An early Newcomb College vase, with freesia, marked 'NC / W / CW46 / MWS', some crazing lines.
1909   *5.75in (14.5cm) high*
$5,500-6,000   **DRA**

A Newcomb College transitional vase, decorated with dogwood, on original carved stand, marked 'NC / JM / 7 / CL / FQ67', the stand incised '1' inside circle.
1913   *with stand 8.25in (21cm) high*
$4,500-5,500   **DRA**

A Newcomb College vase, decorated with paperwhites, marked 'NC / AFS / 147 / JM / QB37'.
1927   *6.75in (17cm) high*
$2,000-2,500   **DRA**

A Newcomb College vase, decorated with live oaks, Spanish moss and sunset, marked 'NC / 4 / RA72 / JM', partial paper label covering other markings.
1928   *5.5in (14cm) high*
$3,500-4,000   **DRA**

A Ridgway Pottery 'Metro' shape part coffee and dinner service, 'Homemaker' pattern, after a design by Enid Seeney, comprising a coffee pot and cover, 2 milk jugs, 2 sugar bowls, 6 cups, 6 saucers, 6 side plates, a vegetable dish and cover with stand or plate, printed backstamps.
c1960-70
$200-250   **BE**

CERAMICS

A 1950s Ronzan Pottery ceramic figural dish, painted maker's marks 'RONZAN / MADE IN ITALY / 1332'.

21in (53.5cm) high

$450-550   L&T

A Royal Albert Beatrix Potter 'The Christmas Stocking' figure, no.BP6A.

$80-100   PSA

A rare Royal Albert Beatrix Potter 'Tomasina Tittlemouse' figure, no.BP6A.

$200-250   PSA

A rare Royal Albert Beatrix Potter 'Old Mr Pricklepin' figure, no.BP6A.

$250-350   PSA

A Royal Cauldon footed dish, by Frederick Rhead, printed marks, some minor rim rubbing.

Frederick Rhead (1856-1933) was a British pottery who spent much of his career in the USA. He was the father of Charlotte Rhead (see page 82) and Frederick Hurten Rhead (see page 126).

12in (30.5cm) long

$50-80   FELL

QUICK REFERENCE - SADLER & SONS

Sadler & Sons was founded in 1882 in Burslem, Stoke-on-Trent. It specialized in teapots, mugs and other tea accessories. At first, it focused on 'Brown Bettys' teapots, made from red clay, finished with a dark Rockingham glaze. In the Interwar period, Sadler & Sons began to produce novelty teapots. These were modeled as cars, buildings and figurines, including one Father Christmas teapot and another modeled as Winston Churchill riding a tank. Production continued at the factory until 2000. Sadler & Sons novelty teapots are increasingly collectible today.

A 20thC Sadler & Sons green coach 'T44' teapot, with '576' impressed to base.

8.25in (21cm) long

$150-200   LOCK

A Royal Dux porcelain figurine, no.1586, impressed model number, pink triangle pad mark, small chip to one leaf of base, some rubbing to paint.

23.5in (59.5cm) high

$400-450   FELL

A 1930s Sadler & Sons teapot, modeled as a racing car with nursery rhyme prints, including 'Wendy Watering', 'Helping Daddy', in the style of Mabel Lucie Attwell, with 'OKT42' number plate, impressed marks.

8.75in (22.5cm) long

$150-200   FLD

An early 20thC Pilkingtons Royal Lancastrian vase, by Richard Joyce, painted and impressed marks, restored.

5.75in (14.5cm) high

$250-350   FLD

A Saturday Evening Girls glazed ceramic honey jar, decorated in cuerda seca with wooded landscape, signed 'S.G. / S.E.G. / 66-7-12', professional restoration to rim of base and small area on edge of lid.

1912   5.25in (13.5cm) high

$1,000-1,300   DRA

A Shelley Pottery Vogue Art Deco tea service, by Eric Slater, 'Chevron' pattern, comprising a sugar bowl, 5 trios, a plate, jug and more, 11775E pattern 756533.

The pottery was founded in 1822 and rebranded as Shelley from 1925. Notable Art Directors include Walter Slater, Eric Slater and Frederick Rhead (1896-1905, father of Charlotte Rhead, see page 82, and Frederick Hurten Rhead, see page 126). The company is best known for its bone china tea sets, produced from the 1920s-40s. It was absorbed by Royal Doulton in 1971.

$2,000-2,500   HAN

A Shelley Pottery 'Queen Anne' part tea-service, 'Balloon Tree' pattern, no.11624, comprising 9 cups and 12 saucers, 12 tea plates, 2 bread and butter plates, cream jug and sugar bowl.

$450-550   KEY

A late Foley Shelley 'Intarsio' pedestal bowl, decorated in the Art Nouveau-style, printed mark.

6.75in (17cm) high

$250-350   FLD

A Shelley Pottery luster bowl, by Walter Slater, model no.8306, with printed mark and facsimile signature.

7.5in (19cm) diam

$350-400   WW

A Shelley Pottery 'I's Shy' 'L.A.9' figure, designed by Mabel Lucie Attwell, with printed green mark, repair to bow.

6.25in (16cm) high

$120-160   WW

A 19thC Sitzendorf porcelain figurine of Juno and her peacock, three baton marks to the base.

8.25in (21cm) high

$60-70   HW

A 19thC Staffordshire model of Potash Farm, on an inscribed plinth base.

6.25in (16cm) high

$250-350   KEY

CERAMICS

QUICK REFERENCE - STAFFORDSHIRE FAKES

Common Staffordshire dogs have proved difficult to sell, particularly as there are many fakes on the market. The main difference between old and new is that old figures were made in press molds; new figures are made in slip molds in the process called slip casting. The larger holes left in the base of slip cast pieces are an easily detected sign of a modern reproduction. Although some original figures were produced by slip casting, they are extremely few in number. Old pieces generally show at least some fine strokes of a paint brush; modern pieces are often colored by swabs or sponges. Most old dogs show at least some painting on the back side; many new pieces have no painting on the back. Old dogs also generally show more detail in the overall molding especially in the tails, legs, ears and modeled hair. Old gold nearly always shows some wear; new gold usually shows none. Most old gold is relatively soft colored with a dull luster; much of the new gold has a highly reflective surface. However, if unsure, it is always better to buy from a reputable source as fakers are getting better!

A Teco jardinière, decorated with irises, Terra Cotta, stamped 'Teco', professional restoration to two handles.

The Teco Art Pottery range was produced from 1902 until the mid-1920s by Gates Potteries, a subsidiary of the American Terracotta & Ceramic Company. Teco pieces were plain and architectural in style, influenced by and sometimes designed by local Chicago architects.

c1910   *14.5in (37cm) wide*
$1,300-1,600   **DRA**

A 1910s lobed and footed Teco vase, impressed 'Teco', a few dark scuffs to body.

9in (23cm) high
$1,600-2,000   **DRA**

A pair of early 19thC Staffordshire red and white mantelpiece dogs.
$60-80   **PSA**

A three-handled Teco vase, stamped 'Teco 287'.
c1910   *11in (28cm) high*
$1,000-1,200   **DRA**

A Teco vase, impressed 'Teco', incised '293'.
c1910   *9.5in (24cm) high*
$800-950   **DRA**

A tapering Teco mat green vase, with impressed mark.
c1910   *9.5in (24cm) high*
$600-650   **DRA**

A bowl decorated with leaves, by Van Briggle, Colorado Springs, CO, USA, unmarked.
c1914   *10in (25cm) diam*
$600-750   **DRA**

A vase, by Van Briggle, with stylized flowers, marked.

c1919   *10.5in (26.5cm) high*

$150-250   DRA

A Villeroy & Boch tile, designed by Otto Eckmann, four radiating stylized fox head motifs, stamped marks.

6in (15cm) square

$100-160   WW

A Karl Ens Volkstedt figure, of a reclining nude female, in the Art Deco style, indistinctly signed, possibly 'Ruis Dasseldf'.

A Karl Ens Volkstedt figure of a pheasant.

10.5in (46.5cm) long

$100-130   DA&H

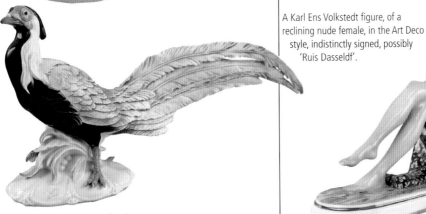

14.75in (37.5cm) wide

$160-200   DA&H

A Charles Vyse figure, modeled as a faun riding on the back of a snail, perched upon a lettuce leaf, impressed 'C.Vyse' and 'Chelsea' to side of base, the tips of the snail's tentacles are missing, fine crazing.

Charles Vyse (1882-1971) was apprenticed at Doulton (see pages 85-97) and trained under Charles Noke. He studied in London and at the Royal College of Art and Camberwell School of Art, before founding a studio with his wife Nell in Chelsea, London, in 1919.

excluding base 8.75in (22cm) high

$1,000-1,300   PW

Hansons
AUGUST AC 2016
1177

A Vienna Ernst Wahliss pot and cover, decorated with a classical maiden.

$60-80   HAN

An Ernst Wahliss Austrian Art Nouveau figural dish, modeled as a nude maiden next to pool with a crab, figure with luster finish, marked 'E', 'W' and 'Turn Wien', small chips.

12in (30cm) diam

$200-250   ECGW

CERAMICS

An early 20thC Weller Coppertone console bowl and flower frog, incised script mark to bowl.

15.5in (39.5cm) long

$250-350　　　　　　　　　　　　　　　　　**DRA**

A Weller 'Dickensware II' vase, unmarked, a few areas of paint loss.

c1900　　　　　　　*12in (30.5cm) high*

$250-350　　　　　　　　　　　**DRA**

A 20thC ceramic sculpture, by Bjørn Wiinblad (1918-2006), Denmark, in the form of a lady wearing a hat, polychrome painted decoration, signed and dated.

1984　　　　　　*20.5in (52cm) high*

$550-650　　　　　　　　　　**ECGW**

A rare 1940s Wilkinson's 'Reginald Mitchell' Toby jug, produced by Clarice Cliff, showing Reginald Mitchell sat in the clouds with God of Mercury and Spitfire's flying below, 'The first of the few' written on the base, no backstamp.

11.75in (30cm) high

$2,000-2,500　　　　　　**PSA**

A Royal Staffordshire Wilkinson Ltd. 'Marshall Foch' World War I character jug, designed by Sir Francis Carruthers Gould, inscribed 'Au Diable Le Kaiser', with printed marks to base, extensive crazing throughout, hairline leading from the rim, the right hand reglued.

11.5in (29.5cm) high

$200-250　　　　　　　　　　**APAR**

A Wood & Sons Toby jug replica, from a limited edition of 500, with certificate.

11in (28cm) high

$40-50　　　　　　　　　　**K&O**

A 1960s Zsolnay Pecs cockerel figure, the stylized figure covered in an eosin luster glaze, printed maker's marks.

7.75in (19.5cm) high

$130-200　　　　　　**L&T**

A late 19thC to early 20thC cold-painted terracotta figure of dog, with glass eyes.

12.25in (31cm) high

$900-1,100　　　　　　**L&T**

A late 19thC walnut and marquetry inlaid wall-mounted musical cuckoo clock, retailed by Camerer, Kuss & Co., with a twin spring driven wooden movement with back-mounted count wheel and anchor escapement with strike on a coiled gong, with a music box playing six airs, some losses and repair to case.

20in (51cm) high

$900-1,100 **KEY**

An early 20thC Black Forest bracket cuckoo clock.

16.5in (42cm) high

$160-200 **HAN**

An early 20thC 'digital' timepiece in the manner of Junghans.

6.25in (16cm) high

$200-250 **HAN**

An early 20thC candle timepiece, brushed brass base.

6.75in (17cm) high

$350-400 **HAN**

QUICK REFERENCE - GUILD OF HANDICRAFT

Charles Robert Ashbee founded the Guild and School of Handicraft in 1888. Based on the model of the medieval workshop, the Guild operated as a co-operative. Style and aesthetics followed the Art and Crafts movement and the Guild produced leather, furniture, metalwork, jewelry and books, with much of the work based on Ashbee's designs. Revival of traditional techniques, education of working people and encouraging satisfaction through work were key principles of the Arts and Craft movement and the Guild. In 1902, the Guild (150 people, including the Guildsmen and their families) moved from East London to Chipping Campden, Gloucestershire. Ashbee believed that living a simple, collective life in rural surroundings would add to the health and well-being of the craftsmen and consequently the work they produced.

Although the work of the Guild was widely exhibited, increasing financial difficulties from 1905 eventually resulted in the voluntary liquidation of the Guild in 1908.

A copper and electroplate mantle clock, attributed to the Guild of Handicraft.

c1895 *11in (27.5cm) high*

$650-950 **CHEF**

A Royal Copenhagen porcelain lace pattern mantel clock, the two-train movement with lever platform escapement, striking on a bell, the dial inscribed 'W.Q. le Maire Kjobenhavn', impressed marks beneath.

11in (28cm) high

$4,000-4,500 **FELL**

An early 20thC novelty mother-of-pearl and silver pocket watch stand and pocket watch, minor losses to the mother-of-pearl, clock in need of attention, maker's mark worn.

1912 *3.5in (9cm) high*

$450-550 **FELL**

A 1960s to 1970s wooden wall clock with brass frame, by Heinrich Tessenow for Deutsche Werkstätten, maker's label reading 'WK MÖBEL DeWEMÖBEL, Deutsche Werkstätten Heinrich Tessenow-Uhr, 1912, 2957'.

designed 1912 *9.75in (24.5cm) high*

$750-800 **QU**

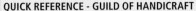

A sheet metal table clock, by Marianne Brandt for Ruppelwerk, marked '1-TAG-WERK, RUPPEL geschützt'.

1929-32 *6in (15.5cm) wide*

$1,000-1,200 **QU**

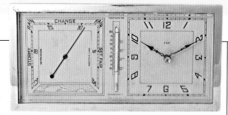

A Smiths Art Deco eight-day mantel clock compendium, impressed marks to rear.
c1930   *9.5in (24cm) wide*
$150-200   **BELL**

An Art Deco Vitascope Bakelite-cased rocking ship clock, printed backstamp for 'Vitascope Industries Ltd Made in Great Britain'.
12.5in (31.5cm) high
$550-650   **LSK**

An Asprey mirrored wall clock, London, dial inscribed 'ASPREY / LONDON'.
c1930   37in (94cm) wide
$800-950   **L&T**

A French Art Deco silver-plated mantel clock, on variegated marble base.
7in (17.5cm) high
$50-70   **LSK**

An Art Deco marble-cased mantel clock, with a cold-painted cast bronze figure of a lady, the dial with 'J C Vickery 145-147 Regent St', some damage, mechanism not working.
8in (20.5cm) wide
$200-250   **FELL**

An Art Deco D'Argyl ceramic mantel clock case, painted signature to base.
20.75in (53cm) wide
$350-400   **WW**

An Art Deco marble clock, with a bronze and ivory figure of a reclining female, marked 'France' to the reverse.
24.75in (63cm) wide
$1,000-1,200   **CHEF**

An Art Deco clock, with spelter figure on onyx and stone base.
11.5in (29cm) high
$150-200   **K&O**

A French Art Deco majolica figural timepiece, with wolves.
15.75in (40cm) long
$70-100   **HAN**

CLOCKS

A 1940s miniature rosewood-cased travel clock, by Van Cleef and Arpels.

5.75in (14.5cm) long

$150-200   **LOCK**

A Neon Electric Clock Company wall clock, Cleveland, OH, USA, in working order, but not PAT tested.

c1950   *22in (56cm) high*

$1,600-2,000   **CHEF**

A Bulova space-age desk clock.

c1960   *6.25in (16cm) high*

$100-120   **FLD**

A 1960s Smiths Noddy and Big Ears alarm clock.

4.5in (11.5cm) diam

$40-50   **LOCK**

A Jaeger LeCoultre brass-cased mantel clock, with back-wound movement, stamped '442' beneath.

Jaeger-LeCoultre were established in 1833 by Charles Antoine Le Coultre in Le Sentier, Vallée de Joux, Switzerland, and obtained the current name after the merger with chronometer maker Edward Jaeger in 1937.

c1970   *7in (18cm) high*

$600-650   **FELL**

A Jaeger LeCoultre gilt-brass-cased mantel clock, stamped 'Swiss' and '530' to back.

5.5in (14cm) high

$350-400   **LSK**

A Jaeger-LeCoultre mantel clock, the eight-day duration timepiece movement with a lever escapement-set within a Perspex case in the form of an aquarium, signed.

7.75in (20cm) high

$750-800   **BE**

A Modernist chrome and rosewood mantel clock, signed 'Aurelio Bosato, Milano'.

9.5in (24cm) wide

$250-350   **DUK**

A Lorna Bailey 'Across The Universe' mantle clock, no.27 of a limited edition of 60.

$130-200   **HAN**

QUICK REFERENCE - 'THE BEANO'

- 'The Beano' is the longest running British children's comic and is published by DC Thomson. It has been published every Thursday since 30 July 1938, with some exceptions during World War II.
- The heyday of 'The Beano' was probably the 1950s, when its weekly circulation was near to 2 million copies. Today it sells around 35,000 copies a week.
- Older weekly editions of 'The Beano', especially pre-war copies, can now fetch high values, especially when in excellent condition. Special issues such as the Christmas, Fireworks and Easter editions are also highly collectible and can fetch two to three times the price of a normal issue.
- 'Beano' books and annuals have dropped in price in recent years, as many have come to market through online auction sites such as eBay. However, they can still command premium prices when in high grade condition.

'The Beano Book', annual no.3, 1942, printed by DC Thomson, featuring characters spinning around Big Eggo and Lord Snooty playing the Bagpipes, 127 pages.
$250-300   AST

'The Magic Beano Book', 1949, featuring Biffo, Big Eggo around Maxy's Taxi.
$50-70   AST

'Beano', no.15, 1938, the first 'Fireworks' issue.
$650-800   PCOM

'The Beano Book', 1955.
$70-80   PCOM

'Dennis the Menace Book', 1956.

Dennis the Menace is probably the best-known Beano character. Dennis had his first annual in 1956, published bi-annually with Beryl the Peril into the 1980s and then every year since.
$120-160   PCOM

'Beano', no.1223, 1965, Christmas issue.
$130-200   PCOM

'Dandy', no.15, 1938.

The first 'Dandy' comic was published by DC Thomson in December 1937. Like 'The Beano', it achieved great popularity in the mid-20thC, with nearly two million sales a week in the 1950s. By the 2000s, weekly circulation was down to under 10,000 and the 'Dandy' ceased printing in 2012. 1930s and wartime 'Dandy' comics are rare. Before wartime shortages, the 'Dandy' comic was 28 pages and cost only 2 pennies.
$350-400   PCOM

'Bully Beef and Chips', original comic artwork by James Hughes for Dandy comic, 1969, mounted.

Rarely seen comic artworks are increasingly sought by collectors. Most original artwork is unique, with only one page of artwork created for every comic strip produced.
$1,200-1,300   PCOM

QUICK REFERENCE - MARVEL COMICS

- Marvel Comics began in October 1939. Its first publication was called simply 'Marvel Comics' and featured The Human Torch. Several other superheroes were added to Marvel's repertoire in the 1940s, including Captain America and Miss Marvel.
- Many Marvel comics were created by Marvel's head writer and editor, Stan Lee, and illustrated by artist Jack Kirby. In the 1960s, they worked together to create famous superhero figures such as the Fantastic Four, The Incredible Hulk, The Amazing Spider-Man and the X-Men.
- Today, Marvel is owned by Disney and continues to publish comics. The success of the Marvel film franchise in recent years has pushed up prices for key comic book issues. This is especially true of comics featuring the first appearances of characters who had previously been comparatively obscure and have been popularized by recent films, such as Rocket Racoon from Guardians of the Galaxy, or Deadpool.
- Condition is key with comics and prices can be substantially higher for comics in high grade condition.

'Tales of Suspense, Iron Man versus Gargantus!', no.40, April 1963, story by Stan Lee, art by Jack Kirby.

This features the first appearance of Iron Man in Mark II armor.

$400-450   AST

'The Amazing Spider-man', no.50, July 1967, artwork by John Romita Sr., featuring the first appearance of Kingpin, Spider-man's origin retold.

Vintage Spider-man comics are consistently popular with collectors; he is one of Marvel's best-known superheroes and there have been six Spider-man films since 2002 alone.

$750-850   AST

'Captain America', no.102, June 1968, published by Marvel Comics.

$80-100   AST

'The Fantastic Four', no.16, July 1963, story by Stan Lee, cover art by Jack Kirby, featuring Doctor Doom and Ant-Man.

$200-250   AST

A CLOSER LOOK AT A MARVEL COMIC

This is the first issue of 'The Mighty World of Marvel', from October 1972. It was the first publication of Marvel UK.

The comic stars the well-known superhero The Incredible Hulk.

'X-Men, The Menace of Merlin', no.78, October 1972, published by Marvel Comics, featuring Thor.

$60-80   AST

'Marvel Spotlight, Ghostrider', no.5, August 1972, published by Marvel, featuring the first appearance of Ghostrider.

$250-300   AST

This UK release reprinted classic US Marvel material from Fantastic Four' no.1, 'The Incredible Hulk' no.1, 'and 'Amazing Fantasy' no.15.

The rarely seen free gift transfer increases the value of this comic considerably.

'The Mighty World of Marvel', no.1, 1972, with free gift transfer.

$150-200   PCOM

COMICS & ANNUALS

'Champion', no.2, 1966, with rare free gift.

'Champion' was a short lived boys' comic. It lasted just 15 issues before it merged with 'Lion'. In general, free gifts are rare, especially those that do not lie flat in the comic, such as this FA Cup Whistle.

$100-130   PCOM

QUICK REFERENCE - DC COMICS

- DC began in the 1930s as National Allied Publications. The name 'DC' comes from the initials of its successful 'Detective Comics' series.
- DC went on to become one of the most successful publishers of superhero comics. It has long been the main rival of Marvel.
- The best-known DC heroes are probably Superman, who first appeared in 1938, and Batman, who first appeared in 1939.
- Today, DC is a subsidiary of Warner Brothers Entertainment. Its films are successful and its comics remain popular, both new issues and collectible vintage editions.

'Superboy Annual', 1953-54, published by Atlas/Top Seller, the first annual in a series of annuals lasting approximately 15 years.

$20-25   PCOM

'Hotspur', no.468, 1968, with a free gift, a spinner in its original packet.

$40-50   PCOM

'Batman', no.200, 1968, published by DC Comics, front cover artwork by Neal Adams.

$40-50   PCOM

'Action Comics', no.373, 1969, published by DC Comics, 80-page edition featuring Supergirl.

'Action Comics' was a long running series that first began in 1938. It was the comic series that introduced Superman.

$20-25   PCOM

'Doctor Who: The Eleventh Doctor', no.5, published by Titan Comics, 2014, signed by Matt Smith.

The longevity of the TV series has inevitably added to the interest and collectible nature of this comic.

$50-60   HC

'Fireball XL5 Annual', 1964.

This comic strip appeared in TV Century 21 science fiction comic. It followed Spaceship Fireball XL5, captained by Steve Zodiac and based on the Gerry Anderson's classic Supermarionation TV Series of the early 1960s.

$60-70   PCOM

'Oor Wullie Annual', 1962, artwork by Dudley Watkins.

The comic strip was published weekly in Scotland's 'The Sunday Post' and bi-annually as annuals, alternating with 'The Broons'.
$90-100   PCOM

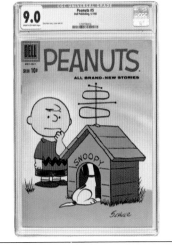

'Star Wars', no.1, July 1977, published by Marvel Comics, art by Howard Chaykin, Roy Thomas adaptation of the movie.

This was the first Star Wars comic. The original series ran 1977-86. A new series of Star Wars comics was launched by Marvel Comics in 2015.
$100-120   AST

'Warlord Summer Special', 1982.

Publishers of weekly comics almost always cashed in on producing a summer special, often at larger format than the regular editions. These are highly collectible. Later issues of Warlord are scarcer due to lower print runs.
$35-40   PCOM

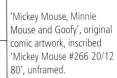

'Peanuts', no.5, published by Dell, 1960, art and story by Dale Hale.

$400-450   HC

'Mickey Mouse, Minnie Mouse and Goofy', original comic artwork, inscribed 'Mickey Mouse #266 20/12 80', unframed.

9.75in (24.5cm) high
$90-110   APAR

'Kid Kong', original comic art work, a two-page storyboard, inscribed verso 'Buster Monster Fun Special 1983', pages 48 and 49', unframed.
11in (28cm) high
$60-80   APAR

'Mickey Mouse and Goofy', original comic art work, inscribed 'Mickey 269 W/E Dec 20th 1980', unframed.
9.75in (25cm) high
$60-80   APAR

COMMEMORATIVES

A Royal Doulton 'Admiral Lord Nelson' Loving Cup, designed by Charles Noke and Harry Fenton, no.54 of an edition of 600, printed marks.

This Royal Doulton loving cup was released in a limited run in 1935 and depicts scenes from the Battle of Trafalgar, 1805, at which Nelson died.

1935   *10.5in (26.5cm) high*

$250-400   **CHEF**

A Continental faience bust of Nelson, the foot with 'AR' monogram.

6.5in (16.5cm) high

$250-350   **CM**

A Wellington commemorative jug, overall crazing, minor glaze faults from firing.

c1812   *4.75in (12cm) high*

$400-450   **PW**

A silver City of London medal, made to commemorate the Great Reform Bill, by B. Wyon, obverse 'REFORM IN THE PRESENTATION OF THE PEOPLE'.

1832

$600-650   **DUK**

A Charles Stewart Parnell carved bog-oak ceremonial baton, surmounted by a silver-plated bust of Charles Stewart Parnell, the baton's upper section carved with ivy and shamrock.

There is only one other example of this baton known. That example bore a plaque inscribed 'Presented to - Mr M.J. Murray - Chief Marshall of the - Parnell Anniversary Demonstration - held 7th Oct. 1890 - by the Parnell Anniversary Committee'. Presumably these ceremonial batons were given to several of the organizers of the demonstration.

1890   *28.5in (72.5cm) long*

$2,000-2,500   **WHYT**

A Daniel O'Connell lusterware commemorative jug, for the Clare by-election, inscribed 'Daniel O'Connell Esq. MP - For The County of Clare - The Man of the People'.

1828   *8in (20.5cm) high*

$1,300-2,000   **WHYT**

A Sir Winston Churchill (1874-1965) gold commemorative medal, by Spink & Sons, reverse showing spirit of England with legend 'Very Well, Alone', cased with certificate, no.384 of a limted edition of 1000.

This was struck to commemorate the death of Churchill in 1965, the reverse was adapted from the famous cartoon by Sir David Low, published in the Evening Standard in 1940, after the retreat from Dunkirk.

1.5in (4cm) diam 1.69oz

$2,500-3,500   **DW**

A Halcyon Days commemorative enamel box, detailed beneath lid 'The Right Honourable The Baroness Thatcher LG, OM, PC, FRS, Prime Minister of the United Kingdom 1979-1990. 13th October 1925 to 8th April 2013. After a photograph by Julian Calder', 'In an edition limited to 87 this is no.12', in box with paperwork.

5.5in (14cm) high

$250-350   **FELL**

A Victoria and Albert marriage mug.

c1840   *4.75in (12cm) diam*

$100-130   **LOCK**

QUICK REFERENCE - ERIC RAVILIOUS

● Eric Ravilious (1903-42) was an English painter and designer. He was born in London and studied at the Eastbourne School of Art and the Royal College of Art, then worked as a designer for Wedgwood 1935-40.

● His designs were highly popular, especially his 1937 coronation mugs, first produced for the coronation of Edward VIII, then for George VI.

● He died in 1942 while serving as a war artist on a Royal Air Force air sea rescue mission off the coast of Iceland.

● After Ravilious's death, Wedgwood continued to use his designs, sometimes adjusting and re-coloring them, as in the case of the Elizabeth II coronation mug, which was re-worked from his 1937 coronation mug designs. His designs remain popular with collectors today.

A Copeland commemorative tyg, 'Victoria Queen and Empress, Comforter of the Afflicted', and 'Brittania Tower of Justice'.

5.5in (14cm) high

$450-600   **PSA**

A Wedgwood Edward VIII Coronation pottery mug, designed by Eric Ravilious.

1937   *4.25in (10.5cm) high*

$1,000-1,200   **DW**

A Wedgwood Elizabeth II Coronation pottery mug, designed by Eric Ravilious.

1953   *4.25in (10.5cm) high*

$200-250   **DW**

A Royal Doulton loving cup, commemorating Elizabeth I and II, no.387 of 1000, with matching certificate.

This loving cup was made in 1953 to commemorative the coronation of Queen Elizabeth II. The reverse shows an image of Queen Elizabeth I.

c1953   *10.5in (26.5cm) high*

$200-250   **PW**

A hand-written note on Buckingham Palace headed paper, signed by HRH Queen Elizabeth II and Prince Philip, thanking Nanny Rattle for 'the splendid silver wedding presents', finishing with 'we have been much touched by your kind and good wishes on the occasion of the 25th anniversary of our wedding'.

9.5in (24cm) high

$350-400   **LSK**

An Aynsley Lion, made to commemorate the Silver Jubilee of Queen Elizabeth II, no.44 of a limited edition of 100, with certificate.

21.75in (55cm) wide

$250-300   **PW**

COMMEMORATIVES

QUICK REFERENCE - THE INVESTITURE OF PRINCE CHARLES

The Investiture of HRH The Prince of Wales took place in July 1969 at Caernarfon Castle in north-west Wales. In this ceremony, Queen Elizabeth II formally awarded Prince Charles, then aged 20, his title of the 21st Prince of Wales. The ceremony was directed by the Constable of the Castle, Lord Snowdon, and Prince Charles was given with the Insignia of his Principality and Earldom of Chester: a sword, coronet, mantle, gold ring and gold rod. The ceremony was attended by 4,000 guests and watched by millions more on television. This 'Welsh Dragon' paperweight was made to commemorate the occasion.

A Royal Crown Derby 'Welsh Dragon' paperweight, no.162 of a limited edition of 250, with box and certificate.
1969
$450-500   HAN

A Christmas greetings card, from HRH Charles, Prince of Wales, and HRH Diana, Princess of Wales, addressed 'Nanny Rattle from Charles' and separately signed 'Diana'.
5in (13cm) long
$750-800   LSK

A HRH Prince Charles and Lady Diana Spencer parcel-gilt wedding goblet, by Stuart Devlin, London, no.40 of a limited edition of 950.
1981   7.5in (19cm) high 10.8oz
$350-400   CHEF

An autograph notecard, signed 'Diana', Kensington Palace, to Dudley Poplak, thanking him for the fascinating book', with the original used postal envelope, addressed to Poplak in Princess Diana's holograph, 2 pages, oblong 8vo.

Dudley Poplak was an interior designer and friend of Princess Diana's mother. He refurbished Highgrove, was commissioned by the Queen, and was a good friend of Prince Charles and Princess Diana.
1991
$1,000-1,200   LSK

A Diana Princess of Wales Christmas card, with HRH Prince William and HRH Prince Harry.
1995
$900-1,100   CHEF

A Christie's sale catalog, 'Dresses from the collection of Diana, Princess of Wales', signed by Diana, Princess of Wales, no.99 of a limited edition of 250, in original packaging.
1997
$2,500-3,500   CHEF

An Elizabeth II gold sovereign and first day cover, no.115 of a limited edition proof of 2002, with case.
2002
$350-400   DA&H

QUICK REFERENCE - COINS

The desirability of a coin depends on three things - condition, age and rarity. Older coins can be worth more, but those in poor condition tend to fetch a fraction of the price of a near mint condition coin from the same year. Collectors will aim to buy coins in the very best condition, and uncirculated coins are highly prized. The condition of a coin is examined and classified in great detail, usually with a series of two to five letter codes, from 'P' for 'poor' to 'UNC' for 'uncirculated' and 'FDC' for 'fleur du coin' or perfect condition. Collectors tend to collect by currency, by country or by specific historical period.

An uncirculated George III shilling, proof-like, toned.
1787
$450-550   DUK

A near fine George III gold spade guinea.
1790
$750-800   CHEF

A George III guinea.
1798
$250-300   HAN

A George III guinea, slight signs of mount at 12.00 o'clock.
1785
$450-550   HAN

An almost uncirculated George III Bank of England issue eighteenpence bank token.
1813
$130-200   DUK

A very fine George III guinea.
1798
$750-800   FELL

A George III sovereign, with attached edge loop.
1817
$550-600   BRI

An almost fine George III sovereign.
1817
$850-950   FELL

A George III half-sovereign.
1817
$200-250   FELL

A George III sixpence.
1817
$60-80　　　　　　　　　　　　　　　　DUK

A George IV crown, 'SECUNDO' on edge.
1822
$450-550　　　　　　　　　　　　　　　DUK

An almost uncirculated Victoria 'Godless' florin, toned.
1849
$450-550　　　　　　　　　　　　　　DUK

A very fine Victoria young head sovereign, die no.14.
1865
$450-550　　　　　　　　　　　FELL

A fine Victoria sovereign.
1893
$400-450　　　　　　　　　FELL

A fine Victoria sovereign.
1896
$400-450　　　　　　FELL

An uncirculated Victoria halfcrown.
1900
$130-200　　　　　　　　　　　　　　DUK

A Victoria florin.
1901
$50-70　　　　　　　　　　　　　　　DUK

A fine Edward VII half-sovereign.
1904
$150-200　　　　　　　　　　　FELL

A fine Edward VII half-sovereign.
1910
$200-250   FELL

A George V sovereign.

This was found in the P&O SS Egypt shipwreck, in original box with certificate of authenticity, Lloyd's from 30 June 1932.
1912
$450-550   DUK

A fine George V sovereign.
1915
$450-550   FELL

An Edward VII enameled half-sovereign, some red enamel scratches, with enamel date.
1923
$200-250   FELL

An uncirculated George V proof crown, raised edge lettering.
1935
$1,000-1,100   DUK

A George VI brass threepence, trace luster.
1949
$150-200   DUK

An Elizabeth II Isle of Man sovereign, reverse the Prince and Princess of Wales, in box of issue, uncirculated.
1981
$350-400   DUK

An almost uncirculated George VI threepence, full luster.
1949
$550-600   DUK

An Elizabeth II fifty pence, uncirculated.
2009
$120-160   DUK

A fine Asian Territories Ceylon George II ar 96-stivers 2-Rix Dollars.

This is a well-stuck coin from this crude series.

1808

$250-350   DUK

An uncirculated Royal Mint The Falkland Islands Government gold 50 coin, cased with certificate.

1979   *1.19oz*

$1,000-1,300   DW

A Mexico gold fifty pesos.

1946

$800-850   BELL

A mint Netherlands Av Ducat Utrecht.

This is from the Vliegenthart shipwreck and is boxed with its certificate and associated paperwork.

1729

$550-650   DUK

A Portugal Joao I gold 4-Escudos, ex-solder mount.

1754   *0.48oz*

$250-400   FELL

An extremely fine USA cent, 'Liberty Cap' type, 'ONE HUNDRED FOR A DOLLAR' on edge, good color with chocolate brown toning.

1794

$4,500-5,500   DUK

A fine USA dollar, 'AMERICA' reverse variety.

1800

$2,000-2,500   DUK

A fine USA Liberty head gold Dollar, some discoloration to obverse, possibly ex-loose mount.

1853   *0.06oz*

$100-130   FELL

A USA gold twenty dollars.

1915

$1,000-1,200   BELL

A mint Cayman Islands 50 dollars, Pick10a Law, dated, numbered 'A1 026960'.

1974

$300-400   LOCK

A mint Djibouti 10000 francs, Pick39b, numbered '64356 / 01964356'.

1984

$90-100   LOCK

A fine France 10000 francs, Pick132d, dated '4-11-1954', numbered 'Y.7471 / 475 / 186772475', one set of staple holes.

1954

$130-200   LOCK

A fine British Guiana one dollar, Pick12c, dated '1st January, 1942', numbered 'G3 03589'.

1942

$150-200   LOCK

A fine early Hibernian Bank one pound token, dated '10 July 1826', numbered '50', signed twice on back, cancelled with ink 'x' over clerk and cashier's signatures.

1826

$1,200-1,300   WHYT

A Republic of Ireland ten dollar bond, numbered '1500-1001', printed signature of John O'Mahony, printed by The Continental Bank Note Printing Company of New York.

These bonds were issued in America to fund the Fenian Rising of 1867 and were 'redeemable six months after the acknowledgement of the Independence of the Irish Nation'. They were redeemed almost 80 years later when Eamon De Valera called the Fenian bonds in. Any outstanding bonds were thereafter valued as collectibles, which today occasionally show up at auction.

$550-650   WHYT

A Bank of Ireland Dublin one pound note, dated '11 October 1917', numbered '1 / 92 36709', printed signature of Baskin.

1917

$400-450   WHYT

A Currency Commission Consolidated Banknote, 'Ploughman' Northern Bank five pounds, dated '8-5-31', numbered '01EK 039558', signed 'Stewart', small edge tear.

1931

$2,500-3,000   WHYT

A Currency Commission Consolidated Banknote, 'Ploughman' National Bank ten pounds, dated '2-10-31', numbered '01NT032597', signed 'Russell', some edge tears with some neatly glued, '900' written on back.
1931
$1,500-2,000   **WHYT**

A fine Currency Commission Consolidated Banknote, Bank of Ireland 'Ploughman' one pound, dated '6-9-37', numbered '75BA 048195/6', signed 'Gargan'.
1937
$900-1,100   **WHYT**

A fine Mahon five pounds, B215, dated '28 May 1927', numbered '032H 74321'.
1927
$450-500   **LOCK**

A Mali 1000 francs, Pick13b, numbered 'H.16 / 50428 / 038250428'.
$90-100   **LOCK**

A Palestine one pound, Pick7c, numbered '0759052', dated '20th April 1939', original.
1939
$850-900   **LOCK**

A Sarawak one dollar, Pick20, dated '1st January 1935', numbered 'A3 108,144', one small edge nick.
1935
$150-200   **LOCK**

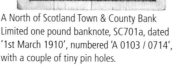

A North of Scotland Town & County Bank Limited one pound banknote, SC701a, dated '1st March 1910', numbered 'A 0103 / 0714', with a couple of tiny pin holes.
1910
$450-550   **LOCK**

A National Bank of Scotland one pound, SC501b, dated '11th November, 1916', numbered 'J694-173'.
1916
$450-500   **LOCK**

A Bahr & Proschild bisque-head doll, with fixed glass eyes, pierced ears, mohair wig, jointed composition body, marked '212'.

11in (28cm) high

$550-650   HT

A Belton bisque-shoulder-head doll, with fixed glass eyes, mohair wig, kid body with bisque hands.

11in (28cm) high

$650-750   HT

A CLOSER LOOK AT A MADAME BARROIS DOLL

This doll was made by Madame Barrois, a maker of French china and bisque dolls, active c1844-77.

The body is made of kid leather, the head of bisque. She has fixed blue glass eyes, a closed mouth and a light brown mohair wig.

Around her neck, the doll wears a cross, a pendant miniature and a pair of spectacles. That these small accessories are still in tact adds to the value.

She wears a cream silk and lace gown and bonnet. The clothing is highly detailed and ornate, mirroring 19thC Parisian fashions.

A Madame Barrois bisque-shoulder-head doll.

23in (58.5cm) high

$1,500-2,000   HT

A bisque-socket-head doll, with glass sleeping eyes, open mouth with teeth, on a original fully jointed wood and composition body, with mohair wig, the head incised '1078 Germany SIMON & HALBIG S&H 15 1/2', in original box, retaining label, marked as a 'C.M. Bergmann' doll.

Charles M. Bergmann ran a German doll company in the early 20thC. The dolls were chiefly modeled as children, with open mouths, sleepy eyes and jointed bodies. Bergmann specialized in doll bodies and some heads were provided by other companies, such as Simon & Halbig.

34in (86cm) high

$600-750   BER

A C.M. Bergmann bisque-socket-head doll, with glass sleeping eyes, open mouth with teeth, on fully jointed composition body, original human hair wig, the head incised 'C.M. Bergmann Simon Halbig'.

25in (64cm) high

$350-400   BER

A Demalcol 'googly eye' doll, mold no.5/0.

9in (23cm) high

$600-650   PW

A French-type DEP girl doll, with molded teeth, pierced ears sleeping eyes and jointed body, with Jumeau shoes marked 'Paris Deposé' with bee, head impressed 'DEP 9', head damaged.

24in (61cm) high

$350-400   BRI

A Grace and Putnam baby doll, with sleeping eyes, shrinkage cracks to the hands.

14.25in (36cm) high

$200-250   PW

A Heubach Koppelsdorf musical doll, 251.2/0, holding a baton and sheet of music.

24in (61cm) high

$2,000-2,500   JN

A Gebruder Heubach bisque-head boy character doll, with glass sleeping eyes, open mouth and teeth, brown mohair wig, jointed composition limbs and body, marked '10532'.

22in (56cm) high

$450-550   HT

QUICK REFERENCE - JUMEAU

- Jumeau was founded near Paris, France, in the 1840s by Pierre-François Jumeau (1811-95) and Louis-Desire Belton.
- It designed and manufactured high-end bisque dolls with elegant and detailed clothing. Its dolls were highly acclaimed, receiving medals at the 1851 London Great Exhibition and the 1878 Exposition Universelle.
- Jumeau dolls remain extremely popular with collectors today and those with good condition original costumes can fetch very high prices.

A Jumeau head character doll, with fixed glass eyes, closed mouth, pierced ears, mohair wig, jointed composition limbs and body, marked 'DEP'.

26in (66cm) high

$2,000-2,500   **HT**

A Kammer & Reinhardt 117n bisque-head character doll, in original clothes, with weighted glass eyes, open mouth and teeth, on a jointed wood and composition body, lacks one finger.

c1910   *23in (59cm) high*

$600-750   **C&T**

QUICK REFERENCE - KESTNER

- Kestner & Co. was founded in 1816 in Thuringia, Germany, by Johannes Daniel Kestner. The company was later taken over by his grandson, Adolphe Kestner.
- It was known for its child dolls, with high quality bisque heads, mohair wigs and blown-glass sleeping eyes. The comparatively rare '200' series, produced c1910, are especially sought after by collectors.
- Kestner dolls were especially popular in the USA, where they were distributed by George Borgfeldt.
- Kestner merged with Kammer & Reinhardt in the 1930s.

A Kestner 192 bisque-head girl doll, with weighted glass eyes, open mouth, upper teeth, later brown wig, on a jointed wood and composition body, teeth repaired, body incorrect.

c1910   *26in (66cm) high*

$200-250   **C&T**

QUICK REFERENCE - KAMMER & REINHARDT

- Kammer & Reinhardt was founded in Waltershausen, Germany, in 1886, by designer Ernest Kammer and entrepreneur Franz Reinhardt.
- Kammer designed the heads until his death in 1901, when Simon & Halbig took over, working from Kammer's designs.
- In 1909-14, Kammer & Reinhardt produced popular character dolls, with painted eyes, closed mouths and mohair wigs. The character child dolls are especially collectible.
- Kammer & Reinhardt merged with Kestner in the 1930s.

A Kammer & Reinhardt 115/A bisque-head character doll, with weighted glass eyes, closed mouth, on a jointed wood and composition toddler body, hairline crack to left side of face.

c1910   *20in (51cm) high*

$350-400   **C&T**

A Kestner bisque-head doll, with glass sleeping eyes, closed mouth, mohair wig, jointed composition limbs and body, marked '14'.

21in (52.5cm) high

$2,000-2,500   **HT**

A Kestner bisque-head doll, with glass sleeping eyes, open mouth and teeth, mohair wig, double-jointed composition limbs and body, marked '167'.

18in (45.5cm) high

$400-450   **HT**

An early 20thC bisque-head doll, attributed to Kestner, with fixed open eyes.

37in (94cm) high

$550-600   **PW**

A Kestner bisque-head doll, with glass sleeping eyes, open mouth and teeth, pierced ears, mohair wig, jointed composition limbs and body, marked '192'.

30in (76cm) high

$900-1,100   **HT**

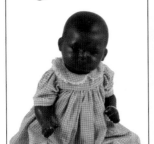

An early 20thC French bisque doll automaton group, the doll incised 'France JB' (possibly Limoges), modeled revealing a further bisque doll's head, winding key to the side.

16.25in (41cm) high

$550-650   BELL

QUICK REFERENCE - ARMAND MARSEILLE

- Armand Marseille was founded in Thuringia, Germany, in 1885 by Armand Marseille (1856-1925). The company manufactured bisque dolls heads until the 1930s.
- The Armand Marseille factory was very prolific, producing doll heads of varying quality, ranging from the high-end to the more commercial. In 1900-30 it was producing nearly 1,000 doll heads every day. The doll bodies were brought in from other manufacturers.
- Marseille dolls remain popular with collectors, although in general prices have fallen. As it is a well-known maker and produced a large quantity of dolls, it is worth examining condition carefully. Look for clean, undamaged heads and high quality examples. To fetch the highest price, dolls should be in mint condition, with their original clothes.

An Armand Marseille bisque-head lady doll, with glass sleeping eyes, closed mouth, mohair wig, composition body and limbs, marked 'M.H. A300M 13/OX'.

8.5in (21.5cm) high

$550-650   HT

A bisque-shoulder-head boy doll, with glass stationary eyes, on leather body, the head incised 'AM 370'.

20in (50cm) high

$80-100   BER

An Armand Marseille 341 black bisque-head 'Dream' baby doll, with weighted glass eyes, closed mouth, on a composition baby body.

c1910   *19in (48cm) high*

$200-250   C&T

An Armand Marseille oriental doll, with cloth body and sleeping eyes, mold no.353/372, signs of age to costume.

15in (38cm) high

$550-600   PW

An Armand Marseille 'Ellar Star' oriental doll, with sleeping eyes, mold no.1/2K, minor chips to neck.

13.5in (34cm) high

$350-400   PW

An Armand Marseille 'googly eye' doll, mold no.323 4/0, small chip to the neck.

8.75in (22cm) high

$600-650   PW

An Armand Marseille oriental baby doll, with sleeping eyes, head marked '353/2K', small chips to fingers and toes.

10.25in (26cm) high

$450-550   PW

A Max Rader bisque-head doll, with glass sleeping eyes, open mouth and teeth, pierced ears, mohair wig, jointed composition limbs and body, marked '5050.14 R. DEP'.

30in (76cm) high

$400-450   HT

DOLLS

A German character boy doll, probably Bruno Schmidt, with glass sleeping eyes, closed mouth, molded hair, jointed composition limbs and body, marked '2048'.

20in (51cm) high

$400-450   HT

An early 20thC German bisque-head Marot jester doll, possibly Schoenau & Hoffmeister, with fixed glass eyes and closed mouth, with internal musical movement, unsigned.

13.5in (34.5cm) high

$60-80   BELL

A Simon & Halbig bisque-head doll, with fixed glass eyes, open mouth and teeth, pierced ears, mohair wig, jointed composition limbs and body, marked '1079 17 S & H DEP'.

Simon & Halbig was one of the most prolific manufacturers of bisque shoulder-heads in the 19thC and early 20thC. It supplied bisque heads to other well-known doll companies, such as Kammer & Reinhardt and Jumeau.

38in (96.5cm) high

$650-750   HT

A Simon & Halbig bisque-head doll, with glass sleeping eyes, open mouth and teeth, pierced ears, mohair wig, jointed composition limbs and body, marked '1339 S & H, LLS, 15'.

34in (86.5cm) high

$600-650   HT

A Nippon bisque-head oriental baby doll, possibly Tajimi Japanese, with weighted glass eyes, open mouth with molded tongue and teeth, painted features, real hair wig, on a five-piece bent limb composition body.

c1920   12.5in (32cm) high

$350-400   C&T

A German bisque-head doll, with painted features, sleeping glass eyes, open mouth with teeth, trembling tongue, head stamped '55 CP'

21.75in (55cm) high

$100-130   WHP

An English bisque-head girl doll, stamped 'Regina D P 56-12' and 'British Made', composition bent limbs, original lace dress and bonnet.

23.25in (59cm) high

$550-650   KEY

A Continental bisque-head automaton violin-playing doll, the violin neck detached from the body of the violin, the mechanism worked by pressing the tummy, the head impressed '103 I'.

13.25in (34cm) high

$550-650   GWA

A German bisque-head 'Three Faces' doll with fixed glass eyes, the faces depicting smiling, crying and sleeping, mohair wig, turned wood knob to top of head, composition arms, compressed cardboard body and legs.

14in (35.5cm) high

$400-450   HT

An original Barbie 850 blonde Bubblecut Doll, in original Barbie Doll Case, with clothing and accessories, with the original Barbie 'doll case' retailers' tag.

Barbie dolls have been produced by Mattel Inc. since 1959.
c1962
$900-1,000   **LSK**

A Gotz plastic headed doll, with 'Gotz' stamp to back, '452-20' stamped to back of neck and 'Lison' to back of shoulders, original wig and glass eyes, open mouth.
22.5in (57cm) high
$80-100   **LOC**

A 1960s Faerie Glen Sally doll, in original outfit.
7.5in (19cm) high
$40-70   **DSC**

A 1960s Faerie Glen Tonie doll, in original outfit.
7.5in (19cm) high
$40-70   **DSC**

A Gotz doll, stamped back of head 'Carlos 372-22', with padded stuffed body, plastic hands and head.
$50-70   **LOC**

A 1970s Flair Havoc Superagent doll.
9in (23cm) high
$50-80   **DSC**

A small 1950s Pedigree costume doll.

Pedigree dolls were produced by Lines Brothers (later known as Tri-ang). Lines Brothers' first composition dolls were released in 1937, and the name Pedigree was registered in the early 1940s. Plastic Pedigree dolls were released after World War II, and soon became one of the most important doll ranges in the UK.
7in (18cm) high
$20-30   **DSC**

A Kammer & Reinhardt celluloid doll, model no.728, with flirty eyes and open mouth, with a broken voice box, marked, 'K & R', '728/9', 'Germany', '50/54'.
22in (56cm) high
$80-100   **LC**

A Kammer & Reinhardt 717 celluloid doll, with weighted glass eyes, open mouth with teeth, on a fully jointed wood and composition 'flapper-style' body, lacks one finger.
c1915   *16in (41cm) high*
$130-200   **C&T**

A small 1950s Pedigree costume doll, boxed.
7in (18cm) high
$20-30   **DSC**

A 1950s Pedigree hard plastic black toddler doll.

20in (51cm) high

$100-130   DSC

A 1960s Pedigree Paul, ref.13MPS, in original box with stand and Sindy set booklet.

Paul was Sindy's boyfriend.

$250-350   C&T

QUICK REFERENCE - SASHA DOLLS

- Sasha dolls are named after their designer, Sasha Morgenthaler (1893-1975). The dolls were produced by the German company Götz in 1965-69 and 1995-2001, and by the British company Trenden in 1966-86.
- Early Sasha dolls, many of which were painted by hand, are rarest and most sought-after. For all Sasha dolls, condition is vital. A playworn Sasha doll will typically fetch less than $70.
- Sasha dolls are very detailed and come in a wide variety of different clothes. They are known for their distinct facial expressions, which differ greatly from the fixed smiles of many other mid to late 20thC plastic dolls.

A 1960s Pedigree Sindy in 'Weekenders', ref.12GSS Auburn, in original box with stand and 'Heart Tokens' leaflet.

Sindy was released by Pedigree in 1963 to compete with Mattel's popular Barbie doll, and was the best-selling toy in the UK in 1968 and 1970. Good condition boxed Sindy dolls from the 1960s-70s are increasingly sought after, but do not tend to fetch the high prices of early Barbie dolls.

$550-600   C&T

A Sasha 'Brunette', with brown painted eyes with painted lashes and features, in tube box.

c1968

$350-400   C&T

A 1980s Pedigree Sindy Pop Star, complete with outfit including belt, headband, guitar and organ.

$60-100   DSC

A Sasha 'Gregor', with painted eyes, pale painted lips.

c1968

$600-750   C&T

A Sasha 'Gregor', with painted eyes and features, in tube box.

c1968

$250-300   C&T

A Sasha Baby, with painted eyes and features, boxed with inner packing and leaflet.

c1970

$100-130   C&T

A large 1930s Ideal composition Shirley Temple doll, USA, with side glancing hazel eyes, lashes and painted feather brows, open mouth with upper teeth and original blonde wig, on a five piece body and wearing original dress with badge, underclothes, socks and shoes.

26in (66cm) high

$400-550   **C&T**

A large 1930s 241 composition 'Dream' baby, German, with weighted eyes, open mouth and painted hair.

24in (61cm) high

$50-70   **C&T**

A 1930s Lenci felt 'Farm Girl' doll, the head with painted side-glancing brown eyes, shaded lips and shoulder length auburn hair, swivel head and jointed at shoulders and hips, wearing original green felt dungarees with white shirt, brown sandals and cloth hat, some mottling to face.

For Lenci ceramics, see page 101.

17in (43cm) high

$100-150   **C&T**

A composition doll, in original clothes to celebrate the Queen's Coronation in 1953, the Steiner Koppelsdorf head with weighted blue eyes, open mouth, upper teeth and brown wig, on a fully jointed wood and composition body.

This doll was dressed for the Coronation of Queen Elizabeth and was displayed in the window of the Mary Lee ladies dress shop in Tunbridge Wells. The clothes were made in the shop workroom.

c1953   *25in (64cm) high*

$100-160   **C&T**

A Lenci felt girl doll, 'Charlotte', no.648 of a limited edition of 999, with painted features, wearing elaborate dress and felt hat and shoes, boxed with certificate.

1985   *19.75in (50cm) high*

$100-150   **C&T**

A Lenci felt girl doll, 'Franca', no.1003 of a limited edition of 1999, with painted features, wearing blue felt dress, hat and shoes, boxed with certificate.

1985   *13in (33cm) high*

$60-100   **C&T**

A pair of American Little Lulu dolls, by Marge, of stuffed cloth, each with three original plastic purses, comprising one red pictorial lettered 'Little Lulu By Marge', one green and one transparent containing toy cosmetics, faces slightly dusty.

It is unusual to find two such Little Lulu dolls complete with their accessories.

c1944   *14in (36cm) long*

$130-200   **DW**

QUICK REFERENCE - BLISS

The R. Bliss Manufacturing Company was established in 1832 in Pawtucket, Rhode Island by Rufus Bliss (1802-80), primarily as producers of wooden screws and clamps for cabinet-making. It was not until the 1870s-80s that Bliss began to produce the high-quality lithographed paper-on-wood dolls' houses it became famous for. Most architectural features, such as carpets, window frames and so on, were illustrated on the lithographs rather than carved from wood. Bliss dolls' houses are known for their high quality and bright colors. Bliss shut down in the 1930s.

A Bliss dolls' house, two rooms on each side with side openings, roof top deck, Bliss Mfg paper litho over wood, minor wrinkling to the lithograph, one chimney missing.

21in (53.5cm) high

$1,000-1,600   **BER**

A lithographed paper-on-wood dolls' house, attributed to Bliss, lacking front porch railing section and one return above the front window, some losses to the interior carpet paper.

19in (48.5cm) high

$650-800   **POOK**

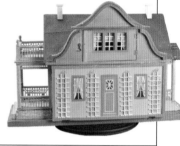

A Gottschalk red roof dolls' house and garden, with a gambrel roof with side porch, balcony and side entrance, front drops down to expose interior of one room with staircase and landing, attic panel opening to reveal a furnished bedroom.

16in (40.5cm) high

$2,000-2,500   **BER**

A Gottschalk red roof dolls' house, with floral topped balconies, an attic room and five interior rooms, electrified retaining mostly original paint, lacking chimneys and front stairs, interior missing most papers.

26in (66cm) wide

$800-950   **POOK**

An early folk art two-room dolls' house, with a front porch with tapered columns, colored and clear glass window panels, brick chimney and carved wood faux bricks and lattice foundation, the rear of the house open, revealing two rooms and an open attic space.

c1900   *30in (76cm) high*

$450-600   **POOK**

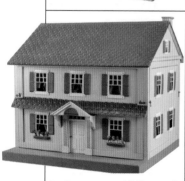

A yellow two story dolls' house, of pressboard construction.

23.5in (59.5cm) high

$400-550   **BER**

Judith Picks

What little girl wouldn't have loved a dolls' house like this one? With its bright colors and unique features, it would have been a joy to play with. It has a balcony and wrap-around porch outside, and a living room, bedroom and attic within. This is a particularly unusual Bliss dolls' house due to the turrets, tables and turned posts. Usually on a Bliss dolls' houses, such architectural features would have been illustrated on the lithographed paper instead. This would have been a very expensive toy at the time.

A rare Bliss lithographed dolls' house.

30in (76cm) high

$2,000-2,500   **BER**

An early 20thC architectural painted wood two-story dolls' house, home made, with glass windows and elaborate rooftop pergolas, electrified with a center light socket, with seven opening doors.

35in (89cm) high

$400-550   **POOK**

An English dolls' house, opening at back in three sections and to the side, with four rooms with hallway and landing, mostly original wall and floor coverings.

c1930   *39in (99cm) high*

$150-200   **C&T**

A Scottish dolls' house, the exterior of painted wood red brick, with façade in three sections with glass fronted door with etched Scotsman in kilt, with ten glazed windows with etched glass, one depicting scene of Edinburgh, all rooms with original papers, and furnished throughout, the dining room including table and four red upholstered chairs, wooden fireplace and surround, writing desk, kitchen with tiled floor, dressers, copper ware, cups, jugs, coffee grinder and more, Salon with chaise longue, display cabinet, piano, fireplace and mantle, two attic rooms with beds, dressing table, chest of drawers, wardrobe and miniature toys.

c1890   *39.25in (100cm) wide*

$6,500-8,000   **C&T**

An English Gothic dolls' house, 'The Dolls Castle', the front opening in one wing to four rooms on two levels, with remains of some original papers, the interior comprising a painted tinplate bath, a wash stand, a kitchen dresser, a table, chairs, a piano, a bed, a cooking range and six bisque-head dolls.

A letter dated 1819 was found in this house.

c1819   *30in (76cm) high*

$550-650   **BELL**

A terraced dolls' house, with white painted brickwork and six windows.

16in (40.5cm) wide

$800-950   **APAR**

A mid-19thC open-fronted dolls' house, 'The Spanish House', rooms retaining their original papers and finishes, one room with landscapes viewed through Gothic arches, the kitchen with original range, shelving and well.

38.75in (98.5cm) high

$400-550   **CHOR**

CHRISTOPHER DRESSER

QUICK REFERENCE - CHRISTOPHER DRESSER

- Christopher Dresser (1834-1904) was born in Glasgow and trained at the Government School of Design in London. He studied to be a botanist but from the 1860s chiefly focused on his work as a designer.
- He is often considered one of the first industrial designers. He aimed to make high quality and beautifully designed products available to the widest audience possible. His designs were intended for mass commercial production, available to many manufacturers and often made with inexpensive materials, such as silver-plate rather than silver.
- Dresser worked with a large number of manufacturers, designing in a range of materials. Amongst others, he designed metal and silverware for Coalbrookdale, Elkington and Hukin & Heath, ceramics for Linthorpe and Minton, and glass for James Couper & Sons.
- His designs were functional and stylized, and combined Victorian technology with traditions from a variety of cultures. He was especially inspired by Japanese design, and spent several months in Japan in 1876-77 on commission from Tiffany & Co. Despite being created over 100 years ago, his designs still look remarkably 'modern' today.

An Elkington & Co. silver-plate cruet stand, by Christopher Dresser, with glass pepper pot, mustard pot and salt, stamped maker's marks 'ELKINGTON & CO. / 17286'.

c1880   *5in (12.5cm) high*

$650-800   **L&T**

A Hukin & Heath silver-plate bon-bon dish, by Christopher Dresser, with a woven wicker-covered handle, stamped maker's marks 'H&H / 2223 / DESIGNED BY DR. C DRESSER'.

c1880   *8.25in (21cm) wide*

$550-650   **L&T**

A Hukin & Heath silver-plate double bon-bon dish, by Christopher Dresser, stamped marks 'H&H / 2523'.

c1880   *10.75in (27.5cm) high*

$2,000-2,500   **L&T**

A Hukin & Heath electroplated toast rack, by Christopher Dresser, stamped marks to base 'H&H / 2556', with registration mark.

c1880   *5.5in (14cm) wide*

$1,300-1,600   **L&T**

A Hukin & Heath silver-plate cruet stand, attributed to Christopher Dresser, stamped maker's marks 'H&H / 2881'.

c1880   *7.75in (19.5cm) long*

$350-400   **L&T**

A Hukin & Heath oak and silver-plate mounted salad bowl and servers, attributed to Christopher Dresser, stamped maker's marks 'H&H / 2447'.

c1880   *13.75in (35cm) wide*

$900-1,100   **L&T**

A Hukin & Heath silver-plated sugar basin, by Christopher Dresser, with inscription 'CBC Sports presented to J. Lewis, June 1884'.

              6.5in (16.5cm) long

$150-200   **APAR**

A Linthorpe pottery vase, by Christopher Dresser, impressed mark with faint signature mark and Henry Tooth monogram, restored.

Henry Tooth ran Linthorpe Pottery in 1879-82, before leaving to found Bretby Art Pottery. During this time, most Linthorpe wares were marked to the bottom with his monogram, a 'H' and 'T' combined into one symbol.

8.75in (22.5cm) high

$250-350   FLD

A Linthorpe pottery vase, by Christopher Dresser, impressed signature mark and Henry Tooth monogram, some damage.

6.25in (16cm) high

$200-250   FLD

A Linthorpe pottery vase, by Christopher Dresser, shape 157, two impressed signature marks and Henry Tooth monogram.

12.25in (31cm) high

$300-400   FLD

A pair of Linthorpe Art Pottery vases, attributed to Christopher Dresser, unmarked.

9.5in (24cm) high

$60-100   HAN

A pair of Aesthetic Movement Minton faux cloisonné porcelain vases, probably from a design by Christopher Dresser, faint impressed marks, hair crack to one, both with crazing.

7.75in (19.5cm) high

$1,000-1,300   BE

A Linthorpe Art Pottery miniature vase, by Christopher Dresser, incised '1631'.

7in (18cm) high

$40-50   HAN

An Aesthetic Movement Minton Persian bottle vase, by Christopher Dresser, on integrated stand, unmarked.

8.5in (21.5cm) high

$350-400   HAN

An Aesthetic Movement Minton tile, by Christopher Dresser, with raised marks.

The British Museum catalogs this tile design as by Christopher Dresser, also known as 'Dresser's Tomtits' or 'Little Birds', and it is recorded in the 1885 Minton tile catalog.

c1880   7.75in (20cm) square

$160-220   HAN

LATER MINTON COMPANY NAMES

Herbert Minton and Co., c1847-62
Minton, c1862-72
Mintons Ltd., c1873-1951
Minton, c1951-68
Mintons, 1968+

ENAMELS

QUICK REFERENCE - MOORCROFT ENAMELS

- In 1998, Moorcroft (see pages 107-118) acquired Kingsley Enamels Ltd., a family company founded in 1904 with a history in decorative metalwork.
- Moorcroft and Kingsley joined together to produce a range of handpainted elegant enamel items, including vases, boxes, tins and jars. Many items were made to mirror Moorcroft ceramics in shape and pattern.
- Patterns were created by Moorcroft designers, as well as by Elliot Hall, great-grandson of the founder of Kingsley Enamels. Hall went on to found his own company, Elliot Hall Enamels, after the closure of Moorcroft Enamels in 2006.
- Moorcroft Enamels are relatively rare, as they were in production for less than eight years.

A Moorcroft Enamels box, decorated with a stylized crane, printed mark, painted 'Trial A. Rose 11.12.02'.

2in (5cm) long

$200-250   FLD

A Moorcroft Enamels box, decorated with handpainted Amazonian animals, printed mark.

2.25in (6cm) long

$350-400   FLD

A Moorcroft Enamels vase and cover, 'Making Tracks' pattern, designed by Fiona Bakewell.

2.75in (7cm) high

$150-200   FLD

A Moorcroft Enamels box, 'Pansy' pattern, printed marks, painted 'Trial 16.12.98'.

2.25in (5.5cm) diam

$200-250   FLD

A Moorcroft Enamels box, 'Peacock' pattern, designed by Rachel Bishop, printed marks.

2in (5cm) diam

$150-200   FLD

A Moorcroft Enamels vase and cover, 'Samburu Giraffe' pattern, designed by Anji Davenport, marked as a second.

2.75in (7cm) high

$200-250   FLD

A Moorcroft Enamels vase, 'Shells' pattern, designed by Peter Graves, printed marks.

1.75in (4.5cm) high

$60-100   FLD

A CLOSER LOOK AT A CHINESE FAN

This Cantonese brisé fan has 26 sticks, all finely carved and pierced.

The fan has three painted panels, each displaying a European landscape. The middle depicts a woman seated in a garden surrounded by flowers.

The front stick is ornately carved, so that the fan is a decorative object both open and closed.

The panels have losses to their painted borders, but the fine detail and early date of this fan assures the price.

A late 18thC Chinese Cantonese brisé 26-stick fan.

Brisé is French for 'broken'. While other fans are held together by a pleated leaf or rivet, on brisé fans the sticks are entirely separate, held together by a pin and fabric band or ribbon.

8in (20.5cm) wide

$2,500-3,500   LA

A Cantonese brisé fan, the leaf painted with figures, their faces ivory and betwen precious objects borders, framed and glazed.

c1840   *open 20in (51cm) wide*

$900-1,000   SWO

A 19thC Chinese fan, with carved ivory guards, the silk embroidered with a floral spray and three birds in flight, with a fitted box.

sticks 12.25in (31cm) long

$900-1,100   LA

A 19thC Cantonese double-side carved ivory brisé fan, the leaves with figures in a pagoda landscape, with similar decorated guards.

7.5in (19cm) long

$900-1,000   BE

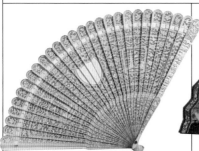

A 19thC Cantonese single-side carved ivory brisé fan, with central shield-shaped cartouche, trailing foliage and pagoda vistas, with solid guards decorated with pagoda landscapes.

10.5in (26.5cm) long

$2,000-2,500   BE

A late 19thC 'Mandarin Hundred Faces' fan, with black lacquer and gilt-guards and sticks decorated with figures, the mount painted with courtly figures in buildings, the figures with ivory faces and silk clothing.

guards 11in (28cm) long

$650-800   APAR

A Cantonese export ivory fan, painted on paper with Oriental figures within a temple, with ivory faces, the ivory sticks and guards carved and pierced with figures, with wooden case.

c1900   *sticks 12.25in (31cm) long*

$1,000-1,200   BELL

FANS

- There is evidence of fans from as early as around 3000 BC. The Greeks and Romans used fixed fans as cooling devices and fans are mentioned in ancient Chinese myths.
- The first folding fans were developed in China and Japan and were brought to Europe by Portuguese traders in the early 16thC.
- They became popular in the 17thC and by the beginning of the 18thC were being made throughout Europe. Increasing numbers were also imported from China. The introduction of printed fans alongside carved and painted fans made fans cheaper and more widely available than previously. Fans continued to be popular throughout the 19thC and early 20thC.
- While fans are no longer a common fashion accessory today, antique and vintage fans are popular with many collectors and can often display high levels of craftsmanship.

A late 18thC painted bone fan, decorated with Mercury holding his caduceus and a purse, with two ladies, mounted in a gilt case.

14.5in (37cm) wide

$650-750   **WW**

A late 18thC European mother-of-pearl silvered and gilt-highlighted 20-stick fan, sticks with trophies and a painted paper panel depicting courting couples, one stick damaged.

11.75in (30cm) long

$250-350   **KEY**

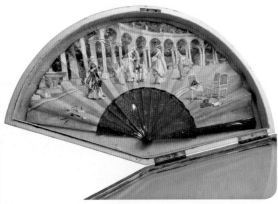

A late 18thC fan, with carved and pierced tortoiseshell sticks and guards, the paper leaf handpainted with figures, in a gilt-glazed frame.

open 23.25in (59cm) wide

$800-850   **DA&H**

A late 18thC to early 19thC Continental carved ivory fan, the paper leaf with Mother Nature and two panels of young lovers, with pierced ivory sticks decorated with figures and urns, the guards decorated with musical trophies and figures.

10.25in (26cm) long

$900-1,100   **BE**

A late 18thC to early 19thC French ivory and painted brisé fan, painted in gouache with a classical Roman scene, the guards and sticks carved and pierced with figures, buildings, flowers and latticework, in case.

20in (51cm) wide

$550-600   **BE**

A late 18thC to early 19thC French ivory and painted fan, with carved and painted ivory and mother-of-pearl guards and sticks, the leaf painted in gouache with lovers, some damage, in glazed case.

19.25in (49cm) wide

$300-350   **BE**

A late 18thC to early 19thC Italian painted chicken-skin Grand Tour fan, with horn sticks and guards, the guard with an enamel clock dial, the fan painted in gouache with the Roman Forum, flanked by eagles and ribbon tied swags and urns, in a glazed case.

12.5in (31.5cm) wide

$2,500-3,000 **WW**

A Regency period ivory fan, with silk leaf with applied sequins, with inlaid and gilt sticks and similar guards.

7.5in (19cm) long

$200-250 **BE**

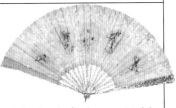

A 19thC bone and gilt decorated fan, the paper leaf decorated with young lovers, the sticks decorated with garlands, with similar decorated guards.

8.5in (21.5cm) long

$200-250 **BE**

A French handpainted paper fan, the watercolor leaf with a pastoral landscape scene depicting figures, dated and indistinctly inscribed, mounted on pierced bone sticks.

1861 *10.5in (27cm) long*

$130-200 **DW**

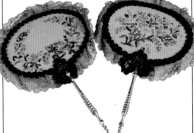

A late 19thC to early 20thC carved and pierced bone 18-stick fan, decorated with mirrored sequins and tri-color gilt highlights, with feather fringing.

10.5in (26.5cm) long

$150-200 **KEY**

A pair of early 20thC embroidered fans, with wooden gilt handles.

15.75in (40cm) long

$80-100 **LOCK**

A Brussels lace fan, the floral gauze painted the four seasons with decorative mother-of-pearl sticks, in a Duvelleroy case, some discoloration.

Provenance: Mary E. Chamberlain, née Endicott, daughter of William Endicott, US Secretary of War, and wife of Joseph Chamberlain, British Politician and Statesman.

14.25in (36cm) long

$550-650 **CHOR**

A Victorian two-piece mourning dress, the bodice with hook and eye-fastening, embroidered with ruched panels, beadwork and sequins.

size 2

$250-300 **FLD**

An Edwardian-style lady's satin evening gown, with small train, with a black bead work on voile overlay with beadwork and fringing to the sleeves and hem.

size 4

$200-250 **FLD**

A 1920s lady's satin evening dress, with beadwork panels.

size 6

$80-100 **FLD**

A 1920s lady's chiffon cocktail dress, with beadwork panels to the bodice and crosshatch beadwork to the skirt.

size 4

$150-250 **FLD**

A 1930s-40s lady's crepe dress and bolero jacket, with embroidered detailing.

size 4

$40-50 **FLD**

A 1950s lady's satin Chinese bed jacket, embroidered with dragon birds and flowers, with fish scale bands to the hem and cuffs.

$450-550 **FLD**

A 1950s brocade wedding dress, with a faint gold pattern and bow detail to the waist.

size 2

$40-50 **FLD**

A Burberry women's classic full-length trench coat, with a notched lapel collar, and buttoned epaulettes.

size 6

$450-550   **FELL**

An Belstaff black leather biker jacket, with silver-tone hardware, engraved stud embellishments, labelled 'Belstaff, size 44'.

size 8

$450-550   **FELL**

A Hermès mustard yellow woollen two-piece outfit, labelled 'Hermès size 40'.

size 6

$60-100   **FELL**

A Hermès women's green wool cashmere jacket, with tan leather trim, lined with silk embossed with maker's 'H' logo, labelled 'Hermès Paris'.

28in (71cm) long size 8

$600-650   **FELL**

A 1970s Horrockses floral maxi dress, zip fastening with button detailing to the front, with original matching belt, labelled.

size 8-10

$40-50   **FLD**

A Stella McCartney girl's cotton military-style jacket, labelled 'Stella McCartney Kids, size 14 years', with maker's original tags attached.

18in (45.5cm) long

$60-80   **FELL**

A long 20thC Paisley coat, hand-made machine-sewn unstructured coat utilizing earlier black and gray Paisley shawl.

48in (122cm) long

$200-250   **DW**

A vintage Valentino two-piece outfit, comprising a crinkled black satin fitted jacket with front button fastening and a waist belt, and a matching knee-length pencil skirt, labelled 'Valentino Night', no obvious signs of wear.

size 6

$130-200   **FELL**

An Alexander Wang embossed crocodile sleeveless fitted top, 'labelled Alexander Wang, size 6', original labels attached.

size 4

$90-120   **FELL**

A 9ct gold compact, hallmarks for Birmingham, lacking mirror, some surface scratches and wear.

1918   *2.25in (6cm) long 1.64oz*

$600-650   **FELL**

An Art Deco silver and enameled compact, by Page, Keen and Page, Birmingham, with applied Royal Navy coronet.

1927   *2in (5cm) diam 1.79oz*

$90-120   **HAN**

An Art Deco silver and enameled compact, applied marcasite and carved coral, import marks for London.

1934   *3in (7.5cm) long 3.29oz*

$130-200   **HAN**

A 1940s Crisford and Norris enameled silver compact.

1946   *3.25in (8cm) diam 4.55oz*

$200-250   **HAN**

A silver powder compact, enameled with cock pheasant, Birmingham.

1961

$300-400   **BRI**

A Cartier enamel compact, decorated with birds amongst scrolls, with three old cut diamonds to the thumb piece, enclosing a mirror and pad inscribed 'Cartier'.

2.75in (7cm) square

$1,300-2,000   **APAR**

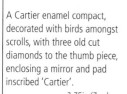

A Continental compact, with engine-turned decoration and green guilloche enamel border, marked 'sterling silver'.

2.25in (5.5cm) diam

$200-250   **FELL**

An Austrian Art Deco silver and Bakelite compact, marked for 900 standard.

2in (5cm) wide 2oz

$130-200   **HAN**

A Cartier 'Must De Cartier' silk scarf, decorated with gold-tone chains and burgundy belts.

33in (84cm) long

$200-250   **FELL**

A Gucci silk scarf, with autumnal leaves on a black background, with maker's label and envelope cover.

34.75in (88cm) wide

$200-250   **FELL**

A Gucci silk scarf, with a floral design, lightly discolored.

34.75in (88cm) long

$60-80   **FELL**

A Hermès 'La Présentation' silk scarf, designed by Christiane Vauzelles, featuring four show horses.

issued 1978   *35.5in (90cm) long*

$150-200   **FELL**

A Hermès 'Memoire d'Hermès' silk scarf, designed by Cathy Latham, with painter motif and portrait of founder Thierry Hermes.

issued 1992   *35in (89cm) long*

$400-450   **FELL**

A Hermès 'Plumes Et Grelots' jacquard silk scarf, designed by Julie Abadie, in maker's box.

issued 1995-96   *35.5in (90cm) long*

$250-350   **FELL**

A Hermès printed silk scarf, in 'Harnais Francais' pattern, in original box.

33.5in (85cm) square

$200-250   **BE**

A Hermès printed silk scarf, in 'Monaco' pattern, in original box.

33.5in (85cm) square

$200-250   **BE**

A Hermès pleated 'Plaza De Toros' scarf, designed by Hubert de Watrigant, in maker's box.

50.75in (129cm) long

$200-250   **FELL**

A Hermès 'Tresors Retrouves' silk scarf, designed by artist Annie Faivre.

35in (89cm) long

$350-450   **FELL**

An Alexander McQueen cream silk and wool blend scarf, with maker's signature and black skull print.

45in (114cm) long

$250-300   **FELL**

A Salvatore Ferragamo silk scarf, with two leopards surrounded by roses, with maker's label.

34.25in (87cm) square

$130-200   **FELL**

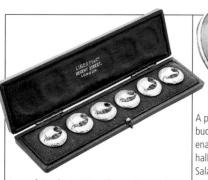

A set of six Liberty & Co. silver and enamel buttons, attributed to Jessie M. King, London, designed as a galleon, stamped 'L&Co', hallmarked for Birmingham, with original box.

1906   each 1in (2.5cm) diam
$1,000-1,200   **L&T**

A pair of silver buckles, with guilloche enamel decoration, hallmarked for Levi & Salaman, Birmingham, light general scratches, in associated Masonic box.

1909   1.75in (4.5cm) wide
$150-200   **FELL**

A half buckle, depicting Colonial Indian architecture, some panels handpainted ivory.

2.5in (6cm) long 1.15oz
$650-800   **FELL**

A mid-20thC silk top hat, manufactured by Christy's London for Austin Reed, in Austin Reed, Belfast hat box.

size 7 1/8
$200-250   **WHYT**

A 20thC novelty brass pig figural lipstick holder, the shaft sliding out to reveal the lipstick.

2in (5cm) long
$90-120   **MART**

An Art Nouveau white metal hand mirror, stamped 'TC' monogram.

7.75in (20cm) long
$150-200   **WW**

A gold mesh-link purse stamped '9'.

0.85oz
$350-400   **BE**

An Art Deco Tiffany & Co. enameled 14ct gold necessary, with rose-cut diamonds in platinum, suspends from lipstick tube, opens to mirrored interior and two hinged chambers, with original cake rouge and powder with puffs, marked.

6.25in (16cm) high 3.72oz
$5,500-6,000   **DRA**

An early 20thC Russian silver purse, maker's mark 'BB', with '835' standard marks.

8in (20.5cm) wide 17.2oz

$450-600   L&T

An Edwardian silver-mounted and tortoiseshell evening bag, by Charles and George Asprey, London, mounts applied with a crowned 'RC', probably for Lady Rachael Cornell.

1909   6.5in (16.5cm) long

$250-400   WW

An Art Deco cream enameled minaudière, set with blue paste jewels, unmarked.

7.25in (18.5cm) wide

$250-400   WW

An Art Deco lady's evening bag, with applied continental silver pierced mounts.

4.5in (11.5cm) long

$200-350   FELL

An Alexander McQueen patent leather 'Elvie' purse, serial no.204991 182054, with maker's dust bag.

15.25in (39cm) wide

$550-650   FELL

An Anya Hindmarch 'Carker' leather purse, with maker's dust bag.

13.75in (35cm) wide

$450-550   FELL

A Cartier 'Must De Cartier' crossbody purse, crafted from maker's signature Bordeaux leather.

11in (28cm) wide

$250-350   FELL

A 1980s Céline ladies leather purse, with gilt-brass mounts.

12.25in (31cm) wide

$100-130   LSK

A vintage Chanel bag, quilted black fabric trimmed with black patent leather, with dust bag.

Chanel was founded by Coco Chanel in Saumur, France, in 1883 and is still creating high-end clothes, jewelry and perfume today.

9in (23cm) wide

$350-400   MOR

A Chanel 'Medium Classic Double Flap' lambskin leather purse, serial no.14434149, with maker's dust bag and authenticity card.

10in (25.5cm) wide

$2,500-3,500   FELL

A Christian Dior 'Gaucho' leather saddle purse.

8.5in (21.5cm) wide

$200-250   FELL

A Coach leather purse with scarf, serial no.F0769-11304.

12.75in (32.5cm) wide

$100-130   FELL

A limited edition Fendi runway 'Queen' baguette snakeskin purse, with maker's dust bag.

10.75in (27cm) wide

$250-350   FELL

A 1940s Fre Mar beaded purse, with paisley design.

$80-100   HAN

A Gucci vintage 'GG Supreme Web' messenger purse, with maker's monogram coated canvas exterior.

Gucci was founded in Florence, Italy, in 1921 and remains a key designer of purses, shoes and accessories today. Vintage Gucci bags are now highly collectible.

9.75in (42.5cm) wide

$400-450   FELL

A Gucci 'Charlotte' purse, serial no.203506 203998, with maker's classic monogram canvas.

17.25in (44cm) wide

$400-450   FELL

A Hermès 'Fourre Tout' canvas purse.

16.5in (42cm) wide

$100-130   FELL

QUICK REFERENCE - HERMÈS BAGS

- Hermès was founded in 1837 and is best-known for its purses, most famously the 'Kelly', designed in the 1930s and used by Grace Kelly from 1956, and the 'Birkin', designed for actress Jane Birkin in 1984, adapted from a 1894 design.
- Hermès bags are produced in a wide variety of different leathers and skins. Depending on the bag and its material, prices can vary from under $100 to over $100,000.
- Condition can affect value considerably. Fakes are common and can be extremely good, so if in doubt it is worth taking a bag to Hermès for identification.

A Hermès black leather briefcase.

14.25in (36cm) wide

$800-1,000   L&T

An Art Deco Knoll and Pregizer silver and paste purse, marked 'KP', with import marks for London.

The German firm of Knoll and Pregizer is best known for it costume jewelry, now highly prized for its classic Art Deco styling.

c1933   *8.75in (22cm) wide*

$600-750   HAN

A Louis Vuitton 'Boulogne' purse, designed in collaboration with Takashi Murakami, original dust bag and carrier bag.

12.25in (31cm) wide

$600-750   CHEF

A Mulberry 'Lily Metallic Maxi Grain' leather purse, serial no.1425602.

Mulberry is a British lifestyle and fashion brand. It was founded in 1971 by Roger Saul and his mother Joan.

8.25in (21cm) wide

$300-400   FELL

A Mulberry yellow crocodile-style suede 'Bayswater' bag, with dust bag.

14.5in (37cm) wide

$350-400   TEN

A Salvatore Ferragamo leather 'Gancini' purse, with maker's box.

7.25in (18.5cm) wide

$80-100   FELL

A Valentino 'Nappa Petale Dome' leather purse, serial no.BF4WB083NAP2, with maker's dust bag.

13.5in (34cm) wide

$150-200   FELL

A Michael Kors leather purse, with maker's dust bag.

14.5in (37cm) wide

$200-250   FELL

A Ralph Lauren 'Ricky' leather purse, with maker's dust bag and product card.

13.75in (35cm) wide

$150-200   FELL

A Zaglani metallic green python skin purse.

16.5in (42cm) wide

$250-350   FELL

A Gucci vintage 'GG Supreme' suitcase, with maker's monogram coated canvas exterior.

22.5in (57cm) wide

$250-350   **FELL**

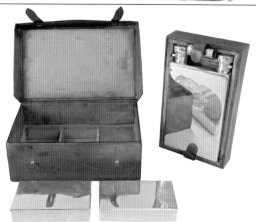

A 1920s Gustave Keller leather-cased travelling drinks set, in a brown pigskin case, the lower section with three plated sandwich tins, with fitted silver double drinks flask.

case 11.5in (29cm) wide

$900-1,100   **ECGW**

A Louis Vuitton monogrammed leather briefcase, serial no.877642, with original paper trade label.

17in (43cm) wide

$900-1,000   **CHEF**

A Louis Vuitton Monogram Serviette Conseiller briefcase, serial no.SR0043, with maker's monogram coated canvas exterior.

15in (38cm) wide

$900-1,000   **FELL**

QUICK REFERENCE - LOUIS VUITTON

- Louis Vuitton is a fashion company and retailer founded by Louis Vuitton (1821-92) in 1854.
- The company's great success sparked from its 'Trianon' trunk, produced in 1858. This trunk was waterproof, canvas-covered and airtight. Previously, trunks had domed or sloping tops to allow water to run off, but Vuitton's trunk was already waterproof and could therefore have a flat top. This allowed it to stack when being transported.
- In 1876, Louis Vuitton introduced beige and brown striped canvas in order to differentiate its products from competitors and imitators. Its checked 'Damier' was introduced in 1888, followed in 1896 by the 'LV' monogram canvas, which is still used by Louis Vuitton today.
- Vintage Louis Vuitton pieces are highly popular today. Specially commissioned pieces or those with niche uses, such as musical instrument cases, can fetch especially large sums.

A vintage 20thC Louis Vuitton case, serial no.975633.

27.75in (70cm) wide

$1,600-2,000   **K&O**

A 1920s Louis Vuitton hard suitcase, serial no.80971[2?], featuring the original hand stencilled monogram canvas exterior, all fastenings functional, lacking key.

29.75in (75.5cm) wide

$2,500-3,500   **FELL**

An early 20thC red Morocco leather government cabinet box, with gilt monogram 'M' and crown for Charles Spencer-Churchill, 9th Duke of Marlborough, lacking key, can open and close but not lock and unlock.

18in (45.5cm) wide

$4,000-4,500   **BELL**

A 'Revenge' Crew T-shirt and cap from Richard Marquand's Star Wars Episode VI Return of the Jedi (1983).

$450-550   PSL

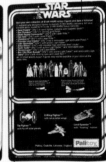

An X-Wing ILM model miniature, from Irvin Kershner's Star Wars Episode V The Empire Strikes Back (1980).

To save time and money, the team at Industrial Light & Magic (ILM) created this Rebel starfighter from a commercially available model kit. Assembled in the ILM workshop by Mike Fulmer, the model was then painted by Wesley Seeds III, approved by Lorne Petersen, and was ultimately shot by Ken Ralston on the motion control stage. After its use on The Empire Strikes Back, this model miniature was gifted to Special Visual-Effects supervisor Brian Johnson.

12in (30cm) long

$150,000-190,000   PSL

A TIE fighter pilot helmet from George Lucas' Star Wars Episode IV A New Hope (1977), designed by John Mollo, with concept art by Ralph McQuarrie.

This is a standard-issue helmet for TIE fighter pilots, worn in many of the film's various dog fights, against the Millennium Falcon after its escape from the Death Star, and in the final battle above the Death Star surface. The helmet is a composite of the Imperial Stormtrooper helmet and the Rebel pilot helmet, of which far fewer were made compared to their Stormtrooper counterparts. Two of the TIE pilot helmets were re-purposed for use by AT-AT crews in The Empire Strikes Back, with the remaining helmets subsequently re-used for the production of Return of the Jedi.

13in (33cm) high

$300,000-350,000   PSL

A CLOSER LOOK AT A 'JAWA' FIGURE

This Palitoy Star Wars 'Jawa' figure has a vinyl cape rather than a cloth cape, making it a rare version.

It was one of a dozen produced in 1978, a year after the release of the first Star Wars film.

The model is held within a bubble, on a 12B un-punched card, with some minimal edge war.

It is in near mint condition. The owner was a former employee of Palitoy and had kept the toy in a cupboard since its release.

A Palitoy Star Wars vinyl cape 'Jawa' figure.

3.75in (9.5cm) high

$30,000-35,000   VEC

A Bespin Security Guard Kenner figure, product no.69640.48-back, 'The Empire Strikes Back', carded, punched.
1982
$80-90   CA

A Logray (Ewok Medicine Man) Kenner figure, product no.70710.77-back, 'Return of the Jedi', carded, punched.
1983
$60-80   CA

A Klaatu Kenner figure, product no.70730.77-back, 'Return of the Jedi', carded, unpunched.
1983
$60-80   CA

An Emperor Palitoy figure, no.79-back, tri-logo, 'Return of the Jedi', carded, unpunched, very slight wear.
1984
$130-200   CA

Batman's Batsuit from Christopher Nolan's The Dark Knight (2008) and The Dark Knight Rises (2012), worn by Christian Bale, designed by Lindy Hemming, created by Graham Churchyard and his team, including key sculptor Julian Murray.

This refined Batsuit is a military-inspired redesign of the Batman Begins outfit, and allowed Batman to fight with increased agility at the expense of the protection afforded by its armor. The most significant design change was an improved cowl, which separated the headpiece from the neck, allowing performers to turn their head in the suit for the first time. Lindy Hemming received a BAFTA Award nomination for her contribution to The Dark Knight.

76.75in (90cm) high

$250,000-350,000   PSL

The Hero Batpod Vehicle from Christopher Nolan's The Dark Knight (2008) and The Dark Knight Rises (2012), conceived by Christopher Nolan, designed by Nathan Crowley with special-effects supervisor Chris Corbould, used in filming largely by stunt rider Jean-Pierre Goy, with the battery, fuel tank and throttle controls removed.

In The Dark Knight, Bruce Wayne used the Batpod to escape his Tumbler vehicle during his battle with the Joker (Heath Ledger), and later used the vehicle in his unsuccessful attempt to save Rachel Dawes (Maggie Gyllenhaal) and in his hunt for Harvey Dent (Aaron Eckhart). In The Dark Knight Rises, Batman and Selina Kyle (Anne Hathaway) used the vehicle during their battles with Bane (Tom Hardy) and the new League of Shadows. The Batpod is designed for a rider in a prone position who steers the vehicle with their arms and shoulders, and features advanced design elements such as an exhaust system integrated within the framework.

149.5in (380cm) long

$400,000-550,000   PSL

A Walt Disney original animation cel, depicting Donald Duck with caterpillar, the mount signed in bold green crayon, 'To W.L. Courtney with best wishes Walt Disney', framed mid-20thC by 'Cohen's Picture Store, Washington D.C.'.

$3,500-4,500   HAN

A Walt Disney original animation cel, used in the production of The Three Caballeros, with the pistol-packing rooster 'Panchito Pistoles', the mount signed in bold blue crayon, 'My Best Wishes, Walt Disney'.

1944

$2,000-2,500   HAN

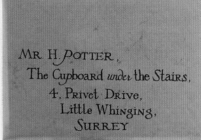

A Walt Disney original handpainted color animation cel, used in the production of Snow White and the Seven Dwarfs, Disney's first full-length animated feature film, original gallery label to verso of frame, 'Ernest Brown & Phillips Ltd, Leicester Galleries, Leicester Square, London', remnants of original 1938 exhibition label to verso.

1937

$16,000-20,000   HAN

Sloth's stunt mask from Richard Donner's The Goonies (1985), one of two masks created for the production, made of polyurethane foam, used by Sloth's stunt double, Randell Dennis Widner.

12in (30cm) high

$45,000-55,000   PSL

Harry Potter's Hogwarts acceptance letter from Chris Columbus' Harry Potter and the Philosopher's Stone (2001), made from marble-effect paper, with Harry's address printed on the front of the envelope and the Hogwarts crest printed on the reverse, with a real red wax Hogwarts seal.

7.25in (18cm) wide

$11,000-13,000   PSL

Judith Picks

The music still makes me clutch the back of the sofa! This clapperboard was used throughout production, including in the final reshoot of the scene in which Hooper (Richard Dreyfuss) finds the severed head of Ben Gardner (Craig Kingsbury) in the remains of his sunken boat. Unable to acquire studio funding to reshoot the scene, Spielberg famously spent $3,000 of his own money to film the underwater sequence. The board's scratches and markings can be matched to a well-published behind-the-scenes promotional photograph of Spielberg holding the clapperboard.

A wood clapperboard from Steven Spielberg's Jaws (1975), marked for use with the production's secondary 'B' camera, with a custom-made set in the shape of sharks' teeth, operated by pulling the top stick vertically.

12.75in (32cm) wide

$110,000-130,000 **PSL**

Richard Attenborough's personal annotated script for Steven Spielberg's Jurassic Park (1993), 140 printed US Legal pages including blue, yellow and pink-colored revisions, filled with Attenborough personal notes and amendments.

11in (28cm) high

$15,000-20,000 **PSL**

Juliet's wedding dress from Richard Curtis' Love Actually (2004), worn by Keira Knightley.

$6,500-8,000 **PSL**

A Leonardo Ninja Turtle costume display from Steve Barron's Teenage Mutant Ninja Turtles (1990), created by Jim Henson's Creature Shop, London, worn by David Forman.

66in (167cm) high

$15,000-20,000 **PSL**

The Terminator's costume from James Cameron's Terminator 2: Judgment Day (1991), worn by Arnold Schwarzenegger.

72in (183cm) high

$40,000-50,000 **PSL**

Rick 'Jester' Heatherly's flight suit from Tony Scott's Top Gun (1986), worn by Michael Ironside, with an array of fighter squadron patches stitched across the arms and chest, with a Western Costume Co. costumiers label at the collar, reading '2507-1; Top Gun; Jester'.

This flight suit screen-matches to the scene in which Jester introduces the new Top Gun recruits to Charlie (Kelly McGillis).

$10,000-11,500 **PSL**

Van Helsing's hero functioning crossbow from Stephen Sommers' Van Helsing (2004), used in the film by Hugh Jackman, with a poster used in the promotion of the film.

The crossbow is still fully functional. The chain-driven action is powered by a 12-volt battery located in the butt stock, which powers the weapon through a connector between the stock and the pistol grip. Pulling the trigger drives a chain which simulates the firing of the bow string, with the spring-loaded magazine rotating with each movement of the action. The weapon disassembles into three components with folding bow arms and sights.

35.5in (90cm) long

$25,000-35,000 **PSL**

FILM & TELEVISION

A Stan Laurel and Oliver Hardy page from album, with stuck in cartoon, signed in ink and inscribed 'Thank You Sandra!'.

$250-300   HT

A Stan Laurel and Oliver Hardy photograph, signed in ink and inscribed 'HELLO SANDRA!'.

$400-450   HT

A Product Enterprise Dr Who Classic Moments resin diorama, of the 'Tomb of the Cyberman', no.35 of a limited edition of 500, with certificate.

$120-160   LSK

A Product Enterprise Doctor Who Classic Moments resin diorama, 'An Unearthly Child', no.205 of a limited edition of 500, with certificate, in original box.

$120-160   LSK

A near mint Corgi Dr Who 40th Anniversary Gift Set, TY96203, from a limited edition of 200, signed by Tom Baker, with certificate.

$100-130   LSK

A framed and glazed signed David Prowse 'GREEN CROSS CODE' T-shirt.

$40-50   LSK

Fox Mulder's FBI Photo ID and Badge from The X-Files (1993-2002), used by David Duchovny in season one.

5in (12.5cm) wide folded

$10,000-12,000   PSL

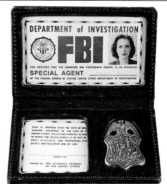

Dana Scully's FBI Photo ID and Badge from The X-Files (1993-2002), used by Gillian Anderson in season two.

6.5in (16.5cm) wide folded

$10,000-11,000   PSL

QUICK REFERENCE - FORNASETTI

Piero Fornasetti (1913-88) was an Italian artist and designer of furniture, ceramics, glass and other homeware. In opposition to the prevailing Modernist and Mid-Century Modern movements of his time, Fornasetti's designs were highly decorative and often made use of Surrealist imagery. Designs were usually in gilt and monochrome or in black and white. He is perhaps best-known for the recurring face of opera singer Lina Cavalieri, whose image he used across numerous works. He was very successful during his lifetime and his work has continued to rise in value since his death, attracting the attention of many collectors.

A set of three Neiman Marcus hot air balloon plates, by Piero Fornasetti.

7in (18cm) diam

$160-200 — HAN

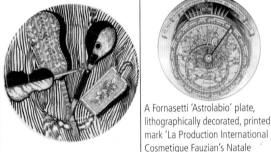

A mid-20thC tray, by Piero Fornasetti, transfer-decorated enameled metal, original paper label, minor chips to enamel.

19.5in (49.5cm) wide

$550-650 — DRA

A 1950s 'Jerusalem' pattern hostess cart, by Piero Fornasetti (1913-88), with brass and lacquered wood frame.

30.25in (77cm) long

$1,300-2,000 — L&T

A Fornasetti 'Strumenti Musicali' plate, printed marks 'S C Richard' and 'Fornasetti Milano'.

9in (23cm) diam

$160-200 — SWO

A Fornasetti 'Astrolabio' plate, lithographically decorated, printed mark 'La Production International Cosmetique Fauzian's Natale 1965', Fornasetti hand and brush mark, 'Made in Italy' and numbered '1'.

9.5in (24cm) diam

$250-350 — SWO

A Fornasetti 'Soli E Lune' silk scarf, designed by Piero Fornasetti, labelled.

35.5in (90cm) long

$200-250 — SWO

A 1950s-70s Fornasetti Milano umbrella stand, transfer-decorated enameled metal, original foil label, with original liner.

27.25in (69cm) high

$3,500-4,000 — DRA

A 1950s Italian lacquered jewelry box, in the manner of Piero Fornasetti, the interior fitted with velvet lined compartments and lift-out tray.

13.5in (34cm) wide

$350-400 — L&T

QUICK REFERENCE - WINE BOTTLES

Wine bottles of a dark green, almost black color were made in Britain from the mid-17thC. These bottles were free-blown, so have no seam lines, and are often asymmetrical in shape. Common forms include the 'onion' or the 'shaft and globe'. The bottles would have been used to serve wine. They were often stamped with a seal or coat of arms to one side, which would have been used at the time to identify the owner of a bottle when it was sent back to the wine merchant to be refilled.

A James II 'sack' onion shaped bottle, excavated in Burma in 1933.

It is believed this bottle belonged to the famous pirate Samuel White who spent his time in Burma. See Maurice Collis, 'Siamese White', Faber and Faber, 2011 (originally published 1936).

8.5in (21.5cm) high

$1,300-2,000   JN

A rare 'Transitional' shaft and globe to onion wine bottle, a chip to the string, some surface degradation.

c1680-90   *5.5in (14cm) high*

$1,000-1,300   WW

A 1720s black glass Dutch horse hoof onion bottle, pontilled kick-up base.

8in (20.5cm) high

$130-200   MART

An English mallet shape wine bottle, with string rim and kick-in base.

c1720   *7.75in (20cm) high*

$400-450   WW

An early 18thC black glass bladder bottle, with string rim, deep kick-up oval pontilled base.

8in (20.5cm) high

$450-600   MART

An early 18thC onion shaped bottle, with green tinted color.

6in (15cm) high

$400-550   APAR

An early to mid-18thC English black glass mallet bottle, with string rim and pontilled kick-up base.

6in (15.5cm) high

$550-650   MART

An 18thC Dutch pig snout case gin bottle, with pontilled base.

9.75in (25cm) high

$60-80   MART

QUICK REFERENCE - BACCARAT

- In 1764, the Compagnie des Cristalleries de Baccarat was founded in the town of Baccarat in north-eastern France.
- Alongside Val St Lambert and St Louis, Baccarat was one of the key European pioneers of mechanically-pressed glass.
- It produced a range of glass products, including vases, bowls and paperweights. Baccarat pieces often have gilt and etched decoration, and can often have gilt or ormolu mounts. Its commonly used 'cranberry' shade of delicate pink is also distinctive.
- It remains a leading manufacturer of glass, and is today owned by Starwood Capital Group.

A Baccarat molded vase, decorated with flowers.
c1865   10in (25.5cm) high
$1,000-1,300   **M&DM**

A Baccarat blown clear chinoiserie vase, with oriental imagery.
c1890   8in (20.5cm) high
$650-850   **M&DM**

A Baccarat molded polychrome vase, decorated with flowers.
c1860   8in (20.5cm) high
$900-1,200   **M&DM**

A Baccarat cranberry 'square' finger bowl.
c1895   4in (10cm) wide
$150-200   **M&DM**

A Baccarat polychrome enamel vase, in classic Japonaise shape depicting wild flowers, gilded.
c1890   5in (13cm) high
$550-650   **M&DM**

A Baccarat enameled and opal snake 'stick' vase.
c1890   6in (15cm) high
$1,600-2,000   **M&DM**

A pair of Baccarat red on pale green gilded cameo 'water lily' vases, signed 'Bourgeois Depose'.

These were made for Emile Bourgeois at the 'Grand Depot' Paris.
c1900   9in (23cm) high
$4,000-4,500   **M&DM**

An early 20thC Baccarat crystal glass decanter, cased in green over clear crystal and polished intaglio, cut with fruiting cherry boughs, below a clear crystal faceted spire-form stopper, unmarked.
16.5in (42cm) high
$600-750   **FLD**

GLASS

QUICK REFERENCE - HARRACH

- There has been a glassworks in Harrachow, Bohemia, since the mid-17thC. In the early 18thC, this was taken over by the Harrach family.
- Throughout the 19thC, Harrach was renowned for its luxury tableware and glassware, which was exhibited throughout Europe. Much of the company's production in the 19thC and 20thC was exported to other European countries.
- By 1900 it had become a pioneer of Art Nouveau glass. It produced glass for important Czech glass companies such as J.&L. Lobmeyr and Moser. Its Art Nouveau wares tend to feature cameo designs of flowers and other natural imagery.

A late 19thC Harrach cameo glass vase, cased in blue over opal and cut with a flowering bough, unmarked.

3.75in (9.5cm) high

$200-250   FLD

A late 19thC Harrach Tapestry glass vase, enameled with flowers.

8.75in (22cm) high

$400-450   FLD

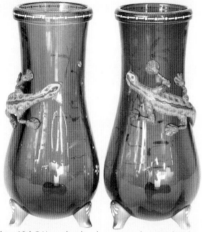

A pair of late 19thC Harrach ruby glass vases, decorated with an applied stylized lizard, with enamel decoration amongst enameled and gilded insects, flowers and foliage, unmarked.

7.75in (20cm) high

$400-450   FLD

A pair of Harrach opal vases, with applied polychrome enamel turtles and icicle drip collars.

c1890   6in (15cm) high

$1,000-1,300   M&DM

A Harrach blue and brick red 'faux porcelain' glass vase, in an Art Nouveau pewter mount.

c1897   9in (23cm) high

$2,000-2,500   M&DM

A pair of pad-footed Harrach 'Lizard' vases, beasts wrapped around crackle glass.

c1898   9in (23cm) high

$1,600-2,000   M&DM

A three-handled Harrach 'Heckla' vase, gilded over polychrome over amber with raised mistletoe.

c1899   6in (15cm) high

$1,500-1,700   M&DM

A Harrach enamel vase, with a green shrimp on dark brown glass.

c1900   4in (10cm) high

$250-350   M&DM

A Kralik purple and amber 'corrugated' bowl, with Secessionist vines and owl cornered brass frame, each owl holding a ring.

Wilhelm Kralik Söhne was one of the largest Bohemian art glass producers in the early 20thC, active from the late 1870s until World War II. It specialized in martelé (hammered) or swirled glass, often decorated with flowers or rigaree trails. Kralik glass can be hard to identify as it is has many similarities to Tiffany and Loetz.

c1897   *5in (12.5cm) wide*
$1,200-1,300   **M&DM**

A Kralik iridised green vase, with Austrian Secessionist brass top with pointed handles.

c1898   *7in (18cm) high*
$1,000-1,200   **M&DM**

A vivid red Kralik vase, with multiple pulls drawn up to four points.

c1900   *9in (23cm) high*
$900-1,000   **M&DM**

A Kralik purple triangular vase, after a Kolomann Moser design, known as 'Streifen und Flecken'.

c1900   *7in (18cm) wide*
$650-800   **M&DM**

A large Kralik copper clad deep purple vase.

c1900   *11in (28cm) high*
$1,200-1,500   **M&DM**

An early 20thC Kralik fluted cylindrical glass vase, unmarked.

                    6.75in (17cm) high
$150-250   **FLD**

A Kralik blue to clear Art Deco landscape cameo vase.

c1925   *10in (25.5cm) high*
$1,000-1,200   **M&DM**

A Kralik dark red to clear tropical Art Deco cameo vase.

c1925   *7in (18cm) high*
$400-550   **M&DM**

A Kralik cased ball vase, decorated with paperweight canes in reds, whites and greens.

c1925   *10in (25.5cm) high*
$600-750   **M&DM**

A pair of Kralik white-cased vases, decorated with paperweight canes in reds, whites and greens.

c1925   *6in (15cm) high*
$1,000-1,300   **M&DM**

GLASS

QUICK REFERENCE - MOSER

- Ludwig Moser (1833-1916) was an Austrian painter, book illustrator, architect, and jewelry, glass, textile and furniture designer.
- He opened a glass workshop in 1857 in Karlovy Vary, Bohemia. It specialized in polishing, engraving and cutting glass. The company began to make its own glass from 1893, when Moser founded a factory in Karlsbad with his sons, Gustav and Rudolf. The company produced clear glass tablewares, decorated with engraved and enameled designs.
- From 1919 Moser's designers began to create colored art glass vases and bowls. The company collaborated with Wiener Werkstätte designer Josef Hoffmann in the 1920s to create glasses and vases depicting animals and jungle scenes, often highlighted with gilt or enamel decoration.
- Moser suffered in the Depression of the 1930s, and the family sold their shares in 1938.

A set of 12 early 20thC reversible glass champagne flutes, in the manner of Moser, each with a lobed bowl, knopped stem and fluted bowl.

9in (23cm) high

$1,000-1,200   L&T

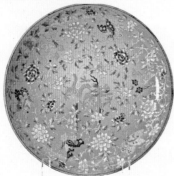

A late 19thC Moser Aesthetic Movement cranberry glass dish, enameled with a Chinese dragon amongst flowers, with gilded highlights, unmarked, some damage.

9.75in (24.5cm) wide

$400-450   FLD

A Moser 'Alexandrit' cut vase, designed by H. Hussman.

c1920   5in (13cm) high

$650-800   M&DM

An early 20thC Wiener Werkstätte for Ludwig Moser & Sons bowl and cover, by Josef Hoffmann, acid marked.

5.5in (14cm) high

$350-450   FLD

A Moser amber/uranium green faceted vase, signed 'Moser WW' for Wiener Werkstätte.

$800-1,000   M&DM

A 1920s Moser vase, the bowl decorated with an Oroplastic gilt band, depicting a classical scene, engraved signature.

Oroplastic refers to dark-colored cut glass with gilded bands of acid-etched decoration. It was first created in c1914-15 by Leo Moser, son of founder Ludwig Moser.

7.75in (19.5cm) high

$650-800   FLD

A Wiener Werkstätte 'bamboo' martini glass, designed by Josef Hoffmann for Ludwig Moser & Sons.

c1922   6in (15.5cm) high

$550-650   FLD

A Moser Animor vase, designed by Rudolf Wels, cut with a frieze of elephants, palm trees and birds, double signature within the decoration and acid signature to the base.

c1926   7.75in (20cm) high

$1,000-1,300   FLD

A deep acid cut back and gilded vase, with palm trees, a chariot and hunted lion, signed.

This was designed by Gustav Moser-Millot for the 1937 Paris Exhibition.

1936   8in (20.5cm) high

$800-1,000   M&DM

A post-war Exbor glass solifleur sommerso vase, designed by Pavel Hlava, unmarked.

Exbor, also known as Egermann-Exbor, was a Czech glassworks founded in 1962, as part of the Bor Glass National Enterprise group. Its key designers include Stanislav Honzik and Josef Rozinek, whose glass fish were popular in the 1960s, and Pavel Hlava, who designed a range of vases and vessels for Exbor, typically of cased column form. The majority of Exbor pieces bear a circular Exbor acid stamp.

9in (23cm) high

$250-400   FLD

A post-war Exbor glass vase, by Pavel Hlava, of sleeve form, cased in citron over clear, unmarked.

10.25in (26cm) high

$350-400   FLD

A post-war Exbor Egermann Glassworks crystal vase, by Pavel Hlava, unmarked, with original box and labels.

4.75in (12cm) high

$250-400   FLD

A Carl Goldberg enamel and intaglio cut 'Fish' vase.

This design was shown at the 1925 Paris Exhibition.

3in (7.5cm) high

$400-450   M&DM

An early 20thC Beyermann of Haida glass vase, with outlines of foxes in woodland, unmarked.

11in (28cm) high

$200-250   FLD

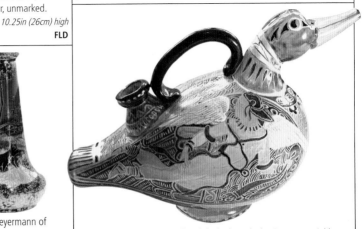

An enamel Fritz Heckert 'jodhpur' duck-shaped Islamic water sprinkler, lacking stopper.

8in (20.5cm) long

$3,500-4,000   M&DM

A Fritz Heckert cameo vase, depicting a windmill, shore and full rigged ships, probably an Otto Thamm design, signed.

c1900   *6in (15cm) high*

$900-1,100   M&DM

A green and white iridised Fritz Heckert vase, designed by Otto Thamm.

This finish has only recently been identified and is called 'Mormopal'.

c1900   *5in (12.5cm) high*

$550-650   M&DM

A Fritz Heckert scissor cut 'King Tut' pattern vase, by Otto Thamm.

c1900   *13in (33cm) high*

$1,300-1,600   M&DM

GLASS

A blue-cased and flash cut wine glass, designed by Otto Prutscher for Meyr's Neffe, unmarked.

Josef Meyr founded Meyr's Neffe in 1815. By the mid-19thC, Meyr's Neffe consisted of seven glassworks, operated by Wilhelm Kralik. After Wilhelm Kralik's death in 1877, two of his sons Karl and Hugo Kralik, continued to trade as Meyr's Neffe, while Heinrich and Johann formed Wilhelm Kralik Söhne. Meyr's Neffe merged with Moser in 1922.

8in (20.5cm) high

$450-600   FLD

A post-war Mstisov Harmony glass, by Frantisek Zemek, unmarked.

9.75in (25cm) high

$100-140   FLD

A 1930s Czech crystal glass vase, by Karel Palda, in the Art Deco taste, unmarked.

8.25in (21cm) high

$130-200   FLD

An Art Nouveau Rindskopf Hyacinthe green glass vase, with iridescent texture.

13.5in (34cm) high

$130-200   LSK

A Rindskopf pleated 'Pepita' fan vase.

c1900   *6in (15cm) high*

$400-600   M&DM

A ribbed blue Rindskopf fan vase.

c1900   *12in (30.5cm) high*

$800-1,000   M&DM

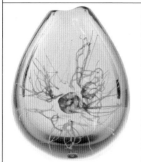

A post-war Skrdlovice glass vase, by Petr Hora, internally decorated with a pink and white splatter design, with original label.

8.25in (21cm) high

$350-400   FLD

An early 20thC Theresienthal drinking glass, in the 'Grape Vine' pattern, unmarked.

8in (20.5cm) high

$130-200   FLD

Judith Picks

There is always added value in a good story. Solid provenance would further add to the value, but the story helps. This was owned by William Henry Cotton (1838-73), India merchant, who by family repute looted this bowl from the Prince of Oudh's palace at Delhi following the Indian Mutiny of 1857.

A mid-19thC Bohemian uranium glass sugar bowl, perhaps for the Indian market, cut with a band of raised diamonds between a scalloped rim and foot.

5.5in (14cm) high

$550-650   MAB

QUICK REFERENCE - D'ARGENTAL

- Inspired by the success of Daum and Gallé, the St Louis glassworks launched its 'D'Argental' cameo range in c1918.
- In 1919, St Louis recruited Paul Nicolas (1875-1952), a protégé of Émile Gallé, to design for the D'Argental brand. He brought with him a group of previous employees from Gallé's factory, and was the main designer for D'Argental in the 1920s-30s.
- D'Argental pieces were usually made of lead crystal, with fine detail wheel-cut into the surface. Pieces are usually dark red, brown and caramel in color.
- Pieces made by Nicolas and his colleagues were usually signed 'St Louis Nancy' or 'D'Argental', with a Cross of Lorraine for the pieces Nicolas made himself. Pieces signed 'Paul Nicolas' rather than 'D'Argental' were made for him to sell.
- Although not as well known as Daum and Gallé, D'Argental's very high quality has lead to an increase in interest and prices in recent years.

A D'Argental cameo vase, by Paul Nicolas, with leafy branches, signed, with Cross of Lorraine.
c1920   *9in (23cm) high*
$1,600-2,000   **M&DM**

A black on orange cameo vase, by Paul Nicolas for the St Louis Glassworks, with grape vines, signed 'D'Argental', with Cross of Lorraine.
c1920   *12in (30.5cm) high*
$3,500-4,000   **M&DM**

A D'Argental cameo vase, by Paul Nicolas, with flowering orchids, signed, with Cross of Lorraine.
c1920   *13.5in (34.5cm) high*
$3,500-4,000   **M&DM**

A D'Argental cameo vase, by Paul Nicolas, with an aquatic scene, signed, with Cross of Lorraine.
c1920   *9in (23cm) high*
$1,600-2,000   **M&DM**

A black and red on orange cameo vase, by Paul Nicolas for the St Louis Glassworks, depicting trailing grape vines, signed 'D'Argental', with Cross of Lorraine.
c1920   *10in (25.5cm) high*
$2,500-3,000   **M&DM**

A D'Argental cameo vase, by Paul Nicolas, with flowering orchids, signed, with Cross of Lorraine.
c1920   *5in (12.5cm) high*
$1,300-1,600   **M&DM**

A cameo vase, by Paul Nicolas for the St Louis Glassworks, depicting the 'Mehun sur Vevre' castle, signed 'D'Argental', with Cross of Lorraine.

This item was part of the Nicolas Exhibition at the École De Nancy 2010 and is supplied with a letter of provenance and signed exhibition book.
c1925   *13in (33cm) high*
$4,000-4,500   **M&DM**

A brown on lime green cameo vase, by Paul Nicolas for the St Louis Glassworks, depicting blooming irises, signed 'D'Argental', with Cross of Lorraine.

This item was part of the Nicolas Exhibition at the École De Nancy 2010.
c1925   *12in (30.5cm) high*
$4,000-4,500   **M&DM**

GLASS

A cameo bowl vase, by Paul Nicolas for the St Louis Glassworks, with clematis flowers, signed 'D'Argental', with Cross of Lorraine.
c1925　　　　10in (25.5cm) wide
$1,600-2,000　　　　**M&DM**

A cameo vase, by Paul Nicolas for the St Louis Glassworks, with yachts with rocky outcrops on water, signed 'D'Argental'.
c1925　　　　7in (18cm) high
$1,600-2,000　　　　**M&DM**

A stylized Art Deco cameo vase, by Paul Nicolas for the St Louis Glassworks, signed 'D'Argental'.
c1925　　　　8in (20.5cm) high
$2,000-2,500　　　　**M&DM**

A purple-red on orange cameo vase by Paul Nicolas, depicting flowering branches in a frieze, signed 'Paul Nicolas'.
c1925　　　　5in (12.5cm) high
$1,600-2,000　　　　**M&DM**

A D'Argental cameo bowl, by Paul Nicolas, with fir cones, signed, with Cross of Lorraine.
c1920　　　　6in (15cm) wide
$1,300-1,700　　　　**M&DM**

A cameo bowl, by Paul Nicolas, with lily of the valley, signed 'Paul Nicolas'.
c1925　　　　5in (12.5cm) wide
$1,600-2,000　　　　**M&DM**

A cameo bowl-vase, by Paul Nicolas for the St Louis Glassworks, with orchids and ginko, signed 'D'Argental', with Cross of Lorraine.

This item was part of the Nicolas Exhibition at the École De Nancy 2010.
c1925　　　　10in (25.5cm) wide
$4,000-4,500　　　　**M&DM**

A cameo lamp base, by Paul Nicolas for the St Louis Glassworks, with blackberries, signed 'D'Argental', with Cross of Lorraine.

These small lamps were intended to have cloth shades.
c1925　　　　5in (12.5cm) high
$1,000-1,300　　　　**M&DM**

A D'Argental cameo atomizer, by Paul Nicolas, with flowering fuchsia, signed, with Cross of Lorraine.

This item was part of the Nicolas Exhibition at the École De Nancy 2010 and is supplied with a letter of provenance and signed exhibition book.
c1920-25　　　　5in (12.5cm) high
$2,500-3,500　　　　**M&DM**

QUICK REFERENCE - DAUM

● The Daum glass studio was founded in Nancy, France, in 1878, by Jean Daum. It rose to prominence under his two sons, Auguste and Antonin, who focused on decorative glassware, partly inspired by the work of Émile Gallé.

● The brothers incorporated natural imagery and Oriental and Far Eastern inspiration into their Art Nouveau and later Art Deco designs.

● Daum used a variety of innovative techniques, using acid to etch, frost or shine surfaces, using wheel-turning to give the glass a 'hammered' look, and using pâte-de-verre, where crushed glass is packed into molds and fused in a kiln, or 'intercalaire', where a powdered glass design is sealed between two layers of glass.

● Daum's key glass artists included Amalric Walter, Charles Schneider and Henri Bergé.

A Daum Frères cameo glass 'Blackberry' goblet, overlaid, acid-etched and enameled with 'Daum Nancy', with Cross of Lorraine.

3.75in (9.5cm) high

$2,500-3,500   **CHEF**

A Daum Frères cameo glass 'Cockscomb' vase, overlaid and etched with 'Daum Nancy', with Cross of Lorraine.

9.75in (24cm) high

$2,500-3,000   **CHEF**

A Daum Frères 'Rosehip' cameo glass vase, etched and enameled, cameo mark 'Daum Nancy', with Cross of Lorraine.

8in (20.5cm) high

$4,000-4,500   **CHEF**

A Daum Frères 'Coeurs de Janette' glass vase, overlaid, acid-etched and enameled, with enameled mark 'Daum Nancy', with Cross of Lorraine.

6.25in (16cm) high

$3,000-3,500   **CHEF**

An unusual Daum Frères 'Falling Maple Leaf' cameo glass vase, overlaid and acid-etched with elliptical rim, signed in the cameo.

9.75in (25cm) high

$5,500-6,000   **CHEF**

A Daum Nancy and Louis Majorelle glass vase, with metal frame and handles, signed 'Daum Nancy France L. Majorelle'.

12in (30cm) high

$3,500-4,000   **JN**

A Daum wheel-carved smoked glass vase, with hunting scenes, wheel-etched 'DAUM / NANCY'.

c1927   *6.75in (17cm) high*

$350-400   **L&T**

A CLOSER LOOK AT A DAUM LAMP

This Daum cameo glass table lamp is in perfect condition.

It is etched and enameled in the intricate 'Summer Trees' pattern.

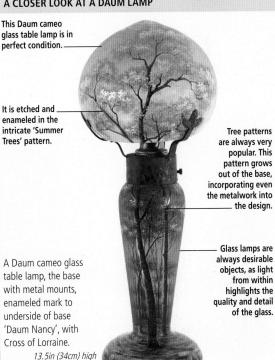

Tree patterns are always very popular. This pattern grows out of the base, incorporating even the metalwork into the design.

Glass lamps are always desirable objects, as light from within highlights the quality and detail of the glass.

A Daum cameo glass table lamp, the base with metal mounts, enameled mark to underside of base 'Daum Nancy', with Cross of Lorraine.

13.5in (34cm) high

$17,000-21,000   **CHOR**

GLASS

QUICK REFERENCE - ÉMILE GALLÉ

- Emile Gallé (1846-1904) was a key Art Nouveau glass designer, born in Nancy, France. He studied botany, chemistry, philosophy, art and glass-making, before joining his father at the family factory in 1867.
- In 1873, he founded his own studio and by 1877 was running his own business.
- Early works were usually clear or transparent glass with gilded and enameled decoration, but after seeing English cameo glass at an exhibition in Paris, Gallé turned his attention to cameo glass. His factory expanded due to the success of his cameo glass and continual innovation.
- After his death in 1904, the company continued to produce class under the supervision of Émile Gallé's widow and son-in-law.

A Gallé 'La Groseille' fire-polished cameo glass vase, acid-etched and polished with redcurrants, cameo signature 'GALLÉ'.
c1900 12.25in (31cm) high
$2,000-2,500   **L&T**

An early 20thC Gallé cameo glass vase, cut with seeding sycamore boughs, cameo signature.
5in (13cm) high
$1,200-1,600   **FLD**

An early 20thC Gallé cameo glass vase, cut with a Virginia creeper, cameo signature to the body.
7.5in (19cm) high
$900-1,300   **FLD**

A Gallé cameo glass vase, acid-etched with flowering orchids, relief-carved cameo signature 'GALLÉ'.
c1910
$1,000-1,600
7.5in (19cm) high
L&T

A Gallé cameo glass vase, acid-etched with flowering fuchsias, relief-carved cameo signature 'GALLÉ'.
c1910
$550-650
7in (17.5cm) high
L&T

A Gallé cameo glass vase, cut with a fruiting vine design, cameo Gallé star mark to the body.

Glass sold after Émile Gallé's death in 1904 was marked with a star added after his cameo signature.

9.5in (24cm) high
$650-800   **FLD**

A Gallé cameo glass vase, cut with fruiting boughs, cameo signature to the body.
4in (10cm) high
$900-1,000   **FLD**

A Gallé cameo glass 'Wisteria' vase, overlaid and acid-etched, signed in cameo.

7.25in (18.5cm) high
$800-1,000   **CHEF**

GLASS

QUICK REFERENCE - LALIQUE

- René Lalique (1860-1945) was an influential Art Nouveau and Art Deco designer. He began his career as a jewelry designer, then opened his first glassworks in 1908.
- The Lalique glassworks produced glass screens, lamps, car mascots, fountains, lights and vases. These were primarily mold-blown or pressed, of frosted white, opalescent glass.
- Colored Lalique pieces can be rare and therefore can fetch higher prices. 'Cire perdu' (lost wax) pieces are extremely rare, and the most eagerly sought Lalique wares.
- Many of Lalique's designs continued to be produced after his death. Pre-1945 pieces tend to be marked 'R. Lalique, France'. Post-1945 pieces are often marked 'Lalique, France'.

A Lalique molded frosted glass 'Bacchantes' vase, with female nude figures in deep relief, engraved 'Lalique France' to foot.
9.75in (25cm) high
$3,000-4,000   **FELL**

A late 20thC Lalique 'Bacchantes' clear and frosted glass vase, with interior label and etched mark 'Lalique, France', boxed.
9.75in (25cm) high
$1,000-1,300   **BELL**

The 'Bacchantes' vase was first designed by René Lalique in 1927. The vase depicts the dancing priestesses of Bacchus, and has been a staple of the Lalique collection since its release up until the present day. It was originally made of glass, but since 1947 has chiefly been produced in crystal. In 2010, for the 150th anniversary of René Lalique's birth, a new version was produced called 'Révélation Bacchantes', set inside a cube of crystal.

A 'Malesherbes' ruby glass vase, no.1014, by René Lalique, molded with overlapping leaves, script etched mark 'R. LALIQUE / FRANCE / NO. 1014'.
designed 1934   9in (23cm) high
$3,500-4,500   **L&T**

A René Lalique 'Christina' black enamel cocktail glass, signed.
1925   5in (13cm) high
$400-550   **M&DM**

A René Lalique amber 'Bahia' lemonade glass, signed.
1931   4.75in (12cm) high
$350-450   **M&DM**

A Lalique 'Danseuse Bras Baisse' frosted and molded glass nude female figure, signed 'Lalique France' to base.
9in (23cm) high
$550-650   **GWA**

A Lalique yellow 'Dindon' glass cendrier, no.287, designed by Rene Lalique, etched 'R Lalique France'.
designed 1925   4in (10cm) diam
$400-550   **WW**

A Lalique cockerel, etched 'LALIQUE FRANCE'.

For an alternative version of this piece, modeled as a car mascot, see page 26.
8.25in (21cm) high
$350-400   **JN**

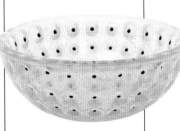

A modern Lalique clear and frosted 'Nemours' glass bowl, no.404, originally designed by Rene Lalique, etched 'Lalique France' to base.
10in (25.5cm) diam
$350-400   **WW**

GLASS

QUICK REFERENCE - LOETZ

- In Klostermühle, Bohemia, in 1836, a glassworks factory was founded by Johann Eisner. It 1852 it was acquired by Susanne Loetz, widow of the glass entrepreneur and maker Johann Loetz. The factory became known as Loetz Witwe (Loetz Widow) and later simply 'Loetz'.

- In 1879, the factory was taken over by Max Ritter von Spaun. His innovative designs, along with those of designers such as Prochaska and Franz Hofstätter, Michael Powolny, Koloman Moser and Josef Hoffmann made Loetz one of the largest glassmakers in Central Europe in the late 19thC and early 20thC. The company closed in 1947.

- Loetz's best-known ranges were iridescent and trailed in the Art Nouveau style. Common forms include ovoid, tapering or baluster-shaped vases, or gourd-like vases with extended necks.

- The factory was very influential and many competitors copied or were inspired by Loetz designs. This can cause problems identifying true Loetz works today. Loetz used various marks, the most common being 'Loetz / Austria' in script.

A Loetz 'Alpengruen' vase, with branches and birds with amber and red beads, three small red beads missing, enamellers codes to base.
1893   *6in (15cm) wide*
$1,600-2,000   **M&DM**

A Loetz pink 'Chine' vase.
c1897   *3in (7.5cm) high*
$350-400   **M&DM**

A pair of Loetz 'Octopus' or 'Victoria' vases, gilded, cased tentacle like air channels, UK importer's registration marks to base of one.

These 'Octopus' vases were renamed 'Victoria' by the British importer, to celebrate Queen Victoria's Jubilee.
1887   *6in (15cm) high*
$5,500-6,500   **M&DM**

A pair of Loetz vases, enameled with berries and branches, enamellers' codes to base.
c1888   *8in (20.5cm) high*
$1,000-1,300   **M&DM**

A Loetz vase, in the 'Creta Chine' pattern, with random whiplash lines.
c1898   *7.5in (19cm) high*
$400-550   **FLD**

A rare Loetz orange 'Phaenomen' 6893 vase, with waved bands of pale gold iridescence.
c1898   *10.25in (26cm) high*
$2,000-2,400   **L&T**

A Loetz Crete green 'Cisel' vase.
c1899   *8in (20.5cm) high*
$350-450   **M&DM**

A Loetz Crete 'Glatt' iridescent glass vase, series II-259, unsigned.
c1900   *7.75in (20cm) high*
$250-350   **WW**

A Loetz 'Candia' silver overlaid and iridescent glass vase, with 'Papillon' gold iridescence overlaid with cyclamen in silver.
c1900   *9.75in (25cm) high*
$1,600-2,000   **L&T**

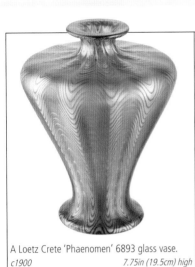

A Loetz Crete 'Phaenomen' 6893 glass vase.
c1900   *7.75in (19.5cm) high*
$1,600-2,000   **L&T**

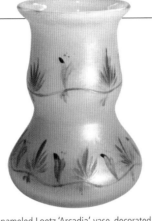

An enameled Loetz 'Arcadia' vase, decorated with lotus flowers.
c1900   *4in (10cm) high*
$350-450   **M&DM**

A Loetz bronze 'Rusticana' vase.

This is in the classic propeller blade shape.
c1900   *12in (30.5cm) high*
$1,200-1,500   **M&DM**

A Loetz 'Papillon' (butterfly wing) vase, with chrome-plate overlays and Secessionist handles.

1900   *11in (28cm) high*
$2,500-3,000   **M&DM**

A Loetz 'Norma' blue vase/bowl, with amber rigorie.
c1900   *4in (10cm) wide*
$800-950   **M&DM**

A Loetz 'Phaenomen' 6893 vase.

This vase is in the very rare orange finish.
c1900   *9in (23cm) high*
$3,000-3,600   **M&DM**

A Loetz Metalic blue and brown 'Pheanomen' 7773 vase.
c1900   *6in (15cm) wide*
$3,500-4,000   **M&DM**

A rare Loetz pink 'Medici' 'Phaenomen' 2/484 three-handled glass vase.
c1902   *5in (13cm) high*
$2,000-2,500   **L&T**

A Loetz blue on pale green 'Orpheus' jug.
c1907   *9in (23cm) high*
$650-800   **M&DM**

GLASS

A Loetz 'Ausfuehrung' 157 vase, in orange glass with black striping, series PN II-7452.

The 'Ausfuehrung' range is often wrongly attributed to Michael Powolny (1871-1954), an Austrian ceramicist and sculptor whose Art Deco glass designs tend to have similar vertical stripes and bright colors.

c1913-26   7.75in (20cm) high
$400-550   **L&T**

A Loetz 'Ausfuehrung' 157 jar and cover, unmarked.

c1914-30   7.75in (19.5cm) high
$350-400   **FLD**

A Loetz 'Ausfuehrung' 157 vase, in orange glass with black striping.

c1914-30   5.25in (13.5cm) wide
$750-850   **L&T**

A Loetz 'Ausfuehrung' 216 bowl vase, with applied tadpole prunts, red over purple.

c1925   7in (18cm) wide
$550-650   **M&DM**

A Loetz cobalt 'Silberstreifen' décor vase.
c1915   7in (18cm) high
$650-850   **M&DM**

A Loetz 'Silberstreifen' Candia amber décor bowl vase.
c1915   7in (18cm) wide
$650-850   **M&DM**

These were only recently identified as Loetz pieces.

A Loetz black on pink tango bowl.
c1925   9in (23cm) wide
$400-450   **M&DM**

A Loetz ball footed cameo open vase, with foliage.
c1925   9in (23cm) wide
$1,000-1,200   **M&DM**

A Loetz cobalt 'Papillon' iridescent twin-handled glass vase, of baluster form with open neck forming the handles, blue with mottled decoration, unsigned.
c1930   10.25in (26cm) high
$800-1,000   **HAN**

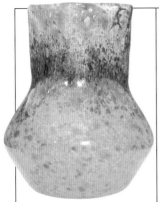

A 1930s Monart glass vase, shape CD, with mottled orange to green with aventurine inclusions.

8.75in (22cm) high

$800-850   **FLD**

A large Monart brown and orange vase, shape SA, size V.

c1935   *8in (20.5cm) high*

$400-450   **M&DM**

Judith Picks

I first came across Monart as a homesick Scot in London. Monart glass was made at the Moncrieff Glassworks in Perth, Scotland, from 1926-61. It was a collaboration between the Spanish glassmaker Salvador Ysart and Isobel Moncrieff, the wife of the factory's owner. 'Monart' comes from 'Moncrieff' and 'Ysart'. Salvador Ysart and his son Paul Ysart (see page 285) designed over 300 shapes, including vases, bowls, dishes and lamps. Most pieces were free-blown, and typically have vibrant colors and mottled patterns. Monart glass is not signed but bears a distinctive pontil mark. Before leaving the factory, every piece was given a sticky paper label. These were very often lost over time, so it is a great treat to a collector to discover one with the original paper label still present.

A 1930s Monart glass vase, shape SA, in pink graduating to amethyst with pulled trails, with original paper label.

9in (23cm) high

$550-650   **FLD**

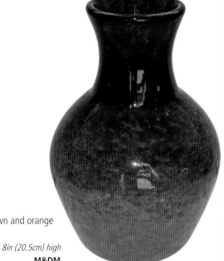

A Monart brown and orange vase, shape V.

c1935   *8in (20.5cm) high*

$400-450   **M&DM**

A Monart green and orange vase, shape OE.

c1935   *8in (20.5cm) high*

$350-400   **M&DM**

A Monart green and pink vase, shape TE.

c1935   *9in (23cm) high*

$450-600   **M&DM**

A Monart orange and black dish, shape MB.

c1935   *4in (10cm) high*

$250-300   **M&DM**

A Monart blue and black vase, shape OJ.

c1935   *6in (15cm) high*

$350-400   **M&DM**

GLASS

QUICK REFERENCE - VENINI

- Venini & C. was founded in Murano, Italy, in 1921 by Milanese lawyer Paolo Venini (1895-1959) and Venetian antique dealer Cappellin. Cappellin left the company a few years later.
- Venini achieved some success in the 1920s-30s and went on to become one of the leading post-war Italian glassworks. It produced decorative colored glass, reviving many traditional Venetian techniques along with new and innovative design.
- Key designers include Napoleone Martinuzzi (1892-1977), Gio Pointi (1891-1979) Carlo Scarpa (1906-78) and Fulvio Baconi (1915-96).
- Venini was acquired by the group Italian Luxury Industries in 2001.

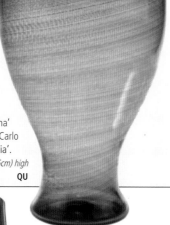

A Venini & C. 'Mezza Filigrana' cup form vase, designed by Carlo Scarpa, engraved 'venini italia'.

c1934   10.75in (27.5cm) high

$1,500-2,500   QU

A Venini & C. 'A Bolle' fish, by Tyra Lundgren, stamped 'venini murano E'.

1937   9.75in (25cm) high

$1,300-2,000   QU

A Venini & C. shell, designed by Tyra Lundgren, stamped 'venini murano ITALIA'.

c1938   8.25in (21cm) long

$800-950   QU

A Venini & C. 'Arlecchino' from the 'Commedia dell'Arte', by Fulvio Bianconi, stamped 'venini murano MADE IN ITALY', label under the stand, repaired fracture lines on the neck and on one arm.

1947-48   14.25in (36.5cm) high

$1,500-2,000   QU

A Venini & C. 'Taschentuch' or 'Fazzoletto' vase, designed by Fulvio Bianconi, marked 'venini 96', original manufacturer's label.

designed c1948-50   9in (23cm) high

$250-350   FIS

A Venini & C. glass vase, with green, aventurine and blue spiral inclusions.

c1950   10.75in (27cm) high

$750-850   L&T

A post-war Venini & C. 'Pezzato' vase, by Fulvio Bianconi, with tesserae in blue, red, green and yellow, acid marked.

11.5in (29cm) high

$2,500-3,500   FLD

A Venini & C. 'Calabase' vase, by James Carpenter, marked to base 'venini 99', original manufacturer's label.

designed c1972   9in (23cm) high

$900-1,100   FIS

A Venini & C. 'Forati' vase, designed by Fulvio Bianconi, marked 'Fulvio Bianconi venini 2000', original manufacturer's label.

2000   12.75in (32.5cm) high

$650-800   FIS

QUICK REFERENCE - BAROVIER & TOSO

- In 1878, four members of the Barovier family founded the company Fratelli Barovier. The family had a long history of glassmaking, and had been involved in the Murano glass industry since the 14thC.

- Ercole Barovier (1889-1974) gave up a career in medicine to join the company in 1919. He worked there for 53 years. He experimented with new methods of bringing color and texture to glass. This led to his 1929 Primavera series, with its distinctive white crackled surfaces and dark trim, his mid-1930s 'colorazione a caldo senza fuisone' technique (literally 'color glass while hot without fusing'), and his 1940s organic textured shapes in thick glass.

- In 1936, Fratelli Barovier merged with another successful glassmaking family company, Ferro Toso. The company was soon known as Barovier & Toso. After the death of Ercole Barovier, his son Angelo (1927-2007) took over the management of the company.

- Today, Barovier & Toso is part of Oikia 3.

A Barovier & Toso 'Diamante' vase, designed by Ercole Barovier, stamped 'barovier e toso murano'.

c1938   *11.5in (29cm) wide*

$2,000-2,500   **QU**

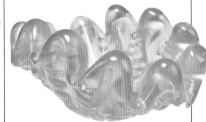

A Barovier & Toso 'big costolature' shell, designed by Ercole Barovier, of iridescent colorless glass.

1942   *15.5in (39.5cm) wide*

$2,000-2,500   **QU**

A Barovier & Toso 'Neolitico' plate, designed by Ercole Barovier.

1954   *12.75in (32.5cm) wide*

$1,300-2,000   **QU**

A Barovier & Toso 'Pezzati' egg vase, designed by Ercole Barovier.

c1956   *7.5in (19cm) high*

$8,000-8,500   **QU**

A Ferro Toso Barovier 'Aventurina' vase, designed by Ercole Barovier, foot with melted gold foil.

1936   *7.5in (19cm) high*

$650-800   **QU**

A Barovier & Toso 'Tessere ambra' cylindrical vase, designed by Ercole Barovier, engraved 'barovier e toso murano'.

1957   *7.25in (18.5cm) high*

$3,500-4,000   **QU**

A Barovier & Toso 'Porpora' vase, designed by Ercole Barovier, with torn, purple gold foil inclusions.

c1959   *11in (28cm) high*

$750-850   **QU**

A Barovier & Toso 'Efeso' cup shape vase, designed by Ercole Barovier, engraved 'barovier e toso murano' with remains of manufacturer's label.

c1964   *15.25in (39cm) high*

$3,000-4,000   **QU**

GLASS

QUICK REFERENCE - ALESSANDRO BARBARO

- Alessandro Barbaro was born in Murano, trained at the Formia factory, and has now been a glassmaker for over 35 years. He is a glass master at Vetreria Artistica Colleoni glassworks, where he works with his assistant Deigo Bardella.
- His figurative pieces are often inspired by animals or the human form, and his work is notable for its attention to detail and color.
- He combines the modern technique of 'massiccio', where large glass objects are shaped and molded whilst hot, with the more traditional technique of 'soffiato', or glass-blowing.
- His work is in the private collections of Elton John and Madonna, and can also be found in hotels and corporate headquarters around the world.

A Murano glass sculpture of three stylized eyes, by Alessandro Barbaro, signed.

18in (47cm) high

$800-950   **CHEF**

A Murano Picasso-style glass head of a girl, by Alessandro Barbaro, on a slate base, signed.

22.75in (58cm) high

$1,200-1,600   **CHEF**

A Murano Picasso-style glass head, by Alessandro Barbaro, modeled wearing a hat, signed.

23.5in (60cm) high

$2,000-2,500   **CHEF**

A Murano Picasso-style glass head, by Alessandro Barbaro, modeled wearing a wide brimmed hat, with aventurine inclusions, signed.

18in (47cm) high

$2,500-3,500   **CHEF**

A Murano Picasso-style double glass head, by Alessandro Barbaro, modeled one atop the other surmounted with a bird, signed.

21.75in (55cm) high

$900-1,100   **CHEF**

A Murano Picasso-style glass head, by Alessandro Barbaro, divided through the vertical, one side surmounted with a bird, signed.

16.25in (41.5cm) high

$900-1,000   **CHEF**

A Murano Picasso-style glass head, by Alessandro Barbaro, surmounted with a bird, on a marbled base, signed.

17in (43cm) high

$1,000-1,200   **CHEF**

A Murano stylized glass model of a horse's head, by Alessandro Barbaro, with deep wheel-cut decoration, signed.

17.25in (44cm) high

$650-800   **CHEF**

A post-war Cenedese vase, engraved signature and label.

13.25in (33.5cm) high

$250-350   **FLD**

An Effetre International 'Rainbow' ball vase, designed by Lino Tagliapietra, marked 'SAITA MURANO', for distributor.

1990   *9.25in (23.5cm) high*

$650-800   **FIS**

A Salviati & Cie flagon with stoppers, engraved 'Salviati'.

c1990   *7.25in (18.5cm) high*

$550-600   **QU**

A Murano glass vase, probably to a design by Carlo Scarpa, indistinct diamond point etched three-line mark.

12.5in (32cm) high

$400-550   **BE**

A Seguso Vetri d'Arte 'Bullicante' flagon with stopper, designed by Flavio Poli.

c1937   *7.25in (18.5cm) high*

$900-1,000   **QU**

A Barovier Seguso & Ferro 'Grigio oro' vase, designed by Flavio Poli and Alfredo Barbini, model no.Z1518.

Barovier Seguso & Ferro was a Murano glassmaker founded in 1933 by three ex-employees of Barovier, who left during the Great Depression: Antonio Seguso, Luigi Ferro and Napoleone Barovier, the cousin of Ercole Barovier (see page 229). The company still exists today as Seguso & C. Vetri d'Arte.

1936   *14.5in (37cm) high*

$5,500-6,000   **QU**

A Seguso Vetri d'Arte 'Sommerso' vase, designed by Flavio Poli, model no.111665.

1957   *11.5in (29.5cm) high*

$650-800   **QU**

A Sommerso Seguso Vetri d'Arte glass bowl, by Flavio Poli, with acid textured corroso finish, unmarked.

13.5in (34cm) wide

$900-1,100   **FLD**

A Seguso Viro 'Acqua' vase, marked 'Seguso Viro 67 / 101 ACQUA;, with manufacturer's labels.

c1995   *11.75in (30cm) high*

$350-400   **QU**

GLASS

A 1950s Gino Cenedese flat aquarium.

8.75in (22cm) wide

$550-600   **QU**

A pair of 1960s Vetreria Archimede Seguso rabbit and squirrel figures, the rabbit with sticker, 'MADE IN ITALY MURANO'.

squirrel 7in (17.5cm) high

$400-450   **QU**

A 20thC sommerso glass fish, in the manner of Cedenese.

11.5in (29cm) high

$100-140   **FLD**

QUICK REFERENCE - VISTOSI 'PULCINI'

- These endearing and quirky 'Pulcini' glass birds were created by Alessandro Pianon (1931-84) for the Vistosi glassworks.
- Vistosi was established in Murano in 1945 by the Vistosi family. In 1956, they hired Alessandro Pianon, a young Venetian architect, to revise the company's designs.
- Pianon's 'Pulcini' series was released in 1962. It consisted of five birds: a spherical orange bird, a cubic olive bird, a tall green/blue bird, a rounded blue/gray bird, and a wedge-shaped blue bird.
- The bodies were made of colored glass, the legs of copper wire and the eyes of circular floret canes. Each bird was hand blown into a mold. Some were then decorated with murrines, slices of multicolored glass. Some had textured surfaces applied after shaping. The beaks and tails were pinched on. The metal sockets for the legs were set in clear glass applied after the making of the body. Each individual bird created was unique.
  - This complicated production process meant that the 'Pulcini' birds were made in limited numbers and were very expensive. When first released in 1962, they could not be bought from a department store but had to be specially ordered. They remain very rare today, and a collection of all five birds is uncommon.

A Vistosi glass bird, designed by Alessandro Pianon, blue glass with applied glass eyes, on copper wire feet.

c1960   *10.5in (26.5cm) high*

$6,500-8,000   **GWA**

A Toso Murano glass model of a leaping fish, signed.

15.25in (39cm) high

$300-400   **CHEF**

A Toso Murano glass stallion, the mane, tail and hooves with aventurine inclusions, etched mark.

17.75in (45cm) wide

$350-400   **CHEF**

An Aureliano Toso swan shell, designed by Dino Martens, model no.6074.

1954   *9.5in (24cm) high*

$1,500-2,500   **QU**

A post-war Murano candelabra, modeled as a blackamoor, with aventurine inclusions.

11.5in (29cm) high

$250-350   **FLD**

A 1950s Kosta clear crystal glass liqueur 'Hen flask' decanter, designed by Vicke Lindstrand, with a stopper in the form of a head with beak and comb, engraved signature 'Kosta LG188'.

7.75in (19cm) high

$250-350   **FLD**

A 1950s Kosta 'Abstracta Lu' vase, designed by Vicke Lindstrand, with random black whiplash lines over blue and green spotting, engraved signature.

11.5in (29.5cm) high

$750-850   **FLD**

A late 1950s Kosta Boda teardrop shape vase, designed by Vicke Lindstrand, with an encased design in amethyst colored glass, marked 'Kosta LH1404'.

9in (23cm) high

$150-200   **LYN**

A mid-20thC Kosta 'Ventana' vase, designed by Mona Morales Schildt.

9.5in (24cm) high

$450-550   **FLD**

A late 20thC Kosta Boda Artists Collection cameo glass bowl, designed by Ulrica Hydman-Vallien, cut with abstract birds, snakes and flowers picked out in enamel, engraved and handpainted signatures, no.33 of a limited edition of 60.

11.5in (29cm) wide

$550-650   **FLD**

A Kosta Boda 'Open Minds' vase, designed by Ulrica Hydman-Vallien, etched mark with 'no.48744', two original labels and painted signature.

$150-200   **DA&H**

A later 20thC Kosta Boda Artists Collection glass, by Ulrica Hydman-Vallien, engraved signature.

4.25in (11cm) high

$80-100   **FLD**

A Kosta 'Colora' vase, designed by Vicke Lindstrand, the green core with blue threads, cased in clear crystal, engraved signature.

c1958   *10.75in (27cm) high*

$1,000-1,200   **FLD**

A later 20thC Kosta Boda Artists Collection glass vase, designed by Bertil Vallien, with a pearlized iridescent ground, engraved signature.

11.5in (29cm) high

$150-200   **FLD**

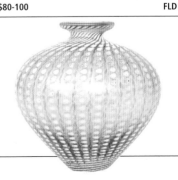

GLASS

QUICK REFERENCE - ORREFORS

- The Orrefors factory was established in 1898 in Småland, Sweden. It began by producing bottles and tableware but from the 1920s increasingly focused on art glass.
- It first experimented with cameo glass, then with 'graal' engraving and, from 1920, with cut and engraved glass produced using a copper wheel. Its pieces were often colorless, engraved with stylized designs inspired by the Swedish landscape.
- Key designers included Simon Gate (1883-1945), Edward Hald (1883-1980), Vicke Lindstrand (1904-83) and Sven Palmqvist (1906-84).
- Orrefors merged with Kosta Boda in 1990.

An Orrefors Secessionist uranium green 'Astrid' wine glass, designed by Simon Gate.
c1922   6.25in (16cm) high
$40-50   **HAN**

A Orrefors spherical form fish graal vase, designed by Edward Hald, marked 'Orrefors, Fish Graal 873P, Edward Hald'.
c1960   5in (12.5cm) diam
$1,000-1,300   **LYN**

A Orrefors teardrop form fish graal vase, designed by Edward Hald for Orrefors, marked 'Orrefors, Fish Graal 1228H, Edward Hald'.
c1954   4in (10cm) diam
$1,000-1,300   **LYN**

An Orrefors 'Ariel' vase, designed by Edvin Öhrström, engraved signature.
c1955   7.75in (20cm) high
$800-1,000   **FLD**

A post-war Orrefors 'Ariel' glass vase, designed by Edvin Öhrström, engraved signature.
5.75in (14.5cm) high
$120-160   **FLD**

An Orrefors 'Kraka' vase, by Sven Palmqvist, cased in clear crystal over a blue to green interior decorated with a fine bubble mesh, engraved signature.
c1955   8in (20.5cm) high
$750-850   **FLD**

An Orrefors 'Sea Life' 'Graal' glass bowl, by Eva Englund, internally decorated with jellyfish, dated, engraved signature.
1968   8.75in (22cm) diam
$4,000-4,500   **FLD**

An Orrefors crystal glass vase, designed by Per Sundberg, of organic shouldered ovoid form, in a satin acid finish, engraved signature.
10.75in (27cm) high
$600-650   **FLD**

A late 1960s Aseda of Sweden decanter, 'oxide' series, designed by Bo Bogstrom, flecked charcoal glass cased in clear.

10in (25.5cm) high

$100-150   **LYN**

A late 1920s Elme pressed glass 'Skyscraper' vase, designed by Edvin Ollers, molded with a stylized architectural landscape.

9.75in (25cm) high

$130-200   **FLD**

QUICK REFERENCE - HOLMEGAARD

- In the early 1820s, Count Christian Danneskiold-Samsøe asked permission from the King of Denmark to establish a glassworks at Holmegaard Mose. He died before receiving the answer, but when the permission came, his widow Countess Henriette Danneskiold-Samsøe founded the glassworks. Production began in 1825. The factory was located on a peat bog, which provided sufficient fuel to heat the kilns.
- Initial production focussed on bottles for beer or spirits, but in the 1830s glassblowers were brought in from Germany and Bohemia to help expand the factory's domestic range.
- Holmegaard continued to produce through the 19thC and 20thC. Its art glass pieces were usually free blown and are generally marked with the designer's mark and date of production.
- Today Holmegaard is part of the Royal Scandinavia group and produces both hand-blown and machine-blown glass.

A Flygsfors free-form non vase, designed by Paul Kedlev, in white red and clear glass, marked 'Flygsfors Coquelle 63', designed mid-1950s.

1963   16in (40.5cm) high

$350-400   **LYN**

A Holmegaard red-cased glass Gulvase or floor vase, designed by Otto Brauer.

c1962   18in (46cm) high

$350-400   **HAN**

A late 1960s Holmegaard Napoli vase, designed by Michael Bang, white, blue and clear glass with trailed decoration, with label.

10in (25.5cm) high

$200-250   **LYN**

A late 1960s Holmegaard Gulvase, designed by Otto Brauer in the late 1950s, white green and clear glass.

10in (25.5cm) high

$250-300   **LYN**

A late 1960s Holmegaard Carnaby case, designed by Per Lutken, yellow glass cased in clear, labelled.

10in (25.5cm) high

$400-450   **LYN**

A late 1960s Holmegaard Carnaby vase, designed by Per Lutken, white red and clear glass, labelled.

The Carnaby range was never marked but only labelled.

8in (20.5cm) high

$150-170   **LYN**

GLASS

An Iittala white ibis, designed by Oiva Toikka, Iittala labels to body, faint etched marks to base, boxed.

2in (5cm) high

$550-650   **PW**

An Iittala mandarin duck, designed by Oiva Toikka, Iittala labels to body, faint etched marks to base, no.19/50, boxed.

4.75in (12cm) high

$200-250   **PW**

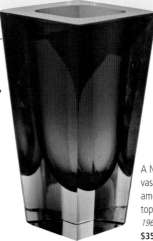

A Nuutajarvi Notsjo 'Prisma' vase, designed by Kaj Franck, the amethyst core cased in a pale topaz, engraved signature.

1960   5.25in (13.5cm) high

$350-400   **FLD**

A mid-20thC Nuutajarvi Notsjo 'GN25' sommerso vase, signed 'G. Nyman' with acid pen.

13.5in (34cm) high

$1,000-1,200   **FLD**

A mid-20thC Nuutajarvi Notsjo 'Pearl Necklace' Helminauha vase, with an oblique string of bubbles, signed 'G. Nyman' with acid pen.

9in (23cm) high

$900-1,000   **FLD**

A Nuutäjarvi mandarin duck, designed by Oiva Toikka, etched marks to base, numbered.

4.5in (11.5cm) high

$150-250   **PW**

A Riihimäki 'Nebulosa' glass vase, designed by Nanny Still.

c1968   7in (18cm) high

$100-130   **PSA**

QUICK REFERENCE - RIIHIMÄKI

- The Riihimäki glassworks was founded by M.A. Kolehmainen and his son A.P. Kolehmainen in 1910 in the town of Riihimäki, Finland. It began by making glass bottles and window glass, but soon expanded its range. By 1927 it was the largest glass factory in Finland.
- Key designers included Aimo Okkolin from 1937, Helena Tynell and Nanny Still from 1949, and Tamara Aladin from 1959. These four were the chief designers for Riihimäki up until the 1970s.
- Riihimäki was purchased by Ahlstrom in 1985 and merged with Karhula in 1988 under the name Ahlstrom Riihimaen Lasi Oy. The Riihimäki factory closed in 1990.

A post-war Riihimäki Harlekini sapphire blue glass liqueur set, designed by Nanny Still.

decanter 11.5in (29.5cm) high

$350-400   **FLD**

QUICK REFERENCE - STEUBEN

- The Steuben Glassworks was founded in Corning, NY, USA, in 1903, by Thomas G. Hawkes and English glassmaker and chemist Frederick Carder.
- In 1904, Carder patented an iridescent glass called 'Aurene', (from 'aurum', Latin for gold) which resembled Tiffany's 'favrile' glass. The 'Aurene' range was produced until 1933 in blue, brown, green and red.
- In 1918, the company was acquired by The Corning Glass Works. New ranges were introduced, including 'Calcite', 'Verre de Soie' and 'Cluthra'. Cameo glass was also made.
- In 1932-33, the factory was reorganized due to financial difficulties and Carder left. '10M', a high-quality, colorless crystal glass was introduced, and colored glass was gradually phased out. Steuben continues today as part of Corning Inc.

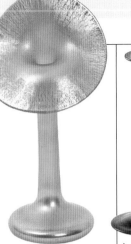

A Steuben Aurene 'Jack in the Pulpit' vase, model no.130, covered in a golden iridescence, etched 'Aurene 130' to base.

It is believed pieces of Steuben marked just 'Aurene' and the model number are some of the earliest examples of production.

7.75in (20cm) high

$1,300-2,000   WW

A pair of early 20thC Steuben blue Aurene candlesticks, both etched 'AURENE 686', one with remnants of foil label.

8in (20.5cm) high

$800-950   DRA

An early 20thC Steuben Aurene glass vase, with a tonal blue iridescence, unmarked.

7in (18cm) high

$400-550   FLD

An early 20thC Steuben blue Aurene glass vase, signed 'Steuben Aurene 923'.

6in (15cm) high

$350-400   DRA

An early 20thC Steuben gold Aurene bowl, on a French silver-plate stand, the stand with repair to one arm.

12in (30.5cm) high

$200-250   DRA

A early 20thC Steuben gold Aurene vase, with vine pattern, etched 'STEUBEN AURENE 6300', few minor scratches.

Provenance: Estate of Georgine Long, Bookkeeper to Gustav Stickley.

10.5in (25.5cm) high

$2,500-3,000   DRA

A 1920s Steuben Cluthra vase, unmarked, a few flecks to base.

10.75in (27.5cm) high

$650-800   DRA

A 1920s Steuben acid cut-back rose over alabaster vase, with fish, unmarked, a couple of scratches and bubbles.

9.5in (24cm) high

$2,000-2,500   DRA

GLASS

QUICK REFERENCE - STEVENS & WILLIAMS

- Stevens & Williams was established in Stourbridge in 1847 and produced high-quality, heavily cut crystal glass.
- In the early 1880s, it appointed John Northwood as manager and art director and Frederick Carder as a designer. Under Northwood's direction, the factory experimented with new techniques to create new art ranges, including 'Su No Ke' glass, a Japanese-inspired range, 'Jewell Glass', 'Verre de Soie', 'Tapestry' and 'Moss Agate'. It also created high-quality cameo glass.
- After Northwood's death in 1902 and Carder's departure in 1903, Stevens & Williams continued to flourish. It received a Royal Warrant in 1919 and changed its name to Royal Brierley Crystal in 1926. Royal Brierley went bankrupt in the 1990s.

A late 19thC Stevens & Williams cameo glass vase, unmarked.

9.5in (24cm) high

$600-650   **FLD**

A late 19thC Stevens & Williams cameo glass vase, cut with a scrolling convolvulus, acid marked 'cameo'.

7in (18cm) high

$600-750   **FLD**

A late 19thC Stevens & Williams cameo glass vase, cut with a flowering apple tree bough, unmarked.

8.25in (21cm) high

$200-250   **FLD**

A late 19thC Stevens & Williams cameo glass powder bowl, cut with convolvulus, unmarked.

3.75in (9.5cm) high

$400-450   **FLD**

A late 19thC Stevens & Williams 'Verre de Soire' vase, with wrythen air trap lines to the magenta interior, unmarked.

8.25in (21cm) high

$400-550   **FLD**

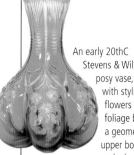

An early 20thC Stevens & Williams posy vase, cut with stylized flowers and foliage below a geometric upper border, unmarked.

5.5in (14cm) high

$250-300   **FLD**

An early 20thC Stevens & Williams double-cased crystal glass vase, cut with a river scene with ducks and flowering boughs with an exotic bird, unmarked.

15.75in (40cm) high

$650-800   **FLD**

A CLOSER LOOK AT A STEVENS & WILLIAMS VASE

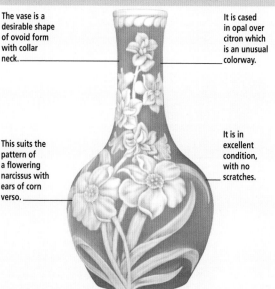

The vase is a desirable shape of ovoid form with collar neck.

It is cased in opal over citron which is an unusual colorway.

This suits the pattern of a flowering narcissus with ears of corn verso.

It is in excellent condition, with no scratches.

A late 19thC Stevens & Williams cameo glass vase, unmarked.

9in (23cm) high

$1,600-2,000   **FLD**

An early 20thC Stevens & Williams spirit decanter, polished intaglio cut with flowers and foliage with clear crystal stopper.

9.5in (24cm) high

$1,200-1,500   **FLD**

An early 20thC Stevens & Williams decanter, with a clear crystal hollow blown loop handle, shallow collar neck with integral spout, unmarked.

11in (28cm) high

$1,000-1,200   **FLD**

An early 20thC Stevens & Williams crystal glass decanter and stopper, with hallmarked silver collar, Robert Pringle & Sons, London.

1901   *9.5in (24cm) high*

$200-250   **FLD**

An early 20thC Stevens & Williams crystal liqueur glass, with a double-cased ovoid bowl flash cut with panels of fruit with floral borders, unmarked.

4.75in (12cm) high

$450-550   **FLD**

An early 20thC Stevens & Williams hock glass, flash cut with strawberry diamond swags between ribbons.

7in (18cm) high

$750-800   **FLD**

An early 20thC Stevens & Williams double-cased crystal glass vase, flash cut with flowers and foliage above a strawberry diamond ground, unmarked.

9.25in (23.5cm) high

$350-400   **FLD**

A 1930s Stevens & Williams 'Rainbow' pattern vase, in the manner of Keith Murray, unmarked, drilled for a lamp base.

10.25in (26cm) high

$100-160   **FLD**

A 1930s Stevens & Williams vase, intaglio cut with floral trailing above engraved berry boughs.

6.75in (17cm) high

$200-250   **FLD**

An early 20thC Stevens & Williams glass vase, flash cut with a stylized flowering foliate scroll, unmarked.

11.5in (29cm) high

$200-250   **FLD**

GLASS

A contemporary studio glass vase, by Claire Kelly, signed and dated.

2005   *6.25in (16cm) high*
$200-250   FLD

A Siddy Langley bowl, with petrol iridescent ground, dated, engraved signature.
1987   7in (17.5cm) diam
$350-400   FLD

A Peter Layton art glass flask vase, in the 'Landscape' pattern, etched signature.

8.75in (22.5cm) high
$250-300   DA&H

QUICK REFERENCE - PETER LAYTON

Peter Layton (b.1937) is an internationally successful glass artist. He was born in Yorkshire, educated at Bradford Art College and then London's Central School of Art and Design. He learnt pioneering techniques of working with hot glass from Harvey Littleton at the University of Iowa, where he worked 1966-69. On his return to Britain, he established his own glass studio in Scotland, a Glass Department at Hornsey College of Art and later the London Glassblowing Workshop, which is still going today.

A Peter Layton studio glass vase, signed, some light scratches to the surface.
9.75in (25cm) high
$450-550   ECGW

A 1970s Mdina studio glass vase, signed.
6.75in (17cm) high
$60-100   HAN

An Okra studio glass vase, Glass Guild Founder Member 1997/1998, no.5, with iridescent wave design, luster effect, signed.

The Okra Glass studio was founded by Richard Golding and Nicola Osborne in 1979.
4.5in (11.5cm) high
$120-160   HAN

A set of six studio pedestal wine glasses, by Karlin Rushbrooke, incised 'Karlin Rushbrooke' and dated '1976' verso.
1976   7.5in (19cm) high
$150-200   LSK

A studio glass bowl, by Anthony Wassell, cut in the 'Delta' pattern in frosted and polished finish, engraved signature, dated.
1995   20.75in (53cm) wide
$400-450   FLD

A studio glass 'Visage' bowl, by Iestyn Davies for Blowzone, engraved signature, dated.

1998   *9.5in (24cm) wide*

$450-550   **FLD**

A late 20thC 'Tutti Frutti' bowl, by Iestyn Davies for Blowzone, cut with elliptical cuts, unsigned.

          9.5in (24cm) wide

$900-1,000   **FLD**

QUICK REFERENCE - SAM HERMAN

- Sam Herman (b.1936) is a designer, painter, glassblower and sculptor, and key figure in the studio glass movement.
- He was born in Mexico and studied Fine Art at the University of Wisconsin, where he was taught by American studio glassmakers Dominick Labino (1910-87) and Harvey Littleton (1922-2013).
- He later moved to Britain, and in 1969 became head of the glass department at the Royal College of Art in London. Here he taught his students to work directly with molten glass, and encouraged glass designers to craft their work themselves.
- In 1969 he and Michael Harris founded the studio Glasshouse in London. In 1974 he set up Australia's first hot glass studio in Adelaide. He also produced designs for Vat St Lambert in Belgium and Rosenthal in Germany.

A Val St Lambert amorphic vase, by Sam Herman, with offset aperture, with pulled glass to the shoulder, metallic oxides, etched signature 'CA.47'.

          12.5in (32cm) high

$600-750   **WW**

A Val St Lambert shouldered form glass vase, by Sam Herman, with swirling green and yellow bands with metallic luster, etched 'V.S.L'.

          8.75in (22cm) high

$450-550   **WW**

A luster glass bottle vase, by Sam Herman with applied whorls and spotted inclusions, etched marks to base 'SAMUEL J. HERMAN / 1972'.

1972   *9.5in (24cm) high*

$1,600-2,000   **L&T**

A shouldered slender elliptical form glass vase, by Sam Herman, surface marvered with metallic oxide waving stripe with blue drip, etched signature and date.

1978   *11.5in (29.5cm) high*

                    WW

$650-800

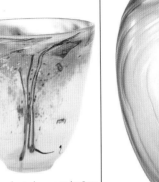

A Val St Lambert glass vase, by Sam Herman, cased in clear glass, acid-etched 'Val St Lambert', etched signature and date.

1979   *11in (28cm) high*

$1,200-1,600   **WW**

A contemporary studio glass 'Contour' vase, by Catherine Hough, engraved signature.

          11.75in (30cm) high

$450-550   **FLD**

GLASS

QUICK REFERENCE - THOMAS WEBB & SONS

- Thomas Webb & Sons was founded by Thomas Webb in Stourbridge in 1837. On the death of Thomas Webb in 1869, the company was taken over by his son, Thomas Wilkes Webb.
- Along with its own team of craftsman, Webb employed freelance glass decorators, such as the skilled French decorator and gilder, Jules Barbe.
- Its rock crystal-style glass, developed by Willian Fritsche in the 1870s, was shaped by deep cutting, wheel engraving and polishing, to imitate the look of natural rock crystal. Opaque yellow and pink Queen's Burmese pieces were manufactured with the permission of the inventors from US Mount Washington Glass Works. Webb's cameo glass was also popular, as was its 'Cameo Fleur' glass, cut by means of chemicals rather than by hand.

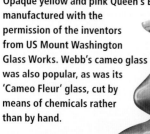

A Thomas Webb & Son Ivory cameo glass vase, engraved with anthemion designs and formal borders.

c1880   5in (13cm) high

$250-350   **WW**

A late 19thC miniature cameo glass vase, by Thomas Webb & Sons, cased in opal over ruby over citron with an opal interior, cut with a flowering blossom bough with butterfly.

2.25in (6cm) high

$450-550   **FLD**

A late 19thC Thomas Webb & Sons cameo glass vase, cut with a geranium and butterfly, unmarked.

5in (13cm) high

$650-800   **FLD**

A late 19thC cameo glass vase, by Thomas Webb & Sons, cased in opal over citron and cut with a flowering fuchsia bough with butterflies, unmarked.

5in (13cm) high

$750-850   **FLD**

A late 19thC Thomas Webb & Sons cameo glass posy vase, cut with a butterfly and flowering fuschia vine, unmarked.

2.75in (7cm) high

$600-750   **FLD**

A late 19thC Thomas Webb & Sons cameo glass vase, cut with a flowering hawthorn branch, unmarked.

5.5in (14cm) high

$750-850   **FLD**

A Webb 'Bronze' glass vase, ovoid with applied loop handles, covered in an iridescent finish, unsigned.

11.75in (30cm) high

$350-400   **WW**

A Webb Corbett enameled vase, depicting bowls of fruit, signed.

Webb Corbett was established in 1897 by Thomas and Herbert Webb, grandchildren of Thomas Webb, and Harry Corbett. The company specialized in cut and engraved glass, and enameled pieces, as well as producing rock crystal-style pieces similar to those of Thomas Webb & Sons. Many of these were designed by William Kny, the son of Frederick Englebert Kny, one of the designers for Thomas Webb. Another key designer, Irene Stevens, joined the firm in 1946.

c1920   4in (10cm) high

$90-100   **M&DM**

QUICK REFERENCE - WHITEFRIARS

- In the late 17thC, a glassworks was founded at Whitefriars, off Fleet Street, London. This glassworks was taken over by James Powell in 1834 and renamed James Powell & Sons.
- From the 1830s, Powell & Sons produced sections of stained glass windows, expanding the business to include domestic wares in the mid-19thC. In 1875, James Powell's grandson, Henry James Powell, joined the works, where he experimented with new colors and heat-resistant glass. Barnaby Powell, James Powell's great-grandson, was a key designer at the firm from the late 1920s, joined by James Hogan in 1932 and William Wilson in 1933.
- Whitefriars struggled financially in the 1970s and closed in the 1980s. Glass produced by the company from the 1830s to 1980 is usually referred to as 'Whitefriars' glass, although the name was not officially adopted until 1962. The Whitefriars brand name is now owned by the Scottish glassmaker Caithness.

A 1930s Whitefriars ribbon-trailed vase, by James Hogan, pattern no.8975.

9.75in (25cm) high

$200-250   FLD

A sea green optic molded glass vase, by William Wilson for James Powell and Sons, Whitefriars.

c1937   *12.25in (31cm) high*

$60-80   HAN

A Whitefriars 'Textured' range vase, by Geoffrey Baxter, pattern no.9667, in tangerine.

Designer Geoffrey Baxter joined the factory in 1954 and created his innovative 'Textured' range in 1967. This included distinctive shapes such as the 'Drunken Bricklayer' and 'Banjo' vases. The glass continued to be hand-blown, but Baxter experimented with unusual techniques, using nails, wire and wood bark to create his prototype molds. The following pieces are all in the 'Textured' range.

An 'Alsatian Blue' vase, by James Powell, Whitefriars, with 'Sea Green' folded foot.

8.5in (21.5cm) high

$150-250   APAR

10.5in (27cm) high

$200-250   FLD

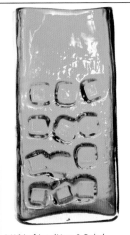

A Whitefriars 'Nuts & Bolts' vase, by Geoffrey Baxter, pattern no.9668, in kingfisher blue.

10.5in (27cm) high

$350-400   FLD

A Whitefriars 'Mobile Phone' vase, by Geoffrey Baxter, pattern no.9670, in tangerine.

6.25in (16cm) high

$200-250   FLD

A Whitefriars 'Mobile Phone' vase, by Geoffrey Baxter, pattern no.9670, in kingfisher blue.

6.25in (16cm) high

$150-200   FLD

A Whitefriars 'Mobile Phone' vase, by Geoffrey Baxter, no.9670, in willow, original label and Design Centre London label.

6.5in (16.5cm) high

$200-250   HAN

A Whitefriars 'Mobile Phone' vase, by Geoffrey Baxter, in willow, unsigned.

10.75in (27cm) high

$300-400   WW

A Whitefriars 'Drunken Bricklayer' vase, by Geoffrey Baxter, pattern no.9673, in meadow green.

13.5in (34cm) high

$1,200-1,600   **FLD**

A Whitefriars 'Drunken Bricklayer' vase, by Geoffrey Baxter, pattern no.9672, in indigo.

13in (33cm) high

$650-800   **FLD**

A Whitefriars 'Drunken Bricklayer' vase, by Geoffrey Baxter, in sage, unsigned.

7.75in (20cm) high

$650-800   **WW**

A Whitefriars 'Drunken Bricklayer' vase, by Geoffrey Baxter, in meadow green, unsigned.

8.5in (21.5cm) high

$550-650   **WW**

A rare Whitefriars 'Drunken Bricklayer' vase, by Geoffrey Baxter, in lavender, unsigned.

8.25in (21cm) high

$1,300-2,000   **WW**

A Whitefriars 'Cello' vase, by Geoffrey Baxter, pattern no.9675, in cinnamon.

7.5in (19cm) high

$150-200   **FLD**

A Whitefriars 'Cello' vase, by Geoffrey Baxter, pattern no.9675, in pewter.

7.5in (19cm) high

$200-250   **FLD**

A Whitefriars 'Cello' vase, by Geoffrey Baxter, pattern no.9675, in meadow green.

7.5in (19cm) high

$200-250   **FLD**

A Whitefriars 'Cello' vase, by Geoffrey Baxter, pattern no.9675, in tangerine.

7.5in (19cm) high

$350-400   **FLD**

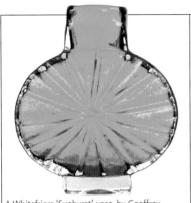

A Whitefriars 'Sunburst' vase, by Geoffrey Baxter, pattern no.9676, in kingfisher blue.

6in (15cm) high

$200-250   **FLD**

A Whitefriars 'TV' vase, by Geoffrey Baxter, pattern no.9677, in meadow green.

6.75in (17cm) high

$250-300   **FLD**

A Whitefriars 'Shoulder' vase, by Geoffrey Baxter, pattern no.9678, in kingfisher blue.

9.75in (25cm) high

$200-250   **FLD**

A Whitefriars 'Hoop' vase, by Geoffrey Baxter, pattern no.9680, in pewter.

11.75in (30cm) high

$250-350   **FLD**

A Whitefriars 'Banjo' vase, by Geoffrey Baxter, pattern no.9681, in willow.

12.5in (32cm) high

$1,000-1,200   **FLD**

A Whitefriars 'Banjo' vase, by Geoffrey Baxter, pattern no.9681, in kingfisher blue.

12.5in (32cm) high

$900-1,000   **FLD**

A Whitefriars 'Banjo' vase, by Geoffrey Baxter, pattern no.9681, in pewter.

12.5in (32cm) high

$1,200-1,500   **FLD**

A Whitefriars 'Banjo' vase, by Geoffrey Baxter, pattern no.9681, in meadow green.

12.5in (32cm) high

$2,500-3,000   **FLD**

A Whitefriars 'Banjo' vase, by Geoffrey Baxter, pattern no.9681, in tangerine.

12.5in (32cm) high

$1,300-2,000   **FLD**

GLASS

A Whitefriars 'Onion' vase, by Geoffrey Baxter, pattern no.9758, in meadow green.

5.5in (14cm) high

$200-250   **FLD**

A Whitefriars 'Onion' vase, by Geoffrey Baxter, pattern no.9758, in kingfisher blue.

5.5in (14cm) high

$200-250   **FLD**

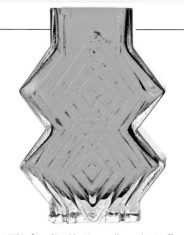

A Whitefriars 'Double Diamond' vase, by Geoffrey Baxter, pattern no.9759, in kingfisher blue.

6.25in (16cm) high

$150-200   **FLD**

A Whitefriars 'Double Diamond' vase, by Geoffrey Baxter, pattern no.9759, in aubergine.

6.25in (16cm) high

$250-300   **FLD**

A Whitefriars 'Double Diamond' vase, by Geoffrey Baxter, pattern no.9759, in meadow green.

6.25in (16cm) high

$250-300   **FLD**

A Whitefriars 'Double Diamond' vase, by Geoffrey Baxter, pattern no.9759, in indigo.

6.25in (16cm) high

$130-200   **FLD**

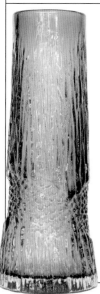

A Whitefriars 'Rocket' vase, by Geoffrey Baxter, pattern no.9825, in sage green.

12.25in (31cm) high

$600-650   **FLD**

A Whitefriars 'Nipple' vase, by Geoffrey Baxter, pattern no.9828, in lilac.

10.5in (27cm) high

$800-850   **FLD**

A Whitefriars 'Nipple' vase, by Geoffrey Baxter, pattern no.9828, in kingfisher blue.

10.5in (27cm) high

$650-800   **FLD**

A pair of Chance Glass handkerchief vases, with a cut linear pattern.

largest 6.25in (16cm) high

$130-200   **FLD**

A 1930s Art Deco Bimini lamp worked glass figure of Diana the Huntress, unmarked.

6in (15cm) high

$250-400   **FLD**

A contemporary Caithness vase, cut and polished with penguins, original label.

9.5in (24cm) high

$120-160   **FLD**

A pair of vases, with pewter mounts, with a spider in a web, signed 'Coquereles' in the pewter.

c1930

$1,300-1,600   **M&DM**

A James Couper & Sons, 'Clutha' glass bottle vase, with aventurine and milky trailed inclusions.

James Couper and Sons was founded in Glasgow in 1855. In the 1890s it patented 'Clutha' glass, a range of usually blown glassware with etched or engraved decorative elements. Christopher Dresser (see pages 192-193) produced designs for the 'Clutha' range. The company closed in 1922.

c1900   *8.25in (21cm) high*

$550-650   **L&T**

A Dartington kingfisher blue glass 'Flower People' face vase, designed by Frank Thrower, no.FT16.

Dartington Glass was established in 1967, in Torrington, Devon, as a manufacturer of quality glassware. It is now called Dartington Crystal and continues to produce crystal and glassware. Frank Thrower was the chief designer and creator of Dartington Glass.

6in (15cm) high

$60-80   **HAN**

12in (30.5cm) high

A Dartington kingfisher blue 'FT52 Head' vase, by Frank Thrower, unmarked.

9in (23cm) high

$120-160   **FLD**

A Dartington kingfisher blue Greek key glass 'FT58' vase, by Frank Thrower.

designed 1968   *9.5in (24cm) high*

$50-70   **HAN**

A Fioretti glass vase, with mezz filigrana-style decoration of cinnamon and lime bands all cased in clear crystal, dated, engraved signature.

1959   *9in (23cm) high*

$150-250   **FLD**

GLASS

A Haida enamel box and lid, enameled with stylized passion flowers.
c1915   *9in (23cm) wide*
$400-450   **M&DM**

A late 19thC graduated set of W.H. Heppell purple malachite glass fish jugs, the smallest with a design lozenge for '24th November 1882'.
tallest 7in (18cm) high
$100-120   **FLD**

A Lamartine cameo landscape vase, signed in cameo.

These were made by ex-Daum workers in French Algeria.
c1920   *9in (23cm) high*
$2,000-2,500   **M&DM**

A small Mdina cased glass fish vase, etched 'Mdina' verso.
6.75in (17cm) high
$80-100   **LSK**

A 1930s glass vase, by Verrerie D'Art de Metz, acid-cut with an abstract Art Deco design, signed 'Verame'.
8.25in (21cm) high
$130-200   **FLD**

An early 20thC Mont Joye Legras & Cie cameo glass vase, gilt shield mark to the base.

Mont Joye Legras & Cie was a glass factory based in Paris from the late 19thC to early 20thC. It produced its first cameo designs in 1900. It ran a glassworks of over 1,000 makers and decorators. After World War II, it merged with Cristallerie de Pantin to form Verreries et Cristalleries de St Denis.
5in (13cm) high
$350-400   **FLD**

An early 20thC Poschinger vase, decorated with lily pads outlined with cream enamelling, over the deep emerald green body with internal aventurine, unmarked.
7.5in (19cm) high
$250-350   **FLD**

A Quezal Art Nouveau 'Aurene' with silver overlay vase, signed.
c1905   *7in (18cm) high*
$2,500-3,500   **M&DM**

A 19thC Richardsons vase, decorated in vitrified enamels in the Etruscan taste with classical dressed figures, printed marks.

10in (25.5cm) high

$150-200 **FLD**

A 1930s Richardsons cameo glass vase, cut with spiral lilies over a planished effect ground, acid marked.

6.25in (16cm) high

$350-400 **FLD**

An early 20thC Riedel Lithyalin vase, intaglio-cut with water-lilies picked out in gold over the marbled red and ocher ground, unmarked.

4.5in (11.5cm) high

$600-750 **FLD**

A purple on green gilded Riedel cameo vase.

This range was first exhibited at the 1900 Paris exhibition.

c1900 *12in (30.5cm) high*

$1,600-2,000 **M&DM**

A Riedel pair of vases enameled and gilded depicting butterflies.

c1890 *12in (30.5cm) high*

$2,000-2,500 **M&DM**

A Sabino pair of opalescent glass bookends, molded as opposed turkeys, etched marks 'Sabino, France'.

c1920 *bookends 7.5in (19cm) long*

$350-400 **L&T**

A Schneider purple to clear ball vase, cut and etched, footed, signed.

Charles Schneider was an Art Deco glass artist working in Paris in the 1910s-30s. After completing his apprenticeship at Daum Frères, Charles Scneider and his brother Ernest opened a family glassworks at Epinay-sur-Seine, France. The company shut in 1933 due to financial difficulties in the economic depression.

c1930 *5in (12.5cm) high*

$400-550 **M&DM**

An early 20thC Schneider Le Verre Français cameo 'Fig' pattern jug, signature cane.

6.75in (17cm) high

$350-400 **FLD**

A 19thC Sowerby malachite pressed glass Gladstone bag flower trough, dated.

1877 *3.5in (9cm) long*

$60-80 **FLD**

GLASS

A 20thC Stourbridge crystal glass bowl, unmarked.

9.75in (24.5cm) wide

$100-130 **FLD**

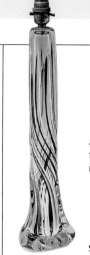

A late 19thC composed Stourbridge glass posy vase tulip garniture.

6.5in (16.5cm) high

$450-550 **FLD**

A Strathearn heavy glass table lamp, raised dolphin mark.

18in (46cm) high

$100-130 **LSK**

An early 20thC Stuart & Sons crystal glass vase.

Frederick Stuart began working at the Red House Glass Cone near Birmingham in 1827 when he was 11 years old. He took over the factory in 1882, forming Stuart & Sons in 1883. The factory is best-known for its fine-quality, clear cut glass.

6.5in (16.5cm) high

$60-80 **FLD**

An early 20thC Stuart & Sons crystal glass vase, with applied emerald green peacock trailing.

5in (13cm) high

$80-100 **FLD**

An Art Deco Val Saint Lambert cased glass vase, by Charles Graffart, with grid pattern and lens arcading, unmarked.

5.5in (14cm) high

$70-80 **HAN**

A 1930s W.M.F. 'Ikora' glass vase, cased in clear crystal over a tonal mottled jade green to red with central band of cinnamon, unmarked.

16.25in (41cm) high

$250-400 **FLD**

A W.M.F. 'Ikora' low flaring form glass bowl, pale yellow glass graduating to aubergine with white spider's web striations, unmarked.

13.75in (35cm) diam

$130-200 **WW**

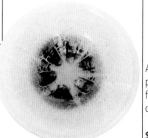

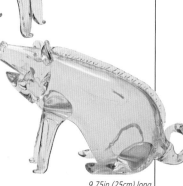

A pair of early 20thC novelty pig decanters, curled tail forming the handle, loss to one ear.

9.75in (25cm) long

$400-450 **BE**

A Burns Brian May Red Special electric guitar, made in Korea, serial no.BHN0xx8.
$550-650   GHOU

A Carvin AC50 electro-acoustic bass guitar, flamed Koa wood finish.
$750-850   GHOU

A Danelectro '56 U3 electric guitar, sparkle finish with some minor blemishes.
$250-400   GHOU

A Mark Griffiths' Fender Jazz Bass guitar, made in USA, serial no.1xxxx9, sold with CITES certificate no.554486/01.

This bass was purchased by Mark Griffiths at Mick's Vintage Guitars, Seattle USA in 1981. The body finish had been removed and the bridge replaced. The pickups were later changed to Seymour Duncans. It was used by Griffiths on many Cliff Richard band tours and the Everly Brothers reunion concerts at The Royal Albert Hall in 1984. It was eventually refinished in Fiesta red and used as a spare on The Shadows' final tour in 2004. This guitar comes with a certificate of authenticity signed by Griffiths, stating these facts.
1955-56
$4,000-5,500   GHOU

A Fender Classic Player Baja Telecaster electric guitar, made in Mexico, MX12xxxxx9.
2012
$550-650   GHOU

A Fender limited edition Donald 'Duck' Dunn Precision bass guitar, crafted in Japan, serial no.0xx8.
$1,600-2,000   GHOU

A Gibson Les Paul Custom '54 Reissue electric guitar, made in USA, serial no.LE774344, with original hard case, replaced bridge, original retained, re-fret.

This guitar was purchased from Becketts of Southampton in 1975 and has had a single owner since.
1972
$7,500-8,000   GHOU

A Gibson Diamond Dot ESDD335 hollow body electric guitar, made in USA, serial no.0xxx6xx6.
2006
$2,000-2,500   GHOU

Judith Picks

Memories of a concert at the Caird Hall in Dundee as a student! This guitar is sold with a buying-in receipt documenting the transaction between Greg Lake and Music Ground Ltd., signed by Greg Lake and dated '19/3/05'. Also included is a headed letter to a previous owner from Music Ground Ltd., confirming that this guitar with original finish, pickups and hardware belonged to Greg Lake of Emerson, Lake and Palmer.

The guitar can also be seen on Greg Lake's official website under the 'Collection' section.

A Greg Lake's Gibson Les Paul Standard electric guitar, made in USA, serial no.5xxxx0, pickup surrounds possibly later, replaced bridge, original retained.
1969
$9,500-10,000   **GHOU**

A Gretsch Eddie Cochran G120W-57 electric archtop guitar, serial no.01xxxxW57-116.
2001
$2,500-3,000   **GHOU**

A Guild F4 HR NT electro-acoustic guitar, made in USA, serial no.AF0xxxx0.
$650-800   **GHOU**

A Ovation Elite Standard 6868 electro-acoustic guitar.
1997
$650-800   **GHOU**

A Paul Reed Smith 20th Anniversary Custom 22 electric guitar, serial no.61xxxx4.
2006
$2,000-2,500   **GHOU**

A Rickenbacker 330 electric guitar, made in USA, serial no.H4xxx9.
1991
$1,500-2,000   **GHOU**

A Taylor T5C2 hollow body electro-acoustic guitar, Koa finish.
2010
$1,600-2,000   **GHOU**

A Watkins Rapier electric guitar, serial no.1120.
38.25in (97cm) long
$750-800   **PW**

A Yamaha SLG-100S silent guitar.
$300-350   **GHOU**

A 9ct gold bar pin, with garnet and seed pearls.

0.1oz

$40-50   LOCK

A 9ct gold amethyst bar pin.

0.1oz

$60-100   LOCK

A 9ct gold bar pin, set with tennis racket and ball.

$80-100   LOCK

A 9ct gold bar pin, set with jade stones.

0.11oz

$50-70   LOCK

A Victorian gold bear pin, with case.

0.35oz

$250-400   BELL

A late Victorian silver and gold pheasant pin, with pavé-set sapphire neck, 0.4ct diamond body and ruby wings and tail.

1.5in (3.5cm) long 0.3oz

$3,200-3,800   FELL

QUICK REFERENCE - ARCHIBALD KNOX

- Archibald Knox (1864-1933) was born on the Isle of Man. In 1897, he moved to London, where he worked at the Silver Studio, which provided designs for Liberty & Co.
- He created a range of Art Nouveau designs for Liberty & Co., including those for textiles, clocks, vases and jewelry. He is best known for his work on Liberty's Cymric silver and Tudric pewter ranges.
- His designs were heavily inspired by the Norse and Celtic rune stones and ruins on the Isle of Man, as can be seen by his use of intricate knot and cross motifs.
- He lived in London and the USA, before returning once more to the Isle of Man in 1913. There he remained until his death in 1933.

An Edwardian garnet set bar pin.

$60-80   HAN

An Art Nouveau silver and enamel bar pin, indistinct stamped marks.

1.5in (3.5cm) wide

$250-350   WW

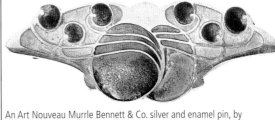

An Art Nouveau Murrle Bennett & Co. silver and enamel pin, by Archibald Knox, stamped 'MBCo / SILVER'.

c1900   *2in (5cm) wide*

$900-1,100   L&T

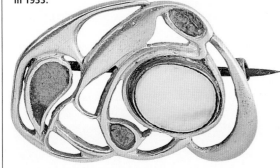

An Art Nouveau Liberty & Co. silver and enamel pin, no.1186e, by Archibald Knox, London, set with mother-of-pearl, stamped 'L&Co. / SILVER'.

c1900   *1.25in (3cm) wide*

$550-650   L&T

An Arts and Crafts Liberty & Co.,'Cymric' silver and enamel pin, by Archibald Knox, London, stamped 'L&Co. / CYMRIC', London.

c1900   *1.25in (3cm) wide*

$650-800   L&T

JEWELRY

A Norwegian silver-gilt and enameled butterfly pin, designed by Hroar Prydz, marked.

2in (5cm) wide

$120-160   HAN

A Norwegian silver and enameled butterfly pin, designed by Hroar Prydz.

1.5in (4cm) wide

$200-250   HAN

A silver and enameled butterfly pin, by J. Aitkin and Son, Birmingham.

1916   *1.25in (3cm) wide*

$130-200   HAN

A Norwegian David Andersen silver-gilt and enameled pin, designed by Willy Winnaess, signed.

1.5in (4cm) wide

$150-200   HAN

A 1940s Birmingham Medal Company silver and enameled leaf pin, marked 'Sterling'.

1in (2.5cm) wide

$40-50   HAN

An 18ct gold Kutchinsky rabbit pin, with sapphire and single-cut 0.15ct diamond eyes and buck teeth, ruby cabochon nose, signed, hallmarks for London.

1971   *2.25in (5.5cm) long 0.94oz*

$2,500-3,500   FELL

QUICK REFERENCE - KUTCHINSKY

- Kutchinsky was founded in London in the 1890s by Hirsch Kutchinsky. He and his family had recently moved to Britain from Poland, where they had historically been jewellers to the court of King Ludwig of Bavaria.
- In the 1930s, the company was taken over by Kutchinsky's grandson, Joseph Kutchinsky. It continued to flourish after World War II.
- It is best known for its designs incorporating semi-precious stones and diamonds, especially its animal pins set with gemstones.
- Kutchinsky was purchased by Moussaieff Jewellers in 1991.

An 18ct gold, 0.3ct diamond, emerald and enamel Kutchinsky tiger pin, signed, hallmarks for London.

1968   *3in (7.5cm) long 1.63oz*

$3,000-3,500   FELL

A yellow metal giraffe pin set, with diamonds and ruby, with indistinct Continental hallmarks.

0.77oz

$650-800   GWA

A gem-set jasper fish pin.

2.25in (6cm) long

$300-350   FELL

A Tiffany & Co. 0.3ct diamond gecko pin, signed, stamped 'PT 950', with maker's case.

1in (2.5cm) long 0.14oz

$1,200-1,300   FELL

QUICK REFERENCE - GEORG JENSEN

- Georg Jensen Co. was founded in 1904 by Georg Jensen (1866-1935), an important Danish silversmith and jewelry designer of the late 19thC and early 20thC.
- Inspired by the Arts and Crafts and Art Nouveau movements, Jensen created a range of detailed jewelry designs over the course of his life. His distinctive pieces were highly success.
- Georg Jensen Co. has employed many talented designers, including Johan Rohde (1865-1935), Harald Nielsen (1892-1977), Henning Koppel (1918-81), and Vivianna Torun Bülow-Hübe (1927-2004). Georg Jensen Co. is still operational today.

A Georg Jensen 'Moonlight Blossom' '283' sterling silver pin, London import mark for 1959.

2.25in (5.5cm) diam 0.92oz

$650-800   **PW**

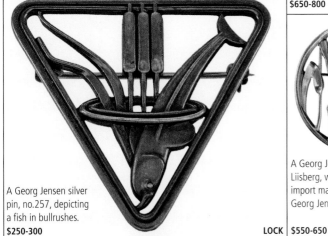

A Georg Jensen silver pin, no.257, depicting a fish in bullrushes.

$250-300   **LOCK**

A Georg Jensen silver pin, by Hugo Liisberg, with a lapwing in reeds, import marks for London 1960, Georg Jensen Ltd., no.297.

2.25in (5.5cm) diam

$550-650   **FLD**

A Georg Jensen silver pin, by Hugo Liisberg, with ducks, import marks for London 1963, Georg Jensen Ltd., no.299.

2.25in (5.5cm) diam

$550-650   **FLD**

An Ivan Tarratt Modernist silver 'Flight' pin, designed c1959 by Ernest A. Blyth.

Tarratt was founded in Leicester, England, in 1913 by George Tarratt. The company specialized in silverware and produced distinctive Art Deco geometric designs in the 1920s-30s. George's son, Ivan Tarratt, later took over and expanded the jewelry and watch lines. The Tarratt shop is still open in Leicester, as is another branch in Rugby.

1965   2.75in (7cm) wide 0.59oz

$130-200   **HAN**

A Georg Jensen silver pin, by Henning Kopel, with enamel decoration, London import marks for 1963, no.315.

1.75in (4.5cm) wide

$650-800   **FLD**

A Modernist silver pin, by Thomas Lynton Mott, Birmingham.

1965   2.25in (6cm) wide

$130-200   **HAN**

A Mexican Modernist Taxco silver fish pin, with an amethyst cabochon eye, stamped '925 JH Gro'.

$120-160   **HAN**

A German Modernist 14ct gold pin, attributed to Kordes & Lichtenfels, stamped 'K&L 585'.

1.5in (4cm) wide 0.16oz

$100-130   **HAN**

A Victorian gold and half pearl-set locket.

0.92oz

$650-800 BELL

A Victorian 15ct gold, opal, half pearl and diamond pendant, later chain.

$350-400 DA&H

An Art Nouveau plique-à-jour enamel pendant, stamped mark '800'.

c1900 *1.5in (4cm) long*

$450-600 L&T

An Arthur and Georgie Gaskin silver and turquoise necklace, with mother-of-pearl panels, unsigned.

pendant 2.5in (6.5cm) long

$1,000-1,200 WW

A Danish silver Bernhard Hertz Art Nouveau pendant, with amber colored cabouchons, stamped 'BH 828 S'.

pendant 2.75in (7cm) long

$650-800 GWA

A gold, rose diamond, seed pearl and green enameled Art Nouveau pendant, ropetwist link neckchain, detailed '15 CT', with case.

c1910

$800-950 BELL

An Art Nouveau Murrle Bennett & Co. silver and enamel pendant, link chain, stamped 'MB&Co / 950'.

Murrle Bennett & Co. was founded in London in 1884 by German Ernst Murrle and Englishman J.B. Bennett. The firm specialized in high quality affordable silver and gold jewelry in the Art Nouveau style. Its jewelry was often inset with turquoises, amethysts and mother-of-pearl. In 1916, the firm was purchased and the business continued under the name White, Redgrove & Whyte.

c1900 *pendant 1.75in (4.5cm) long*

$1,600-2,000 L&T

An Arts and Crafts Liberty & Co. silver and enamel pendant, by W.H. Haseler, Birmingham, stamped 'W.H.H.'.

1908 *1.25in (3cm) diam*

$900-1,100 L&T

An Arts and Crafts silver and enameled pendant, on later silver chain.

1.25in (3cm) diam

$90-100 HAN

QUICK REFERENCE - SUFFRAGETTE JEWELRY

- Suffragette jewelry was produced in the 1900s and made of purple, white and green semi-precious stones.
- Although the pieces were to an extent subtle, purple, white and green were widely known to be the colors of The Women's Social and Political Union and of the suffragette movement. Flags were made for demonstrations in these colors and protestors were encouraged to dress in similar shades. Wearing jewelry made in purple, white and green would have therefore been a brave statement at the time.
- Jewellers Mappin & Webb included five pieces of dedicated 'Suffragette Jewelry' in their Christmas 1908 catalog, each set in gold, with emeralds, pearls and amethysts.
- Fakes are common, as are unrelated purple, white and green jewelry marketed as suffragette jewelry. Nonetheless, true suffragette jewelry is highly collectible today and, due to its unique historical context, can fetch high prices.

An early 20thC suffragette pendant, set with an amethyst within a border of garnets and seed pearls, suspending an amethyst and garnet in yellow gold, cased.

2.25in (6cm) long

$1,200-1,600 **WW**

A three string coral bead necklace, with a 9ct gold clasp.

$130-200 **LOCK**

A James Fenton silver and enamel pendant necklace, Birmingham, marked.

1908 *1.75in (4.5cm) long*

$250-350 **WW**

A Smith & Ewan silver and enamel pendant necklace, Birmingham, marked.

1908 *1.5in (3.5cm) long*

$200-250 **WW**

A gold and moonstone set necklace, on an oval link neckchain, with a boltring clasp.

c1910

$650-800 **BELL**

An Edwardian gold seed pearl and diamond spaced memoriam locket.

$800-950 **TRI**

A coral and vari-gem pendant, with emerald, sapphire and ruby highlights, stamped '18k', some surface wear.

2.5in (6cm) long 1.28oz

$600-750 **FELL**

A Tiffany & Co. tag pendant, engraved 'Please Return to Tiffany & Co. New York M27137', signed 'Tiffany & Co. 925'.

33.75in (86cm) long 0.91oz

$80-100 **FELL**

A 20thC 18ct gold circling fish collar necklace, unmarked.

7in (18cm) long 4.31oz

$4,500-5,500 **DRA**

An Etruscan revival bangle, set with diamonds and a red gem.

inner 2.75in (7cm) diam

$650-800   GWA

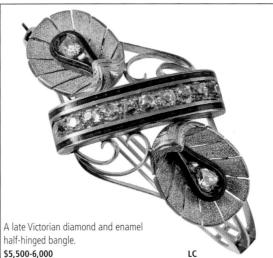

A late Victorian diamond and enamel half-hinged bangle.

$5,500-6,000   LC

A late 19thC to early 20thC Etruscan-style yellow metal bangle, set with a cabochon-cut amethyst with small diamonds and pearls.

2.5in (6cm) wide 0.77oz

$1,000-1,200   LOC

An early 20thC 18ct gold and ruby serpent bracelet, open mouth and fangs, stamped '750', 'B3'.

7.5in (19cm) long 1.39oz

$3,000-4,000   DRA

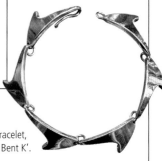

A 1950s Danish Modernist silver bracelet, by Bent Knudsen, marked 'Sterling Bent K'.

Bent Knudsen (1924-97) was a Danish decorative artist and silversmith. He and his wife Anni founded a silversmith workshop in 1956 and from there produced simple, elegant Modernist jewelry.

6.75in (17cm) long

$200-250   HAN

A pair of 18ct yellow gold, mabe pearl and enamel ear clips, by De Vroomen.

1.5in (3.5cm) diam

$1,600-2,000   APAR

A pair of Norwegian silver and enamel ear clips, by Einar Modahl, stamped '925 S EM, STERLING, NORWAY'.

Einar Modahl began his career as the apprentice of the Norwegian silversmith Marius Hammer. Modahl is known for his Modernist designs of silver jewelry in the 1960s-70s.

0.5in (1.5cm) diam

$90-120   DA&H

An Arts and Crafts 'Cymric' silver and enamel ring, stamped 'L&Co. / CYMRIC'.

c1900   *0.75in (2cm) wide*

$400-450   L&T

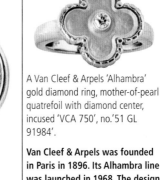

A Van Cleef & Arpels 'Alhambra' gold diamond ring, mother-of-pearl quatrefoil with diamond center, incused 'VCA 750', no.'51 GL 91984'.

Van Cleef & Arpels was founded in Paris in 1896. Its Alhambra line was launched in 1968. The design is inspired by the four-leaf clover and is supposed to be a symbol of good luck.

size 6 0.23oz

$2,000-2,500   DRA

A Danish Modernist silver and opalescent blue cabouchon ring, by Carl Ove Frydensberg, marked.

size N - N 1/2 1.25in (3cm) long

$60-80   HAN

A pair of near matched 9ct gold cufflinks, with engraved floral and foliate motif, hallmarks for Birmingham.

1897/1903   *0.75in (2cm) long 0.33oz*

$200-250   **FELL**

A pair of George VI 9ct gold champlevé enamel cufflinks.

0.21oz

$400-450   **MOR**

A pair of Cartier 'Trinity' cufflinks, signed 'Cartier, 969040', in case.

0.5in (1.5cm) long 0.47oz

$900-1,200   **FELL**

A pair of 18ct gold and diamond cufflinks, each side set with an old cut 0.4ct diamond.

0.5in (1.5cm) long

$1,000-1,200   **GWA**

A pair of Alfred Dunhill silver and enameled cufflinks, with 'D' logo, boxed.

$90-100   **HAN**

A pair of gold and enameled cufflinks, with golfer motifs, detailed '750' and a gold and similar stick pin, detailed '750', with a case.

together 0.54oz

$650-800   **BELL**

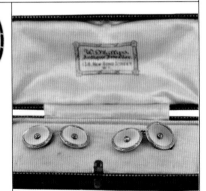

A pair of 18ct gold mother-of-pearl cufflinks, in a Phillips fitted case.

$300-350   **LOCK**

A pair of diamond- and sapphire-set dress cufflinks, by Lucien Piccard.

$400-550   **BELL**

A pair of gold and enameled cufflinks, enameled with foxes masks, some damage.

0.26oz

$550-650   **BELL**

A pair of white enameled gold and rose diamond cufflinks, inset with monograms.

0.35oz

$800-850   **BE**

JEWELRY

A 1920s Theodor Fahrner sterling silver marcasite pin.

$500-550   GRV

A 1940s Marcel Boucher rhodium-plated, rhinestone, paste and faux pearl parure, including a pin and earrings.

$400-450   GRV

A 1950s Creation French enameled ceramic and gilt-metal pin, in the form of a poodle.

1.5in (4cm) wide

$25-40   HAN

A 1930s Theodor Fahrner silver and turquoise pin.

$750-800   GRV

A 1980s Stanley Hagler gilt-metal, glass and rhinestone parure, including a pin and earrings.

$500-550   GRV

A 1960s Miriam Haskell gilt-metal and rhinestone parure, by Robert Clark, including a pin and earrings.

$450-500   GRV

QUICK REFERENCE - JOSEFF OF HOLLYWOOD

- Eugene Joseff (1905-48) began his career in the early 1920s in Chicago as a graphic artist in an advertising agency, designing jewelry in his spare time. By 1927, he was training as a jewelry designer in Los Angeles.
- From 1931, Joseff was commissioned to design and produce unique and historically accurate jewelry for Hollywood studios. He created pieces for numerous films, including The Wizard of Oz and Gone with the Wind. He rented these out to the studios, ensuring they were returned to him afterwards for potential re-hire.
- In 1935, he opened a shop, Sunset Jewelry, in Hollywood, and founded the Joseff of Hollywood company. From 1937, he produced replicas of his cinema original jewelry for retail, a move highly popular with cinema-loving customers.
- Eugene Joseff died in a plane crash in 1948. The company was continued by his widow and is still operational today.

A Christian Dior gold-tone metal and glass pin, by Henkel and Grosse, Germany.

1962

$300-350   GRV

A 1940s Joseff of Hollywood 'Russian gold' and glass parure, including a pin and earrings.

$600-650   GRV

A 1940s Joseff of Hollywood 'Russian gold' and rhinestone parure, including earrings and a pin.

$600-650   GRV

A 1940s Joseff of Hollywood flower pin, in red molded tenite, with silver-colored metal and rhinestone center, signed 'Joseff Hollywood'.

3in (7.5cm) long

$130-200   **PC**

A 1930s KTF Trifari rhodium-plated rhinestone pin, sold by Asprey, in original box.

$650-750   **GRV**

A Trifari rhinestone and faux sapphire pin with enamel detailing, probably from an Alfred Spaney design, signed crown 'Trifari'.

c1941   *2.5in (6.5cm) long*

$130-200   **PC**

Judith Picks

Alfred Phillipe was one of Trifari's most influential and interesting designers. Previously a designer of precious jewelry at Van Cleef & Arpels and Cartier, he moved into more affordable costume jewelry in the wake of the Great Depression. He approached costume jewelry with the same attention to detail as he had fine jewelry, and replicated methods he had developed at Van Cleef & Arpels, such as the invisible setting technique, in which stones are fixed from the back so that the mount is hidden from the front. Phillipe worked with Swarovski crystals and sterling silver, often plated with gold. His elegant designs were very popular in the 1930s-50s, especially his notable Tifari 'Crown' pins and his Lucite 'Jelly Bellies'.

A pair of Trifari Moghul 'Jewels of India' fan pins, designed by Alfred Philippe with green melon carved 'Jello Mold' stone, signed crown 'Trifari Pat, Pend'.

designed 1949   *0.75in (2cm) long*

$550-650   **PC**

A pair of early 1950s Trifari rhodium-plated, rhinestone and faux pearl earrings, designed by Alfred Philippe.

$300-350   **GRV**

A 1960s Trifari gold-tone base metal and enamel parure, including a pin and earrings.

$300-350   **GRV**

A 1960s Weiss silver-tone base metal and rhinestone parure, including a pin and earrings.

$170-200   **GRV**

A 1940s gilt-metal, plastic and glass parure, including a bracelet and pin, unsigned.

$170-200   **GRV**

A pair of 1950s Bogoff silver-tone base metal and rhinestone earrings.

$200-250   **GRV**

A pair of Christian Dior gilt-metal and rhinestone earrings, by Mitchel Maer.

1952-56

$300-350   **GRV**

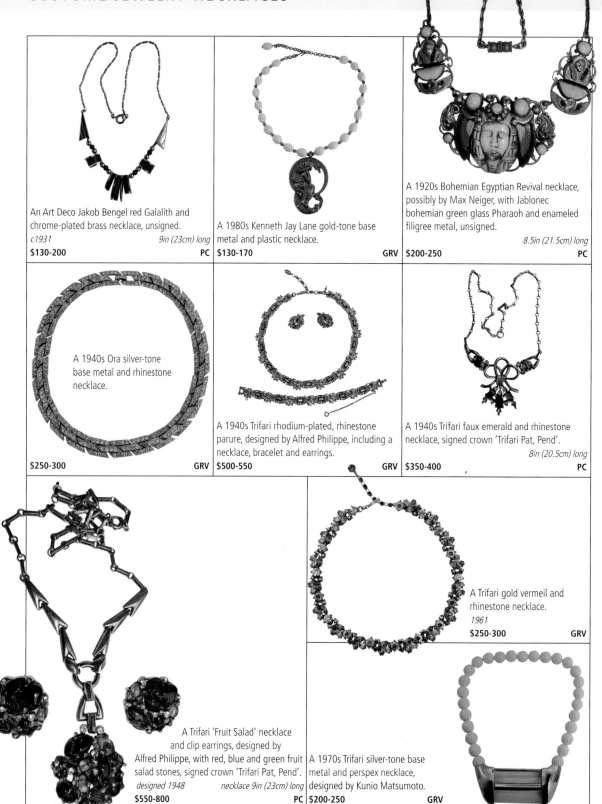

An Art Deco Jakob Bengel red Galalith and chrome-plated brass necklace, unsigned.
c1931   *9in (23cm) long*
$130-200   **PC**

A 1980s Kenneth Jay Lane gold-tone base metal and plastic necklace.
$130-170   **GRV**

A 1920s Bohemian Egyptian Revival necklace, possibly by Max Neiger, with Jablonec bohemian green glass Pharaoh and enameled filigree metal, unsigned.
8.5in (21.5cm) long
$200-250   **PC**

A 1940s Ora silver-tone base metal and rhinestone necklace.
$250-300   **GRV**

A 1940s Trifari rhodium-plated, rhinestone parure, designed by Alfred Philippe, including a necklace, bracelet and earrings.
$500-550   **GRV**

A 1940s Trifari faux emerald and rhinestone necklace, signed crown 'Trifari Pat, Pend'.
8in (20.5cm) long
$350-400   **PC**

A Trifari gold vermeil and rhinestone necklace.
1961
$250-300   **GRV**

A Trifari 'Fruit Salad' necklace and clip earrings, designed by Alfred Philippe, with red, blue and green fruit salad stones, signed crown 'Trifari Pat, Pend'.
designed 1948   *necklace 9in (23cm) long*
$550-800   **PC**

A 1970s Trifari silver-tone base metal and perspex necklace, designed by Kunio Matsumoto.
$200-250   **GRV**

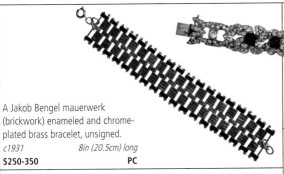

A Jakob Bengel mauerwerk (brickwork) enameled and chrome-plated brass bracelet, unsigned.
c1931   *8in (20.5cm) long*
$250-350   **PC**

A 1930s Knoll and Pregizer silver and rhinestone bracelet.
$1,000-1,300   **GRV**

A 1960s Kramer rhodium-plated rhinestone bracelet.
$200-250   **GRV**

A 1960s Matisse Renoir copper and enamel parure, including a bracelet and earrings.

Matisse Renoir specialisd in hand-worked solid copper jewelry, often in the Arts and Crafts style. The company was founded in 1948 as Renoir of Hollywood and established the subsidiary company Matisse Ltd. in 1952. Matisse pieces combined copper with colorful enamels. Production ceased in 1964.
$200-250   **GRV**

A 1940s Trifari gold vermeil and rhinestone bracelet.
$130-170   **GRV**

A 1950s Napier rhodium-plated, rhinestone ring.
$170-200   **GRV**

A 1930s Ciro sterling silver and rhinestone ring.
$200-250   **GRV**

A 1950s Trifari gilt-metal and paste bracelet, with interlocking leaf design, marked to the clip.
6.75in (17cm) long
$50-80   **HAN**

A 1960s Panetta gold vermeil, faux opal and rhinestone ring.
$130-170   **GRV**

A Trifari rhinestone fur clip with faux opal and ruby cabochons, designed by Alfred Philippe, signed crown 'Trifari Des, Pat No 119103'.
designed 1940   *2.75in (7cm) long*
$150-250   **PC**

QUICK REFERENCE - EILEEN GRAY

Eileen Gray (1878-1976) was born in Ireland and grew up in London. She was one of the first female students to attend Slade School of Art. In the 1900s, she moved to Paris and soon established herself as one of the leading designers of lacquered screens and Art Deco decorated panels. In 1922, she opened a gallery to showcase her work, the Galerie Jean Desert. Her designs extended to furniture, lighting and architecture. After World War II, her work was relatively forgotten, until the London-based furniture company Aram acquired the rights to her designs in the 1970s.

A table lamp, by Eileen Gray.

c1945-50s   19in (48.5cm) high

$800-950   JN

A 1960s Harvey Guzzini Perspex and chrome table lamp, the height adjustable shade with two bulb fitting.

23.5in (60cm) high

$350-400   HAN

A 1950s Joseph Lucas Ltd. Perido radio lamp, cream plastic and gilt-brushed metal.

See J. Hill, 'Old Radio Sets', Shire Publications, 2009, for an illustrated example of this model. This is one of only a handful of known examples, apparently never put into commercial production.

$250-350   HAN

An Art Deco metal model 'Popular' heat lamp, by The Barber Polykymatic, with original flex, tilt mechanism.

15.75in (40cm) high

$70-80   LSK

A 1930s Art Deco figural table lamp, with crackle glass shade.

$150-200   HAN

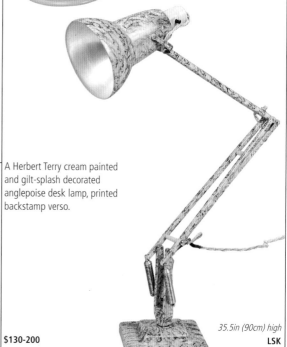

A Herbert Terry cream painted and gilt-splash decorated anglepoise desk lamp, printed backstamp verso.

35.5in (90cm) high

$130-200   LSK

An Art Deco-style chromium-plated bi-plane desk or table lamp.

17.75in (45cm) long

$250-300   FLD

An early 20thC brass newel post lamp, with metal and multicolored simulated shell shade in the form of a gramophone horn, foot later mounted on an oak base as a standard lamp, electrically powered.

56in (142cm) high

$400-550   **DA&H**

A Liberty & Co. Art Deco walnut standard lamp and shade, Liberty & Co. label under the lead weighted base, minor damage.

68.5in (174cm) high

$1,000-1,200   **KEY**

Judith Picks

Nothing makes a statement in a room like a Castigloini lamp! The Castiglioni brothers, Livio (1911-79), Pier Giacomo (1913-68) and Achille (1918-2002), all studied at the Polytechnic Institute of Milan. Livio and Pier set up a design studio in 1938 and were joined by their younger brother in 1944. The brothers produced innovate designs for furniture and lighting. Along with their distinctive 'Allunaggio' (moonlanding) seat from 1966, the 1962 'Arco' lamp remains one of their most memorable designs. It was designed by Achille Castiglioni and produced by the Italian lighting company Flos.

A Flos 'Arco' marble and chromed metal floor lamp, by Achille Castiglioni (1918-2002).

designed 1962   76.5in (194cm) high

$1,300-2,000   **L&T**

An early 20thC hall lantern, with leaded glass panel sides, within repoussé work foliate borders.

lantern 12.5in (32cm) high

$200-250   **FLD**

A 1960s glass pendant light shade, neon orange opaque glass, with aluminum fitting.

11.75in (30cm) diam

$90-110   **HAN**

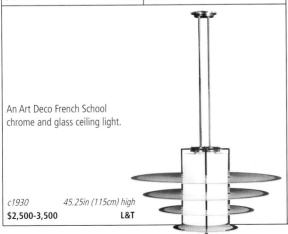

An Art Deco French School chrome and glass ceiling light.

c1930   45.25in (115cm) high

$2,500-3,500   **L&T**

A 'Fun 1' ceiling light, by Verner Panton for J. Lüber AG.

1964   23.5in (60cm) high

$650-800   **QU**

A 1970s Murano glass chandelier, with four graduated tiers of trefoil section drops in clear, amber and smoked glass with three electric lamp holders.

13in (33cm) diam

$450-550   **DA&H**

MECHANICAL BANKS

- Mechanical banks are toy banks in which coins are deposited via a mechanical process.
- The first US mechanical bank was patented by James Serrill in 1869 and the idea soon spread. Mechanical banks were widely produced from the 1870s to the 1930s. They were chiefly made from cast iron, with the addition of spring-driven and wind-up mechanisms.
- Mechanical banks were partly a product of the growth of the middle classes over the 19thC. Parents often purchased them for their children, with the aim of encouraging them to save pocket money.
- Kyser and Rex Co., founded in Pennsylvania in 1879, was one of the USA's most significant producers of mechanical banks. Another key maker was J. & E. Stevens Co., founded in Connecticut in 1843. Similar banks were produced in Germany by Bing and Saalheimer & Strauss.

A Kyser & Rex cast iron 'Coin Registering-1890' mechanical bank.
$4,000-4,500   POOK

A Kyser & Rex cast iron 'Boy Stealing Watermelons' mechanical bank, non-functional, original key lock trap, no key.
$3,500-4,000   POOK

A Kyser & Rex cast iron 'Zoo' mechanical bank.
$1,200-1,600   POOK

A Kyser & Rex cast iron 'Organ Grinder and Bear' mechanical bank, break on the bear's hat.
$2,500-3,500   POOK

A Saalheimer & Strauss Mickey Mouse 'Smile Please' tinplate mechanical bank, made in Germany, registration no.508041, with ear pull action causing tongue to come out for coin placement as the eyes roll back, inscribed 'Ideal Films Ltd' to the side panel.

7in (17.5cm) high
$6,500-7,500   PW

A J. & E. Stevens cast iron 'Boy Scout Camp' mechanical bank.
$2,500-3,500   POOK

A J. & E. Stevens cast iron 'Home' mechanical bank with dormers.
$1,300-2,000   POOK

An Ives cast iron palace still bank, finial attached with screw for stability.

7.75in (19.5cm) high
$800-950   POOK

A Swiss 'The Britannia' Sainte-Croix mahogany and satinwood inlaid polyphon disc musical box, in the form of a smoker's cabinet, with a timepiece, inscribed 'Star Silver Depot, London', and a group of 9in (23cm) discs, in working order.

$1,300-2,000 APAR

A late 19thC Clariona by Merritt Gally 14-note mechanical American reed organ, fitted with double bellows, with one paper roll of Christmas carols, in a mahogany case, bellows restored, in working order.

13.5in (34cm) high

$400-450 W&W

A late 19thC Schutz-Marke German symphonion, with oak case, with double comb, with 22 discs, in working order.

19.75in (50cm) wide

$1,700-2,000 APAR

A 'Peter Pan' miniature travel gramophone, in a mahogany case.

6.25in (16cm) long

$550-600 WHP

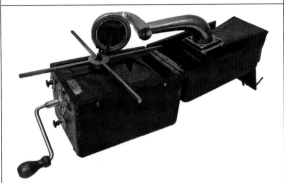

A 'Peter Pan' 'camera' gramophone, leather covered wood case, wind-up motor, speaker horn, nickel-plated interior fittings.

open 19in (48.5cm) long

$400-450 HT

An 'Americana' CD jukebox, echoing the enduring 'Bubbler' design by Rock-Ola, manufactured in England by Juke Box Greats 'Sound Leisure', with solid chrome case, two large pillasters displaying 'The Emblem of the United States and Lady Liberty'.

67in (170cm) high

$2,000-2,500 JN

QUICK REFERENCE - TIFFANY METALWARE

Tiffany & Co. began in 1837, primarily as a stationary shop. It went on to become one of the leading jewellers and design houses in America. In the 1870s, Tiffany developed a range of metal hollowware, often inspired by Japanese objects or designs. Favrile glass, also used with great success in Tiffany's lamps, was incorporated into many metalwork pieces. More experimental enameled metal pieces were added to the ranges from 1899; Tiffany Studios produced vases, boxes, bowls and ink wells using this technique.

A Tiffany Studios lidded box with 'Pine Needle' design, gilt-bronze and caramel slag glass, marked 'TIFFANY STUDIOS NEW YORK 816', tight hairline to side.

1899-1920   *6.75in (17cm) long*

$550-600   **DRA**

A Tiffany & Co. mixed metal caster, hammered sterling silver body with floral and insect motif in mixed metals, marked, light wear.

c1879   *4.75in (12cm) high 2.74oz*

$1,300-1,600   **DRA**

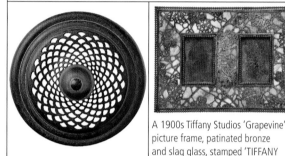

A 1900s Tiffany Studios patinated bronze heat cap, faint scratches.

5.5in (14cm) high

$1,000-1,200   **DRA**

A 1900s Tiffany Studios 'Grapevine' picture frame, patinated bronze and slag glass, stamped 'TIFFANY STUDIOS NEW YORK', one crack to one piece of glass.

10.25in (26cm) wide

$3,500-4,000   **DRA**

A 1900s Tiffany Studios 'Pine Needle' thermometer, patinated bronze, slag glass and original mercury, stamped 'TIFFANY STUDIOS NEW YORK'.

8.75in (22cm) high

$1,300-2,000   **DRA**

An early 20thC Tiffany & Co. patinated bronze Kangaroo vessel, stamped 'TIFFANY & CO', some light wear.

9.75in (25cm) high

$1,000-1,300   **DRA**

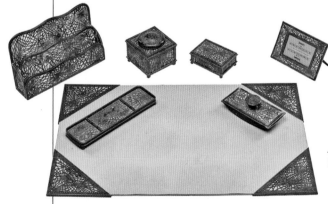

An early 20thC Tiffany Studios 'Pine Needle' desk set, comprising a letter holder, a pen tray, a rocker blotter, a calendar holder, an inkwell, blotters and utility box, each piece 'TIFFANY STUDIOS NEW YORK', with its respective number, crack to glass in pen tray, box lid detached with cracks in one glass pane.

letter holder 10in (25.5cm) wide

$1,600-2,000   **DRA**

A pair of 1920s Tiffany Studios candlesticks, acid-etched gilt-bronze and enamel, both stamped 'LOUIS C. TIFFANY FURNACES, INC. 41A', with circular Tiffany Studios cipher, with original bobeches.

4.25in (11cm) high

$1,200-1,600   **DRA**

A 20thC Tiffany Studios bronze inkwell, in the 'Modeled' pattern, marked and numbered 'TIFFANY STUDIOS 1112', glass insert has minor chips.

5in (13cm) diam

$550-600   **DRA**

A matched pair of 19thC brass 'Cupid' doorstops.

17.75in (45cm) high

$600-750 **WW**

A pair of Victorian brass doorstops, modeled with the infant Hercules strangling a snake, stamped with registration number '53035', with weighted bases.

16in (40.5cm) high

$600-650 **WW**

A Victorian brass 'Classical Lady' doorstop.

A Victorian brass 'Dolphin' doorstop.

14in (35.5cm) high

$200-250 **WW**

17.25in (43.5cm) high

$550-650 **WW**

A Victorian brass 'Lion's Paw' doorstop.

15in (38cm) high

$250-300 **WW**

A Victorian painted cast iron 'Fox Head' doorstop.

14.5in (37cm) high

$550-600 **WW**

A late 19thC to early 20thC brass 'Fox Head' doorstop, with riding crop handle, stamped 'PEERAGE ENGLAND 19478'.

18in (45.5cm) high

$600-750 **WW**

A brass 'Fox Head' doorstop, with a lead weighted base.

18.25in (46.5cm) high

$550-650 **WW**

A wrought iron and lead 'Swan' doorstop, attributed to Morgan Colt, New Hope, PA, USA, some scratches to base.

c1920 *17.25in (44cm) high*

$550-600 **DRA**

METALWARE

A cast iron weather vane, of a farmer with his dog shooting a rabbit, with traces of red paint.

31.75in (80.5cm) wide

$900-1,000   **WW**

A zinc 'Arrow' weathervane, with wear.

c1900   *23.25in (59cm) long*

$550-600   **POOK**

A 'Swell Bodied Cow' weathervane.

c1900   *27.25in (69cm) long*

$150-250   **POOK**

A pair of Liberty & Co. 'Tudric' pewter candlesticks, by Archibald Knox, cast with stylized Celtic decoration, stamped 'TUDRIC / 0221 / 3'.

For Archibald Knox's jewelry, see page 253.

5.75in (14.5cm) high

$550-800   **L&T**

A Liberty & Co. 'Tudric' pewter tulip vase, marked, poor repair where shaft meets base.

c1905   *10in (25.5cm) high*

$150-200   **DRA**

A copper spirit kettle, by W.A.S. Benson, (1854-1924), with brass fittings and stand with burner, Hammersmith, London, stamped 'BENSON'.

c1880-1920   *10.25in (26cm) high*

$100-130   **DRA**

An Arts and Crafts copper and cast iron coal scuttle, with beaten finish and riveted straps to the angles.

c1900   *21.25in (54cm) long*

$400-450   **L&T**

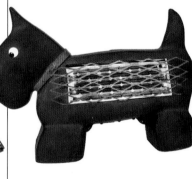

An Art Deco cast metal Zooray Scottie dog electric room heater.

$350-400   **MART**

A pair of 20thC cast brass door pulls, stamped verso 'W. & R. LEGGOTT LTD. LONDON & BRADFORD'.

14.5in (37cm) long

$80-100   **FELL**

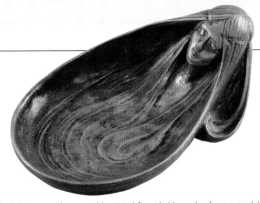

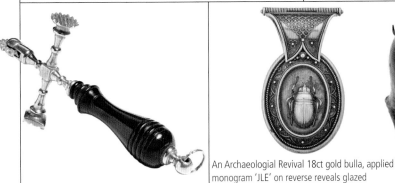

An Art Nouveau bronze cold-painted figural vide poche, from a model by Gustave Gurchner, of a maiden with flowing hair, unmarked.

8in (20cm) long

$1,000-1,200   ECGW

A W.M.F. silver-plated dish, modeled as a young boy kneeling, looking at a frog, impressed marks and numbered '349', heavy rubbing and wear.

8.25in (21cm) wide

$200-250   FELL

An early 19thC brass alloy pastry jigger, with a turned treen handle, possibly laburnum.

9in (23cm) long

$250-350   WW

An Archaeologial Revival 18ct gold bulla, applied monogram 'JLE' on reverse reveals glazed chamber, applied mark 'Innocenti', for Leopoldo Innocenti, Piazza Trinita Dei Monti, Rome.

c1875   *2.25in (6cm) high 1.03oz*

$3,200-3,800   DRA

An early 20thC cast metal 'Pig' desk bell, registered mark '153419'.

6in (15.5cm) long

$250-300   APAR

A 19thC brass hand warmer, pierced and engraved with birds, the interior with gimbal mounted burner.

3.5in (9cm) diam

$350-400   BE

A 20thC Spanish ship's cast alloy bell, inscribed 'DELFIN DEL ATLANTICO LAS PALMAS', general knocks, has been polished, lacks clapper.

12.5in (32cm) high

$200-250   FELL

A white metal show collar of champion Irish Red Setter Garryowen, engraved 'Garryowen - The Champion - Irish Red Setter - Owner, JJ Giltrup', with 23 discs, each engraved with one of Garryowen's show honors.

Garryowen was an Irish Setter with a significant sporting and show career. He was born in 1876, bred by H.S. Moore of Dublin, sired by Champion Palmerston out of Champion Belle. He was owned by James J. Giltrap, a law agent. He won 37 firsts, both champion and challenge prizes, and won the Grand Prix de Honeur of the Belgian Kennel Club as the best of 978 sporting dogs of all breeds. He is mentioned in James Joyce's 'Ulysses' and gave the name to a brand of Plug tobacco produced by the Spillane's family. This collar was worn by Garryowen at the Dog Show held at the Royal Zoological Society in Dublin in August 1884, where he won first prize in the champion class of Irish Setter dogs.

1879-84

$9,500-10,000   WHYT

A Waterloo medal, inscribed to 'Corp. John Wilson, 1st Batt. 71st Reg', with original ring and ribbon.

$3,500-4,000   **CHEF**

A India General Service medal, with Pegu clasp, impressed 'ASSISTT SURGEON I.T. WILLIAMS 9TH REGT N.I.'.

1854

$650-800   **DUK**

A Victorian Crimea medal, Sebastopol, Inkermann, Balaklava, awarded to Private John Cornish, Scots Fusilier Regiment of Foot Guards.

Private John Cornish joined the Guards at Stratton in 25 June 1850 at 19. He was discharged 28 October 1856.

$650-800   **DUK**

A Foreign Services Sea Gallantry silver medal, reverse engraved 'For Saving The Lives of British Subjects 1841, To Louis Rapin from The British Government'.

1841   *1.75in (4.5cm) diam*

$300-400   **LOCK**

An Indian Mutiny medal, with two clasps 'Lucknow' and 'Relief of Lucknow', awarded to John Sharp, 9th Lancers.

1858

$400-450   **TEN**

Judith Picks

General Rowland Hill was born in 1772 at Hawkstone Hall, near Prees, Shropshire, the second son of Sir John Hill, 3rd Baronet. He was educated at The King's School in Chester, then quickly rose through the army ranks. By 1793 had been made a captain and by 1800 was a colonel. He led armies in battle in Egypt, Spain, Portugal and France, in some of the most important battles of the early 19thC. He served in the Napoleonic Wars as a brigade, division and corps commander under the command of the Duke of Wellington. At Waterloo he was Commanding Officer of II Corps. He later became Commander-in-Chief of the British Army in 1828, succeeding Wellington. He was known as 'Daddy Hill' by his troops due to his caring nature and the kindness with which he treated his soldiers.

General Rowland Hill died at Hardwicke Grange, Hadnall, Shropshire, in 1842 at the age of 70.

This unique bar pin was commissioned by the General himself and would have been hand-crafted for him.

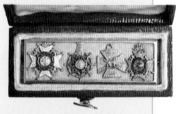

A unique miniature pin bar, belonging to General Rowland Hill, 1st Viscount Hill GCB GCH (1772-1842), with miniature enamel representations of medals, the Order of the Most Honourable Order of the Bath KCB Neck badge, the Portuguese Order of the Tower and Sword, the Peninsular Cross, and the Hanoverian Guelphic Order, in a fitted padded case.

2in (5cm) long

$12,000-13,000   **HAN**

A Canada General Service Medal, with Finian Raid 1866 clasp (later clasp), re-engraved 'Capt & Adjt E M H Vieth 15th Regt N.S.M.'.

Edmund Montgomery Harris Vieth served with Halifax Volunteer Battalion 63rd Bn (Nova Scotia Militia).

$200-250   **LOCK**

A Queen's South Africa medal, with Cape Colony, Transvaal, Wittebergen clasps, impressed '2709 PTE W. DEVEREUX, S. STAFFORD. REGT'.

$160-200   **DUK**

A World War II Nazi agricultural medal, struck in 'AE'.

2in (5cm) diam

$120-130   **DUK**

An Elizabeth II Royal Observer Corps medal, with clasp, impressed 'OBSERVER. L.J. GUILDING.'

$300-400   **DUK**

A late Victorian officer's cast WM pouch belt badge of the 2nd Madras Infantry, battle honors for Carnatic, Mysore, China, Nagpore and Assaye.
$130-200   W&W

A Scottish Gordon Highlanders officers silver cap badge, Edinburgh, reads 'BYDAND' below stag.
1913
$300-400   DUK

An Imperial German Air Service Commemorative badge, stamped 'C E Juncker, Berlin', with crescent and '800'.

This badge was authorized in 1914 for officers, NCOs and other men in the Imperial German Air Service who were, on mobilization, no longer required in the air service.
$350-400   W&W

A Surbiton Junior Cadet Corps badge, possibly World War I period.
$100-120   LOCK

A World War I City of London Volunteer Corps VTC badge.
$60-80   LOCK

A World War II Third Reich Ostfolk Award, first class in Gold with Swords.
$200-250   HAN

A German Nazi Luftwaffe badge, silver and gold-plated, stamped 'PLEUGER &VOSS LUDENSCHEID'.
$650-750   DUK

A World War II Polish 32nd Masovian Infantry Regiment silver and enamel breast badge.
$90-100   LOCK

A World War II Home Front S.B. (Voluntary Stretcher Bearers) Emergency Hospital Scheme badge.
$50-60   LOCK

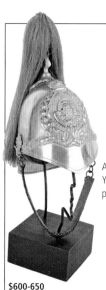

A 1st West Yorkshire Yeoman Cavalry silver-plated dress helmet.

$600-650   APAR

A 17th Lancer Officer's lance cap, the left side with a gold bullion rosette embroidered 'VR' cipher with a gilt-plume cup and white stitched swan feather plume, the gilt cap plate mounted with silver Royal Coat of Arms above the 17th Lancers' Skull emblem.

$4,500-5,500   HT

A late 19thC green cloth spiked helmet, with badge inscribed 'Third Vol R Battn South Staffordshire', inscribed 'Sergt Piper, A Company, 2nd Vol. Battn. York and Lancaster Regiment', in hat box.

$650-800   APAR

A leather and brass mounted pickelhaube, with large winged eagle insignia, with associated trunk.

$350-400   APAR

A cloth and leather trimmed pickelhaube, in associated trunk inscribed 'Major Corbett'.

$450-550   APAR

An early 20thC blue cloth spiked helmet, with badge insignia, inscribed 'D. Jones late Milton & Jones, Military Outfitters, 136, Deansgate, Manchester', in associated hat tin.

$350-400   APAR

An aluminum BMW Works fireman's helmet, with the factory decal and 'Luftschutz' emblem.
1939-45

$250-350   HW

A Merryweather Hemel Hempstead brass fire brigade helmet.

9in (23cm) high

$550-600   **FLD**

A Merryweather Marsh and Baxters Brierley Hill nickel-plated officer's fireman's helmet.

9.75in (25cm) high

$750-800   **FLD**

A late 18thC to early 19thC Norwich Union Insurance leather fireman's helmet, with liner.

9in (23cm) high

$750-800   **FLD**

A Merryweather pattern fire officer's nickel-plated helmet.

9.75in (25cm) high

$600-650   **FLD**

A Merryweather pattern leather and part brass Andover Fire Brigade fireman's helmet.

9.5in (24cm) high

$1,200-1,300   **FLD**

A late 19thC dragon pattern nickel-plated officer's Gloucester fireman's helmet.

9.75in (25cm) high

$650-750   **FLD**

A Merryweather pattern Windsor Castle George V brass fireman's helmet.

9.75in (25cm) high

$900-1,100   **FLD**

A Birmingham fire brigade chrome-plated ceremonial helmet.

9.75in (25cm) high

$1,000-1,200   **FLD**

A 1920s Scottish chief officer's leather and silver-plated helmet, by Jas Hendrey Glasgow.

9in (23cm) high

$800-950   **FLD**

ORIENTAL

A pair of 20thC Chinese ginger jars and covers.
7.5in (19cm) high
$100-120 **PW**

A Chinese blue and white vase.
c1880 *5in (13cm) high*
$80-100 **K&O**

A Chinese ginger jar and cover, with twelve panels of flowers, underglaze blue six character mark to base.
13.5in (34cm) high
$450-550 **DA&H**

A 20thC Chinese porcelain Rouleau vase, in the Kangxi style.
18.25in (46cm) high
$550-600 **JN**

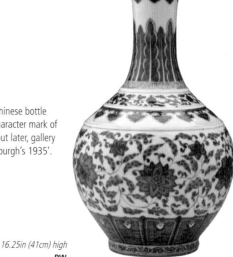

A 20thC Chinese bottle vase, six character mark of Qianlong but later, gallery label 'Edinburgh's 1935'.
16.25in (41cm) high
$600-650 **PW**

A 20thC Chinese porcelain ewer, in the Yuan style, the base unglazed.
13.25in (33.5cm) high
$130-200 **JN**

A Chinese Kangxi period dish, the base with a six-character Chenghua mark.
c1700 *5.5in (14cm) wide*
$350-400 **JN**

A Chinese Kangxi period porcelain teapot stand, the base unglazed.
c1700 *5.25in (13.5cm) square*
$250-300 **JN**

A late Qianlong Chinese dish, painted with peonies, rockwork, birds and a lattice fence.
14.5in (37cm) wide
$250-350 **BE**

QING DYNASTY REIGNS

Kangxi,
1662-1722
Yongzheng,
1723-35
Qianlong,
1736-95
Jiaqing,
1796-1820
Daoguang
1821-50
Xianfeng,
1851-61
Tongzhi,
1862-74
Guangxu,
1875-1908
Xuantong,
1909-11
Hongxian,
1915-16

A pair of late 19thC Canton famille rose vases, panted with mandarins, precious objects, birds, fruit and figures, with applied serpents, one chipped to hind leg.

Until 1842, all European trade with China was confined to the port of Guangzhou (Canton). European traders would travel up the Pearl River from Macau and Hong Kong to reach the port. Canton porcelain was exported from and sometimes decorated in Guangzhou, but had often been made elsewhere in China.

17.5in (44.5cm) high

$2,000-2,500   **GWA**

A 19thC Canton famille rose vase and cover, two chips to the rim with extensive glued repairs to the body.

The famille rose color palette was created in the early 18thC, at the end of the Kangxi period. It includes opaque pink, carmine, white and yellow, colors that had originated in Europe. The style was widely copied in European countries.

25.25in (64cm) high

$550-600   **BELL**

A 19thC Chinese famille rose vase, painted with reserves of deer, fungus and pine trees.

13in (33cm) high

$350-400   **HW**

A 20thC Chinese famille rose porcelain vase, apocryphal Qianlong seal mark, chips to rim.

13in (33cm) high

$100-130   **BE**

A Chinese Kangxi famille verte porcelain plate.

9.5in (24cm) diam

$400-450   **JN**

A late 19thC Chinese porcelain famille rose dish, enameled with a prunus tree, pierced rocks, blooms and song birds.

11.75in (30cm) diam

$200-250   **BE**

A Chinese famille verte porcelain bowl, the sides painted with warriors and a deity.

c1900   *15.25in (38.5cm) diam*

$450-550   **JN**

A Chinese famille rose porcelain snuff bottle, painted with a Court Lady, the reverse with a poem by Jin Jingde, Xianfeng mark, cover probably matched.

3.25in (8cm) high

$300-400   **BE**

A Chinese famille rose Qianlong porcelain figure, restored.

7.5in (19cm) high

$800-950   **BE**

ORIENTAL

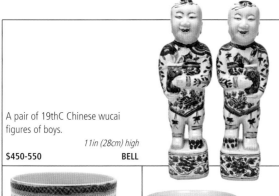

A pair of 19thC Chinese wucai figures of boys.

11in (28cm) high

$450-550   BELL

A Chinese Qianlong porcelain mug, painted with a floral spray within a 'sunburst' medallion.

4.25in (11cm) high

$130-200   BE

A Chinese Imari Kangxi period porcelain tankard.

c1700   3.5in (9cm) high

$400-450   JN

A CLOSER LOOK AT A WUCAI VASE

This vase is painted in the wucai five-color palette of blue, red, green, yellow and white.

The vase depicts figures and a crane by a fence.

It has ornate boards to the top and bottom of the vase.

The wucai style began in the Ming period and continued into the Qing period. This vase dates from the 17thC Transitional period between the two dynasties.

A Chinese Transitional wucai vase, degradation to green enamels, rim frits.

6.75in (17cm) high

$900-1,100   BE

A late Qing Dynasty Chinese ginger jar, made by Wang Bingrong, with a molded seal mark, with a carved wood stand and cover.

8.75in (22cm) high

$550-600   BE

A 19thC Chinese Yixing teapot and cover, stamped marks, glued repairs to spout, the cover broken into four pieces and glued.

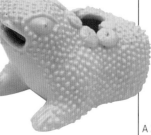

From the early 16thC, clay teapots were produced in Yixing, in the Eastern province of Jiangsu. These were very popular with the upper classes. The clay would absorb the aroma and flavour of the tea, meaning that after using a Yixing teapot for many years, you could brew tea simply by pouring boiling water into the empty pot.

6.25in (16cm) high

$400-450   BELL

A mid-20thC Chinese glazed ceramic statue, repaired.

7in (18cm) high

$40-50   LOCK

A 19thC Chinese porcelain 'warty toad' brush washer.

2.5in (9cm) long

$300-350   BE

A 20thC Chinese flambé glazed Fanghu porcelain vase, the base unglazed.

10in (25.5cm) high

$400-450   JN

QUICK REFERENCE - SATSUMA

- Satsuma ceramics were produced in the towns of Satsuma and Kyoto from the mid-19thC.
- These highly decorative earthenwares were cream in color, with finely crackled glazes and thickly applied enameled and gilded decoration.
- Satsuma ceramics are often decorated with panels depicting miniature everyday scenes, people, animals and landscapes, surrounded by ornate borders.
- Satsuma ware was first shown outside Japan at international exhibitions, creating a huge demand for Satsuma items in the West. This increased production, meaning that Satsuma pieces can vary considerably in quality, from high craftsmanship to items of poorer quality intended for department stores.

A pair of Japanese Satsuma vases, marks in gold and red.

6in (15cm) high

$130-200   JN

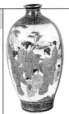

A 20thC Japanese Satsuma porcelain vase, painted with warriors in sea landscape, on carved hardwood stand, some minor rubbing.

vase 19.75in (50cm) high

$130-200   APAR

A pair of Satsuma vases, with elephant handles, with panels of figures, marks in gold and red.

18in (45.5cm) high

$550-650   JN

A Japanese Meiji period Satsuma vase, painted with figures and branches, marked, minor rubbing.

6in (15.5cm) high

$80-100   APAR

A Japanese Meiji period imperial Satsuma earthenware koro and cover, the cover with a shi-shi finial, the base with a Satsuma mark.

8.25in (21cm) high

$300-400   JN

A Japanese Meiji period Satsuma jar and cover, with figures in landscapes, signed, rubbing to gilding and two hairline cracks to the rim.

17.25in (44cm) high

$150-200   APAR

A Japanese Meiji Period Satsuma moon flask, by Sozan.

c1890   *6in (15cm) high*

$550-600   K&O

A CLOSER LOOK AT A SATSUMA EWER

This is a good signed Japanese Meiji period imperial piece of Satsuma.

It is by the renowned artist Seiuntai Kouzan and is highly decorative.

It is molded with a dragon spout and handle, the sides with gilt Tokugawa mon.

The base has a gilt signature and red and gilt artist's seals.

A Satsuma earthenware ewer and cover.

10.5in (26.5cm) high

$900-1,100   JN

ORIENTAL

A Hirado blue and white porcelain shi-shi with a ball.

5in (13cm) long

$250-350   **PW**

A 20thC Japanese blue and white jardinière, with geishas.

15in (38cm) diam

$300-400   **JN**

A Japanese blue and white stick stand.

24in (61cm) high

$300-400   **JN**

A Japanese late Meiji Imari charger, painted with panels of garden scenes.

Imari porcelain takes its name from the Japanese port from which it was shipped to Europe from the 17thC. It was traditionally made in the town of Arita and took inspiration from Japanese textiles. Imari imagery often features landscapes, trees, birds and depictions of women in detailed kimonos, often in a palette of blue, reddish-orange and gold.

19in (48cm) diam

$130-200   **PW**

A pair of Japanese late Meiji Imari vases, molded with dragons.

12.25in (31cm) high

$300-350   **PW**

A Japanese Meiji period Kutani porcelain vase.

Kutani pottery dates back to the 17thC village of Kutani and enjoyed great popularity in the 19thC. Kutani ceramics were typically decorated with overglaze painting in vivid blues, greens, yellows, purples and reds. Wares often feature bird motifs. In the Meiji era, much Kutani pottery was exported to Europe.

14.75in (37.5cm) high

$90-110   **APAR**

A Japanese Kutani figure of a 'bijin'.

14.25in (36.5cm) high

$150-200   **PW**

A Kutani figure of a samurai on horseback, in full armor with a daikyu.

9.75in (25cm) high

$300-350   **PW**

A Kutani figure of Fukurokuju.

Fukurokuju is one of the Seven Lucky Gods in Japanese mythology. He is the God of wisdom and longevity, usually portrayed as bald with long whiskers, and an abnormally high forehead. The sacred scroll in his right hand either contains the lifespan of every person on earth or a magical scripture.

10.25in (26cm) high

$100-120   **CHEF**

QUICK REFERENCE - NETSUKE

- Netsuke are Japanese miniature sculptural objects that have been crafted since the 16thC.
- They are a practical part of traditional male Japanese dress. As kimonos had no pockets, men carried their tobacco, pipe, purse and other personal items, on a silk cord passed under their sash, or obi. These hanging objects were together called sagemono and often consisted of a small container called an inro. The netsuke was attached to the top of the chord to keep it in place and an ojime bead strung on to the chord to allow access.
- Netsuke are highly decorative, with forms often inspired by mythology and popular religion. They were usually made of ivory or wood.

A 19thC Japanese ivory netsuke, depicting a bearded Daruma carrying a gourd on his shoulder, signed 'Tomoyuki'.

3.25in (8cm) high

$650-800 WW

A 19thC Japanese wood netsuke, depicting a boy with dimples laughing, the eyes inlaid, signed 'Masakazu'.

2in (5cm) high

$2,000-2,500 WW

A 19thC Japanese wood netsuke, depicting a man on a mat with a basket of mushrooms, the reverse signed 'Toyomasa'.

1.75in (4.5cm) high

$1,000-1,600 WW

A Japanese cloisonné vase, decorated with a pheasant, within white metal rim mounts, with pine box.

7.25in (18.5cm) high

$450-550 GWA

A Meiji Japanese ivory netsuke, of a tall man playing a ceremonial drum, wearing a leaf engraved robe and inro, signed 'Yoshiyuki'.

3.75in (9.5cm) high

$900-1,100 MOR

A 19thC Japanese lacquer and ivory netsuke, of an actor wearing a long red wig and a dragon mask, the eyes inlaid in horn, his leg signed 'Jugyoku'.

1.5in (4cm) high

$3,500-4,000 WW

A 19thC Japanese ivory netsuke, of a rat eating a spray of millet, with a smaller pup on its back, the eyes inlaid, signed 'Okatomo'.

1.75in (4.5cm) high

$5,500-6,500 WW

A Japanese carved ivory ojime, in the form of a human skull, engraved 'SIC ER I'.

An ojime is a sliding bead that was strung on a chord hung from the sash in traditional Japanese dress.

1.5in (3.5cm) wide

$300-400 BE

Judith Picks

What impresses me here is the incredible quality of the craftsmanship on what would have been a very everyday object. An inro, literally 'seal-basket', is a small container hung from the waist in traditional Japanese clothing. It consists of several sections held together by a cord. At the top, the cord is pulled through an ojime bead, then passed behind the waist sash, or obi, and fastened to a netsuke. Inros would have been used and worn on a daily basis, and yet are often beautifully detailed and ornate.

A Japanese four-case gold lacquered inro, decorated with two rats, with floral ojime bead and finely carved wood netsuke in the form of two birds feeding on wheat resting on a rattan mat, signed on the inro.

3in (7.5cm) high

$4,000-4,500 GWA

QUICK REFERENCE - BACCARAT PAPERWEIGHTS

- Although paperweights were first made in Murano, it was France that became the leading producer of paperweights in the 19thC, with Clichy, St Louis and Baccarat as the leading companies in the 1840s-50s.
- The Compagnie des Cristalleries de Baccarat was founded in Baccarat, France, in 1765. Baccarat produced paperweights during three periods: 1845-60, 1920-34 and 1953-2001
- Many were made from clear crystal with canes cut to create floral designs. Millefiori paperweights were also common. 'Millefiori' is Italian for 'thousand flowers' and refers to designs of densely packed stylized decoration often found in paperweights. These designs would often appear over a white ground known as 'muslin'.
- Some Baccarat paperweights contain a signature cane, marked with the date the paperweight was made.

An early Baccarat 'Pansy' paperweight, star-cut base, some minor chips.

2.5in (6.5cm) diam

$800-950   POOK

An antique Baccarat wallflower paperweight, minor scratches to underside, tiny seeds to clear glass.

2.5in (6.5cm) wide

$1,000-1,300   JDJ

A Baccarat glass 'garlanded butterfly' paperweight, bruised.

3.25in (8cm) diam

$1,500-2,000   BE

An antique Baccarat red clematis paperweight, one bubble at center of flower, one to right leaf, base possibly re-cut.

2.75in (7cm) wide

$1,700-2,000   JDJ

A Baccarat close-packed millefiori mushroom paperweight, star-cut base.

c1850   *2.75in (7cm) diam*

$600-650   BELL

A contemporary Baccarat scattered millefiori paperweight, signed on base, small bruise in crown, with accession numbers.

3in (7.5cm) diam

$100-130   POOK

A 19thC French paperweight, set with a posy of millefiori flowers, some faults.

3in (7.5cm) diam

$600-750   WW

A 19thC scramble glass paperweight, probably French, with oriental wood stand, small chips to the foot, and dome.

3.25in (8cm) diam

$90-120   PW

QUICK REFERENCE - CLICHY PAPERWEIGHTS

- Clichy was founded by Joseph Maës in 1837 and went on to become one of the great French glassworks of the 19thC.
- Clichy produced paperweights from the 1840s to c1880. These are rarely dated, usually marked only with a 'C'. They were mostly flat with a concave base.
- Millefiori patterns were common, as were colored swirls and flowers. One common design was a small rose-shaped cane that became known as the 'Clichy rose'.

An antique Clichy paperweight, scattered minor surface imperfections.

2.5in (6.5cm) diam

$100-160   POOK

A Clichy scrambled millefiori paperweight, with a fragment of a Clichy rose cane.

3in (7.5cm) diam

$300-350   POOK

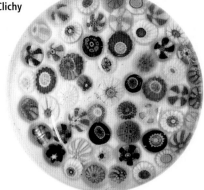

A late 19thC Clichy paperweight, set with millefiori canes, scratches to the dome and sides.

3.5in (9cm) diam

$1,500-2,000   PW

QUICK REFERENCE - ST LOUIS PAPERWEIGHTS

- The glassworks at St Louis, Lorraine, started producing clear crystal wares in the 1780s.
- St Louis began production of paperweights c1842-45.
- Many St Louis paperweights were made with a 'latticinio' ground, with threads of glass arranged in a lattice design, usually in pink or white. 19thC St Louis paperweights tend to have star-cut bases and high domes.
- The St Louis factory still produces glassware, including paperweights, today.

A St Louis three-flower paperweight, one flower signed 'SL 1971', with a paper sticker, six and one facet, in original box.

1971   3in (7.5cm) wide

$250-350   JDJ

A 19thC St Louis garland butterfly paperweight.

3in (7.5cm) wide

$1,000-1,200   FLD

A St Louis harlequin paneled paperweight, with central cane signed 'SL 1989', in original box, with certificate of authenticity.

1989   3in (7.5cm) wide

$650-750   JDJ

A St Louis paperweight, center cane signed 'SL 1991', in original box, some light wear to box.

3.5in (9cm) diam

$1,000-1,200   JDJ

A St Louis Cristal glass paperweight, inset with a grouper fish, in presentation box with blue 'SL' date cane, dated.

1997   3in (7.5cm) diam

$250-400   WW

PAPERWEIGHTS

A late 19thC Old English paperweight, with concentric millefiori cane work.

3in (7.5cm) wide

$200-250   **FLD**

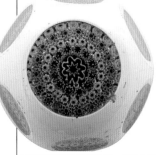

A late 19thC Old English paperweight, with concentric millefiori cane work, within a clear crystal glass dome, with one top printie window and six side windows.

2.25in (6cm) wide

$450-550   **FLD**

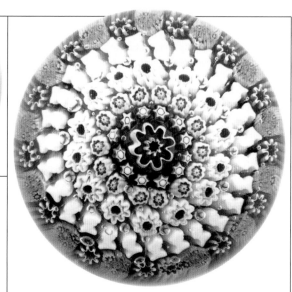

A 19thC Old English paperweight, possibly Bacchus, with a concentric millefiori cane work, with an outer ring of Queen Victoria profile canes.

3.25in (8cm) wide

$1,000-1,200   **FLD**

An early 20thC John Walsh paperweight.

3in (7.5cm) wide

$150-200   **FLD**

A Whitefriars Christmas paperweight, designed by Geoffrey Baxter, signature and date cane.

Whitefriars was one of Britain's leading glassworks in the 19thC and 20thC (see pages 243-246). In the years 1975-80 Whitefriars produced special Christmas paperweights, decorated with festive scenes and motifs. These were designed by Geoffrey Baxter (1922-95), who worked at Whitefrairs from 1954 until the factory's closure in 1980.

1976   *3in (7.5cm) wide*

$120-160   **FLD**

A Whitefriars commemorative paperweight, designed by Geoffrey Baxter, celebrating silver jubilee of the Coronation of Her Majesty Queen Elizabeth II, signature and date cane.

1977   *3in (7.5cm) wide*

$80-100   **FLD**

A Whitefriars Christmas paperweight, designed by Geoffrey Baxter, decorated with Mary and Joseph, signature and date cane.

1978   *3in (7.5cm) wide*

$120-160   **FLD**

A Whitefriars Christmas paperweight, designed by Geoffrey Baxter, with a partridge surrounded by pears, signature and date cane.

1979   *3in (7.5cm) wide*

$150-200   **FLD**

A Whitefriars Christmas paperweight, designed by Geoffrey Baxter, signature and date cane.

1980   *3in (7.5cm) wide*

$200-250   **FLD**

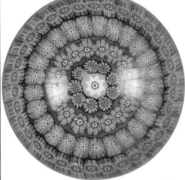

A later 20thC William Manson paperweight, 'Elizabeth of Glamis', no.45 of a limited edition of 200, with box and certificate.

William Manson was Paul Ysart's apprentice at Caithness Glass in the 1960s and later his colleague at Harland. Manson returned to Caithness in 1974 and remained there until he set up his own studio, the William Manson Paperweights Studio, in 1997. The studio is now based in Perth, where Manson and his family continue to create limited edition paperweights.

$100-130   FLD

A glass paperweight, by William Manson, signed to the underside and 'WM' cane to the inside.

2.25in (6cm) diam
$60-100   HAN

An Ysart glass paperweight, by Paul Ysart, decorated with a butterfly and dragonfly, with 'PY' cane.

3.25in (8cm) diam
$350-400   WW

QUICK REFERENCE - PAUL YSART

Paul Ysart (1904-91) is considered one of the most important 20thC paperweight makers. He was son of Salvador Ysart, a Spanish glassmaker who worked at Monart in Perth. Paul Ysart worked with his father at the Moncrieff glassworks until 1963, then moved to Caithness Glass where he worked until 1970. He then opened his own paperweight studio in Harland, Wick, which he ran until his retirement in 1979. His paperweights are complex and detailed in design, often signed with 'PY' or 'H' canes.

An Ysart glass dahlia head paperweight, by Paul Ysart, with 'PY' cane.

See Ian Turner and Frank Andrews, 'Ysart Glass', Volo Edition, page 143, catalog no.171, for a comparable weight illustrated.

3in (7.5cm) diam
$250-350   WW

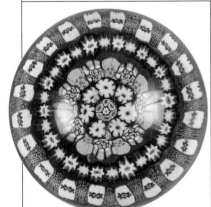

A concentric millefiori paperweight, attributed to Paul Ysart.

3.25in (8.5cm) diam
$200-250   POOK

A concentric millefiori paperweight, attributed to Paul Ysart, marked with accession numbers.

2.5in (6.5cm) diam
$200-250   POOK

A late 20thC Perthshire Paperweight, 'Bouquet Overlay', with a top printie window and eighteen side facets, no.45 of a limited edition of 300, with box and certificate.

$250-350   FLD

PAPERWEIGHTS

A waterlily paperweight, by Rick Ayotte, red dragonfly bottom left, signed near foot 'Rick Ayotte 1 of 3 2011'.

2011   *4in (10cm) diam*

$1,000-1,200   JDJ

A coiled red rose paperweight, by Ray Banford.

3in (7.5cm) diam

$200-250   POOK

A bouquet paperweight, by Chris Buzzini, signed in a cane 'Buzzini 88' and inscribed to exterior 'Buzzini 88 MB17'.

3in (7.5cm) wide

$900-1,100   JDJ

A contemporary paperweight, by Jim D'Onofrio, depicting a turtle with plants, rocks and sand, signed in script 'Jim D'Onofrio 93' and '0284'.

The four-digit number, '0284', represents the sequential number of paperweights made in his career.

3.5in (9cm) diam

$650-750   JDJ

A Millville red crimp rose footed paperweight, by Emil Larsen.

Millville, New Jersey, was home to a number of glass factories in the 19thC and 20thC. Many Millville glassworks produced frit paperweights, using loose glass powder to create a design inside the weight. Another popular design was a glass rose within a clear crystal globe. This rose became the trademark symbol of Millville in 19thC and usually came in red or pink.

3.5in (9cm) diam

$900-1,100   POOK

A coiled rose pedestal paperweight, by Charles Kaziun Jr., with signature cane.

1.75in (4.5cm) high

$250-300   POOK

A 19thC scramble paperweight, possibly New England Glass Company, some damage.

2.25in (6cm) wide

$130-200   FLD

A 'woodland red salamander' paperweight, by Cathy Richardson, signed in script 'C. Richardson 2007 WS-002'.

3.75in (9.5cm) wide

$600-750   JDJ

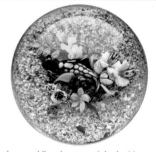

A red spotted lizard paperweight, by Mayauel Ward, signed in script 'Mayauel Ward 2007' and possibly 'PWRLM'.

2007   *3in (7.5cm) wide*

$450-550   JDJ

QUICK REFERENCE - FOUNTAIN PENS

- The first commercial fountain pens date from the 1880s, but the 'golden' age of the fountain pen was the 1910s-50s.
- Most collectors aim to collect one period or brand of fountain pen. The collectors' market for fountain pens has long been dominated by pens produced in the first half of the 20thC, by big names such as Parker, Waterman, Montblanc and Dunhill Namiki. However, these pens have become less common in recent years, prompting some collectors to focus on lesser-known brands and contemporary limited edition pens.
- The rarity, quality and material can all affect value. Unusual celluloids or pens with complex metal overlays can be popular, as can classic models, such as the Parker 51 or 75. Limited editions, such as Montblanc's 'Lorenzo de Medici' of 1992, are also highly sought after.
- Condition is paramount. To ensure value, a pen must come with its original packaging and paperwork. Most collectors do not use the pens, or even unpack them. Uninked pens in mint condition, and pens still sealed in their cellophane, tend to fetch the highest prices.

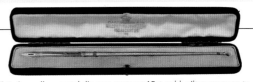

A Victorian yellow metal dip pen, tests as 15ct gold, gilt monogram to lid, in original case, by 'Carrington & Co, Goldsmiths & Jewellers 130 Regent St.'.

7.5in (19cm) long 0.21oz

$350-400   **LOCK**

A Louis Cartier sterling silver fountain pen, marked with French control marks, with 18ct gold nib, no.024075.

$400-450   **HAN**

A Louis Cartier fountain pen, the silvered fluted body with gold colored clip and banding, stamped '18K 750', marked 'Plaque OR G', in maker's box.

5.5in (14cm) long

$150-200   **FELL**

A Louis Cartier fountain pen, the red marble effect body with red cabochon terminal, the nib stamped '18K 750', in maker's fitted case.

5.5in (14cm) long

$350-400   **FELL**

A Panthère de Cartier gold-plated and enamel fountain pen, nib stamped '18K 750', some scratches and dents, in maker's case.

5in (13cm) long

$250-350   **FELL**

A Cartier Diabolo ball point pen, with blue cabochon terminal, some light surface wear, in fitted maker's case and card outer sleeve.

5.5in (14cm) long

$150-200   **FELL**

A Conway Stewart 27 gray hatch fountain pen, in original box.

Conway Stewart & Co. was a British distributor and maker of fountain pens, founded by Frank Jarvis and Tommy Garner in London in 1905. In its first decade, it chiefly imported and sold fountain pens from the United States. It later designed and manufactured its own fountain pens, often cased in colorful plastic. The company went into administration in 2014.

$80-100   **LOCK**

A Conway Stewart no.22 fountain pen, with floral printed lacquer with Greek key cap ring, 14ct gold no.5 nib, and lever filler.

$250-350   **HAN**

A Conway Stewart Red Whirl Silver Duro fountain pen, boxed with paperwork.

2010

$400-450   **HAN**

A Cross 10ct rolled gold fountain pen, in original case.

$50-70   **LOCK**

PENS & WRITING

A Dunhill Namiki fountain pen, maki-e lacquer barrel and cap with raised and gilt-leaf and praying mantis decoration, 14ct gold nib, lever filling, the nib and clip marked 'Dunhill'.

The Namiki Manufacturing Company was founded by Ryosuki Namiki in Japan in 1915. It launched its successful range of 'Pilot' fountain pens in 1918. From 1930, Namiki worked closely with Alfred Dunhill, a British distributor, to sell Namiki's pens around the world under the trade name Dunhill Namiki. The partnership ended when World War II broke out.

c1930   *5.25in (13.5cm) long*

$4,500-5,500   HAN

A Dunhill Namiki fountain pen, with lacquered decoration, lid with two 14ct gold bands, one band engraved with initials and dated.

1931   *4.25in (10.5cm) long*

$1,300-2,000   LOCK

An MM Co. Ltd. 'Spot' fountain pen, with two 9ct gold bands.

5.5in (14cm) long

$80-100   LOCK

A Montblanc fountain pen, the banded black resin body with silvered cap, with 18ct white gold nib, in box, with a black leather pouch with Montblanc refills.

5.5in (14cm) long

$250-350   FELL

A Montblanc Meisterstuck Classique 144 fountain pen, gold-plated trim, 14ct gold nib, cartridge filling, HC137887.

$250-350   HAN

A Montblanc jumbo pen.

$350-400   JN

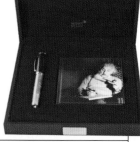

A Montblanc Albert Einstein fountain pen, no.1410 of a limited edition of 3000, the platinum-plated body engraved with scientific equations, nib stamped '4810 18K', in maker's display box with small hardcover book 'Albert Einstein Famous Quotes', a Montblanc fabric pouch and two Montblanc writing inks.

$4,000-4,500   FELL

Judith Picks

In an age when letter writing has been virtually superceded by emails, there is still something deeply satisfying about using a splendid vintage fountain pen. Montblanc was founded in 1906 in Hamburg. It placed a white tip, later a rounded star, at the top of its pen caps, to represent the top of Europe's highest mountain, Montblanc, after which it was named. The firm achieved great popularity, notably with its successful Meisterstück, or Masterpiece, range. Montblanc continues today as part of the Richemont group. Vintage Montblanc pens are highly collectible.

A Montblanc Meisterstuck fountain pen, Agatha Christie, no.28363 of a limited edition of 30000, with silver mounts and 18ct gold engraved nip, boxed.

5in (14cm) long

$800-1,000   BELL

A limited edition Donation Montblanc Leonard Bernstein fountain pen, with 18ct gold nib.

1996

$650-750   HAN

A Montblanc Meisterstuck ball point pen.

5.25in (13.5cm) long

$90-100   LOCK

A Montblanc Meisterstuck ball point pen, stamped '925', some signs of wear.

5.5in (14cm) long

$300-400   FELL

A Parker sterling silver Gisele fountain pen.

Founded in 1889 by George Parker, Parker became popular with its 'Lucky Curve' fountain pens, which greatly reduced the possibility of leaks. Its 1911 Jack Knife Safety pen was also a success; the cap could be screwed down to the pen's body to prevent leakages when the pen was not in use. The company continues today as part of Newell Brands.

5in (13cm) long

$100-130   LOCK

A Parker 75 Sterling Silver fountain pen and ballpoint pen set.

$150-200   LOCK

An 18ct gold Swan self-filling fountain pen, lever filler, screw cap, in leather Mabie, Todd and Co. Ltd. box.

4in (10cm) long

$300-400   HAN

A Waterman silver pinstipe fountain pen, no.2 nib.

In New York in 1884, Lewis Waterman (1837-1901) patented a metal nib with hair-thin grooves to allow air to circulate the ink reservoir, thus allowing a smooth and steady flow of ink and reducing leaks. He founded the L.E. Waterman Pen Company in 1888 and within the first year sold 5,000 pens. By his death in 1901, the company was selling nearly 1,000 pens a day. The company survives today as Waterman S.A. and is based in Paris.

c1915

$150-200   HAN

A Parker Duofold Senior red streamline fountain pen.

1929

$130-200   HAN

A boxed Parker Vacomatic oversize gray pearl fountain pen.

1935

$200-250   HAN

A Parker Vacumatic green fountain pen, marked '17'.

c1937   *5in (13cm) long*

$90-100   LOCK

A 1950s Sheaffer Snorkel saratoga fountain pen, made in Australia, 14ct gold nib with platinum mask.

$50-70   HAN

A Swan Leverless self-fill fountain pen, iridescent green snakeskin, 14ct gold nib.

1937

$90-120   HAN

A Waterman 452 silver overlay basket weave fountain pen.

c1924

$250-350   HAN

QUICK REFERENCE - S. MORDAN AND CO.

- Sampson Mordan (1790-1843) was a British silversmith. In 1822, he and his associate Joseph Isaac Hawkins patented the first ever mechanical pencil.
- Mordan then went into partnership with Gabriel Riddle, a stationer with whom he manufactured and sold silver propelling pencils. The partnership dissolved in 1837, and Mordan continued to sell his pencils under the trading name of S. Mordan and Co.
- After his death in 1843, his sons Sampson and Augustus inherited the firm, which continued to produce metalware until World War II.
- S. Mordan and Co. manufactured a wide variety of products, including locks, whistles, boxes and inkwells - but they were chiefly known for their propelling and telescopic pencils. S. Mordan and Co.'s silver and gold-cased 'Everpoint' pencils remain popular with collectors today, as do its novelty propelling pencils. These pencils were often shaped as animals, figures, tools or everyday objects. They were usually made in silver or gold.

A Victorian telescopic pencil, by S. Mordan and Co., with design lozenge, the body formed by a nutmeg, with a ring attachment.
1856   *1.25in (3cm) long*
$1,700-2,000   **WW**

A Victorian silver plumb bob pencil, manufactured by S. Mordan and Co., with a William Thornhill registration mark for 1873, with a six section telescopic pencil, with a ring attachment.
1873   *extended 4.25in (11cm) long 0.6oz*
$550-650   **WW**

A Victorian dumb bell telescopic silver pencil, by S. Mordan and Co., with a design lozenge.
1875   *closed 1.75in (4.5cm) long 0.6oz*
$650-750   **WW**

A Victorian ivory telescopic pencil, probably made by S. Mordan and Co., retailed by W. Thornhill and Co., with a registration lozenge, modeled as a girl, in the Kate Greenaway manner.
1881   *closed 1.75in (4.5cm) long*
$1,000-1,200   **WW**

A Victorian silver and porcelain 'walnut' pencil, with a part opened shell to reveal the interior nut, by S. Mordan and Co., registration mark.
1885   *1.25in (3cm) long*
$800-950   **WW**

A 9ct gold S. Mordan and Co. pencil.
2.5in (6.5cm) long
$200-250   **FELL**

A Victorian silver gold 'salmon' pencil, by S. Mordan and Co., the tail pulling out to reveal a pull-out extending pencil, unmarked.
2.25in (5.5cm) long 0.2oz
$450-600   **WW**

A Victorian gold and silver-gilt pencil, probably by S. Mordan and Co., enameled with a carnation head, unmarked.
2in (5cm) long
$450-550   **WW**

A Victorian silver 'Ally Sloper' telescopic pencil, probably by S. Mordan and Co., unmarked.

Alexander 'Ally' Sloper is the fictional character of the comic strip 'Ally Sloper'. He is one of the earliest comic strip characters and is regarded as the first recurring character in comics. Red-nosed and blustery, this archetypal lazy schemer is often found 'sloping' through alleys to avoid his landlord and other creditors. He was created for the British magazine 'Judy' by writer and fledgling artist Charles H. Ross, and inked and later fully illustrated by his French wife Émilie de Tessier. The strips, which used text narrative beneath unbordered panels, premiered in the 14 August 1867 issue of 'Judy', a humor-magazine rival of the famous 'Punch'.

closed 2.25in (5.5cm) long 0.8oz
$2,000-2,500   **WW**

A Victorian gold and enamel pencil, by
S. Mordan and Co.

closed 1.75in (4.5cm) long

$600-750   WW

A Victorian 18ct gold
and enamel telescopic pencil,
by S. Mordan and Co., enameled
with the Queen of Spades playing card.

2.25in (6cm) long

$450-550   WW

A Victorian 'church warden's pipe'
pencil, by S. Mordan and Co., porcupine
quill body, ivory bowl.

2.25in (6cm) long

$250-300   WW

A Victorian silver
'gin bottle' pencil, probably
by S. Mordan and Co., with an
enameled label 'Genuine Hollands, GENEVA,
J.D.K.&Z, Rotterdam', unmarked.

closed 1.5in (4cm) long 0.4oz

$400-450   WW

A Victorian silver
'champagne bottle'
pencil, by S. Mordan and Co.,
faded enamel label, 'Zoedone,
non-alcoholic aerated iron beverage,
brain and nerve tonic, sole manufacturer
The Zoedone Co. Wrexham'.

1.75in (4.5cm) long 0.5oz

$550-600   WW

A Victorian silver 'anchor' pencil, 'Faith, Hope
and Charity', by S. Mordan and Co.

1.75in (4.5cm) long 0.2oz

$850-900   WW

A Victorian silver 'mug' pencil,
by S. Mordan and Co.

closed 1in (2.5cm) long 0.5oz

$750-800   WW

A Victorian hound's head silver
pencil, retailed by Clarke and Co.,
New Bond Street, lacking body.

closed 1.75in (4.5cm) long 0.2oz

$250-300   WW

A Victorian gold whistle pencil, unmarked.

3.25in (8cm) long 0.42oz

$550-600   WW

A Victorian gold 'plumb bob' pencil, made by
Walter Thornhill, retailed by Asprey and Son,
maker's mark 'WT', marked 'M', possibly for
Mordan, with an arrow and a lozenge mark.

**Plumb bob pencils were also known
as spinning tops and peg tops. This pencil
was one that Thornhill and Mordan co-operated in.
See K. Bull, 'The KB Collection of Pencils', 2012, pages 68-69.**

1873

$2,000-2,500   WW

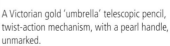

A Victorian gold 'umbrella' telescopic pencil,
twist-action mechanism, with a pearl handle,
unmarked.

closed 2in (5cm) long 0.14oz

$450-550   WW

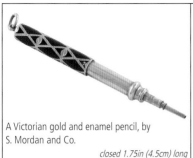

PENS & WRITING

A Victorian silver-plated 'dog's head' Inkwell, by Elkington & Co., set with glass eyes and with a hinged cover.

6in (15cm) wide

$350-400   **TEN**

A Japanese Meiji bronze and copper 'fish basket' inkwell, decorated with crabs, clams, a snail and other shells, with a glass lined well.

c1868-1912   2.75in (7cm) wide

$900-1,100   **WW**

A late 19thC French carved 'bulldog' inkwell, his head moving on a hinge to reveal a well.

4.5in (11.5cm) high

$450-550   **WW**

A late Victorian brass 'teapot' inkwell, the hinged lid revealing a glass liner, the brass rim inscribed 'STOCKLEY 44 NEW BOND ST LONDON'.

3.5in (9cm) wide

$130-200   **WW**

A late 19thC carved wood 'Moor's head' inkwell, with a hinged top, previously mounted.

4.5in (11.5cm) high

$600-750   **WW**

A late 19thC Swiss bone 'chalets' inkstand, the roofs hinged to reveal a white metal inkwell and a sander.

4.5in (11.5cm) wide

$250-300   **WW**

A late 19thC Scottish polished specimen agate 'curling stone' inkwell, with revolving handle enclosing a central well.

2.75in (7cm) diam

$850-900   **BE**

A late Victorian copper and brass Isobath constant-level inkwell, by Thomas De La Rue, the patent for W.T. Shaw.

1891 *4.5in (11.5cm) high*

$250-350 **WW**

A late 19thC pottery 'rugby ball' inkwell, with a hinged gilt-metal lid in the form of a cap, registration no.167875, first registered in 1891.

3in (7.5cm) wide

$250-350 **WW**

A German Art Nouveau bronze inkstand, with a pen rest, on a polished black base.

7in (17.5cm) wide

$60-100 **WW**

A late 19thC cold-painted metal inkwell, modeled as Dan Leno, the hinged lid revealing a ceramic well, with a book inscribed 'DAN LENO'.

George Wild Galvin (1860-1904), better known as Dan Leno, was the greatest Victorian Music Hall comedian and is best known for his dame roles in pantomimes.

4.5in (11.5cm) high

$160-200 **WW**

An Edwardian 'Slouch hat' travelling inkwell, marked 'CIV' (City Imperial Volunteers), the gilt-metal interior with inner cap and original glass inkwell.

3in (7.5cm) long

$200-250 **MART**

An Edwardian silver and clear cut glass inkwell, by William Comyns, London, decorated with Reynold's cherubs below hinged cover.

1903 *4in (10cm) diam*

$250-350 **FLD**

A Doulton Lambeth stoneware and silver 'Suffragette Movement' inkwell, silver well by Grey & Co., Chester.

1910 *3.5in (9cm) high*

$550-600 **BE**

A George V silver inkwell and perpetual calendar, with ivorine cards, by Wilmot Manufacturing Co. Birmingham.

1921 *5in (13cm) wide*

$120-150 **APAR**

A postcard, of Coulsdon station.
$60-80   LOCK

A postcard, of the Great Northern Ireland Railway, with a horse pulling a carriage along the track at Fintona Junction.
$50-70   LOCK

A postcard, showing people getting water at Midland Station, with handwritten words 'LINCOLN TYPHOID OUTBREAK 1905/ DRAWING WATER AT MIDLAND STATION'.
$90-100   LOCK

A postcard, of Lincoln station interior, with horse attached to carriage and staff.
$80-100   LOCK

A postcard, of Yarm-on-Trees railway station interior, with printed words 'YARM-ON-TREES RAILWAY STATION. NO. 1547'.
$60-80   LOCK

A postcard, no.1272, of 'The Station Abertillery' interior, from the F. Viner collection.
$80-100   LOCK

A postcard, no.510, of Penpych and Blaenrhondda station, Treherbert, from the F. Viner collection.
$60-80   LOCK

A postcard, depicting Walton station interior.
$80-100   LOCK

A postcard, of Kings Lynn station exterior in the snow.
$120-160   LOCK

QUICK REFERENCE - POSTCARDS

- Postcards have their origins in the mid-19thC, but their 'golden' age was arguably 1890-1910. Postcards continued to be sent throughout the 20thC, but today have largely fallen out of fashion due to the rise of mobile phones and the internet.
- As well as being used as greetings cards, postcards in the late 19thC and early 20thC were used as a method of spreading news. People regularly sent commemorative postcards and postcards featuring 'news' photographs, depicting fire and mining disasters, shipwrecks and train crashes.
- Postcards were so commonly sent and received in the 20thC that most vintage postcards are worth very little, sometimes only a few pence. It is only very rare postcards that can today fetch higher prices. These include postcards depicting rare or now closed railway stations, postcards of the Titanic, and postcards by key designers such as Louis Wain.

A postcard, by G. Courtney, of the SS Titanic being pulled by tugs from Southhampton on its maiden voyage in April 1912.
$300-400 LOCK

A postcard, of RMS Titanic.
$100-130 LOCK

A postcard, by G. Courtney, reading 'S.S."TITANIC" leaving Southhampton on her Maiden Voyage April 10th 1912'.
$400-450 LOCK

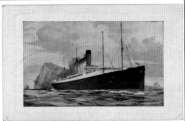

A postcard, of RMS Carpathia, which picked up survivors of the Titanic.
$60-80 LOCK

A postcard, Viner's series no.21, of the launch of a lifeboat at Weston-super-Mare.
$20-25 LOCK

A postcard, of trawlers in Grimsby Dock during the lock out in 1901.
$25-30 LOCK

A postcard, of RMS Carpathia at Fiume.
$100-130 LOCK

A postcard, of Pugh's Wholesale Fruit Market, 511 Dudley Road, Wolverhampton, dated '24.3.1917'.

1917

$70-80   **LOCK**

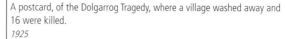

A postcard, of the Dolgarrog Tragedy, where a village washed away and 16 were killed.

1925

$40-50   **LOCK**

A postcard, of 'Britannia Colliery, Pengam, 1934', from F. Viner collection.

$35-40   **LOCK**

A Rugby League postcard, of New Zealand 1947 Rugby League Tourists, taken at Fartown 22 November 1947, with player's legend.

$40-50   **LOCK**

A postcard, of J. Nelson & Sons Butchers' shopfront in St Oswald Street, Old Swan, Liverpool.

$60-70   **LOCK**

A postcard, of Pegram's shopfront and staff on Derby Road, Bootle.

$50-70   **LOCK**

A postcard, no.433, of Viner's shop front, Broad St, Wrington, with delivery cart.

$60-70   **LOCK**

A postcard, Viner's series no.442, of Lewis Merthyr Colliery.

$60-80   **LOCK**

A postcard, from the F. Viner collection, of men ascending a pit in Wales.

$60-80   **LOCK**

A silk postcard, for the Australian Commonwealth Militiary Forces.
$40-50   LOCK

A silk postcard, for Royal Sussex Regiment.
$50-70   LOCK

A silk postcard, for Machine Gun Corps, sewn words 'Greetings from Grantham'.
$60-70   LOCK

A postcard, of the ventriloquist Geo F. Ford with his puppet.
$25-30   LOCK

A Wiener Werkstätte postcard, no.561, 'Beauty', by Maria Likarz.
$100-130   LOCK

A Louis Wain postcard, 'THE PHOTOGRAPHER ON THE SANDS', from the Wrench Series.
$120-160   LOCK

A Louis Wain Salmon postcard, 'Cat knitting', 3021.
$70-80   LOCK

A Louis Wain Cats & Dogs postcard, 'CONTENTED / Christmas Greetings', 9501.
$60-80   LOCK

A Louis Wain postcard, 'STOP THERE TILL MY MATE COMES, AND I'LL SUMMONS YOU BOTH FOR FURIOUS DRIVING AND ASSAULT', from the Wrench Series.
$120-160   LOCK

QUICK REFERENCE - CIGARETTE CARDS

- Cigarette cards emerged in the USA in the 1870s, originally as a means of stiffening cigarette packs.
- They were blank to begin with, but cigarette companies soon took advantage of the space to print advertisements. By the 1890s, most cigarette companies included cards within their packs, featuring photographs or illustrations of monarchs, actors, sportsmen, soldiers and much more.
- Like postcards, most cigarette cards are worth very little. They were made and marketed as items to be collected - and people did just that! Cigarette cards were produced in vast quantities and complete collections are very common. It is only very rare cigarette cards that attract higher prices today.
- See P. Lynch and M. Murray, 'Murray's Guide to Cigarette & Trade Values', for more information.

An Allen & Ginters 'Commodore's Pennant Denmark' card, from the 'Naval Flags' series.
$25-35   **LOCK**

A Barratt 'Felix Pictures' card, no.11.

Priced at £35 ($47) in P. Lynch and M. Murray, 'Murray's Guide to Cigarette & Trade Values'.
$250-300   **LOCK**

A Duke & Son 'FAIR DAY - Wales' card, from the 'Holidays' series.
$15-20   **LOCK**

A Buchner 'CAPT. JOSEPH B. EAKINS' card, from the 'Police Inspectors & Captains' series.
$50-60   **LOCK**

A Cameron & Cameron 'Fireman' card, from the 'Occupations for Women' series.
$60-80   **LOCK**

A Faulkner 'Hands' card, from the 'Football Terms' 1st series, for Grenadier Cigarettes.
$45-55   **LOCK**

A Franklyn Davey 'CERF' card, from the 'Beauties' series, for Loadstone Cigarettes, slightly grubby.
$35-40   **LOCK**

A Gail & Ax 'ALABAMA' card, from the 'Industries of the States' series, reading 'COTTON, IRON, COAL AND THEIR MANUFACTURES'.
$45-55   **LOCK**

A Glass & Co. 'FECKSA' card, from the 'Beauties' series, slight staining.
$80-100   **LOCK**

A Harvey & Davey '1st Bengal Lancers' card, from the 'Colonial Troops' series.

$80-100   LOCK

A Hignett 'ARABIAN STALLION' card, from the 'Animal Pictures' series, for Butterfly Cigarettes.

$25-35   LOCK

A Hill's Cigarettes 'Maj-Gen R.S.S. Baden Powell' card, from the 'Boer War Generals-Campaigners' series.

$30-40   LOCK

A Hill's Cigarettes 'Queensland Mounted Rifles', from the 'Colonial Troops (Leading Lines)' series.

$20-25   LOCK

A Hill's Cigarettes 'Lieut-Col H.C.O.PLUMER' card, from the 'Boer War Generals-Campaigners' series.

$25-35   LOCK

A Lambert & Butler card, from the 'Types of the British Army & Navy' series, brown specialities back.

$80-90   LOCK

A Major Drapkin 'The South Wales Borderers' card, from the 'Soldiers & their Uniforms' series, for Drapkin's Cigarettes.

$35-40   LOCK

A Phillips 'General Lord Kitchener' card, from the 'Colonial Troops' series.

$25-35   LOCK

A Player's '78th Highlanders Piper 1814' card, no.47, from the 'Old England's Defenders' series.

$15-20   LOCK

QUICK REFERENCE - TRAVEL POSTERS

- Travel posters boomed in the early 20thC as changing economic circumstances and technical advancements allowed more people to take holidays and to travel to farther destinations. They were used to promote railways, cruise liners, airlines, ferries and buses, and to present particular locations around the world as desirable holiday destinations.
- The 'golden' age of travel posters was the 1910s-30s, where railway and cruise liner posters were especially common. After World War II, travel posters began to decline in significance as television, radio and magazines took over as the main source of advertisements. Airline posters from the 1950s-70s remain popular, as do post-war Russian posters, but other post-war posters tend to be less sought after.
- Posters with bright, saturated colors depicting evocative attractive scenes tend to fetch the highest prices. Posters designed in the Modernist or Art Deco style are also popular with collectors.
- The brand can affect value. Posters produced by the 'Big Four' British railway companies - Great Western Railway (GWR), London, Midland and Scottish Railway (LMS), London and North Eastern Railway (LNER) and Southern Railway (SR) - are usually popular, as are major cruise liners such as White Star, or airlines such as Air France. A poster's value can also increase if it is the work of a well-known designer such as Jean Carlu, Cassandre (Adolphe Mouron) or Tom Purvis.
- Condition is also important. Many posters have been stored folded, and while such folds can be professionally removed, tears, scuffing and other damage to the image will often more dramatically reduce the value.

'WHITBY / IT'S QUICKER BY RAIL', designed by K. Hauff, for LNER, professionally restored and mounted on linen.
$1,600-2,000 TEN

'STRATFORD-UPON-AVON', designed by Michael Reilly, printed by J. Weiner Ltd., London, paper, large loss in upper right corner and image, losses.
50in (127cm) wide
$800-850 SWA

'EDINBURGH SOUTHERN RAILWAY', designed by Fred Taylor, for the LNER & LMS companies, slight fold tears, oval indelible railway approval stamp.
c1935 39.75in (101cm) long
$450-600 BELL

'Marblethorpe / TRUSTHORPE AND SUTTON-ON-SEA', designed by Tom Eckersley, for the Eastern Region, folded.
1960
$300-350 TEN

'ESSEX / SAFFRON WALDEN / SEE BRITAIN BY TRAIN', designed by Savage, for the Eastern Region, folded, with a few small tears.
$250-350 TEN

'MORECAMBE AND HEYSHAM / BE SURE TO GO BY TRAIN', designed by Lander, for the London Midland Region, folded.
$200-250 TEN

'NORTHUMBERLAND / SEE BRITAIN BY TRAIN', designed by J.G. Fullerton, for the North Eastern Region, some wear.
$800-950 TEN

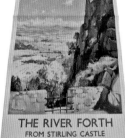

'THE RIVER FORTH FROM STIRLING CASTLE', designed by Jack Merriott, for the Scottish Region, folded.
$650-750 TEN

'The New Sunset Limited / SUNSET ROUTE', paper, speckling in margins and image, pin holes in margins and corners.
1924   *23in (58.5cm) high*
$1,300-2,000   **SWA**

'AUSTRIA', designed by Erich Von Wunschheim, printed by Christoph Reisser, Austria, minor repaired tears, replaced loss in corner.
                    37.25in (94.5cm) high
$750-800   **SWA**

'Schoellenen / GOESCHENEN-ANDERMATT / SWITZERLAND', by Otto Baumberger (1889-1961), printed by J.E. Wolfensberger, Zurich, minor creases.
1934   *39.75in (101cm) high*
$550-600   **SWA**

A CLOSER LOOK AT A POSTER

'Étoile du Nord' (The North Star) was revolutionary in advertising when it first appeared. It is a travel poster with no landscape, no destination and no train.

The design is simple, stark and structured, which adds to the power of the image.

The scene is viewed from a low angle, a common technique of the poster's well-known designer, Adolphe Mouron Cassandre (1901-68).

There are some repaired tears and creases, with overpainting in the margins and along the folds.

'ÉTOILE DU NORD', printed by Hachard & Cie, Paris, foxing in image.
1927   *41.5in (105.5cm) high*
$2,500-3,500   **SWA**

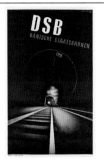

'DSB / DÄNISCHE STAATSBAHNEN', designed by Aage Rasmussen (1913-75), printed by Andreasen & Lachmann, tape on verso.

Rasmussen was a Danish illustrator and poster designer. This poster, considered to be his best, uses the perspective created by the tracks to draw the viewer's eye to the horizon from which a train approaches at full speed. The asymmetric typography is organized perpendicularly to the meter that shows the speed: 120 kmh.
1937   *39in (99cm) high*
$900-1,100   **SWA**

'STEAM POWER / THE NEW HAVEN R.R.', tears at edges, creases in image.
                    41.5in (105.5cm) high
$800-950   **SWA**

'TURBOTRAIN / PARIS-CAEN', designed by Raoul 'Eric' Castel (1915-97).

Raoul 'Eric' Castel created bold, bright and often abstract advertisements in the 1950s-70s. In his innovative posters for the French Railway, he was able to imply speed through the dynamic use of sharp colors.
1972   *39in (99cm) high*
$550-600   **SWA**

POSTERS

'SPORTS D'HIVER À CHAMONIX / CACHAT'S-MAJESTIC', designed by
Cândido Aragonese de Faria (1849-1911), printed by Atelier Faria, Paris.
c1910   *61.25in (155.5cm) wide*
$4,000-4,500   **SWA**

'ST. MORITZ / ENGADIN', designed by Carl Moos (1878-1959), printed
by Fretz, Zurich, repaired tear at right edge, into central image, archival
tape on verso.
                                            38.5in (98cm) high
$6,000-6,500   **SWA**

'KANDERSTEG / SWITZERLAND',
designed by Willy Trapp (1905-84),
printed by Wolfsberg, Zurich, some
foxing and staining, tears and pin
holes, margins trimmed.
                        40in (101.5cm) high
$450-550   **SWA**

'LE SKI DANS LA CÉLÈBRE STATION
THERMALE DE BARÈGES', designed
by Gaston Gorde (1908-95), printed
by Les Affiches Touristiques-Gorde
& Boudry, Denfort, restored losses,
repaired tears in margins.
1934   *39.25in (99.5cm) high*
$3,000-3,500   **SWA**

'MONT. REVARD / TÉLÉPHÉRIQUE TÉLESKI',
designed by Paul Ordner (1900-69), printed
by M. Déchaux, Paris, minor restoration.

**Mount Revard, in the Aix-les-Bains region,
was one of the oldest ski resorts in France.
Skiing began there c1908.**
c1935   *39in (99cm) high*
$650-750   **SWA**

'Let's go skiing!
/ use THE NEW
HAVEN R.R.
Snow Trains',
designed by
Sascha Maurer
(1897-1961),
printed by
Latham Litho
Co., Inc., Long
Island City.

**The New Haven Railroad's Snow Trains,
which began operating in 1933, were
self-contained ski trips on wheels in which
the train itself was used as a ski lodge and
people ate in the dining car.**
1936   *22in (56cm) high*
$1,300-2,000   **SWA**

'NORWAY / A FISTFUL OF FUN / FLY THERE BY
SAS', designed by Inger Skjensvold Sørensen
(1922-2006), printed by Grøndahl & Søn,
Norway.
1956   *39.25in (99.5cm) high*
$1,000-1,200   **SWA**

'MONT SAINT-MICHEL', designed by Leon Constant-Duval (1877-1956), printed by Champenois, Paris.

c1920   41.25in (105cm) high

$2,000-2,500   **SWA**

'ONE WAY TO PLEASURE-BY MOTOR-BUS', designed by Christopher R.W. Nevinson (1889-1946), printed by Avenue Press, London.

Nevinson studied art at the Academie Julian in Paris. He was involved in the Italian Futurist movement through his friendship and collaboration with Marinetti. This image is one of a series of four he designed for the London Transport in 1921. The series shares the common design element of the red border.

1921   40.25in (102cm) high

$900-1,000   **SWA**

'WARSZAWA', designed by Stefan Norblin (1892-1952), printed by K. Kozianskich, Warsaw, tears and creases.

c1925   39in (99cm) high

$1,300-2,000   **SWA**

'LAC D'ANNECY', designed by Roger Broders (1883-1953), printed by Lucien Serre & Cie, Paris, mounted on Japan, matted and framed, repaired tears.

1930   39.25in (99.5cm) high

$4,000-4,500   **SWA**

'LAGO DI GARDA RIVA', designed by Antonio Simeoni, printed by Barabino & Graeve, Genova, extensively overpainted margins, tears at edges, some affecting image.

This is one of only two posters designed by Simeoni.

1926   39.5in (77.5cm) high

$2,000-2,500   **SWA**

'EUROPA-AMERICA DEL SUD IN 2 GIORNI', staining in image, creases and abrasions.

This is the Italian version of a rare and unusual air-mail poster.

c1930   26.25in (66.5cm) high

$650-800   **SWA**

'THE TADOUSSAC / HOTEL AND FISHING CAMPS / in FRENCH CANADA', designed by Roger Couillard (1910-99), 1950s, silkscreen, restored, repaired tears, creases, overpainting.

Situated at the confluence of the St Lawrence and Saguenay rivers, Tadoussac (Montagnais Indian for 'nipple' - referring to the shape of the nearby hills) celebrated its 400th anniversary in 2000. It was the site of the first fur trading post in Canada.

35.75in (91cm) high

$2,000-2,500   **SWA**

POSTERS

'San Francisco / UNITED AIR LINES', designed by Stanley Walter Galli (1912-2009), repaired tears at upper edge.

Galli, born in San Francisco and a lifelong resident of Northern California, was a painter, prolific illustrator and printmaker. Although a member of the New York and California Society of Illustrators, and the designer of numerous wildlife conservation stamps for the United States Postal Service in the 1960s-70s, he is best remembered for the series of posters he designed for United Airlines in the 1950s-60s.

40in (101.5cm) high

$1,000-1,200   SWA

'STOCKHOLM', designed by Iwar Donnér (1884-1964), framed, creases, minor restored losses and restoration in image.

1936   38.25in (97cm) high

$900-1,100   SWA

'PRAGER MESSE', designed by Vilem Heiten, printed by M. Schulz, Prague, minor repaired tears.

1948   37.25in (94.5cm) high

$550-600   SWA

'VENEZIA', designed by Adolphe Mouron Cassandre (1901-68), printed by Calcografia & Cartevalori, Milan, minor losses.

In a style more consistent with his stage designs, Cassandre depicts a tranquil vista on a Venetian canal. In 1954, this image was reissued with additional text at the bottom to promote a Graphic Industries conference in Venice.

1951   39.25in (99.5cm) high

$2,000-2,500   SWA

'SOUTHERN California VIA UNITED AIR LINES', designed by Stanley Walter Galli (1912-2009).

40in (101.5cm) high

$3,500-4,000   SWA

'UNITED AIR LINES / NEW ENGLAND', designed by Joseph Binder (1898-1972), minor losses.

1957   40in (101.5cm) high

$600-750   SWA

'Ireland / FLY IRISH AIRLINES', designed by Raymond T. Cowern, printed by Browne & Nolan Ltd., 1960s, showing Glendalough, Co. Wicklow.

40in (101.5cm) high

$250-350   WHYT

QUICK REFERENCE - FILM POSTERS

● Film posters can be popular with collectors, especially popular blockbusters or cult classics. The market for science fiction and horror posters is especially vibrant.

● Many collectors buy posters based on the film they depict, but others may focus on films by key directors, or collect the work of one designer.

● Common poster sizes include the American one-sheet - 27in (68.5cm) by 41in (104cm) - and the UK quad - 30in (76cm) by 40in (84cm). Posters from other countries are often in different sizes and include alternative artwork from the UK and US editions. Posters from the film's country of origin tend to be preferred by collectors.

● Film posters with memorable styling or images of key scenes or characters from the film tend to be the most popular. Rare versions of posters, such as 'teaser' posters produced before the release of the film, are widely sought after. Value can vary with trends, and a modern re-boot of an old classic will usually push up prices of posters for the original film.

'AT MAD MULE CANYON' a one sheet poster, 101 Bison Films/ Universal Films, folded.
1913   *41.75in (106cm) high*
$150-200   **FLD**

'Bulldog Drummon's Third Round' 'by Sapper', a two sheet poster, starring Jack Buchanan, Astra-National Productions, printed litho J. Weiner Ltd., folded.
1925   *88.5in (225cm) high*
$450-550   **FLD**

'THRILLING YOUTH', a six sheet poster, starring Billy West, Gloria Grey and George Bunny, Rayart Pictures, Wardour Films Ltd., printed by W.E Berry Ltd., folded.
1926   *88.5in (225cm) high*
$250-300   **FLD**

'CAFE DE PARIS', designed by René Péron (1904-72), printed by Baudin, Paris, repaired tears, creases.

In the USA, the film studios largely produced anonymous posters to promote their films. The French, on the other hand, employed recognized poster artists. René Péron was one of the leading figures of French film poster design, and over the course of his 50-year career, designed more than 2,000 posters.
1938   *62.75in (159.5cm) high*
$2,000-2,500   **SWA**

'BREAKFAST AT TIFFANY'S', designed by Robert McGinnis (b.1926), printed by Paramount Pictures Corp., creases, rippling throughout.

1961   *40in (101.5cm) high*
$7,500-8,000   **SWA**

'PSYCHO', Paramount, British quad poster, style B, corner pinholes and light creasing.

Far rarer than the Janet Leigh version, this poster shows Hitchcock warning cinema-goers to be punctual and that they will not be admitted after the start of each performance.
1960   *40in (101.5cm) wide*
$1,000-1,200   **DW**

'DR. NO', James Bond film poster, Eon Productions, staring Sean Connery and Ursula Andress, 'Printed in England - Stafford and Co., Ltd. Netherinfield Nottingham and London', folded.

1962   *38in (96.5cm) wide*
$7,500-8,000   **CAPE**

POSTERS

'I WANT YOU FOR THE NAVY', designed by Howard Chandler Christy (1873-1952), printed by Forbes, Boston, creases, overpainting in margins.
1917   *40.5in (103cm) high*
$800-850   **SWA**

'ENLIST / On Which Side of the Window are YOU?', designed by Laura Brey, printed by National Printing & Eng. Co., Chicago, tears, creases, losses.
1917   *38.75in (98.5cm) high*
$1,300-2,000   **SWA**

'IF I FAIL HE DIES / WORK for the RED CROSS', designed by Arthur G. McCoy, printed by J.J. LeTourneau Printing Co., Duluth, tears in margin.
1918   *28in (71cm) wide*
$1,000-1,300   **SWA**

'EVERY GIRL PULLING FOR VICTORY / VICTORY GIRLS / UNITED WAR WORK CAMPAIGN', designed by Edward Penfield (1866-1925), tears in margin, into image.

Best known for his extensive series of turn-of-the-century American literary posters, Penfield also designed four posters for the American war effort.
c1918   *27.75in (70.5cm) high*
$650-800   **SWA**

'FOOD FOR FREEDOM / YOUR FARM CAN HELP', printed by the US Government Printing Office, Washington, DC.

This was one of a spate of USA World War II posters that took advantage of some of the prevailing avant-garde design techniques, such as photomontage. The cinematic style of this image suggests it might be a still taken from a 1941 government documentary called 'Food, printed by Freedom'.
1941   *39.75in (101cm) high*
$450-550   **SWA**

'ADOLF WAS A PAINTER TOO, designed by Robert S.E. Coram (Maroc), London, the Royal Academy.
1941   *29.25in (74cm) high*
$1,600-2,000   **CHEF**

'DON'T KEEP A DIARY', printed by H. Manly & Son Ltd., London.
c1942   *14in (35.5cm) high*
$650-800   **SWA**

'LA DAME AUX CAMELIAS', designed by Alphonse Mucha (1860-1939), printed by Chaix, Paris, some staining.
1898 *15.5in (39.5cm) high*
$2,000-2,500 **SWA**

'SAY IT WITH RESULTS', designed by Willard Frederic Elmes (1900-56), printed by Mather & Company, Chicago, repaired tears in margins.
1927 *47.5in (120.5cm) high*
$1,800-2,200 **SWA**

'bal du grand prix á l'opera', designed by Charles-Félix Gir (1883-1941), printed by Lapina & Fils, Paris, restored losses and overpainting.

Charles Gir was a painter and poster designer who worked, for various theaters and music halls promoting performers and performances. He also did sketches, drawings and even sculptures based on the opera and ballet.
1929 *23in (58.5cm) high*
$650-800 **SWA**

'THÉÂTRE DU VAUDEVILLE / RÉJANE', designed by Leonetto Cappiello (1875-1942), printed by Vercasson & Cie., Paris, repaired tears.
1902 *52in (132cm) high*
$1,200-1,300 **SWA**

'HAGENBECK-WALLACE CIRCUS / WILD WEST CHAMPIONS', 1930s, printed by Erie Litho & Ptg. Co., Erie, repaired tears, abrasions.
40.25in (102cm) wide
$350-400 **SWA**

A CLOSER LOOK AT A POSTER

This poster was created to advertise the International Exposition in Brussels in 1910.

It emphasizes a new mode of transportation, the dirigible airship, depicted hovering over the city's Town Square.

The image of Brussels' Town Square features the historic Grand Palace, the Town Hall and Brewer's Hall.

The poster is designed by Henri Cassiers (1858-1944), a painter from Flanders, also notable for his posters for the Antwerp-based Red Star Line ship company.

'BRUSSELS UNIVERSAL AND INTERNATIONAL EXHIBITION', printed by J.E. Goosens, repaired tears, creases, minor losses, tape on verso.
1910 *47in (119.5cm) high*
$1,300-2,000 **SWA**

'CORSETS LE FURET', designed by Roger Pérot (1908-76), printed by Etablts Delattre, Paris.
1933 *54.5in (138.5cm) high*
$800-850 **SWA**

POSTERS

'WORKERS OF ALL COUNTRIES, UNITE!', designed by D. Moor (Dmitry Stakhievich Orlov, 1883-1946) & Sergei Senkin (1894-1963), printed by State Publishing House, Moscow, creases in margins and image.

This poster is a photomontage of a large rally of workers under 'the great and invincible banners of Marx, Engels, Lenin and Stalin'.

1939   36.75in (93.5cm) high
$4,000-4,500   SWA

'JIM CROW IS HIS ENEMY-AMERICA'S ENEMY-MY ENEMY', designed by Symeon Shimin (1902-84), printed by L.I.P. & B.A., NY, USA, tape along tear from bottom edge into text.

This is Henry A. Wallace presidential campaign poster was published by the Progressive Party. Wallace was the Progressive Party Presidential candidate in 1948. He was the former Secretary of Agriculture and Vice President for Franklin Roosevelt's third term. After his unsuccessful Presidential run, the party disbanded in 1950.

c1948   46in (117cm) high
$3,500-4,000   SWA

'RACISM CHAINS BOTH', designed by Hugo Gellert (1892-1985), printed by Typographical Union Label, Dunnelen, NJ, USA, for the National Black Liberation Commission.

1970   22.5in (57cm) high
$550-600   SWA

'KENNEDY FOR PRESIDENT', small format, printed by Allied Printing, Washington DC, paper, minor tear.

1960   20.75in (52.5cm) high
$1,300-2,000   SWA

'VIII OLYMPIC WINTER GAMES / SQUAW VALLEY / FEBRUARY 18.28 / 1960', minor creases and restoration at edges.

This is the second of two official posters designed for the Squaw Valley Winter Olympic Games. The first one was issued before the exact dates of the games were determined. This second poster appeared in 1959 and aimed to show the location of Squad Valley in relation to the USA and provide the dates of the Games. Walt Disney was chairman of the pageantry committee, which put him in charge of the opening and closing ceremonies. Vice President Richard Nixon officially opened the games. The poster was printed in five different languages. This is the English version.

1960   35.75in (91cm) high
$2,000-2,500   SWA

'IWERNE MINSTER / Please use your correct address', designed by John Minton (1917-57), issued by the G.P.O., framed and glazed.

c1955   36in (91.5cm) wide
$650-800   DW

'La coopération inter-européenne pour un niveau de vie plus élevé', designed by Gottfried Honegger-Lavater (1917-2016), Switzerland, minor repaired tears.

c1950   28.75in (73cm) high
$1,000-1,300   SWA

A 'BROADWATER TUNBRIDGE WELLS' enamel sign, in railway-style totem design.

See page 300 for British Railway posters.

$25-40   LSK

A Southern Railway 'REEDHAM' target sign, believed to be Kent location.

This sign is in poor condition, with corrosion losses around edges and attempted restoration to center of sign. However it is rare - hence the price.

$200-250   LSK

A 'Derby Midland' totem sign, some rust.

Again although in need of restoration, this is a desirable sign.

36in (92cm) wide

$550-600   HAN

A BR Southern Region station totem sign, 'PADDOCK WOOD'.

This is desirable as it is a well-known Kent commuter station.

$600-750   LSK

An enameled iron railway platform number sign.

23.75in (60.5cm) wide

$250-300   DA&H

A LMS railway small home signal arm.

$60-80   LSK

An LNER signal lamp, outer case only, repainted.

$100-120   LSK

A locomotive two-aspect headlamp, Eastern Region of British Rail, brass-plated, reading 'G.Polkey Ltd Birmingham'.

$200-250   LSK

A mid-19thC South Eastern Railway (SER) three-aspect head lamp, missing red aspect glass, with an 'S. R. A. G 3724' plaque to neck of lamp.

$90-110   HAN

A GW railway large brass locomotive whistle, mounted on stand.

$120-150   LSK

QUICK REFERENCE - THE BEATLES

The Beatles were one of the most popular bands in music history. Formed in Liverpool in 1960 and disbanded in 1970, their albums have sold over 800 million albums worldwide since the 1960s. The band's unparalleled popularity meant that a large quantity of memorabilia was produced during their active years, including clothing, jewelry, stationary, grooming products, musical instruments, trading cards and tableware. Original records, posters and concert tickets are also popular with collectors.

A 'Beatles for Sale' original UK mono LP, by The Beatles, PMC 1240, matrix numbers XEX 503-3N and XEX 504-4N, yellow and black Parlophone labels reading 'The Parlophone Co...', 'Sold in U.K.' and 'Recording First Published 1964', MT tax code on side 1 label.

The track listing shows the song Kansas City as 'KANSAS CITY (Lieber & Stoller)', in later versions this was changed to 'Medley: (a) Kansas City (Leiber/Stoller) (P)1964 Macmelodies Ltd./KPM. (b) Hey, Hey, Hey, Hey! (Penniman) Venice Mus. Ltd. (P)1964' after the attorneys for Venice Music complained.

1964
$60-100   DW

A 1960s Yatton (Avalon) Furniture Beatles ottoman, the vinyl padded cover above paneled sides transfer-decorated with images of the band and their facsimile signatures.

39.25in (100cm) wide
$800-950   CHEF

An autograph letter from George Harrison (1943-2001), signed 'George', written in Bombay to Joe Marchini at his home in Henley, in blue ballpoint pen with 'Hare Krishna' printed to lower left corner, mentioning Kumar (nephew of Ravi Shankar) and his mother, the singer Lakshmi, also mentioning Ted and Doreen, possibly Ted Doran and Doreen Dahl, two pages, 8vo, together with the original postmarked envelope addressed in block capitals in black felt tip pen by Harrison.

Kumar Shankar was George Harrison's recording engineer on the 'Dark House' LP made in 1974 (as well as subsequent recordings).

1974
$2,000-2,500   DW

A 'Help!' original first pressing UK mono LP, by The Beatles, PMC 1255, matrix numbers XEX 549-2 and XEX 550-2, yellow and black 'Parlophone labels, MT tax code on side 1 label.

1965
$60-100   DW

A 'Revolver' original UK mono LP, by The Beatles, PMC 7009, early mono pressing with matrix numbers XEX 605-2 and XEX 606-3, yellow and black Parlophone labels, KT tax code on side 2 label.

1966
$100-130   DW

A 'Margo of Mayfair With The Beatles' novelty powder tin and contents, printed with photographic portrait images of the band members, some rubbing, surface scratches and wear, some light rusting to base.

7.5in (19cm) high
$100-130   FELL

A CLOSER LOOK AT A BEATLES POSTER

This bill poster for the Llandudno Odeon features The Beatles as the headline act, along with Billy J. Kramer and The Dakotas, The Lana Sisters, Billy Baxter, Tommy Wallis and several other supporting acts.

Many early Beatles gig posters were simply thrown away, meaning this early poster is a rare and very valuable find.

It is dated Monday 12 August 1963, just before the band was propelled into huge fame by their 23 August 1963 single 'She Loves You'.

It has some losses and tears, but the rarity of the poster ensures a high value.

A quad size bill poster for the Llandudno Odeon, printed by Electric Printing Co. Ltd., Manchester standard British Cinema.

This poster was owned by Welsh folk singer Mary Hopkin, who was one of the first signatures to The Beatles' Apple label and later represented the UK in the 1970 Eurovision Song Contest. It is believed that she took the poster from the venue at the concert itself.

1963   *41.25in (105cm) wide*
$45,000-55,000   JON

An autographed Abba Polar Music 'Chiquitita' picture postcard, signed in black pen by all four group members.

$250-350   SAS

A 'The Man Who Sold the World' record, by David Bowie, Mercury, with the withdrawn banned cover of David Bowie wearing a dress, with black/silver label, cat.6338 041.

1971

$3,000-3,500   AST

An 'Are You Experienced' record, by Jimi Hendrix, on Track 612 001, sleeve laminated on front, mat on reverse with tape marks.

1967

$80-100   AST

A 'The Division Bell' LP record, by Pink Floyd, original UK release, EMD 1055 with inner sleeve.

1994

$150-200   SAS

An 'Out of Our Heads' export LP, by The Rolling Stones, with USA track listing, labelled 'MONO DECCA LK4725'.

$200-250   AST

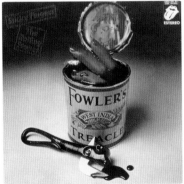

A 'Sticky Fingers' LP, by The Rolling Stones, Spanish production, Madrid, some damage to the sleeve, record with minor scratch to 'A' side.

1971

$90-100   CAPE

A Sex Pistols 'Punk' limited edition print, no.4 of 50, depicting the group at The EMI Offices, Manchester Square, London.

$200-250   SAS

An original The Who flyer, for their concert at The Hammersmith Palais, 'Thurs.. 29th October 1970 at 9.30 p.m'.

$150-250   SAS

SCENT BOTTLES

A mid-Victorian novelty scent bottle, modeled as a lantern with clear glass liner and screw-thread detachable cover, missing loop handle, signed 'S. Mordan & Co. Makers', some general scratches.

Sampson Mordan & Co. was most notable for its mechanical pencils, see pages 290-291.

2.75in (7cm) high

$600-650   FELL

A late Victorian silver-mounted ceramic egg scent bottle, by S. Mordan and Co., London, plain screw-off cover.

1886   *2.25in (6cm) long*

$450-550   WW

A silver-mounted ceramic shell scent bottle, by S. Mordan and Co., London, plain screw-off cover.

1888   *2.25in (5.5cm) long*

$250-350   WW

A silver and glass owl scent bottle, by S. Mordan and Co., London, the screw-top with inset glass eyes.

1894   *2.25in (5.5cm) high*

$450-550   BE

A silver-mounted glass owl scent bottle, by S. Mordan and Co., London, the screw-off head with textured feathers and set with glass eyes.

1894   *3.25in (8cm) long*

$900-1,000   WW

A Thomas Webb & Sons cameo glass lay down scent bottle, Stourbridge, with internal glass stopper and screw-fitted silver-gilt cover, hallmarks for Frederick Bradford McCrea, London.

1884   *10.25in (26cm) long*

$1,600-2,000   WW

A Thomas Webb & Sons cameo glass scent bottle, Stourbridge, the repoussé silver cover with a screw fitting, marked for Theodore Starr of New York.

c1885   *9.25in (23.5cm) long*

$1,500-2,000   WW

A Thomas Webb & Sons cameo glass laydown scent bottle, Stourbridge, the silver-mounted hinged cover with original glass stopper, hallmarked for London.

1887   *4.25in (10.5cm) long*

$900-1,100   WW

A late 19thC Baccarat scent bottle, acid-etched in the Art Nouveau style, unmarked.

7.75in (20cm) high

$130-160   **FLD**

An Art Nouveau D'Argental cameo glass scent bottle, carved with a wooded lakeside scene, mounted on gilt-metal with atomizer, signed in the glass.

4.75in (12cm) high

$650-800   **HAN**

A 20thC Daum crystal glass scent bottle, the metal fittings decorated with an applied pâte-de-verre flower, engraved signature, lacking atomizer.

5in (13cm) high

$90-120   **FLD**

A Schneider hot applied 'tea rose' scent bottle, signed.

c1923   *2.5in (6.5cm) high*

$2,500-4,000   **M&DM**

A late 19thC Stevens & Williams cameo glass scent bottle, with a clear crystal lapidary stopper.

6.25in (16cm) high

$350-400   **FLD**

A Victorian glass scent bottle, lobed ovoid form blue milk glass body with polychrome marbled effect overlay, with later applicator and stopper.

5in (12cm) high

$150-200   **MART**

A set of three 19thC glass scent bottles, with gilt decoration, in a wooden case.

5in (13cm) long

$160-200   **WW**

An early 20thC Continental glass and enamel scent flask, with a small glass stopper beneath the gilt-metal mounted cover.

3in (7.5cm) high

$300-400   **WW**

A yellow metal scent bottle, decorated with repoussé scrollwork.

2in (5cm) long

$1,800-2,200   **FELL**

An early 19thC pocket globe, with hand-colored paper gores, in original fish skin case, with internal hand-colored celestial map inscribed 'A Correct Globe with New Constellations of Dr Halley & Co', the globe inscribed 'A Correct Globe with New Discoveries', case spilt.

3in (7.5cm) diam

$3,500-4,000   **GWA**

A terrestrial desk globe, with 12 tinted culottes, signed and inscribed 'Smith Terrestrial Globe Exhibiting The Whole of The Discoveries To The Present Time, London Smith & Co. 63 Charing Cross'.

c1870   *globe 3.5in (9cm) diam*

$750-850   **CM**

A Husun star globe, by Henry Hughes & Son, London, with maker's label signed as per title, in original box with brass meridian and horizon rings.

c1920   *globe 7in (18cm) diam*

$1,000-1,300   **CM**

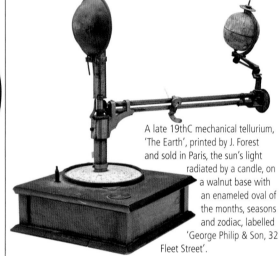

A mid-20thC Philips terestrial globe, on a mahogany base.

globe 14in (35.5cm) diam

$250-350   **LOCK**

A late 19thC mechanical tellurium, 'The Earth', printed by J. Forest and sold in Paris, the sun's light radiated by a candle, on a walnut base with an enameled oval of the months, seasons and zodiac, labelled 'George Philip & Son, 32 Fleet Street'.

base 9.5in (24cm) wide

$2,500-3,000   **PW**

A Victorian boxwood sundial and compass, by Cox of Newgate Street London, with paper dial, pen work degrees, the lid with original paper instructions.

3in (7.5cm) long

$250-350   **DW**

An ex-Royal Naval ship's binnacle, of brass and teak construction, complete with compass, soft iron spheres missing.

56.25in (134cm) high

$1,000-1,200   **PW**

A steering hub or helm station, manufactured by Brown Bros. Company, Edinburgh, ships wheels attached to heavy cast iron and brass pedestal supporting central rudder indicator, flanked by four pressure gauges for hydraulic rudder control and twin propeller cylinder.

41in (104cm) high

$2,500-3,500   **PW**

A brass microscope, by J.B. Dancer, Manchester, with rack-and-pinion/thumb wheel focussing, plano/concave mirror, in original mahogany case with accessories.

9.5in (24cm) high

$650-800   **TEN**

A 19thC lacquered brass monocular compound microscope, by Baker, London, with rack-and-pinion coarse and fine focusing, mechanical stage, plano/convex mirror, on a Y-shaped base, with accessories, in a mahogany case.

$450-600   **TEN**

A Leitz Wetzler brass binocular microscope, no.164752, with course/fine focusing, three lens turret, three way adjustable stage, Ogilvy condenser and adjustable width eyepieces, cased, with accessories.

$250-400   **TEN**

An early 19thC pull pocket telescope, in ebony and silvered metal, in leather box.

2.5in (6cm) diam

$300-400   **CHOR**

A pair of silver mounted binoculars or opera glasses, hallmarked for Barnet Henry Adams, Birmingham, inset compasses between lenses.

1890   *4.75in (12cm) wide*

$80-100   **MART**

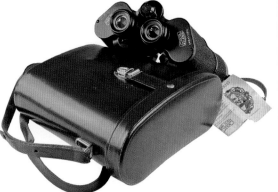

A cased pair of Carl Zeiss Jena Jenoptem 10 x 50 binoculars.

$200-250   **LOCK**

A pair of Carl Zeiss Wien M 9/13 Z Feldstecher 6 fach binoculars, serial no.556119, in original case.

$70-80   **LOCK**

Judith Picks

A wonderful link with an historic event! Alexander Fleming discovered penicillin in 1928. However it was not until the 1940s that the scope of its properties really began to be recognized. The seller's parents lived opposite Alexander Fleming and had intervened when they saw burglars trying to break into Fleming's home. In recognition of this Fleming sent Mr and Mrs Bax a letter on 8 March 1955 (three days before he passed away at his home of a heart attack). The letter thanks the neighbours for assisting with 'scaring the burglars' and notes how he does not now 'trust the safe' and will now protect all his medals by putting them in the bank. Elizabeth Montgomery, a former next-door neighbour of Fleming and believed to be his housekeeper, sent Mr and Mrs Max the mold as a 'souvenir of the Fleming family' following his death. She notes at the bottom of the letter, 'As though you didn't know - but just in case - this said affair is a blob of the original mould of penicillin, not to be confused with gorgonzola cheese!!!'

A specimen of the mold which produces penicillin, mounted on paper and under glass, signed on the reverse 'Alexander Fleming', with a thank you letter written by Fleming dated 8 March 1955 to the current owner's parents, and a letter from Elizabeth Montgomery.

1954 *2in (5cm) diam*

$7,500-8,500 **SOU**

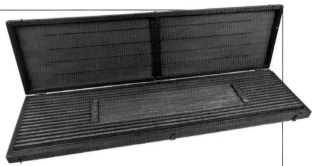

An early 20thC Hannygton (Astronomical) slide rule, designed by Major General John Caulfield Hannygton (1807-86), impressed makers names 'Aston and Mander', in mahogany box.

1917

$900-1,100 **DA&H**

QUICK REFERENCE - TRIUNIAL MAGIC LANTERN

- The 'Magic Lantern' was a forerunner of the slide projector. One of the first produced was the Sturm lantern in 1676.
- The Sturm lantern was a simple projector, but by the late 19thC, the technology was much more sophisticated. A Triunial magic lantern was able to produce impressive technicolor lantern displays and moving picture effects, which proved a popular entertainment in the 1880s.
- The 'Docwra Triple' was the invention of Colin Docwra. In 1888 it won a gold medal at the Crystal Palace photographic exhibition, and from 1889 was sold by W.C. Hughes Manufacturers of London.

A late 19thC mahogany and rosewood-cased Triunial Magic Lantern, by W.C. Hughes, Manufacturers, Mortimer Road, Kingsland, London, with three brass rack and pinion lenses, plaque to base, 'The Docwra Triple', with a small group of lenses and a long magic lantern slide.

39in (99cm) high

$40,000-45,000 **BRI**

An Ica AG (Dresden) stereoviewer, in mahogany case with three fan-fold slide holders with slides.

$150-200 **TEN**

A late 19thC English stereoscopic slide viewer, 'The Magic Stereoscope no.229', by Negretti & Zambra, 59 Cornhill, London, the walnut slide box with twin lenses individually focussed and two slide boxes.

16in (41cm) high

$2,500-3,500 **TRI**

QUICK REFERENCE - LORENZL

- Josef Lorenzl (1892-1950) was born in Austria and went on to become one of the most talented sculptors of the Art Deco Period.
- He worked as a designer and sculptor for several Austrian manufacturers, including Vienna Arsenal and Goldscheider, creating ceramic figures or statuettes in bronze, ivory or chryselephantine (usually bronze and ivory).
- His sculptures were usually small and tended to depict single female figures, often dancers or gymnasts. His figures were often nudes, usually with the bobbed hair and slender figures fashionable in the 1920s-30s.
- Lorenzl's sculptures were often finished with patinated silver or gilt, and placed on a plain green or black onyx or marble base.

A patinated bronze of a nude girl, by Josef Lorenzl, on onyx base, signed in the bronze 'Lorenzl 381'.

11.5in (29cm) high

$1,000-1,200　　　　ROS

An Art Deco scarf dancer table lighter, by Josef Lorenzl, bronze patinated spelter on a marble base, unsigned.

10.75in (27cm) high

$450-600　　　　ECGW

A gilt and cold-painted bronze female dancer, by Josef Lorenzl, on an onyx base, signed 'LORENZL'.

c1925　　6.5in (16.5cm) high

$800-950　　　　TEN

A CLOSER LOOK AT A LORENZL FIGURE

This Lorenzl figure is modeled as a young female nude standing on tip-toe, her arms outstretched.

Her figure is slim and her hair cropped in a 1920s-30s style, as is common in Lorenzl's figures.

She holds blue and red spotted scarves attached to an Egyptianesque waistband.

The image of the scarf dancer was popular with Lorenzl, both in his bronze figures and in his ceramic work for Goldscheider.

An Art Deco silvered and cold-painted bronzed figure, by Josef Lorenzl, foot signed 'R. Lor.', on onyx base.

5in (12.5cm) high

$1,600-2,000　　　　HT

An Art Deco bronze figure of a young female nude, after Lorenzl, unmarked, on an onyx base.

11.25in (28.5cm) high

$1,000-1,200　　　　HT

A 1980s Lindsey B Art Deco-style ceramic bust of a woman, underglaze painted, unsigned.

12.5in (31.5cm) high

$160-220　　　　LSK

An Art Deco bronzed figure of a young male athlete, on marble plinth.

10.5in (27cm) high

$150-200　　　　HW

An Art Deco bronze and ivory figure of a young female, unmarked, on an onyx base.

10in (25.5cm) high

$1,000-1,200　　　　HT

An Art Deco spelter and marble group, of a mother and child and German Shepherd dog, on a slate base.

23.25in (59cm) wide

$130-200　　　　DA&H

SCULPTURE

A bronze and enamel Frogman 'Polly Wogg' model, by Tim Cotterill, no.17 of a limited edition of 200, with certificate, signed by the artist.

Tim 'Frogman' Cotterill was born in Leicester, England, in 1950. He first trained in engineering, then began to work with metal in the 1970s-80s, creating experimental wheeled vehicles and metal sculptures of animals and birds. In 1990 he relocated to California and set up Frogman Foundry, from which he creates a range of bronze bird, fish and reptile sculptures.

An Hagenauer ebonized bust of an African figure, modeled as a female to one side and as a male to the other, stamped marks, possibly overpainted.

12.25in (31cm) high

$550-650   CHEF

An Hagenauer skier, stained wood and gilt, with impressed marks.

5in (13cm) high

$550-650   SWO

A painted bronze elephant mobile sculpture, in the manner of Alexander Calder.

13.75in (35cm) high

$650-800   CHEF

3.5in (9cm) high

$600-650   BE

QUICK REFERENCE - HARRY PHILLIPS

Harry Phillips was Head of the School of Sculpture and Pottery at Leeds College of Art from 1950. His well-known works include 'Christ Triumphant' at St George's Church, Norton, Letchworth (1963); 'St Michael' at St Michael's Church, Lewes, Sussex (1976); and 'Saint Christopher' from St Christopher's Church, Hinchley Wood, Surrey (1975). He is the subject of the song 'In the Gallery', by Dire Straits, whose lead singer Mark Knopfler played with Phillips' musician son Steve.

A painted steel mobile sculpture, by Manuel Marin, Spain, signed 'M Marin'.

Manuel Marin (1942-2007) was a bull fighter and sculptor who created vibrant and colorful works over the course of his life. Born in Spain, he later came to London to work in an art gallery, then became the assistant of Henry Moore. Marin later moved to New York. He associated with many artists, including Andy Warhol, who became a personal friend. Today his work is displayed in many private collections.

20in (51cm) high

$2,000-2,500   SWO

A mixed metal sculpture, 'Street Light', by Andre Wallace (b.1947), on a wooden plinth.

Born in Taunton, Wallace studied at the Somerset College of Art from 1965-67. He continued his studies, attending the Royal College of Art from 1971-73, when he was awarded the Sainsbury Prize for Sculpture. In subsequent years he has been commissioned to create sculptures for public spaces in the UK and has held solo exhibitions.

21.25in (54cm) high

$550-600   SWO

A patinated bronze 'The Dancer' figure, by Harry Phillips (1911-76), the figure in a Native American Indian-style head dress, unsigned.

18.5in (47cm) high

$450-550   CHEF

A polished bronze figure of a dancer, by Hattakitkosol Somchai (1934-2000), Thailand, signed and dated '79'.

1979   25.5in (65cm) high

$550-650   CHEF

QUICK REFERENCE - SEWING

- Most sewing accessories available to collectors date from the 19thC and early 20thC. Items from the 18thC and earlier, before mass production made these sewing accessories common, are especially prized.
- Collectors tend to focus on one type of sewing tool or accessory, such as thimbles, pin cushions or needle cases. Pin cushions were very widely produced and remain popular with collectors, in part due to the aesthetic appeal of novelty pin cushions, often modeled as animals, clothing, vehicles and toys. Pieces that are finely handcrafted as opposed to factory made, and those with a high level of detail, are often the most valuable.
- Sewing accessories and tools were made from a range of materials, including silver, gold, ivory, bone, mother-of-pearl, tortoiseshell and wood. Silver pieces became increasingly common in the Edwardian period as the price of silver dropped.
- For sewing boxes, see pages 38-39.

A silver-framed pin cushion, modeled as a vessel, maker's mark 'CS FS', Chester.
1893   *2in (5cm) high*
$450-550   JN

A silver pin cushion, of two swans, by Hilliard & Thomason, Birmingham.
1896   *2.5in (6.5cm) wide*
$450-550   PW

A silver jockey cap pin cushion, with leather base, maker's mark 'CS & FS', Birmingham.
1897   *2.25in (6cm) long*
$350-400   JN

A silver shoe pin cushion, maker's mark 'A. & L. LTD', Birmingham.
1897   *6.5in (16.5cm) long*
$120-150   JN

An 'owl on a cauldron' pin cushion, by Walker & Hall, Sheffield.
1901   *3.25in (8.5cm) high*
$450-550   JN

A silver hen pin cushion, later velvet cushion, with import marks for Chester, importer's mark of S. Landeck.
1901   *4.25in (11cm) long*
$800-950   WW

A silver pin cushion, modeled as a shoe with a ribbon lace and set with three colored stones, replacement cushion, by Adie & Lovekin, Birmingham.
1903   *2.5in (6.5cm) long*
$400-450   WW

A silver miniature chick pin cushion, maker's mark 'L. & S.', Birmingham.
1903   *1.25in (3cm) high*
$200-250   JN

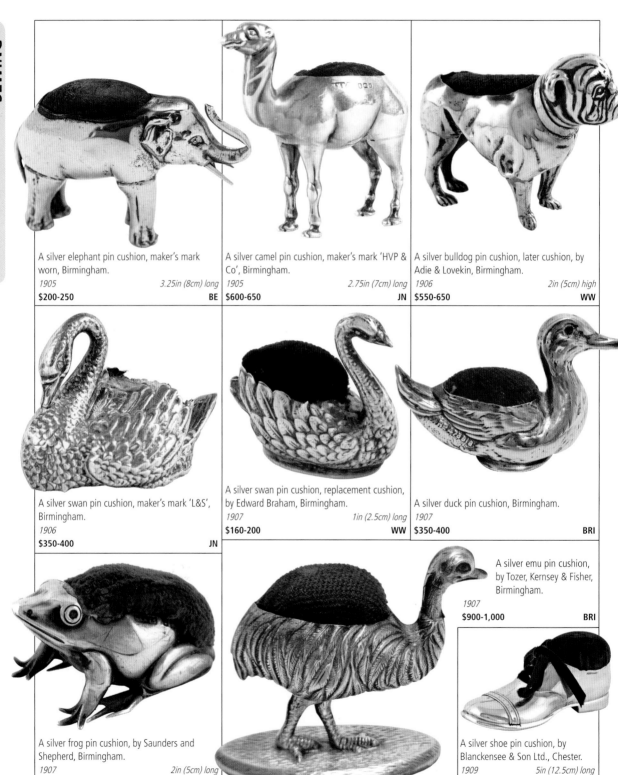

A silver elephant pin cushion, maker's mark worn, Birmingham.
1905   *3.25in (8cm) long*
$200-250   **BE**

A silver camel pin cushion, maker's mark 'HVP & Co', Birmingham.
1905   *2.75in (7cm) long*
$600-650   **JN**

A silver bulldog pin cushion, later cushion, by Adie & Lovekin, Birmingham.
1906   *2in (5cm) high*
$550-650   **WW**

A silver swan pin cushion, maker's mark 'L&S', Birmingham.
1906
$350-400   **JN**

A silver swan pin cushion, replacement cushion, by Edward Braham, Birmingham.
1907   *1in (2.5cm) long*
$160-200   **WW**

A silver duck pin cushion, Birmingham.
1907
$350-400   **BRI**

A silver frog pin cushion, by Saunders and Shepherd, Birmingham.
1907   *2in (5cm) long*
$550-600   **WW**

A silver emu pin cushion, by Tozer, Kernsey & Fisher, Birmingham.
1907
$900-1,000   **BRI**

A silver shoe pin cushion, by Blanckensee & Son Ltd., Chester.
1909   *5in (12.5cm) long*
$300-350   **CHOR**

A silver roller skate pin cushion, by Crisford & Norris Ltd., Birmingham.

1909   *2.75in (7cm) long*
$450-600   **BE**

A silver teddy bear pin cushion, by H.V. Pithey & Co., Birmingham.

This is an unusual example, having jointed limbs, and is highly desirable.

1909   *3in (7.5cm) long*
$1,000-1,300   **BE**

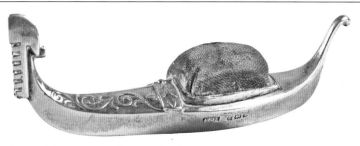

A silver pin cushion, modeled as the ship 'Royal George', missing propeller, by S. Blanckensee & Sons Ltd., Chester.

1910   *5in (13cm) long*
$350-400   **GWA**

A silver Humpty Dumpty pin cushion, maker's mark 'L&S', Birmingham.

1910
$400-450   **JN**

A silver gondola pin cushion, maker's mark 'A&Z', Birmingham.

1910   *3.75in (9.5cm) long*
$250-350   **JN**

A silver pin cushion, modeled as a naval officer's hat, Chester.

1910   *4in (10cm) long*
$450-550   **JN**

A pin cushion, modeled as a young lady, with silver head and shoulders and carrying a fan, maker's mark 'CS*FS', Birmingham.

1911   *2.5in (6.5cm) high*
$350-400   **JN**

A silver chauffeur's cap pin cushion, maker's mark 'A.L. LTD.', Birmingham.

1914   *2in (5cm) long*
$350-400   **JN**

SEWING

A Victorian two-color gold thimble.
c1840 *0.14oz*
$150-200 BELL

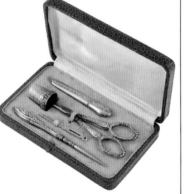

A Victorian yellow metal thimble, unmarked, testing as 14ct, in original velvet carry case.
1in (2.5cm) high 0.2oz
$160-200 LSK

A 9ct gold thimble, 'Coronation hallmark', by James Swann & Son, Birmingham.
1952 *0.18oz*
$200-250 LOCK

A Victorian sewing set, comprising a mother-of-pearl penknife, a ribbon hook, a thimble, a pair of scissors and a bodkin, in a wooden case.
$120-160 WW

A French silver-gilt sewing set, comprising a thimble, a needle case, a pair of scissors, a bodkin and a spike, in a fitted case.
$160-200 WW

A bone pincushion/needlebook, the cover inscribed 'Bazaar', with flannels and tie.
1.75in (4.5cm) long
$150-200 BLEA

A CLOSER LOOK AT A SEWING COMPENDIUM

This novelty sewing compendium is formed as a bicycle lamp, with the lamp serving as a magnifying lens.

It has folding handles, a clip fitted to the back, and a hinged conical top that opens to reveal the contents.

The exterior attachment rings are somewhat misshapen and the pull-out compendium and lid are loose, but the price reflects its rarity.

Inside is a tape measure, an associated foreign thimble and a cotton/needle holder, with the outer interior rim pierced to hold needles.

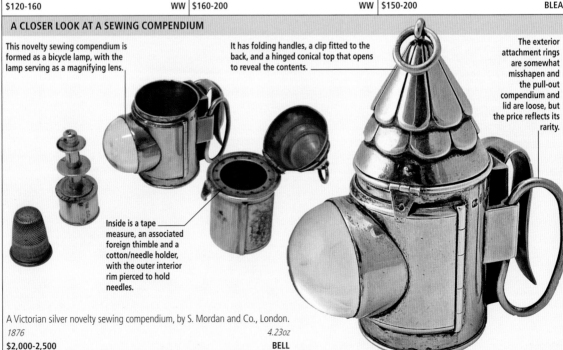

A Victorian silver novelty sewing compendium, by S. Mordan and Co., London.
1876 *4.23oz*
$2,000-2,500 BELL

QUICK REFERENCE - SILVER

- The relatively strong value of silver in the 2000s and 2010s caused many larger silver items, such as tea sets, to be melted down for scrap and lost forever. This has strengthened the value of smaller silver items from the 18thC, 19thC and 20thC, whose 'scrap value' is low, but historical and collectible value can be high.
- Small silver items remain appealing to collectors, in part due to their high level of detail, interesting novelty designs and small size, which make even large collections relatively easy to store. Most collectors focus on one type of item, such as caddy spoons, vinaigrettes or card cases.
- The vast majority of British silver is hallmarked, as are many silver items from other countries. It is worth consulting a guide and learning to recognize the marks of key makers such as Nathaniel Mills, Walker & Hall, Hester Bateman, Joseph Willmore and S. Mordan and Co., or important retailers such Thornhill or Leuchars.
- High quality and detailed pieces are more likely to fetch higher prices. Additional features, such as enamelling or inset stones, can also raise the value. Silver pieces with a broader market, such as those also of interest to collectors of railway or sporting memorabilia, can be especially valuable.
- Always check an item's condition carefully, as silver is a relatively soft metal and pieces are often well-used. It is possible for damage such as dents or splits to be professionally repaired, but this can be expensive. Polishing or cleaning removes microscopic layers of silver, so should not be done too often or it may damage a piece's detail.

An Arts and Crafts silver caddy spoon, probably by Archibald Knox, Liberty & Co., Birmingham.
1903
$1,600-2,000   FLD

An Art Nouveau silver and enamel caddy spoon, by Liberty & Co., Birmingham.
1909   *3in (7.5cm) long 0.6oz*
$800-950   WW

A silver and silver-gilt caddy spoon, naturalistically modeled in the form of a fish, by Thomas Bradbury and Sons Ltd., Sheffield.
1909
$600-650   FLD

An Arts and Crafts silver caddy spoon, with spot-hammered decoration, the handle with pierced wire-work decoration and with six hanging rings, by The Sandheim Brothers, London.
1916   *4in (10cm) long 1.3oz*
$550-600   WW

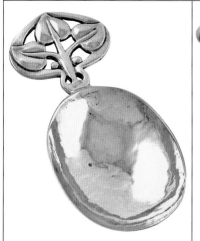

An Arts and Crafts silver caddy spoon, with spot-hammered bowl, by Davis Limited, Birmingham.
1916   *3.75in (9.5cm) long 0.9oz*
$750-800   WW

An Arts and Crafts silver caddy spoon, spot-hammered bowl, seal-top handle with a foliate terminal, by A.E. Jones, Birmingham.
1919   *2.5in (6.5cm) long 0.5oz*
$400-550   WW

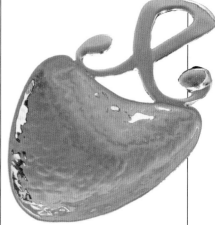

An Arts and Crafts silver caddy spoon, with a heart-shaped planished bowl, by Winifred King and Co., Birmingham.
1926
$450-500   FLD

SILVER

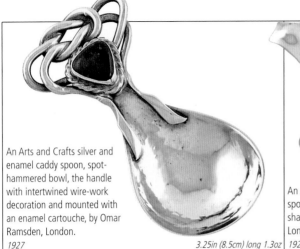

An Arts and Crafts silver and enamel caddy spoon, spot-hammered bowl, the handle with intertwined wire-work decoration and mounted with an enamel cartouche, by Omar Ramsden, London.

1927

3.25in (8.5cm) long 1.3oz

$3,500-4,000   WW

An Arts and Crafts silver caddy spoon, with spot-hammered bowl, shaped handle, by Charles Horner, London.

1927   *2.75in (7cm) long 0.3oz*

$200-250   WW

An Arts and Crafts silver caddy spoon, the hammered bowl below a pierced handle with apple tree motif, by Bernard Instone, Birmingham.

1928

$800-950   FLD

A Scottish Ballater provincial caddy spoon, with embossed view of Balmoral castle with 'BALMORAL' below, the thistle handle with lion rampant within crowned shield as finial, William J. Fraser, Edinburgh.

After William Robb's death, his Ballater shop was left to his daughter and she continued to run it for a short time. Within two years, William J. Fraser had taken over and continued to produce the most popular ranges of Robb's work.

1928   *3.25in (8.5cm) long 0.62oz*

$550-650   L&T

A silver caddy spoon, with chased intertwined basket-weave decoration, stamped '3181', by Liberty & Co., Birmingham.

1936   *3.25in (8.5cm) long 0.9oz*

$450-550   WW

A silver caddy spoon, modeled as a hand, by Thomas Bradbury and Sons Ltd., Sheffield.

1943   *2.75in (7cm) long 0.7oz*

$80-100   FELL

An Arts and Crafts commemorative silver caddy spoon, bowl inscribed 'ST. PAUL'S CATHEDRAL', the handle with a depiction of the Cathedral, by Bernard Instone, Birmingham.

1950   *3.25in (8cm) long 0.7oz*

$750-800   WW

A silver caddy spoon, with circular bowl and parcel-gilt flat hammered loop handle, by Stuart Devlin, London.

1975

$650-750   FLD

QUICK REFERENCE - NATHANIEL MILLS

● Card cases were popular among polite society from the late 18thC to early 20thC, when a 'calling card' was used to announce an impending visit or arrival. Among the most popular card cases were silver 'castle-top' card cases, depicting architectural scenes. Notable makers of these include Joseph Wilmore, Taylor & Perry, Edward Smith and, most importantly, Nathaniel Mills.

● Nathaniel Mills (1746-1840) set up a silver workshop in Caroline Street, Birmingham, in the early 1800s. His son, also called Nathaniel Mills (1811-73), later took over the business.

● Father and son specialized in highly detailed 'castle-top' boxes, card cases, snuff boxes and vinaigrettes, featuring scenes of castles, cathedrals and other key buildings, including Buckingham Palace, Balmoral Castle and the Crystal Palace. These were sold as tourist souvenirs. The business was very successful and the younger Nathaniel Mills died in 1873 as a rich man, leaving $40,000 in his will.

● Nathaniel Mills 'castle-top' card cases and vinaigrettes are highly collectible today. Some obscure buildings, and even some scenes of well-known buildings, are very rare, which can increase desirability and price.

A silver 'castle-top' card case, with a view of Warwick castle, by Nathaniel Mills, Birmingham.
1840   3.5in (9cm) high 2.29oz
$1,000-1,200   **DN**

A silver 'castle-top' card case, with a view of St Paul's Cathedral, some general scratches, marks, wear and tarnishing, hinge loose, by Nathaniel Mills, Birmingham.
1845   4in (10cm) long 2.6oz
$1,300-2,000   **WW**

A silver 'castle-top' card case, possibly depicting Exeter Cathedral, by Frederick Marston, Birmingham.
1847   3.5in (9cm) long 1.6oz
$2,500-3,500   **WW**

A silver engraved 'castle-top' card case, depicting St Columb's Cathedral, Londonderry, from the river Foyle, with a chain and ring attachment, by Nathaniel Mills, Birmingham.
1847   4in (10cm) long 2.6oz
$6,000-6,500   **WW**

A silver engraved 'castle-top' card case, depicting The High Level Bridge, Newcastle, by Nathaniel Mills, Birmingham.
1850   4in (10cm) long 2oz
$6,000-6,500   **WW**

A silver engraved 'castle-top' card case, depicting Norton Hall, Sheffield, the reverse engraved with a crest, by H. Wilkinson, Sheffield.
1851   4in (10cm) long 3.2oz
$6,000-6,500   **WW**

A silver engraved 'castle-top' card case, depicting Aberystwyth sea front, by Yapp and Woodward, Birmingham.
1852   4in (10cm) long 2.1oz
$2,500-3,000   **WW**

A silver and enamel card case, the fitted leather interior with an ivory aide-mémoire, a pencil and compartments for cards and stamps, with import marks for Henry Greaves, London.
1902   4.25in (10.5cm) high
$450-550   **WW**

SILVER

A pair of silver owl pepper pots, the pull-off heads with red glass eyes, textured feathers, by George Richards, London.

1851 *2.75in (7cm) high 2.9oz*

$1,000-1,200 **WW**

A Continental silver cat pepperette, with import marks for Berthold Muller, Chester.

1910 *3.25in (8cm) high 4.14oz*

$450-550 **BE**

A composite silver frog cruet, with naturalistic skin and inset glass eyes, the mustard with gilded spoon forming the tongue, by Richard/ William Comyns, London.

1959 *21oz*

$2,500-3,000 **HT**

A pair of Norwegian sterling silver and enameled owl condiments, by David Andersen, detailed 'D-A NORWAY STERLING 925 S'.

5.5in (14cm) high 1.76oz

$600-650 **BELL**

A pair of silver mastif dog heads menu card holders, by S. Jacobs, London.

1900 *2in (5cm) long 2oz*

$800-950 **WW**

A set of four silver owl menu holders, by S. Mordan and Co., Chester.

1904 *3in (7.5cm) high*

$850-900 **JN**

A set of six George V silver and stained mother-of-pearl menu holders, by Richard Martin and Ebenezer Hall, Birmingham.

1912 *2.25in (5.5cm) high*

$550-650 **BE**

A set of four Far Eastern silver-gilt and glass Sage menu card holders, importer's mark of Cohen and Charles, London.

c1928 *1.5in (4cm) high*

$300-400 **WW**

A George III silver nutmeg grater, by Samuel Meriton, London.

In 18thC Britain, nutmeg was an expensive and popular spice, prized for its medicinal properties. During the Napoleonic Wars, Britain gained control of Run Island, then the only source of nutmeg in the world. Nutmeg production was expanded, which lowered the price at home and made nutmeg accessible to a greater number of people.

c1775
$750-850

1.75in (4.5cm) high 0.5oz
WW

A George III silver nutmeg grater, by Hester Bateman, London.

1784
$1,600-2,000

1.75in (4.5cm) long 0.9oz
WW

A George III silver nutmeg grater, by Samuel Pemberton, Birmingham.

1792
$400-450

1.25in (3cm) high 0.4oz
WW

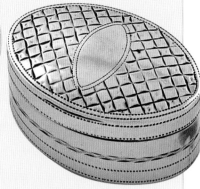

A George III silver nutmeg grater, the base later inscribed 'To Lady Tryon, Isabel Carden, 1964', by Samuel Pemberton, Birmingham.

1801
$1,200-1,300

1.5in (4cm) long 0.8oz
WW

A George IV silver nutmeg grater, engraved with a monogram, by John Shaw, Birmingham.

1821
$900-1,100

1.5in (4cm) long 1.1oz
WW

A William IV silver nutmeg grater, by Joseph Willmore, Birmingham.

1832
$650-800

3in (7.5cm) long 2.2oz
WW

A silver shell nutmeg grater, with textured decoration, the interior with a hinged grater, by Hilliard & Thomason, Birmingham.

1863
$2,500-3,500

1.75in (4.5cm) long 0.7oz
WW

SILVER

QUICK REFERENCE - VINAIGRETTES

Vinaigrettes are small boxes containing a sponge soaked in smelling salts, pleasant smelling oils, perfume or vinegar. Georgian and Victorian ladies or gentlemen would use the cleansing smell to combat against the smell of sewers in major cities of the time, or use the smelling salts to revive faintness. Vinaigrettes were often cased in silver, while the interior was washed in gold to prevent damage or staining from the liquid. The lid, or entire box, would often be decorated with motifs, scenes or landscapes. 'Castle-top' vinaigrettes by makers such as Nathaniel Mills (see page 325) are highly sought after.

A George IV silver vinaigrette, hallmarks rubbed but still clearly legible, grille not hallmarked, maker's mark 'TS' probably for Thomas Shaw, Birmingham.
1828   3.in (9cm) long 0.63oz
$200-250   **FELL**

A silver vinaigrette, by Edward Smith, Birmingham.
1848-49   1.25in (3cm) wide
$160-220   **TRI**

A George III silver reticulated fish vinaigrette, by Joseph Willmore, Birmingham.
1818   3.5in (9cm) long 0.4oz
$850-900   **WW**

A silver vinaigrette, hallmarked, by Nathaniel Mills, Birmingham.
1850   1.5in (4cm) long 0.81oz
$200-250   **FELL**

A silver vinaigrette/ whistle, by S. Mordan and Co.
1870   2in (5cm) long 0.4oz
$400-450   **WW**

A CLOSER LOOK AT A VINAIGRETTE

It is by the respected maker Nathaniel Mills of Birmingham, which increases the value.

The interior contains a high-quality silver-gilt pierced and engraved foliate scroll grille.

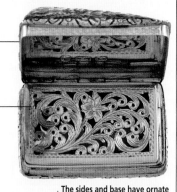

The lid of this 'castle-top' vinaigrette depicts Malvern Abbey in Worcestershire.

The sides and base have ornate engine-turned decoration.

A Victorian silver 'castle-top' vinaigrette, by Nathaniel Mills, Birmingham.
1843   1.5in (4cm) long 0.9oz
$10,000-12,000   **WW**

A Victorian silver whistle/vesta case, the hinged cover with a striker, by S. Mordan and Co., London.

1884 *2.5in (6.5cm) long 0.4oz*

$350-400 **WW**

A silver whistle, with a ring attachment, by S. Mordan and Co., London.

1888 *5.5in (14cm) long 0.6oz*

$150-200 **WW**

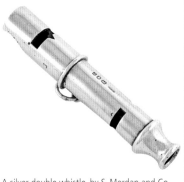

A silver double whistle, by S. Mordan and Co., London.

1919 *4.25in (10.5cm) long 1.2oz*

$250-300 **WW**

A set of silver postage scales, the dial with 'Inland Letter Post', by Levi and Salaman, Birmingham.

1902 *3.25in (8.5cm) high*

$300-400 **WW**

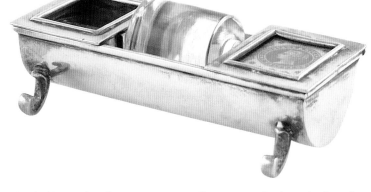

A silver double stamp box/glass stamp moistener, with stamps set under glass and a glass roller, by James Deakin and Sons, Chester.

1902 *3.5in (9cm) long 1.7oz*

$300-400 **WW**

A set of silver postage scales, by Levi and Salaman, Birmingham.

1907 *3.25in (8cm) long*

$250-350 **WW**

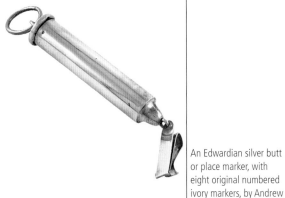

A set of American silver letter scales, by Tiffany & Co.

3.5in (9cm) long 0.5oz

$150-200 **WW**

An Edwardian silver butt or place marker, with eight original numbered ivory markers, by Andrew Barrett & Sons, London, over-striking another.

1907 *2in (5cm) high*

$1,200-1,500 **TEN**

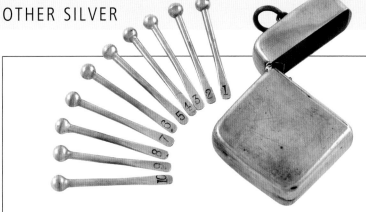

A silver butt marker, with ten unmarked numbered pegs, by Grey & Co., Chester.

1921 *2in (5cm) long 1.1oz*

$650-800 WW

A cast silver horse's head stirrup cup, with maker's mark 'JRB, London'.

4in (10cm) long

$550-650 JN

A silver butt marker, opening to reveal ten numbered ivory pegs, by Asprey and Co., Chester.

1924 *1.75in (4.5cm) long 1.5oz*

$1,000-1,200 WW

A set of three silver 'hounds head' stirrup cups, with maker's mark 'JRB, London'.

3.25in (8.5cm) long

$1,700-2,000 JN

An Austro-Hungarian silver elephant toothpick holder, with a Howdah pierced for toothpicks, maker's mark 'JJ'.

c1870 *5in (13cm) high 6.5oz*

$450-550 WW

A silver fish-shaped toothpick holder, with import marks for London and year cipher.

1897 *0.74oz*

$150-200 PSA

A silver toothpick holder, modeled as a bandaged hare with toothache, on crutches and with a basket on his back, bearing spurious Russian marks for Kostroma.

4in (10cm) long

$550-600 WW

A pair of silver-plated chick toothpick holders.

$80-100 APAR

A Russian silver hare's head top or handle, unknown assay master, maker 'HM'.

3.75in (9.5cm) high 6.86oz

$550-600 BE

A pair of George IV silver scissor snuffers, by Abstinando King, London.

1824 *6.25in (17cm) long 4.38oz*

$450-550 TEN

A silver beehive honey pot, of skep form, with a clear glass liner, by Francis Dexter, London.

A skep is a man-made beehive or basket, used for catching and transporting bees. The swarm is shaken off the branch so that they fall into the skep, then turned upside down, propped on a stone, and transported. In the late 18thC and 19thC, many honey pots were made in the form of skeps.

1844 *4.25in (11.5cm) high 6.5oz*

$4,000-5,000 WW

A Victorian silver-gilt sauce label, incised 'FRENCH VINEGAR', by William Summers, London.

1864 *1in (2.5cm) long 0.2oz*

$400-450 WW

A silver parcel-gilt posy holder, with patent spring-loaded jaws to grip the flowers, maker's mark only, struck twice, by B.H. Joseph & Co., Birmingham.

c1875 *4.5in (11cm) long 1.8oz*

$1,000-1,200 LC

A silver pig pen wipe, by Levi and Salaman, Birmingham.

1904 *2in (5cm) long*

$550-600 WW

A silver 'cat in a shoe' case, the shoe with an oak underside, Birmingham.

1913

$400-450 BELL

SMOKING

A silver presentation cheroot case, with a depiction of the Crystal Palace, with a presentation inscription 'Presented to T C Mills Esq by the Gentlemen connected with the L & NW Railway, 1851', in a fitted leather case, by Cronin & Wheeler & Co., Birmingham.

T.C. Mills was the London Freight Manager of the London & North West Railway Company and was responsible for moving from the Midlands to Hyde Park the 1.5 million square feet of glass and thousands of tons of iron required for the construction of the Crystal Palace which was designed by Joseph Paxton for the Great Exhibition of 1851.

1850   *4.75in (12cm) long 3.6oz*

$3,500-4,000   **WW**

A Russian silver-gilt and enamel cigarette case, the body with cloisonné enamel, with Russian assay marks, Cyrillic maker's mark attributed to Sergei Shaposhnikov, Moscow, and Kokoshnik mark.

1896-1908   4in (10cm) long 5.15oz

$1,000-1,200   **FELL**

A silver cigarette case, by Goldsmiths & Silversmiths Co. Ltd., London.

1913   3.25in (8cm) high 3.94oz

$160-200   **FELL**

An Art Deco enameled silver cigarette case, Birmingham.

1929   3.25in (8cm) long 2.97oz

$130-200   **HAN**

A 1950s silver and enameled cigarette case, designed by Henry Clifford Davis, the interior gilded.

1959   3.25in (8.5cm) wide 4.6oz

$350-400   **HAN**

A Russian niello-decorated cigarette case, depicting buildings and a motor car, detailed '84'.

3.46oz

$250-350   **BELL**

QUICK REFERENCE - AQUARIUM BOX

Very few of these aquarium boxes were produced. This box was commissioned by Sir Bernard and Lady Docker along with a similar, larger cigar box for Sir Winston Churchill. Margaret Bennett, the maker, was only told of the recipient once the box had been completed. The Dockers were notorious socialites in the post-war period. Sir Bernard was the chairman of BSA group, whilst Lady Docker was appointed as a director of the coach builder Hooper & Co. to advise on style. This resulted in numerous extraordinary motor cars including 'The Golden Car' (a golden Daimler), 1951, a car covered in 7000 gold stars, and 'The Golden Zebra', 1955, with gold-plated trim, an ivory dashboard and zebra trim upholstery. Lady Docker also owned a yacht 'Shemara'.

A Japanese silver and mixed metal cigarette case, decorated with a house by a lake.

3.25in (8cm) high 2oz

$130-200   **DA&H**

A rare Dunhill Aquarium perspex cigarette box and cover, by Margaret Bennett, commissioned by Lady Docker (1906-83), reverse-painted with exotic and tropical fish, the cover an aerial view of a pond, cedar lining, unsigned, the cover missing hinge.

7.25in (18.5cm) long

$12,000-15,000   **WW**

A Japanese silver and copper cigarette case, stamped 'Sterling'.

4.25in (11cm) wide 2.79oz

$200-250   **HAN**

QUICK REFERENCE - VESTA CASES

- Match cases, commonly called vesta cases, were popular from the 1830s until the 1920s, when pocket lighters began to replace matches. The name came from an early brand of match, named after Vesta, the Roman goddess of the hearth.
- Early matches were likely to ignite accidentally when they rubbed against each other, so were placed in a small box, usually made of metal, to prevent damage to clothing or property. Vesta cases also usually contained a textured surface to strike matches on.
- Vesta cases are very popular with collectors today. A vast quantity and wide range has survived, and plain examples from the late Victorian and Edwardian periods are readily available at relatively low prices. Finely made silver vesta cases, or those with interesting novelty or figural forms, tend to fetch the highest prices.

A silver vesta box, with domino enamel decoration, some scratches, marks and wear, the interior worn, by Thomas Johnson II, London.
1885   *2in (5cm) long 1.27oz*
$650-800   **FELL**

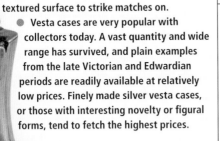

A Victorian vesta case and slow match holder, in the form of a high-buttoned boot with a strap-on roller skate, by Jane Brownett, retailed by Leuchars, 38-39 Piccadilly, London.
1876 2.25in (6cm) high 1.75oz
$4,000-4,500   **LC**

A silver and enamel vesta case, enameled with a lady in a landscape setting, by L. Emmanuel, Birmingham.
1887   *1.5in (4cm) long 0.6oz*
$450-550   **WW**

A silver and enamel vesta case, with a huntsman on horseback, by Edmonds and Johnson, London.
1890   *1.75in (4.5cm) long*
$750-850   **WW**

A silver-framed match box, with a miniature chamber stick, with Moroccan leather liner with striker, possibly by Thomas Wheeler, London.
1892   *3.25in (8cm) long 1.97oz*
$200-250   **APAR**

A silver and enamel vesta case, enameled with a jockey, by Wright and Davies, London.
1896   *2.25in (5.5cm) long 1.8oz*
$900-1,100   **WW**

A silver vesta case, enameled with a golfer, base inscribed 'Wearside Golf Club D M McAuslan from R L Rennison, 1898, Keep Your Eye on the Ball', by S. Mordan and Co., London.
1891   *2.25in (6cm) long*
$3,500-4,000   **GWA**

An Edwardian silver vesta case, enameled with a grandstand and horse race, by Andrew Barrett and Sons, London.
1901   *2.25in (5.5cm) long 1.2oz*
$1,000-1,200   **WW**

A silver vesta case combined with a sealing wax holder, the interior of the lid with a striking plate, by William Hornby, London, retailer's mark for 'JC Vickery, 181 & 183 Regent Street'.
1902   *2.25in (5.5cm) long*
$350-400   **BELL**

SMOKING

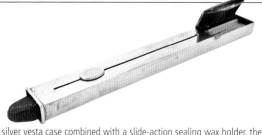

A silver vesta case combined with a slide-action sealing wax holder, the interior with a striking plate, by Stuart Clifford & Co., London.

1907   *6.5in (16.5cm) long*

$400-450   **BELL**

A patented silver wind-proof vesta case, one flap detached, by J.C. Vickery, Birmingham.

1914   *2in (5cm) long 2oz*

$250-350   **PW**

A silver vesta case, enameled with a 'Morland's England's Glory' matchbox, by Henry Plant, Birmingham.

1905   *2.25in (5.5cm) long 1.3oz*

$600-650   **WW**

An early 20thC French silver vesta/ cigar cutter combination, with smaller lidded compartment, makers initials 'G.C'.

2.25in (6cm) long 1.43oz

$150-200   **APAR**

QUICK REFERENCE - DUNHILL

- Dunhill was founded in London in 1893 by Alfred Dunhill. He took over his father's saddler business and focused instead on producing luxury car accessories.
- After the 1905 success of Dunhill's 'Windshield Pipe', a pipe designed to be smoked while driving or cycling, Dunhill moved into the tobacco business, producing pipes and smoking accessories such as vesta cases and lighters. Vintage Dunhill smoking accessories are now highly collectible.
- The Dunhill brand survives today as part of Richemont. Its product lines include menswear, men's jewelry, writing instruments, gifts and games.

A 9ct gold vesta case, hallmarked for Birmingham, 'HM' possibly for Henry Matthews, some surface scratches.

c1920   *2in (5cm) high*

$450-550   **FELL**

A 14ct gold Dunhill watch 'unique lighter' with roller mechanism and hinged arm, with inset watch, marked 'Dunhill Swiss', the interior with dedication and stamped '14C, PAT No 143752', some scratches, dents, and rubbing, watch face worn and faded.

2in (5cm) high

$2,500-3,500   **FELL**

A Dunhill Aquarium table lighter, designed by Margaret Bennett, the Perspex panels reverse-painted with a blue Japanese fighting fish and a Zebra fish, cast marks.

4in (10cm) wide

$3,500-4,000   **WW**

An 18ct yellow metal and blue enamel lighter, the body of Rollagas type, stamped beneath '750', marked 'Dunhill', some enamel losses to cover and body.

2.5in (6.5cm) high

$750-800   **FELL**

An 18ct yellow metal lighter, of 'Rollagas' type attributed to Dunhill, the body later-set with small diamonds, stamped beneath '750', marked 'Dunhill' beneath cover only, superficial scratching.

2.5in (6.5cm) high

$2,500-3,500   **FELL**

A German 'American jeep' table lighter, by W. Baier, the jeep with trailer which acts as an ash tray, engraved to top 'Germany 1950'.

9in (23cm) long

$100-140 **LOCK**

An 18ct yellow metal Cartier lighter, later-set with 'laque de chine' panel and two lines of small diamonds, stamped beneath 'Cartier Paris 99029F' and '750'.

2.75in (7cm) high

$1,600-2,000 **FELL**

An S.T. Dupont gold-plated 'laque de chine' lighter, stamped '16GGL41', minor losses, untested, in original leather pouch.

2.5in (6cm) high

$150-200 **FELL**

A S.T. Dupont gold-plated engine-turned lighter, in case.

$70-80 **HAN**

An Art Deco Ronson 'Touch Tip' lighter desk tray, of chrome and oxidized metal, the removable lighter flanked by two cedar lined cigarette boxes.

12.25in (31cm) wide

$400-450 **HAN**

An Art Deco chrome 'airplane' desk lighter, stamped 'Patent' verso.

7.5in (19cm) wide

$100-120 **LSK**

An early 20thC cold-painted spelter table lighter, modeled as a Moorish rug seller with an attendant.

7.5in (19cm) high

$350-400 **DA&H**

SMOKING

A tobacco jar, cover and plunger, 'The Smokers and Jolly Topers', with 'Thos. Bear Tobacco' manufacturer's stamp, cover restored.

5.25in (13.5cm) high

$450-600   H&C

A pair of late 19thC H.F. & Sons London stoneware tobacco jars and tin covers, with panels for 'CAVENDISH' and 'BEST SHAG'.

7.75in (20cm) high

$250-300   DN

A Wild Woodbine Cigarettes coin-operated dispensing machine, with plaque 'British Automatic Vendors Limited - Machine no.1782'.

31.5in (80cm) high

$400-450   DA&H

An early 20thC wood and copper mounted cigarette dispenser, modeled as a house, missing match striker to one side.

5.25in (13.5cm) wide

$90-100   APAR

A Henry Howell & Co. ebony and phenol resin YZ Pelican and patinated copper novelty pipe bowl, stamped 'YZ'.

This YZ Pelican bird was illustrated in 'Motor Commerce', 23 October 1926, without the bowl as a car mascot.

7in (18cm) high

$450-550   WW

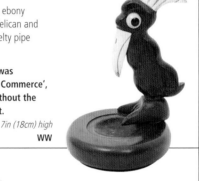

A CLOSER LOOK AT A SMOKER'S COMPENDIUM

This Art Deco smoker's compendium is modeled as a stylized airplane.

Novelty smoking accessories are always highly collectible.

A silver combination penknife pipe tool, including pipe cleaner, tamper, cigar cutter, fork and blade, some minor wear, by Saunders and Shepherd, Chester.

1894   *3.25in (8.5cm) long*

$250-350   HAN

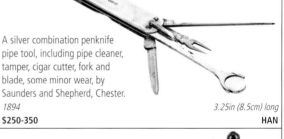

The wings are cigarette cases, the turret a vesta case and the central fuselage a cigar box.

It is unmarked, but is probably by J.A. Henckels, a German metalware and knife manufacturer.

A 1930s Art Deco 'airplane' silver-plated smoker's compendium.

9.75in (25cm) long

$3,500-4,000   GWA

A Norwegian silver and enamel cigar cutter, by Marius Hammer, blade marked 'MH 830S'.

2in (5cm) long

$150-200   LOCK

QUICK REFERENCE - SPORTING MEMORABILIA

- Sporting memorabilia is collected all over the world. Most collectors focus on one sport, and often on particular items within it, such as golf clubs, tennis rackets or signed football jerseys. Football (or soccer), golf, baseball, cricket and tennis tend to be the most popular sports with collectors.
- The large quantity of collectors can often push up prices for sporting memorabilia. The date, the fame of any connected player or team, and the importance of any connected event, game or match, all affect the value substantially. Condition is always important, and framed and mounted pieces are popular.
- Signed clothing, kits, balls, clubs, bats and rackets are popular. However, many signed pieces from the later 20thC were signed in bulk and not necessarily worn or owned by the signee. Items worn by a player in an event or match tend to be the most valuable objects. Collectors will aim to buy these accompanied by authoritative documentation and photographic evidence to confirm the connection between the item and the player.
- Printed and paper memorabilia, such as football programs and match tickets, can also be valuable, especially for cancelled games or significant matches. Photographs, books, posters and novelty items are also enjoyed by collectors.
- Early memorabilia can be very rare and highly desirable, so it is worth knowing the history of the sport. Early examples of items such as golf clubs or tennis rackets, which changed in shape and design over time, are very popular. It is also worth looking out for pieces relating to female players, as this area is growing in importance and appeal.

A Tommy Crawshaw purple England v Scotland cap.

Thomas Henry 'Tommy' Crawshaw (1872-1960) was born in Sheffield and spent most of his career at Sheffield Wednesday. Between 1894 and 1909, he played 492 games and won two F.A. Cup and two League Championship medals. He appeared 10 times for England. This cap was awarded for the match v Scotland at Celtic Park 4 April 1896. Scotland won 2-1.

1895-96

$1,500-2,000 GBA

A West Bromwich Albion shirt, worn by Bert Trentham in the 1935 F.A. Cup Final, inscribed '1934-35', the neck with a tag inscribed in ink 'H. TRENTHAM'.

Herbert Francis 'Bert' Trentham (1908-79), nicknamed 'Corker', was a full-back born in Chirbury, Shropshire, who joined West Bromwich Albion from Hereford United in April 1929. He won an F.A. Cup winner's medal in 1931 and a runners-up medal in 1935.

$3,500-4,000 GBA

A Kenny Morgans Manchester United navy blue player's blazer, Manchester United wirework club badge to breast pocket, with a letter of provenance.

Kenneth Godfrey Morgans was born in Swansea on 16 March 1939. He signed for Manchester United in 1955 and played on the youth team's outside-right position. Morgans made his first professional team debut on 21 December 1957, aged 18, against Leicester City. He was the last survivor to be rescued from the Munich Air Disaster on 6 February 1958, but suffered only minor injuries. He returned to Wales and played for Swansea Town, Newport County and Barry Town before becoming player/manager at non-League Cwmbran Town in 1968. He later became a pub landlord, then ship's chandler, and died in Swansea on 18 November 2012.

c1960

$1,300-1,600 GBA

A George Best Northern Ireland No.7 jersey, worn in the World Cup qualifier v Switzerland at Windsor Park, Belfast, 14 October 1964, with a letter of provenance.

Northern Ireland won the match 1-0, through a goal by Sunderland's Johnny Crossan. George Best won a total of 37 Northern Ireland international caps 1964-77. The Switzerland match at Windsor Park was his 4th cap. In the away leg in Lausanne, Best scored the first of his nine international goals.

$25,000-35,000 GBA

An England 1966 World Cup final spare shirt, no.16, with two letters of provenance.

This shirt was issued to Martin Peters for the 1966 World Cup final. It was given to Sid Brown the coach driver by Bobby Moore and at the same time Moore gave his shirt to Harold Shepherdson.

$12,000-13,000 GWA

A Matt Le Tissier match-worn Southampton jersey, inscribed 'MATTHEW LE TISSIER, TESTIMONIAL, 14th MAY 2002', mounted in a frame, signed in black marker pen and inscribed 'BEST WISHES', with the receipt for the shirt following a charitable donation toward the Matt Le Tissier Testimonial Year.

42in (100cm) high

$3,500-4,000 GBA

A Liverpool No.28 jersey, worn by Steven Gerrard on his first full competitive start for the club in the UEFA Cup 3rd Round 2nd Leg tie v Celta Vigo played at Anfield on 8 December 1998, with two provenance documents featuring this shirt.

Steven Gerrard was born in Whiston, Merseyside on 30 May 1980. He joined the Liverpool Academy aged nine. Gerrard signed his first professional contract with Liverpool on 5 November 1997 and made his first-team debut as a last minute substitute in the Premier League game v Blackburn Rovers at Anfield on 19 November 1998.

An Eduardo Arsenal No.9 match-issued Champions League away jersey.
2009-10
$200-250   GBA

$4,500-6,000   GBA

A Steven Gerrard England 2014-15-style replica jersey, signature in black marker pen.
$150-200   GBA

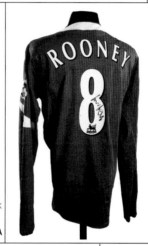

A Thierry Henry signed Arsenal No.14 replica 2003-04 'invincibles' season home jersey, signed in black marker pen in the shirt number.
$150-200   GBA

A Wayne Rooney Manchester United No.8 match-issued Premier League jersey, from his first season at Old Trafford, signed in black marker pen to the '8'.
2004-05
$800-950   GBA

A pair of Frank Lampard Adidas Adipure X-TRX SG football boots, both signed in black marker pen, both boots inscribed 'MUM' and '8', the left boot additionally inscribed 'ISLA', the right 'LUNA'.
$550-600   GBA

A Cristiano Ronaldo signed Nike Mercurial football boot, signed in blue marker pen.
$200-250   GBA

A pair of Eden Hazard platinum and yellow Nike Mercurial Vapor XI Elite football boots, both signed in black marker pen.
$600-650   GBA

A Glasgow Rangers Football Club Sports Day trophy, with a plaque inscribed 'RANGERS FOOTBALL CLUB, AMATEUR SPORTS, 1 MILE H'CAP, 1st PRIZE, WON BY, JOHN MILROY, MAYBOLE, SCOTLAND, 6th AUGUST 1892'.

20.5in (52cm) long

$550-650　　　　　　　　　　　GBA

A 9ct gold and enamel 1904 Glasgow Charity Cup winner's medal, awarded to Alex Smith of Rangers F.C..

Alexander Smith (1876-1954) was born in Darvel and signed for Glasgow Rangers in April 1894. He played at Ibrox for 21 years. He was a member of the four consecutive League Championships team in 1899-1902. The winger was also capped for Scotland on 20 occasions.

$1,600-2,000　　　　　　　　　GBA

A silver-plated football trophy shield roundel.

1920　　　　　　　6.25in (16cm) high

$150-200　　　　　　　　　　　GBA

A 1923 German National Football Championship gilt-bronze winner's medal, awarded to Otto Carlsson of Hamburger SV, inscribed 'DEM DEUTSCHEN FUSSBALL MEISTER, 1923, BERLIN, 10. JUNI 1923'.

In 1923, Hamburger SV were officially crowned German National Champions for the first time. Otto Carlsson was born in Sweden 16 December 1901. He later moved to Germany and joined Hamburger SV in 1922.

6in (15cm) long

$2,500-3,000　　　　　　　　　GBA

A 9ct gold St Vincent de Paul Charity medal, awarded to Celtic goalkeeper John Thomson.

1927-28

$6,000-6,500　　　　　　　　　GWA

A 9ct gold Harry Nuttall Football League representative medal, inscribed 'THE FOOTBALL LEAGUE, ENGLAND v SCOTLAND, GLASGOW, NOVEMBER 2nd 1929, RESERVE', in original case.

Nuttall was the reserve for the Football League. This match was played at Ibrox. The Scottish League won 2-1.

$350-400　　　　　　　　　　　GBA

A 9ct gold 1965 F.A. Cup winner's medal, awarded to Willie Stevenson of Liverpool F.C., inscribed 'THE FOOTBALL ASSOCIATION, CHALLENGE CUP, WINNERS, W. STEVENSON', sold with an example of Stevenson's autograph.

In the final Liverpool beat Leeds United 2-1 after extra-time.

$13,000-16,000　　　　　　　　GBA

A 9ct gold and enamel GAA Football Interprovincial medal, awarded to a Co. Down player on the Ulster team.

1966

$600-650　　　　　　　　　　　WHYT

A West Ham United program, from the first season in the Football League 1919-20, Second Division fixture v Coventry City, 13 December 1919, worn.

$650-800 GBA

An 1921 F.A. Cup Final program, Tottenham Hotspur v Wolverhampton Wanderers, played at Stamford Bridge, some folds.

$1,500-2,000 GBA

A CLOSER LOOK AT A FOOTBALL PROGRAM

This program is from the 1924 F.A. Cup Final. Memorabilia from significant matches is always more valuable.

The game was played between Aston Villa v Newcastle United on 26 April 1924. Newcastle won the match 2-0, with goals scored by Neil Harris and Stan Seymour.

The program illustration depicts an Aston Villa player in the club's usual colors. However, the other player is not in Newcastle's traditional colors but in their rival Sunderland's - this mistake by the printer adds to the value.

It rained heavily on the day of the match and few programs survived in tact, making this one of the most valuable Wembley cup final programs.

An F.A. Cup Final program, 26 April 1924.

$5,500-6,000 GBA

An England v Scotland 'Wembley Wizards' international program, 31 March 1928, an area of paper with surface damage.

$250-300 GBA

A 1932 F.A. Cup Final program, Arsenal v Newcastle United, result written on center page, slight foxing inside program, scribbles to pages 6 and 7.

$350-400 HAN

A Clapton Orient v Sportklub Rapid full Orient program, for friendly match played on 28 August 1934.

Rapid won the game 3-2.

$100-120 LOCK

An Arsenal v Glasgow Rangers program, 12 September 1934, friendly match.

$150-200 GBA

A George Best signed Manchester United program, from his debut season in 1963-64, signed on the line-ups page for the League fixture v Birmingham City, 11 January 1964, additionally signed by United's Willie Anderson and Birmingham's Terry Hennessy.

$130-200 GBA

A football ticket, for the Ireland v England international match played at the Balmoral Show Grounds, 22 March 1902.

This match was settled by an England goal scored by Jimmy Settle in the 86th minute.
$1,200-1,500   GBA

An F.A. Cup final ticket counterfoil stub, Barnsley v West Bromwich Albion at the Crystal Palace, 20 April 1912.
$1,200-1,300   GBA

A 1930 World Cup ticket stub, for the Uruguay v Yugoslavia semi-final played at the Centenary Stadium, 27 July 1930.
$250-300   GBA

A Red Devils souvenir, with center team, photo signed by 11 players including Tommy Taylor, Roger Byrne, David Pegg.
1956-57
$450-550   CAPE

A Hendon Hall dinner menu, signed by the England squad for the match v Spain at Wembley, 3 April 1968, 25 signatures including all 11 1966 World Cup winners, plus manager Ramsey and trainers Shepherdson and Cocker, other autographs including match starters Knowles, Mullery and Summerbee.
$600-750   GBA

A postcard, of Alfred Di Stefano, Real Madrid, Spain, Argentina, signed.

Alfred Di Stefano was probably most famous for his European Cup Final with Real Madrid.
5.5in (14cm) high
$70-80   LOCK

A 1960s Bobby Moore West Ham and England signed color magazine page.
16in (40.5cm) high
$150-250   LOCK

An England v Wales magazine cut out, on card, signed by Milne, Norman, Banks, Charlton, Armfield, Smith and Wilson.
1963   *9in (23cm) wide*
$35-40   LOCK

An official Football League team-sheet, for the Liverpool team to play Manchester United in the F.A. Cup semi-final, 13 April 1985, signed by Ronnie Moran on behalf of L.F.C.
$1,000-1,200   GBA

An official FIFA pennant for the 1966 World Cup.

19.75in (50cm) long

$350-400

GBA

An Alan A'Court England U-23 shirt badge, England v Czechoslovakia 1957.

This match was played in Bratislava, 30 May 1957. England won 2-0. Both goals were scored by Duncan Edwards.

$80-100

GBA

A silver snuff box, inscribed 'Presented by the Committee of the Clapton F.C. to S.B. Jose Esq. in recognition of his valuable service as President 1909/10', by George Unite, Birmingham.

1908   *2.59oz*

$450-550

HAN

An Austrian silver cigarette case, with enamel decoration of a football match, inscribed 'PRESENTED TO MR EDGAR CHADWICK AS A MEMENTO OF FRIENDSHIP, GRATITUDE AND HIGH ESTEEM, FROM THE DEUTSCHER FUSSBALLCLUB, MAY 1900, PRAGUE', Austrian .900 silver mark, in original case.

In May 1900 Edgar Chadwick was a Burnley player. He joined Southampton in August. He also played for Everton from 1888-99, during which time he won 7 England international caps. This cigarette case was presented to him in Prague, where he was coaching players during the English close season.

3.25in (8cm) long

$12,000-13,000

GBA

A Pioneer white leather football, formerly owned by Geoff Hurst, with the 22 signatures of the England 1966 World Cup squad and manager Alf Ramsey, in a display case, with key, the blue biro signatures faded but legible.

$1,500-2,000

GBA

A gentlemen's Longines 9ct gold automatic wristwatch, inscribed 'PRESENTED TO R.D. BLANCHFLOWER (CAPTAIN) BY TOTTENHAM HOTSPUR F.C. ON WINNING THE FOOTBALL LEAGUE AND THE F.A. CUP, 1961', the gold strap 18ct, with original Harrods retail case and a signed letter of authenticity from Gayle Blanchflower.

1960

$12,000-13,000

GBA

A rare Tottenham Hotspur cockerel mascot smoker's clay pipe, inscribed 'SPURS, PLAY UP', small chip, beak missing.

$400-550

GBA

A spelter figure of a footballer, with bronze patina, signed 'Ruffony' and stamped 'FRANCE' to the base.

23.25in (59cm) high

$550-650

GBA

An early Cassius Clay publicity photograph, signed in blue ink, with a dedication 'TO TED'.
1963
$900-1,100 GBA

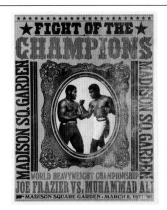

A Muhammad Ali v Joe Frazier 'Fight of the Champions' program, at Madison Square Garden, New York, NY, USA, 8 March 1971, front cover a little worn.
$150-200 GBA

A program for the Muhammad Ali v Jean-Pierre Coopman World Heavyweight Championship fight in Puerto Rico, 20 February 1976.
$1,200-1,500 GBA

An official program for the Muhammad Ali v Jimmy Young Heavyweight Championship fight at Landover, MD, USA, 30 April 1976, the undercard featuring Ken Norton v Ron Stander.
$650-800 GBA

A pair of Muhammad Ali signed boxing gloves, signed in black marker pen, somewhat faded, one glove is dedicated 'To Jerry, From Muhammad Ali', the other inscribed 'Floats Like a Butterfly Stings Like a Bee!', both dated '5/7/91', with a certificate of authenticity and hologram.
$650-800 GBA

A pair of signed and annotated Muhammed Ali Lonsdale branded boxing gloves, with plaque titled 'Received at a tribute dinner for Muhammad Ali, 8th August 1983, The Albany sporting club'.
$1,300-2,000 FLD

The Everlast boxing trunks worn by Muhammad Ali during his World Heavyweight Title fight v Jimmy Young, on 30 April 1976 in Landover, MD, USA, the trunks reading 'Made Expressly For MUHAMMAD ALI', with a file of authenticity documentation.

Muhammad Ali won his fight against Jimmy Young through a 15-round unanimous decision. The three judges awarded the decision to Ali by scores of 72-65, 70-68 and 71-64. In c1972 boxing equipment manufacturer Everlast began to supply Muhammad Ali with specially made equipment, produced exclusively for Ali by the company with special tagging.
$30,000-35,000 GBA

A full ticket for the John L. Sullivan v 'Gentlemen Jim' Corbett Heavyweight Championship of the World fight, at the Olympic Club, New Orleans, 7 September 1892, the reverse stamped 'PRESS'.
$2,500-3,000 GBA

SPORTING

An India v England Test Series signed shirt, signed by 15 England players: Kevin Pietersen, Tim Ambrose, James Anderson, Ian Bell, Stuart Broad, Paul Collingwood, Alastair Cook, Andrew Flintoff, Stephen Harmison, Monty Panesar, Matt Prior, Owais Shah, Ryan Sidebottom, Andrew Strauss and Graeme Swann, with certificate of authenticity, glazed and framed.

$550-650   TEN

A team-signed Marcus Trescothick England Test Match cricket shirt, the shirt numbered with cap '603', the left-sleeve initialed 'TM', signed by Trescothick and 11 of his England team-mates in black marker pen, including Vaughan, Giles, Strauss, Anderson, Harmison, Flintoff and others.

Marcus Trescothick played in 76 Test Matches between 2000-06. During the 2005 Ashes Series he became the fastest player to reach 5,000 Test runs.

$150-250   GBA

An Ian Johnson Australia cricket blazer from the 1948 Tour of England, by Farmer's of Sydney, inscribed in pen 'IAN JOHNSTON'.

Ian William Geddes Johnson CBE (1917-98) was an Australian cricketer who played 45 Test Matches as a slow bowler 1946-56. Johnson captured 109 Test wickets at an average of 29.19 and as a lower order batsman made precisely 1,000. He captained the Australian team in 17 Tests. Johnson was part of Bradman's 1948 'invincibles' tour of England and played in 4 Tests, taking 7 wickets, scoring 51 runs and taking 5 catches.

1948

$1,600-2,000   GBA

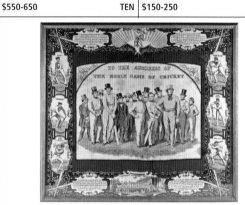

A Victorian printed cotton panel, titled 'TO THE ADMIRERS OF THE NOBLE GAME OF CRICKET', with famous cricketers including Lillywhite, Felix, Hillyer and Dorrington, the border with cartouches inscribed with the rules of cricket, in an oak glazed frame.

34in (86.5cm) long

$400-550   WW

A 'Freddy Truman's 150th Test' presentation cricket stump, inscribed 'PRESENTED BY ROTHMANS OF PALLMALL, FREDDY TRUMANS 150TH TEST WICKET ENGLAND - S. AFRICA TEST EDGBASTON 1960...'

34.75in (88cm) long

$250-300   WW

A Victorian Staffordshire pottery mug, decorated with molded figures believed to be Lillywhite, Pilch and Box.

3.5in (8.5cm) high

$150-200   WW

A bronze figure of W.G. Grace, inscribed 'W.G. Grace', on a marble plinth.

11in (28cm) high

$400-550   GBA

QUICK REFERENCE - HARDY

- In 1872, brothers William and John James Hardy set up a shop selling guns and metalware in Alnwick, Northumberland.
- From 1874, the brothers added fishing tackle to their stock. Originally they bought in most of the tackle they sold, but as the firm expanded they began to produce their own. In 1891 Hardy launched its 'Perfect' reel, which quickly became a success.
- Other reels made by Hardy include the Fortuna (1921-66), the Cascapedia (1932-39), the Alma multiplier (1925-37), the Zane Grey multiplier (1928-57) and the Jock Scott multiplier (1938-52). Vintage Hardy reels are highly collectible today.
- Hardy opened a shop in London in the 1890s and continued successfully into the 20thC. For over a century the firm passed down through the generations. After the retirement of director James Leighton Hardy in 1992, the firm moved out of the family. Today Hardy continues today as part of Pure Fishing Ltd.

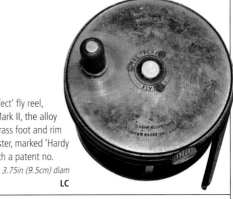

A Hardy 'Perfect' fly reel, Duplicated Mark II, the alloy reel with a brass foot and rim tension adjuster, marked 'Hardy Bros Ltd', with a patent no.

3.75in (9.5cm) diam

$250-300   LC

A Hardy 'Perfect' fishing reel, with an ivorine winder, stamped 'Hardy Bros Ltd, Alnwick, Patent Perfect Reel'.

3.75in (9.5cm) diam

$200-250   LC

A Hardy 'Perfect' fishing reel, the alloy reel with rim tension regulator and brass foot, marked 'Hardy Bros Ltd.'.

3.75in (9.5cm) diam

$200-250   LC

A Hardy's salmon 'Perfect' reel with ivorine handle, stamped marks.

4.5in (11.5cm) diam

$1,000-1,300   BELL

A Hardy 'The Husky' fly fishing reel, in case.

3.25in (8.5cm) diam

$120-150   BRI

A leather-cased early brass C. Farlow fishing reel, with a ivorine winder, the reel and case both stamped 'HRH', the reel stamped 'Cha Farlow & Co, Makers 191 Strand, London, HRH'.

4.5in (11.5cm) diam

$250-350   LC

A leather-cased early C. Farlow reel, made in mahogany and brass and with an ivorine winder, the reel and case stamped 'HRH', the reel marked 'Cha Farlow, Maker 191 Strand, London'.

4in (10cm) diam

$350-400   LC

A George V carved wood and painted half-block model of a salmon, attributed to the Fochabers Studio, mounted on a stained pine plaque and inscribed '36 LBS, BRIDGE POOL, DELFUR, 1ST OCT.1924', with photographs of the fisherman who caught the salmon.

52in (132cm) wide

$8,000-8,500   WW

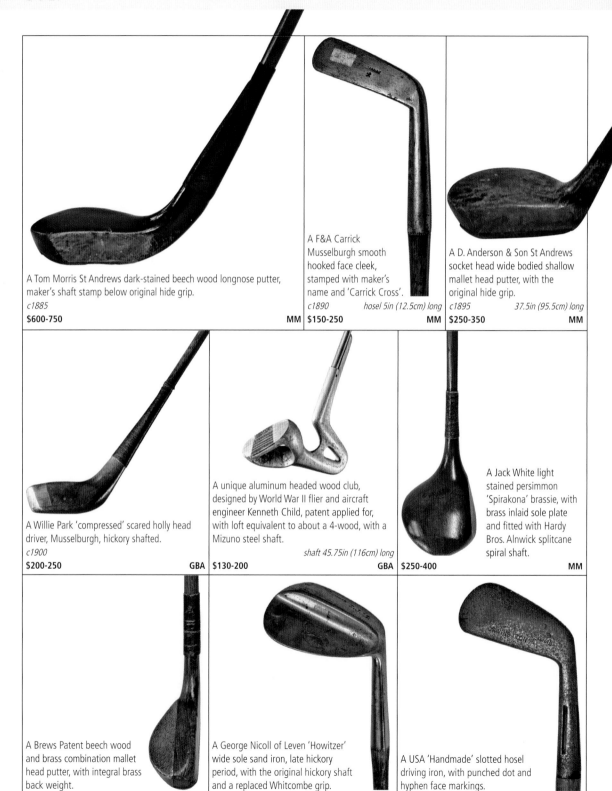

A Tom Morris St Andrews dark-stained beech wood longnose putter, maker's shaft stamp below original hide grip.
c1885
$600-750   MM

A F&A Carrick Musselburgh smooth hooked face cleek, stamped with maker's name and 'Carrick Cross'.
c1890   *hosel 5in (12.5cm) long*
$150-250   MM

A D. Anderson & Son St Andrews socket head wide bodied shallow mallet head putter, with the original hide grip.
c1895   *37.5in (95.5cm) long*
$250-350   MM

A Willie Park 'compressed' scared holly head driver, Musselburgh, hickory shafted.
c1900
$200-250   GBA

A unique aluminum headed wood club, designed by World War II flier and aircraft engineer Kenneth Child, patent applied for, with loft equivalent to about a 4-wood, with a Mizuno steel shaft.
shaft 45.75in (116cm) long
$130-200   GBA

A Jack White light stained persimmon 'Spirakona' brassie, with brass inlaid sole plate and fitted with Hardy Bros. Alnwick splitcane spiral shaft.
$250-400   MM

A Brews Patent beech wood and brass combination mallet head putter, with integral brass back weight.
$200-250   MM

A George Nicoll of Leven 'Howitzer' wide sole sand iron, late hickory period, with the original hickory shaft and a replaced Whitcombe grip.
$450-550   MM

A USA 'Handmade' slotted hosel driving iron, with punched dot and hyphen face markings.
$50-70   MM

A Rory McIlroy signed golf cap, white Nike, signature to the brow in black marker pen.

$400-450　　　　　　　　　　　　　　GBA

A Tiger Woods signed Titleist golf visor, with a certificate of authenticity and a color photograph showing Woods in a similar visor.

Due to scandals surrounding his personal life, Tiger Woods memorabilia has declined in value in recent years.

$150-250　　　　　　　　　　　　　　GBA

A 9ct gold S. Mordan and Co. for Asprey score card, with telescopic pencil and penknife, dents and rubbing.

3in (7.5cm) long

$800-950　　　　　　　　　　　　　　FELL

A set of four mechanical toy golfers, by the A. Schoenhut Company, Philidelphia, with three bunkers, a putting green and a set of nine miniature golf clubs to attach to each golfer toy.

1922　　　　*36.5in (93cm) long*

$550-650　　　　　　　　　　　　　　GBA

An early 20thC Scottish silver-plated mantel timepiece, with drum movement, with a golfer and decorated with thistles, clubs and balls, the back with registration number '214577', the base stamped 'GW N188 0AJ'.

12.5in (32cm) high

$1,500-2,000　　　　　　　　　　　　WW

A rare 'Snowdrop' mesh pattern gutty golf ball, showing one strike mark.

$200-250　　　　　　　　　　　　　　MM

A Gary Player 1968 Carnoustie Open Golf Champion signed photograph, no.114 of a limited edition of 250, copyright Allsports, issued for the Sir Vivian Richards Foundation.

21.5in (54.5cm) wide

$80-100　　　　　　　　　　　　　　MM

A Worplesdon Golf Club 9ct gold medal, for 'Scratch Mixed Foursomes', engraved on the reverse 'Miss D.R Fowler' (1925 English Ladies Champion) and 'E Noel Leighton', both International Players, in original case.

1924　　　　*0.89oz*

$550-650　　　　　　　　　　　　　　MM

A Lewis Hamilton and Nico Rosberg signed AMG Petronas 2016 F1 cap.

$250-300   GBA

A gentleman's TAG Heuer Swiss limited edition wristwatch, watch reference CAI7114, serial no.REQ8354, supplied to Mclaren Racing Ltd., in original case, signed by Lewis Hamilton.

$1,600-2,000   JN

Grand Prix Monaco 78
6/7 MAI

A 1978 Monaco Grand Prix original Formula 1 poster, featuring the 1977 F1 World Champion Niki Lauda leading the field in his Ferrari, artwork after Alain Giampaoli, in a clip frame.

23.5in (60cm) high

$250-300   GBA

A 2007 'La Ferrari' cover, signed by Michael Schumacher, Felipe Massa, Kimi Raikkonen and Luca Badoer, the annual 60-page souvenir magazine celebrating the marque's 60th anniversary, Italian and English text.

In 2007, Michael Schumacher had an advisory role at Ferrari, having retired at the end of 2006. Kimi Raikkonen replaced the seven-time World Champion behind the wheel and he too then took the F1 title, while Felipe Massa missed out by a single point to Lewis Hamilton the following year.

laFerrari2007

1947-2007

11.75in (30cm) high

$450-550   GBA

A 2011 German GP program, signed by Michael Schumacher, Lewis Hamilton and seven others, including Sebastian Vettel, Fernando Alonso, Jenson Button, Nico Rosberg, Felipe Massa, Rubens Barrichello and Mark Webber, with German and English text.

11.75in (30cm) high

$200-250   GBA

A Michael Schumacher signed 2004 F1 World Champion cap.

In 2004 Ferrari and Speedline's official merchandising labels marked Michael Schumacher's seventh F1 World Championship title, five of them with Ferrari.

$250-350   GBA

An Arai 1:1 full-scale replica of the Nigel Mansell Quantum helmet, with Labatt's and Canon sponsor decals.

9.75in (25cm) high size M

$250-300   PW

A signed Pierre Fix-Masseau poster, 'Monte Carlo', featuring motor racing, signed by the artist in pencil lower right and dated '1988', published by Renecasha.

Monte-Carlo

39.25in (100cm) high

$450-550   GBA

A London 1908 Olympic Games competitor's badge, by Vaughton of Birmingham, silvered bronze and enamel, head of Athena, inscribed 'COMPETITOR'.
$650-800 **GBA**

A Cortina 1956 Winter Olympic Games helper's badge, gilt-metal and enamel, inscribed 'AIUTANTE, VII GIOCHI OLIMPICI, INVERNALI, CORTINA, 1956, ITALIA'.
$250-350 **GBA**

A Cortina 1956 Winter Olympic Games participant's bronze medal, by C. Affer.
1.75in (4.5cm) diam
$400-450 **GBA**

A Rome 1960 Olympic Games bronze badge, with uninscribed orange enamel bar.

This is one of 63 badges issued to the Japanese Olympic Delegation for the Tokyo 1964 Games.
$350-400 **GBA**

A Tokyo 1964 Olympic Games gold-plate and enamel official's badge, inscribed 'OFFICIAL', in original case.
$300-400 **GBA**

A Sarajevo 1984 Winter Olympic Games bearer's torch, manufactured by Nippon K. under the supervision of Mizuno Corp, stainless steel cylinder in silver-colored aluminum alloy, bowl gold-colored with 'Sarajevo 84' legend.
22.75in (57.5cm) high
$3,500-4,000 **GBA**

A 1964 Tokyo Olympic Games participation medal, designed by T. Okamoto and K. Tanaka, reverse with Olympic Rings and legend in Japanese and English.
$250-300 **GBA**

A Usain Bolt signed Jamaica Puma athletics vest, signed by Bolt in silver marker pen.
$350-400 **GBA**

A rowing blade, signed by the Great Britain 2000 Sydney Olympic Games coxless fours gold medal winners, Steve Redgrave, Matthew Pinsent, James Cracknell and Tim Foster.
$300-400 **GBA**

A Scottish rugby cap, believed to be Melrose RFC and first awarded in 1900-01, by Tress & Co., London, retailed by W.J. Milne, Aberdeen, with eight successive season dates between 1900-01 and 1907-08.

$350-400   GBA

A Gloucestershire county Rugby Union representative cap, awarded to Don Cummins of Bristol RFC, dated.

Don Cummins represented Gloucestershire at no.11 in the match v Somerset played at Kingsholm, 23 October 1937.

1937-38

$650-800   GBA

A Harry Dyer Rugby League Yorkshire County representative cap, dated.

Leeds's Harry Dyer played in the Roses match v Lancashire at Rochdale, 12 February 1939.

1938-39

$450-550   GBA

A Michael Bradley Ireland No.9 international Rugby Union jersey, by Umbro, with IRFU badge.

Scrum-half Michael Bradley captained Ireland in 1993, during which they won the Millennium Trophy with a 17-3 victory over England at Lansdowne Road. Bradley won 40 Irish caps, 15 as captain, and scored 40 points 1984-95. He is now a coach.

1993

$2,000-2,500   GBA

A signed Dream Lions rugby shirt, signatures in black marker pen, comprising Johnny Smith, Keith Wood, Fran Cotton, Richard Hill, Willie John McBride, Martin Johnson, Finlay Calder, Dean Richards, Gareth Edwards, Barry John, Jeremy Guscott, Scott Gibbs, J.J. Williams, Gavin Hastings, Ian McGeechan and Ieuan Evans, framed and glazed, with a certificate of authenticity and pictures of the Lions at the signing.

35in (89cm) high

$200-250   GBA

A framed England rugby shirt, signed by the England 2003 World Cup winners, signatures in black marker pen including Johnson, Wilkinson, Greenwood, Dallaglio, Robinson Dawson, Back, Corry and Hill.

37in (94cm) high

$750-850   GBA

A French vintage rugby poster, titled 'Gd. Match de Football Rugby', signed Van Hasselt, published by Kossuth, Paris, backed on linen.

47.25in (120cm) wide

$3,500-4,000   GBA

A tilt-top tennis racket, stamped 'Chas. Ward, Heckmondwike, Yorkshire', with original unbroken stringing.

c1880

$1,000-1,200   **GBA**

A 'Tournament 3' lawn tennis racket by Bussey & Co., with a striking fishtail.

This racket was possibly never strung when it was first made. The present stringing in is modern gut.

c1896

$350-400   **GBA**

A late 1920s Birmal patent aluminum lawn tennis racket, patent no.219535, with a wooden grip, piano wire stringing, probably a prototype, scratch signed by Eric Cross to the grip in the form 'ERIC.A.X'.

This racket was once owned by Eric A. Cross, Tennis Director, Consultant and Wimbledon competitor, who received it from Birmal after he had suggested the use of aluminum for rackets.

$550-650   **GBA**

QUICK REFERENCE - BORG V MCENROE

The tennis players Bjorn Borg and John McEnroe had a legendary rivalry, heightened by the fact their temperaments contrasted so dramatically; McEnroe the brash New Yorker, Borg the ice-cool Swede. 1981 proved to be the pivotal year when McEnroe gained supremacy over the Swede, beating him in both the Wimbledon and US Open finals, latterly in four sets at Flushing Meadow. Borg all but retired after this match, making just fleeting appearances on the circuit thereafter.

A 1930s Lightning Tennis Ball Cleaner, by Suffolk Iron Foundry, in cast iron.

This was designed to accept up to four tennis balls at a time.

$400-550   **GBA**

A Roger Federer signed tennis shirt, cap and bandana, each Nike item individually signed and framed and mounted under glass.

These items are understood to have been tournament worn.

35.75in (91cm) high

$400-550   **GBA**

A Donnay Borg Pro Personal Model tennis racket, used by Bjorn Borg in the 1981 US Open Final v John McEnroe, signed by Borg and inscribed in Swedish 'basta halsningar' (Best Regards), with original head cover, with information on provenance.

$8,500-9,500   **GBA**

A 'Welcome' banner from the 2010 Wimbledon Lawn Tennis Championships, printed on green vinyl.

78.75in (200cm) high

$250-350   **GBA**

A pair of 19thC French spelter figures, with the unusual subject of 'jeu de balle au tambourin', each signed 'Lauergne'.

14.5in (37cm) high

$350-400   **GBA**

SPORTING

A set of five die-cut embossed baseball cards, of players from Boston, Indianapolis, New York, Philadelphia, Detroits, by Rafael Tuck & Sons (R&S) Baseball Diecuts, mounted together.

1888   *15in (38cm) wide*

$200-250   **WHYT**

A pair of early 20thC painted cast iron baseball player andirons, stamped 'R.B.S.', billet bars replaced.

19.25in (49cm) high

$5,500-6,000   **POOK**

A Michael Jordan signed Nike Air Jordan basketball shoe, mounted in an acrylic case, fitted for electricity.

9in (23cm) long

$750-800   **GBA**

A croquet set on a hardwood stand, with brass mounts and with an applied metal plaque, inscribed 'J. SALTER & SONS, ALDERSHOT, ENGLAND, MADE IN ENGLAND'.

39.25in (99.5cm) high

$900-1,300   **WW**

A silver-plated basketball trophy, on a marble base.

9.5in (24cm) high

$200-250   **GBA**

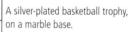

A CLOSER LOOK AT A RACING SUBSCRIBERS TICKET

This is a silver Subscribers Ticket to the Liverpool racecourse. These entitled the bearer to free admission, and would have been issued in return for financial contributions to building a racecourse.

The reverse is marked 'SUBSCRIBERS TICKET / THE EARL OF SEFTON'.

A Doncaster silver ticket, showing the grandstand, backstamped '125', maker's stamp 'WC'.

Doncaster is one of the oldest established centers for horse racing in Britain. There are records of regular race meetings being held there in the 16thC and a racecourse was marked out as far back as 1614. By the 1760s the meetings were increasing in importance and in 1776 the St Leger, the world's oldest classic horse race, was first run.

It is intricately engraved. The front depicts three horses cantering past the grandstand.

It belonged to William Molyneux, 2nd Earl of Sefton, Whig MP for Droitwich and later Baron Sefton of Croxteth, an enthusiastic sportsman who leased land to help establish what is now Aintree racecourse.

A Liverpool silver Subscribers Ticket.

A Staffordshire pottery plate, commemorating the jockey Fred Archer, from the Wallis Gimson and Co. Portrait Series, registered design no.41050.

c1886   *9.5in (24cm) diam*

$250-350   **GBA**

2in (5.5cm) high 0.41oz

$2,000-2,500   **DNW**

$1,000-1,300   **DNW**

1.5in (4cm) diam 0.85oz

QUICK REFERENCE - TAXIDERMY

- Stuffed and mounted animals were commonly displayed in homes from the mid-Victorian to the Edwardian eras, typically in glazed wooden cases, decorated with a naturalistic background. Taxidermy began to go out of fashion in the 1930s and, by the 1970s, had mostly died out.
- There has been a renewed interest in taxidermy in the 21stC, both in old and newly created examples. Part of this is driven by a rise in 'eclectic' interests and by the new tastes of interior decorators. This means the visual appeal and condition of a piece is now key.
- The type, species and size of animal, as well as how it has been stuffed and mounted, all affects the value. Realistic, detailed animals and scenes are preferable. Pieces by well-known taxidermists, such as Peter Spicer, John Cooper and Rowland Ward, can often be valuable. Domestic animals or common wild animals, such as pheasants or geese, are common and tend to fetch lower prices. More exotic animals, such as polar bears, tigers or giraffes, are rarer and can be considerably more expensive.
- The sale and movement of many stuffed animals is strictly controlled, particularly those made after 1947 and those of exotic or endangered species. Buyers and sellers should familiarize themselves with the relevant national and international laws.

A Harris hawk (Parabuteo unicinctus).

21.25in (54cm) high

$400-450   CHEF

A heron, a snipe, a golden plover, a cock teal and a wigeon, by T.E. Gunn, paper trade label to the reverse.

35.75in (91cm) high

$900-1,100   CHEF

An African giant kingfisher (Megaceryle maxima), under a modern glass dome.

20in (51cm) high

$550-650   CHEF

An early 20thC brace of Cuckoos.

23.25in (59cm) wide

$400-450   CHEF

A common male ostrich (Struthio camelus).

80in (203cm) high

$1,600-2,000   TEN

A modern female snowy owl (Bubo scadiacus), with Article 10 Certificate.

24in (62cm) high

$900-1,100   BRI

An early 20thC stuffed Lady Amherst pheasant, with an ivorine plaque inscribed 'ROWLAND WARD 167 PICCADILLY'.

42.25in (107.5cm) high

$750-850   WW

TAXIDERMY

A trout, by John Cooper & Sons, case with 'Caught by J. Fred Ray in the Test Sept 1891 3lbs', internal trade label.

22.75in (58cm) wide

$1,000-1,300   SWO

An Edwardian trout, with a trade label inscribed 'PRESERVED BY J. COOPER & SONS, 28 Radnor Street, ST. LUKE'S, LONDON E. C.', case inscribed 'TROUT Caught below Fisherton Mills.Sep. 26th 1907. Weight 10lb's 9oz's. length 28 1/2in's. girth 18in's'.

The value is enhanced by a framed facsimile photograph of the fisherman who caught the fish.

35.25in (89.5cm) wide

$2,000-2,500   WW

A dace, case inscription 'Dace, Caught by J Upton, River Thames, Pangbourne, 5th July 1910 Weight 1lb 2oz'.

17.25in (44cm) wide

$1,000-1,200   SWO

A stuffed pike, case marked 'Pike caught by J. Ryall, March 1922, weight 15lbs', remnants of paper label to rear.

43.5in (110cm) long

$550-650   BELL

A brown trout, cased, with worn dated inscription, with Cooper label.

1934   *case 26.5in (67cm) long*

$900-1,000   TEN

A mirror carp, label reads 'Caught by J.S. Wilkinson, River Nene 1935'.

34in (86.5cm) long

$250-400   BRI

A Crucian carp, case with paper label inscribed 'Carp, Caught by Billy Mills, Stratford-on-Avon, 1940'.

14.25in (36cm) wide

$350-400   SWO

A baboon, snarling, on an ebonized and rugged base.

45in (114cm) long

$1,700-2,000　　　　　　　　　　　　MEA

A mid-20thC wild boar (Sus scrofa), on carved wood shield.

24.75in (63cm) long

$600-650　　　　　　　　　　　　　TEN

A late 20thC Hungarian red deer (Cervus elaphus), gold medal class.

37.5in (95cm) long

$1,700-2,000　　　　　　　　　　　TEN

QUICK REFERENCE - VAN INGEN & VAN INGEN

Van Ingen & Van Ingen were Indian taxidermists located in Mysore, South India, best known for their tiger and leopard taxidermy trophy mounts. The firm was established by Eugene Van Ingen in the 1890s. His sons later ran the business until it closed in 1999. Van Ingen & Van Ingen served the highest international nobility as well as the Maharajas of India, preserving their 'shikar' hunting trophies in lifelike poses, with great attention to detail. Examples of Van Ingen & Van Ingen taxidermy are still found today throughout the world in the form of head mounts, full mounts, flat animal rugs and rug mounts with heads attached.

An elk head and antlers, mounted with a wooden board, with a label on the back and license details.

42.25in (107cm) high

$1,700-2,000　　　　　　　　　　　LC

A mid-20thC Ibex shoulder mount, on carved wood shield.

left horn 35.5in (90cm) long

$650-800　　　　　　　　　　　　TEN

An African lioness head (Panthera leo), on an oak shield inscribed 'BAHR-EL-ZERAF August 1914'.

Provenance: Shot by the 4th Lord Raglan in Sudan, August 1914. With two photographs of the shot lioness being carried by natives.

sheild 22.75in (58cm) high

$2,000-2,500　　　　　　　　　　　LC

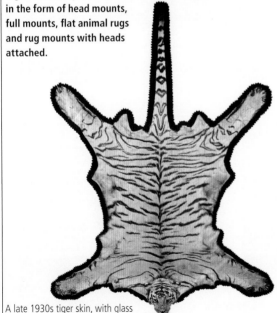

A late 1930s tiger skin, with glass eyes and an open mouth, stamped 'VAN INGEN & VAN INGEN / MYSORE', with a paper label.

101.25in (257cm) long

$4,500-5,500　　　　　　　　　　　L&T

A Bennett's Wallaby (Macropus rufogriseus).

39.25in (100cm) long

$650-800　　　　　　　　　　　　TEN

TECHNOLOGY

QUICK REFERENCE - TELEPHONES

- The telephone was first patented by Alexander Graham Bell in 1876.
- The earliest telephones were wooden wall-mounted 'coffin' telephones. With the exception of very early handmade models, these tend to be less popular with collectors today, as few remember growing up with them.
- 'Skeleton' or 'Eiffel Tower' telephones, developed by Lars Magnus Ericsson in 1890, were the world's first phones put into mainstream production, and are more popular with collectors. Later 'Pyramid' telephones used from the 1930s onward tend to fetch lower prices.

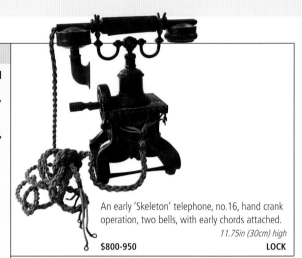

An early 'Skeleton' telephone, no.16, hand crank operation, two bells, with early chords attached.
11.75in (30cm) high

$800-950   LOCK

An Ericsson 'Skeleton' telephone, designed by Lars Magnus Ericsson.
1892   *11.5in (29.5cm) high*

$750-850   SWO

A late 19thC to early 20thC Ericsson 'Eiffel Tower' or 'Skeleton' cradle telephone, on a shaped cast iron base above twin bells.
11.5in (29.5cm) high

$550-650   FLD

A mid-20thC Mickey Mouse telephone, Walt Disney productions, marked 'EET 78/1' to base, untested.
14.5in (37cm) high

$80-100   LOCK

A telephone box coin-operated A and B button machine, with Bakelite telephone, advertising Christmas Greetings Telegrams and Emergency Calls, modern fitting and two keys.
25.5in (65cm) high

$650-800   DA&H

A late 20thC replica of vintage GPO green telephone, 300 series with base drawer.
base 7in (18cm) wide

$250-350   KEY

A Bakelite EKCO A.D 64 radio, by Serge Chermayeff.

Bakelite was developed by the Belgian-American chemist Leo Baekeland (1863-1944) in Yonkers, New York, in 1907. Marketed as the 'material of a thousand uses', Bakelite was a type of resin that set hard on heating and could be molded under pressure into complex shapes. Its low cost and versatility prompted its success. Bakelite was the first modeled plastic to be used in radios and was commonly used throughout the 1930s.

introduced 1933   *15.75in (40cm) high*

$150-200   **FLD**

An Art Deco Bakelite EKCO A.D 76 radio, by Wells Coates, some damage.

introduced 1935   16.25in (41cm) high

$400-450   **FLD**

A Bakelite Philco 444 'People's Set' radio.

introduced 1936   16.25in (41cm) high

$150-200   **FLD**

A Modernist Fada 1000 amber catalin radio, bullet form, paper labels to base.

10.25in (26cm) wide

$550-650   **WW**

An Art Deco Philips Pancake speaker, by Louis Kalff, with two Bakelite concave discs, unmarked, bearing remnants of a gold sticker to the reverse, some damage.

17in (43cm) high

$160-220   **FLD**

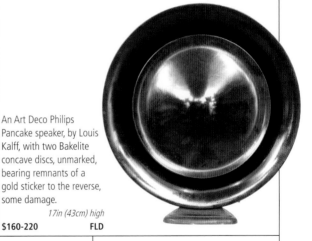

A 1920s-30s 'Underwood Noiseless Portable' typewriter, manufactured by John T. Underwood, NY, USA, with Swedish keyboard, in original transport box.

12in (30.5cm) wide

$250-300   **QU**

An early 20thC American cash register, by The National Cash Register Company, the chromium-plated case embossed with Art Nouveau motifs, size 37.5-DD, serial no.547278.

17.25in (43.5cm) high

$450-550   **DA&H**

A Curta Calculator, Type II, no.534529, with gray barrel, in plastic case, in original box.

$1,000-1,200   **TEN**

TEDDY BEARS

QUICK REFERENCE - STEIFF BEARS

- Steiff was founded by Margarete Steiff (1847-1909) in Giengen, south Germany, in 1880. Margarete Steiff suffered from poliomyelitis and used a wheelchair for the majority of her life. Despite constant pain in her right hand, she completed her training as a seamstress and went on to found what remains one of the world's most successful soft toy companies.
- Margarete's nephew Richard Steiff (1877-1939) joined the company in 1897. In 1902 he designed his 'Steiff Bär 55 PB', the first soft toy bear with jointed arms and legs. Over 3,000 bears were sold at the first trade fair, and Steiff's new 'Teddy' bear was an international success. The name 'Teddy' bear supposedly comes from an incident on a 1902 hunting trip, where president Theodore 'Teddy' Roosevelt refused to kill an injured bear tied to a tree.
- Although the market has softened in recent years, early 20thC Steiff bears can sell for high prices, and modern limited edition bears tend to fetch good prices. Materials, color, form and labels can all be used to identify and accurately date bears. Check for the distinctive 'Button-in-Ear' trademark, which Steiff used from 1904 to distinguish its bears from those of its rivals.
- Condition is always important. Damaged bears can usually be restored by professionals, but tears, stains, replaced pads or worn fur can all reduce value.

A Steiff original apricot mohair teddy bear, with shoebutton eyes, stitched nose, center seam, with major hair loss, one pad redone, three repaired.

16in (40.5cm) high

$550-650   **BER**

A padless Steiff peach teddy bear, with block-printed trailing to button, some thinning on stomach.

8in (20.5cm) high

$1,000-1,200   **BER**

A 1950s Steiff white plush mohair teddy bear.

18in (45.5cm) high

$650-800   **BER**

An apricot Steiff teddy bear, with original eyes and nose, one paw pad replaced.

c1908   *10in (25.5cm) high*

$1,000-1,200   **BER**

A Steiff teddy bear.

c1910-20

$1,300-2,000   **MITC**

A golden Steiff teddy bear, with glass eyes and button with remnants of red tag, remnants of original nose, missing stuffing and right hand pad.

c1920   *24in (61cm) high*

$1,800-2,200   **BER**

A blond mohair Steiff 'Dickie' teddy bear, glass eyes, light brown stitched nose, working squeaker, velvet pads, stomach and back showing bare spots.

10in (25.5cm) high

$1,300-2,000   **BER**

A CLOSER LOOK AT A STEIFF BEAR

This bear is made from plush mohair of cream coloring, with a red and black ribbon around his neck.

He is an early bear and in near mint condition, which increases the value.

He has a detailed face, with shoebutton eyes and a stitched nose and mouth.

He has a blank Steiff button in his ear and the owner's initials stitched onto each paw.

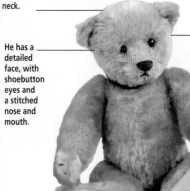

A Steiff teddy bear, with original pads.

c1907   *12in (30.5cm) high*

$1,200-1,500   **BER**

A Steiff mohair teddy bear, '1920 Classic Teddy Bear', with golden stud in ear, internal growler, moveable limbs and felt paw pads.

In the 1990 and 2000s, Steiff produced several limited edition bears that were replicas of older bears. Although still collectible, these should not be confused with the originals. Check the labels and inspect the bears carefully. Original bears tend to have a distinctive smell in comparison to newer bears.

13.5in (34cm) high

$80-100   **LOCK**

A boxed limited edition Steiff teddy bear, 'Teddy Boy 1905, Hellblond 50', no.2712 of 6000 produced, in its box, with certificate.

1998   *18in (46cm) high*

$130-200   **LC**

A Steiff olive-color mohair teddy bear, '1907 Classic teddy Bear', with golden stud in ear, internal growler, moveable limbs and felt paw pads.

13.5in (34cm) high

$60-80   **LOCK**

A boxed limited edition Steiff teddy bear, 'Bar 55 LB 1902', no.3072 of 7000 produced, in its box, with certificate.

21in (53cm) high

$130-200   **LC**

A Steiff 'Cinnamon, The £110,000 Bear', no.663864, retailed by Danbury Mint, with numbered tag to ear, no.174 of a limited edition of 1994, with Steiff certificate and cinnamon velvet Steiff dust bag.

2010   *18in (46cm) high*

$100-130   **APAR**

A limited edition Steiff bear on wheels, 'Bar auf Radern 1921', no.520 of 1500 produced, with a growler, in its box, with certificate.

17.5in (44cm) high

$150-250   **LC**

A teddy bear on wheels, possibly Steiff, plush mohair, original collar.

10in (25.5cm) high

$550-600   **BER**

An early 20thC Steiff mohair elephant, with jointed arms and legs, with a plain button, boot button eyes, black stitched claws.

This has a handwritten stitched label to the reverse, reading 'Jim Ingilby', a relation of the Ingilby baronets of Ripley Castle in North Yorkshire.

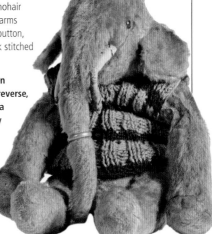

A Steiff 'Four-in-hand Beer Coach', no.232 of a limited edition of 500, on original beech base with plaque and perspex cover, certificate and instructions.

base 37in (94cm) wide

$450-550   **DA&H**

1904-05   *16.25in (41cm) high*

$1,500-2,000   **TEN**

A 1950s Chiltern 'Hugmee' blond plush teddy bear, with plastic nose.

16.25in (41cm) high

$250-350   FLD

A Farnell white plush teddy bear, with glass eyes, black stitched nose, pronounced hump, pads and mohair.

London manufacturer J.K. Farnell produced the first British teddy bear in 1906 and soon became one of the leading teddy bear manufacturers, patenting its 'Alpha TM' bear in 1925. J.K. Farnell's teddy bears were expensive at the time due to the high quality of the material used.

22in (56cm) high

$300-400   BER

A 1930s English golden mohair teddy bear, probably Farnell 'Alpha', with glass eyes, swivel neck, jointed at shoulders and hips with stitched claws and rexine pads, pads worn.

20in (51cm) high

$200-250   C&T

An Ideal golden mohair straw-filled teddy bear, with boot button eyes, stitched nose and mouth and swivel head, jointed at shoulders and hips and with felt paw pads, eyes and nose stitching replaced, pads re-covered.

12.5in (32cm) high

$120-160   C&T

An American 'Kanickerbocker' musical teddy bear, glass eyes, working music box, some hair loss.

c1920-30   *13in (33cm) high*

$150-250   BER

An Old Bexley Bears teddy bear, by Rosita Lynn, 'Tickle' teddy bear, from a limited edition of four, with movable limbs and padded paws, with swing tag certificate.

14.5in (37cm) high

$50-70   LOCK

A 1950s Pedigree blond plush teddy bear, with brown eyes, black stitched nose and felt pads.

15.75in (40cm) high

$100-130   FLD

A German Petz teddy bear, in early worsted wool, with shoebutton eyes, stitched nose and paws, made for the American market.

c1908   *14in (35.5cm) high*

$130-200   BER

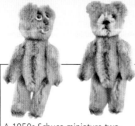

A 1950s Schuco miniature two-faced Janus teddy bear.

Schuco was founded in 1912 in Nuremberg by Heinrich Müller and Heinrich Schreyer. The company was famous for its innovative novelty and mechanical bears, including teddy bear perfume bottles, where the head was removed to reveal a glass phial within. Schuco bears were usually made of metal covered in plush, and were often miniature in size.

3.5in (9cm) high

$160-220 APAR

A Schuco plush teddy bear, with mechanical 'yes/no' action and growler.

21in (53.5cm) high

$750-850 BER

QUICK REFERENCE - STRUNZ

Wilhelm Strunz founded the Wilhelm Strunz Felt Toy Co. in Nuremberg, Germany, in 1902. It made soft toys and fabric dolls. The company soon began to copy Steiff mohair bears, first the rod-jointed 'Bar 28 PB', then other models. The firm purchased Steiff products, took them to pieces, noted the method of assembly, then used the parts to create patterns to produce exact copies. It also copied Steiff's 'Button-in-Ear' trademark. The two companies held a fierce legal dispute until 1908, when Strunz was forced to withdraw the ear button, replacing it with a stapled paper tag. From 1910, Strunz bears were marked 'Prasident', referring to Teddy Roosevelt.

An early 20thC English gold mohair jointed teddy bear, replacement pads and later-stitched eyes, somewhat threadbare, a few holes and repairs.

26.5in (67cm) high

$120-130 DW

A 1940s English fully-jointed bear, in blond mohair.

28.75in (73cm) high

$60-80 WHP

A Strunz Rod teddy bear, with shoebutton eyes, leather pads and stitched nose, copied from the Steiff Rod teddy bears, eyes possibly replaced.

20in (51cm) high

$2,500-3,500 BER

A blond baby teddy bear, with stitched nose, pads and lush.

c1950 *13in (33cm) high*

$400-450 BER

A mid-20thC musical teddy bear, with glass eyes, hand-stitched snout, plush golden fur, with a winding key.

17.75in (45cm) high

$80-100 BELL

A French pink cotton plush teddy bear, with boot button eyes, stitched nose and mouth and cupped ears, swivel head, jointed at arms and legs, with stitched claws and cream pads.

19in (48.5cm) high

$90-110 C&T

A 1920s West German tinplate Arnold 'TIN LIZZY' remote controlled car, in original box.

9.5in (24cm) wide

$350-400 HW

A Bing tinplate clockwork liner, single small funnel with fixed key, some paint loss, both masts missing.

7in (18cm) long

$200-250 W&W

An early 20thC Burnett tinplate clockwork pram, pushed by woman with walking action, stamped 'Burnett Limited, London, Made in England', minor scratches, chips and wear to the enamel overall, the clockwork motor winds and unwinds working the front wheel.

Burnett was set up in London in 1914, at a time when the huge dominance of German-made tinplate toys was clearly going to disappear. It appears to have sub-contracted the manufacturing of its designs to a Mansfield company. Burnett went out of business at the start of the World War II, Chad Valley taking over its operation in 1939.

5.5in (14cm) wide

$1,600-2,000 PW

QUICK REFERENCE - BING

- In c1863-64 brothers Ignaz and Adolf Bing founded Bing in Nuremberg, Germany.
- By the early 20thC, Bing had become one of the largest toy companies in the world, with over 5,000 employees. It produced teddy bears, tinplate toys and model trains (see page 387).
- Toys were made of tin-plated steel ('tinplate'), a malleable material that could be stamped or printed with designs. Germany was the global center for tinplate toy production in the 19thC and early 20thC.
- World War I crippled Bing's export market. The death of Ignaz Bing in 1918 and the economic depression of the late 1920s caused further disruption. The company was dissolved in 1933.

A Bing rear entrance Tonneau car, lacking clockwork motor.

10.5in (27cm) long

$1,500-2,000 SWO

A CIJ Alfa Romeo P2 tinplate light green racing car, front axle broken off.

$6,500-8,000 BRI

A 1920s German tinplate penny toy 'GENERAL' double decker bus, possibly by Fischer, with 'GENERAL' to sides, and 'NS80' to engine cover sides.

4.5in (11.5cm) long

$200-250 W&W

A Gunthermann EHN tinplate and clockwork musical clowns, with fixed key operation and an on and off lever, in working order.

$90-120 LSK

A Hausser tinplate horse-drawn field ambulance, comprising a two-horse team and rider, tinplate ambulance with two riders, canvas screens, two-man stretcher party and wounded man.

$250-350 W&W

A late 1950s German JNF large 1:24-scale tinplate Mercedes Benz 300, a late friction-powered example, with Tarleton-style seats, fitted with plated parts, Ackermann steering, tinplate wheels and rubber tires.

$150-200   W&W

An early 20thC Lehmann tinplate zig-zag wagon, patent USA 2 January 1906.

5in (13cm) diam

$350-400   TRI

A Lehmann tinplate clockwork novelty toy, 'THE PERFORMING SEA-LION', in original box, some wear to box, wear and losses to tail.

7.5in (19cm) long

$550-650   FELL

A CLOSER LOOK AT A MARKLIN BOAT

This is a 1930s tinplate 'Put-Put'-style steam powered boat, in very good condition.

It is beautifully detailed with the hull in two-stone gray, with a light brown deck, and superstructure with cream sides.

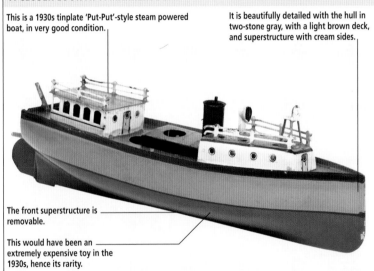

The front superstructure is removable.

This would have been an extremely expensive toy in the 1930s, hence its rarity.

A Marklin boat, with engine vent, crows-nest and railings, single small funnel painted black, support for jack flag to aft is missing, two exhaust vents and rudder, stamped 'MARKLIN GERMANY'.

10.25in (26cm) long

$19,000-21,000   W&W

A Marx Merrymakers tinplate mouse band.

10.25in (26cm) wide

$750-850   CHOR

A Minimodels tinplate and clockwork model of the Railton land speed record car, with 'John Cobb' signature transfer, with key, in original box.

$250-350   LSK

A rare late 1930s tinplate Minic Scale Model Series clockwork Rolls Tourer (35M), the clockwork motor in working order, in a rare box.

$1,000-1,200   W&W

A German OROBR tinplate and clockwork limousine, with chauffeur, permanent fixed key, in working order.

$650-800   LSK

A Schuco tinplate wind-up motorbike racer, with red framed bike, yellow overalls and a white six vest.

$100-130   LOC

A rare Shackleton model, 'DAVID BROWN Trackmaster 30' crawler tractor, a heavy die-cast and tinplate wind-up, box reading 'Constructional Model Mechanically Driven', painted red, in working order, weak spring mechanism, head lights missing, in a well-worn and damaged box.

This is believed to be one of only 50 produced.

$2,000-2,500   W&W

A scarce early Sutcliffe tinplate clockwork naval ship, 'GRENVILLE MODEL DESTROYER', in early box, some wear overall, clockwork motor in working order.

12.5in (32cm) long

$550-650   W&W

A 1950s Technofix German 'Cable Car' toy, with tinplate base with 'mountain' pressing attached to one end, with clockwork mechanism to two cable cars and with two cars that run down the mountain and into a tunnel where they are lifted to re-run the route, in original box.

$120-160   W&W

A German Tipp & Co. tinplate six wheel tipper delivery lorry, with driver, fixed single key mechanism in working order, number plate '10962', requires restoration.

$80-100   LSK

A scarce late 1920s to early 1930s German Tipp & Co. tinplate clockwork penny toy petrol tank wagon, 'SHELL MOTOR SPIRIT' livery, clockwork motor in weak working order.

4in (10cm) long

$100-120   W&W

A CLOSER LOOK AT A 'FUHRER WAGON'

This is a rare mid-1930s car, fitted with black rubber tires.

This tinplate clockwork toy is painted in black with Ackermann steering.

It is complete with composition Elastolin/Lineol Hitler with driver.

The condition is good for its age.

A Tipp & Co. 'Fuhrer Wagen', German Mercedes-Benz open topped Hitler's Staff Car, with '11A=19357' registration numbers.

$1,000-1,200   W&W

A Chinese tinplate and clockwork MS857 tractor and driver, with original key in all card box.

$90-100   LSK

QUICK REFERENCE - CORGI TOYS

- In 1956, the Mettoy company launched a range of diecast models, in part inspired by the success of Dinky Supertoys (see pages 369-370). Diecast toys are made from a metal alloy that can be cast in a mold, also known as a die.

- Corgi cars were more realistic than Dinky cars, with clear windows, detailed interiors, 'Glidamatic' suspension and opening doors and trunks.

- Corgi produced many models in the 1960s and 1970s inspired by popular TV programs and films, including Chitty-Chitty Bang Bang, James Bond and Batman. These are often highly sought-after by collectors. One of Corgi's best-known models is James Bond's Aston Martin DB5, first produced in 1965.

- Unusual colors increase price, as do unusual combinations of wheel, interior and body colors.

- Condition is important for collectors of Corgi cars. Mint boxed examples tend to fetch the highest prices.

A near mint Corgi Toys 'CHEVROLET CORVETTE STINGRAY', no.310, in metallic silver, with lemon interior and wire wheels.

$200-250   LSK

A mint Corgi Toys 'CHEVROLET CORVETTE STINGRAY', no.300, with golden jacks and take-off wheels.

$150-200   LSK

A Corgi Toys 'ASTON MARTIN D.B.4', no.218, in original box.

$100-120   LOCK

A near mint Corgi Toys '1968 Winter Olympics CITROEN SAFARI', no.499, with yellow roof-rack, two skis, two poles with toboggan, both figures apparent, in original window box with header card, with instruction sheet.

$350-400   LSK

A Corgi Toys 'FERRARI 206 DINO SPORT', no.344, with racing no.'23', in original window box.

$80-100   LSK

A Corgi Toys 'FORD THUNDERBIRD', no.214S, in original box.

$150-200   BRI

A near mint Corgi Toys 'FORD CORTINA GXL', no.313, no front number plate, with figure, right hand drive version, whizzwheels version, in original window box, window pierced.

$150-200   LSK

A near mint Corgi Toys 'BRM FORMULA 1 GRAND PRIX RACING CAR', no.152S, racing no.7, in original box, with leaflet and adhesive sheets.

$160-220   LSK

A Corgi Toys 'E TYPE JAGUAR' competition model, no.312, racing no.2, with driver, in original box.

$120-160   W&W

A Corgi Toys 'LAND ROVER 109 WB', no.438, in original box.
$120-160
LSK

A Corgi Toys 'LINCOLN CONTINENTAL EXECUTIVE LIMOUSINE', no.262, with unused illuminating screen sheet.
$250-350
LSK

A Corgi Toys Rambler 'MARTIN SPORTS FASTBACK', no.263, in original box.
$100-130
LSK

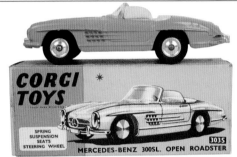

A Corgi Toys blue 'MERCEDES BENZ 300SL ROADSTER', no.303S, in original box.
$150-200
BRI

A Corgi Toys 'MERCEDES BENZ 600 PULLMAN', no.247, windscreen wipers, in original box, with leaflet.
$130-150
LSK

A Corgi Toys red 'MONTE CARLO B.M.C. MINI COOPER S', no.339, with roof rack with two wheels, in original box.
$150-200
LOCK

A Corgi Toys 'SIMCA 1000' competition model, no.315, racing no.8, with minor fading to stripes, in original box.
$100-120
W&W

A Corgi Toys 'STUDEBAKER GOLDEN HAWK', no.211, in original box.
$150-200
LSK

A Corgi Toys 'DRIVING SCHOOL TRIUMPH ACCLAIM', no.278, in original window box with header card.
$80-100
LSK

A Corgi Toys Bedford 'UTILECORN' Ambulance, no.412, first type with split windows in cream, 'AMBULANCE' within banner to sides, in early box, minor wear.
$130-200   W&W

A CLOSER LOOK AT A CORGI GIFT SET

This Gift Set 11 is desirable to collectors.

It has the yellow and metallic blue body with matching trailer, with flat spun hubs.

It is in the original all card box with sliding tray interior.

It also has a pack of adhesive decals, which adds to its desirability.

A Corgi Toys 'E.R.F. DROPSIDE LORRY AND PLATFORM TRAILER', with cement and plank loads.
$650-800   LSK

A Corgi Major Series diecast model of a 'DECCA AIRFIELD RADAR', no.1106, in original box.

$100-130   LOC

A Corgi Toys, 'FORWARD CONTROL JEEP', no.470, in original Corgi Toys window box.

$80-100   LSK

A Corgi Toys 'MASSEY FERGUSON 165 TRACTOR AND SHOVEL', no.69, with driver, in original box, with original packing piece.
$130-200   LSK

A Corgi Toys 'VOLKSWAGEN KOMBI', no.434, in original box.
$250-300   LSK

A Corgi Toys 'RICE'S BEAUFORT DOUBLE HORSE BOX', no.112, with foal figure, in original box.
$50-70   LSK

A Corgi Toys, 'LONDON TRANSPORT ROUTEMASTER BUS', no.468, spun hubs with 'Church's Shoes' livery, in original box.
$350-400 LSK

A Corgi Toys 'CORGI CARS' Ford articulated car transporter, no.1138, with 'Corgi Cars' to sides, in original sliding tray diorama box, with one packing piece.
$200-250 LSK

A Corgi Toys 'DAKTARI' set, gift set no.7, with Land Rover in green and black Zebra Stripe, five figures, in original window box, Whizzwheels version.
$150-200 LSK

A Corgi Toys London Transport Set, gift set no.11, comprising 'Austin Taxi', no.418, 'Outspun' Routemaster Bus', no.468, a policeman on a stand, and a 'Morris Mini-Minor', no.226, in original box.
$250-350 LSK

A Corgi Toys 'CONSTRUCTOR SET', gift set no.24, comprising two Commer 3/4 ton cab and chassis units, four interchangeable bodies, milkman figure, brown plastic bench, in original picture box with lift-off lid and polystyrene tray.
$90-110 LSK

A Corgi Toys 'Mini 1000 Camping Set', gift set no.38, with cream mini with red interior, two figures, plastic tent and BBQ, in original window box, with inner display stand.
$200-250 LSK

A Corgi Toys Fairground Attractions Boxed Group, including no.CC20401 'The South Down Gallopers', no.CC07041 'Land Rover and Trailer', no.CC20303 'Garrett Showmans Tractor', no.CC10802 'Foden S21 8 Wheel Platform Lorry and Coldcast Box', no.CC10303 'AEC Ergomatic Pole Truck', no.CC20103 'Fowler Showmans Locomotive', no.CC55104 'Diamond T Ballast Generator and Trailer', no.CC10705 'Scammell Highwayman Ballast and Caravan', and a Boxed Corgi Classics 'Billy Smart's Scammell Highwayman and Trailers'.
$400-450 LSK

QUICK REFERENCE - DINKY TOYS

- Dinky toys began in 1931 as 'Model Miniatures', designed to accompany the Hornby railway sets. The majority of models were produced in a scale of 1:48.
- The first car, no.23a, was produced in 1934. In the same year, the range was renamed 'Dinky'.
- After World War II, Dinky launched a new range of lorries, their 'Supertoys' series. Several vans were added to the range from 1950 onward. Supertoys were sold in blue and white horizontally striped boxes.
- Supertoys are considered very desirable by many diecast collectors, with rare variations and models fetching especially high prices. Pre-war Dinky models are also highly sought after.
- Dinky ceased production in the 1970s.

A Dinky Supertoys 'FODEN FLAT TRUCK', no.502, with very light chipping, in early utility-style box, with minor wear and corner tape repair.

$400-450   W&W

A Dinky Supertoys 'FODEN FLAT TRUCK WITH TAILBOARD', no.903, second type cab, some wear on hard edges, chips on cab roof.

$120-130   LSK

A Dinky Toys 'FODEN FLAT TRUCK', no.502, first type denim blue cab, in original buff labelled box, some chips and scratches.

$350-400   LSK

A Dinky 'FODEN FLAT TRUCK WITH CHAINS', no.905, second type cab, in original Supertoys box.

$250-300   LSK

A Dinky Foden 'FLAT TRUCK WITH CHAINS', no.905, second type cab, in original Supertoys box, with some chipping.

$200-250   LSK

A Dinky Foden 'DIESEL 8-WHEEL WAGON', no.901, second type cab, in original Supertoys box, some areas of chipping.

$150-200   LSK

A Dinky Supertoys 'FODEN DIESEL 8-WHEEL WAGON', no.501, with some light chipping, in early utility-style box, with some minor wear.

$250-350   W&W

A Dinky Toys 'FODEN 14-TON REGENT TANKER', no.942, playworn example in original Supertoys box.

$180-220   LSK

A Dinky Toys 'FODEN 14 TON MOBILGAS TANKER', no.941, in original Supertoys box, some playwear.

$200-250   LSK

A CLOSER LOOK AT A DINKY SUPERTOYS GUY VAN

This is a mint scarce Dinky Supertoys Guy Van.

It has the Tomato Ketchup bottle and 'Heinz 57 Varieties' to both sides.

A Dinky Toys 'BIG BEDFORD HEINZ VAN', no.923, 'HEINZ 57 VARIETIES' livery with Baked Beans can transfer, in original Supertoys box, some chipping to paint work.
$350-400   LSK

It is in the early blue striped box without illustration.

Although the box has some wear and tape damage, this is a rare desirable van and highly collectible.

A Dinky van, no.920, with red cab and chassis, yellow body and wheels.

This is much rarer than the van 'Big Bedford Heinz Van' (see top right) and is also in mint condition.
$1,600-2,000   W&W

A Dinky Toys 'PRESSURE REFUELLER', no.642, RAF blue body and hubs, in original Supertoys box, some playwear.
$100-130   LSK

A Dinky Toys 'LEYLAND OCTOPUS WAGON', no.934, in original Supertoys box.
$150-200   LSK

A Dinky Toys 'SLUMBERLAND MATTRESSES GUY VAN', no.514, in original box, some surface chips to model.
$300-350   LSK

A Dinky Supertoys 'B.B.C T.V ROVING EYE VEHICLE', no.968, with camera and operator on roof, and plastic aerial.
$160-200   LSK

A Dinky Toys 'EVER READY GUY VAN', no.918, second type cab, with spare wheel and 'EVER READY' livery, in original Supertoys box.
$450-550   LSK

A Dinky Toys 'BIG BEDFORD LORRY', no.922, with minor playwear, in original Supertoys box.
$250-300   LSK

A Dinky Supertoys 'LEYLAND COMET LORRY', no.531, a few very light chips, in original box, with only minor wear and marking.
$130-200   W&W

QUICK REFERENCE - FRENCH DINKY

- French Dinky began in Bobigny, Paris, in the early 1930s.
- At first, model trains and cars were produced in line with its British parent company, but French Dinky's range became increasingly different, focusing on French commercial vehicles, aircraft and cars by makers such as Citroen, Peugeot and Renault.
- It continued production into the 1970s after Dinky had declined in England. Some of its most prized models, such as the 'Citroen Presidentielle', were produced between 1969 and 1972. Production was transferred to the Pilen factory in Spain in 1977 and the company closed in 1981.

A French Dinky Toys 'CITROEN 2CV MODELE 61', no.558, in original box.
$150-200   LSK

A rare French Dinky 'Peugeot 402 TAXI 24L', taxi meter to front passenger side, with a black painted tinplate base.
$260-300   W&W

A French Dinky Toys 'CITROEN DS19', no.530, in original box, with viewer hole.
$150-200   LSK

A French Dinky Toys 'MASERATI SPORT 2000', no.22a, white figure driver, in original box.
$200-250   LSK

A French Dinky 'CAMIONNETTE CITROEN 1200 Kg' H van, no.25CG, in cream C.H.Gervais livery, minor wear to box.
$130-160   W&W

A French Dinky 'CAMIONNETTE CITROEN 1200 Kg' H van, no.561, with 'CIBIE' transfers, with sliding door, in original worn box.
$250-300   LSK

A French Dinky Toys 'CAMION UNIC BENNE MARREL' skip Lorry, no.38A, unglazed, box with base packing, areas of paint loss and paint flaking to rear.
$120-150   LSK

A French Dinky Toys 'ROULEAU COMPRESSEUR RICHIER', no.90A, with driver, in original box with lift-off lid.
$160-200   LSK

A French Dinky 'CAMION G.M.C. MILITAIRE DEPANNAGE' Army Recovery Truck, no.808, vehicle in mint condition, in original box with packing.
$200-250   W&W

A Dinky Toys '38 series Sunbeam Talbot', no.38b, a few chips, one retouched.
$200-250   W&W

A Dinky Toys 'AUSTIN SEVEN COUNTRYMAN', no.199, in original box.
$200-250   LSK

A Dinky Toys 'Morris Oxford' saloon, no.159, in original type 3 box with in-correct color spot.
$250-300   LSK

A Dinky Toys 'PONTIAC PARISIENNE', no.173, in original box.
$130-200   LSK

A rare Dinky Toys 'Standard Vanguard 40e', some substandard casting paintwork.
$1,600-2,000   W&W

A rare Dinky Toys 'Royal Air Mail Service Car 34a' and an 'Air Mail' post box, the post box sign present but detached, some minor wear.
$600-650   W&W

A Dublo Dinky 'ROYAL MAIL VAN', no.68, with original box.
$160-200   LSK

A Dinky Toys 'COMET WAGON WITH HINGED TAILBOARD', no.532, in original box.
$250-300   LSK

A Dinky Toys 'LYONS GUY VAN', no.514, in original box, some playwear.
$450-550   LSK

A scarce 1930s Meccano Dinky Toys 'Motor Truck no.22C,' minor wear for age.
$750-800   W&W

A Dinky Toys 'PATHE NEWS CAMERA CAR', no.281, with cameraman, in original box with packing ring.
$300-400   **LSK**

A Dublo Dinky Toys 'LAND ROVER AND HORSE TRAILER WITH HORSE', no.73, and with a tan horse.
$150-200   **LSK**

A rare 'MECANNO DINKY TOYS' set no.33, comprising 'Mechanical Horse and Five Assorted Trailers', horse in red with blue wheels, box van with 'Meccano Engineering for Boys' to sides, Flat Truck, Petrol Tank, 'ESSO' on trailer, Dust Wagon on trailer and an open wagon, in original box with yellow card insert, minor wear and light chipping.
1935-37
$1,000-1,300   **W&W**

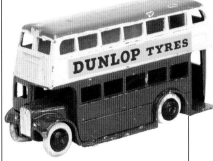

A Dinky Toys 'Gift Set No.4 RACING CARS', comprising Cooper-Bristol in green no.6, Alfa Romeo in red no.8, Ferrari in blue with yellow nose and wheels no.5, H.W.M. in light green no.7 and Maserati in red with white stripe no.9, in original display box with insert, some minor chipping.
$4,500-5,500   **W&W**

A late 1930s scarce Dinky Toys Double Deck bus, no.29C, some chipping mainly to roof.
$350-400   **W&W**

A rare Dinky Toys Caravan, no.30g, wire drawbar fitted upside down.
$300-350   **W&W**

A scarce 1930s Meccano Dinky Toys Farm Tractor, no.22e, with hook, with light wear only.
$150-200   **W&W**

A Dinky Toys 'EMPIRE FLYING BOAT', no.60R, 'CANOPUS' on body, 'G-A' and 'DHL' to wings, with gliding loop, in original box, with leaflet.
$250-350   **LSK**

QUICK REFERENCE - MATCHBOX TOYS

- The Matchbox range was introduced by Lesney Products in 1953.
- It was called 'Matchbox' because its miniature die-cast toys were originally sold in boxes similar in size to matchboxes. Cars and trucks were produced at a 1:75-scale and the toys were usually smaller than 4.5in (11.5cm) long.
- Matchbox toys were very popular with children and by 1960 Lesney was producing around 50 million Matchbox vehicles a year. The 'Yesteryear' range, aimed at adult collectors, was also successful.
- The Matchbox range struggled after the release of Mattel's small die-cast Hot Wheels range in 1968. The 'Superfast' range was introduced to compete with Hot Wheels, but Lesney went into bankruptcy in 1982. The Matchbox brand was taken over by Mattel in 1997.

A Matchbox Superfast Pre-Production Prototype model, 'Alfa Carabo', no.75, made from resin and polymers, with single sheet drawing of this model.

$550-600　　　　　　　　　　　　LSK

A Matchbox Regular Wheels Thames Trader Wreck Truck, no.13C, in original type D color picture box.

$130-200　　　　　LSK

A Matchbox Series 'Morris Minor 1000', no.46, minor wear.

$130-200　　　　　　　　　　　　W&W

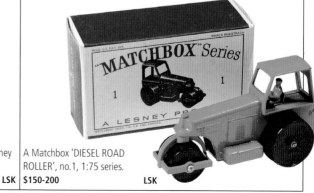

A Matchbox Superfast Prototype model of a 'Stretcher Fetcha/Delivery Van', constructed from resin and brass, with a brass back with a slide out hand operated serving hatch, unusual idea of a Matchbox Model, with original drawing of a Bread Van that probably relates to this example, all on headed Lesney Products Paper.

$200-250　　　　　　　　　　　　LSK

A Matchbox Triumph T110 motorcycle, no.4, 1-75 series, in original box.

$130-200　　　　　LSK

A Matchbox Lesney Moko '745D MASSEY HARRIS' tractor, with chimney and exhaust, some paint loss.

$200-250　　　　　　　　　　　　LSK

A Matchbox 'DIESEL ROAD ROLLER', no.1, 1:75 series.

$150-200　　　　　LSK

QUICK REFERENCE - BRITAINS

- The William Britain Company manufactured lead mechanical toys from 1845. In 1893, William Britain Jr. developed a method of hollow-casting lead die-cast toys, dramatically decreasing the cost of production of toy soldiers.
- By 1900, Britains had produced over 100 different sets of toy lead figures. These were very popular and sold especially well through Gamages department store in London.
- Although best known for its diecast lead toy soldiers, Britains also made toy cars and diecast military trucks. After World War I it created civilian figures, such as footballers, Salvation Army models and Disney characters and began its 'Home Farm' series of large pieces inspired by rural life.
- From the 1950s, Britains increased focused on plastic soldiers and the production of lead hollowcast figures ceased in 1966. The company was acquired by the Dobson Park Group in 1986 and after a series of further acquisitions is now owned by The Good Soldier LLC in Ohio.

A Britains Clockwork Series 'Fordson Major TRACTOR' and trailer set, no.139F, tractor with seated driver with a mechanical trailer with load, in original box and with divisions.

$800-950   CHOR

A rare 1950s Britains 'CIVILIAN 4-WHEELED LORRY', no.59F, with tipping rear loadbed, opening drivers door, with an original civilian driver, with 8 Britains metal milk churns, most with their lids, with light chipping only, in original box.

$550-650   W&W

A scarce Britains Model 'FARM FORDSON MAJOR TRACTOR', no.127F, complete with driver, with only light chipping, in original box.

$200-250   W&W

A Britains Mechanise Transport of the British Army 'BEETLE LORRY', no.1877, with driver, in mint condition, in original box with packing and returns slip.

$150-200   W&W

A Britains 'FINA' Petrol Pump Set, with three plastic hoses and nozzles, in original box.

$350-400   LSK

A Britains 'VOLUNTEER CORPS AMBULANCE', no.1315, with driver, missing patient and stretcher, in original box.

This is a scarce post-war issue.
$550-600   LSK

A Britains 'PONTOON SECTION ROYAL ENGINEERS', no.203, pulled by a four-horse team, two mounted with drivers, with minor wear and chipping, in original box.

$250-300   W&W

A late 1930s Britains, 'Underslung Lorry with Driver', set no.1641, with leaflet, requires restoration to front storage box, one tire missing, in original box.

$150-200   LSK

QUICK REFERENCE - BRITAINS BOXED MILITARY SETS

● The first set of toy soldiers produced by Britains in 1893 was the Mounted Lifeguards, the household cavalry of the Queen.
● These were quickly followed by further British troops, both mounted and on foot. World War I saw the introduction of foreign forces to the range.
● Foot soldiers were a standard size of 2in (5.5cm) high.
● Britains only began to label and then mark their figures after 1900, in response to the wealth of forged exact copies appearing on the market.
● Britians boxed military sets remain highly collectible today. Packaging, marks, condition and even the way the box is tied can effect a set's value.
● Early figures are the most desirable, especially those from the 1890s. Early naval figures, guardsmen, and first khaki troops from the Boer War are especially valuable. Figures made between 1938-41 are highly sought after.

A Britains 'Officers of the Gordon Highlanders', set no.437, with very minor chips only, in an early TOBA box, with some wear.

$200-250   W&W

A CLOSER LOOK AT A 'ROYAL MARINE ARTILLERY' SET

The box reads 'Per Mare, Per Terram', ('By Sea, By Land'), the motto of the Royal Marine Artillery.

The original box, although damaged and repaired, increases the value.

Despite some paint chipping, general wear and the absence of the officer's sword, this set retains a reasonable price due to its early date.

Britains' fine attention to detail in the uniform set it ahead of its competitors.

A Britains 'Royal Marine Artillery', set no.35, comprising one officer and seven marines.

c1908

$300-400   W&W

A rare Britains 'French Matelots', set no.143, comprising eight running figures, an officer with sword and seven matelots, with insert, contents have been re-tied, with a few minor chips, in original box.

1948-49

$250-350   W&W

A rare set of Britains 'Royal Air Force Personnel (Side Caps)', set no.240, eight figures in first style uniforms, two officers, plus six aircrew personnel, some light chipping to two, one head loose, one some significant paint loss, re-tied into ROAN box for display.

1940-41

$250-350   W&W

A Britains 'Indian Army Service Corps', set no.1898, comprising one British officer, four Indian soldiers, mule with handler, contents loose on replacement insert, in ROAN box with minor wear and splits to base.

1940-59

$150-200   W&W

A Britains 'Royal Air Force Color Party', set no.2171, comprising an Officer, Color bearer with standard and 2 Color Sergeants, all marching, tied into an adapted box.

This is a rare set produced in 1958 only.

1958

$750-850   W&W

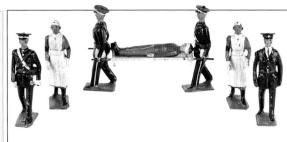

A rare set of Britains 'St. John Ambulance Stretcher Party', from set no.1426, comprising an officer, orderly, two stretcher bearers, with stretcher and casualty, plus two nurses, with light chipping and paint wear.
$450-500 W&W

A scarce Britains 'British Army Presentation Case', set no.73, comprising a Royal Horse Artillery gun team at the walk, six horses, three mounted with Officer, plus seven 17th Lancers including Officer, seven Royal Scots Greys including Officer, Regimental Trumpeter on gray horse, six Life Guards including Officer, mounted Field Marshall with binoculars, plus piper and ten Highlanders marching with Officer, the Royal Norfolk Regiment Officer and eleven other ranks with rifles at the slope, also a band of the line, eleven bandsmen and Drum Major, with a few minor chips, in display box, with some wear, and some damage to lid.
$800-950 W&W

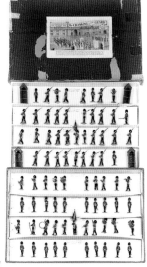

A scarce Britains 'Changing of the Guard at Buckingham Palace', set no.1555, comprising 79 Guards figures including Scots Guards, four officers, bandsmen, two standard bearers with four sentry boxes, minor chips, there is some wear to the box, damage to the lid.

This appears to be an assembled set as there are color variations to the scarlet tunics.
$450-550 W&W

A Britains 'Arabs of the Desert', set no.2046, 12 pieces including 4 mounted on horseback, 4 running and 4 marching, some minor wear and splitting, with insert, contents have been re-tied, in original box.
1950-66
$150-200 W&W

A Britains 'United States Army Band', set no.9478, comprising 25 figures marching, 24 playing instruments, complete with drum major, a few very minor chips only, in original box.
$350-400 W&W

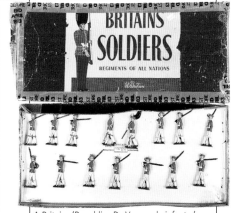

A Britains 'Republica De Venezuela infantry', from set no.2099, showing 13 marching infantrymen, plus a standard bearer and an officer with sword, with minor chips only, in original box.
$150-200 W&W

QUICK REFERENCE - SCALEXTRIC VINTAGE RACING CARS

- Scalextric cars were released in 1957 by the British company Minimodels. Amongst their first models were a C54 Lotus and a C55 Vanwall.
- Scalextric cars are slot cars, electrically powered model racing cars that are able to run on slotted tracks.
- Minimodels was sold to Line Brothers (who traded as Tri-ang) in 1958. The company is now owned and distributed by Hornby.
- Scalextric vintage cars are highly collectible. The models are usually made at a 1:32 scale and feature a range of car brands from the last sixty years.

A Scalextric C68 Aston Martin GT, French issue, in original box.
$150-200   WHP

A Scalextric C65 Alfa Romeo, racing no.5, in original box.
$120-150   WHP

A Scalextric C53 tinplate Austin Healey, in original box.
$600-650   WHP

A Scalextric C68 Aston Martin DB4 GT, converted to a 'Marshal' car.
$250-300   WHP

A Scalextric C69 Ferrari GT 250 Berlinetta, racing no.7.
$850-900   WHP

A Scalextric Offenhauser, racing no.3.
$300-400   WHP

A Scalextric C17 Lamborghini, racing no.2, USSR issue.
$650-800   WHP

A Scalextric Aston Martin DB2, tinplate clockwork model, in original box.
$120-150   WHP

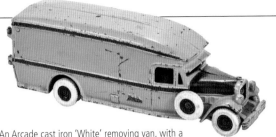

An Arcade cast iron 'White' removing van, with a nickel-plated driver and rubber-tired wheels, including side mounts.

13in (33cm) long

$2,500-3,000   POOK

QUICK REFERENCE - HUBLEY CAST IRON TOYS

- The Hubley Manufacturing Company was founded by John E. Hubley in 1894 in Lancaster, Pennsylvania, USA.
- Hubley's first success was in the production of electric toy trains, but the focus shifted in the early 20thC to cast iron toys and novelties. The company produced a popular range of motorized and horse-drawn vehicles, as well as gun caps, military figures and mechanical banks.
- Production of cast-iron toys ceased during World War II, and Hubley shifted to die-cast metal and later plastic.
- Hubley toys are highly sought after as collectibles today, especially in the USA, although condition can dramatically affect value.

A Hubley cast iron 'Popeye Patrol' motorcycle.

8.5in (21.5cm) long

$2,500-3,000   POOK

A Hubley cast iron 'Harley Davidson hillclimber' motorcycle, the driver wearing embossed Harley Davidson jacket, the tank embossed on one side '45', some loss to tank decal, sporadic paint loss to bike and driver.

8.5in (21.5cm) long

$6,500-7,500   POOK

A Hubley cast iron 'Ingersoll Rand' compressor utility truck, with a painted driver.

This is a very scarce example, probably due to the complexity of the castings and assembly.

8in (20.5cm) long

$4,000-4,500   POOK

A CLOSER LOOK AT A HUBLEY 'PENN YAN' BOAT

There was limited production of this model, said to be due to licensing issues with the Penn Yan boat Company.

It has four passengers and a driver.

This is an extremely scarce Hubley speed boat.

Even with the damage - some paint loss, flat spots on rear tires, two figures replaced, and a missing propeller - the rarity accounts for the value.

A Hubley cast iron 'Penn Yan' speed boat pull toy.

14in (35.5cm) long

$5,500-6,500   POOK

A scarce Kenton cast iron 'City Telephone' utility truck, with a painted driver, sporadic minor paint loss, distressed original tires, loose rear tire.

9.5in (24cm) high

$2,500-3,500   POOK

A Pratt & Letchworth cast iron horse drawn dray wagon, with a driver.

17in (43cm) long

$1,300-2,000   POOK

A Brooklin Models white metal model of a 1967 Ford Mustang, model no.ROD10, 1:43-scale, in original foam packed box.

$90-100   **LSK**

A Fairylite plastic and friction drive Jaguar Mark Ten, with horse box and horse figure, in original box, damage to rear tail gate, and bonnet mascot missing from car.

$250-300   **LSK**

A rare Hornby Series Modeled Miniatures Open Sports Car 22a, some light chipping.

$350-400   **W&W**

A Meccano No 2 Motor Car Constructor, with driver, lacking spare wheel cover and side lamp, with instructions, in original box in poor condition.

$850-900   **GWA**

An O.K. Toys Silver Wraith Rolls Royce and Caravan, with friction drive and plated parts, with bonnet mascot, in original box.

$250-350   **LSK**

A Spot On Models Jaguar MK 10, no.218, with luggage in suitcase.

$450-550   **LSK**

A Tekno Volkswagen Saloon 'PTT', no.819, in original box.

$600-650   **LSK**

A near mint 1950s Morestone Series scale model 'ROAD SERVICE' vehicle, Land Rover series 1 SWB, with drop down tailgate, removable metal aerial, driver and passenger with removable heads, in original box with minor wear.

$250-350   **W&W**

A Tri-ang Minic delivery van, with 'Carter Paterson' decals, in original box.

$100-120   **WHP**

A Spot-On Routemaster double-decker bus, with 'Ovaltine' adverts to sides, route no.284, with picture and information sheet, and Owners Club sheet, with minor wear, in original box.

$350-400   **W&W**

A Tri-ang Minic clockwork single-decker bus, in original box.

$100-130   **BELL**

A rare 1930s Tri-ang Minic tinplate clockwork single deck bus (52M), in London Transport deep red and stone livery, with 'Dorking' header board, clockwork motor in working order, in original box, one outer end flap missing.

$300-350   **W&W**

A Hornby Series Modeled Miniature Farm Tractor 22e, with hook, minor chips.

$600-650   **W&W**

A pair of Minichamps 1:35-scale Military Tanks, 'US M1A2SEO Abrams Iraq 2003' and 'Russian T-72M1', in original boxes.

$300-350   **LSK**

A unique child's ride-in toy car, modeled as a Mercedes SLR 722S, set with thousands of Swarovski 'Crystals', with 12V rechargeable battery, input for MP3 player, working LED lights, key start with sound effects, and remote control if the child cannot reach the pedals.

This car was commissioned several years ago as a one-off example at a cost of $24,000. Overall condition is good as this has not been used by a child but was a business 'prop' at fairs.

46in (117cm) long

$3,000-4,000   **APAR**

A mid-20thC Austin Pathfinder pedal car, originally built by disabled Welsh Miners from 1949 onward, with pressed steel body, the removable bonnet panel housing four spark plugs, and a chromed rear bumper.

61.5in (156cm) long

$4,500-5,500   **DUG**

A 1930s Lines Brothers Triang pedal car, working horn, originally sold by Libertys, Regent Street, London, with number plate 'LIB 4242', restored.

32in (83cm) long

$850-900   **LOCK**

A Daiya tinplate and battery operated 'SPACE CONQUEROR ROBOT', missing antenna, in original worn box.

Daiya was formed in Tokyo in the 1950s and was active in the toy industry until the late 1970s. It produced a range of tinplate toys including space ships, robots, cars and novelty items. Like many other Japanese companies of the time, its tin toys were often mechanical, either clockwork or battery operated.

11in (28cm) high

$600-650   LSK

An early post WWII Japanese produced tinplate clockwork U-Boat-style submarine, produced by CK Koshibe, fixed wind-up handle, rudder stamped 'FOREIGN'.

'FOREIGN' is often found on just post-war Japanese and German toys of the period.

12.5in (32cm) long

$120-150   W&W

A Nomura 'MYSTERY ACTION EMERGENCY SERVICE', 'TN Toys Japan', tinplate battery operated truck, with driver, in original box.

Nomura, founded in the 1940s, was one of Japan's largest makers of tinplate toys during the 1950s and 1960s. It was purchased by Hasbro in 1992. 'TN' stands for 'Toys Normura' and is found on many of their toys.

$250-300   LSK

A Daiya tinplate and battery operated Highway Patrol 'POLICE CAR', in original box.

$100-120   LSK

A Japanese tinplate toy, remote control smoking 'PA PA BEAR', by Marusan (SAN), battery operated, in original box.

Marusan is a Japanese model and toy company founded in 1947 and still operational today.

$35-45   LOCK

A mid-20thC Japanese tinplate clockwork toy, 'Toyland See-Saw', made by 'S Fine Toys', pat. no.31-36112.

7in (17cm) long

$60-80   LOCK

A scarce Japanese 'ramblin' Mickey Mouse' waddler, Walt Disney Enterprises, George Borgfeldt Distribution, with long wire tail, one ear replaced.

George Borgfeldt Distribution were an American company who pioneered toy licensing and acquired exclusive rights to a variety of copyrighted toys, including several lines produced in Japan. The Japanese toy industry was increased and supported by many American distributors, such as Rosko, Cragstan and George Borgfeldt, who sold Japanese toys in the USA.

c1934   *7.5in (19cm) high*

$800-950   BER

A Masudaya tinplate and battery operated Mickey Mouse Space Ship, in original box, with card insert.

Masudaya was founded in 1924 and is still operational today. It was one of the leading Japanese manufacturers of tinplate toys post-1945 and was distributed in the USA by Cragstan of New York.

$35-40   LSK

A Yonezawa Japanese tinplate battery operated 'SPACE EXPLORER', no.802, in original box.

Yonezawa was a prolific toy manufacturer in Japan in the 1950s-70s. It manufactured a range of different battery and mechanical tinplate toys and was best known for its sci-fi toys, including robots and space ships.

11.5in (29cm) high

$1,000-1,200   LOCK

A full size Punch and Judy tent, with board announcing 'Prof. Lazarus Traditional Punch and Judy', with puppets of Punch, the crocodile, the baby and a set of gallows, with carrying case and guy ropes.

$250-350 APAR

An 1890s toy theater, 'Excursions on Land & Sea: the World's Wonders, Birmingham: Joseph Walker', 32 transparent colored scenes on a paper scroll, each titled below image, mounted on two rollers turned by a wooden handle, back illuminated by a central candle.

Provenance: From the collection of Percy H. Muir. Joseph Walker applied for a US patent for his imitation show panorama in 1894. A rare survival.

7in (18cm) high

$1,000-1,200 DW

A rare 1950s 'Fish Footman SE Series' Pelham puppet, from the Pelham Puppet Alice In Wonderland range, with original box, stamped 'SE Fish' on the end of the box.

The famous 'Alice In Wonderland Fish Footman' puppet is perhaps the most sought after of the entire catalog of Pelham Puppets. Released in 1950, the puppets were one of the first fairytale ranges ever released. Alice is the most popular, but the Frog Butler and Fish Footman characters were the least sellable of the collection. Pelham factory records show that in the whole year of 1954, they sold only two Fish Footmen puppets. This is only the second Fish Footman known to come to auction.

$900-1,100 EBA

A 1950s French miniature post office, the lid lettered 'Super-Poste' and 'Transcar, Paris', in gilt, inside lid with toy bank notes and unused printed stationary, interior compartmented and with drawers, with a telephone, a metal balance, a globe, an ink blotter, ink stamps on a stand and an ink pad, bottles of ink, toy coins, and stamps.

15.5in (39.5cm) wide

$130-200 DW

A working model of a chair-o-planes funfair attraction, scratch built with wood, paper and balsawood, electrically operated.

22in (55cm) high

$150-200 LSK

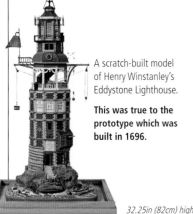

A scratch-built model of Henry Winstanley's Eddystone Lighthouse.

This was true to the prototype which was built in 1696.

32.25in (82cm) high

$450-550 TEN

A mid-20thC ventriloquist's dummy, attributed to Leonard Insull, the papier mâché head with moving eyebrows, eyes and lips.

Leonard Insull was the maker of the famous 'Archie Andrews' dummy used by ventriloquist Peter Brough in the 1950s and 60s. He was considered Britain's leading ventriloquist figure maker of the 20thC and made numerous figures for the magic shop, Davenports.

39.5in (100cm) long

$2,500-3,500 CHOR

A late 19thC French miniature sedan chair.

13.5in (34cm) high

$250-300 CHOR

TOYS & GAMES

A reproduction 'horse' velocipede, or tricycle, with polychrome painted carved wood, faux leather saddle, and wrought iron framework.

32in (81cm) high

$400-650   **BELL**

A 19thC-style painted rocking horse.

48in (122cm) long

$150-250   **ECGW**

An early 20thC rocking horse, painted dapple gray, with glass eyes, with leather tack and saddle, on a pine base.

42in (107cm) wide

$1,000-1,200   **PW**

Judith Picks

'Toffee' has been in the same family since he was made in 2000, and has rarely been ridden. His owners commissioned a number of rocking horses from Geoff Martin, to sell in the USA under the name of their family business 'The Mayflower Trading Company'. They decided to keep Toffee for the family. Geoff Martin's exquisitely-detailed rocking horses, each of which is unique, are highly sought-after. They rarely come on the market, tending to remain in the same family as heirloom pieces. Geoff Martin hand-carves only a small number of rocking horses every year in his Leicestershire workshop, each horse taking between six and eight weeks to manufacture. They are strong enough to be ridden by adults as well as children.

A mid-20thC rocking horse, dapple gray horse with a leather saddle on a pine stand.

52in (132cm) high

$1,000-1,300   **KEY**

A chestnut rocking horse, hand-crafted by Geoff Martin, Horsecraft, with glass eyes, with long mane and tail made of horsehair, original leather saddle, bridle, and martingale, with brass furniture, matching wooden swing stand with twin spiral-turned pillars and side-rails, metal rockers, stretcher with brass plaque 'The Mayflower Trading Co. (407) 957-3296'.

2000   *59.5in (151cm) long*

$1,300-2,000   **DW**

A rocking horse, painted dapple gray on pine base, small chips, scuffs and signs of use and play, some small paint touch-ups, some shrinkage cracks to the paintwork, all joints stable.

53.25in (135cm) wide

$550-650   **PW**

A late 19thC wooden painted Noah's Ark, comprising approximately 120 animals and people, within 3 plastic boxes, some damage.

18in (46cm) long

$2,500-3,000   **HAN**

A mint 'Les Soldats de Plomb Paris' Mignot set, French WW1 period hay wagon with straw load, with four horse team, two mounted with drivers, in original box.

$120-150   **W&W**

QUICK REFERENCE - CHESS

- Chess is thought to have originated in 6thC India. Several variations of the game were played in Asia before chess came to Europe in the 10thC.
- Chess as we know it today developed in Italy in the 15thC, but did not achieve mass popularity until the 19thC.
- Most sets available to collectors today are from the 19thC and 20thC. Many of these were made in China and India, although British, German and French examples are also often found.
- Collectors aim to buy complete sets, as it is very difficult to find matching replacements. Sets with extremely detailed carved pieces tend to fetch the highest value.

A 19thC Indian 'Pepys'-type ivory chess set, with elaborately carved decoration, raised on foliate decorated circular bases, kings and queens with pierced and galleried baluster knops, bishops with pierced miters, knights with arched horses heads, rooks with rusticated decoration and spire finials, the pawns with foliate decoration.

king 4.5in (11.5cm) high

$2,500-3,000 BE

A 19thC Indian Muslim-pattern ivory chess set, the pieces of domed form.

king 1.75in (4.5cm) high

$2,000-2,500 BE

A mid-19thC English bone chess set, the bases inscribed 'CS', some damage and wear.

king 3in (8cm) high

$600-650 DW

A mid-19thC incomplete French carved bone and ivory 22-piece chess set, from Dieppe, the natural side with finely carved king and queen.

king 3in (8cm) high

$800-950 DW

A late 19thC to early 20thC Jaques & Son Staunton boxwood and ebony chess set, in a mahogany box with a sliding lid, both kings stamped 'JAQUES LONDON', the rooks and knights stamped with crown mark, with a label inscribed 'THE STAUNTON CHESSMEN TWO PRIZE MEDALS AWARDED, 1862. H.S. Staunton, JAQUES & SON, LONDON'.

king 3.5in (9cm) high

$750-800 WW

A Russian wooden chess set, by Oleg Raikis, in a carved wood box with chessboard cover.

This chess set was made in 1994 for the Chess Collectors Congress in St Petersburg and was later used in the 2000 film The Luzhin Defence, directed by Marleen Gorris, based on the book by Vladimir Nabokov.

c1994 *board 14in (35.5cm) square*

$550-650 DW

An early 20thC mahogany travelling chess set, with carved bone pieces, with a rosewood and sycamore board.

8in (20.5cm) wide.

$100-130 DW

A late 19thC coromandel-cased games compendium, with a carved bone chess set, bone chequers set, folding board, bridge, painted lead horses, turned fruitwood shakers and die.

12.5in (32cm) wide

$400-550 BELL

A Victorian 9ct gold-mounted tortoiseshell games box, with enameled playing cards, the mounts hallmarked for James Deakin & Sons, Birmingham.

1894   *6.25in (16cm) wide*

$650-800   BELL

An Indian ivory and horn games box, with a cribbage board, with bone-topped dominoes with spare tiles.

                                  9.5in (24cm) long

$300-400   PW

A 19thC box of alphabet spelling tiles, comprising 130 bone alphabet tiles, both sides of each with an incised letter stained black, plus 5 complete blank tiles, in original mahogany box.

                              box 9.25in (23.5cm) wide

$1,600-2,000   DW

A rare set of cards, 'The Scripture Alphabet Embellish'd', comprising 26 vignettes, by R. Miller, 27 alphabet cards (2 duplicates), in original wooden box, some with penciled notes in a juvenile hand.

c1820   *cards 2.5in (6.5cm) high*

$3,500-4,000   DW

A rare German hand-colored lithographed pastime game, 'Der Blumengarten' ('The Flowergarden'), with standing cut-outs either folded or on wooden bases, base with inscription 'Frederick Pearson the gift of Mrs Cooper April 1841', in original box.

c1841

$1,600-2,000   DW

A late 19thC marble helter-skelter game, with helter-skelter attachment in the form of a figure, with fifty marbles.

                              8.5in (21.5cm) high

$450-550   DW

A near mint SNK Corporation 'NEOGEO POCKET COLOR', unused, boxed as issued.

$90-100   LSK

An Ideal Toy Corporation 'Tin Can Alley' game, in original box.

$40-50   LSK

A Bing Live Steam '2-2-0 Locomotive', with tender, and 30 pieces of track.
10.5in (27cm) long
$1,000-1,200   DUG

A Bing GW 4-6-0 c/w loco, 'WINDSOR CASTLE', no.460, some chips and scratches, with 6-wheel 'Great (Crest) Western' tender.
$400-450   LSK

A Bing electric LNWR 4-4-0, 'GEORGE THE FIFTH', chips and scratches, front buffer beam repainted, with 6-wheel tender, missing center pair of wheels.
$250-350   LSK

A Bing LNER c/w 0-6-0 tank loco, no.47480, some chips.
$300-350   LSK

A Bing Midland Railway freelance engine and tender, no.1000, with 2 first/third and a brake van, 4-wheel coaches.
$130-200   LSK

A Bing GI LNWR 2-4-0, lithographed 'KING GEORGE V' with '1902', small chips touched in, with 4-wheel 'LNWR' tender.
$550-600   LSK

A Bing 1921 series GWR brake third coach, small chips to roof.
$150-200   LSK

A Bing LMS bogie coach, roof repainted, bowing to acetate glazing.
$100-120   LSK

A Bing bogie Pullman car 'Minerva', acetate windows, interior replaced.
$100-120   LSK

A Bing lithographed road engine shed, requires refixing.
$90-120   LSK

TOYS & GAMES

A Bing for Bassett-Lowke 1931 series LMS brake third coach.
$120-130   LSK

A Bassett-Lowke Corgi 99014 British Railways Princess Royal class engine and tender, no.46205, 'Princess Victoria', from a limited edition of 100, with instructions.
$650-800   LSK

A Bassett-Lowke standard 0-6-0 tank engine electric, no.41611.
$400-450   LSK

A Bassett Lowke and Corgi BL99032/C LNER black class J39 goods engine and tender.
$600-650   LSK

A Bassett Lowke LNER 'Duke of York' engine and tender, electric, touching-in to paintwork and over varnishing.
$300-400   LSK

A Bassett Lowke LMS 'Duke of York' clockwork engine and tender, touching-in and overvarnished to locomotive, tender repainted.
$150-200   LSK

A Bassett-Lowke BR red and cream corridor first coach, no.3995, and third class, no.9272, blemishes and small scratches to both.
$350-400   LSK

A Marklin Continental Steam Outline 0-4-0 electric loco, with smoke deflectors, and 4-wheel tender with '889/0' on rear.
$90-120   LSK

A Marklin G1 'Bo-Bo' diesel locomotive, in DB blue, no.212-227-3.
$350-400   LSK

A Marklin ticket rack with tickets.
$300-400   LSK

QUICK REFERENCE - HORNBY

- Hornby began in 1901, when Frank Hornby (1863-1936) applied for a patent for 'Improvements in Toy or Educational Devices for Children and Young People'. He went on to found Meccano Ltd. in 1907.
- Meccano produced toy trains from 1920. These Hornby Trains were made of metal and were '0' gauge in size. They were powered first with a clockwork motor, joined by an electric range in 1925.
- Hornby Dublo, of '00' gauge, was launched in 1938. These models had diecast metal bodies and were often decorated in the liveries of the then four largest British railway companies, Great Western Railway, London, Midland and Scottish Railway, London and North Eastern Railway and Southern Railway.
- In the 1950s, Hornby began to struggle in an increasingly competitive market and was ultimately purchased in 1964 by Lines Bros., the parent company of Tri-ang railways. Trains continued to be produced as Tri-ang Hornby, renamed Hornby Railways once more in 1972.
- Hornby is now once more an independent company and still produces model trains.
- Condition strongly affects prices and collectors aim to buy boxed models. Pre-war models tend to be the most highly sought after.

A pre-war Hornby clockwork 0 Gauge train set, 'Goods Set', in original box.
$550-600   MITC

A Hornby Dublo 3234 class 8F engine and tender, no.48094, with test tag, minor paint loss.
$200-250   LSK

A Hornby Dublo 3221 'LUDLOW CASTLE' engine and tender.
$450-550   LSK

A French Hornby '2 car 20 volt SNCF' railcar.
$200-250   LSK

A pre-war Hornby Dublo EDL7 'LMS' tank engine, some corrosion marks.
$150-200   LSK

A Hornby Dublo EDL7 3-rail LNER tank engine, with guarantee.
$90-100   LSK

A Hornby SR clockwork 0-4-0 no.1 special loco, 'no.A179', with 4-wheel, no.1, special tender, chips and scratches.
1931-35
$150-200   LSK

A Hornby Dublo 3231 3-rail diesel shunter, no.D3763, two piece coupling rod.
$160-220   LSK

A Hornby Dublo 'CITY OF LIVERPOOL', no.3226, engine and tender.
$300-400   LSK

A CLOSER LOOK AT A HORNBY LOCOMOTIVE

This is a 2-rail class AL1 3300HP 'Bo-Bo' electric locomotive, E3002 (2245).

It is in blue livery with white roof and fitted with twin pantographs.

It is boxed, with paper packing, and the contents are in very good condition.

Even though the pantographs have surface rusting, it is still a desirable model.

A Hornby Dublo locomotive.
$650-800   W&W

A Hornby Railways 3.5in gauge 'Stephenson's Rocket' set, with locomotive, tender, track, instruction leaflet, funnel, appears unused, in original box with outer box.

$250-400   LSK

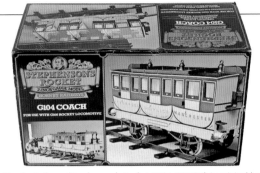

A Hornby Railways 'Stephenson's Rocket G104 COACH', in original box with polystyrene packing pieces, with transfers.

$200-250   LSK

A Hornby signal cabin, some losses to printing.

1928

$40-50   LSK

A Hornby engine shed, no.E2E, missing track, lamp and gutter ends, corrosion to roof.

1935-41

$130-200   LSK

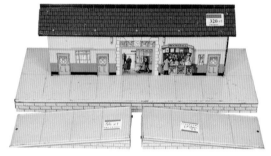

A Hornby no.3 station, some scratches and other playwear.

$40-50   LSK

A Hornby 2E 'Windsor' station, detached from platform but would refix as tabs present, no electric lights.

$70-80   LSK

A Hornby Railway Accessories, no.1 set, comprising truck with cast wheels, three trunks, small green suitcase, in a 'Meccano' box lid.

1931-33

$70-80   LSK

A Hornby signal gantry, no.2E, with green bridge lining, lighter blue bases, ladder and finials, red levers and red distant arms, with a 1934-39 water tank, no.2, with light green base and column, yellow tank with red inside.

1935-36

$130-200   LSK

QUICK REFERENCE - WRENN TRAINS

- G&R Wrenn was founded by brothers George and Richard Wrenn in 1950 in Lee Green, South London, and at first specialized in producing track for model railways. A third brother, Cedric Wrenn, joined the company in the late 1950s. In 1955, the company moved to Basildon in Essex.
- Its first line was the '00-gauge' model railway, which consisted of two- and three-rail track for '00' gauge models. Wrenn later produced two-rail track for 'TT' gauge model railways. Wrenn track was compatible with model trains from a range of other manufacturers, such as Hornby, Marklin, Rivarossi, Tri-ang or Trix.
- In 1965, Lines Brothers Ltd. (who traded as Tri-ang) bought a controlling share in Wrenn. Under their direction, Wrenn made and distributed Horby Dublo models and Tri-ang's 'TT' line, under the name 'Tri-ang Wrenn'.
- In 1972, after the collapse of Lines Brothers Ltd., Wrenn started to produce its own die-cast models as well as trackwork, aiming not at the mass toy market but primarily at collectors. By the end of 1973, Wrenn had released over 40 new '00' gauge wagons, 3 coaches and 20 locomotives. They soon produced '00' gauge, '0' gauge and 'N' gauge models.
- Wrenn was purchased by Dapol in 1992. Production continued until 2001, when the company and its resources were purchased by three avid Wrenn collectors.
- Wrenn trains tend to fetch consistenty good prices, with the majority of locomotives likely to sell for well over $250. Their high quality, detailed paintwork and compatibility with other tracks ensure higher prices and a steady market. Many models were only produced in limited numbers, which likewise raises prices.
- See Maurice Gunter, 'The Story of Wrenn - From Binns Road to Basildon', Irwell Press, 2003.

A Wrenn W2213A NE wartime black A4 4-6-2, no.4900, 'GANNET'.
$350-400   LSK

A Wrenn W2221 BR experimental light green Castle class 4-6-0, no.5023, 'BRECON CASTLE'.
$300-400   LSK

A Wrenn W2261A LMS Royal Scot 4-6-0, no.6160, 'QUEEN VICTORIA'S RIFLEMAN', ref. no.02241, packer no.1.

Only approximately 200 of this model were produced.
$550-600   LSK

A Wrenn W2262 BR Royal Scot 4-6-0, no.46110, 'GRENADIER GUARDSMAN', packer no.2.
$400-450   LSK

A Wrenn W2265AX SR Bulleid 'Spamcam' 4-6-2, no.21C155, 'FIGHTER PILOT', ref. no.11345, packer no.3.

Only approximately 250 of this model were produced.
$450-500   LSK

A Wrenn W2209A LNER green A4 4-6-2, no.4495, 'GREAT SNIPE', packer no.6.
$400-450   LSK

A Wrenn W2269 BR green Rebuilt Bulleid 4-6-2, no.34053, 'SIR KEITH PARK'; with Golden Arrow insignia, ref. no.901251, packer no.2.

Only approximately 500 of this model were produced.
$450-550   LSK

A Wrenn W2271 LNER standard class 4 2-6-4T, no.9025, ref. no.05832, packer no.3.

Only approximately 144 of this model were produced.
$550-600   LSK

A Wrenn W2274 5 pole motor LMS red Royal Scot 4-6-0, no.6125, 'LANCASHIRE WITCH', ref. no.04415, packer no.3.

Only approximately 300 of this model were produced.
$400-450   LSK

A Wrenn W2276X/5P SR Malachite green Bulleid 'Spamcam' 4-6-2, no.21C101, 'EXETER', with 5-pole motor, ref. no.06832, packer no.3.

Only approximately 185 of this model were produced.
$600-650   LSK

A Wrenn W2281 War Department Gray 8F 2-8-0, no.302, ref. no.81146, packer no.2.

Only 207 of this model were produced.
$900-1,100   LSK

A Wrenn W2285 LMS Duchess class 4-6-2, no.6221, 'QUEEN ELIZABETH', ref. no.320892, packer no.2.

Only 243 of this model were produced.
$600-650   LSK

A Wrenn W2288 Royal Scot 4-6-0, no.46159, 'THE ROYAL AIR FORCE'.

Only 112 of this model were produced.
$650-800   LSK

A rare Wrenn Railways Southern Railway Merchant Navy W2289 21C5 class 4-6-2 tender locomotive Canadian Pacific, in 'War Time' unlined black livery, in original box with packing and paperwork.
$650-800   W&W

A Wrenn W2302 Streamlined Coronation Class 4-6-2, no.6244, 'KING GEORGE VI', ref. no.01506, packer no.3.

Only approximately 200 of this model were produced.
$850-950   LSK

A Wrenn W2304 BR Duchess class 4-6-2, no.46244, 'KING GEORGE VI', with optional etched number plates for 'CITY OF LEEDS', ref. no.91312, packer no.2.

Only approximately 166 of this model were produced. The real locomotive was original 'City of Leeds' and renamed in honor of the King.
$550-650   LSK

A limited edition Wrenn W2407, SR streamline engine and tender, 'TAVISTOCK', no.189 of a limited edition of 250, with instructions.
$400-450   LSK

A limited edition Wrenn W2410 SR RI 0-6-0T, no.1047, no.49 of a limited edition of 350.
$450-550   LSK

A limited edition Wrenn W2414 BR Duchess Class 4-6-2, no.46251, 'CITY OF NOTTINGHAM', no.26 of a limited edition of 250, ref. no.90311, packer no.2.
$650-750   LSK

A limited edition Wrenn W2415 BR Rebuilt Bulleid 4-6-2, no.34052, 'LORD DOWDING', no.86 of a limited edition of 250, ref. no.90939, packer no.3.

This model was made for the 50th Anniversary of the Battle of Britain.
$550-600   LSK

A mint LGB/Aster Gauge 1 limited edition Ex-South African Railways NGG13 class 2-6-2 + 2-6-2 Garratt Locomotive, fitted with sound, model no.20922, in Schinznacher Baumschulbahn Dark Red livery as no.NG 60 'Drakensberg', in wooden presentation case, made in Japan, no.335 of a limited edition of 600, with certificate.

The Aster Hobby Co. Inc. of Yokohama, Japan, has been producing gauge 1 live steam locomotives since 1975. The majority of its model trains are made at a 1:32 scale.
$3,500-4,000   LSK

An Aster/Fulgurex Gauge 1 K4S 4-6-2 Locomotive and 8-wheel Tender 'PENSILVANNIA' no.5475, electric version, limited production in original box and card outer box.
$1,600-2,000   LSK

A kit-built brass Connoisseur Models finescale 2 rail class J71 0-6-0 LNER tank engine, no.8254, fitted with can motor.
$250-350   LSK

A metal/brass kit built O gauge electric Drummond class T9 4-4-0 tender locomotive, 'Greyhound' in Southern lined green livery, RN289, with its four-wheeled 'Watercart' bogie tender.

This model is based on one of five examples (RN285-289) that came out of the Nine Elms factory in London in 1900, the second year of production. They were put into service by LSWR, Southern and in later life by BR. Production stopped in 1901 with one, RN30120, in preservation.
$400-450   W&W

A Graham Farish 00 gauge American 4-6-4 tender locomotive, with its 12-wheeled bogie tender, RN5405, in original box.
$200-250   W&W

A late 1930s 4-6-4 tank locomotive Meccano model, in the style of a Baltic tank locomotive as operated by the pre-grouping railways in the UK, operating motion and wheels.

The model comes with period typed information stating that this model was displayed in 1938 in Hamleys, the famous London Toy Shop based in Regent Street.
39.5in (100cm) long
$650-800   W&W

A Reeves Casting's and LBSC designs 0-4-0 tank locomotive 'TICH', in 3.5in (9cm) gauge, back head fittings with hand water pump, no boiler certificate, with a folder of drawings.
$1,000-1,200   LSK

A metal/brass kit built O gauge electric Stroudley class E1 0-6-0 tank locomotive, with a 'Brighton' tool box, lamps, driver and fireman, safety valve, dome and chimney, RN32138.
$300-350   W&W

A mint Sunset Models H0 brass 'Santa Fe' 825 class 0-8-0 and tender, made in South Korea by Samhongson.
$350-400   LSK

TOYS & GAMES

QUICK REFERENCE - NAPOLEONIC PRISONER-OF-WAR

- During the Napoleonic Wars, captured French prisoners were kept in Great Britain, some for as long as ten years. They were not kept alongside other convicts, but confined to separate prison camps, some purpose-built, others adapted from dockyards, castles and unused buildings.
- They had some liberty within these prison camps and were encouraged by their captors to set up artisan guilds and produce small items to sell at the regularly held civilian markets. Many of these prisoners of war were highly skilled craftsmen, who before the wars had specialized in fields such as ivory carving, silversmithing and cabinet-making.
- Among the objects they made and sold were models of naval ships of the era. The prisoners constructed these from cattle bone, boxwood, baleen and any other materials they could buy.
- These prisoner-of-war model boats were skilfully crafted to a high level of accuracy and detail, meaning that they are highly sought after by collectors today.

An early 19thC Napoleonic French prisoner-of-war bone and baleen model for a 64-gun ship, with later rigging.

14in (35.5cm) long

$5,500-6,500   **CM**

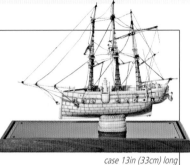

A stylized bone model of a 'Man O'War', possibly Portuguese, in later case.

c1860

$550-650

case 13in (33cm) long
CM

A model of the 'Barque Manila', with masts with yard and foot ropes, standing and running rigging, mounted on two brass supports, in glazed wooden case.

c1880   11in (28cm) long

$1,600-2,000   **CM**

A ship builder's mirror-backed model, with a typed card 'Baghdadi, 1,635 tons gross, Built 1885 by Wigham - Richardson & Co Newcastle, Owned and managed by Persian Gulf S.S Company. Length 255 feet Breadth 35 feet 1 inch Depth 17 feet', in original mahogany case.

1885   78.75in (200cm) wide

$2,500-4,000   **ECGW**

A scale waterline model, with detailed superstructure and fittings, with silver plaques engraved 'R.M.S. QUEEN MARY, CUNARD WHITE STAR LINE, LENGTH 1019' 6", SCALE 1" TO 60', MODEL BY E.E. BURRAGE'.

c1937   30in (76cm) wide

$1,600-2,000   **CM**

A precision model of the steam launch 'Bat', no.016, built by Keith N. Townsend of Annan, Dumfriesshire, 1:8-scale, the gas-fired live steam Townsend Marine Plant especially designed for 'Bat', closely resembling the original plant, the engine scale whistle and steering operated by remote control.

case 50.75in (129cm) long

$6,500-8,000   **SWO**

A 1:192 scale recruiting office waterline model of the aircraft carrier 'H.M.S. Hermes', as configured for her service as flagship during the Falklands War, the deck with three Sea King helicopters, one embarking, with soldiers, in perspex case.

52in (132cm) long

$2,000-2,500   **CM**

A radio-controlled steam-powered 1:8 scale model of the 'Windermere Launch Bat', modeled by Keith Townsend, with builder's certificate, historic data, instructions, tools and spare parts.

1987   47.5in (120.5cm) long

$7,500-8,000   **CM**

QUICK REFERENCE - BRIAN KING

Brian King has dedicated his life to model boats. He was born in the 1920s in Northampton and educated at Twickenham Junior Technical School, before completing a craft apprenticeship with Lagonda Cars. He worked for many years as a draughtsman at a gear-cutting firm and went on to teach engineering at Carshalton Technical College. Throughout his career, he has spent his free time crafting complex model ships. Since 1959, his work has earned him several gold medals and much international acclaim.

A model of the 'H.M.S Victoria', with a plaque, 'H.M.S. Victoria Launched Elswick 1897. 340ft x 70ft x 26.6ft / 29ft = 10470 ton. 2-110 Ton & 1-29 ton Guns. Mediterranean Flagship. Sunk in Collision with Camperdown of Tripoli in 1893. Model by Brian King', cased.

In 1987, this model won the Gold Medal at Naviga World Championship at Rouen and a Gold Medal and Earl Mountbatten Award at MEE.

39.5in (100cm) wide

$5,500-6,000   **ECGW**

A model of the 'H.M.S Empress of India, Royal Sovereign Class 1890', by Brian King, with an information card.

1982   *46in (117cm) wide*

$7,500-8,000   **ECGW**

A model of the 'H M Cutter Speedy', by Brian King, with a plaque, 'H M Cutter 'Speedy'. Launched Pembroke dock, 25-6-1828, length on dock 63ft 9in, burden 122 Tons Scale 1/48', cased.

This model won the Gold Medal in the 58th Model Engineer and Modelling Exhibition.

30in (76cm) wide

$1,300-2,000   **ECGW**

A model of the 'HMS Belfast 1939', with a plaque, 'H.M.S Belfast (Edinburgh Class) 32 knots 6" Cruiser. Shown after 1959 refit. Builders Harland and Wolff, Length overall 613ft 6in 1:150 model built at Weybridge by Brian King 1988 -1991', cased.

The 'HMS Belfast' was initially part of the British naval blockade against Germany, but following damage by a German mine in 1939 had to undergo extensive repairs. She returned to action in November 1942 and in June 1944 took part in Operation Overlord supporting the Normandy landings. In the 1970s she was moored in London on the River Thames and opened to the public.

1988-91   *48.75in (124cm) wide*

$7,500-8,000   **ECGW**

A model of the 'HMS Glorious', with a plaque, 'H.M.S Glorious (Pre World War II Carrier.) Shown circa 1936 length overall 786ft. displacement 23250 tons, scale 1:192, Built at Weybridge 1994/95 by Brian King', cased.

This model boat won the Gold Medal and Earl Mountbatten at MEE 1997 and the Silver Medal at Naviga at Mons 2000.

1994-95   *50in (127cm) wide*

$4,500-5,500   **ECGW**

A model of the 'HMS Tabard' submarine, with a plaque reading, 'HMS Tabard T Class submarine, length 273.5ft, launched 21/11/45, eleven 21 inch torpedo tubes, modeled by Brian King 1999', cased.

1999   *33.75in (86cm) wide*

$1,000-1,200   **ECGW**

A model of the 'USS Hornet', with a plaque 'USS Hornet (CB8) scale 1:200, launched December 1940, sunk by Japanese October 1942. Aircraft F4F Wildcat fighters, SBD Dauntless Divebombers, TBD Devastator Torpedo bombers. Kit by Trumpeter built by Brian King 2014', without case.

The USS Hornet took part in the Battle of Midway in June 1942 but was subsequently lost during the Battle of The Santa Cruz Islands four months later.

A model of the 'HMS Campanula', with a plaque, 'HMS Campanula, Flower Class Corvette scale 1:72. Kit by Revell, built by Brian King 2014', cased.

2014   *33.5in (85cm) wide*

$650-800   **ECGW**

2014   *48in (122cm) wide*

$400-550   **ECGW**

TOYS & GAMES

QUICK REFERENCE - POND YACHTS

Pond yachts have been built in Britain since as early as the 18thC. Throughout the 19thC, they were raced on the lakes of the Royal Parks of London. The London Model Yacht Club was founded in 1846, bringing with it rules, races and trophies, and other clubs soon sprung up. The oldest of these clubs that is still active today is the Model Yacht Sailing Association, which was founded in 1876 and whose members have been sailing model yachts in Kensington Gardens for nearly 150 years.

An early 20thC 'Frebelle' pond yacht, the mid-deck inscribed 'FREBELLE / S.M.Y.C.', on a wood stand.

This pond yacht, the 'Frebelle' was built in the 1930s by John (Ian) Morrison, who was serving his apprenticeship with local yacht-builders James N. Miller in St Monans. In 1940 he joined the Royal Navy where he worked as a shipwright/carpenter, before he left to continue his career as a builder of both model and fishing boats in Scotland.

52.5in (133cm) long

$250-400　　　　　　**L&T**

A large plank-on-frame Bermudian pond yacht, on a stand.

73in (187cm) high

$550-650　　　　　　**BELL**

A Bermudian cutter rigged pond yacht, with lead keel, on an oak stand.

25.5in (70cm) high

$600-650　　　　　　**BELL**

A commercial pond model of a small dinghy, on a mahogany stand.

33.5in (85cm) high

$550-650　　　　　　**BELL**

A wooden model sailing boat, with a lead keel, on a wooden stand.

25.5in (65cm) wide

$250-350　　　　　　**BELL**

A sailing model of the Marblehead class pond yacht 'Pocahontas', modeled by R. Foster, the hull and deck with access hatch to battery and rudder/sailing servos compartment, with stand, plans and remote control.

71in (180cm) long

$2,000-2,500　　　　　　**CM**

A model rowing boat, 'Badger', of stained beech, with mechanical automated oars, on a wooden stand.

28in (71.5cm) wide

$2,000-2,500　　　　　　**BELL**

A Frog flying scale model airplane, interceptor MkIV, silver body with RAF roundels to sides and outer wings, repaired, in original box, with instructions.

$80-100   LSK

A model biplane, possibly a Gypsy Moth, no.G-ATBL.

59in (150cm) wide

$350-400   BELL

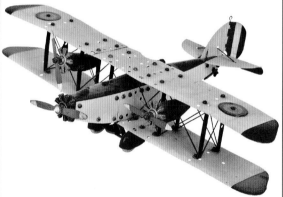

A Meccano no.1 constructors biplane, a pilot with 3 propellers and RAF roundels to wings, with a clockwork motor to power the central propeller, with key.

$200-250   LSK

A Meccano made-up construction aircraft, as 3-engine triplane airliner, unpowered.

$100-160   LSK

A late 20thC model biplane, no.NC14041.

59in (150cm) wide

$250-350   BELL

A near mint Mercury Fiat G.212 Airplane, no.402, silver with 3 propellers, with Italian Air Force markings, in original box.

$120-160   LSK

A balsa wood model of a 'F-1 Single Engine Hydroplane', kit-built, later adapted to be remote controlled, powered via motor and fitted with rudder servo.

$90-120   LSK

A limited edition 1:43-scale Bassett Lowke kit-built model of a Bell Type Traction Engine, no certificate, with plinth and packaging.
$150-200   **LSK**

A limited edition 1:43-scale Bassett Lowke kit-built model of a 1911 LGOC B Type Motor Bus, no.B340, with certificate and literature, in original packaging.
$120-150   **LSK**

A 1:43-scale Bassett Lowke kit-built model of a Burrel Type Steam Roller, with certificate and literature, no.302 of a limited edition of 2000.
$250-300   **LSK**

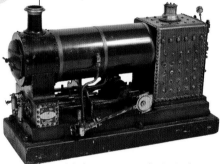

A model of a non-compound twin simple cylinder undertype steam engine, possibly by Bassett Lowke and later adapted, coal-fired example, free running example.
$1,600-2,000   **LSK**

An early Bing plated vertical steam engine, with single oscilating cylinder, sight glass, whistle, safety and filler cap, single wick spirit burner, free running.

$200-250   **LSK**

A ESL of England 'Standard' stationary steam plant, no.1540, tin housed boiler with steam take off to power a single cylinder horizontal engine, with small spoked flywheel, free running.
$60-80   **LSK**

A Fleishmann stationary steam plant, with sight glass, whistle and safety, with burner, powering a single cylinder engine fitted with dummy governor, raised on a tin base, missing the boiler chimney.
$100-130   **LSK**

A Twin Cylinder Marine steam engine, by Krick of Germany.
$150-200   **LSK**

A Mamod 'TE1A Live Steam Traction Engine', with steering rod, burner and scuttle, in original box.
$90-120   **LSK**

A 1:8-scale model of a Fowler BB1 Class Ploughing Engine, mainly constructed from Meccano components but fitted with a non-Meccano 12V motor.

30in (76cm) long.

$600-650 LSK

A 1920s Meccano Steam Engine, with spirit fired vertical boiler, with filler safety valve, lever for steam output, powering a single oscillating cylinder with opposing un-spoked fly wheel, in original box, with reproduction leaflet.

$550-650 LSK

A D.R. Mercer precision-engineered 'Burrell-Black Prince' miniature live steam road locomotive, Birmingham, with specifications, boxed, with accessories.

14.25in (36cm) long

$900-1,100 HAN

A vertical steam engine, no.10, by Stuart Turner, free running.

$250-350 LSK

A horizontal single cylinder mill engine, no.8, by Stuart Turner, the metal lagged cylinder 1in (2.5cm) bore by 1in (2.5cm) stroke, fitted eccentric driven steam valve, free running.

$250-350 LSK

A scratchbuilt stainless steel and copper coal fired boiler, requires finishing.

$250-300 LSK

A copper and wooden clad vertical steam boiler, appears scratchbuilt.

$250-350 LSK

An early 20thC single cylinder hot air engine, with secondary cylinder, free running.

$400-450 LSK

TREEN & CARVINGS

Judith Picks

As with all Black Forest carvings, this bear group is full of character! 'Black Forest' carvings were once thought to have been made in the Black Forest region of Bavaria, Germany - hence the name. In fact, many were produced in Brienz, Switzerland, over the course of the 19thC. These carvings were a key part of the town's economy and were highly popular with tourists.

The craftsmen of Brienz carved figures, furniture, boxes and clock cases from tree trunks, often linden or walnut. The most popular subjects were bears. Many carved bear figures were depicted engaging in human activities - playing musical instruments, socializing or, as in this carving, going on a hike.

A Black Forest carved wooden bear group, a large bear carrying a barometer on his back.

14in (35.5cm) long

$550-650   **JN**

A Black Forest carved bear, one hand holding a dish, the other raised with leafage-carved jardinère stand.

48in (122cm) high

$4,000-5,500   **BRI**

A 19thC Black Forest bear glass holder, carrying a basket on his back.

11in (28cm) high

$900-1,000   **JN**

A Black Forest carved wooden desk stand, with fitted ceramic glass inkwell and pen tray, the base split and glued, the ink pot chipped and damaged.

8.25in (21cm) wide

$90-110   **FELL**

A carved wooden Black Forest owl tobacco jar, with hinged head and glass eyes.

11in (28cm) high

$600-650   **JN**

A large carved wooden Black Forest fox's head tobacco jar, with hinged head and glass eyes.

13in (33cm) high

$550-650   **JN**

A Black Forest seated dog, his paw on a plaque.

19in (48.5cm) long

$650-800   **JN**

QUICK REFERENCE - MAUCHLINE WARE

- The term Mauchline ware refers to the wooden souvenirs produced in Mauchline and its surrounding towns in South West Scotland over the 19thC and early 20thC.
- Mauchline ware chiefly consisted of snuff boxes and other small wooden items, many of which were transfer-printed or carved with patterns and scenes. Pieces were chiefly made of sycamore, as its light color was a useful background for black transfers.
- Production stopped in 1933, after the last operational factory in Mauchline burnt down.
- Mauchline ware is highly collectible today.

A 19thC Mauchline ware root and pen work table snuff box, with Burn's Cottage and Craignethen Castle, unmarked.

3.5in (9cm) long

$450-550   WW

A 19thC Mauchline ware sycamore and pen work snuff box, by J. Cowan, Tarbolton, decorated with a woman with tartan shawl, entitled 'Woe Burn's Lord Gregory'.

This depicts a scene from Robert Burns' 1793 poem 'Lord Gregory'.

3in (7.5cm) long

$450-550   WW

A 19thC Mauchline ware root and pen work table snuff box, the sides with thistle decoration, with a Highland soldier at the mouth of a cave, with the motto 'We are this day in Arms for a Broken Covenant, and a Persecuted Kirk', unmarked.

3.5in (9cm) long

$650-800   WW

A 19thC Mauchline ware sycamore and pen work snuff box, by Laurie, Cumnock, with a drinking scene after Burns' picture entitled, 'It is the moon I ken her horn,' the sides with tartan decoration.

3.5in (9cm) long

$400-450   WW

A 19thC Mauchline ware sycamore and pen work snuff box, by Smith, Mauchline, with a St Bernard with a child asleep on its back, titled 'Le Chien de l'Hospice'.

3.25in (8.5cm) long

$250-350   WW

A 19thC Mauchline ware sycamore and pen work snuff box, by McKerrow, Cumnock, with a portrait of Lord Byron, surrounded by thistle decoration.

3.25in (8cm) long

$600-650   WW

A 19thC Mauchline ware sycamore and pen work snuff box, by Laurie, Cumnock, with a scene after 'The Rent Day' by Sir David Wilkie, entitled, 'Poor tenant bodies, scant o cash'.

3.25in (8cm) long

$450-550   WW

An early 19thC Mauchline ware sycamore and pen work snuff box, by Crawford, Cumnock, with a grouse shoot, with thistle decoration.

3.25in (8.5cm) long

$400-450   **WW**

A 19thC Mauchline ware sycamore and pen work snuff box, by Crichton, Cumnock, with a set of arms on a stylized thistle ground, the arms of Broun Coulston, with the motto of 'BOYD, Cumnock'.

3.25in (8.5cm) long

$450-550   **WW**

A 19thC Mauchline ware sycamore and pen work snuff box, by Crawford, Cumnock, with an Arabic script frame on a seaweed/ribbon ground.

3.25in (8cm) long

$450-550   **WW**

A 19thC Mauchline ware sycamore and pen work snuff box, by Smith, Mauchline, with a vignette of an Arabian horseman.

3.5in (9cm) diam

$350-400   **WW**

A 19thC Mauchline ware sycamore and pen work snuff box, by P. Crichton, Cumnock, with a vignette of two pointers, with black 'strung' border, with plain incurved corner.

4in (10cm) long

$200-250   **WW**

A Mauchline ware snuff box, with printed scene titled 'Come away do, what are you staring at?', 90% foil interior and stamped 'W.H. Pierce And Co, Manchester'.

2.25in (6cm) wide

$100-120   **BLEA**

A 19thC Mauchline ware puzzle box, with a scene of Skegness Pleasure Gardens, with a puzzle slide base.

3in (7.5cm) long

$50-70   **FLD**

A 19thC Mauchline ware miniature sketch pad, with Burns' Monument, marked 'Made of wood grown on the banks of the Doon', with original pencil.

2.5in (6.5cm) long

$60-70   **FLD**

A pair of 19thC Mauchline ware book boards, attached to 'The Lady of the Lake' by Walter Scott, the back board with The Hermitage, Dunkeld, the book printed Adam and Charles Black, Edinburgh.

The verse 'From the Athole Plantations, Dunkel / Should auld acquaintance be forgot, and never brought to min, should auld acquaintance be forgot, and the days o'lang syne'.

1874   *5.75in (14.5cm) high*

$130-200   **FLD**

A Victorian Mauchline ware egg cruet, decorated with transfer-printed scenes and faux eggs, the base inscribed 'MADE OF WOOD GROWN ON THE DOOR OF THE DOON'.

10.5in (26.5cm) high

$200-250　　　　　　WW

A 19thC Mauchline ware egg timer, with scenes of Clevedon Pier and Walton Castle.

3.5in (9cm) high

$40-50　　　　　　FLD

Judith Picks

The verse is from one of Scotland's favorite poems and reads 'And at his elbow, Souter Johnny, His ancient, trusty, drouthy crony; Tam lo'ed him like a vera brither, They had been fou for weeks thegither!'
And to translate, in Scots 'drouthy' is used for those who have a particular fondness for drink, particularly alcohol. Tam loved him like a very brother and they had been drunk for weeks together!

A 19thC Mauchline ware needle case, formed as a darning mushroom, with Tam O'Shanter and Souter Johnny.

4in (10cm) long

$80-100　　　　　　FLD

A 19thC Mauchline ware miniature tape measure, with St Mary's Church, Eastbourne.

1.5in (3.5cm) high

$60-80　　　　　　FLD

A 19thC Mauchline ware telescope needle case, with a scene of Morpeth.

4in (10cm) high

$90-100　　　　　　FLD

A 19thC Mauchline ware cotton spool holder, with Broxmouth House, Dunbar.

3in (7.5cm) high

$80-100　　　　　　FLD

A 19thC Mauchline ware pocket watch stand, with Carlisle Parade and Robertson Terrace, Hastings.

3.75in (9.5cm) high

$60-80　　　　　　FLD

A 19thC Mauchline ware box and cover, with National Monument to the Forefathers, Plymouth, Mass, the cover a pin cushion, with a 'J&P Coats' paper label.

3.25in (8.5cm) high

$80-100　　　　　　FLD

A 19thC Mauchline ware miniature train, locomotive with the Wallace Monument, a coal tender with the New Municipal Building Glasgow and a freight wagon marked 'Luggage Van', with the Esplanade, Redcar.

Provenance: The Alex Wilson Collection of Mauchline ware.

locomotive 7.5in (19cm) long

$550-650　　　　　　L&T

TREEN

QUICK REFERENCE - TUNBRIDGE WARE

- The term Tunbridge ware refers to turned wooden items made in Tonbridge and Tunbridge Wells in Kent, England during the 19thC.
- Tunbridge ware included boxes, toys, jewelry, furniture and more and was often sold to tourists.
- By using a variety of woods, including oak, holly, yew, sycamore and maple, Tunbridge craftsmen were able to create distinctive decorations. Tunbridge ware is known for its inlaid woodwork, where small pieces of differently colored wood are arranged to form a pattern, as in a mosaic.
- Production of Tunbridge ware had collapsed by 1927.

A 19thC Tunbridge ware nutmeg grater.

1.5in (4cm) high

$90-110   FELL

A 19thC treen spice box and cover, enclosing eight smaller spice pots and covers with black printed labels.

7.25in (18.5cm) diam

$600-650   BE

A Victorian treen turned lignum vitae egg cruet.

8.5in (21.5cm) high

$200-250   WW

A treen table snuff box, the lid containing original arsenic green label with provenance to Temeraire, Trafalgar and Beatson's Yard.

This was made from wood recovered from H.M.S. Temeraire which increases its value considerably.

3.5in (9cm) wide

$1,600-2,000   CM

A Victorian Tunbridge ware and rosewood inkstand, the interior with four divisions, and a glass well with a white metal lid.

3.25in (8.5cm) diam

$200-250   WW

A topographical Scottish penwork snuff box, the lid with a view of a terrace of buildings on a waterfront with a sail boat, foil interior 60%, full length wooden hinge.

3.25in (8cm) wide

$350-400   BLEA

A Scottish penwork snuff box, the lid with penwork scene of dancing figures, devil, skeleton and horse and rider, full length wooden hinge, slight rubbing.

3.25in (8cm) wide

$350-400   BLEA

A CLOSER LOOK AT A TUNBRIDGE WARE SPICE BOX

This is a rare and large early 19thC painted Tunbridge ware spice box.

It is in the form of a circular cottage, the side painted with door, trellis windows, and vegetation.

It incorporates a nutmeg grater.

The interior has four divisions with printed herb labels and is centered by a wooden circular box with a tin grater.

A Tunbridge ware spice box.

5.5in (14cm) diam

$17,000-20,000   BLEA

QUICK REFERENCE - TRIBAL ART

- The term Tribal Art is used to describe the cultural, ritual and functional items produced by the indigenous peoples of Africa, Oceania, South East Asia, Australasia and the Americas. Many of these items were originally made for use rather than decoration. Today, pieces are collected both for their historic and ethnographic interest and for their visual impact and appeal. Many collectors choose to focus on one tribe or region or one type of item.
- Interest in tribal pieces began in the Western world in the 18thC and 19thC as explorers reached new places and cultures. This interest grew in the early 20thC due to the influence tribal art had on European artists such as Pablo Picasso.
- Pieces from the 19thC and before with verifiable history tend to be the most valuable. Look for signs of use and age, such as wear or patina, but examine carefully, as patina can be easily faked. From the early 20thC, some tribes made large quantities of items purely for export or to sell as souvenirs; these pieces can be variable in quality and tend to be less valuable.
- In the past 20 years, the value for tribal art has been steadily rising, especially at the higher end of the market. Older pieces with clear provenances are often only accessible to wealthy collectors or museums.

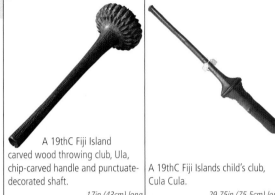

A 19thC Fiji Island carved wood throwing club, Ula, chip-carved handle and punctuate-decorated shaft.

17in (43cm) long

$2,000-2,500　　SK

A 19thC Fiji Islands child's club, Cula Cula.

29.75in (75.5cm) long

$900-1,100　　SK

An early 19thC Fiji Island chief's staff, with dark patina.

47in (119cm) long

$1,000-1,200　　SK

A Gilbert Islands wood cloth beater, the main side with crosshatch and other carving, three sides with plain lines, the handle crosshatch carving all round.

14.5in (37cm) long

$2,000-2,500　　JN

A Maori carved hardwood fiddle hand club, with concentric bands to a pierced and figural handle.

15in (38cm) long

$650-800　　KEY

A Maori carved wooden paddle, with two mother-of-pearl eyes either side.

57in (145cm) long

$2,500-3,500　　JN

A 19thC Maori carved wood billhook hand club, Wahaika, New Zealand, the curved blade with deeply carved scroll designs and recumbent tiki on the inside, the handle end in the form of a stylized mask.

15.25in (38.5cm) long

$8,000-9,500　　SK

A mid-to-late 19thC Marquesas Islands coconut, with stylized carving overall, the cord with carved bone tiki and kukui nut beads, the coconut bottom previously broken and repaired.

5.75in (14.5cm) diam

$2,000-2,500 SK

Two Massim carved wood finger drums, with stylized birds at the handle, one with tympanum.

16in (40.5cm) high

$600-650 SK

A Micronesian triton shell trumpet, the sound hole on the side.

12.25in (31cm) long

$130-200 SK

A New Ireland carved shell 'kap kap'.

3.25in (8cm) diam

$450-550 SK

A Papua New Guinea fibre pectoral, edged in nassa shells, with two shell terminals, patina of long use.

14in (35.5cm) square

$400-450 SK

A New Guinea carved wood food platter, from the Murik Lakes area, with abstract faces in a four-point star design, some cracks.

18.5in (47cm) diam

$400-450 SK

A late 19thC Polynesian fish-shaped wood bowl, with geometric chip-carving, one old repaired crack.

18.25in (46.5cm) long

$1,600-2,000 SK

A Baule wood mask, Ivory Coast, with horns and a carved arch coiffure, with a short beard.

12.5in (32cm) high

$600-750   **WW**

A Dan carved wood dance mask, Liberia, with woven plant fibre and braided cord hair, with cowrie shells.

12.5in (32cm) high

$450-550   **CHEF**

A Dan mask, Ivory Coast, wood with a plaited fibre coiffure.

8.75in (22.5cm) high

$450-550   **WW**

A Kamba wood maternity figure, Kenya, with inlaid eyes and an aluminum earring, the mother sitting in a tripod stool and with an infant on her lap.

12in (30.5cm) high

$650-800   **WW**

A hide Masaai shield, Kenya, inscribed '112972 Vosseler' and other faint inscriptions.

Provenance: Heimat-Museum, Hof, Germany, collected before 1914.

38.25in (97cm) high

$2,000-2,500   **WW**

A Yoruba Ibeji, Nigeria, wood, with a bead necklace, signed with a concentric triangle motif.

10.25in (26cm) high

$250-350   **WW**

A Yoruba beadwork and cloth crown, Nigeria, decorated masks and symbols, with detachable bird finial.

without fringe 22in (56cm) high

$600-650   **WW**

A Yoruba wood female Ibeji, Egbe, Yagba, Nigeria, with remains of Reckitt's Blue to top.

11.5in (29cm) high

$2,000-2,500   **WW**

A Zulu wood staff, South Africa, wood, with an open wheel finial with a burnished exterior and with a part-spiralled handle.

21.25in (54cm) long

$650-800   **WW**

TRIBAL ART

A mid-20thC Apache olla, with figurative and geometric decoration.

13.25in (33.5cm) high

$550-650   **POOK**

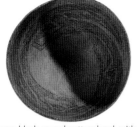

A Mono basketry bowl, with 'quail going to water' design.

Traditionally, the Mono people lived along the Sierra Nevada and in the San Joaquin Valley in what is now central California. Today they mostly live in the Big Sandy and Cold Springs Rancherias, in the Tule River Reservation, or elsewhere in northern California. Basket making and beadwork are amongst Mono traditional arts. Baskets were traditionally used for storage, transportation of goods and carrying infants. The Sierra Mono Museum in North Fork, California, is home to a large collection of Mono Indian basketry.

c1900   *17.5in (44.5cm) diam*

$4,500-5,500   **SK**

A late 19thC Navajo Third Phase Chief's blanket, with stepped diamond and cross devices, a few small repairs.

66in (167.5cm) long

$20,000-27,000   **SK**

A Tusayan black-on-red pottery bowl, with abstract design, restored from pieces.

Tusayan Ware was one of the earliest widespread pottery types in southwest America. Although a few types were localized, most are found over a large area, including in northwestern New Mexico, southern Utah, and northeastern Arizona.

c1050-1150   *9.75in (25cm) diam*

$1,000-1,300   **SK**

A pair of late 19thC Ute man's beaded hide moccasins, with buffalo hide soles.

11in (28cm) long

$1,000-1,200   **SK**

A 19thC Northwest Coast carved whale tooth amulet, the female figure giving birth, two stylized whales at the lower sides and back, incised detail.

4.5in (11.5cm) high

$9,000-11,000   **SK**

A late 19thC Southwestern Native American pottery animal, with chip to ear, cracks to exterior glaze.

9.5in (24cm) long

$250-350   **POOK**

An early presentation-style pipe tomahawk, with hand-forged head and ash handle with silver inlays, including the mouthpiece.

17.75in (44.5cm) long

$16,000-20,000   **SK**

QUICK REFERENCE - INUIT ART

- Much of what is considered 'Inuit Art' today has been made since the 1950s, when the work of Alaskan and North Canadian artists and sculptors was promoted by a young Canadian artist called James Houston. In the last few decades, the market has dramatically increased in size.
- Many sculptures are carved in local soapstone, then embellished with whalebone, ivory, antler, sinew and other materials.
- It is chiefly the artist that brings value to a work of Inuit Art, although the visual appeal also plays a key role. Sculptures tend to be signed on the base, sometimes in Roman letters or syllabics, but often with a combination of numbers and letters assigned to the artist as an identifier, as there is no tribal tradition of written language.

A stone figure, 'Kinngait goose', by Aqjangajuk Shaa RCA (b.1937), E7-1065, Cape Dorset, signed in syllabics.

7in (18cm) high

$250-400   **WAD**

A stone, bone and sinew model, 'Kugluktuk camp scene', by John Evaglok (b.1965), W21102, Coppermine.

10.5in (26.5cm) wide

$750-850   **WAD**

A stone figure, 'Iqaluit polar bear', by Henry Evaluardjuk, Frobisher Bay, signed in syllabics with Roman.

4.75in (12cm) long

$550-600   **WAD**

A stone and antler figure, 'Iqaluit musk ox', by Seepee Ipeelie (1940-2000), E7-511, Frobisher Bay.

7in (18cm) long

$350-400   **WAD**

A stone figure, 'Kinngait crouching bear', by Kaka Ashoona (1928-96), E7-1101, Cape Dorset, signed in syllabics.

4in (10cm) long

$150-200   **WAD**

A stone and leather figure, 'Magic Man', by Kiawak Ashoona OC, RCA, Cape Dorset, signed in syllabics.

1989   *21in (53.5cm) high*

$6,500-8,000   **WAD**

A CLOSER LOOK AT AN INUIT SCULPTURE

This sculpture is made from stone, wooly mammoth ivory and anhydrite

It was inspired by artist Billy Gauthier's own observations while seal hunting.

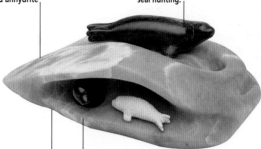

The detail of the interesting scene presented adds to the value of the piece.

It depicts a snow den under the ice, with a breathing hole to the top and bottom, in which a seal pup is safely hiding. The mother seal has sensed the vibrations of the unfamiliar seal above, and so puts her head through the lower breathing hole, to calm and warn the pup within.

A model, 'We have a visitor', by Billy Gauthier (b.1978), Happy Valley Goose Bay, Labrador, signed in Roman, dated.

2016   *5.5in (14cm) long*

$1,300-2,000   **WAD**

TRIBAL ART

A 1980s stone, bone and antler figure, 'Falcon Swooping Toward Prey', by Charlie Ugyuk, Spence Bay, Taloyoak.

14.25in (36cm) high

$3,500-4,000　　　　　　　　**WAD**

A stone and antler model, 'Kinngait reclining caribou', by Lukta Qiatsuk (1928-2004), Cape Dorset.

12.5in (32cm) long

$800-950　　　　　　　　**WAD**

A stencil and stonecut, 'Kinngait ravens shield the owl', by Kenojuak Ashevak CC RCA (1927-2013), E7-1035, Cape Dorset, no.42/50, framed.

1984　　　　　　　*32in (81.5cm) wide*

$800-950　　　　　　　　**WAD**

A stone and bone figure, 'Falcon Hunting', by Pitseolak Qimirpik (b.1986), Lake Harbour.

10.5in (26.5cm) wide

$800-950　　　　　　　　**WAD**

A felt tip drawing, 'Kinngait bird shaman', by Kingmeata Etidlooie (1915-89), E7-895, Cape Dorset, signed in syllabics.

c1970　　　　　　　*26in (66cm) wide*

$650-800　　　　　　　　**WAD**

A stonecut, 'Kinngait Umiakuta (long boat)', by Sheojuk Etidlooie, Cape Dorset, no.45/50.

Sheojuk Etidlooie began print-making late in life after Jimmy Manning suggested she try drawing. Her contributions to the Cape Dorset print releases 1994-99 include direct yet abstract depictions of birds, skin boats and tents isolated against their backgrounds.

1997　　　　　　　*28in (71cm) wide*

$350-450　　　　　　　　**WAD**

A stonecut, 'Qamani'tuaq man hunting spirit animals', by Myra Kukiiyaut (1929-2006), E2-210, Baker Lake, no.7/50.

1978　　　　　　*29.75in (75.5cm) wide*

$100-120　　　　　　　　**WAD**

Two wood and ivory shaman masks, unidentified, King Island/Ugiuvak, AK, USA.

The King Island shaman masks represent the good and the bad shaman. The bad shaman is characterized by the thick lower lip and the good shaman by a thick upper lip.

11in (28cm) high

$3,500-4,000　　　　　　　　**WAD**

A 9ct hallmarked J.W. Benson crown-wind half-hunter pocket watch, Birmingham.
1927   *3.35oz*
$650-800   **FLD**

A Victorian hallmarked silver pair cased verge pocket watch, with a painted scene of a steam train with factory buildings, back plate signed 'James Davenport, Macclesfield, Birmingham'.
1840
$750-850   **FLD**

A Rolex military issue crown-wind pocket watch, dial marked 'B 11130' and crow's foot to reverse.
$650-800   **FLD**

A pocket watch, by Saunders & Jacob, London, with 18ct yellow gold case, signed, key-wind full plate fusee and chain movement with ratchet tooth lever escapement, dial a replacement, some scratches.
1882   *1.5in (4cm) diam 1.73oz*
$550-650   **FELL**

A pocket watch, by Zenith, Edinburgh, in 9ct yellow gold case, signed keyless wind movement with ratchet tooth lever escapement, some scratches.
1952   *2in (5cm) diam 3.42oz*
$600-650   **FELL**

A gilt-metal key-wind lever pocket watch, made for the Chinese market.
$350-400   **FLD**

An Ingersoll chrome-cased 'Dan Dare' pocket watch, with automaton arm movement, Eagle Comics emblem.
$250-300   **LOC**

A 1950s Ingersoll Jeff Arnold chrome-plated pocket watch, from the Eagle comic.
$60-100   **LOCK**

WATCHES

QUICK REFERENCE - WATCHES

- Over the last two decades, interest in vintage wristwatches, and in wristwatches in general, has grown. The trend has been prompted in part by men's magazines and the popularization of formal appearance and retro looks in men's fashion. Watches can be status symbols as well as investment pieces.

- Although wristwatches were produced in small quantities earlier, they became popular shortly after World War I and by the 1930s had almost entirely replaced the pocket watch.

- Watches can be dated from the case, hands, numbers and general design of the watch. Wristwatches that resemble pocket watches with wire 'lugs' to attach the clock to the strap usually date from the early 20thC. Rectangular watches and sparkling lady's cocktail watches tend to be from the late 1920s or 1930s. Simple, circular styles with pared down dials were popular in the 1950s. Bulkier, more sculptural and futuristic watches are often from the late 1960s-70s.

- The maker, complexity of the movement, the date of manufacture and the material used all affect the value of a wristwatch. High-end well-known brands such as Rolex, Cartier and Omega remain popular due to their high quality. Watches with extra features or 'complications', such as chronographs, sun and moon phases, alarms or calendars, tend to be more valuable.

- Condition is important, as damage can be expensive to repair. Watches should always be repaired professionally.

An 18ct gold Ingot wristwatch, ref.14400, lever movement, signed 'Corum', Corum strap, gilt-metal buckle and pouch.

This watch was the property of Robert Hardy CBE, the British actor notable for playing Siegfried Farnon in All Creatures Great and Small, and Cornelius Fudge in the Harry Potter films. He died 3 August 2017, aged 91.

c1985   *1.5in (4cm) long*

$1,600-2,000   TEN

A lady's Hermès 'Roque' bracelet watch, quartz movement, bangle signed 'Hermès', reference no.L01.210, serial no.1071228.

case 0.75in (2cm) wide

$250-350   FELL

A lady's 18ct yellow gold Baume & Mercier quartz wristwatch and chain, set with diamonds, in original Garrard box.

$1,000-1,300   JN

A gentleman's cased Chopard Luna D'oro calendar quartz wristwatch, the signed circular white dial with subsidiary dials for day of the week, date of the month and moonphase.

$1,300-2,000   BELL

A gentleman's steel Breitling Old Navitimer II bracelet wristwatch, the dial with three subsidiary dials, date of the month aperture, with the original purchase invoice from Mappin & Webb.

1999   *1.5in (4cm) diam*

$3,500-4,000   BELL

A Heuer 'Automatic Calendar Chronograph' wristwatch, ref.750.501, (calibre 7750) lever movement, signed 'Heuer', with a Heuer box and warranty booklet.

Heuer was founded by Edouard Heuer in Switzerland in 1860. It first manufactured pocket watches and chronographs for sportsmen, and from 1913 also produced wristwatches. Heuer's watches were notably accurate, meaning that Heuer was selected as the official timekeeper for the Olympic Games in 1920, 1924 and 1928. It continues today as TAG Heuer.

c1982   *1.75in (4.5cm) wide*

$2,500-3,500   TEN

A gentleman's TAG Heuer '2000' series quartz mid-size stainless steel wristwatch.

dial 0.75in (2cm) diam

$130-200   LOCK

A CLOSER LOOK AT A MICKEY MOUSE WATCH

Ingersoll's 'Mickey Mouse' watch was first released in 1933. It was priced at $3 and was so successful that it saved the company from bankruptcy, reputedly selling over 11,000 at Macy's in New York on the first day it was released.

The watch features Mickey Mouse in the center, his gloved hands rotating and acting as the hour and minute hands of the clock.

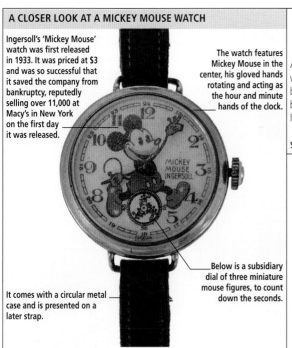

It comes with a circular metal case and is presented on a later strap.

Below is a subsidiary dial of three miniature mouse figures, to count down the seconds.

A 1930s American 'Mickey Mouse' wristwatch, by Ingersoll, produced for the British market, celluloid dial.

$450-550   **MAB**

A military issue Jaeger Le Coultre wristwatch, waterproof, the backplate marked 'no.285136', broad arrow, WWW, F.14477, tan leather strap.

1.25in (3cm) diam

$2,000-2,500   **HAN**

A gentleman's Jaeger Le Coultre Military issue wristwatch, the back marked 'A.M 6B / 159 1001 / 42'.

$3,500-4,000   **LOCK**

A chrome-plated BBC Correspondent Chronograph wristwatch, lever movement, signed 'Lemania', screw back engraved 'BBC 5844', the case backstamped with 'BBC' and serial number.
c1975   *1.5in (4cm) wide*

$1,000-1,200   **TEN**

A gentleman's Omega RAF Military issue stainless steel wristwatch, numbered on back '6645 10100 6B / 542 3016 / 53', on a modern leather strap.

Omega's first wristwatch was released in 1900. During World War I, Omega produced wristwatches for the British Royal Flying Corps and the communications troops in the US Army. It has continued to be an innovator in watch design since. It created the first calendar watch with time, date, day, month and moon phase in 1947. It is still operational and based in Switzerland.
c1953

A gentleman's Longines 9ct gold-cased wristwatch, on a later strap.

$350-400   **LOCK**

A gentleman's Longines wristwatch, Air Ministry issue, in stainless steel screw back case, sixteen jewel lever movement no.6651631, engraved to case 'AM 6B / 159 4121 / 56'.
c1955   *1.5in (4cm) diam*

$1,300-2,000   **MOR**

$8,000-9,500   **LOCK**

WATCHES

A 1960s gentleman's steel Omega 'Speedmaster Professional' wristwatch, integral Omega steel bracelet, movement apparently not operative.

The 'Speedmaster', a chronograph watch with a strong reputation for accuracy and reliability, was first released in 1956. It is sometimes know as the 'Moon Watch', as one was worn by Neil Armstrong on the moon landing of 1969.

1.5in (4cm) diam

A gentleman's 9ct gold-cased Omega wristwatch, on a later strap.

$400-450   LOCK

$4,000-4,500   HAN

A gentleman's gold Omega 'Automatic' wristwatch, jeweled lever movement, Omega logo to the winding button, the case back '18k 0,750 146304 16434 S.C', the gold bracelet with Omega logo and detailed '0,750', with case.

2.33oz

$2,500-3,500   BELL

A CLOSER LOOK AT A 'PRINCE' WATCH

The Rolex 'Prince' wristwatch was popular in the late 1920s and thorough the 1930s and remains highly collectible.

The '8092' fifteen jeweled lever observatory quality movement is timed in six positions, to cope with all climates.

Its slender, rectangular form and dual dial ensured its popularity. This example is in silver, with mat silvered dials.

The clock face has black Arabic shadow numerals and blued steel swallow skeleton hands.

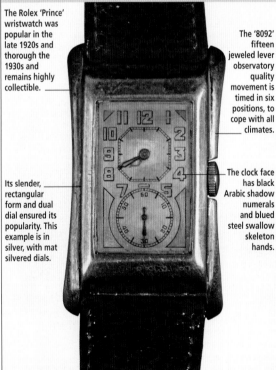

A gentleman's Rolex 'Prince' wristwatch, signed to dial, movement and case no.74664971u, Glasgow import mark.
c1930
$5,500-6,500   MOR

A lady's gold Omega 'De Ville' bracelet wristwatch, on a woven mesh link bracelet, with an Omega foldover clasp, detailed '750'.

5.75in (14.5cm) long 1.52oz

$1,200-1,300   BELL

A gentleman's Rolex 9ct gold wristwatch, the movement inscribed '15 jewels unicorn', case with import marks for Dublin, numbered '117159' and stamped 'R.W.C.Ltd'.

Rolex was founded in London in 1905 as Wilsdorf and Davis. In 1920 it relocated to Geneva, from where it still operates today. It created the 'Oyster', the first waterproof watch, in 1926, and the 'Bubbleback', the first automatic wristwatch for commercial use, in the 1940s. Its vintage 'Oyster' and 'Bubbleback' watches, alongside its 'Paul Newman Daytonas', remain highly collectible today.

1927   case 1.25in (3cm) diam 0.85oz

$900-1,000   BE

A gentleman's steel Rolex 'Oyster Perpetual' bracelet wristwatch, Rolex crown to the winding button, case back detailed 'R.C', on an oyster bracelet, with a Rolex foldover clasp.
c1965
$3,500-4,000   BELL

A gentleman's Rolex stainless steel 'Oyster Date Precision' wristwatch, design no.6694, watch number '2406818', with non-Rolex strap.
c1968   *1.5in (3.5cm) long*
$1,000-1,300   **GWA**

A gentleman's Rolex 'Oyster Perpetual Superlative Chronometer Officially Certified' wristwatch, design no.1002, marked '2809867' between the lugs, case inscribed 'G.Y.E 2.8.1972' on leather strap.
$1,300-2,000   **BE**

A gentleman's Rolex 'Tudor Oyster Prince' wristwatch, on a Rolex bracelet.
$650-800   **LOCK**

A Rolex 18ct pink gold diamond bracelet watch, cover star set with 76ct TW diamonds, Rolex Precision 17 jeweled movement, Rolex case no.4940, one diamond replacement, the dial worn.
                                    7in (18cm) long
$6,500-8,000   **DRA**

A gentleman's 9ct gold Rotary Maximus wristwatch, Birmingham, with a jeweled lever movement, numbered '99933 36635', on a gold bracelet, the clasp detailed 'Chaincraft 9ct'.
1946   *0.89oz*
$450-550   **BELL**

A 1970s Sorna Jacky Ickx gentleman's manual wind chronograph 'Easy Rider' wristwatch, case no.2651, with later black strap.
$350-400   **FLD**

A gentleman's gold Vacheron & Constantin automatic bracelet wristwatch, detailed '750 Swiss Made'.
                                    7in (18cm) long 2.65oz
$2,500-3,500   **BELL**

WINE & DRINKING

QUICK REFERENCE - WINE LABELS

- Wine labels came into popular use in the mid-18thC. They fell out of fashion in the 1860s, when wine was increasingly served straight from the bottle in which it had been bought, after new legislation permitted the sale of single bottles of wine with paper labels.
- 18thC and 19thC wine labels were generally made of silver or silver-plate, although enamel, pottery, porcelain, ivory, bone or mother-or-pearl were also used. More than 500 silversmiths are recorded as having made labels.
- Some collectors choose to focus on the maker, while others focus on a particular style of design or place of manufacture.

An early 19thC silver Anti-Corn Law League wine label, by Mordan, with the word 'FREE' on each side, pierced 'CYPRUS'.

2.25in (5.5cm) long 0.3oz

$450-550   WW

A George IV silver Armorial wine label, pierced 'SHERRY', crest of Harrison, of London and North, Riding, no maker's mark.

1825   *2.25in (6cm) long 0.8oz*

$300-400   WW

A rare mid-18thC Battersea enamel wine label, with two cupids in front of tents, holding a banner, titled 'CLARET', some damage.

c1755   *2.5in (6.5cm) long*

$750-850   WW

A Victorian provincial silver wine label, 'PAXARETE', by Barber and North, York.

c1845   *2.25in (6cm) long 0.7oz*

$650-800   WW

A Scottish silver 'cut-out letter' wine label, by J. and W. Mitchell, Glasgow.

1847   *2.25in (6cm) long 0.8oz*

$200-250   WW

A provincial silver wine label, incised 'CLARET', by James and Josiah Williams, Bristol and Exeter.

1868   *2in (5cm) long 0.2oz*

$400-450   WW

A silver armorial wine label, modeled as a fox, pierced 'MADEIRA', maker's mark worn, London.

1929   *2.25in (6cm) long 1.1oz*

$900-1,100   WW

A silver wine label, with a crown finial, mounted with two lions, incised 'KELDER', by Leslie Durbin, London.

1953   *2.25in (6cm) long 0.9oz*

$200-250   WW

A silver wine label, modeled as an Imperial lion, pierced 'CLARET', by Michael W. Druitt, London.

1973   *3.25in (8cm) long 1oz*

$150-200   WW

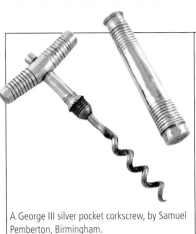

A George III silver pocket corkscrew, by Samuel Pemberton, Birmingham.

c1800   3.25in (8cm) long

$400-450   **WW**

A corkscrew, probably George III, with a base metal screw and mother-of-pearl handle, maker's mark possibly 'IC'.

3.5in (9cm) long

$150-200   **FELL**

A George III silver pocket corkscrew, with stained ivory handle, unmarked.

c1800   3in (7.5cm) long

$300-400   **WW**

A Dutch silver pocket corkscrew, marked with a Dutch tax mark and French import mark.

c1800-20   closed 2.75in (7cm) long

$250-350   **WW**

A Charles Hull 1864-patent Royal Club single lever corkscrew, roller type, patent no.480, with plaque marked 'C. Hull Patentee Birmingham Royal Club Corkscrew'.

9.75in (25cm) long

$1,300-2,000   **DA&H**

A Georg Jensen silver Art Deco corkscrew, detailed '925 Sterling Denmark', import mark with date letter indistinct.

$400-450   **BELL**

A Folk art marine ivory 'bird' corkscrew.

5.75in (14.5cm) long

$350-400   **WW**

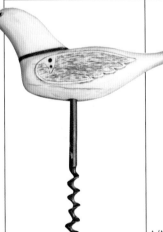

A 'Master Incolor' cocktail shaker, by Raphael & Lawson Clarke, British, red Bakelite and silver-plated metal.

c1930   10.5in (27.5cm) high

$1,600-2,000   **BELL**

A 19thC clear glass 'pistol' spirit flask.

9in (23cm) long

$90-120   **FLD**

E very item illustrated has a letter code that identifies the dealer, auction house or private collector that owns or sold it.

APAR
ADAM PARTRIDGE
www.adampartridge.co.uk

AST
ASTON'S
www.astonsauctioneers.co.uk

BE
BEARNES, HAMPTON &
LITTLEWOOD
www.bhandl.co.uk

BELL
BELLMANS
www.bellmans.co.uk

BER
BERTOIA
www.bertoiaauctions.com

BLEA
BLEASDALES
www.bleasdalesltd.co.uk

BLO
DREWEATTS & BLOOMSBURY
www.bloomsburyauctions.com

BRI
BRIGHTWELLS
www.brightwells.com

C&T
C&T AUCTIONEERS AND
VALUERS
www.candtauctions.co.uk

CA
CHISWICK AUCTIONS
www.chiswickauctions.co.uk

CAPE
CAPES DUNN
www.capesdunn.com

CHEF
CHEFFINS
www.cheffins.co.uk

CHOR
CHORLEY'S
www.chorleys.com

CM
CHARLES MILLER
www.charlesmillerltd.com

DA&H
DEE ATKINSON & HARRISON
www.dee-atkinson-harrison.co.uk

DN
DREWEATTS & BLOOMSBURY
www.dreweatts.com

DNW
DIX NOONAN WEBB
www.dnw.co.uk

DRA
RAGO ARTS
www.ragoarts.com

DSC
BRITISH DOLL SHOWCASE
www.britishdollshowcase.co.uk

DUG
DAVID DUGGLEBY
www.davidduggleby.com

DUK
DUKE'S
www.dukes-auctions.com

DW
DOMINIC WINTER
www.dominic-winter.co.uk

EBA
EAST BRISTOL AUCTIONS
www.eastbristol.co.uk

ECGW
EWBANK'S
www.ewbankauctions.co.uk

FELL
FELLOWS
www.fellows.co.uk

FIS
DR FISCHER
KUNSTAUKTIONEN
www.auctions-fischer.de

FLD
FIELDINGS
www.fieldingsauctioneers.co.uk

FOR
FORUM AUCTIONS
www.forumauctions.co.uk

GBA
GRAHAM BUDD AUCTIONS
www.grahambuddauctions.co.uk

GHOU
GARDINER HOULGATE
www.gardinerhoulgate.co.uk

GRV
GEMMA REDMOND VINTAGE
www.gemmaredmond
vintage.co.uk

GWA
GREAT WESTERN AUCTIONS
www.greatwesternauctions.com

H&C
HISTORICAL & COLLECTABLE
www.historicaland
collectable.com

HALL
HALLS
hallsgb.com/fine-art

HAN
HANSONS
www.hansonsauctioneers.co.uk

HANN
HANNAM'S
www.hannamsauctioneers.com

HC
HERITAGE AUCTIONS
www.ha.com

HT
HARTLEYS
www.hartleysauctions.co.uk

HW
HOLLOWAY'S
www.hollowaysauctioneers.co.uk

JDJ
JAMES D. JULIA INC.
jamesdjulia.com

JN
JOHN NICHOLSON'S
www.johnnicholsons.com

JNEW
JOHN NEWTON ANTIQUES
www.johnnewtonantiques.com

JON
ROGERS JONES & CO.
www.rogersjones.co.uk

K&O
KINGHAM & ORME
www.kinghamandorme.com

KEY
KEYS
www.keysauctions.co.uk

L&T
LYON & TURNBULL
www.lyonandturnbull.com

LA
DAVID LAY FRICS
www.davidlay.co.uk

LC
LAWRENCES CREWKERNE
www.lawrences.co.uk

LHA
LESLIE HINDMAN
www.lesliehindman.com

LOC
LOCKE & ENGLAND
www.peacockauction.co.uk/
locke-england

LOCK
LOCKDALES
www.lockdales.com

LSK
LACY SCOTT & KNIGHT
www.lsk.co.uk

LYN
LYNWAYS
www.lynways.com

M&DM
M&D MOIR
www.manddmoir.co.uk

MAB
MATTHEW BARTON LTD.
www.matthewbartonltd.com

MART
MARTEL MAIDES
www.martelmaides.co.uk

MEA
MEALY'S
mealys.ie

MITC
MITCHELLS
www.mitchellsantiques.co.uk

MM
MULLOCK'S
www.mullocksauctions.co.uk

MOR
MORPHETS
www.morphets.co.uk

PC
PRIVATE COLLECTION

PCOM
PHIL-COMICS AUCTIONS
www.phil-comics.com

POOK
POOK & POOK INC.
www.pookandpook.com

PSA
POTTERIES AUCTIONS
www.potteriesauctions.com

PSL
PROP STORE
www.propstore.co.uk

PW
PETER WILSON
www.peterwilson.co.uk

QU
QUITTENBAUM
www.quittenbaum.de

RE
RICHARD EDMONDS
AUCTIONS
richardedmondsauctions.com

RHA
RITA HASDELL
rita.hasdell@btinternet.com

ROS
ROSEBERYS
www.roseberys.co.uk

SAS
SPECIAL AUCTION SERVICES
www.specialauctionservices.com

SK
SKINNER INC.
www.skinnerinc.com

SOU
CATHERINE SOUTHON
www.catherinesouthon.co.uk

SWA
SWANN AUCTION GALLERIES
www.swanngalleries.com

SWO
SWORDERS
www.sworder.co.uk

TEN
TENNANTS
www.tennants.co.uk

TOV
TOOVEY'S
www.tooveys.com

TRI
TRING MARKET AUCTIONS
www.tringmarketauctions.co.uk

VEC
VECTIS
vectis.co.uk

W&W
WALLIS & WALLIS
www.wallisandwallis.co.uk

WAD
WADDINGTON'S
www.waddingtons.ca

WHP
W&H PEACOCK
www.peacockauction.co.uk

WHYT
WHYTE'S
www.whytes.ie

WM
WRIGHT MARSHALL
www.wrightmarshall.co.uk

WW
WOOLLEY & WALLIS
www.woolleyandwallis.co.uk

The following list of general antiques and collectibles centers, markets and shops has been organized by region. Any owner who would like to be listed in our next edition, space permitting, or who wishes to update their contact information, should email info@millers.uk.com.

USA

ALABAMA
Antique Attic
www.antiqueatticdothan.com

ALASKA
Duane's Antique Market
www.duanesantiquemarket.com

The Pack Rat Antiques
+1 907-522-5272

ARIZONA
American Antique Antiques
www.americanantiquemall.com

Brass Armadillo
www.brassarmadillo.com

ARKANSAS
Mid-Towne Antique Mall
www.midtownantiquemall.com

CALIFORNIA
Ocean Beach Antique Mall
www.antiquesinsandiego.com

COLORADO
A&J Antiques Mall
www.ajantiques.com

Brass Armadillo
www.brassarmadillo.com

CONNECTICUT
The Antique & Artisan Gallery
www.theantiqueandartisangallery.com

DELAWARE
Lewes Mercantile Antiques
www.antiqueslewes.com

FLORIDA
Avonlea Gallery
www.avonleamall.com

Wildwood Antique Malls
wildwoodantiquemalls.com

GEORGIA
Kudzu Antiques + Modern
www.kudzuantiques.com

HAWAII
Antique Alley
www.portaloha.com/antiquealley

IDAHO
Antique World Mall
www.antiqueworldmall.com

ILLINOIS
Second Time Around Antique Market
www.2xaroundantiques.com

INDIANA
Exit 76 Antique Mall
www.exit76antiques.com

Manor House Antique Mall
www.manorhouseantiques.com

IOWA
Brass Armadillo
www.brassarmadillo.com

KANSAS
Flying Moose Antique Mall
www.flying-moose.com

Paramount Antique Mall
www.paramountantiquemall.com

KENTUCKY
Preservation Station
www.visitpreservationstation.com

LOUISANA
Magazine Antique Mall
www.magazinestreet.com/
merchant/magazine-antique-mall

MAINE
Cornish Trading Company
www.cornishtrading.com

MARYLAND
The Antique Center
www.antiquecentersavage.com

MASSACHUSETTS
Showcase Antiques Center
www.showcaseantiques.com

MICHIGAN
Collette's
www.collettesvintage.com

Michiana Antique Mall
www.michianaantiquemall.com

MINNESOTA
Staples Mill Antiques
www.staplesmillantiques.com

MISSISSIPPI
Flowoods Antique Flea Market
www.flowoodantiquefleamarket.com

MISSOURI
Relics Antiques Mall
www.relicsantiquemall.com

River Market Antiques
rivermarketantiquemall.com

MONTANA
The Montana Antique Mall
www.montanaantiquemall.com

NEBRASKA
Platte Valley Antique Mall
www.plattevalleyantiquemall.com

NEVADA
Cheshire Antiques
www.cheshireantiques.com

NEW HAMPSHIRE
Antiques at Colony Mill Marketplace
www.facebook.com/colonymillantiques

NEW JERSEY
Lafayette Mill Antiques Center
www.millantiques.com

Somerville Center Antiques
www.somervilleantiques.net

The Yellow Garage Antiques Marketplace
www.yellowgarageantiques.com

NEW MEXICO
Antique Connection Mall
www.antiqueconnectionmall.com

NEW YORK
L.W. Emporium Co-op
www.lwemporium.com

The Manhattan Art and Antiques Center
www.the-maac.com

Showplace
www.nyshowplace.com

NORTH CAROLINA
Fifteen Ten Antiques
www.1510-antiques.com

Granddaddy's Antique Mall
www.granddaddys.com

The Red Door Antiques
reddoorantiquesoflincolnton.com

Sleepy Poet Antique Malls
sleepypoetstuff.com

NORTH DAKOTA
Plain and Fancy Antique Mall
www.facebook.com/plain-and-fancy-antique-mall-261127253910701

OHIO
Grand Antique Mall
www.grandantiquemall.com

Hartville Market Place and Flea Market
www.hartvillemarketplace.com

Heart of Ohio Antique Center
www.heartofohioantiques.com

OKLAHOMA
Antique Co-op
www.antiqueco-op.com

OREGON
Old Town Antique Mall
www.grantspassantiques.com

PENNSYLVANIA
Antiques Showcase & German Trading Post
www.blackhorselodge.com

RHODE ISLAND
Rhode Island Antiques Mall
www.riantiquesmall.com

SOUTH CAROLINA
The Old Mill Antique Mall
www.oldmillantiquemall.com

SOUTH DAKOTA
4 Seasons Flea Market
www.4seasonsfleamarket.com

TENNESSEE
Goodlettsville Antique Mall
www.goodlettsvilleantiquemall.com

TEXAS
Antique Pavilion
www.antique-pavilion.com

Forestwood Antiques Mall
www.forestwoodantiquemall.com

Montgomery Street Antiques
www.montgomerystreetantiques.com

Snider Plaza Antique Shop
www.sniderplazaantiques.net

Uncommon Objects
www.uncommonobjects.com

UTAH
Capital City Antique Mall
www.capitalcityantiquemall.com

VERMONT
The Vermont Antique Mall
www.vermontantiquemall.com

VIRGINIA
Antique Village
www.antiquevillageva.com

Factory Antique Mall
factoryantiquemall.com

WASHINGTON
Seattle Antiques Market
www.seattleantiquesmarket.com

Thorp Fruit and Antique Mall
www.thorpfruit.com/antiques

WEST VIRGINIA
South Charleston Antique Mall
www.southcharlestonantique.com

WISCONSIN
Red Shed Antiques
www.redshed.biz

WYOMING
Antiques Central
www.antiqescentralonline.com

CANADA
Antique Market
www.antiquesdirect.ca

Finnegan's Market
finnegans-market.hudson-village.com

Green Spot Antiques
www.greenspotantiques.com

Post Office Antique Mall
www.postofficeantiquemall.com

Old Strathcona Antique Mall
www.oldstrathconamall.com

One-of-a-Kind Antique Mall
www.oneofakindantiquemall.com

Toronto Antiques on King
www.torontoantiquesonking.com

Vanity Fair Antique & Collectables Mall
+1 250-380-7274

SPECIALISTS

If you wish to have any item valued, it is advisable to contact the dealer or specialist in advance to check that they will carry out this service and whether there is a charge. While most dealers will be happy to help you with an enquiry, do remember that they are busy people with businesses to run. Telephone valuations are not possible. Please mention the 'Miller's Collectibles Handbook & Price Guide' by Judith Miller when making an enquiry.

ADVERTISING
Awsum Auctions
www.awsumauctions.com

ANTIQUITIES
Frank & Barbara Pollack
Email: barbarapollack@comcast.net

AUSTRIAN BRONZES
European Bronze
www.europeanbronze.com

AUTOMOBILIA
Automobilia Auctions
automobiliaauctions.com

Dunbar's Gallery
www.dunbarsgallery.com

BOOKS
Abebooks
www.abebooks.com

Aleph-Bet Books
www.alephbet.com

Bauman Rare Books
www.baumanrarebooks.com

CAMERAS
Brooklyn Film Camera
www.brooklynfilmcamera.com

Houston Camera Exchange
hcehouston.com

CANES
Tradewinds Antiques
tradewindsantiques.com

CERAMICS
Charles & Barbara Adams
Email: adams_2430@msn.com

Mark & Marjorie Allen Antiques
www.antiquedelft.com

HL Chalfant Antiques
www.hlchalfant.com

British Collectibles
www.britishcollectibles.net

Jill Fenichell
jillfenichellinc.com

Cynthia Findlay
www.torontoantiquesonking.com

Pam Ferrazzutti Antiques
www.pamferrazzuttiantiques.com

Samuel Herrup Antiques
www.samuelherrup.com

Mellin's Antiques
www.mellinsantiques.com

Pascoe & Company
www.pascoeandcompany.com

Rago Arts
www.ragoarts.com

Philip Suval, Inc
Email: jphilipsuval@aol.com

TOJ Gallery
www.tojgallery.com

CLOCKS
Kirtland H. Crump
www.kirtlandcrumpclocks.com

RO Schmitt Fine Art
www.roschmittfinearts.com

COMICS
Carl Bonasera
www.allamericancomicshops.com

Comic Connect
www.comicconnect.com

Comic Gallery Collectibles
www.stores.ebay.com/comic-gallery-collectibles

Heritage Auctions
comics.ha.com

Metropolis Collectibles
www.metropoliscomics.com

CURRENCY
Gemini
www.geminiauction.com

Goldberg
www.goldbergcoins.com

DOLLS
All Dolled Up
www.alldolledup.ca

Sara Bernstein Dolls
www.rubylane.com/shop/sarabernsteindolls

Theriault's
www.theriaults.com

FASHION
Lofty Vintage
www.loftyvintage.com

Vintage Swank
www.vintageswank.com

FILM & TV
Wonderful World of Animation
www.wonderfulworldofanimation.com

The Prop Store
propstore.com

Julien's Auctions
www.juliensauctions.com

GLASS
Brookside Art Glass
www.wpitt.com

The End of History
www.theendofhistoryshop.blogspot.com

Cynthia Findlay
www.torontoantiquesonking.com

Holsten Galleries
www.holstengalleries.com

Antiques by Joyce Knutsen
Tel: 315 637 8238 / 352 567 1699

Lillian Nassau
www.lilliannassau.com

Jeffrey F Purtell
www.steubenpurtell.com

Paul Reichwein
Tel: 717 569 7637

Retro Art Glass
www.retroartglass.com

Paul Stamati Gallery
www.stamati.com

GUITARS
Norman's Rare Guitars
www.stamati.com

JEWELRY
Ark Antiques
Tel: 203 498 8572

Deco Jewels Inc.
Tel: 212 253 1222

Fraleigh Jewellers
www.fraleigh.ca

Leah Gordon Antiques
www.leahgordon.com

Jeweldiva
www.jeweldiva.com

Fiona Kenny Antiques
www.fionakennyantiques.com

Arthur Guy Kaplan
Email: rkaplan8350@comcast.net

Macklowe Gallery
www.macklowegallery.com

Melody Rodgers LLC
www.melodyrodgers.com

Roxanne Stuart
Email: gemfairy@aol.com

Bonny Yankauer
Email: bonnyy@aol.com

LIGHTING
Chameleon Fine Lighting
www.chameleon59.com

Lillian Nassau
www.lilliannassau.com

MECHANICAL MUSIC
Mechantiques
www.mechantiques.com

The Music Box Shop
www.themusicboxshop.com

METALWARE
Wayne & Phyllis Hilt
www.hiltpewter.com

MILITARIA
Faganarms
www.faganarms.com

International Military Antiques
www.ima-usa.com

ORIENTAL
Hellios Auctions
www.heliosauctions.com

Polly Latham Asian Art
pollylatham.com

Marc Matz Antiques
www.marcmatz.com

Mellin's Antiques
www.mellinsantiques.com

Mimi's Antiques
www.mimisantiques.com

PAPERWEIGHTS
L.H. Selman Ltd.
www.theglassgallery.com

The Dunlop Collection
Tel: 704 871 2626 or (800) 227 1996

PENS & WRITING EQUIPMENT
Fountain Pen Hospital
www.fountainpenhospital.com

Go Pens
www.gopens.com

David Nishimura
www.vintagepens.com

Pendemonium
www.pendemonium.com

POSTCARDS
Vintage Postcards
www.vintagepostcards.com

POSTERS
Chisholm Larsson Gallery
www.chisholm-poster.com

Poster Connection Inc.
www.posterconnection.com

Posteritati
www.posteritati.com

Vintage Poster Works
www.vintageposterworks.com

ROCK & POP
Hein's Rare Collectibles
www.beatles4me.com

Julien's Auctions
www.juliensauctions.com

SCIENTIFIC
Barometer Fair
www.barometerfair.com

George Glazer Gallery
www.georgeglazer.com

The Olde Office
www.branfordhouseantiques.com

Tesseract
www.etesseract.com

SCULPTURE
Valerio Art Deco
www.valerioartdeco.com
Olde Hope Antiques
www.oldehope.com

SILVER
Alter Silver Gallery Corp.
Email: aftersilvergallery@mac.com

Argentum
www.argentum-theleopard.com

Chicago Silver
www.chicagosilver.com

Richard Flensted-Holder
By appointment only Tel: 416 961 3414

Imperial Half Bushel
www.imperialhalfbushel.com

Jonathan Trace
Tel: 914 658 7336

Louis Wine Ltd.
www.louiswine.com

SMOKING
Vintage Lighters NJ
vintagelightersnj.net

Elegant Lighters
www.elegantlighters.com

SPORTING MEMORABILIA
Larry Fritsch Cards Inc.
www.fritschcards.com

Golf For All Ages
www.golfforallages.com

Hall's Nostalgia
stores.ebay.com/Halls-Nostalgia

Ingrid O'Neil Sports & Olympic Memorabilia
www.ioneil.com

TECHNOLOGY
Harry Poster
www.harryposter.com

TEDDY BEARS
The Calico Teddy
www.calicoteddy.com

TOYS & GAMES
Bertoia
www.bertoiaauctions.com

The Old Toy Soldier Home
oldtoysoldierauctions.com

Trains & Things Hobbies
www.traversehobbies.com

TREEN
Steven Powers
www.stevenspowers.com

TRIBAL ART
Arte Primitivo
www.arteprimitivo.com

Marcy Burns American Indian Arts
www.marcyburns.com

Morning Star Gallery
www.morningstargallery.com

Myers & Duncan
Email: jmyersprimitives@aol.com

Elliott & Grace Snyder
www.elliottandgracesnyder.com

Steven Powers
www.stevenspowers.com

Trotta-Bono American Indian Art
www.trottabono.com

Waddington's
www.waddingtons.ca

WATCHES
Matthew Bain Inc.
www.matthewbaininc.com

The Antique Watch Co.
www.antiquewatchco.com

WINE & DRINKING
Donald A. Bull
www.bullworks.net

Steve Visakay Cocktail Shakers
www.visakay.com

The following list of auctioneers who conduct regular sales by auction is organized by region. Any auctioneer who would like to be listed in our next edition, space permitting, or to update their contact information, should email info@millers.uk.com.

USA

ALABAMA
Buddy's Antique Auction
www.buddysantiqueauction.com

High as the Sky Auction Company
www.highastheskyauction
company.com

Tucker Auctions
tuckerauctions.com

ALASKA
Alaska Auction Co.
www.alaskaauction.com

ARIZONA
Altermann Galleries & Auctioneers
www.altermann.com

The Stein Auction Company
www.garykirsnerauctions.com

Brian Lebel's Old West Show & Auction
www.oldwestevents.com

J Levine
www.jlevines.com

Old World Mail Auctions
www.oldworldauctions.com

ARKANSAS
Ponders Auctions
www.pondersauctions.com

CALIFORNIA
Bonhams
www.bonhams.com

Goldberg
www.goldbergcoins.com

I.M. Chait Gallery/Auctioneers
www.chait.com

Clark's Fine Art Gallery & Auctioneers
www.estateauctionservice.com

Clars Auction Gallery
www.clars.com

D.G.W Auctioneers
www.dgwauctioneers.com

Heritage Auctions
www.ha.com

Julien's Auctions
www.juliensauctions.com

Michaan's Auctions
www.michaans.com

John Moran
www.johnmoran.com

L.H. Selman Ltd.
www.paperweight.com

Ingrid O'Neil Sports & Olympic Memorabilia
www.ioneil.com

P.B.A. Galleries
www.pbagalleries.com

Poster Connection Inc.
www.posterconnection.com

Profiles in History
www.profilesinhistory.com

Nate D Sanders
www.natedsanders.com

San Rafael Auction Gallery
www.sanrafael-auction.com

Robert Slawinski Auctioneers
www.slawinski.com

Stacks Bowers Galleries
www.stacksbowers.com

Treasureseeker Auctions
www.treasureseekerauction.com

COLORADO
Pacific Auction Companies
www.pacificauction.com

CONNECTICUT
ATypicalFind
www.atypicalfind.com

Automobilia Auctions
automobiliaauctions.com

Greenwich Auction
www.greenwichauction.net

Heckler
www.hecklerauction.com

Litchfield County Auctions
litchfieldcountyauctions.com

Lloyd Ralston Gallery
www.lloydralstontoys.com

Shannon's Fine Art Auctioneers
www.shannons.com

Winter Associates Inc.
www.auctionsappraisers.com

DELAWARE
Angola Auction Services
auctionangola.nova-antiques.com

Reagan-Watson Auctions
www.reagan-watsonauctions.com

FLORIDA
Auctions Neapolitan
www.auctionsneapolitan.com

Burchard Galleries
www.burchardgalleries.com

Fine Art Auctions
www.faamiami.com

Leslie Hindman
www.lesliehindman.com

Kincaid Auction Company
www.kincaid.com

Kodner
www.kodner.com

A.B. Levy's
www.ablevys.com

Palm Beach Modern Auctions
www.modernauctions.com

TreasureQuest Auction Galleries Inc.
www.tqag.com

Turkey Creek Auctions
www.antiqueauctionsfl.com

GEORGIA
Ahlers & Ogletree Auctions
www.aandoauctions.com

Great Gatsby's
www.greatgatsbys.com

Red Baron's Antiques
www.rbantiques.com

HAWAII
Malama Auctions
www.malamaauctions.com

IDAHO
The Coeur D'Alene Art Auction
www.cdaartauction.com

ILLINOIS
Aspire Auctions
www.aspireauctions.com

Bunte Auction Servies
www.bunteauction.com

Hack's Auction Center
www.hacksauction.com

Heritage Chicago
www.ha.com

Leslie Hindman
www.lesliehindman.com

Rock Island Auction Company
www.rockislandauction.com

Susanin's Auctions
www.susanins.com

John Toomey Gallery
www.johntoomeygallery.com

Wright
www.wright20.com

INDIANA
Antique Helper & Ripley Auctions
www.antiquehelper.com

Schrader Auction
www.schraderauction.com

Stout Auctions
www.stoutauctions.com

Strawser Auctions
www.strawserauctions.com

IOWA
Jackson's
www.jacksonsauction.com

Tom Harris Auctions
www.tomharrisauctions.com

Tubaugh Auctions
www.tubaughauctions.com

KANSAS
Woody Auction
www.woodyauction.com

KENTUCKY
Hays & Associates
www.haysauction.com

The Sporting Art Auction
www.thesportingartauction.com

LOUISIANA
Crescent City Auction Gallery
www.crescentcityauctiongallery.com

Neal Auction Company
www.nealauction.com

New Orleans Auction Galleries
www.neworleansauction.com

MAINE
James D Julia Auctioneers Inc.
www.jamesdjulia.com

Thomaston Place Auction Galleries
www.thomastonauction.com

MARYLAND
Alexander Historical Auctions
www.alexautographs.com

Guyette & Deeter
www.guyetteanddeeter.com

Hantman's Auctioneers & Appraisers
www.hantmans.com

Richard Opfer Auctioneering
www.opferauction.com

Sloans & Kenyon
www.sloansandkenyon.com

Theriault's
www.theriaults.com

MASSACHUSETTS
James R Bakker Antiques
www.bakkerproject.com

Douglas Auctioneers
www.douglasauctioneers.com

Eldred's
www.eldreds.com

Fontaine's Auction Gallery
fontainesauction.com

Grogan & Company
www.groganco.com

Willis Henry Auctions
www.willishenry.com

Kaminski
www.kaminskiauctions.com

Marion Antiques
www.marionantiqueauctions.com

Rafael Osona
www.rafaelosonaauction.com

Simond & Oakes
www.simondoakes.com

Skinner Inc.
www.skinnerinc.com

Tremont Auctions
www.tremontauctions.com

White's Auctions
www.whitesauctions.com

Willis Henry Auctions Inc.
www.willishenry.com

MICHIGAN
American Auctions
www.americanaauctions.com

Chamberlain's Auction Gallery
www.chamberlainsgallery.com

DuMouchelles
www.dumouchelles.com

MINNESOTA
Luther Auctions
www.lutherauctions.com

MISSISSIPPI
Edens
www.edensauctions.com

European Antique Auction Gallery
www.europeanauctiongallery.com

Stevens Auction Company
www.stevensauction.com

MISSOURI
Link Auction Galleries
www.linkauctiongalleries.com

Regency Superior
www.regencystamps.com

Selkirk Auctioneers & Appraisers
www.selkirkauctions.com

Simmons & Company Auctioneers
www.simmonsauction.com

Soulis Auctions
dirksoulisauctions.com

MONTANA
Allard Auctions Inc.
www.allardauctions.com

NEBRASKA
The Auction Mill
www.theauctionmill.com

Omaha Auction Center Ltd.
omahaauctioncenter.com

Wasner Auction Service
wanserauction.com

NEVADA
Auctions Imperial
auctionsimperial.com

Lightning Auctions, Inc.
www.lightningauctions.com

NEW HAMPSHIRE
Amoskeag Auction Company
www.amoskeagauction.com

The Cobbs
www.thecobbs.com

Gallery at Knotty Pine
www.knottypineantiques.com

Paul McInnis Inc. Auction Gallery
www.paulmcinnis.com

Northeast Auctions
www.northeastauctions.com

William A Smith
www.wsmithauction.com

Withington Auction
www.withingtonauction.com

NEW JERSEY
Bertoia
www.bertoiaauctions.com

Bodnar's Auction
www.bodnarsauction.com

Dennis Auction Service
www.dennisauction.com

Nye & Co.
www.dawsonandnye.com

Rago Arts
www.ragoarts.com

Time and Again Auction Gallery
www.timeandagaingalleries.com

Waterfords
www.waterfordsauction.com

NEW MEXICO
Altermann Galleries & Auctioneers
www.altermann.com

Manitou Galleries
www.manitougalleries.com

NEW YORK
Antiquorum
www.antiquorum.com

Auctionata
auctionata.com

Bonhams
www.bonhams.com

Carlsen Gallery
www.carlsengallery.com

Christie's
www.christies.com

Clarke
www.clarkeny.com

Comic Connect
www.comicconnect.com

Copake Auctions
www.copakeauction.com

Cottone Auctions
www.cottoneauctions.com

Doyle New York
www.doylenewyork.com

Guernsey's Auctions
www.guernseys.com

Heritage Auctions
www.ha.com

Hellios Auctions
www.heliosauctions.com

Hesse Galleries
www.hessegalleries.com

William J Jenack Auctioneers
www.jenack.com

Keno Auctions
www.kenoauctions.com

Kestenbaum & Company
www.kestenbaum.net

Mapes Auction Gallery
www.mapesauction.com

Phillips
www.phillips.com

Roland Antiques
www.rolandsantiques.com

Shapiro Auctions
www.shapiroauctions.com

Sotheby's
www.sothebys.com

Stair Galleries
www.stairgalleries.com

Swann Galleries
www.swanngalleries.com

Philip Weiss Auctions
www.weissauctions.com

NORTH CAROLINA
Brunk Auctions
www.brunkauctions.com

Leland Little
www.lelandlittle.com

Raynor's Historical Collectible Auctions
www.hcaauctions.com

NORTH DAKOTA
Curt D Johnson Auction Company
www.curtdjohnson.com

Haugland's Action Auction
hauglandsactionauction.com

OHIO
Apple Tree Auction Center
www.appletreeauction.com

Aspire Auctions
www.aspireauctions.com

Cincinnati Art Galleries LLC
www.cincinnatiartgalleries.com

The Cobbs Auctioneers LLC
www.thecobbs.com

Cowan's Historic Americana Auctions
www.cowanauctions.com

Rachel Davis Fine Arts
www.racheldavisfinearts.com

Early Auction Company
earlyauctionco.com

Garth's Auctions
www.garths.com

Gray's Autioneers
www.graysauctioneers.com

Treadway Toomey Auctions
www.treadwaygallery.com

OKLAHOMA
Buffalo Bay Auction Co.
www.buffalobayauction.com

AUCTIONEERS

OREGON
Antique & Auction Company of Southern Oregon
www.oregonauctionhouse.com

O'Gallerie
www.ogallerie.com

PENNSYLVANIA
Alderfer Auction & Appraisal
www.alderferauction.com

Aspire Auctions
www.aspireauctions.com

Noel Barrett
www.noelbarrett.com

Briggs Auction, Inc.
www.briggsauction.com

William H. Bunch Auctions
www.bunchauctions.com

Concept Art Gallery
www.conceptgallery.com

Cordier Auctions & Appraisals
www.cordierauction.com

Dargate Auction Galleries
www.dargate.com

Freeman's
www.freemansauction.com

Hunt Auctions
www.huntauctions.com

Kamelot Auctions
www.kamelotauctions.com

Morphy Auctions
www.morphyauctions.com

Pook & Pook Inc.
www.pookandpook.com

Stephenson's
www.stephensonsauction.com

Witman Auctioneers
www.witmanauctioneers.com

RHODE ISLAND
Bruneau & Co. Auctioneers
bruneauandco.com

Web Wilson
www.webwilson.com

SOUTH CAROLINA
Charlton Hall
www.charltonhallauctions.com

Wooten & Wooten
www.wootenandwooten.com

SOUTH DAKOTA
Fischer Auction Company
www.fischerauction.com

Girard Auction & Land Brokers, Inc.
www.girardauction.com

TENNESSEE
Berenice Denton Estate Sales and Appraisals
www.berenicedenton.com

Case Antiques
caseantiques.com

Kimball M Sterling Inc.
www.sterlingsold.com

TEXAS
Altermann Galleries & Auctioneers
www.altermann.com

Austin Auction Gallery
www.austinauction.com

Dallas Auction Gallery
www.dallasauctiongallery.com

Gallery Auctions Inc.
www.galleryauctions.com

Houston Auction Company
www.houstonauctionco.com

Simpson Galleries
www.simpsongalleries.com

Heritage Auctions
www.ha.com

UTAH
Silcox Auctions
www.silcoxauction.com

VERMONT
Townsend Auction Gallery
townshendauctions.com

Uriah Wallace Auction Service
www.uriahwallace.com

VIRGINIA
Bremo Auctions
bremoauctions.com

Jeffrey S. Evans & Associates
www.jeffreysevans.com

Ken Farmer & Associates
www.kfauctions.com

Freeman's
www.freemansauction.com

Green Valley Auctions & Moving Inc.
www.greenvalleyauctions.com

Old World Auctions
www.oldworldauctions.com

Phoebus Auction Gallery
www.phoebusauction.com

Quinn's Auction Galleries
www.quinnsauction.com

WASHINGTON
Mroczek Brothers
www.mbaauction.com

Pacific Galleries Auction House
www.pacgal.com

WASHINGTON DC
Seattle Auction House
www.seattleauctionhouse.com

Weschler's
www.weschlers.com

WEST VIRGINIA
Adkins Auctions
www.adkinsauction.com

Cozart Auction Service
cozartauctions.com

WISCONSIN
Leslie Hindman
www.lesliehindman.com

Krueger's Auctions
www.kruegersauctions.com

WYOMING
Auction in Santa Fe
www.auctioninsantafe.com

Great Western Auctions
www.wyoauctions.com

CANADA

ALBERTA
Hall's Auction Services Ltd.
www.hallsauction.com

Hodgins Art Auctions Ltd.
www.hodginsauction.com

Lando Art Auctions
www.landoartauctions.com

BRITISH COLUMBIA
Augeo Gallery
augeogallery.com

Bolylin Auction
www.bolylin.com

Gosby Antiques
gosby.ca

Heffel Gallery Ltd.
www.heffel.com

Kilshaw's Auctioneers
www.kilshaws.com

Maynards Fine Art Auction House
www.maynards.com

Waddington's
www.waddingtons.ca

Westbridge Fine Art
www.westbridge-fineart.com

ONTARIO
888 Auctions
www.888auctions.com

A Touch of Class
www.atouchofclassauctions.com

Auction Network
auctionnetwork.ca

Dupuis
dupuis.ca

Eins Auction
www.einsauction.com

Empire Auctions
www.toronto.empireauctions.com

The Great Estate Sale
www.thegreatestatesale.com

Heffel Gallery Inc.
www.heffel.com

Ritchies
www.ritchies.com

Sotheby's
www.sothebys.com

Waddington's
www.waddingtons.ca

Walkers
www.walkersauctions.com

A.H. Wilkens
ahwilkens.com

QUEBEC
Empire Auctions
www.montreal.empireauctions.com

Enchères Champagne
champagneauctions.ca

Iegor - Hôtel des Encans
www.iegor.net

Kavanagh Auctions
kavanaghauctions.com

Montréal Auction House
pages.videotron.com/encans

Valeona Gallery Inc.
valeona.com

The following list is organized by the type of collectible. If you would like your club, society or organization to appear in our next edition, or would like to update your details, please contact us at info@millers.uk.com.

CLUBS & SOCIETIES

GENERAL
The North American Collectibles Association
www.nacacollectors.com

ADVERTISING
Antique Advertising Association of America
www.pastimes.org

Coca-Cola Collectors Club
www.cocacolaclub.com

ANTIQUITIES
Association of Dealers & Collectors of Ancient & Ethnographic Art
adcaea.wildapricot.org

BOOKS
Antiquarian Booksellers' Association of America
www.abaa.org

CAMERAS
The American Society of Camera Collectors
cameracollectors.wordpress.com

The Ohio Camera Collector's Society
historiccamera.com

CANES
International Association of Antique Umbrella and Cane Collectors
www.antiquecaneworld.com

CERAMICS
American Art Pottery Association
www.aapa.info

American Ceramic Circle
www.americanceramiccircle.org

Tansferware Collectors Club
www.transcollectorsclub.org

Homer Laughlin China Collectors' Association
www.hlcca.org

M.I. Hummel Club
www.hummelgifts.com

National Shelley China Club
www.shelleychinaclub.com

Royal Doulton Collectors Club
www.royaldoultoncollectorsclub.com

Southern Folk Potter Collectors Society
www.southernfolkpotterysociety.com

CLOCKS
National Association of Watch & Clock Collectors
www.nawcc.org

COMICS & ANNUALS
CGC Collectors Society
comics.www.collectors-society.com

COMMEMORATIVES
American Political Items Collectors
www.apic.us

CURRENCY
American Numistmatic Association
www.money.org

American Nusimastic Society
numismatics.org

International Bank Note Society
www.theibns.org

The Scripophily Society
www.scripophily.org

NGC Collectors Society
coins.www.collectors-society.com

PMG Collectors Society
notes.www.collectors-society.com

DOLLS
Annalee Doll Society
www.annalee.com

National Antique Doll Dealers Association
www.nadda.org

United Federation of Doll Clubs
ufdc.org

FANS
Fan Association of North America
fanassociation.org

FASHION
The Costume Society of America
www.costumesocietyamerica.com

International Organization of Lace
www.internationalorganizationoflace.org

FILM & TV MEMORABILIA
Disneyana Fan Club
www.disneyanafanclub.org

GLASS
American Carnival Glass Association
www.myacga.com

National Imperial Glass Collectors' Society
www.imperialglass.org

JEWELRY
American Hatpin Society
www.americanhatpinsociety.com

Costume Jewely Collectors International
www.costumejewelrycollectors.com

Jewelcollect
www.jewelcollect.org

LIGHTING
Historical Lighting Society of Canada
www.historical-lighting.org

National Association of Aladdin Lamp Collectors Inc.
www.aladdincollectors.org

MECHANICAL BANKS
Mechanical Bank Collectors of America
www.mechanicalbanks.org

MECHANICAL MUSIC
The Musical Box Society International
www.mbsi.org

The Automatic Musical Instrument Collectors' Association
www.amica.org

MILITARIA
Association of American Military Uniform Collectors
www.aamuc.org

Medal Collectors of America
www.medalcollectors.org

The Society of American Bayonet Collectors
bayonetcollectors.org

PAPERWEIGHTS
Paperweight Collectors Association Inc.
www.paperweight.org

PENS & WRITING
The American Pencil Collectors Society
www.pencilcollector.org

Pen Collectors of America
www.pencollectorsofamerica.com

The Society of Inkwell Collectors
soicmember.com

POSTCARDS
San Francisco Bay Area Post Card Club
www.postcard.org

POSTERS
The International Vintage Poster Dealers Association
www.ivpda.com

SCENT BOTTLES
International Perfume Bottle Association
www.perfumebottles.org

SEWING
Thimble Collectors International
thimblecollectors.com

SILVER
International Association of Silver Art Collectors
thesilverbugle.com

CLUBS & SOCIETIES

SMOKING
The North American Society of Pipe Collectors
www.naspc.org

On The Lighter Side
www.otls.com

SPORTING MEMORABILIA
Golf Collectors' Society
www.golfcollectors.com

National Fishing Lure Collectors' Club
www.nflcc.com

Society for American Baseball Research
www.sabr.org

Tennis Collectors of America
tenniscollectors.org

TECHNOLOGY
Antique Wireless Association
www.antiquewireless.org

TEDDY BEARS
The Steiff Club
www.steiffusa.com

TOYS & GAMES
Antique Toy Collectors of America
www.atca-club.org

Canadian Toy Collectors Society
www.ctcs.org

Chess Collectors' International
chesscollectormagazine.sharepoint.com

The Lionel Collectors Club of America
www.lionelcollectors.org

Miniature Figure Collectors of America
www.mfcashow.com

National Model Railroad Association
www.nmra.org

The Train Collectors Association
www.traincollectors.org

TRIBAL ART
www.atada.org
Antique Tribal Art Dealers Association

WATCHES
Early American Watch Club
www.nawcc-ch149.com

National Association of Watch & Clock Collectors
www.nawcc.org

WINE & DRINKING
International Correspondence of Corkscrew Addicts
the-icca.net

INTERNET RESOURCES

Miller's Antiques & Collectables
www.millersguides.com

1stdibs
www.1stdibs.com

ADA
www.adadealers.com

Antique Trail
www.antiquetrail.com

The Antiques Trade Gazette
www.antiquestradegazette.com

Auction.fr
www.auction.fr

BADA
www.bada.org

Barnebys
www.barnebys.co.uk

Bid Square
www.bidsquare.com

Collector's Weekly
www.collectorsweekly.com

eBay
www.ebay.com

Go Antiques
www.goantiques.com

La Gazette du Drouot
www.drouot.com

LAPADA
www.lapada.org

Live Auctioneers
www.liveauctioneers.com

Maine Antique Digest
www.maineantiquedigest.com

Rubylane
www.rubylane.com

Rubylux
www.rubylux.com

The Saleroom
www.the-saleroom.com

WorthPoint
www.worthpoint.com